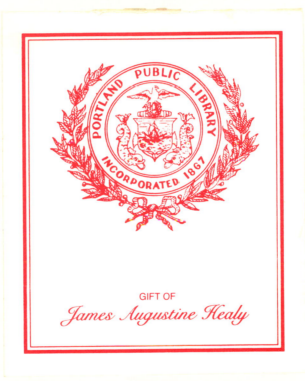

Modern
Irish Writers

MODERN IRISH WRITERS

A Bio-Critical Sourcebook

Edited by Alexander G. Gonzalez

Emmanuel S. Nelson, Advisory Editor

Greenwood Press
Westport, Connecticut • London

Library of Congress Cataloging-in-Publication Data

Gonzalez, Alexander G.
    Modern Irish writers : a bio-critical sourcebook / edited by
Alexander G. Gonzalez.
        p. cm.
    Includes bibliographical references and index.
    ISBN 0–313–29557–3 (alk. paper)
    1. English literature—Irish authors—Bio-bibliography—
Dictionaries. 2. English literature—Irish authors—Dictionaries.
3. Ireland—Intellectual life—Dictionaries. 4. Authors, Irish—
Biography—Dictionaries. 5. Ireland—Biography—Dictionaries.
I. Title.
PR8727.G66 1997
820.9'9415'03—dc20
    [B]   96–30581

British Library Cataloguing in Publication Data is available.

Library of Congress Catalog Card Number: 96–30581
ISBN: 0–313–29557–3

First published in 1997

Greenwood Press, 88 Post Road West, Westport, CT 06881
An imprint of Greenwood Publishing Group, Inc.

Printed in the United States of America

The paper used in this book complies with the
Permanent Paper Standard issued by the National
Information Standards Organization (Z39.48–1984).

10 9 8 7 6 5 4 3 2

For my family, on both sides of the Atlantic

Contents

Contents

Preface

This book is intended to serve as a reference work for scholars studying modern Irish authors, whether those scholars be entirely new to the field or experienced researchers simply moving on to study the work of authors new to them. Arranged alphabetically, the entries are written by contributors who are experts on their authors and who are fully up to date on the latest research available relevant to their entries. Each entry contains a brief biography, a concise, detailed discussion of the author's major works and themes, a review of the author's critical reception, and a bibliography of primary and secondary sources. Appended to the book is a main bibliography that lists the most significant secondary sources in the field, from broad literary histories to books and articles specifically written on fiction, drama, and poetry.

I still remember well my own initial foray into research in Irish studies. An enthusiastic graduate student at the University of Oregon, I had to prepare for a comprehensive examination in Irish literature armed only with a list of authors with whose work I was required to make myself intimately familiar. I had reasonable knowledge of Yeats and Joyce, the latter of whom I had determined would be the eventual subject of my doctoral dissertation. I had, in fact, elected to take this particular examination as what I saw as a sensible way of gaining background knowledge on Joyce. Little did I realize that Irish studies would soon become the passion of my intellectual life, replacing Joyce as my specific focus.

Playing overwhelmingly the most significant role in the development of this passion was the then-recent appearance of Richard Fallis's literary history, *The Irish Renaissance*. At last I had a road map, so to speak, lending coherence to an alphabetical list of authors, most of whose names—Patrick Kavanagh, Seumas O'Kelly, Paul Vincent Carroll, for example—I had never seen before. In addition to this "map," which helped me to place authors chronologically and by genre, the book was also a guide that made evaluations, provided literary-historical connections, and listed sources for further study. With a revised edition in preparation, it remains the single most important book for the beginner in Irish studies and is still indispensable for many advanced researchers. It is appropriate, then, that Richard Fallis, whom I have come to know in recent years, be the first person to whom I express gratitude in this preface.

I would also like to thank the many scholars who made recommendations—most expressed with great passion—about what authors this volume should include. I would have accommodated all of their suggestions but was unable to do so only because of space limitations. No doubt reviewers will find fault with some of my decisions, but tough choices had to be made. If I indulged any bias, it was to include authors whose reputations are resurging over those whose reputations are only of very recent birth. I also tended to include figures whose literary-historical importance warranted their inclusion, even though in some cases their literary output may not be extraordinarily significant (e.g., Edward Martyn). The following authors either were on my original list of 100 that had to be reduced or were suggested to me by scholars in the field of Irish literature: Nuala Archer, Sebastian Barry, Sam Hanna Bell, Patrick Boyle, Ita Daly, Seamus Deane, Teresa Deevy, Greg Delanty, Anne Devlin, Eilis Dillon, L. D. Doyle, Roddy Doyle, Anne Enright, Peter Fallon, Eamon Grennan, Michael Hartnett, Aidan Higgins, Douglas Hyde, Neil Jordan, Brendan Kennelly, Hugh Leonard, Edward Lysaght, Patrick McCabe, Thomas McCarthy, Donagh MacDonagh, Patrick McGinley, Bernard MacLaverty, Michael MacLiammoir, Val Mulkerns, Joseph O'Connor, T. P. O'Mahoney, Janet O'Neill, Maurice Leitch, Deidre Madden, Eilis Ní Dhuibhne, Gerald O'Donovan, Eimar O'Duffy, Standish O'Grady, Stewart Parker, Padraic Pearse, Forrest Reid, George Shiels, Colm Toibin, Robert Tressell, Mervyn Wall, Anthony C. West, and Jack Yeats. Iris Murdoch, G. B. Shaw, and Oscar Wilde were not included because too little of their writing concerns Ireland.

Some of these writers only narrowly missed well-deserved inclusion. Others are excellent writers but relatively early in their careers. Dozens more could be listed, and it is manifestly obvious that a second volume could have been—and at some point ought to be—published. The richness of the Irish literary scene continues to be remarkable.

I have others to thank. Robert Rhodes was very helpful during the difficult process of selecting the authors to be included. Cóilín Owens provided valuable advice regarding the book's bibliographies. Bernard McKenna must receive special thanks for his willingness to write essays on short notice when the original contributors were either unable or unwilling to honor their commitments. The Linen Hall Library was extremely helpful to Bernard and deserves both his thanks and mine. Patricia Hazard of Cortland College also deserves thanks, especially for helping me to prepare the volume's various bibliographies. For putting me in touch with needed contributors I am grateful to Tony Bradley,

Jim Cahalan, Anne Colman, Audrey Eyler, Deborah Fleming, Michael Patrick Gillespie, Dillon Johnston, and Ann Owens Weekes. I had not anticipated many of the problems involved in preparing a volume such as this; it was gratifying to see so many friends, both old and new, coming together to enable it to become a reality.

A Note on Using This Book

To avoid the frequent repetition of book citations in the secondary-source bibliographies of individual entries, most books are listed only once—in this volume's main bibliography.

Once a researcher has located his or her author's entry and consulted both its "Critical Reception" component and its bibliography of secondary sources, the researcher ought next to consult the literary-histories bibliography, the general bibliography, and the genre bibliography appropriate for his or her author. In many cases, this volume's entries cite the most important general sources beyond the immediate scope of their selected authors' bibliography; those sources cited are listed in the appropriate sections of the main bibliography.

Introduction

As John Wilson Foster makes clear in his *Fictions of the Irish Literary Revival: A Changeling Art* (1987), a distinction exists between the terms "Irish Literary Revival" and "Irish Renaissance." The Revival, which was based in large part on reestablishing Ireland's literary connections to its Celtic past and which included authors reacting against such an agenda, began around 1885 and ended somewhere between 1925 and 1940, according to what seems to be a consensus among critics and scholars. The Irish Renaissance, however, arguably has continued to the present day and shows no signs of flagging, let alone ending. The first scholar to imply that the Irish Renaissance was continuing to flourish was Richard Fallis in his groundbreaking book, *The Irish Renaissance* (1977), a literary history that included literature after 1940 with no apology relative to the Revival literature in which the book was predominantly grounded. Fallis's book is necessarily becoming dated, but it remains the most important book to consult first for anyone beginning an exploration of Irish literary studies. Ranging comfortably among the acknowledged greats of Irish literary history, the book is equally at home in its discussion of important but lesser-known figures, who fully deserve the attention Fallis gives them. It is a very thorough literary history, even though it does not—and, of course, cannot—cover every major work by every single author. I am glad to report that a revised edition is in the works and will probably have already appeared by the time this sourcebook is published.

An equally valuable book is A. Norman Jeffares's *Anglo-Irish Literature* (1982), another literary history, distinguished not only by the author's highly respected intellect but also by his trademark graceful prose. Between this book and Fallis's very few significant texts go unexamined. Other noteworthy literary histories are Ernest Boyd's *Ireland's Literary Renaissance* (1916; rev. 1922),

which is especially useful in gaining a sense of the critical reception given to
many works upon their first appearance; Frank O'Connor's well-loved but
highly idiosyncratic *A Short History of Irish Literature: A Backward Look*
(1967); Maurice Harmon's *Modern Irish Literature 1800–1967: A Reader's
Guide* (1967); Allan Warner's *A Guide to Anglo-Irish Literature* (1981); Roger
McHugh and Maurice Harmon's *A Short History of Anglo-Irish Literature from
Its Origins to the Present Day* (1982); and the most recent book of this kind,
Seamus Deane's outstanding *A Short History of Irish Literature* (1986; rev.
1994).

Once a researcher has established a firm literary-historical framework, the
next step ought to be to consult Richard Finneran's thorough bibliographic
study, *Anglo-Irish Literature, a Review of Research* (1976), and its supplement,
Recent Research on Anglo-Irish Writers (1983). Although these two books are
also, necessarily, becoming dated, they are still highly significant contributions
to scholarship. Each volume is a series of bibliographic essays composed by
some of the most highly respected scholars working in Irish studies. Chapters
on general works, nineteenth-century writers, Oscar Wilde, George Moore,
George Bernard Shaw, W. B. Yeats, J. M. Synge, James Joyce, four Revival
figures (Lady Gregory, AE, Oliver St. John Gogarty, and James Stephens), and
Sean O'Casey appear in each volume. A chapter on modern drama in the original book is expanded into three chapters in the supplement: one each on modern
drama, modern fiction, and modern poetry.

In addition to literary-historical studies, certain texts of general interest are
widely consulted by researchers. Various dictionaries exist, such as Brady and
Cleeve's *A Biographical Dictionary of Irish Writers* (1967; rev. 1985), Henry
Boylan's *A Dictionary of Irish Biography* (1978; rev. 1989), and, perhaps the
most useful among these, Robert Hogan's *Dictionary of Irish Literature* (1979;
rev. 1996). Even after twenty-five years, Malcolm Brown's seminal *The Politics
of Irish Literature* (1972) remains the most important book on its subject, though
Peter Costello's *The Heart Grown Brutal: The Irish Revolution in Literature,
from Parnell to the Death of Yeats, 1891–1939* (1977) is also an impressive
work, probably most useful for its commentary on Irish fiction. David Cairns
and Toni O'Brien Johnson's *Gender in Irish Writing* (1990) is widely cited as
an important contribution to the ongoing debate on the role of gender in Irish
literature, and Ann Owens Weekes's *Irish Women Writers: An Uncharted Tradition* (1990) is an excellent guide to the fastest-growing area of literary study
about Ireland. William J. McCormack's widely hailed *Ascendancy and Tradition
in Anglo-Irish Literary History from 1739–1939* (1985), the definitive scholarly
work on its subject, is required reading for anyone undertaking any study of
Ireland's former upper class as it is represented in literature.

Jacqueline Genet's *The Big House in Ireland: Reality and Representation*
(1991) is a collection of scholarly essays that, as its title indicates, addresses
the Big House as theme and symbol from both historical and literary perspectives, including various kinds of romanticization. Edward Hirsch's substantial

essay "The Imaginary Irish Peasant" (1991) applies a similar approach to its subject.

Regarding comedy in Irish literature, four books distinguish themselves. Vivian Mercier's *The Irish Comic Tradition* (1962) is a classic. David Krause's *The Profane Book of Irish Comedy* (1982) is also approaching classic status, and Maureen Waters's *The Comic Irishman* (1984) is an excellent book that seems similarly destined. Theresa O'Connor's *The Defiant Spirit: Comedy in the Works of Irish Women Writers* (1995) is an outstanding collection of essays with the narrower focus indicated by its title.

If the researcher's project leads to a focus in a particular genre, certain scholarly texts stand out as milestones. In the general study of Irish fiction, John Wilson Foster's *Fictions of the Irish Literary Revival* (1987) is the preeminent work, even though its scope is restricted to a broad-ranging study of the Revival and does not concern itself with fiction written afterward. In fact, Foster uses the idea of the Revival as a unifying principle in surveying virtually every conceivable kind of fiction produced during the period. He includes authors such as James Joyce, George Moore, Daniel Corkery, and Brinsley MacNamara by showing how they reacted against the Revival movement. Benedict Kiely's *Modern Irish Fiction* (1950) is still quite valuable, as is—and this will surprise some readers—Vivian Mercier's Trinity College, Dublin, doctoral dissertation, "Realism in Anglo-Irish Fiction 1916–1940" (1943). One example of Mercier's insightfulness is that he is the only reviewer even to have noticed that Seumas O'Kelly used a page or two of interior monologue in his novel *The Lady of Deerpark* (1917). Foster's *Forces and Themes in Ulster Fiction* (1974) remains the only quality study specifically focused on the fiction of the North.

The other major studies of Irish fiction focus exclusively on either the novel or the short story. John Cronin's *The Anglo-Irish Novel* (1980) is a good introduction to the genre, but James Cahalan's *The Irish Novel: A Critical History* (1988) is more thorough and is generally considered the definitive reference work on the novel. Also outstanding are Patrick Rafroidi and Maurice Harmon's *The Irish Novel in Our Time* (1976) and Rudeger Imhof's *Contemporary Irish Novelists* (1990); each collection of essays concentrates on the novel after Joyce. The definitive survey of the Irish historical novel remains Cahalan's *Great Hatred, Little Room: The Irish Historical Novel* (1983). For an essentially comprehensive study of the novel in modern Irish, Alan Titley's *An tUrscéal Gaeilge* (1991) is an indispensable resource, covering virtually every novel written in Irish for the past century. Patrick Rafroidi and Terence Brown's *The Irish Short Story* (1979) is a collection of essays that surveys the best-known writers of the short story up to about 1978, concluding with John McGahern. Deborah Averill's *The Irish Short Story from George Moore to Frank O'Connor* (1982) is insightful in its survey of the short story from its start through to the 1960s, and Thomas F. Kilroy's *The Irish Short Story: A Critical History* (1984) contains, in addition to the general introduction, five lengthy essays: on the nineteenth century, on Moore and Joyce, on the 1920s and 1930s, on the story at midcentury, and on the contemporary short story (up to 1980). Though Irish fiction outside of Joyce's has long been considered inferior relative to the drama and poetry, these and other fine studies have more than shown that Irish fiction—always in the short story and especially recently in the novel—needs no apology in terms of literary merit.

Modern Irish drama is the genre for which the Revival is most famous, and Ireland continues to produce plays of strikingly original complexity and power. An excellent, comprehensive history of the Abbey Theatre through 1928 is Andrew E. Malone's *The Irish Drama* (1929), but even after fifty-six years and a long history of detractors, Una Ellis-Fermor's *The Irish Dramatic Movement* (1939; rev. 1954) remains the most-quoted book on its subject. Robert Hogan, both alone and with various coauthors, has produced a very useful six-volume history of the Irish theater from its modern foundations in 1899 to about 1966. Hugh Hunt's *The Abbey, Ireland's National Theatre, 1904–1978* (1979) provides a fairly comprehensive history of the Abbey during the period indicated in its title. The most recent, and widely considered to be currently the definitive literary history of the genre, is D. E. S. Maxwell's outstanding *A Critical History of Modern Irish Drama, 1891–1980* (1984). This ambitious book—admirably thorough in surveying the plays and playwrights that have shaped the course of Ireland's dramatic history—not only ranges broadly but also brings remarkable intellectual depth to its study of both major and minor authors and works. The reputation of not a few "minor" authors is significantly enhanced. For a focused look at drama produced in the North from 1902 until about 1970, Sam Hanna Bell's *The Theatre in Ulster* (1972) is the only available extended study.

It is perhaps because of Yeats's long shadow that, relatively speaking, far fewer books have appeared that tell the general history of Irish poetry in this century. The best books on the earlier poetry are Robert Farren's *The Course of Irish Verse* (1948), Michael Smith's *Irish Poetry: The Thirties Generation* (1983), and Robert Welch's *Irish Poetry from Moore to Yeats* (1980). On the later poetry, two texts tower over the rest: Dillon Johnston's *Irish Poetry after Joyce* (1985) and Robert F. Garratt's *Modern Irish Poetry: Tradition and Continuity from Yeats to Heaney* (1986). These books are an essential starting point for anyone beginning work on modern Irish poetry. Erudite, thorough, and eminently readable, they cover a remarkable amount of ground, though their relatively brief treatment of women poets is a regrettable flaw. To compensate for this, researchers ought to consult Patricia Boyle Haberstroh's long awaited *Women Creating Women: Contemporary Irish Women Poets* (1995). Another recent book, which is still unavailable for review at press time and which would seem to complement Haberstroh's, is Anne Colman and Medbh McGuckian's *The Grateful Muse: Poems by Irish Women, 1716–1939* (1996). It is apparently an anthology with biographical sketches. On recent Irish poetry in general, Elmer Andrews's *Contemporary Irish Poetry* (1992) and Michael Kenneally's *Poetry in Contemporary Irish Literature* (1995) are outstanding collections of essays. Still important in the study of nationalism in Irish poetry, even though dated, is Richard J. Loftus's *Nationalism in Modern Anglo-Irish Poetry* (1964). And the remarkable output of high-quality poetry from the North is admirably covered in Terence Brown's *Northern Voices: Poets from Ulster* (1975) and, more recently, Neil Corcoran's *The Chosen Ground: Essays on the Contemporary Poetry of Northern Ireland* (1992) and Clair Wills's *Improprieties: Politics and Sexuality in Northern Irish Poetry* (1993).

The interest in studying Irish literary culture seems to be increasing even as bright new playwrights, poets, and fiction writers continue to appear. Publishers establishing Irish series or expanding their offerings—such as the University of Kentucky Press, Dufour Editions, Whitston Publishers, and Greenwood Press (there are many more)—are becoming more numerous, while the old reliables—Syracuse University Press, Catholic University of America Press, and Colin Smythe, among others—continue their high-quality output unabated. Doctoral dissertations on Irish writers continue to be produced at a dizzying pace; Irish-studies organizations such as the American Conference for Irish Studies and the International Association for the Study of Irish Literature are expanding rapidly; and Irish-studies programs, such as the venerable one at Boston College or the exciting new program at the University of Notre Dame, are contributing vital new scholars. All the signs would indicate a renaissance continuing to flourish and a remarkable culture from a small island that continues to draw international attention and exhibit universal appeal. When W. B. Yeats, Lady Gregory, and Edward Martyn sat down to plot the course of their Irish National Theatre in the 1890s, they could not possibly have envisioned that the effects of the movement they launched would continue with such energy for a hundred years. As the second hundred years begins, no end is even remotely in sight.

AE (*George William Russell*)

(1867–1935)

Noelle Bowles

BIOGRAPHY

AE was born George William Russell in Lurgan, County Armagh, on April 10, 1867, to a Protestant bookkeeper, Thomas Elias Russell, and his wife, Marianne Armstrong Russell.

He studied art at the Metropolitan School of Art in Dublin, where he met and befriended William Butler Yeats in 1884. Always of a spiritual and introspective nature, Russell found a kindred soul in Yeats, and through this friendship he was introduced to the Theosophical Society of Dublin. His association with the theosophists was tentative at first, but through his contact with them he came to read Eastern philosophical texts such as the Indian *Vedas* and *Upanishads*. In his search for an intimate connection with the divine, Russell developed his pseudonym "AE" in 1888 as a means of establishing a spiritual identity separate from the material world. The original version of the name was "aeon," a Gnostic word meaning the first of mankind created by God, but a publisher's misprint shortened it to simply AE. Although AE began as a visual artist, his greatest influence on Irish culture and politics was through his writings, the first of which, published in 1894, was a volume of poems, *Homeward: Songs by the Way*.

AE eventually joined the Theosophical Society in 1890 and moved from his parents' home in 1891 into the residence of Frederick and Anne Dick, a couple who opened their home to members of the society. In the Dicks' home AE met Violet North, who was to become his wife in 1898. In order to support himself while he studied art and theosophy, AE worked as a clerk for Pim Brothers, a Dublin draper, from 1891 until 1897, when he accepted a position as a bank organizer with the Irish Agricultural Organizational Society (IAOS).

His involvement with the IAOS sparked AE's social conscience and helped to turn him from a dreamy artist into a social reformer. During his lifetime, he edited *The Irish Homestead* (1905–1923), a newspaper to aid Irish farmer and worker cooperative efforts, and then *The Irish Statesman* (1923–1930), when *The Irish Homestead* merged with *The Irish Statesman*.

His work as a newspaper editor led him further into politics, and in 1917 he joined the Irish Home Rule Convention in the hopes of finding a peaceable settlement to the conflicts dividing Ireland; however, he resigned the following year convinced that neither the pro-English Protestants nor the Republican Catholics were willing to accept anything less than a full victory. Although AE withdrew from personal involvement in politics, he continued to lobby for peaceful change in Ireland, and, as a spiritualist with connections to neither Protestantism nor Catholicism, he was able to reach out through his writings to Unionists, Sinn Fein, and the British.

After a lingering and debilitating illness, AE died of colon cancer in July 1935. Even his funeral provided a moment of reconciliation, for it brought together political rivals such as William Cosgrove and Eamon de Valera, and Catholics and Protestants alike mourned his passing (Summerfield 285).

MAJOR WORKS AND THEMES

Literary scholars have often dismissed AE as a mystic whose vaguely defined philosophies are more suited to metaphysical romanticism than substantive critical analysis. However, such a stand ignores the considerable contributions AE made to the Irish Literary Revival and to Ireland's nascent national identity. He desired to make Ireland great in its own eyes as well as in those of other nations, and he used Irish mythology to instill a sense of hereditary pride in his readers.

AE's first and only play, *Deirdre*, was performed to admiring crowds in the spring of 1902. AE considered the Deirdre legend equal in beauty and tragedy to that of Helen of Troy, and, by insisting upon this comparison, he sought to elevate the status of Irish literature. The performance of this play, in conjunction with Yeats's *Cathleen ni Houlihan*, was one of the first times an Irish audience heard the names of its mythic heroes spoken in public. AE's sympathetic representation of ancient Irish characters in both his writing and his art helped to revitalize the Irish heritage and countered the common English assertion that Ireland and its inhabitants were culturally deficient barbarians.

Most of AE's works, from the 1912 publication of *Co-operation and Nationality*, to the demise of *The Irish Statesman* in 1930, address the political causes that racked and ultimately divided the nation. AE sympathized with the plight of Irish workers exploited by the Anglo-Irish aristocracy, and he foresaw the social unrest of the 1913 Dublin strike as well as its brutal suppression. His poem ''Michael'' (1919) memorializes the tragic events of the 1916 Easter Rising and the ideals for which Patrick Pearse was martyred. Although AE sympathized with the peasants and lower classes, he did not advocate violence or revolution as a solution to Ireland's problems. As *The Interpreters* (1922) reveals, his own vision for healing the troubles of Ireland lay not in military conflict or terrorism but in redemption of the individual and society through spiritual enlightenment. Brehon, the mediator for the ideological dialogue between the prisoners of war, represents AE's own position toward political strife when he states that humankind will resolve its differences only when it is able to imbue politics with spiritual consciousness.

His ideological novel, *The Avatars* (1933), builds upon the precepts set forth in *The Interpreters*; however, this work reveals AE's own disappointment and sense of isolation. As he wrote in his introduction, "*The Avatars* has not the spiritual gaiety I desired for it. The friends with whom I once spoke of such things are dead or gone far from me. . . . As it is, I have only been able to light my way with my own flickering lantern" (vii). Although AE strove to enlighten the whole of Irish society, he acknowledged the impossibility of this in *The Avatars*, in which the state stands in opposition to the spiritual rebirth represented by the avatars Aodh and Aoife. In the end, the protagonists realize that political change will come but slowly, and they turn their attentions inward, focusing on personal spirituality as the means to reform society.

AE did not abandon his hope for political and social harmony in Ireland, but his later writings reveal what he felt to be the futility of attempting change on a national scale. He came to believe at last that only individuals could free themselves from Ireland's cycles of bloodshed and martyrdom.

CRITICAL RECEPTION

Much of the critical examination of AE's work focuses on the problems raised by the esoteric nature of his writing. In his introduction to *The Living Torch*, a selection of essays from AE's writings in *The Irish Statesman*, Monk Gibbon concedes the difficulty of determining the precise extent to which theosophy influenced his work. Gibbon gives theosophy qualified credit for AE's spiritual awakening and states that "[t]heosophy unquestionably developed and disciplined his mind, but its influence upon his style was bad, and some of his worst and vaguest writing belongs to the days when he regarded himself an apostle of the cause" (51). Gibbon notes that AE's involvement with the movement "enabled him to adopt the Celtic mythology and make use of it for his own purpose" (47). However, Henry Summerfield complains of the repetitive nature of AE's imagery and writes that "the arcane significance of an image does not necessarily justify its continual recurrence" (73).

Indeed, much of AE's early poetry and prose is, quite literally, purple. Considered the most spiritual of the colors by the theosophists, blues and purples predominate in his poetry and painting. AE's adoption of theosophical symbolism and its inaccessibility to the uninitiated leads A. Norman Jeffares to observe that "[m]any of AE's poems . . . like many of his paintings, can be diffuse and imprecise, lacking in continuous craftsmanship" (*Anglo-Irish Literature*, 169). According to Jeffares, AE's primary significance rests in his encouragement of other writers of the Irish Literary Renaissance such as Padraic Colum, Susan Mitchell, James Joyce, and Patrick Kavanagh.

Because AE was an artist, journalist, poet, philosopher, and social reformer, critics have often judged the man himself as a dabbler not worthy of serious consideration in any of the fields he practiced. Gibbon recognizes this critical tendency and defends AE from such perceptions, stating, "A.E.'s life had a single objective, and . . . the objective was not supremacy in a particular craft but . . . a complete perfecting of the self" (5).

BIBLIOGRAPHY

Works by AE

The Avatars: A Futurist Fantasy. London: Macmillan, 1933.
The Candle of Vision. London: Macmillan, 1918.
Collected Poems. London: Macmillan, 1913.
The Divine Vision and Other Poems. London and New York: Macmillan, 1904.
The Earth Breath and Other Poems. London: John Lane, 1897.
The House of the Titans and Other Poems. London and New York: Macmillan, 1934.
Homeward: Songs by the Way. Dublin: Whaley, 1894.
Imaginations and Reveries. Dublin and London: Maunsel, 1915. (Contains *Deirdre*).
The Interpreters. London: Macmillan, 1922.
Letters from AE, ed. Alan Denson. London: Abelard and Schuman, 1961.
The Living Torch, ed. and with an introduction by Monk Gibbon. New York: Macmillan, 1937.
The National Being: Some Thoughts on Irish Polity. Dublin and London: Maunsel, 1916.
Selected Poems. London and New York: Macmillan, 1935.
Song and Its Fountains. London and New York: Macmillan, 1932.
Vale and Other Poems. London and New York: Macmillan, 1931.
Voices of the Stones. London and New York: Macmillan, 1925.

Studies of AE

Davis, Robert Bernard. *George William Russell ("AE").* Boston: Twayne, 1977.
Kain, Richard M., and James H. O'Brien. *George Russell (A.E.).* London: Associated University Presses; Bucknell University Press, 1976.
Malcolm, Richardson. "AE's *Deirdre* and Yeats's Dramatic Development." *Eire-Ireland* 4 (1985): 89–105.
Summerfield, Henry. *That Myriad-Minded Man.* Totowa, NJ: Rowman and Littlefield, 1975.

Samuel Beckett

(1906–1989)

Phyllis Carey

BIOGRAPHY

Born in Foxrock, Ireland, on Good Friday, April 13, 1906, Samuel Beckett attended Earlsfort House School in Dublin (1912–1919), Portora Royal School in Northern Enniskillen (1920–1923), and Trinity College (1923–1927), where he developed a lifelong interest in Dante and earned his B.A. in modern languages. From 1928 to 1930, he taught on a fellowship at l'École Normale Supérieure in Paris, where he met James Joyce, wrote a respectable piece of literary criticism on *Finnegans Wake*, and won a poetry competition with his poem on Descartes, "Whoroscope." He also wrote a monograph on Proust (1931). After a brief stint at Trinity College, where he taught French and finished his M.A. (1930–1931), a nearly three-year stay in London (1934–1937), and several short trips to Germany, Beckett returned to Paris, his lifelong principal place of residence. In his early years he produced poetry, a number of critical pieces, and several works of fiction written in English with Irish characters and often Irish settings. In 1938, he met Suzanne Deschevaux-Dumesnil, whom he later married (1961).

During World War II Beckett worked in the French Resistance (for which he was later awarded the Croix de Guerre). In 1945, he served as interpreter for an Irish Red Cross unit in Saint-Lô, Normandy. In the postwar years, Beckett increasingly wrote originally in French and then translated or rewrote many of the texts in English. He also wrote drama. In the 1950s and 1960s, particularly because of *En attendant Godot* (1952) (*Waiting for Godot*, 1954) and the plays that followed (*Endgame* [1958], *Krapp's Last Tape* [1958], *Happy Days* [1961]), Beckett's writing career came into its own, bringing him widespread recognition—an honorary doctorate from Trinity College (1959), the International Publisher's Prize (1961), and the Nobel Prize in literature (1969). In addition to fiction and drama, Beckett's works from the late 1950s and 1960s include pieces written specifically for radio, television, and film.

Beckett continued to write in French and in English almost to the end of his life and in the 1970s and 1980s directed a number of his own plays. Although considered a recluse, he was assiduous in answering his mail, accessible to many directors, sometimes involved in the staging of his plays, concerned about productions that took liberties with stage directions, and frequently responsive to requests from various individuals and groups.

In late 1988, Beckett moved from his apartment on the Boulevard St. Jacques to a nearby nursing home, where he lived in a small room until his last illness. He died on December 22, 1989. His last reported work, a poem entitled "Comment dire" (What Is the Word), was published shortly after his death. His second play, *Eleutheria* (originally written in 1947), was published in 1995.

MAJOR WORKS AND THEMES

The story has been widely told in Beckett critics' circles that Beckett, being interviewed by a French reporter, was asked, "You are English, are you not?" and replied simply, "Au contraire." Beckett may not have flaunted his Irish origins, but neither did he deny them. While James Joyce, the most famous exile from Ireland, used the particularities of his Irish heritage to encompass more and more of human experience, Beckett increasingly distilled from his Irish background traces of a primordially human experience beneath and beyond the trappings and disasters of modern civilization. He was able, moreover, to channel his early alienation from his own country into an artistic rendering of the homelessness of modern humanity.

As a young writer, Beckett had formulated his desire to get beneath the surface materiality of words to the "all or nothing" that underlies the spoken and the seen. His probings of language, nevertheless, are punctuated by a black humor reminiscent, at times, of Swift. Beckett's writing follows a minimalist curve that ironically becomes increasingly universal as the use of words diminishes. As Bruce Arnold wrote in *The Irish Independent* shortly after Beckett's death, "His . . . is an Irish voice deriving from an Irish vision, yet spread across the human dilemma in such powerful and universal terms as to make him a world writer of enduring impact" (*The Beckett Circle* 11.2 [Spring 1990]: 2).

Beginning his publishing career with an essay (1929) on *Finnegans Wake* in progress and his monograph on *Proust* (1931), Beckett explored, among many other things, the challenge and difficulty of artistic representation in language. His early poems, "Whoroscope" and a collection published as *Echo's Bones and Other Precipitates* (1935), reveal a strong Dantean influence as well as an increasingly recurring questioning and skepticism about the modern project— especially the Cartesian legacy of scientific rationality. Beckett's aborted first novel, *Dream of Fair to Middling Women* (1932), published posthumously

(1992), embodies his early attempts to express silence through his protagonist, Belacqua, a Dantean paradigm who reappears in various guises in Beckett's writings at least until the early 1980s. This character becomes Belacqua Shuah of *More Pricks than Kicks* (1934), a collection of short stories set against a Dublin background.

Beckett's novels in English, *Murphy* (1938: French version, 1947) and *Watt* (1943–1945, first published in 1953; French version, 1968), employ Irish characters who—unlike Stephen Dedalus and his burdens of history, religion, and nationalism—instead suffer primarily from the legacies of Cartesian rationalism and logical positivism. Murphy wants to escape the "mercantile gehenna" of the big world and enter his own mental world, while Watt actively pursues the reasonable and the logical into the house of Knott, where reason and logic continually break down.

While the earlier works of fiction in English retain several specifically Irish scenes, Beckett's *Trilogy*, originally written in French, excavates the human experience with language in a more universal landscape. (Beckett's first French novel, *Mercier et Camier*, written in 1946, was not published until 1970.) Although the characters in the *Trilogy* have Irish names—Moran, Molloy, Malone, Macmann—they seem increasingly to be disintegrating forms of an indefinably human element in language that devolves further into Mahood, Worm, and, finally, the Unnamable. In the *Trilogy*, Beckett effectively deconstructs the notion of a perceiving self in control of language, in the process dissolving clear-cut distinctions among subject, object, and verb.

As Beckett's fiction moved from social and philosophical satire to an intense exploration of language and the self, his drama translated those major themes into the existential plight of modern humanity. While Joyce had concentrated on Ireland as a matrix of paralysis in *Dubliners*, depending on the particular to convey the universal, Beckett's dramatic characters—Vladimir, Estragon, Pozzo, Lucky, Hamm, Clov, Krapp, Winnie—while retaining occasional Irish allusions and "Irishisms" in speech, exhibit primarily universal qualities in their general paralysis, their common home being "this bitch of an earth" (*Waiting for Godot*, 37). Significantly, Beckett's ability to universalize the alienation of contemporary humanity in highly poetic and at times humorous terms, as well as his gift for highlighting the absurdities to which humans adapt, made his drama popular not only for an intellectual elite but also for prisoners and for those living under various forms of totalitarianism.

Of Beckett's radio plays, written during the same period as the major stage plays, his first, *All That Fall* (1956), exhibits most clearly his abstraction from and universalizing of Irish sources. In Maddy Rooney's journey to the railroad station and the mysterious delay of her blind husband, Dan, Beckett transforms the provincial into questions about human deterioration and death, about meaning, about divine existence and providence. Likewise, in adapting Robert Pinget's *La Manivelle* into English as *The Old Tune* (1963), Beckett made the characters, setting, and idiom clearly Irish while achieving a universal theme.

Beckett's continual experimentation with language, sound, and image led him eventually to *Film* (1963), where there are no words, to his television plays, such as *Eh Joe* (1966), where the protagonist does not speak, and, later, to *Quad* (1984), which focuses on image and movement. The transition to the later works comes in the experimental prose-poetry of the 1960s and early 1970s, *How It Is* (1964), *Imagination Dead Imagine* (1965), and *The Lost Ones* (1972), where, in Dantean fashion, earthy images generate imaginative realities.

In the early 1980s, Beckett produced a series of short plays and prose pieces that complement each other and distill his major themes to their purest and most poetic expression. *Catastrophe* (1982) and *What Where* (1983) suggest more overtly the political implications and questioning of power that have been subtle parts of Beckett's writing from the beginning. *Company* (1980), *Ill Seen Ill Said* (1981), *Worstward Ho* (1983), and the playlets *Footfalls* (1975), *Rockaby* (1981), and *Ohio Impromptu* (1981) evoke austere landscapes peopled with disembodied voices, which by now have become strangely familiar as "the Beckett country," both Irish and universal, both of, and not of, this world.

CRITICAL RECEPTION

As Lance St. John Butler notes, over 100 books devoted to Beckett were published during his lifetime, and this number does not include books containing single chapters on Beckett. Although there were mixed reviews of his early works in the 1930s by such writers as Edwin Muir, Dylan Thomas, and Kate O'Brien, the production of *Waiting for Godot* began the stream of Beckett criticism that has since become a torrent and that has increasingly become more adulatory. While reviews of Beckett's works in the 1950s came predominantly from French critics such as Maurice Nadeau, Georges Bataille, and Jean Anouilh, criticism in English in the 1950s and 1960s, beginning with Ruby Cohn, Raymond Federman, Lawrence Harvey, Frederick Hoffmann, Hugh Kenner, Melvin Friedman, John Fletcher, Martin Esslin, and Richard Coe, has exceeded in quantity its French counterpart, has burgeoned in a second generation of critics, and shows no sign of abating with a third. Partially because of Beckett's close ties with Germany and the many important productions of his plays there, German criticism of Beckett has been substantial, including well-known essays by Theodor Adorno and Wolfgang Iser. Recent guides to research (Murphy et al. and Locatelli) will be of great assistance for future critical discussion. Although Irish criticism on Beckett is minimal before the 1970s, it has grown considerably in the last few decades, spurred on in part by recent discussions about cultural revisionism.

The increasing abstractness of Beckett's writing, the metaphysical overtones of his texts, and his perennial experimentation with language and genre have, in turn, contributed to the versatility literary critics have shown when confronted with Beckettian texts. Although the earlier criticism consists primarily of close readings, the critical commentary on Beckett's works has expanded in recent years to include insights from speech-act theory, reader-response approaches, psychoanalysis, structuralism, semiotics, feminism, deconstructionism, Marxism, and poststructuralism. P. J. Murphy notes that contemporary criticism seems to focus primarily on three questions: (1) "whether Beckett is a Modernist, Late Modernist, or Postmodernist, or perhaps some alternative label altogether," (2) to what extent he is an "Irish" writer, particularly in the context of current nationalist and postcolonial discussions, and (3) what political dimensions can be detected in his works.

If the highest form of critical recognition is imitation, Beckett has to be considered one of the leading writers of the twentieth century. In drama alone, many prominent playwrights of the last thirty years such as Harold Pinter, Václav Havel, Tom Stoppard, Sam Shepard, and Edward Albee openly acknowledge their various debts to Beckett. Though he had no children, Samuel Beckett's literary heirs are numerous indeed and extend far beyond Ireland's shores.

BIBLIOGRAPHY

Selected Works by Samuel Beckett

As the Story Was Told: Uncollected and Later Prose. London: Calder, 1990.
Cascando and Other Short Dramatic Pieces. New York: Grove, 1970.
Collected Poems in English and French. New York: Grove, 1977.
Company. New York: Grove, 1980.
The Complete Dramatic Works. London: Faber and Faber, 1986.
Disjecta: Miscellaneous Writings and a Dramatic Fragment. Ed. Ruby Cohn. New York: Grove, 1984.
How It Is. New York: Grove, 1964.
Ill Seen Ill Said. New York: Grove, 1964.
The Lost Ones. New York: Grove, 1972.
More Pricks than Kicks. 1934. New York: Grove, 1970.
Murphy. 1938. New York: Grove, 1957.
Proust. 1931. New York: Grove, 1957.
Three Novels. New York: Grove, 1965 (*Molloy, Malone Dies, The Unnamable.*)
Watt. 1953. New York: Grove, 1959.

Studies of Samuel Beckett

Bibliographies, Source Materials

Admussen, Richard L. *The Samuel Beckett Manuscripts. A Study*. Boston: Hall, 1979.
Andonian, Cathleen Culotta. *Samuel Beckett: A Reference Guide*. Boston: Hall, 1989.
The Beckett Circle. (Newsletter of the Samuel Beckett Society, published biannually; carries notices of recent and forthcoming critical works on Samuel Beckett as well as reviews of performances.)
Bryden, Mary, James Knowlson, and Peter Mills, eds. *The Samuel Beckett Collection*. Reading, PA: Whiteknights, forthcoming.

Butler, Lance St. John, ed. *Critical Essays on Samuel Beckett*. Critical Thought Series. Hants, England: Scolar, 1993.

Federman, Raymond, and John Fletcher. *Samuel Beckett: His Works and His Critics*. Berkeley: University of California Press, 1970.

Graver, Lawrence, and Raymond Federman. *Samuel Beckett: The Critical Heritage*. London: Routledge and Kegan Paul, 1979.

Hessing, Kees. *Beckett on Tape: Productions of Samuel Beckett's Work on Film, Video and Audio*. Leiden: Academic Press, 1992.

Journal of Beckett Studies. (Contains essays, reviews of books and play productions, photographs, and bibliography.)

Knowlson, James, S. E. Gontarski, and Dougald McMillan, eds. *The Theatrical Notebooks of Samuel Beckett*. London: Faber and Faber, 1992–.

Lake, Carlton. *No Symbols Where None Intended: A Collection of Books, Manuscripts and Other Materials*. Austin: Humanities Research Center, University of Texas, 1984.

Locatelli, Carla. "An Outline of Beckett Criticism in Italy." *Journal of Beckett Studies* 3.1 (1993): 39–57.

Murphy, P. J., Werner Huber, Rolf Breuer, and Konrad Schoell. *Critique of Beckett Criticism: A Guide to Research in English, French, and German*. Columbia, SC: Camden House, 1994.

Murray, Christopher. "Beckett Productions in Ireland: A Survey." *Irish University Review* 14.1 (1984): 103–25.

Perspectives on Beckett as an "Irish Writer"

Bair, Deirdre. " 'No-man's-land, Hellespont or Vacuum': Samuel Beckett's Irishness." *The Crane Bag* 1.2 (1977). In *The Crane Bag Book of Irish Studies (1977–81)*, ed. Mark Patrick Hederman and Richard Kearney. Dublin: Blackwater Press, 1982, 101–6.

Ellmann, Richard. *Four Dubliners: Wilde, Yeats, Joyce, and Beckett*. London: Hamish Hamilton, 1987.

Harrington, John P. *The Irish Beckett*. New York: Syracuse University Press, 1991.

Kennedy, Sighle. "Spirals of Need: Irish Prototypes in Samuel Beckett's Fiction." In *Yeats, Joyce, and Beckett: New Light on Three Modern Irish Writers*, ed. Kathleen McGrory and John Unterecker. Lewisburg, PA: Bucknell University Press, 1976, 153–66.

Kiberd, Declan. "Beckett and Kavanagh: Comparatively Absurd?" *Hermathena* 141 (1986): 45–55.

Kinsella, Thomas. "Poems of Samuel Beckett." *Journal of Beckett Studies* 2.2 (1993): 15–18.

Mays, J. C. C. "Beckett and the Irish." *Hibernia* 23 (November 7, 1969): 14.

———. "Young Beckett's Irish Roots." *Irish University Review* 14.1 (1984): 18–33.

Mercier, Vivian. *Beckett/Beckett*. New York: Oxford University Press, 1977.

———. "Samuel Beckett and the Sheela-na-gig." *Kenyon Review* 23 (Spring 1961): 299–324.

O'Brien, Eoin. *The Beckett Country: Samuel Beckett's Ireland*. Monkstown, County Dublin: Black Cat, 1986.

Rose, Marilyn Gaddis. "The Irish Memories of Beckett's Voice." *Journal of Modern Literature* 2 (1971): 127–32.

Sharkey, Rodney. "Irish? Au Contraire!: The Search for Identity in the Fictions of Samuel Beckett." *Journal of Beckett Studies* 3.2 (1994): 1–18.

Brendan Behan

(1923–1964)

James McNamara

BIOGRAPHY

Brendan Behan was born on February 9, 1923, in Dublin. Noted as much for drunken displays as he was for his writing ability, Behan was never fully appreciated by the critics of his day, who largely dismissed him as a raconteur who happened to be able to write an entertaining tale every once in a while, at least when he was sober.

The eldest of the five children of Stephen and Kathleen (Kearney) Behan, Brendan was introduced early on to the two influences that would produce the foundation of his writing career: reading and politics. Both parents enjoyed reading aloud to their children, and Brendan developed, both at home and at school, a love of reading literature and history. This interest in the written word would carry him through the loneliness of multiple stays in prison. Irish politics also dominated discussions at the Behan household, which was entirely committed to the nationalist cause, and Brendan was a fledgling member of the Irish Republican Army (IRA) by fourteen.

As much as Behan liked to tell of his humble, working-class origins, his family was far from a destitute slum tribe. For example, while his family did reside in a tenement, the building was owned by Behan's paternal grandmother, Christina English. Behan also seems to have enjoyed watching his Uncle Paddy, P. J. Bourke, take part in music hall reviews and melodramas; Bourke ran the Queen's Theatre, "the poor man's Abbey" (Boyle 18). Behan's love of theater combined with his appetite for the written word to produce the desire to communicate with an audience of his own. Behan consumed a steady diet of literature and history, both of his native land and of its usurpers, the English. Behan would eventually teach himself Gaelic and become so proficient that he would write a number of works first in that tongue before translating them into English.

Behan's run-ins with the law are also of paramount importance in the development of his sensibility as a writer. His first major clash with the authorities occurred in 1939, when he was arrested for possessing gelignite with the express purpose of blowing up an English battleship. Behan was sentenced to three years in reform school, which is the basis for his autobiographical "novel" *Borstal Boy* (1958). On Easter Sunday 1942, Behan again found himself on the wrong side of the law: accused of discharging a weapon after a Republican parade, he was sentenced to fourteen years in prison. After serving four years at Mountjoy and other institutions, Behan was released in the general amnesty of 1946. While he was to suffer through many other minor altercations with the authorities, his only other major offense was the ill-advised attempt to help a fellow Dubliner, Dick Timmons, escape from a British prison. This incident marked the end of Behan's active participation in the IRA; while he continued to support the cause financially and remained on the rolls to his death, he did not take a part in operations again.

After prison, like his father, Behan worked as a house painter. He then also tried his hand at writing professionally, producing a column for the *Irish Press* from 1954 to 1956. He married in 1955 and for the next four years probably experienced the greatest joy and success of his ill-fated life.

Behan's first major theatrical production was *The Quare Fellow* (1956). During a promotional event for the London opening of the play, Behan appeared drunk on the BBC in an interview with Malcolm Muggeridge. Perhaps unfortunately, the audience loved him; the inebriated playwright had upstaged his own play, and Behan was to repeat the performance time and again before numerous theater and pub audiences. Behan the writer was never again as interesting as Behan "the wild young Irishman."

After the success of *The Quare Fellow*, Behan followed with *The Hostage*, a translation of his Gaelic drama *An Giall* (1958). Both English-language plays were produced for the British stage by Joan Littlewood, who is often given an undue amount of credit for Behan's two most ambitious theatrical presentations. While he produced several more works, these two pieces represent the climax of his writing career. Behan was rarely able to transcend his reputation as a carouser whose exploits were given extensive coverage by the press on both sides of the Atlantic. His last years were spent entertaining others with his wit, and often that wit was heavily influenced by alcohol. Despite poor health, including the onset of diabetes, Behan continued to drink to excess until his death on March 20, 1964, from "fatty degeneration of the liver."

MAJOR WORKS AND THEMES

To appreciate the complexity of Behan's three major works, one must first look at a number of lesser offerings that show the promise of the artist he was, for at least a short time, to become. Three early works by Behan trade on his ability to present a slice of Irish life, but they begin to reveal, as well, his desire to satirize the conventions that make life so difficult and demanding. His novel *The Scarperer* (1964) actually appeared serialized in the *Irish Times* in 1953. The story concerns several attempts made by shady characters to double-cross each other for monetary profit. The Scarperer plans to help two prisoners escape from jail, only to use one of them as a decoy to suggest another felon's death. The plot ultimately fails, not through the device of good conquering evil but because several individual hoodlums make mistakes. Behan does not seem to question human behavior or offer alternatives to particular actions; rather, his characters seem apathetic to improving society as a whole. They are concerned only with improving their own condition, and all they can do is laugh at their circumstances. The novel stresses the lack of control one has over the environment.

Hold Your Hour and Have Another is a collection of the best essays that Behan composed during his tenure writing for the *Irish Press*. While the collection did not appear in print until 1963, the essays themselves were composed from 1954 to 1956 and as such should be placed in relation to the other writing that Behan was producing at that time. The articles were originally written to entertain a reading audience, and they accomplish that task admirably. The individual offerings often investigate the curious manner people have with language, and the observations provide a glimpse into Behan's love of human beings and the various ways that they attempt to communicate with each other, often with disastrous results.

Behan's first major success came with the 1956 production of *The Quare Fellow*, which established Behan's reputation as a writer of note. Originally titled *Casadh Sugain Eile* (The Twisting of Another Rope), the play concerns the reactions of a prison community to the impending execution of a murderer. The play's theme might be distilled into an examination of how humans react to the presence of death, and the action considers such universal topics as sex, politics, and religion. The action begins with the revelation that the prisoners are no better or worse than their captors; Dunlavin, the central figure of the first half of the play, would rather have a wife-murderer in the next cell than a sex offender. As the mantle passes to Warder Regan in the second half of the performance, Behan's critique of capital punishment comes to the forefront; Regan is a cynic who expresses antipathy to the execution. While his fellow warders do not completely understand or trust him, his gentleness is a comfort to the prisoners: he is usually the officer requested to stand the last watch the night before an execution. His comments while he trains a warder new to the experience of sharing a man's last night reveal the hypocrisy of the entire penal system.

Behan's third short radio play, "The Big House," which was first produced in 1957, might be viewed as allegorical in that Ireland, the Anglo-Irish aristocracy, British commercial interests, and Irish natives of all persuasions are all ridiculed. An estate is looted by an opportunistic Irish manager, and the drama becomes a critique of all parties involved in Irish history. The play represents "a transition from the 'slice of life' realism of *The Quare Fellow* to what Alan Simpson has called the 'non-representational abstract' of *The Hostage*" (Porter 33).

Behan's second major dramatic success, *The Hostage*, was also originally written in Gaelic. The translation of *An Giall* is a music-hall romp in the best tradition of Queen's Theatre, but the ridiculous nature of the action hides the underlying seriousness of the theme. The plot concerns the abduction of a British soldier, Leslie, to serve as a hostage to gain the release of an IRA man sentenced to be executed the next day in Belfast. The hostage is held in a brothel owned by Monsewer, an Englishman by birth who is more fanatically Irish than his entourage; Pat, who served with Monsewer in the civil war and who manages the brothel, is no longer a fanatic. The other zany characters who inhabit the house act out a number of dance hall scenes to comic effect, but the idea that death is close at hand is never far removed from the action. Even a love affair that develops between one of the residents and Leslie is doomed by this undercurrent of destruction; Leslie is, in fact, killed by a stray bullet in the climactic scene. The play criticizes this ridiculous loss of human life and attempts to establish the sanctity of all life, no matter what the nationality.

Behan's autobiographically inspired *Borstal Boy* is difficult to categorize. The work, which recounts Brendan's experiences in reform school, was begun during his stay in Mountjoy. The book represents the author's attitudes toward his British warders. The "novel," if it may be viewed as such, tells the story of young man with too much bravado and arrogance confronting a world that values neither. Behan and his friend, Charlie, an English sailor, are able to transcend their native differences; they remain human through all of the inhuman treatment that they both receive and witness. The book also reveals that the one institution that should have offered the possibility of solace in prison, the church, fails to do so. Behan's excommunication denied him the spiritual comfort he so desperately needed.

The final four works attributed to Behan actually include one compilation of previously published material, two pieces that were transcribed from tape recordings that Behan made in the last years of his life, and one play that was left unfinished at the time of his death. *Brendan Behan's Island: An Irish Sketchbook* (1962) contains a number of essays, grouped geographically, that Behan had published in various venues. These sketches provide little information about the country or its people. *Brendan Behan's New York* (1964) and *Confessions of an Irish Rebel* (1965) were both edited by Rae Jeffs from tapes that Behan recorded. The former is noteworthy for the inclusion of letters from Mary and Patrick Kearney that detail the life of an Irish immigrant in America during the nineteenth century; the latter was to serve as the sequel to *Borstal Boy*, but it falls short, primarily because Behan was too far gone in his alcoholism to provide anything but incoherent anecdotes that are disjointed at best.

In the play *Richard's Cork Leg* (1973) Behan wanted to include a little of everything that had proven successful in *The Hostage*; once again, prostitutes would play a major role in the plot, and the action includes a number of music-hall interludes. The title comes from a story that "James Joyce, having had a play rejected as too gloomy, remarked that he might have fared better had he given Richard, one of the characters, a cork leg" (Kearney 141). Such an obvious oversight would have never occurred to Behan, who was unable to finish the play before his death. It was ultimately edited and produced by Alan Simpson in 1972.

CRITICAL RECEPTION

Far too often, criticism of Behan's creative work becomes subordinate to a critique of Behan the man. Scholars seem naturally to gravitate toward a discussion of his alcoholism or his public persona, lamenting that such an obviously talented individual could not overcome his addiction and produce many more solid works of genius. In Ted E. Boyle's monograph, this approach is followed to a limited extent, but Boyle goes beyond mere reproach to offer some valuable insights into Behan's successful major works. Boyle argues that the reader should look beyond the fact that Behan was "merely a drunken funny man" and recognize that "Behan's plays portray the hysteria which overcomes the human being caught in a situation over which he has no control" (55).

In Raymond J. Porter's book, the author reminds the reader that Behan's work was not always of the highest quality, but that "his best was quite good" (3). Porter notes that Behan's writing often dealt with "serious themes" in a humorous fashion. While several of the shorter sketches are meant merely to entertain the audience, works such as *The Quare Fellow* offer conflicting emotions that must be dealt with; even while "one laughs at the deftly delivered witticisms," one must "sense, in the midst of laughing, the presence of pain" (21).

In his study, Peter Rene Gerdes acknowledges the difficulty of separating Behan the entertainer from Behan the author. Gerdes would like to concentrate on the latter and claims that his purpose is "to counterbalance the image of the showman, which is such a handicap to objective judgment" (10). What follows is a step-by-step analysis of the plays *The Quare Fellow, An Giall*, and *The Hostage* and the autobiographical hybrid novel, *Borstal Boy*. Of the last of these, Gerdes notes that it falls within the category of prison literature and that "in proportion to its population Ireland has produced more [of it] than any other country" (93).

Both Bert Cardullo and Michael Patrick Gillespie give consideration to what is perhaps Behan's most misunderstood major work, *The Hostage*. Cardullo argues that to search for logical coherence in the play becomes a flaw in the audience, not the playwright: "[T]he culmination of the play's intermingling of the tragic and the comic is itself affectionate mockery of conventional dramatic form, of conventional dramatic seriousness" (143). Gillespie points out that all of the energy of the play might have "as its central aim the depiction of clashing political, cultural, and social sentiments within each character" (104). The result is an amalgamation that attempts to represent for the characters "the dilemma of the Ireland that they inhabit" (104).

BIBLIOGRAPHY

Works by Brendan Behan

The Quare Fellow. New York: Grove, 1957.
The Hostage. New York: Grove, 1959.
The Borstal Boy. New York: Knopf, 1959.
"The Big House." *Evergreen Review* 5.20 (1961): 40–63.
Brendan Behan's Island: An Irish Sketch-Book. New York: Geis, 1962.
Brendan Behan's New York. New York: Geis, 1964.
Hold Your Hour and Have Another. Boston: Little, Brown, 1964.
The Scarperer. Garden City, NY: Doubleday, 1964.
Confessions of an Irish Rebel. New York: Geis, 1965.
"Moving Out" and "A Garden Party": Two Plays of Brendan Behan. Ed. Robert Hogan. Dixon, CA: Proscenium, 1967.
Richard's Cork Leg. Ed. Alan Simpson. New York: Grove, 1973.
Brendan Behan: The Complete Plays. Ed. and Intro. Alan Simpson. New York: Grove, Weidenfeld, 1978.

Studies of Brendan Behan

Ahrens, Ruediger. "National Myths and Stereotypes in Modern Irish Drama: Sean O'Casey, Brendan Behan, Brian Friel." *Fu Jen Studies: Literature and Linguistics* 21 (1988): 89–110.
Behan, Dominic. *My Brother Brendan*. New York: Simon and Schuster, 1965.
Bordinat, Philip. "Tragedy through Comedy in Plays by Brendan Behan and Brian Friel." *West Virginia University Philological Papers* 29 (1983): 84–91.
Boyle, Ted E. *Brendan Behan*. New York: Twayne, 1969.
Cardullo, Bert. "*The Hostage* Reconsidered." *Eire-Ireland* 20.2 (1985): 139–43.
Culbertson, Diana. "Sacred Victims: Catharsis in the Modern Tradition." *Cross Currents* 41.2 (1991): 179–94.
de Burca, Seamus. *Brendan Behan, A Memoir*. Newark, DE: Proscenium, 1971.
Esslin, Martin. "Brecht and the English Theatre." *Tulane Drama Review* 11.2 (1966): 63–70.
Gerdes, Peter Rene. *The Major Works of Brendan Behan*. Bern: Herbert Lang, 1973.
Gillespie, Michael Patrick. "Violent Impotence and Impotent Violence: Brendan Behan's *The Hostage*." *Eire-Ireland* 29.1 (1994): 92–104.
Hays, H. R. "Transcending Naturalism." *Modern Drama* 5.9 (1962): 27–36.
Jeffs, Rae. *Brendan Behan: Man and Showman*. Cleveland: World, 1968.
Kearney, Colbert. *The Writings of Brendan Behan*. New York: St. Martin's, 1977.
Kiely, Benedict. "The Great Gazebo." *Eire-Ireland* 4.4 (1969): 143–57.
McCann, Sean. *The World of Brendan Behan*. New York: Twayne, 1965.

Mikhail, E. H. *Brendan Behan: An Annotated Bibliography of Criticism*. New York: Barnes and Noble, 1980.

————, ed. *Brendan Behan: Interviews and Recollections*. 2 vols. Totowa, NJ: Barnes and Noble, 1982.

————. *The Letters of Brendan Behan*. Montreal: McGill-Queens University Press, 1992.

O'Connor, Ulick. *Brendan*. Englewood Cliffs, NJ: Prentice-Hall, 1970.

Porter, Raymond J. *Brendan Behan*. New York: Columbia University Press, 1973.

Rollins, Ronald G. "O'Casey, Yeats and Behan: A Prismatic View of the 1916 Easter Week Rising." *The Sean O'Casey Review* 2.2 (1976): 196–207.

Schrank, Bernice. "Brendan Behan's *Borstal Boy* as Ironic Pastoral." *Canadian Journal of Irish Studies* 18.2 (1992): 63–74.

Trilling, Ossia. "The New English Realism." *Tulane Drama Review* 7.2 (1962): 184–93.

————. "The Young British Drama." *Modern Drama* 3.2 (1960): 168–77.

Wall, Richard. "*An Giall* and *The Hostage* Compared." *Modern Drama* 18.2 (1975): 165–72.

Eavan Boland

(1944–)

Patricia J. Ferreira

BIOGRAPHY

Born the daughter of Irish diplomat Frederick H. Boland and painter Frances Kelly, Eavan Boland lived the majority of her childhood in London and New York before returning to Dublin, her place of birth, in the early 1960s to attend the Convent of the Holy Child, a boarding school in Killiney, and later, Trinity College. Her father's career meant that Eavan lived in diplomatic housing throughout most of her childhood and adolescence. Despite her privileged upbringing, Boland often characterizes her younger years as unhappy because her family was without a living arrangement of its own choosing. The absence of a self-made home fostered feelings of displacement and uprootedness early in Boland's consciousness that would later surface as a major theme in some of her strongest poetry.

Exile for Boland, however, has never functioned solely as a poetic metaphor. The force of leaving Ireland also exacted an enduring toll on her that manifests itself in nonliterary ways. Whenever she writes about the experience, she describes it through instances and moments that serve as concrete demonstrations of distress and discomfort. Such uneasiness did not take long to materialize. When Boland was five years old and she and her mother first journeyed on a plane to London from Ireland to meet her father at his new post as Irish ambassador, she vomited. Later, in poems such as "After a Childhood Away from Ireland," "An Irish Childhood in England: 1951," and "In Which the Ancient History I Learn Is Not My Own," Boland would write specifically of the rupture that occurred in her life when she left for England.

The sense of dislocation is also apparent in Boland's prose. In essays Ireland is resigned to memories of summer with lilac bushes and boys diving into the

Liffey from the lock near Leeson Street. London, in contrast, is figured within the slow death of autumn. Instead of a house built for an "Irishman, his wife, and five children," the Bolands inhabited an embassy where the only reminder of Ireland was the "formal carpets," embossed with the emblems of the four provinces, that covered the building's interior. A "dark, closed-in courtyard" in the city replaced a garden that edged out into the fields of the Irish country-side. A "sparse playroom" and "blank television" located on a remote top floor supplanted a "raggy brown-and-white terrier called Jimmy."

Boland's partial reprieve from life as a diplomat's daughter came from her mother. Most important to Eavan were the elements in Frances Kelly's own background that lent themselves to mystery and imagination. Her father was a sea captain who drowned in the Bay of Biscay, and her mother died shortly after she was born. Frances, in turn, was raised by a foster mother who was a "wonderful story-teller." The combination of factors and events, according to Eavan, produced in her mother a sense of "the unrational, the inexplicable, the eloquent fragment" that fueled her own artistic inclinations and storytelling abilities and subsequently assisted Eavan in coping with her aversion to life away from home. The circumstances surrounding Frances's life and Frances herself instilled within her daughter the ability to envision a sense of place from which she could glean nourishment rather than alienation.

Not surprisingly, another important touchstone for Boland was her journey back to Ireland as a teenager to attend school. Her spirits, however, were buoyed as much by the mood of the country as they were by her return to her place of birth. Like other cities during the 1960s, Dublin exuded a sense of energy. One indication of its vitality, as well as of the life emanating from Ireland as a whole, is the generation of poets who began their careers during this period. Boland's contemporaries included Derek Mahon, Brendan Kennelly, Michael Longley, Eamon Grennan, Eiléan Ní Chuilleanáin, Seamus Heaney, and Seamus Deane.

Boland herself has described the era as "exhilarating." It was not uncommon to see Patrick Kavanagh around Dublin, and she often met aspiring poets closer in age, such as Mahon and Kennelly, in coffee shops, cafés, and pubs to talk and argue. Although Boland was only nineteen, she was a woman more self-assured than most at her age. There were sessions in O'Neill's, Jammet's, and the old Royal Hibernian Hotel, where the young literati of the day, including Mahon and Boland, met to engage in a variety of discussion and arguments on language and literature.

Surviving as a testament to the period are poems that Boland dedicated to Grennan, Kennelly, and Longley in her first formal collection, fittingly called *New Territory* (1967). Through the trope of Spanish explorers, the title poem itself alludes to the camaraderie she and other students shared at the time. She also evokes their sense of anticipation with regard to their literary objectives. Boland figures she and her contemporaries as New World discoverers, poised to make a fresh contribution to Ireland's literary landscape.

MAJOR WORKS AND THEMES

With all of its attendant advantages and aura, Eavan Boland's career cannot solely be characterized within the ebullient hallmarks of her undergraduate associations. Although she has consistently voiced the importance of friendships she established while at Trinity as well as the general climate of the time, which nurtured young writers, she has also articulated her profound sense that something was missing during that period. Exactly what or who was absent would not become clear until after she graduated; however, along with Boland's recollections of intellectual and artistic blossoming are memories of ambivalence that resulted in her initial reluctance to conceive of herself as a poet. With her marriage to novelist Kevin Casey, their subsequent move to the Dublin suburbs of Dundrum, and the birth of their two daughters, Sarah and Eavan Frances, Boland came to realize that her hesitancy to "name" herself as a poet, despite her mounting recognition, was the result of limitations imposed on women by the Irish poetic establishment.

Such restrictions, according to Boland, manifested themselves in three predominant ways, which she would later outline in her formidable essay, "A Kind of Scar." The first involves the historic portrayals of women in Irish poetry combined with the importance of nation as an ideological construct in Ireland. Although women were used to project the all-powerful political structures of the country, mostly in "Aisling" poems that figure Cathleen Ní Houlihan, Dark Rosaleen, and the Old Woman of the Roads as Ireland, such a tradition reduced women to the mythic, emblematic, and ornamental. Meanwhile, Boland saw that the suffering of Irish women throughout history, their "human truths of survival and humiliation," and their "true voice and vision" were "routinely excluded" from Irish literature.

Subsequently, the second constraint involved the terrain of women's lives. Boland has often observed that because the real world of women was neglected in Irish writing, so too was the "lived vocation" of women, how they spent their time and how they felt about their experiences. For instance, when Boland herself left Dublin proper for the suburbs to marry and raise a family, she found she was outside the conventional topography of the Irish poem. If she stayed within the city, there was a possibility of becoming "an honorary male poet." In fact, when she traveled in the literary circles of Dublin, she was told that the "best thing" about her work was that one would never know "it was by a woman." Because she left the customary world of an Irish writer, however, for a life of marriage and family, the usual signifiers of womanhood, she was perceived to have relinquished writing.

The task for Boland was to fashion her existence as well as the lives of additional Irish women into the realm of Irish poetry. A third constraint, however, was that the very occupation of writing was seen as incompatible with a woman's life. Even writers who were women and came before Boland went largely unrecognized in the literary discourse pertaining to Ireland. Therefore, it became necessary for Boland not only to record in her poems the reality of women's lives as she saw it but also to create a critical stance from which her interpretations could be understood. In doing so, she has not divorced herself from themes often equated with Irish poetry. Instead, established motifs, such as exile, famine, and war, have figured in the domains and personae of Irish women.

A new direction would be lent to Irish poetry through Boland's work as well as the endeavors of additional contemporary Irish poets; however, it was a gradual shift. In her own poetry, inklings of a change can be heard in her second book, *The War Horse* (1975), through the title poem as well as "Child of Our Time" and "Suburban Woman," among others. In these pieces, Boland writes of the Troubles in the north of Ireland, yet the conflict erupts in the Republic, on small neighborhood streets and in children's bedrooms and back gardens while people lean on windowsills, sing lullabies, and gossip with neighbors. Moreover, she recreates the terror through particular iconography and action customarily connected to women. Figures hemorrhage, births are stillborn, even tights run.

The connection between the Irish poem and Irishwomen would be established further in subsequent collections, respectively titled *In Her Own Image* (1980) and *Night Feed* (1982). Rather than stemming from conventional notions of Irish politics, the poems in both books are connected to the often unrevealed and undisclosed aspects of women's lives. *In Her Own Image* relies, in part, upon the mutilations exacted upon a woman's body, by herself and others, that reflect her vulnerability as well as destruction, especially when such disfiguring is a response to a man's desire. For instance, "Anorexic" portrays a woman burning away "her curves and paps and wiles" so that she can return to her man "thin as a rib." In "Mastectomy" a male surgeon serves as the perpetrator when he removes a woman's breast as an act of misogyny. By moving such private aspects of women's experiences into the public space of poetry, and by showing the involvement of men in such instances, Boland broadens the political territory of the Irish poem to include the subjugation of women.

The poems in *Night Feed* continue to demonstrate the reality of women's lives, yet rather than positioning women as powerless, Boland lends their experience more control and value. In pieces such as "Degas's Laundresses," "Daphne with Her Thighs in Bark," "Woman Posing," "The New Pastoral," and "Domestic Interior," she uses the world of the painter to evoke her vision. The intentions of the artist, though, as he gazes on the female pose, are not Boland's focus. Instead, she gives voice to the women being painted as well as to the women who view the work. For instance, a woman hanging wash is cautioned by a female onlooker not to become an idealized form. Likewise, Daphne warns her sisters that perfection is not in the stilted world of "virtue" but in virtue transgressed. The everyday tasks of women, buying washing powder and tending to the boiling kettle, are kept routine in these poems, yet the unglorified becomes honored. Moreover, the women who speak are transformed from helpless objects into compelling subjects.

Boland's fifth collection, *The Journey* (1986), continues to empower women and the worlds they inhabit; however, she also demonstrates the complications and complexities of such an undertaking. In the title poem, the speaker at first laments that male poets are "wasting" their meters by writing about women as objects. The speaker then slips into sleep, only to be met by Sappho, who, like Daphne of *Night Feed*, tells of the richness of ordinary women. In response, the speaker infers that she will bear witness to such experience, but Sappho warns that it will be difficult for her not to reduce women back into objects. In another poem, "Envoi," Boland's speaker declares that her muse must be better than those of men, "who made theirs in the image of their myth." Sappho's advice and Boland's assertions ultimately bespeak another difficulty that women negotiate as poets as they transform their lives into the creative.

In *Outside History* (1990), Boland works to preserve the poems from a gaze of fantasy and illusion. The world of the ideal is seen as a wound. The speaker on several occasions affirms that she needs "flesh" and "history" to create her sense of truth. Toward this purpose coffee mugs shatter, poetic harmonies produce discord, early spring is lost to frost, picked wildflowers possess bad luck, speech is gladly imperfect. Such defects are "human," "mortal," part of an "ordeal" in which the poet chooses to reside.

Boland's seventh collection, titled *In a Time of Violence* (1994), also relies upon the unsettling. Disturbances, however, are made more uncomfortable because they have been omitted from history's record. For instance, dirt roads on the edges of Connacht, which were built by the "starving Irish," have been left unmapped because they remain unfinished. What is presented as truth, the map in this case, Boland relentlessly insists is corrupt. Such sentiment is fully realized in "The Pomegranate," where the speaker, through the myth of Persephone, yearns to protect her daughter from reality with all of its blemishes and pain. To do so, however, would be to shield her from authenticity. It would also implicate the speaker in the position of being a cartographer of a faulty map. Given the distance Boland has traveled, to live life other than through the recognition of difficulty and sorrow would be disingenuous.

CRITICAL RECEPTION

Despite the political objectives for women and Irish poetry that she established early in her writing career, Boland has always held that poetry "is a place of experience and not a place of convictions." Her evocation of experience through precise lyric verse has consistently been praised as a hallmark of her work. Even *New Territory*, Boland's first formal collection, demonstrates her uncompromising attention to the poetic. In a special issue of the *Irish University Review* (*IUR*) devoted exclusively to Boland, Jody Allen-Randolph remarks that Boland's debut poems reveal a poet who is "exceptionally well-grounded in formal techniques; her love of craft is everywhere" (Murray 5). Nevertheless, most of the critical attention paid to Boland has focused on the way she has broadened the political paradigm in Ireland, through poetry and prose, to include and address feminist concerns. In fact, Medbh McGuckian, also in the *IUR*, rightly claims that Boland revises the tradition of poetic language in Ireland to "explore . . . the rawness of the female experience" (30). Likewise, Terence Brown in an essay on *The War Horse* notes that although many of the pieces in the collection resemble "well-made English poems of the 1960s, deploying a cautious, exact syntax in lines of controlled logic . . . , they also bear witness to violent eruptions of emotion which are not easily contained within the contortions of a metaphysical conceit" (36).

Boland has also been appraised in terms of how her work compares with that of other poets from Adrienne Rich to Seamus Heaney. Victor Luftig, for the *IUR*, writes of how the work of both Rich and Boland quells skeptics who doubt "first-rate poetry's ability to reach and stir a public" (57). He counters Dana Gioia's lament that poetry no longer possesses efficacy in popular discourse. The very status that Rich and Boland have achieved, argues Luftig, lies precisely in their "relation to rather than isolation from" country and world (61). Such a relationship figures as "poetic responsibility" for Boland and Rich.

Sheila Conboy (in *Éire-Ireland*) also deftly writes of Boland's connection to the world. Rather than using the work of another poet as a parallel, however, Conboy contrasts Boland's objectives with those of Seamus Heaney. She argues that Heaney gains his "aesthetic authority" by moving outside territory whereas Boland, as an Irishwoman, is "dispossessed" without ever leaving. She moves "within the poem," Conboy writes, to being "its maker" (140). Such experiential intimacy lends her own voice power as much as it has empowered an up-and-coming generation of Irish poets.

BIBLIOGRAPHY

Works by Eavan Boland

Books

23 Poems. Dublin: Gallagher, 1962.
Eavan Boland Poetry/Prose Joseph O'Malley. Dublin: Gallagher, 1963.
Autumn Essay. Dublin: Gallagher, 1963.
New Territory. Dublin: Allen Figgis, 1967.
W. B. Yeats and His World. With Micheál Mac Liammóir. London: Thames, 1971.
The War Horse. London: Gollancz, 1975; Dublin: Arlen House, 1980.
In Her Own Image. Dublin: Arlen House, 1980.
Introducing Eavan Boland. Princeton: Ontario Review Press, 1981.
Night Feed. Dublin: Arlen House, 1982; London: Boyars, 1982; Manchester: Carcanet, 1994.
The Journey. Dublin: Gallery, 1982.
The Journey and Other Poems. Dublin: Arlen House, 1986; Manchester: Carcanet, 1987.
Selected Poems. Manchester: Carcanet, 1989.

Outside History. Manchester: Carcanet, 1990.

Outside History: Selected Poems 1980–1990. New York: Norton, 1990.

In a Time of Violence. New York: Norton, 1994; Manchester: Carcanet, 1994.

Object Lessons: The Life of the Woman and the Poet in Our Time. New York: Norton, 1995; Manchester: Carcanet, 1995.

Essays

"Precepts of Art in Yeats's Poetry." *Dublin Magazine* 4.1 (Spring 1965): 8–13.

"Aspects of Pearse." *Dublin Magazine* 5.1 (Spring 1966): 46–55.

"The Attributes We Seek." *Dublin Magazine* 5.3-4 (Autumn/Winter 1966): 47–52.

"The Innocence of Frank O'Connor." In *Michael/Frank: Studies on Frank O'Connor*, ed. Maurice Sheehy. Dublin: Gill and Macmillan, 1969.

"That Lady: A Profile of Kate O'Brien 1897–1974." *The Critic* 34.2 (Winter 1975): 16–25.

"Religion and Poetry." *The Furrow* 33.12 (December 1982): 743–50.

"The Woman Poet: Her Dilemma." *Midland Review* 44.1-2 (Winter 1986): 97–109.

"The Woman Poet in a National Tradition." *Studies* (Summer 1987): 148–58.

"An Un-Romantic American." *Parnassus* 14.2 (1988): 73–92.

A Kind of Scar: The Woman Poet in a National Tradition. Dublin: Attic, 1989.

"Outside History." *American Poetry Review* 19.2 (March/April 1990): 32–38.

"The Woman, the Place, the Poet." *Georgia Review* 44.1-2 (Spring/Summer 1990): 97–109.

"The Need to Be Ordinary." In *Invisible Dublin: A Journey through Dublin's Suburbs*, ed. Dermot Bolger. Dublin: Raven Arts, 1991.

"Truthful Tears (Karl Shapiro and David Ignatow)." *Parnassus* 16.2 (1991): 125–42.

"In Defense of Workshops." *Poetry Ireland Review* 31 (Summer 1991): 40–48.

"Time, Memory and Obsession: Elizabeth Bishop." *PN Review* 18.2 (November/December 1991): 18–24.

"Broken Trust." *PN Review* 19.1 (September/October 1992): 25–28. (Biographies of women poets)

"The Serinette Principle: The Lyric in Contemporary Poetry." *Parnassus* 15.2: 7–25; *PN Review* 19.4 (March/April 1993): 20–26.

"Making the Difference: Eroticism and Aging in the Work of the Woman Poet." *American Poetry Review* 23.2 (March/April 1994): 27–32.

"Compact and Compromise: Derek Mahon as a Young Poet." *Irish University Review* 24.1 (Spring/Summer 1994): 61–66.

"Writing the Political Poem in Ireland." *Southern Review* 31.3 (Summer 1995): 485–98.

Studies of Eavan Boland

Allen-Randolph, Jody. "Ecriture Feminine and the Authorship of Self in Eavan Boland's *In Her Own Image*." *Colby Library Quarterly* 27.1 (March 1991): 48–59.

———. "Finding a Voice Where She Found a Vision." *PN Review* 21.1 (September/October 1994): 13–17.

Cannon, M. Louise, "The Extraordinary within the Ordinary: The Poetry of Eavan Boland and Nuala Ni Dhomhnaill." *South Atlantic Review* 60.2 (May 1995): 31–46.

Conboy, Sheila. "Eavan Boland's Topography of Displacement." *Éire-Ireland* 29.3 (Fall 1994): 137–46.

———. " 'What You Have Seen Is beyond Speech': Female Journeys in the Poetry of Eavan Boland and Eiléan Ní Chuillianáin." *Canadian Journal of Irish Studies* 16.1 (July 1990): 65–72.

Haberstroh, Patricia Boyle. "Literary Politics: Mainstream and Margin." *Canadian Journal of Irish Studies* 18.1 (July 1992): 181–91.

Hagen, Patricia L., and Thomas W. Zelman. " 'We Were Never on the Scene of the Crime': Eavan Boland's Repossession of History." *Twentieth Century Literature* 37.4 (Winter 1992): 442–53.

Henigan, Robert. "Contemporary Women Poets in Ireland." *Concerning Poetry* 18.2 (1985): 103–15.

Klauke, Amy. "Toward Her Own Image." *The Northwest Review* 25.1 (1987): 55–61.

McElroy, James. "Night Feed: An Overview of Ireland's Women Poets." *American Poetry Review* 14.1 (1985): 32–39.

Matthias, John. "Inside and Outside History: Seamus Heaney, Eavan Boland and Contemporary Irish Poetry." *Reading Old Friends: Essays, Reviews, and Poems on Poetics 1975–1990*. New York: State University of New York Press, 1992.

Murray, Christopher, Anthony Roche, and Jody Allen-Randolph, eds. "Special Issue: Eavan Boland." *Irish University Review* 23.1 (Spring/Summer 1993).

Ní Dhomhnaill, Nuala. "What Foremothers?" *Poetry Ireland Review* 36 (Fall 1992): 18–31.

Reizbaum, Marilyn. "Canonical Double Cross: Scottish and Irish Women's Writing." In *Decolonising Tradition: New Views of Twentieth-Century "British" Canons*, ed. Karen Lawrence. Carbondale: Illinois University Press, 1992.

Robertson, Kerry E. "Anxiety, Influence, Tradition and Subversion in the Poetry of Eavan Boland." *Colby Quarterly* 30.4 (December 1994): 264–78.

Sarbin, Deborah. " 'Out of Myth into History': The Poetry of Eavan Boland and Eiléan Ní Chuilleanáin." *Canadian Journal of Irish Studies* 19.1 (July 1993): 86–96.

Stevenson, Anne. "Inside and Outside History." *PN Review* 18.3 (January/February 1992): 34–38.

Weekes, Ann Owens. " 'An Origin like Water': The Poetry of Eavan Boland and Modernist Critiques of Irish Literature." *Bucknell Review* 38.1 (1994): 159–76.

Wills, Clair. "Contemporary Irish Women Poets: The Privatisation of Myth." In *Diverse Voices: Essays on Twentieth-Century Women Writers in English*, ed. Harriet D. Jump. London: Harvester Wheatsheaf, 1991.

Elizabeth Bowen

(1899–1973)

Barbara A. Suess

BIOGRAPHY

Although she was revered more for her "Anglo" works than her "Irish" works, Elizabeth Bowen's Anglo-Irish upbringing in the early twentieth century provided her a unique position from which to view—and write about—Ireland. Bowen's Irish works, the large body of short stories, novels, reviews, and essays devoted to Irish subjects, characters, and settings, are an impressive literary legacy that needs no apology.

Born in 1899 in Dublin, Bowen spent a part of each of her first seven years in that city and at her family's ancestral home, Bowen's Court, in County Cork. When she was seven, her father suffered a mental breakdown; as a result, she and her mother moved to England to stay with relatives on the Kent coast. After her mother died of cancer when Bowen was thirteen, Bowen lived with aunts and then with her father and his second wife at Bowen's Court. Like the semiautobiographical character Lois Farquar, of *The Last September*, here Bowen had a short-lived engagement with a British officer stationed in Ireland, then went to London to study art. While in London Bowen discovered her call to be a writer.

Bowen began writing short stories when she was about twenty but did not find a sympathetic patron until she met Rose Macaulay, who helped Bowen get her first collection, *Encounters*, published in 1923. In the same year, Bowen married Alan Cameron. Their marriage, which lasted until his death in 1952, was affectionate and nurturing, although not necessarily passionate.

Most of the early years of their marriage were spent in Old Headington while Cameron was secretary of education for the city of Oxford. Here, Bowen began to build a solid social and professional base, associating with the Oxford set and writing. In 1930, a year after her first Irish novel, *The Last September*, was published, Bowen's father died; Elizabeth Bowen now owned Bowen's Court—and the heavy financial and progenitorial responsibilities that went along with it. In 1935, a move to London helped Bowen to expand further her writing career and social circles. In addition to novels and short stories, Bowen wrote reviews for *The New Statesman* and *The Tattler* and befriended many of the London literati, including Virginia Woolf, Rosamond Lehmann, and others both within and without the Bloomsbury group.

World War II was a turning point in Bowen's life and career. In 1942, as the release of two autobiographical works, *Seven Winters* (about Bowen's first seven years in Ireland) and *Bowen's Court* (a history of her ancestral home), indicates, Bowen's attention turned momentarily toward her homeland. However, as a functionary of the Ministry of Information—she gathered data in Ireland—as well as an Air Raid Patrol (ARP) warden, Bowen was actively involved in the war. After the war, because of Cameron's poor health and in response to the general feeling of depression that permeated postwar London, Bowen and her husband began to spend more time at Bowen's Court. She published her second Irish novel, *A World of Love*, in 1955.

In 1960, Bowen sold her family's ancestral home in the hopes that it would continue to exist as a "Big House"; however, the new owner had the home demolished. In the last years of her life, Bowen spent much of her time lecturing, particularly in the United States. Living in a small cottage on the Kent coast, Bowen continued to write and was working on her autobiography, *Pictures and Conversations*, at the time of her death, of cancer, in 1973.

MAJOR WORKS AND THEMES

Bowen published ten novels, over seventy short stories, and hundreds of reviews and periodical essays; her most widely read works are her English novels, *The Death of the Heart* (1938) and *The Heat of the Day* (1949). Her Irish works have received relatively little critical attention, with the exception of the novels. Like many of her English novels, Bowen's Irish novels depict the coming-of-age of a young, Anglo-Irish woman during times of political and social upheaval. *The Last September*'s Lois Farquar and *A World of Love*'s Jane Danby must come to terms with their respective, changing positions in a Big House society that, having reigned for centuries, is coming to an end. For Bowen, the lamentable downfall of this elite group is closely tied to her notions of time and place, by which her characters often feel trapped—trapped for example by the period of naive girlhood and by the awkward position of being Anglo-Irish in a society scarred by civil and world war and obsessed with its more glorious past. *The Last September*, in particular, deals with this latter issue, most obviously through its depiction of an Anglo-Irish family torn between sympathy for the Conners (their politically active, Irish Catholic neighbors) and their social/

political obligation to entertain the culturally arrogant British soldiers who have descended on Ireland to battle people like the Conners.

Many of the novel's characters—Hugo Montmorency, Gerald, Lois—represent the impotence and apathy of this society for which the past is simultaneously a burden and an Eden. Lois, however, attempts to escape this stagnant world: her fascination with the cosmopolitan Marda leads her to follow the older woman above and beyond her (rather uninspiring) romance with a British soldier into a more passionate adventure in which they protect an Irish gunner in hiding. Later in the novel, Lois goes on to experience the "real" world of the Continent, leaving behind the Big Houses of Anglo-Ireland that are, within a year, "executed," like Lois's own willful innocence.

Bowen's personification of the Big House lends us another clue about the important use of place to reflect—and to help to create—the mood of the characters in her novels and short stories. The mood created by the Big House, for example, reveals Bowen's own conflicting reverence for, and political embarrassment about, the Big House society. For, although Bowen (nostalgically) respects the society's gentility, self-discipline, and manners, at the same time, her characters display the difficulty of the Anglo-Irish position—somewhere between colonized and colonizer.

Bowen's later Irish novel, A World of Love, also follows the progress of a young woman whose entrance into society requires disillusionment. Jane claims that the past, "as an idea," bores her—yet, out of old letters found in an attic, she creates an imaginary romance that is nonetheless very real to her. Less political than most of Bowen's novels, A World of Love reflects Bowen's belief, as described in her 1950 essay "The Bend Back," that after World War II, people looked to the past to retain a "life illusion"—the illusion that life is, indeed, worth living. Jane's life is one in which, she feels, "[n]othing was to be known. One was on the verge, however, possibly, of more." Thus, she turns to letters from the past and, like Lois, to an older, more experienced woman visitor for inspiration. These experiences do help Jane acquire knowledge and also its frequent partner, disillusionment.

Bowen's characters often use the past in an attempt to find meaning in their present, war-torn lives. Many of the short stories collected and edited by Victoria Glendinning—such as "Her Table Spread," "A Love Story," "The Happy Autumn Fields," "A Day in the Dark," and "Sunday Afternoon"—portray characters who, like Lois and Jane, see into the past, only to find themselves disillusioned and discontented with the present. Bowen's other Irish short stories range in theme from a ghost story to the effects of war on civilian life. However, although themes remain relatively constant throughout most of her fiction, Bowen saw her short stories as "visionary" pieces, more like poetry than novels; in them, she pays less attention to analyzing realistic facts, and the themes are more focused, centered around a "valid central emotion."

Bowen's nonfiction pieces provide a rich tapestry of knowledge about both her personal and her country's sociopolitical past. In Seven Winters, Bowen's childhood is rendered with an early awareness of the difficulties of being Anglo-Irish, a theme that she continues in *Bowen's Court*, a history of the Bowen family and house. Here Bowen moves beyond autobiography into political history; her story of the Bowen family is also the story of Ireland, of the history of Anglo-Irish relationships with the Irish and the English. Bowen expresses an explicit consciousness of the powerless position into which the Irish have been pushed by the two groups that have dominated Ireland for centuries. *The Shelbourne Hotel* (1951), which is a history of that prestigious Dublin edifice, *Collected Impressions* (1950), and the autobiographical *Pictures and Conversations* provide more glimpses into her views on the life, history, and literature of her times.

CRITICAL RECEPTION

Most of the critical readings of Bowen's Irish works focus on her treatment of the decline of the Protestant Ascendancy. Stylistically, critics most often place her in the modern comedy of manners and realist traditions. Victoria Glendinning sees Bowen's style as a link between Virginia Woolf and later writers such as Muriel Spark and Iris Murdoch. Similarly, William Trevor describes Bowen as one who belongs to the past yet is also a forerunner of modern fiction writing.

Most critics focus on Bowen's novels. In *Elizabeth Bowen: An Estimation*, Hermione Lee writes that *The Last September* displays the "conflict between inexperience and disenchantment," yet its nostalgia is more political than in *A World of Love*, which presents a more sentimental, benign picture of the loss of youthful innocence. Similarly, Phyllis Lassner notes that Bowen's most frequent themes are lost innocence and nostalgia for the past, a fact that she ties to Bowen's marginalization as a woman, as an Anglo-Irish individual, and as the female inheritor of a patrilineal estate (*Elizabeth Bowen* 1990). Heather Bryant Jordan also believes that Bowen's identity (and that of her characters and of Ireland) was formed by the fact of being Anglo-Irish, of occupying a "space-between." The marginality of this position, Jordan argues, was further accentuated by the damage that war perpetrated on the twentieth-century individual's ability to believe in familial and social continuity. John Coates, on the other hand, charges this critical focus on the Anglo-Irish crisis with being too narrow. In his essay (1990) Coates offers a reading of the novel's "architecture"—a structured series of comings and goings—that he believes highlights the generational differences regarding the ability to maintain stable personal relationships (e.g., the younger set, represented by Lois and Laurence, find emotions "awkward" whereas the Naylors find comfort in their longtime, personal commitments).

Bowen's Irish short fiction has received even less critical attention than the novels. As Phyllis Lassner points out in *Elizabeth Bowen: A Study of the Short Fiction*, her short stories are most often praised for their economical treatment and for the impressionistic form that heightens the subject matter. Attempts have been made to place her within various traditions of the short story: William Trevor identifies Bowen with the modernists in "Between Holyhead and Dun Laoghaire," and in "Elizabeth Bowen's 'Her Table Spread': A Joycean Irish Story," Alexander G. Gonzalez places Bowen within the Irish tradition.

Many of Bowen's works revolve around the experiences of women characters, yet her Irish fiction has attracted inadequate attention from feminist circles. One exception to this is Phyllis Lassner's discussion of Bowen's manipulation of gender roles and her treatment of women's sexuality in *Elizabeth Bowen*. Lassner views many of Bowen's female characters as representative of women who rail against domestic codes even while they embody those same codes. Renee C. Hoogland, who approaches Bowen's works from a poststructuralist, lesbian-feminist point of view, sees the author as a "truly radical, innovative, and critically practicing feminist."

BIBLIOGRAPHY

Works by Elizabeth Bowen

The Last September. London: Constable, 1929.
To the North. London: Gollancz, 1932.
The House in Paris. London: Gollancz, 1934.
The Death of the Heart. London: Gollancz, 1938.
Bowen's Court. London: Longmans, Green, 1942.
Seven Winters. Dublin: Cuala, 1942.
The Heat of the Day. New York: Knopf, 1949.
Collected Impressions. London: Longmans, Green, 1950.
The Shelbourne Hotel. New York: Knopf, 1951.
A World of Love. New York: Knopf, 1955.
Eva Trout, or Changing Scenes. New York: Knopf, 1968.
Pictures and Conversations. New York: Knopf, 1975.
Elizabeth Bowen's Irish Stories. Intro. Victoria Glendinning. Dublin: Poolbeg, 1978.

Studies of Elizabeth Bowen

Coates, John. "The Recovery of the Past in *A World of Love*." *Renascence* 40 (Summer 1988): 226–46.
———. "Elizabeth Bowen's *The Last September*: The Loss of the Past and the Modern Consciousness." *Durham University Journal* 51 (July 1990): 205–16.
Glendinning, Victoria. *Elizabeth Bowen*. New York: Knopf, 1978.
Gonzalez, Alexander G. "Elizabeth Bowen's 'Her Table Spread': A Joycean Irish Story." *Studies in Short Fiction* 30.3 (Summer 1993): 343–48.
Hoogland, Renee C. *Elizabeth Bowen: A Reputation in Writing*. New York: New York University Press, 1994.
Johnson, Toni O'Brien. "Light and Enlightenment in Elizabeth Bowen's Irish Novels." *Ariel* 18 (April 1987): 47–62.

Jordan, Heather Bryant. *How Will the Heart Endure: Elizabeth Bowen and the Landscape of War*. Ann Arbor: Michigan University Press, 1922.

Lassner, Phyllis. "The Past Is a Burning Pattern: Elizabeth Bowen's *The Last September*." *Eire-Ireland* 21.1 (Spring 1986): 40–54.

———. *Elizabeth Bowen*. Savage, MD: Barnes and Noble, 1990.

———. *Elizabeth Bowen: A Study of the Short Fiction*. New York: Twayne, 1991.

Lee, Hermione. *Elizabeth Bowen: An Estimation*. Totowa, NJ: Barnes and Noble, 1981.

McGowan, Martha. "The Enclosed Garden in Elizabeth Bowen's *A World of Love*." *Eire-Ireland* 16.1 (Spring 1981): 55–70.

O' Eaolain, Sean. *The Short Story*. Dublin: Mercier, 1972.

Scanlan, Margaret. "Rumors of War: Elizabeth Bowen's *The Last September* and J. G. Farrell's Troubles." *Eire-Ireland* 20.2 (Summer 1985): 70–89.

Sellery, J'nan M., and William O. Harris. *Elizabeth Bowen: A Bibliography*. Austin: University of Texas Press, 1981.

Trevor, William. "Between Holyhead and Dun Laoghaire." *Times Literary Supplement*, February 6, 1981: 131.

Paul Vincent Carroll

(1900–1968)

John D. Conway

BIOGRAPHY

Paul Vincent Carroll was born at Blackrock in County Louth on July 10, 1900. His father, Michael Carroll, was the dominant influence in Carroll's formative years and the boy's teacher until he entered St. Mary's College, Dundalk, and eventually St. Patrick's Training College, Dublin, a preparatory school for teachers.

At St. Patrick's during those turbulent years culminating in the Easter Rising, Carroll became fascinated with the theater. He "haunted the pit of the Abbey," where he learned the basics of play making as art and as business and came to regard the Abbey as the center for the "spiritual rebirth of the Irish race."

Before Carroll left Dublin in 1920, he observed at first hand killing in the streets, raids by the Black and Tans, tanks maneuvering on O'Connell Street, searches at gunpoint, and life lived under martial law and a curfew. It is not surprising that upon his return to Blackrock, he found his hometown a provincial backwater where no one had heard of the Abbey Theatre or the Irish Dramatic Revival, where clerical control of education was stifling, and where teachers' wages were low. He returned to Dublin and sailed out on a cattle boat for Scotland.

Arriving in Glasgow in 1921, he taught in the state schools in the poorer sections of the city and devoted his spare time to working on his plays, publishing short stories, and reviewing for the Glasgow *Herald*. In 1923 he married Helena Reilly, with whom he had three daughters. In 1930, *The Watched Pot*, a flawed but promising little one-act play, received experimental production at the Abbey's Peacock Theatre. Carroll had gained the attention of W. B. Yeats and Lennox Robinson, and his dramatic career was beginning to take shape.

The 1930s would be the most successful decade of Carroll's career. His home-town and Dublin and his study of Ibsen, Tolstoy, the Augustans, and Synge provided him with both the material and tone for his early plays. Viewing his native Ireland through the eyes of a rebel and teacher, he saw much that needed correcting, especially in education and in the clergy. His focus sharpened, and so did his craft. In 1921 *Things That Are Caesar's* won an award at the Abbey Theatre; in 1938 *Shadow and Substance* won both the Casement Award of the Irish Academy of Letters and the New York Drama Critics Award; and in 1939 *The White Steed*, rejected by the Abbey Theatre, also received the New York award. In fewer than ten years after his first experimental production at the Abbey, the schoolmaster's son, who refused to teach under "the unbearable clerical yoke" in Ireland, would be recognized as a playwright of international stature.

Carroll remarried in 1944 and in 1945 moved to Bromley, Kent, in England. The second marriage (his first wife was deceased) produced a son. Carroll wrote movie scenarios and television scripts for the BBC. In 1955 *The Wayward Saint*, his most compelling work since *Green Cars Go East* (1947), was produced and published. He died on October 20, 1968, in Kent, from a heart condition.

MAJOR WORKS AND THEMES

Shadow and Substance is the play most frequently associated with Carroll, for good reason. Together with *The White Steed* it is recognized by both the academic and theatrical community as his most durable achievement. Its success, first in Dublin and then on Broadway, enabled Carroll to become a full-time playwright at a crucial time in his career. It is a four-act play, with the entire action taking place in Canon Skerritt's parochial house in County Louth.

The principals in the play represent the essentials of Carroll's best dramas: a canon, curates, a servant girl, a schoolmaster, and a village of busybodies and fools dominated by clerical rule. The play is in the mold of the Ibsen well-made play, and its leading character, Canon Skerritt, is based on Jonathan Swift. What distinguishes *Shadow and Substance* from other Carroll dramas with similar characters is the fire of the playwright's rebellion. It is fully realized in the character of the canon, who lacerates every embodiment of ignorance with the cultured arrogance of a man who finds himself an alien among bumbling curates, fatuous parishioners, a rebellious schoolmaster, and a young peasant girl of incorruptible ideals.

The theme that weaves its way throughout *Shadow and Substance* and other major Carroll dramas is protest against what Skerritt calls "the steady vulgari-zation of our life." Carroll exposes whatever he believes to be unreasonable, pompous, or bloated, in the clergy or out of the clergy. It should be noted, however, that if the playwright is often critical of clerical abuse, he is not anti-Catholic. His canons and schoolmasters and young maiden rebels rail against authority, often in the person of imbecilic administrators. With the exception of

Shadow and Substance, however, Carroll's parlor rebellion is stunted. It is as if the schoolmaster's son could not escape the church and "the clerical yoke" that so obsessed him.

Nevertheless the charge that there is but one canon in the Carroll rectory can easily be disproved by *The White Steed*, another of his internationally acclaimed dramas. This play is more extensive in scope than *Shadow and Substance*, as it is based on the Celtic legend of Ossian. Nora Fintry, the rebellious girl around whom the play is built, is Carroll's dramatic link with the legend. Canon Matt Lavelle, elderly and infirm and about to be replaced, becomes her wily ally and a foil to the austere Father Shaughnessy.

Nora, dreaming of Ireland's heroic past, finds present-day Ireland teeming with bigoted priests, intimidated schoolmasters, morals committees, ignorant and spineless peasantry—little people who do not hear the call of Ossian or Niam or Maeve. She is a spiritual descendant of Yeats's peasant: a wonder-struck girl who rides her pagan steed to seek the Ireland of warriors and poets and heroes.

The New York success of *The White Steed* marked the high point of Carroll's dramatic career, and it provided the Irish dramatic movement, which seemed moribund with the approaching death of Yeats in 1939, with new vigor and direction.

The most notable plays to follow *Shadow and Substance* and *The White Steed* include *The Old Foolishness* (1944) and *Green Cars Go East*, which supports its author's contention that he could write a better slum play than Brendan Behan. *The Devil Came from Dublin* (1951), a rollicking "satirical extravaganza," was performed in both Dublin and London with considerable success. The play, earlier titled *The Chuckeyhead Story*, is the happiest and merriest Carroll ever wrote. Its atmosphere of uproarious hilarity bears an affinity in tone to his short story "Me Da Went Off the Bottle!" In 1955 *The Wayward Saint*, a more characteristic Carroll play with Canon McCooey as something of a latter-day St. Francis, received critical praise. In 1958 Devin-Adair issued *Irish Stories and Plays*, which contains the best of Carroll's short fiction, his most charming children's play, and the three-act *The Devil Came from Dublin*, among other selections.

CRITICAL RECEPTION

It is now commonplace to assert, as both scholars and theatrical critics have, that Carroll never lived up to the early technical brilliance of *Shadow and Substance* and *The White Steed*. Various reasons are offered: too indebted to the realism of Ibsen, too cowed by the church, too timid a rebel, too lacking in lyricism, too limited in theme, and too provincial a thinker. Indeed, his most compelling apologist and friend, Robert Hogan, laments in *After the Irish Renaissance* that Carroll is "one of the great failures of Irish letters: after a brilliant beginning he foundered" (53).

It must be remembered, however, that when Carroll began his attack on narrow-minded clerics in *Things That Are Caesar's* (1932), he was all alone. Those who, with some cause, consider his rebellion too timid should consider the Ireland of the early 1930s: a land of censorship and rigid rule by the Catholic Church. Further, no other Irish playwright of Carroll's stature was so persistent in beating the drum of clerical abuse in so hostile an environment, and he did so with a sharp wit and a satire "shot through with savage laughter."

Much more can be attributed to Carroll than *Shadow and Substance*, *The White Steed*, and canons, curates, schoolmasters, and peasant girls. *Green Cars Go East, The Old Foolishness, The Devil Came from Dublin*, a few short satires, and selected children's plays will all reward close study.

To date, Carroll still awaits the comprehensive critical attention he deserves, although Robert Hogan has as we have seen, written with insight and firsthand knowledge of the playwright. Paul Doyle provides a useful introduction and concludes with the observation that "any overall estimate of Carroll's career must indicate that he well deserves a permanent place in contemporary Irish and English drama" (108). In *Age of Yeats* George Brandon Saul places Carroll in the context of the Irish Literary Renaissance and remarks about his plays that "*Shadow and Substance* and *The White Steed* remain preeminent: sufficient justification for any dramatist's career" (363). It is generally acknowledged that Carroll has few peers among Irish playwrights in portraying the Irish clergy, as John Mason Brown makes clear in *Broadway in Review*: "[W]hen it comes to his drawing of Canon Matt Lavelle and Father Shaughnessy he works with a master's skill" (208). Other critics who have helped establish a balanced perspective concerning Carroll's dramatic achievements include George Jean Nathan, Anne Gertrude Colman, Drew Pallette, Christopher Fitz-Simon (in *The Irish Theatre*), and John D. Conway.

Nevertheless, Carroll has in recent years received little attention from either the academic or theatrical community. His adherence to the concept of the well-made play, his belief in a divine plan, and his insistence on the necessity of both innocence and love are easily dismissed in a secular age. Within the context of the Irish Dramatic Revival he remains, however, a compelling voice. His characterizations, his technical brilliance, his wit, and his satirical attack on sham wherever he finds it reveal him as a worthy successor to Yeats, Synge, and the early O'Casey.

BIBLIOGRAPHY

Works by Paul Vincent Carroll

Plays

The Watched Pot (produced Peacock Theatre, Dublin, 1930). Unpublished.
Things That Are Caesar's. London: Rich and Cowan, 1934.
The White Steed and *Coggerers* (later retitled *Conspirators*). New York: Random House, 1939.

Plays for My Children. New York: Messner, 1939.

Kindred (produced Abbey Theatre, Dublin, 1939). Unpublished. Rev. form: *The Secret Kindred*. Unpublished.

The Old Foolishness. London: French, 1944.

Three Plays: The White Steed; Things That Are Caesar's; The Strings, My Lord, Are False. London: Macmillan, 1944. [Rev. version of *Things That Are Caesar's*.]

Green Cars Go East. London: French, 1947.

Interlude. London: French, 1947.

Conspirators. London: French, 1947.

The Wise Have Not Spoken. London: French, 1947.

The Wayward Saint. New York: Dramatist Play Service, 1955.

The Devil Came from Dublin (as *The Chuckeyhead Story*, produced Pavilion Theatre, Bournemouth, 1950; rev. version as *The Border Be Damned*, produced 1951; further rev. version, as *The Devil Came from Dublin*, produced John Drew Memorial Theatre, East Hampton, New York, 1951). In *Irish Stories and Plays*, 1958.

Farewell to Greatness. Dixon, CA: Proscenium, 1966.

Goodbye to the Summer [earlier version titled *Weep for Tomorrow*]. Newark, DE: Proscenium, 1970. Rev.

We Have Ceased to Live. *Journal of Irish Literature* 2.1 (January 1972).

Screenplay

Saints and Sinners (with Leslie Arliss), 1949.

Studies of Paul Vincent Carroll

Brown, John Mason. "Ireland and *The White Steed*." *Broadway in Review* (1940): 205–8.

Colman, Anne G. "Paul Vincent Carroll's View of Irish Life." *Catholic World* 192 (1960): 87–93.

Conway, John D. "Paul Vincent Carroll's Major Dramatic Triumphs." *Connecticut Review* 6.2 (1975): 61–69.

———. "Paul Vincent Carroll and the Theatre in Scotland." *Eire-Ireland* 12.4 (1977): 125–32.

———. "The Satires of Paul Vincent Carroll." *Eire-Ireland* 8.3 (1972): 13–23.

Doyle, Paul A. *Paul Vincent Carroll*. Lewisburg, PA: Bucknell University Press, 1971.

Nathan, George Jean. "The Devil Came from Dublin." *Theatre Arts* 35 (1951): 66–67.

Pallette, Drew B. "Paul Vincent Carroll—Since *The White Steed*." *Modern Drama* 7 (1965): 375–81.

Ciaran Carson

(1948–)

Maryann Donahue

BIOGRAPHY

Born in Belfast in 1948, Ciaran Carson grew up in an Irish-speaking family. His father had left school at a young age but had retained a passion for reading and storytelling that he passed on to his children in the form of nightly bedside stories. Based on folktales and popular novels or created entirely from his own imagination, these stories shaped Carson's childhood and influenced the form that his poetry would later take. At the age of eleven, Carson learned to play the tin whistle and the mouth organ, and he began to write poetry in his teens. He was educated at a Christian Brothers school and then at Queen's University, Belfast, where he participated in a literary group founded by Philip Hobsbaum in the 1960s and influenced by the work of Seamus Heaney. After graduating from Queen's, he worked as civil servant, teacher, and musician. In 1975 he became traditional arts officer for the Northern Ireland Arts Council, a position that involves collecting, recording, and playing Irish music. Carson continues to reside in Belfast, where he now serves as literature and traditional arts officer of the Arts Council.

MAJOR WORKS AND THEMES

The New Estate (1976) is a collection of carefully crafted lyric poems organized chronologically from medieval to modern subjects. The first poems and the translations of Welsh and early Irish lyrics scattered throughout the book display Carson's thorough engagement with traditional Irish culture. They express the beauty of that culture while providing an ironic, often humorous, commentary on its limitations. Subsequent poems display Carson's fascination with the ordinary, cyclical events, such as housepainting and chimney cleaning, that characterize modern domestic life. The varied collection is held together by Carson's interest in work and craftsmanship. His use of craft as subject matter in poems such as "Linen," "Belleek," and "The Casting of the Bell" is accentuated by his own precisely wrought lines and by the reproductions of old woodcuts, depicting potters, builders, and masons, that appear throughout the book. The poems are also unified by their exploration of what Carson describes as "dialects of silence" (22). Critics tend to focus on the differences in form and style between *The New Estate* and *The Irish for No* (1987), thus overlooking the continuities between the two. In "An Early Bed," as in the poems of the later volume, a sensory detail causes the narrator to recall an earlier event. Haiku-like poems such as "House-Painting" and "Moving In," which contain epiphanies whose full meanings ultimately elude the reader, anticipate the resistance to unified "truth" and the play with multiple possibilities of meaning that characterize Carson's more experimental work.

The Irish for No signals a drastic change in Carson's style. In this book, he draws from his musical experiences, creating unusually long lines that approximate the movements of an Irish reel as well as the flow of chatter that accompanies a pub session. Of the volume's three parts, the first and third contain long, often humorous narratives in which Carson combines the oral and the literary by integrating rich allusions with the rhythms and syntax of ordinary speech. In poems such as "Whatever Sleep It Is" and "Calvin Klein's *Obsession*," he reveals the impact of the imagination on memory through his narrators' recollections of past events. In these longer poems, he also explores the creative process, using digression triggered by sensory impressions to move his stories in unexpected directions. The middle section contains shorter pieces that address the Troubles more directly and provide a political context for the longer narratives. A virtual catalog of army paraphernalia, consumer products, and place-names, these poems display Carson's obsession with the material fragments of Belfast. Through them he pieces together an intricate map of the city in its state of violence and decay.

Belfast Confetti (1989) represents a development of the themes and techniques of *The Irish for No*. Carson again uses his characteristic long lines, combining extended narrative and nine-line poems with prose passages and translations of Japanese haiku. Although varied in form, the individual pieces are drawn together by the complex set of symbols that Carson weaves into the work. The image of confetti, associated in various poems with gunfire, blood, snow, urban debris thrown by rioters, and Carson's own words, holds in creative tension the book's conflicting themes of violence, decay, and celebration. Like its predecessor, *Belfast Confetti* is firmly rooted in the topography of Carson's native city, and images of the mutilation, enclosure, and surveillance to which its inhabitants are subjected dominate the book. As always, the pessimistic tone conveyed in these poems is offset by Carson's wry wit and ironic sense of humor. Much of the volume is devoted to an exploration of the ambiguous relationship between language and external reality. The changing physical landscape of Belfast evades symbolic representation, and language itself takes on a material existence when used to describe a conflict that is, Carson believes, "as much a war of words as anything" (Ormsby 6).

First Language (1993) is more experimental and less tied to the realistic depiction of contemporary Belfast than Carson's previous books. Here he attempts to make the familiar unfamiliar by introducing elements of surrealism and science fiction into his representation of the Ulster dialect and locale. As the title of the volume indicates, *First Language* displays Carson's continuing fascination with linguistic limitations and possibilities. In poems such as "Second Language," "*Tak, Tak,*" and others, he describes the process of language acquisition, explores the complexities of translation, and asserts the primacy of linguistic representation. Pictured on the cover, the Tower of Babel is a recurrent image of the breakdown in communication that has occurred in Carson's world, where the inability of different sides to reach an agreement has had devastating consequences. Yet *First Language* is not simply an indictment of the violence that erupts when verbal communication fails. Babel also recalls an oppressive attempt to impose a single ideology on a diverse group of people. By dismantling traditional literary forms and fracturing language to expose its inherent ambiguities, Carson playfully forces the reader to acknowledge the multiplicity of meanings both in his work and in the world beyond its pages.

CRITICAL RECEPTION

The critical response to Carson's work has been overwhelmingly positive both in Ireland and abroad. *The New Estate* has received praise from reviewers for its formal, aesthetic beauty as well as for its novelistic attention to the details of domestic life. There has, however, been some disagreement about the book's cohesiveness. Tom Paulin praises the realism of the later poems and concludes that the "flimsy" efforts on early Irish subjects "don't really belong to the volume" (*Honest Ulsterman* [January/April 1976]: 86–89). In contrast, Mark Ford sees the entire work as a successful attempt to connect meaningfully "the sprawl of modern living" and traditional Irish culture (*London Review of Books* [January 19, 1989]: 14).

Critics agree that the enormous potential displayed in Carson's first book is realized in *The Irish for No* and *Belfast Confetti*. Several have recently explored the creative tensions that make these works compelling. Gerald Dawe applauds the contrast between Carson's "Eliot-like vision" of "the collected life in the literally deconstructed city of Belfast" and the traditional storytelling methods he employs to convey this vision (*Linen Hall Review* 4.3 [1987]: 24–25). In *The Chosen Ground*, Neil Corcoran notes the "high degree of well-shaped formality" that accompanies the "apparently wanderingly digressive thread" of its narratives (218).

Scholars have also attempted to situate *The Irish for No* and *Belfast Confetti* in relation to postmodern critical theory and practice. Guinn Batten explores Carson's postmodern development of the themes and techniques of Louis Mac-Neice's poetry, while Corcoran and Rand Brandes describe his work as a departure from the modernist poetics of Seamus Heaney. Sean O'Brien aligns Carson with postmodernism yet distinguishes *Belfast Confetti* from other recent collections of poetry in its "sense of the capacity and obligation of language to refer outwards as well as to know itself" (*Honest Ulsterman* 1991: 93–97).

Arguably more postmodern in its outlook, *First Language* has attracted critical attention for its ironic approach to "authentic" experience, for which it has been compared with the work of Paul Muldoon. Thus far, most critics have followed the developments in Carson's oeuvre with delight, praising his increasingly experimental form and style. Clair Wills stands out in her opposition to the direction Carson has taken in his most recent work, which she finds "disappointingly contrived and overloaded" in its "thoroughgoing fragmentation" (*Times Literary Supplement* [March 25, 1994]: 23).

BIBLIOGRAPHY

Works by Ciaran Carson

The New Estate. Belfast: Blackstaff, 1976.
The Pocket Guide to Irish Traditional Music. Belfast: Appletree, 1986.
The Irish for No. Dublin: Gallery, 1987.
Belfast Confetti. Dublin: Gallery, 1989.
The New Estate and Other Poems. Dublin: Gallery, 1989.
First Language. Dublin: Gallery, 1993.
Letters from the Alphabet. Dublin: Gallery, 1995.

Studies of Ciaran Carson

Batten, Guinn. "Ciaran Carson's Parturient Partition: The 'Crack' in MacNeice's 'More than Glass.' " *The Southern Review* 31.3 (1995): 536–56.
Brandes, Rand. "Ciaran Carson." *Irish Review* 8 (1990): 77–90.
———. "The Dismembering Muse: Seamus Heaney, Ciaran Carson, and Kenneth Burke's 'Four Master Tropes.' " *Bucknell Review* 38.1 (1994): 177–94.
Ormsby, Frank. "Interview with Ciaran Carson." *Linen Hall Review* (April 1991): 5–8.

Austin Clarke

(1896–1974)

Shawn Holliday

BIOGRAPHY

Augustine Joseph Clarke was born in Dublin on May 9, 1896, of both Celtic and Catholic heritage. His father was a civil servant with nationalist leanings, while his mother adhered strictly to Catholicism and stern Victorian values. At age seven, he entered Belvedere College, the school later made famous in Joyce's *Portrait* (1916). During the 1909–1910 school year, Clarke left Dublin for County Limerick, where he studied at another Jesuit institution, Mungret College. While there, Clarke heard poetry being read aloud for the first time. He had such a positive emotional response to the intricate sounds of language that at the precocious age of fourteen, Clarke decided that he wanted to become a poet. Upon his return to Dublin and Belvedere College, he began attending Annie Horniman's Abbey Theatre, which would provide the impetus for his later interest in poetic drama based on Irish myth and tradition. In his mid- to late teens, Clarke saw plays by George Moore, Lady Gregory, and Yeats. The only things spoiling Clarke's life at this time were his first serious attacks of depression, a problem that would plague him the rest of his life.

In 1916, the year of the Easter Rising, Clarke received his B.A. from University College, Dublin. Only one year later, he graduated from the same institution with a first-class honors M.A., having written his thesis on playwright John Ford. These five years at the university were active ones for Clarke. Besides continuing his studies of literature written in English, he also began learning Gaelic, becoming competent enough to read the old Irish myths in the original—something Yeats never learned to do. Upon his graduation in 1917, University College offered Clarke a three-year teaching position as lecturer in English. In this same year, Clarke began his literary career by publishing his first book of poems, *The Vengeance of Fionn*. Despite this auspicious literary beginning, Clarke's personal life began slowly to fall apart. Between 1917 and 1919, the poet's father unexpectedly died, and Clarke's love for fellow novelist and playwright Lia Cummins remained unrequited. Troubled again with bouts of depression, Clarke had a nervous breakdown in 1919. For over a year, he was hospitalized for treatment in St. Patrick's Hospital. After his release, Cummins agreed to marry Clarke. However, the couple stayed together for only ten days, and their marriage was not consummated. When AE flatly criticized Clarke's third book of poetry, *The Sword of the West* (1921), the poet could no longer stand living in Ireland. Clarke fled to London in 1922, where he earned most of his living writing book reviews for major English newspapers and journals. He would spend most of the next fifteen years in self-imposed exile.

While in England, Clarke published three books of verse, put together his first volume of *Collected Poems* (1936), and wrote many early plays and his first two prose romances. Much to the author's chagrin, his novels *The Bright Temptation* (1932) and *The Singing Men at Cashel* (1936) were banned in Ireland for being obscene and sacrilegious. Ironically, both were published in England without incident. On a return trip home to visit his mother and sisters, Clarke met Nora Walker and married her in 1930. Upon their permanent return to Ireland in 1937, the author settled at Bridge House, Templeogue, only to find his literary reputation waning: *The Singing Men at Cashel* had fallen apart in the final chapters, and Yeats had omitted Clarke from his *Oxford Book of Modern Verse* (1936). When the poet published *Night and Morning* (1938), it was his last volume of poetry to appear for seventeen years. With the added pressure of financially supporting a growing family, Clarke experienced recurrent bouts of depression and had another nervous breakdown in 1939.

During the 1940s, the author stayed active by turning his attention to verse drama. Along with Robert Farren, Clarke helped to establish the Dublin Verse Speaking Society and the Lyric Theater Company. With these two organizations, he read dramatic poetry over Radio Eireann and produced many of his plays at the Abbey and Peacock Theatres. By accepting his nomination for membership in the Irish Academy of Letters in 1941, Clarke became an ever increasingly important public man and began writing weekly book reviews for the *Irish Times*. In 1955, Clarke returned to poetry with the satiric volume *Ancient Lights*. Although he suffered a heart attack in 1959, he still managed to foster his newfound concern for Ireland's public affairs. In 1966, he wrote what many consider to be his most important contribution to modern poetry, *Mnemosyne Lay in Dust* (1966), a poem that recounts the horrors of his first mental breakdown. Late in his life, Clarke produced several more volumes of poems and was barraged with many literary awards and honors, among which was a nomination for the Nobel Prize in literature. Clarke died in 1974, shortly before the Dolmen Press would publish his *Collected Poems*, thus putting an end to a highly troubled, but eclectic, literary career.

MAJOR WORKS AND THEMES

Much of Austin Clarke's early verse reflects his preoccupation with the major themes and concerns of the Irish Literary Revival. Like Yeats, Douglas Hyde, and George Russell, Clarke relied on the Irish mythological cycles for much of his early subject matter. With his highly acclaimed first book, *The Vengeance of Fionn* (1917), Clarke relies on the story of Diarmuid and Grainne to express his concern for the impossibility of ideal love, while his narratively troubled third book, *The Sword of the West* (1921), does little but feed Clarke's fascination with Irish mythology by romanticizing the tales of Cuchulain.

Although medieval Ireland would continue to provide the setting for many of his verse plays, in *Pilgrimage and Other Poems* (1929) Clarke moved from the romantic poetry of the Revival to focus on the more relevant issue of Catholic guilt. His main concern at this time seems to be the ongoing conflict between private conscience and church orthodoxy. This theme manifests itself in *Pilgrimage* simply as a conflict between man's sexual desire and clerical teaching. However, by the time Clarke wrote the overly confessional *Night and Morning* (1938), he extended his concern to the struggle between reason and faith by focusing on the human need for intellectual freedom. Although he abandoned poetry during the 1940s, Clarke continued to grapple with these issues in his three prose romances and in many of his verse plays. With these works, he did not refer directly to the current issues of Irish society. Instead, Clarke often used the setting of medieval Ireland to show how an unenlightened church can cause mental confusion and individual suffering for its congregation.

With *Ancient Lights* (1955), Clarke returned to poetry by creating a more public voice that addressed a wide range of contemporary social issues. He used short, satiric poems to focus on political injustice, and he returned to long, narrative poems to address the development and exploration of his own life. After the poet visited Mount Parnassus in Greece during 1962, he began a ten-week writing frenzy that resulted in *Flight to Africa* (1963), considered by many to be his best book of verse. By having slowly rebuilt his confidence through late poetic success, Clarke was eventually able to address his nervous breakdown of 1919 by writing his magnum opus, *Mnemosyne Lay in Dust*. For the first time in his career, Clarke fully addressed, in a single poem, the issues that so adversely dominated his young life: sexual repression, Catholic guilt, racial confusion, and intellectual despair. However, after 1966, Clarke's work shows a marked decline in power. For many readers, his later poetry remains obscure due to his intense focus on daily events, leaving us with little reference to universal concerns.

CRITICAL RECEPTION

Many of Clarke's contemporaries cite his successful attempt at incorporating Gaelic assonance into English poetry as the author's major accomplishment. In

A Tribute to Austin Clarke (1966), John Montague claims that the elder poet helped the younger generation "to learn how to write English poetry, with an Irish accent" (10). Christopher Ricks, in the same volume, agrees that Clarke's verse is "exquisite to the ear," but he also believes that the poet's extensive use of anagrams makes his work more "revealing to the eye, too" (18), thus successfully linking the aural and visual elements of written poetry. However, being more judgmental, Thomas Kinsella admits that Clarke's writing is often "uneven" and poor in quality. In his introduction to Clarke's *Selected Poems* (1976), Kinsella cites the poet's powers of observation, his attention to sensory details, and his quest for intellectual freedom to be the most engaging aspects of his work.

Although Clarke's poetry came to overshadow the plays during his lifetime, today's scholars are turning much of their attention to the author's verse dramas in an attempt to establish him as an important modern playwright. Unlike many verse plays, Clarke's works are not considered closet dramas. Audiences need to experience them in the theater to understand fully the author's metrical innovations with sound, especially his use of assonance and lyrics spoken to music.

A good place to start investigating Clarke's work is Maurice Harmon's *Austin Clarke: A Critical Introduction* (1989). Besides giving a thorough discussion of the author's poetry, plays, and novels, Harmon provides a helpful introductory section that places Clarke's work within the contexts of the Irish Literary Revival and modern Irish history. Also interesting is Donald Davie's discussion of Clarke and Padraic Fallon in Dunn's *Two Decades of Irish Writing: A Critical Survey* (1975). In his chapter, Davie discusses how the poet dealt with the troubled legacy and influence of Yeats, while also focusing on the "irresponsible and inexcusable" obscurity of Clarke's later work (47).

BIBLIOGRAPHY

Selected Works by Austin Clarke

Novels

The Bright Temptation: A Romance. London: Allen and Unwin, 1932; New York: Morrow, 1932.
The Singing Men at Cashel. London: Allen and Unwin, 1936.
The Sun Dances at Easter: A Romance. London: Melrose, 1952.

Selected Poetry

Ancient Lights: Poems and Satires. Dublin: Bridge, 1953.
The Cattledrive in Connaught. London: Allen and Unwin, 1925.
Collected Poems. Ed. Liam Miller. Dublin: Dolmen, 1974; London, Oxford, and New York: Oxford University Press, 1974.
Flight to Africa. Dublin: Dolmen, 1963.

Mnemosyne Lay in Dust. Dublin: Dolmen, 1966; London: Oxford University Press, 1966;
   Chester Springs: Dufour, 1966.
Night and Morning: Poems. Dublin: Orwell, 1938.
Pilgrimage. London: Allen and Unwin, 1929; New York: Farrar and Rinehart, 1930.
Selected Poems. Ed. Thomas Kinsella. Dublin: Dolmen, 1976; Winston-Salem, NC:
   Wake Forest University Press, 1976.
Selected Poems. Ed. Hugh Maxton. Winston-Salem, NC: Wake Forest University Press,
   1991.
The Sword of the West. Dublin: Maunsel and Roberts, 1921.
Tiresias, a Poem. Dublin: Bridge, 1971.
The Vengeance of Fionn. Dublin: Maunsel, 1917.

   Plays

Collected Plays. Dublin: Dolmen, 1963.

Studies of Austin Clarke

Halpern, Susan. *Austin Clarke: His Life and Works*. Dublin: Dolmen, 1974.
Harmon, Maurice. "Ancient Lights in the Poetry of Austin Clarke and Thomas Kin-
   sella." *Eire-Ireland* 29.1 (1994): 123–40.
———. *Austin Clarke: A Critical Introduction*. Totowa, NJ: Barnes and Noble, 1989.
Liddy, James. " 'Pity and Love beyond Our Buoys': The 'Simple Tale' of Austin
   Clarke's Poetics." *Concerning Poetry* 14.2 (1981): 47–75.
Lucy, Sean. "The Poetry of Austin Clarke." *Canadian Journal of Irish Studies* 9.2
   (1983): 5–12.
Lyne, Gerard. "Austin Clarke—A Bibliography." *Irish University Review* 4 (1974): 13–
   25.
Montague, John, ed. *A Tribute to Austin Clarke on His Seventieth Birthday*. Dublin:
   Dolmen, 1966.
Shirmer, Gregory A. " 'A Mad Discordancy': Austin Clarke's Early Narrative Poems."
   Eire-Ireland 16.2 (1981): 16–28.

Mary M. Colum

(1884–1957)

Taura S. Napier

BIOGRAPHY

Mary Colum was born in Collooney, County Sligo, on June 13, 1884. She attended the National University in Dublin, where she was one of Yeats's student advocates. After graduating, she cofounded the *Irish Review* with David Houston and three of her colleagues from Pearse's teaching staff: James Stephens, Thomas MacDonagh, and her future husband, the author Padraic Colum. In 1914, she and Padraic moved to the United States, where they would permanently reside and where she would establish her reputation as a literary journalist and woman of letters.

During her career, Mary Colum wrote over 160 articles and reviews for a host of important newspapers and journals. During the 1930s she was literary editor of *Forum* magazine; during the 1940s she originated and edited the poetry review column of *The New York Times Book Review*. Colum also published short stories in European and American collections, lectured throughout the United States on literature and criticism, and ended her career with a course in comparative literature at Columbia University that she co-taught with Padraic, while writing her reminiscences of Joyce, until her death. In addition to *Our Friend James Joyce* (1958), Mary Colum produced two other books: *From These Roots: The Ideas That Have Made Modern Literature* (1937), a work that is still hailed as the first book of comparative criticism, and her autobiography, *Life and the Dream* (1947).

MAJOR WORKS AND THEMES

The *Irish Review* was founded to make the works of Revival artists known in Ireland, Europe, and America; it quickly became an outlet for new works of

Irish literature and art, including the first of Stephens's short stories, Pearse's poems in Irish, and artworks of Jack B. Yeats. According to Padraic Colum, Mary held the "office of critic-in-chief," but in her autobiography she remembers her position differently:

I was the only girl in this group, and being some years younger than the men, I was well bossed and patronised by them. They were determined to write the body of the magazine themselves—the poetry, the stories, the plays, the articles, and the editorial notes. But they decided to let me do some book reviewing in the back pages in small type. (*Life and the Dream* 137)

Such relegation did not discourage her. For the first issue of the journal in March 1911, she wrote an essay review of the *Collected Works of John Synge*, which had just been published.

"John Synge" marked Mary's entrance into the spotlight of literary Dublin. It attracted the attention of academics and general readers alike for its unconventionality, comparing great artists with makers of melodrama and serial shockers in that both find their audience not in rarefied cliques but among the multitudes, "strong men and thieves and deacons." She writes: "An audience of these full blooded folk was what Synge looked to. Every great artist desires such an audience. Every great artist in the end gets it." She refers to the *Playboy* riots, angry that "a howling multitude of the fine buoyant folk of the pit hissed and outraged [the *Playboy*]. . . . This is one of the things for which their children's children will be ashamed of their forebears." Conversely, she reserves special praise for Synge's female characters:

They are the most live women in modern drama. [Synge] scorned the psychological minuteness of what are called the intellectual dramatists, who break up into little pieces the souls of their personages for examination. . . . None of Ibsen's painfully analysed women are as live and natural as Nora Bourke, or Deirdre, or Pegeen Mike. (39)

From this point, Mary was in fact critic-in-chief of the *Irish Review*. Before the journal ceased publication, she wrote six features, in addition to various review articles. In these, her first critical pieces, she attempted to revolutionize what she describes in her autobiography as "that thoughtless and patronising praise that passes for criticism in Dublin" and would continue to revolutionize the arena of literary criticism throughout the modernist period.

Colum's career was characterized by writing techniques that befitted the experimental nature of modern writing, yet that, unlike the works of most of her contemporaries, were concerned with making usually inaccessible modernist literary styles comprehensible to the reading public. Her audiences consisted of what Woolf described as "common readers," those who were not interested in purely academic articles and who found popular writing beneath their intellectual abilities. As she charted the trends that shaped modern writing through the eighteenth and nineteenth centuries in *From These Roots* and continued to do so for the modernist period in her articles, Colum spoke simply and eloquently to readers outside the academic arena. As she writes of her audience in *Life and the Dream*: "I never underestimated the intelligence of my readers which is, I think, a great fault with editors" (413).

Colum's articles combine the book review, literary history, editorial, position paper, and essay in a discussion of five or six contemporary books, a method of writing that John Gross identifies as particular to the early twentieth century, when critics sought to bridge the gap between the artist and the reading public by approaching the text from several interdisciplinary angles. Colum often acted as a "double agent" between the literary establishment and the intelligent reader, at once enticing her audience with straightforward descriptions of new books and discussing their literary/historical influences. She defines the purpose of criticism in a *Forum* article, "On Thinking Critically":

Criticism is a principle through which the world of ideas renews itself. At its highest . . . literary criticism is the creation of profound, informing, and transforming ideas about life as well as literature, for no man can understand literature without a comprehension of life, the subject of literature.

Colum believed that education should be an ongoing endeavor and that it could best take place when readers turned to works outside their own discipline in order to develop a balanced view of the world or just to make sense of it. Her works reflect this: *Life and the Dream* can be identified at once as a literary autobiography, a history of political and intellectual Dublin in the early twentieth century, and a portrait gallery for personages from Yeats to Eleanor Roosevelt. *From These Roots* is at once comparative criticism and historical drama. *Our Friend James Joyce* is memoir and critical commentary; coauthored with Padraic, it further illuminates Joyce as a writer and comrade.

CRITICAL RECEPTION

In a 1935 letter to *Forum*, Eugene O'Neill named Colum as "one of the few true critics of literature writing in English." William Benét wrote of her, "Everyone of sapience knows that Mary M. Colum is the best woman critic in America. There is no one in her class." J. Donald Adams maintained, "Mrs. Colum reminds us of the propulsive force behind creative critical ideas, how they have molded the literature of modern times, how greatly they are needed to mold the literature of the immediate future."

Colum's autobiography was praised by Edmund Wilson for its detailed portraits of twentieth-century *littérateurs* whom Colum had known, among them Yeats, Maud Gonne, and Lady Gregory. He further commended Colum on "an insight into people and societies at once so sympathetic and so shrewd, and so humane an outlook on so large a slice of the world." Other critics have named

Life and the Dream as an essential component of the literary history of Dublin, London, New York, and Chicago during the early twentieth century. Although Colum's works have remained out of print and are used primarily as source-books for other writers, their interest and readability endure.

Mary Colum grew and flourished with the Irish Literary Revival. She would spread the ideas forged in Ireland throughout the world, gaining fame, like her friend James Joyce, by writing from the viewpoint of the self-exile and by fostering the exchange of ideas and writing methods between two continents.

BIBLIOGRAPHY

Works by Mary M. Colum

Books

From These Roots: The Ideas That Have Made Modern Literature. New York: Scribner's, 1937.
Life and the Dream. New York: Doubleday, and London: Macmillan, 1947.
Our Friend James Joyce. New York: Doubleday, 1958.

Periodical Selections

"John Synge." *The Irish Review* 1.1 (March 1911): 39–43.
"Life and Literature" column. *Forum* (December 1933–April 1940).
"The New Books of Poetry" column. *The New York Times Book Review* (November 1941–March 1943).

Studies of Mary M. Colum

Adams, J. Donald. "The Ideas That Have Made Modern Literature." Rev. of *From These Roots. The New York Times Book Review* (December 19, 1937), 2.
Benét, William Rose. "A Colum as Columnist." *The Saturday Review of Literature*, (October 28, 1933), 221.
Napier, Taura. "Critic as Artist: Mary Colum and the Ideals of Literary Expression." *The Canadian Journal of Irish Studies* 19.1 (July 1993): 54–66.
Rimo, Patricia A. "Mollie Colum and Her Circle." *Irish Literary Supplement* 4.2 (Fall 1985): 27–28.
Wilson, Edmund. "The Memoirs of Mary Colum." Rev. of *Life and the Dream. The New Yorker* (March 22, 1947), 109–13.

Padraic Colum

(1881–1972)

Sanford Sternlicht

BIOGRAPHY

Padraic Colum prided himself in telling people that of his generation of Irish writers he was the only one who was peasant-born and Roman Catholic. He meant, of course, that he was deeply rooted in the Irish soil. Colum was born on December 8, 1881, the first of eight children of Patrick Collumb, last of an ancient line of the peasant farmers but a graduate of the National School and a teacher in, and later master of, the Longford workhouse. His mother, Susan McCormack Collumb, was the daughter of a gardener. Colum loved to tell people that he was born in a workhouse but neglected to mention that his father was running the place.

At seventeen, with only eight years of formal education, Padraic Colum passed an examination for a clerkship in the Irish Railway Clearing House on Kildare Street in Dublin. After a nine-hour workday in a six-day workweek, he wrote poetry and plays. Soon Arthur Griffith, the publisher, Sein Fein leader, and later first president of the free Ireland, was his patron.

Griffith published poems and short plays by Colum, one of which, "The Saxon Shillin'," won a prize for a drama that would discourage young Irishmen from enlisting in the British army. As a result, Colum was invited by Frank and Willie (W. G.) Fay to join the newly formed Irish National Dramatic Company as both playwright and actor; soon the company joined with the Irish Literary Theater founded by Yeats, Lady Gregory, George Moore, and Edward Martyn. Under the new name, the Irish National Theatre Company, the great Irish national theater, the Abbey, was established.

Colum's first full-length play was *Broken Soil*, later rewritten as *The Fiddler's House*. But his second, *The Land*, which opened at the newly acquired Abbey

Theatre on June 9, 1905, gave the theater its initial triumph. Unfortunately, the headstrong young man quarreled with Yeats and the Fays and quit the company. The Abbey performed Colum's last successful commercial play, *Thomas Muskerry*, in 1910, and although Colum continued to write plays for the rest of his life and always considered himself a playwright first, his continuing significance as a writer lay in poetry, folklore, and children's books.

Colum's first book of poetry, *Wild Earth*, was published in 1907 and well received. At the age of twenty-six Padraic Colum was an important, recognized playwright and poet. In 1912 Colum married Mary Gunning Maguire. Unable to earn a satisfactory livelihood as writers in Dublin, the couple emigrated to the United States in 1914, settling in New York City. There Colum continued to write poetry and plays but earned his primary living as a writer of books for children.

In 1916 *Wild Earth and Other Poems* was published in New York, and it established Colum as an important voice on the American poetry scene. The collection was revised and added to in 1922, 1927, and 1950. In the 1920s the Colums visited their friends the Joyces in Paris, and Colum typed some of *Finnegans Wake*. Later, Padraic and Mary would write *Our Friend James Joyce* (1958). The Hawaiian legislature invited Colum to come and codify the folklore of the islands, resulting in *At the Gateways of the Day* (1924), *The Bright Islands* (1925), and the compilation of the two: *Legends of Hawaii* (1937).

Colum tried fiction, but his two novels, *Castle Conquer* (1923) and *The Flying Swans* (1957), were not commercially successful. Poetry collections such as *Dramatic Legends and Other Poems* (1922), *Creatures* (1927), *Old Pastures* (1930), and *Poems* (1932) were more successful. His reputation as a poet waned in the 1940s and 1950s, when he published *The Collected Poems of Padraic Colum* (1953). But in his old age Colum returned to Irish themes and a renewed celebrity with *Irish Elegies* (1958, 1961, 1966), *Images of Departure* (1969), and four Noh plays on Irish subjects, based on the Yeats model.

Mary Colum died in 1957. Padraic Colum died in Enfield, Connecticut, on January 11, 1972. He is buried in St. Finton Cemetery, Sutton, County Dublin, in the same grave with his beloved Molly.

MAJOR WORKS AND THEMES

Padraic Colum was an Irish patriot and lover of the country people and the land itself. His play *The Land* established the peasant play as a staple of the Irish national theater. His third play, the tragedy *Thomas Muskerry*, has been called the *King Lear* of Irish drama.

But it is as a lyric poet that Colum will be best remembered. The beauty and discipline of his verse, his concentration on small subjects like flowers, his surety, and his unquestioning belief in God are the foundations of his achievement as a poet.

The Wild Earth established his early reputation, and as long as he was emotionally, if not geographically, close to Ireland, his poetry was highly effective and well regarded—thus the success of *Dramatic Legends* and *Old Pastures* and the revisions and additions to *Wild Earth*. As he settled fully into the New York scene and the international literary set, his work suffered so that his collection of *Creatures, Flowers Pieces*, and *The Vegetable Kingdom* did not advance his reputation.

In his last years, after his wife died and he took her body back to Ireland, Colum renewed his bonds to his mother country, producing in a series of *Irish Elegies* powerful and poignant biographical poems about deceased friends who had contributed to the winning of Irish independence or to the creation of Ireland's international reputation for art and literature.

Images of Departure, Colum's last work, is his farewell to Dublin, Ireland, his friends, his memories, and his life. It is one of the finest Irish poetry collections of the last half of the twentieth century.

Colum conceptualized the early modern Irish poet as a peasant bard, a preserver of the oral tradition, a storyteller with dramatic skill, a codifier of mores, and a conveyer of cultural values. Today Colum's lyrics are read and memorized by thousands of Irish schoolchildren yearly, though often they do not learn or remember the author's name. They know only that the poet is from "olden times," while the beautiful poems tell them of, and teach them about, the past. Thus, Padraic Colum has become both a national poet and an anonymous bard. It is exactly as he would have wished.

CRITICAL RECEPTION

Padraic Colum has long been recognized as an early contributor to the development of the Irish national theater and one of the significant Irish poets of the twentieth century. The poet Padraic Fiacc wrote: "Colum was a link to me, a younger writer, with an Ireland that had so withered already it might never have existed. . . . About the man himself is always the boy who stood at the workhouse window and watched the wandering, rootless Ireland of the children of the great hunger."

Yeats said of the young Colum, "He has read a great deal, especially of dramatic literature, and is I think, a man of genius in the first dark gropings of thought." Unlike Yeats, Colum never groped deeply in thought. He was content to feel deeply about his country, his wife, his friends, and the poor, hardworking people of the rural Ireland of his youth.

BIBLIOGRAPHY

Works by Padraic Colum

Poetry

Wild Earth. A Book of Verse. Dublin: Maunsel, 1907.
Wild Earth, and Other Poems. New York: Holt, 1916.

Dramatic Legends and Other Poems. New York and London: Macmillan, 1922.
Creatures. New York: Macmillan, 1927.
Old Pastures. New York: Macmillan, 1930.
Poems. New York and London: Macmillan, 1932.
The Story of Loury Maen. New York and London: Macmillan, 1937.
Flower Pieces. Dublin: Orwell, 1938.
The Collected Poems of Padraic Colum. New York: Devin-Adair, 1953.
The Vegetable Kingdom. Bloomington: Indiana University Press, 1954.
Ten Poems. Dublin: Dolmen, 1957.
Irish Elegies. Dublin: Dolmen, 1958, 1961 1966 (later additions with changes.)
The Poet's Circuits. Collected Poems of Ireland. London: Oxford University Press, 1960.
Images of Departure. Dublin: Dolmen, 1969.
Selected Poems of Padraic Colum. Ed. Sanford Sternlicht. Syracuse: Syracuse University
    Press, 1989.

Drama

The Land. Dublin: Abbey Theatre, 1905.
The Fiddler's House. Dublin: Maunsel, 1907.
Thomas Muskerry. Dublin: Maunsel, 1910.
The Desert. Dublin: Devereux, 1912.
Mogu the Wanderer. Boston: Little, Brown, 1917.
Three Plays. The Fiddler's House, The Land, Thomas Muskerry. Dublin: Maunsel, 1917.
Balloon. A Comedy in Four Acts. New York: Macmillan, 1929.
Moytura: A Play for Dancers. Dublin: Dolmen, 1963.
Selected Plays of Padraic Colum. Ed. Sanford Sternlicht. Syracuse: Syracuse University
    Press, 1986.

Fiction

Studies. Dublin: Maunsel, 1907.
Castle Conquer. New York: Macmillan, 1923.
Three Men. London: Elkin Matthews and Marrot, 1930.
The Flying Swans. New York: Crown, 1957.
Selected Short Stories of Padraic Colum. Ed. Sanford Sternlicht. Syracuse: Syracuse
    University Press, 1985.

Nonfiction

My Irish Year. London: Mills and Boon, 1912.
The Road round Ireland. New York: Macmillan, 1926.
Cross Roads in Ireland. New York and London, 1930.
A Half-Day's Ride: or, Estates in Corsica. New York and London, 1932.
Our Friend James Joyce (with Mary Colum). Garden City, New York: Doubleday, 1958.
Ourselves Alone: The Story of Arthur Griffith and the Origin of the Irish Free State.
    New York: Crown, 1958.
Story Telling, Old and New. New York: Macmillan, 1961.

Selected Children's Books and Folklore

A Boy in Eirinn. New York: E. P. Dutton, 1913.
The King of Ireland's Son. New York: Macmillan, 1916.

The Island of the Mighty. Being the Hero Stories of Celtic Britain Retold from the Mabinogion. New York: Macmillan, 1924.
Orpheus. Myths of the World. New York and London: Macmillan, 1930.
The Big Tree of Bunlaby. Stories of My Own Countryside. New York: Macmillan, 1933.
Legends of Hawaii. New Haven, CT: Yale University Press, 1937.

Studies of Padraic Colum

Bowen, Zack, *Padraic Colum: A Biographical-Critical Introduction.* Carbondale: Southern Illinois University Press, 1970.
Sternlicht, Sanford. *Padraic Colum.* Boston: Twayne, 1985.

Daniel Corkery

(1878–1964)

Laurie Champion

BIOGRAPHY

Daniel Corkery was born on February 14, 1878, in northern Cork. His father, William, came from a family of generations of carpenters. Daniel's mother, Mary (Barron) Corkery, was raised at sea. Daniel was one of four children. His sister, Mary, remained a close companion to Daniel throughout his life. Corkery's left leg was shorter than his right leg, apparently due to an undiagnosed case of polio.

In his early youth, Corkery attended Presentation Brothers Elementary School in Cork, where he received a King's Scholarship and eventually taught as a monitor. He also taught at St. Patrick's National School, where he resigned in 1921 because he was declined the headmaster position. While there, he taught Seamus Murphy and Frank O'Connor.

In 1908 Corkery helped organize the Cork Dramatic Society. His involvement in the organization led to the production of his plays *The Embers, The Eternal Longing, The Woman of Three Cows*, and *The Hermit and the King*.

The years 1916 through 1921 were fruitful for Corkery. In 1916 *A Munster Twilight*, Corkery's first collection of short stories, was published, followed by *The Threshold of Quiet* (1917), his only novel. Corkery's play *The Labour Leader* was produced by the Abbey Theatre (1919; published in 1920). During this time, Corkery helped develop the Munster Fine Arts Society. In 1920 *The Yellow Bittern* was produced by the Abbey Theatre, and *The Yellow Bittern and Other Plays* was published, establishing Corkery as a leading Irish dramatist. Corkery's second collection of short stories, *The Hounds of Banba* (1920), and his only book of poems, *I Bhreasail* (Isle of the Blessed) (1921), also appeared. During the early 1920s, Corkery taught art in various Cork schools and taught literature and drama to employees of the County Vocational School Educational Committee.

Between 1923 and 1928, Corkery worked as a clerical assistant to County Cork "inspector of Irish." *The Hidden Ireland* (1925), the work Corkery considered his most important, established him as a voice for Irish cultural nationalism.

In 1929 his third collection of short stories, *The Stormy Hills*, was published, and he received his master of arts, with honors, from the National University of Ireland. In 1931 *Synge and Anglo-Irish Literature* was published, and Corkery became Professor of English at University College, Cork. In 1939 *Earth Out of Earth* appeared, and *Fohnam the Sculptor* was produced by the Abbey.

Although Corkery retired from University College in 1947, he continued to publish his works until 1954. In 1948, the year *The Philosophy of the Gaelic League* appeared, he received his honorary D.Litt. from the National University of Ireland. In 1950 *The Wager and Other Stories*, an edition of selected, previously published short stories, appeared. Between 1951 and 1954, he served as a member of the prestigious Seanad Éireann. Corkery's last published book was *The Fortunes of the Irish Language* (1954).

Corkery died on December 31, 1964, in Cork and was buried in St. Joseph's Cemetery. Seamus Murphy designed Corkery's tombstone, honoring Corkery's request that only his name and dates appear on the engraving.

One of the most important roles Corkery plays in the Irish short story tradition is his role as mentor to younger writers such as Frank O'Connor and Sean O'Faolain. Because of his literary diversity, Corkery served as a model, encouraging younger writers to explore various literary genres. Additionally, Corkery was the first important fiction writer to portray Cork realistically and depict the particular lifestyle of its population, including the surrounding rural districts where traditional rural Irish life remained. Corkery was also the first significant fiction writer to depict rural Irish dialect without using it as a means for humor.

MAJOR WORKS AND THEMES

Daniel Corkery was one of the leading contributors to the Irish Renaissance. He upheld the traditional philosophy of the Gaelic League, with the idea that the Irish language would have to revive as the predominantly written and spoken language of Ireland. He believed that through restoration of the Irish language, the Irish people would maintain their own identity.

Corkery consistently portrays themes that reflect rural Irish traditions such as the Gaelic Irish oral storytelling tradition, including religion, superstitions, and folktales that depict the speech and behavior of the people of rural Ireland. Setting is vitally important in Corkery's works, as he demonstrates thorough knowledge of the isolated Cork hillsides and farms, superbly portraying the Irish landscape and rural Irish dialect. In his descriptions of Cork, Corkery often alludes to the water, frequently characterizing sailors and victims of drownings.

Major similarities can be found between Joyce's fiction and Corkery's. In Joyce's portrayal of Dublin and Corkery's portrayal of Cork, both writers use setting to portray particular lifestyles that reflect specific times and places. More significantly, both writers saw paralysis in their nation; however, their perspectives contrast sharply—Joyce encouraged exile, while Corkery admired the courage of those who stayed in Ireland (Gonzalez, "Re-Evaluation").

A *Munster Twilight* consists of twelve stories, including a loose short story sequence, "The Cobbler's Den." The most critically acclaimed stories in the collection are "The Ploughing of Leaca-na-Naomh" and "The Cry." In the former, Corkery depicts a landowner who persuades a fool to plough the saints' ancient burial ground, thus violating both religion and tradition. The latter represents a sort of mystical story, where the main character will not leave the road where generations of people have placed stones where a man died. Other stories in the collection portray sailors, blind men, widows, and poets, characters who struggle with lack of money and means to achieve desired goals.

The nine stories collected in *The Hounds of Banba* are set during the years after 1916. Frequently reflecting obvious rhetorical devices that make the stories seem propagandistic, the stories portray political motifs concerning the Irish Revolution. Six of the stories involve a Volunteer officer's attempt to reorganize Volunteers in Cork; the other three stories portray various aspects of the violence.

All but one of the fourteen stories in *The Stormy Hills* have rural settings, often portraying Gaelic-speaking characters. The subjects of this collection include many elements of Irish culture, including superstitions and ancient tales, as in "The Rivals," in which Corkery portrays a rivalry between two folk storytellers. "The Wager," one of Corkery's best-known stories, is about a drunken member of the ascendancy and his jockey, who throws a prized horse off a ledge to defend his family's honor. "The Priest," one of Corkery's greatest stories, is about a man who faultlessly performs his clerical duties but does nothing to uplift the lives of this parishioners on a day-to-day basis. The story involves one of Corkery's most finely crafted epiphanies. Another well-known story in the collection, "Rock-of-the Mass," portrays a farmer's reflection on the struggles his new farm in the lowlands has caused his wife, his older children, and himself. He remembers the old farm in the hills, recalling a rock where mass had been said during the days of the old penal laws. Ironically, the farmer finds comfort in thinking about the rock but is unaware that the rock has been destroyed to extend a road: the old farm as he remembers it no longer exists. The conflict between tradition and modernity is a common theme in the collection.

Ten years later, *Earth Out of Earth* was published. One of its few memorable stories is "Death of the Runner," which depicts a father–son conflict. " 'There's Your Sea!' " involves a man's desire to return to the mountains. In "Refuge," an old writer finds solace in speaking as if he were one of the characters in a sequel to a romance novel he wrote fifty years earlier.

Unlike the rural setting of most of his short stories, Corkery's only novel, *The Threshold of Quiet*, portrays Cork's urban middle class. The novel's title refers to Thoreau's famous statement that "the mass of men lead lives of quiet desperation." The characters in the novel are frustrated and paralyzed, reflective of the spiritual emptiness found in Irish middle-class life. The plot involves acquaintances and family of Frank Bresnan, who has drowned himself in the river Lee. A conflict between two brothers is one subplot; another involves a romance between a man and a woman and his struggle to accept her devastating decision to enter a convent.

Although Corkery is most recognized for his achievements in the short story genre, his plays also significantly contributed to Irish literature. His most important are collected in *The Yellow Bittern and Other Plays*, a collection of the three one-act plays, *The Yellow Bittern, King and Hermit*, and *Clan Falvey*. Central concerns in these plays are Irish folklore and the traditional Irish way of life.

In addition to his short stories, poems, and plays, Corkery wrote literary criticism, which is still controversial. Most famous are *The Hidden Ireland* and *Synge and Anglo-Irish Literature*, works in which Corkery attempted to establish a national Irish literary tradition and revive the Irish language.

CRITICAL RECEPTION

Although Corkery wrote in many genres, he will be best remembered for his novel and short stories. He is firmly established as the forerunner for the second generation of Irish writers such as Frank O'Connor and Sean O'Faolain. Almost all critics observe that Corkery's disciples have surpassed him artistically. As one critic notes, "The fact that he was the mentor of two younger, much more significant, Cork writers is usually the second, if not indeed the first, thing now said about Corkery" (Sherry 299).

Contemporary critics find Corkery's most valuable contributions in his novel and his two major short story collections, *A Munster Twilight* and *The Stormy Hills*. These critically acclaimed works are esteemed for Corkery's superb realistic portrayal of Cork and Kerry life and his poetic treatment of nature.

Since its publication, *The Threshold of Quiet* has received mixed assessments from critics. Initially, some reviewers praised it, comparing Corkery with Joyce. Even some contemporary critics see *The Threshold of Quiet* as a significant Irish novel and as Corkery's finest literary achievement. G. B. Saul, however, has found the novel tedious, uninteresting, sentimental, and didactic (30–31). Sean O'Faolain called it "a lovely novel, and for many even a perfect novel. Almost aggressively regionalist, it admits no view of life but the local, Irish view" (50).

Generally, most of Corkery's short story collections initially received favorable reviews. Recently, Francis Doherty has claimed that Corkery's best stories have "a special quality about them, the power of restraint, of understatement, of the unresolved, of the otherness of people, their mystery" (38). Although *A*

Munster Twilight initially received almost unanimously favorable reviews, some more recent critics see Corkery as a propagandist who preaches to his audience. Patricia Hutchins notes that most of the collection's stories are "based on a sense of weather, season; even when he is dealing with people whose whole lives have been spent in the streets of Cork one is aware of them moving through sunshine or hurrying under the rain" (43). *The Hounds of Banba* is considered one of his poorest collections, some critics viewing it as overly rhetorical and political. Hutchins notes, "Throughout these stories there runs the pity of the man who can understand the motives behind violence but can never be wholly with it" (44). *The Stormy Hills* is one of Corkery's greatest works. Saul says it "is a remarkable collection of exceptional, in several cases superlative, tales. . . . Character is rich in variety and presented with great subtlety of implication; colloquialism and local idiom are admirably handled" (46). *Earth Out of Earth*, Corkery's commercially least successful collection, has been faulted for its inadequate exposition, but Saul praises four stories from the collection, "Death of the Runner," "Silence," " 'There's Your Sea!' " and "Refuge," calling them "superlative items" (58).

Since *The Wager and Other Stories* (1950) contains sixteen stories from previously published collections, critical assessments of the collection provide a reevaluation of Corkery's stories. Initially, the collection received unanimously favorable reviews in America and is still considered remarkable. Critics point to Corkery's short stories as evidence that he belongs among prominent Irish writers. More recently, Alexander G. Gonzalez and Richard Bonaccorso have established Corkery's place among modern Irish writers, reassessing his fiction. In the second full-length study of Corkery, *"Life that Is Exile": Daniel Corkery and the Search for Irish Ireland*, Patrick Maume portrays Corkery far more positively than does Saul. Considering Corkery a central figure of the Irish Ireland movement, Maume combines biographical information and analytical interpretation.

Corkery's only published collection of poems, *I Bhreasail* (1921), initially received favorable reviews but today is almost ignored by critics. Corkery's plays received a similar initial greeting; however, critics still consider *The Yellow Bittern and Other Plays* artistically significant.

The Hidden Ireland and *Synge and Anglo-Irish Literature* have stirred much controversy. Most critics disagree with Corkery's role as a cultural philosopher, in which, as O'Faolain observes, he uses a politician's approach instead of a critic's (55). Corkery's cultural and political ideas are usually regarded as racist and dogmatic. He is also criticized for his "verbose marshaling of defective scholarship and more-than-questionable critical and aesthetic judgment" (Saul 44), especially in *The Hidden Ireland*.

Despite the weaknesses of Corkery's scholarly works and his unpopular political views, he is firmly established in the literary canon as an important Irish writer, as his creative works helped establish a tradition for younger writers to follow. Corkery's short stories, his novel, and the plays collected in *The Yellow*

Bittern and Other Plays are still considered important works of high literary merit.

BIBLIOGRAPHY

Works by Daniel Corkery

A Munster Twilight. Dublin and Cork: Talbot, 1916. (Short stories.)
The Threshold of Quiet. Dublin and Cork: Talbot, 1917. (Novel.)
The Hounds of Banba. Dublin and Cork: Talbot, 1920. (Short stories.)
The Labour Leader. Dublin: Talbot, 1920. (Play.)
The Yellow Bittern and Other Plays. Dublin: Talbot, 1920.
I Bhreasail: A Book of Lyrics. Dublin: Talbot, 1921.
The Hidden Ireland: A Study of Gaelic Munster in the Eighteenth Century. Dublin: Gill, 1925. (Scholarly book.)
The Stormy Hills. Dublin: Talbot, 1929. (Short Stories.)
Synge and Anglo-Irish Literature. London and New York: Longmans, Green, 1931. (Scholarly book.)
Earth Out of Earth. Dublin and Cork: Talbot, 1939. (Short stories.)
The Philosophy of the Gaelic League. Dublin, 1948. (Scholarly book.)
The Wager and Other Stories. New York: Devin-Adair, 1950.
The Fortunes of the Irish Language. Dublin: Fallon, 1954. (Scholarly book.)

Studies of Daniel Corkery

Bonaccorso, Richard. "Tales from the Cork Lanes: Another Daniel Corkery." *Eire-Ireland* 21.4 (1986): 29–35.
Cullen, L. M. "*The Hidden Ireland*: Re-Assessment of a Concept." *Studia Hibernica* 9 (1969): 7–47.
Doherty, Francis. "Daniel Corkery and the Isolate." *Journal of the Short Story in English* 8 (1987): 35–49.
Gonzalez, Alexander G. "A Context for Joyce: Seumas O'Kelly, Daniel Corkery, and the Nationalist View of the Irish Expatriate." *Etudes Irlandaises* 16.2 (1991): 33–41.
———"A Re-Evaluation of Daniel Corkery's Fiction." *Irish University Review* 14 (1984): 191–201.
Hutchins, Patricia. "Daniel Corkery, Poet of Weather and Place." *Irish Writing* (December 1953): 42–49.
Maume, Patrick. "*Life That Is Exile*": Daniel Corkery and the Search for Irish Ireland*. Belfast: Institute of Irish Studies, 1993.
O'Faolain, Sean. "Daniel Corkery." *Dublin Magazine* (April–June 1936): 49–61.
Saul, George Brandon. *Daniel Corkery*. Lewisburg: Bucknell University Press, 1973.
Sherry, Ruth. "Fathers and Sons: O'Connor among the Irish Writers: Corkery, AE, Yeats." *Twentieth Century Literature 36* (1990): 275–302.

Denis Devlin

(1908–1959)

Jack Morgan

BIOGRAPHY

Devlin was Ireland's ambassador to Italy at the time of his death in 1959, concluding a long diplomatic career going back to the mid-1930s when he joined the Irish Department of Foreign Affairs, a career during which he served in a number of foreign capitals. He was born of Irish parents, Ian and Margaret Devlin, in Greenock, Scotland, in 1908, the firstborn of nine children. Following the family's move to Dublin when he was twelve, he was educated at a Christian Brothers school, followed by Jesuit schooling at Belvedere College, Dublin. In 1926 he began formal training for the Catholic clergy at the diocesan seminary in Cloniffe but left the following year to pursue full-time academic work at University College, Dublin (UCD), where he devoted himself to modern languages and law, completing undergraduate studies in 1929. He then pursued an M.A. in French at UCD and spent the summer of 1930 in the Blasket Islands to improve his fluency in Irish. In September of that year, he coauthored *Poems* with Brian Coffey, marking what would prove a lifelong literary and personal friendship.

Devlin and Coffey had in common middle-class Dublin backgrounds that ill suited them to the prevailing fashion in Irish poetry at the time—rurally based, technically conservative, and little affected by the literary ferment ongoing in contemporary Europe. Doing post-M.A. work at the Sorbonne in the early 1930s, Devlin became—along with Coffey, Thomas McGreevy, Samuel Beckett, Niall Montgomery, Mervyn Wall, and others—associated with the expatriate Irish literary circle in Paris, a group of writers drawn, generally speaking, to the urban-modernist example established by Joyce and averse to the provincial-antiquarian Irishness of the Revival tradition. Devlin and Coffey thereby became exemplars for later Irish poets who likewise felt disinclined to write patently "Irish" poetry as narrowly defined. In an interview with Michael Smith, Mervyn Wall remembered Devlin's resistance to writing about the Irish countryside: " 'I hate scenery' was a constant saying of Devlin's" (Smith, *Irish Poetry: The Thirties Generation* 85).

Places, however, interested him greatly, and his writing reflects his wide-ranging travels. In the 1930s he toured English and Scottish cathedral towns and later lived and worked in Italy, New York, Washington, London, and Turkey. Devlin was appointed first secretary of the Irish legation to Washington in 1940. Robert Penn Warren met him there in 1944 and, like so many who knew Devlin, remarked about his exceptional charm, his "invincible elan" complementing a natural reserve and politeness:

I remember most distinctly an evening in the little back garden of Katherine Anne Porter's home in Georgetown. . . . It was a gay evening, with war and politics, for a moment, far away. It was then that I first got a real sense of Denis's quality—the easy wit without malice or egotism, the flashes of learning, gaiety that was about to burst into song, and most of all, the gift of making other people break from their preoccupations and discover their own gaiety. (Quoted in Downey 107).

In 1946 Devlin married an American, Maria Caron Radon, and published his major collection, *Lough Derg and Other Poems*. During the late 1940s and early 1950s, he continued to publish poetry in periodicals, including "The Colours of Love, "The Passion of Christ," and his long poem, "The Heavenly Foreigner." The latter, evidencing his previously noted fascination with places, is divided into sections by locale: St. Malo, Chartres, Geneva, Galway, Ile-St.-Louis, and Dublin, among others. His work in translation continued too—in 1949 he published *Exile and Other Poems*, translations of work by his fellow diplomat/poet St.-John-Perse. Devlin made numerous literary friends internationally in the course of his diplomatic work, including, besides Warren, Allen Tate (to whom "The Passion of Christ" is dedicated) and Ignazio Silone (to whom "The Tomb of Michael Collins" is dedicated). Devlin died in Dublin in 1959 after a long battle with cancer. He had commanded greater literary attention than any other writer of the 1930s expatriate Irish group except Beckett, and he continues to do so.

MAJOR WORKS AND THEMES

The bulk of Devlin's poetic corpus is, as earlier remarked, not identifiably Irish; rather, it is experimental and European-metropolitan in nature, often given over to translation, and often elliptical. Among his translations, however, are extensive renderings (with Niall Montgomery) of modern French poetry—Nerval, Rimbaud, Mallarmé, Apollinaire—into Irish, and the present-day poets associated with the Dedalus and New Writers Presses in Ireland particularly acknowledge Devlin's influence. Dedalus editor John Deane notes that for these poets, who share with the 1930s poets an interest in "a wider world with its global problems and its artistic concerns, . . . Denis Devlin becomes a father figure" (Qtd. in Sirr 7).

Devlin's lack of interest in specifically Irish subject matter also owed to the fact that, along with Coffey, he stood in the scholarly/Scholastic Irish-Catholic tradition that assumed a strong connectedness with classical European culture; indeed, his devout, learned Catholicism is perhaps one of Devlin's most Irish traits. It was not a matter of rejecting Ireland or Irish culture, and, for all its internationalist focus, his poetry is not without its Irish overtones, intermixing Irish imagery, landscape, and history with foreign ones. One of Devlin's better-known poems is a tribute to the Irish hero Michael Collins, commander in chief of the Irish Free State Army, who was killed in an ambush in 1922 and who had been a close friend of the Devlin family and a frequenter of Denis's father's Parnell St. pub (Downey 141). An uncharacteristically "public" poem and clearly less than Devlin's best, it nevertheless reveals his concern for Ireland and its fortunes, celebrating Collins the guerrilla leader who "[f]ought a week of Sundays and by night" and evoking earlier Irish heroes whom the poet, twelve at the time, remembered on the occasion of Collins's death—Edward the Bruce, Wolf Tone, Silken Thomas, and Red Hugh O'Donnell.

Most notably, Devlin's best-known poem, "Lough Derg," is Irish in setting and subject matter—a meditation on the Donegal pilgrimage site, a penitential island going back to the early Middle Ages and one Devlin visited with his mother when he was in his midteens (Downey 107). The legendary Lough Derg served as subject matter for Carleton (*Lough Derg Pilgrim*, 1829), Thackeray, and other writers and more recently for poems by Yeats ("The Pilgrim"), Patrick Kavanagh ("Lough Derg"), and Seamus Heaney ("Station Island"). Devlin's reaction to the scene is distress and, at the same time, compassion. The bleak island embodies the bitter ironies inherent in faith entangled in "the phantasmagoria of history" (Coffey's phrase, "Distance" 142) and bound up with a "shattered" European culture. The prayers of the tired pilgrims are drab and habitual. Religious faith has been vulgarized and blunted, "blurbed" by the market, until no one can "mend or explain the good and the broke."

CRITICAL RECEPTION

Perhaps the perceived Eliotesque chord struck in "Lough Derg" (first published in *The Southern Review*, 1942) resonated for the New Critical fraternity in the United States and led to Devlin's being promoted by Allen Tate and Robert Penn Warren. Devlin had published poems, reviews, and translations through the mid- and late 1930s and a collection, *Intercessions*, in 1937. In 1934 Samuel Beckett had praised him, along with Brian Coffey, as "without question the most interesting of the youngest generation of Irish poets" (quoted in Deane's *Field Day Anthology*, vol. 3, 225). But the sponsorship of Tate and

Warren greatly enhanced and broadened Devlin's reputation, especially in the United States. *Lough Derg and Other Poems* (1946) was widely and mostly positively reviewed by major American critics like Arthur Mizener, Selden Rodman, Babette Deutch, and others. An exception, though, was Randall Jarrell's commentary in *Partisan Review* (since reprinted in *Poetry and the Age*, 1953), which was unenthusiastic, noting too many echoes of MacNiece and criticizing Devlin's "rather poor and arbitrary ear" (225).

Since his death, Devlin has been well served by the small community of sympathetic critics, poets, and editors willing to address his less-than-easily-accessible oeuvre. Tate and Warren edited *Selected Poems* (1963), and Brian Coffey, until his death in 1995, was a particularly devoted worker on behalf of Devlin's literary reputation. In his essay "Denis Devlin: Poet of Distance," he carefully takes issue with Jarrell's criticisms of Devlin. Coffey also edited a Denis Devlin special issue of *University Review* (1963) and *The Complete Poems* (1964). Michael Smith and Stan Smith have written extensively on the importance of the 1930s generation in general and Devlin in that context. J.C.C. Mays has edited *Collected Poems of Denis Devlin* (1989), a book that offers a long and thoroughgoing introduction as well as extensive and useful textual notes. It is not, however, an exhaustive collection; a true *Complete Works* has yet to appear.

Dillon Johnston's chapter "Devlin and Montague" in his *Irish Poetry after Joyce* (1985) is a significant study. Like J.C.C. Mays, Johnston is willing to venture into Devlin's more elusive poems and does not confine himself to "Lough Derg" and the other now-familiar ones alone. He aptly sums up Devlin's contribution to Irish poetry: "an eclectic receptivity toward literature and philosophy, an Irish-Catholic sensitivity toward the flesh, a modernized Mariolarity in which women offer access to the divine" (168). John Montague has contributed a valuable essay to the corpus of Devlin criticism: his chapter "The Impact of International Modern Poetry on Irish Writing" in *The Figure in the Cave* focuses mainly on the poetry of Devlin, whom he sees as "the most dedicated poet of his generation, and one whose work suggests possibilities for the future" (213).

BIBLIOGRAPHY

Works by Denis Devlin

Poems (with Brian Coffey). Dublin: Alex Thom, 1930.
Intercessions. London: Europa, 1937.
Lough Derg and Other Poems. New York: Reynal and Hitchcock, 1946.
Selected Poems. Ed. Allen Tate and Robert Penn Warren. New York: Holt, Rinehart, Winston, 1963.
The Complete Poems. Ed. Brian Coffey. Dublin: Dolmen, 1964.
The Heavenly Foreigner. Ed. Brian Coffey. Dublin: Dolmen, 1967.

Collected Poems. Ed. J.C.C Mays. Winston-Salem, NC: Wake Forest University Press, 1989.

Studies of Denis Devlin

Coffey, Brian. "Denis Devlin: Poet of Distance." In *Place, Personality and the Irish Writer*, ed. Andrew Carpenter. Gerrards Cross: Colin Smythe, 1977, 137–57.
————, ed. "Denis Devlin Special Issue." *University Review* (Dublin) 11 (1963).
Downey, William G. "Thinking of Denis Devlin." *Eire-Ireland* 14 (Spring 1979): 102–14.
Jarrell, Randall. "Poets." *Poetry and the Age.* New York: Knopf, 1953, 220–36.
Montague, John. "The Impact of International Modern Poetry on Irish Writing." *The Figure in the Cave and Other Essays.* Syracuse: Syracuse University Press, 1989, 208–20.
Sirr, Peter. "Beyond Dancehalls and Farmyard Intrigues." *The Irish Literary Supplement* 12 (Fall 1993): 6–7.

Paul Durcan

(1944–)

Bernard McKenna

BIOGRAPHY

Paul Durcan was born in Dublin on October 16, 1944. His father, John, an attorney, was raised in the town of Turlough, County Mayo, in the Irish west. His mother, the former Sheila MacBride, was a relation to Yeats's great love, Maud Gonne. Through his parents, he was able to achieve a sense of access to Irish history, geography, and tradition—a sense that informs much of his work. Before beginning his career at university in 1971, Durcan lived in London and published, with Brian Lynch, a collection of poems titled *Endsville*, edited a literary journal called *Two Rivers*, married Nessa O'Neill, and nurtured a love for drama and art, experiences that also inform his work. In 1973, he received a first-class honors degree from University College, Cork. However, he began his work in Cork studying poetry until, after his first arts exam, he was told that he "did not have a proper understanding of poetry." Subsequently, he read archaeology and medieval history, often drawing detailed plans and sketches of artifacts and ancient sites. He studied under M. J. O'Kelly, the excavator of Newgrange, who used to take Durcan and his fellow students on tours of the sacred geography of ancient Munster, giving them a sense of communion with the past. Early in his career, Durcan sought to carry forward to his audiences this sense of connectedness with art and history that he obtained in London, Dublin, and Cork. He began to organize public readings of his work, to perfect his skills as a performer, and strongly to advocate that the Arts Council organize poets' and artists' readings and exhibitions in schools at all levels to give the students a sense of direct connection with creative production. His work and the work of the other poets of his generation who did cultivate a love and appreciation for a living poetic tradition have done much to foster the continuing literary Renaissance in Ireland. To date, Durcan has published seventeen volumes of poetry including fourteen collections of new work, a special issue of a single poem, and two collections of previously published work. In addition, he served as editor of the *Cork Review*.

MAJOR WORKS AND THEMES

Durcan counts among his poetic influences Eliot, Pound, and Hopkins. Among Irish writers, Durcan's poetic ancestry traces its way from contemporaries like Michael Hartnett back to Patrick Kavanagh and W. B. Yeats and even to ancient Irish-language writers. Durcan's poetry is in fact designed for oral appreciation. Like Hartnett, Hopkins, and Kavanagh, Durcan focuses on the individual's reactions to sometimes overwhelming and overpowering forces, attempting to empower individuals and to give them a sense of possibility and dignity in the face of those forces by holding them up to scrutiny, sometimes savage, satiric scrutiny.

Although he was the recipient of the Patrick Kavanagh Poetry Award in 1975, Durcan first achieved wide critical and popular recognition for his work with the publication of *The Selected Paul Durcan* (1982). Containing selections from his early publications, the collection directs attention to the best of Durcan's poetic achievement and brings into focus his major themes, including his contempt for the alliance between the Catholic Church and politics in the Irish republic, for the oppressive English government in Northern Ireland, and for the IRA. He also satirizes the Irish popular press and, to a certain extent, public aspirations and demands that drive these forces. In addition, this work highlights his efforts to build a new Irish poetic tradition unburdened from the shadow of received images and metaphors. Durcan attempts to construct an Irish poetry that is free from the Anglo-Irish tradition, headed by Yeats, that tends to overwhelm young developing artists and to strangle their unique poetic voices. Durcan does not criticize the received traditions as much as he condemns their dominance over contemporary Irish thought.

In 1985, Durcan's *The Berlin Wall Cafe* was the Poetry Book Society Choice. Much of its poetry focuses on Durcan's deteriorating relationship with his wife, who provided financial and emotional support during his early years as a student and writer. At their best, the poems in this selection speak to the tragedy of growing separateness and change; to the fact, rather than necessity, of healing or forgetfulness; and to instants of remembered wrong, virtually unbearable in their momentary intensity.

Daddy, Daddy, Durcan's most widely acclaimed work and winner of the 1990 Whitebread Poetry Prize, though largely exploring the poet's relationship with his father, also focuses attention on the received notions of Irish poetic and cultural convention, themes that Durcan continues to probe in his three published volumes since 1990. The poems, which carry forward the complex study of relationships begun in *The Berlin Wall Cafe*, alternatingly castigate and praise his father, study the painful associations between father and son, draw parallels between such a relationship and a marriage, and examine a son's growing understanding of his father.

CRITICAL RECEPTION

Currently, Paul Durcan is considered one of the leading and most strikingly unique voices in contemporary Irish poetry and art. Writing about his work, Maurice Elliott (in Kenneally's *Poetry in Contemporary Irish Literature*) suggests that Durcan's "poetic ancestry is honourable, but . . . slightly unusual, because his tradition is one of which the last successful exponent . . . was Thomas Moore: poetry as oratory." Elliott further suggests that Durcan is a "musician, a popular and occasional poet, a story-teller drawing on primitive and native sources, a public voice, a bard who . . . can spellbind and enrapture" (305). Although Elliott may perhaps have overplayed Durcan's originality—certainly, James Simmons shares many of these characteristics, and many contemporary Irish artists and writers draw on primitive and native sources—Durcan is one of the leading modern proponents of the oral poetic tradition, and, as Elliott correctly observes, Durcan's voice has its origins in Irish-language literary convention. Specifically, as Gerald Dawe observes, Durcan uses his unusual poetic voice to "expose hypocrisy, deceit and repression that underlie . . . power" relationships. Dawe goes on to suggest that Durcan's poetry is "one way, perhaps *the* way, of redistributing justice and praise in favour of those who defy the courts of convention" (Dawe, *Against Piety* 183). Indeed, as Edna Longely proposes (in Brown and Grene's *Tradition and Influence*), "Paul Durcan's poetry is already liberatingly post-post-colonial . . . [H]e stages a . . . personal psycho-drama, tracking social brutalities to the individual heart and mind" (177). He "builds in . . . models of loving kindness, prospects of sexual-spiritual redemption" (178). Durcan does so in forms that emphasize "the cross-pollination of the visual arts with poetry. . . . His poetry is a record of 'collaborations' between verbal, visual and musical media. . . . His interest in film and painting has led him to experiment with methods of translating not only the content, but also the form, of visual works into poetry" (McCracken, "Canvas and Camera" 18). Significantly, his collaborations with, and admiration for, the painting of modern artists and composers R. B. Kitaj, Manual Salamanca, Mary Farl Powers, and Micheal O'Suilleabhain have prefigured a recent trend in Irish writing to develop interrelations between art and poetry.

BIBLIOGRAPHY

Works by Paul Durcan

Endsville. Dublin: New Writer's, 1967.
O Westport in the Light of Asia Minor: Poems. Dublin: Anna Livia, 1975.

Teresa's Bar. Dublin: Gallery, 1976.
Jesus, Break His Fall. Dublin: Raven Arts, 1980.
Drug Swoops at Sligo Festival. Sligo: Pleiades, 1980. (Single poem.)
Sam's Cross: Poems. Portmarnock: Profile Poetry, 1980.
Ark of the North. Dublin: Raven Arts, 1982.
The Selected Paul Durcan. Belfast: Blackstaff, 1982.
Jumping the Train Tracks with Angela. Dublin: Raven Arts, 1983.
The Berlin Wall Cafe. Belfast: Blackstaff, 1985.
Going Home to Russia. Belfast: Blackstaff, 1987.
In the Land of Punt. Dublin: Clashganna Mills, 1988.
Jesus and Angela: Poems. Belfast: Blackstaff, 1988.
Daddy, Daddy. Belfast: Blackstaff, 1990.
Crazy about Women: Poems. Dublin: National Gallery of Ireland, 1991.
A Snail in My Prime: New and Selected Poems. Belfast: Blackstaff, 1993.
Give Me Your Hand: Poems. London: Macmillan, 1994.

Studies of Paul Durcan

Gorman, Damien. "Dreams at Work: Damien Gorman Meets Paul Durcan." *Belfast Review* 13 (1986): 9.
Hannan, Dennis J. "A Note on Paul Durcan's 'The Wreck of the Deutschland.' " *Canadian Journal of Irish Studies* 15.1 (July 1989): 101–5.
McCracken, Kathleen. "Canvas and Camera Translated: Paul Durcan and the Visual Arts." *Irish Review* 7 (Autumn 1989): 18–29.
———. "Masks and Voices: Personas in the Poetry of Paul Durcan." *Canadian Journal of Irish Studies* 13.1 (June 1987): 107–20.
Mahon, Derek. "Orpheus Ascending: The Poetry of Paul Durcan." *Irish Review* 1 (Autumn 1986): 15–19.
Melchiori, Barbara Arnett. "Browning, Yeats, and Paul Durcan: Men and Masks." In *Yeats Oggi: Studi e Ricerche*, ed. Carla DePetris. Rome: Terza Universita Degli di Roma, 1993.
Stuart, Francis. "A Special Kind of Writer." *Cork Review* 2.1 (1981): 27–38.
Toibin, Colm. *The Kilfenora Teaboy: A Study of Paul Durcan*. Dublin: New Island, 1996.

Desmond Egan

(1936–)

Jim McWilliams

BIOGRAPHY

Until he became the first European to win the prestigious National Poetry Foundation of America Award in 1983, Desmond Egan was little known outside his native Ireland. Since that year, however, his reputation has grown steadily. By 1994, for example, his poems had been translated into more than a dozen languages, including Japanese and Russian, and he had won a wide following through his readings and lectures around the globe.

Born in Athlone, Ireland, on July 15, 1936, Egan grew up believing in the power of the written word, for his mother—a primary school teacher—taught him how to read when he was just three years old. His subsequent formal education was long and rigorous. After attending primary school and the Marist Brothers College (both in Athlone), Egan boarded at St. Finian's, a diocesan secondary school in Mullingar, from 1950 to 1955. There, he learned Irish, Latin, and Greek, eventually becoming fluent in all three languages. From 1955 to 1962, he studied at St. Patrick's College, Maynooth, graduating with honors. After a few years of teaching Greek at St. Finian's, he left to further his education at University College, Dublin, where he earned an M.A. with exceptionally high marks. He then returned to St. Finian's and taught Greek and English from 1965 to 1971. During these years, Egan also began to write poetry. He founded his own publishing house—Goldsmith Press, which also published Patrick Kavanagh's posthumous novel, *By Night Unstarred*, as well as poetry by Michael Hartnett and Desmond O'Grady—to print his first, slender collection of poems, *Midland* (1972). He continued to teach at different schools until 1987, when he became a full-time writer. In 1981, he married the author Vivienne Abbott, with whom he has two daughters.

MAJOR WORKS AND THEMES

Egan intends his poetry to challenge a reader. While his themes are provocative in themselves, his style—heavily influenced by modernist techniques—presents special difficulties. Typically, for example, Egan fails to punctuate his verse or even to capitalize letters at the beginnings of his sentences. He eschews conjunctions and frequently uses a disjointed rhythm and/or unexpected enjambments, both of which force a reader to rush headlong through the poem and experience it as a whole instead of stopping to savor individual lines or stanzas. He has argued in essays and interviews that a century without a unifying structure demands poetry without a unifying structure, that a modern poet must not be afraid to invent new poetic forms. "And when one is more aware of meaninglessness than of meaning, when the traditional props of religion and of society seem to have failed," he states in an essay, "Poetry and the Abyss," "the writer is thrown back to an unprecedented degree on his/her own resources. . . . To write in iambic pentameter nowadays (unless for effect) would in my view imply insensitivity" (*The Death of Metaphor* 1990). Egan's predominant mentors in his quest to "make it new" are Ezra Pound and John Berryman, to both of whom he pays homage in his poetry and prose.

Egan's introspective first book, *Midland* (1972), seems to lack polish, leading some of his critics to complain that his early poems want maturity. Actually, his elliptical prosody in *Midland* is a deliberate echo of imagism, while his colloquial phrasing shows Patrick Kavanagh's influence. Many of the poems in the collection anticipate his later work in that they focus upon personal loss and the relentless passage of time. Indeed, these poems about the midlands of Ireland can be read as an attempt to stop time, to delay mutability, much as a painting freezes a moment in time that will never occur again. *Leaves* (1974), his second collection, shifts perspective from landscape to people, although the themes of loss and of time passing continue to dominate. A primary image in the collection is that of a woman, and the best poems in *Leaves* are pensive lyrics that show the effect of a break in the relationship between the speaker and that woman.

The political poems of *Siege* (1976) mark a new direction for Egan since his style becomes even more difficult with its use of epigraphs, an appendix, and quotations from other languages. These poems about an Irish Republican Army (IRA) kidnapping and the subsequent British manhunt for the kidnappers show Egan's despair about violence in Northern Ireland and hint at his belief that the ideal of Irish nationalism has been betrayed by the vulgarity of senseless violence. Although some of the poems in *Siege* are powerful, on the whole the collection seems overly contrived. His fourth collection, *Woodcutter* (1978), shows a wider thematic range than before, but its most memorable poems remain lyrics about coping with death and loss. Especially significant is "Late But! One for Ezra," Egan's moving elegy for Pound.

Athlone? (1980) is among Egan's best work. Consisting of a series of twenty-two poems about his hometown and its people, each individual poem functions much like a snapshot, while collectively the poems serve as a complete photo album of a single town at one particular moment. When asked by an interviewer why he placed a question mark at the end of his title, Egan responded that it would be presumptuous of him to claim to know everything about Athlone, adding, "The question mark has a little touch of humor in it, because midlanders don't claim to be all that sure about anything, even about whether the ground will open in front of your feet ten yards down the road."

In 1983, Egan published *Snapdragon*, a collection of love poems to his wife, and *Seeing Double*, a work in which he first experiments with a new poetic structure: on the left-hand margin of a page he places the poem itself, while on the right margin he adds an italicized commentary upon the poem. These commentaries, often more lyrical than the poem, resemble the marginal glosses found in medieval texts, and, like the glosses, they offer ways to interpret the poem. This innovative structure attracted a great deal of attention from critics and helped Egan win a larger audience for his poems. His frequent readings of his work, in such countries as the United States, Russia, Japan, Italy, France, Belgium, and Germany, also added to his fame. Consequently, his *Collected Poems* (1983) found a receptive audience ready to acknowledge Egan's place in contemporary Irish letters.

Since 1983, Egan has published *Poems for Peace* (1986), a collection that asks for an end to the conflict in Northern Ireland; *A Song for My Father* (1989), a collection about individuals—including his father—whom Egan admires; *Peninsula* (1992), a series of poetic meditations about the Dingle Peninsula, Kerry; *In the Holocaust of Autumn* (1994), nine poems about the Jewish experience in Ireland; and *Poems for Eimear*, a series of ten elegies for a young girl. He has also published *The Death of Metaphor* (1990), a collection of personal essays, criticism, and reminiscences.

CRITICAL RECEPTION

Respect and appreciation for Desmond Egan's poetry have grown considerably since 1983. Hugh Kenner has championed Egan as "the first Irish poet to have broken free from the need to sound 'Irish.' " Brian Arkins, author of the first book-length study of Egan's work, argues further that Egan has "married the local intensity of Kavanagh to the knowledge of Yeats" and, consequently, must be considered a major Irish poet of the twentieth century. Dozens of other critics have also noted Egan's achievements; many of their essays are collected in *Desmond Egan: The Poet and His Work* (1990). In 1985, the special-collections division of the Georgetown University Library began purchasing Egan's papers, which include early drafts of published poems, unpublished poems and essays, and correspondence to and from Egan.

BIBLIOGRAPHY

Works by Desmond Egan

Midland. Newbridge: Goldsmith, 1972.
Leaves. Newbridge: Goldsmith, 1974.
Siege!. Newbridge: Goldsmith, 1976.
Woodcutter. Newbridge: Goldsmith, 1978.
Athlone?. Newbridge: Goldsmith, 1980.
Snapdragon. Newbridge: Goldsmith, 1983.
Seeing Double. Newbridge: Goldsmith, 1983.
Collected Poems. Orono, ME: National Poetry Foundation, 1983; 2d ed., Newbridge:
    Goldsmith, 1984.
Poems for Peace. Dublin: Afri, 1986.
A Song for My Father. Newbridge: Kavanagh, 1989.
The Death of Metaphor. Savage, MD: Barnes, 1990.
Peninsula. Newbridge: Kavanagh, 1992.
Selected Poems. Ed. Hugh Kenner. Omaha, NE: Creighton University Press, 1992.
In the Holocaust of Autumn: A Sequence in Eight Parts with an Epilogue. Newbridge:
    Goldsmith, 1994.
Poems for Eimear. Little Rock: Milestone, 1994.
Elegies. Newbridge: Goldsmith, 1996.

Studies of Desmond Egan

Arkins, Brian. *Desmond Egan: A Critical Study*. Little Rock, AR: Milestone, 1992.
De Kamp, Peter Van. "Desmond Egan: Universal Provincialist." In *The Crows behind
    the Plough: History and Violence in Anglo-Irish Poetry and Drama*, ed. Geert
    Lernout. Atlanta: Rodopi, 1991.
Kenner, Hugh, ed. *Desmond Egan: The Poet and His Work*. Orono, ME: Northern Lights,
    1990.

John Eglinton

(1868–1961)

Rebecca Creasy Simcoe

BIOGRAPHY

William Kirkpatrick Magee, who took the pseudonym John Eglinton, was born in Dublin, where he attended the High School with William Butler Yeats. Eglinton became an influential essayist and commentator on the Irish Literary Revival, finding himself the critical adversary of its most influential leader, his former schoolmate. He engaged Yeats and others in debate about the aims and scope of a national literature; going against the grain of the Revivalist project, he advocated the rejection of local themes and promoted more universal, cosmopolitan writing. In 1898 the *Daily Express* published a series of letters written by Eglinton, Yeats, AE (George Russell), and William Larminie, later published in book form as *Literary Ideals in Ireland*, which identified the lines of contention in this debate.

Philosophically, Eglinton characterized himself as a humanist and transcendentalist and was, although neither theosophist nor mystic, often compared to his friend AE. With Fred Ryan he edited the twelve issues of *Dana*, which ran from May 1904 to April 1905. As the Irish correspondent to *The Dial* from 1921 to 1929, he wrote a series of "Dublin Letters," which kept alive the debate over "literary nationalism" in Irish writing and profiled the major personalities involved in the controversy, such as Yeats, AE, and George Moore.

Eglinton worked in Dublin as an assistant librarian at the National Library of Ireland until 1922. In 1923 he left Ireland for Bournemouth, England, where he lived in exile until his death in 1961.

John Eglinton, self-declared renegade of the Irish Literary Revival, was immortalized by the writers who respected him—philosophical friends and foes alike. Yeats personally selected the pieces included in *Some Essays and Pas-*

sages by John Eglinton. "John Eglinton" makes an appearance in the "Scylla and Charybdis" episode of Joyce's *Ulysses* and also frequents the pages of George Moore's *Hail and Farewell*, where he is dubbed the "Thoreau of the suburbs" and nicknamed "Contrairy John" [*sic*].

MAJOR WORKS AND THEMES

John Eglinton's earliest essays were published in the two collections *Two Essays on the Remnant* (1894) and *Pebbles from a Brook* (1901). In the former he explores the individualist's need to be in solitude with nature and warns that civilization and the modern state pose a constant threat to independent thinkers. The latter also takes up the subject of man's relationship with nature and is filled with Eglinton's individualistic philosophy. Of particular importance for Eglinton, as it was for his American counterpart, Ralph Waldo Emerson, is the role of the poet in history and in the modern world.

"The De-Davisisation of Irish Literature," probably Eglinton's most famous essay, appears in *Bards and Saints* (1906), which reprints some of his best work from *Dana*. In the essay Eglinton asserts that the many writers who followed the teachings of Thomas Davis were wrongly guided by the single-minded desire to exalt the excellence of their own race rather than by the need to explore the soul of an individual consciousness apart from any interpretation of nationality.

Anglo-Irish Essays (1917) is an eclectic collection that includes essays on the Irish language and Irish mythology, the philosophy of the Celtic movement, the ecology of reforestation, Thomas Moore, and Friedrich Nietzsche. In his preface Eglinton asserts that his subject matter is, broadly speaking, the preoccupations of the Anglo-Irish minority in Ireland. He points his readers to the fact that there is something in Ireland older than racial and religious distinctions, history, even archaeology: "Mother Nature herself, in whose presence the poet can forget the squalid animosities of race and creed" (9).

After leaving Ireland for England in 1923, Eglinton edited two volumes of George Moore's letters and published *A Memoir of AE* (1937). Among the famous biographical sketches in *Irish Literary Portraits* (1935) are "Yeats and His Story" and "A. E. and His Story." His brief autobiographical work, *Confidential; or, Take It or Leave It* (1951), is written in both poetry and prose. This, his last published work, begins with the essay "Apologia," in which he discusses his "inferiority complex," the result of the highly esteemed literary company he kept. Though he wrote verse all of his life, the thirty-three poems published in *Confidential* constitute the only poetry collection he ever published.

CRITICAL RECEPTION

Ernest Boyd included an enthusiastic appraisal of John Eglinton in *Ireland's Literary Renaissance*, a work that Eglinton reviewed favorably in *The Dial*. Boyd ranks him "with the finest English essayists," asserting that "[i]t seems as if John Eglinton can write only when manner and matter have blended into an exquisite harmony, making of each essay a well-embroidered tissue of ideas'' (245). This early account of Eglinton's work to 1916 is an excellent introduction to the essayist's themes and preoccupations. Published one year later, Boyd's *Appreciations and Depreciations: Irish Literary Studies* includes a chapter entitled ''An Irish Essayist: John Eglinton,'' a revision of his piece in *Ireland's Literary Renaissance*.

Daniel S. Lenoski defends Yeats against charges of artistic ''insincerity'' in a response to Eglinton's portion of the newspaper debate published as *Literary Ideals in Ireland* (1899). Working from the premise that ''Eglinton accused Yeats of worshipping an art that interested itself in life and man for the sake of art only'' (94), Lenoski is concerned primarily with determining Yeats's alliance with aestheticism and only marginally with illuminating Eglinton's perspective.

In '' 'Our One Philosophical Critic': John Eglinton,'' Mary E. Bryson quotes Yeats's phrase for Eglinton in the title of her introduction to the writer and his ideas. In Bryson's estimation, Eglinton ''contributed to the main thrust of the Revival towards an establishment of standards for a national literature'' (88) and spoke prophetically of the international significance of the writers who emerged after the Revival. She rightly considers Eglinton's lack of critical attention the result of a general neglect of his genre, the essay, as well as the fate of ''the fugitive literature of the periodical'' (83). Her suspicion, though, is that his neglect was also the product of a lingering resentment among his surviving contemporaries: ''The Revival and its aftermath were times of chauvinistic nationalism,'' and Eglinton's ''iconoclastic views on certain sacred Revival values were hardly pleasing to enthusiasts'' (83). In a later article, ''Dublin Letters,'' Bryson herself goes a long way toward keeping his work alive. In her well-researched study of his contributions to *The Dial* she reveals Eglinton to be as much a social historian as literary critic in her outline of his developing ideas.

BIBLIOGRAPHY

Works by John Eglinton

Two Essays on the Remnant. Dublin: Whaley, 1894.

Literary Ideals in Ireland (with W. B. Yeats, AE, and W. Larminie). London: Unwin; Dublin: Daily Express Office, 1899. Reprinted, New York: Lemma, 1973.

Pebbles from a Brook. Kilkenny and Dublin: Standish O'Grady, *Some Essays and Passages by John Eglinton*. Selected by W. B. Yeats. Dublin: Dun Emer, 1905.

Bards and Saints. Dublin: Maunsel, 1906.

Anglo-Irish Essays. Dublin: Talbot; London: Unwin, 1917.

Ed. and trans. *Letters to Edouard Dujardin*, by George Moore. New York: Crosby Gaige, 1929.

Irish Literary Portraits. London: Macmillan, 1935. Reprinted, Freeport, NY: Books for Libraries, 1967.

A Memoir of A. E. London: Macmillan, 1937.

Ed. *Letters of George Moore, with an Introduction by John Eglinton, to Whom They Were Written.* Bournemouth: Sydenham, 1942.

Confidential; or, Take It or Leave It. London: Fortune, 1951.

Studies of John Eglinton

Bryson, Mary E. "Dublin Letters: John Eglinton and *The Dial*, 1921–1929." *Éire-Ireland* 24.4 (Winter 1994): 132–48.

———. " 'Our One Philosophical Critic': John Eglinton." *Éire-Ireland* 10.2 (Summer 1975): 81–88.

Kain, Richard. "Irish Periodical Literature: An Untilled Field." *Éire-Ireland* 7.3 (Autumn 1972): 93–99.

Lenoski, Daniel S. "Yeats, Eglinton, and Aestheticism." *Éire-Ireland* 14.4 (Winter 1979): 91–108.

Darrell Figgis

(1882–1925)

Maryanne Felter

BIOGRAPHY

Born in 1882 in Rathmines, Figgis spent his early childhood in India. After working for a London tea merchant, he eventually became an editor for Dent. Figgis saw himself as a writer, but he was a vastly important political figure as well. With Erskine Childers and Roger Casement, he ran guns from Germany to Howth for the Irish Volunteers in 1914 and was the arms deal's chief liaison, resulting in a stint in jail. His involvement in Irish political events of the day as well as his contemporary literary reputation led him to a seat on the committee that drafted the Irish Constitution, and he wrote a series of articles for *The Irish Independent* to explain the new constitution to the Irish people. Figgis stood as an independent for south Dublin in 1922, but the eventful campaign ended when "two Republicans [broke] into his flat at gun-point one night and trimmed off half of his neat auburn beard" (Costello, *The Heart Grown Brutal* 265). In 1922, "he and his wife were attacked by political opponents," says Dunn, and "the blow that Millie received may eventually have led to her suicide in November of 1924" (37). A year later, after the death of a new love, Rita North, resulting from an abortion, Figgis, too, committed suicide on October 27, 1925. He left only the manuscript of *Recollections of the Irish War* to be published posthumously and a large, already published literary legacy that has been almost ignored until recently.

MAJOR WORKS AND THEMES

Broken Arcs (1911), Figgis's first novel, has a conventional plot and does not approach the quality of his later fiction; it is largely uneven, potboiling sensationalism. *Broken Arcs* established, however, certain themes that recur in Figgis's fiction and is therefore worth some attention. The defiance of social convention, the importance of soul communion, the presence of a mentor-character who understands greater truths and who helps the younger characters move beyond the conventionalities of their society, and the writer-character who has difficulty establishing himself in the London literary world and who is quickly disillusioned by the politics of that world are all present. Interestingly, this is the only one of Figgis's novels that is not at least partially set in Ireland. Perhaps for this reason his otherwise constant theme of spiritual connection with the earth is absent.

Only after living in the west of Ireland could Figgis write the novels after *Broken Arcs*. Communion with the land becomes all-important. In Figgis's second novel, *Jacob Elthorne* (1914), the land inspires, teaches, and succors; the relationship with the land supersedes all others in this life. The theme becomes from this point, constant in his work.

In his third novel, *Children of Earth* (1918), Figgis develops the idea of communion with the earth. The two main characters have the kind of love that transcends ordinary love; it is a spiritual connection that, rooted in the earth, goes beyond what "normal" people experience. The novel is also remarkable for its accurate depictions of folk customs on a small Irish island.

The House of Success (1922), his only historical novel, has a sense of realism as well as political purpose. Parnell himself forms a shadowy backdrop as the novel progresses through to the Easter 1916 rebellion.

In his last novel, *The Return of the Hero* (1923), Figgis merges Ireland's heroic past with its modern, or recent, past. Here, Oisin returns from Tir na nOg to find himself in a debate with Saint Padraic and the bishops about contemporary religion. Padraic is forced to attempt to explain to Oisin how God could condemn a hero like Finn to hell, but Padraic, whose open mind and generous heart make him sympathetic, cannot override the authority of the other bishops and finally is unable to temper Christianity enough to allow it to embrace the code of the older hero.

Figgis's first book of poems, *A Vision of Life* (1909), is an odd collection, unremarkable in terms of theme or style. His rhythms are fairly regular but overtly strained, his ear tending in both rhythms and other sound senses toward the obvious. His rhymes are glaring and take away from meaning rather than enhancing beauty.

Two years later, Figgis published *The Crucibles of Time and Other Poems* (1911). Although the themes and subjects of the poems are conventional, never moving beyond typical Romantic love poems, nature poems, and odes to beauty, Figgis's control of form has improved considerably. His rhythms as well as his rhyme schemes are subtler and more deftly handled. His use of such poetic techniques as alliteration, assonance, and consonance, as well as his ear for sound in general, has also improved so that the poetry is more mellifluous. His

1913 play *Queen Tara*, however, was not as successful as the earlier "Teigue," but it is the only one of Figgis's plays that was performed.

CRITICAL RECEPTION

Not many people have written about Darrell Figgis, but of those who have, one thing is clear: all see him as an undeservedly neglected, talented writer who is long overdue for serious appreciation—all but Yeats, that is, whose comment about Figgis was that "he is the most chuckled-headed, tongue-clotted of writers" (Dunn 32). Although Figgis is mentioned in passing in various critical sources, only two works of any length have been devoted to him. Alexander G. Gonzalez's *Darrell Figgis: A Study of His Novels* treats at length the first four novels and gives background on Figgis. Maryanne Felter's "Darrell Figgis: An Overview of His Work" is a general critical introduction that places all of Figgis's writings into the context of his life and times. Clearly, Darrell Figgis is no Yeats, Joyce, or Synge. But Figgis does deserve far more attention than he currently receives.

BIBLIOGRAPHY

Works by Darrell Figgis

AE (George Russell): A Study of a Man and a Nation. New York: Dodd, Mead, 1916.
Broken Arcs. London: Dent, 1911.
Bye-Ways of Study. Dublin and London: Talbot, 1918.
Children of Earth. Dublin and London: Maunsel, 1918.
A Chronicle of Jails. Dublin: Talbot, 1917.
The Crucibles of Time and Other Poems. London: Dent, 1911.
The Economic Case for Irish Independence. Dublin and London: Maunsel, 1920.
The Gaelic State in the Past and Future or "The Crown of a Nation." Dublin and London: Maunsel, 1917.
The Historic Case for Irish Independence. Dublin and London: Maunsel, 1918.
The House of Success. Dublin: Gael Co-operative, 1922.
"Introduction" In *The Foundations of Peace*, by Seamus Burke. Dublin and London: Maunsel, 1920.
The Irish Constitution (Explained by Darrell Figgis). Dublin: Mellifont, [1922].
Jacob Elthorne. London and Toronto: Dent, 1914.
The Mount of Transfiguration. Dublin and London: Maunsel, 1915.
The Paintings of William Blake. New York: Scribner's, 1925.
Queen Tara. London: Dent, 1913.
Recollections of the Irish War. London: Benn, 1927.
The Return of the Hero. New York: Boni, 1930.
A Second Chronicle of Jails. Dublin: Talbot, 1918.
Shakespeare: A Study. London: Dent, 1911

Studies and Appreciations. London: Dent, 1912.
A Vision of Life. London: John Lane (Bodley Head), [1909].

Studies of Darrell Figgis

Deane, Paul. "The Death of Greatness: Darrell Figgis's *Return of the Hero.*" *Notes on Modern Irish Literature* 3 (1991): 30–36.

Dunn, John. "Darrell Figgis, a Man Nearly Anonymous." *Journal of Irish Literature* 15.1 (January 1986):33–42.

Felter, Maryann. "Darrell Figgis: An Overview of His Work." *Journal of Irish Literature* 22.2 (May 1993): 3–24.

Gonzalez, Alexander G. *Darrell Figgis: A Study of His Novels*. Modern Irish Literature Monograph Series. Butler, PA: Kopper, 1992.

———. "Darrell Figgis's *The House of Success*: A Forgotten Historical Novel." *Eire-Ireland* 26.4 (Winter 1991): 118–25.

———. "The Achievement of Darrell Figgis's *Children of Earth*: Realism and Folk Custom." *Eire-Ireland* 22.3 (Fall 1987): 129–43.

Griffin, Gerald. *The Dead March Past: A Semi-Autobiographical Saga*. London: Macmillan, 1937.

Holt, Edgar. *Protest in Arms: The Irish Troubles 1916–1923*. New York: Coward-McCann, 1960.

Lanters, Jose. "Darrell Figgis, *The Return of the Hero*, and the Making of the Irish Nation." *Colby Quarterly* 31.3 (September 1995) 204–13.

O'Malley, Ernest. *On Another Man's Wound*. Dublin and London: Maunsel, 1936.

Brian Friel

(1929–)

Mary Fitzgerald-Hoyt

BIOGRAPHY

Brian Friel was born on January 9, 1929, in Killclogher, near Omagh, County Tyrone, and was raised in a Catholic, nationalist family. The complex issues of identity and language that inform Friel's plays were apparent even at his birth. Birth certificates were issued for both January 9 and 10, and Ulf Dantanus notes that whereas the parish register listed Friel with the Irish name Brian Patrick O'Friel, the civil birth certificate designated him as the Anglicized Bernard Patrick Friel.

When Friel was ten, his family relocated to Derry. After attending both Long Tower School and St. Columb's College, Friel entered the seminary at St. Patrick's College, Maynooth, an experience he found traumatic. Although he completed a B.A. there, he did not enter the priesthood. After attending St. Mary's Training College (now St. Joseph's) in Belfast, Friel taught school in Derry from 1950 to 1960. In 1954, he married Anne Morrison; the couple has five children.

Friel first achieved recognition as a short story writer, and so favorably received was his work that in 1960 he retired from teaching to write full-time. By the late 1950s he had begun writing plays. In 1963 Friel spent several months observing Sir Tyrone Guthrie's directing in Minneapolis and soon thereafter abandoned short story writing for drama.

In 1980 Friel and actor Stephen Rea founded the Field Day Theatre Company in an attempt to bring new cultural life to Northern Ireland. As well as revitalizing Irish theatre, Field Day has widened its intellectual concerns through the publication of pamphlets and the monumental *Field Day Anthology of Irish Writing*.

Friel's artistic achievement has been recognized through numerous honors, including an appointment to the Irish Senate and membership in the Irish Academy of Letters. He currently resides in Greencastle, County Donegal.

MAJOR WORKS AND THEMES

In his short stories, Friel depicts the world of his childhood, the Catholic populace in northwestern Ireland on both sides of the border. Constrained by poverty and limited opportunities, his characters seek solace from narrow lives by indulging in ultimately disappointing illusions.

Of Friel's early plays, several of which were written for radio broadcast, the most notable is *The Enemy Within*, which premiered at the Abbey Theatre in 1962. The play's protagonist, St. Columba, torn between his allegiance to Ireland and his monastic duties in Iona, illustrates Friel's increasing concern with characters caught between inner conflicts and social demands.

Friel's first play to win international acclaim, *Philadelphia, Here I Come!* (1964), was set in the imaginary town of Ballybeg (Baile Beag), Donegal, the backdrop for many of Friel's later plays. Gareth O'Donnell, a young man on the eve of emigrating to America, is split into two roles, private and public, to portray the difference between the inarticulate young man familiar to the community and the imaginative inner man torn between the unknown world of America and his beloved, though dissatisfying, Irish home. The play ends with the bewildered Gar wondering why he must leave his home for an uncertain future. His is not only a deeply personal dilemma but also a reflection of the plight of so many Irish emigrants.

Friel's next play, *The Loves of Cass McGuire* (1966), which began life as a radio production in 1961, reflects Friel's frequent practice of writing "tandem" plays that explore similar issues from different angles. Cass McGuire, unlike Gar, is returning to Ireland after a long residence in America. Her homecoming is painful, for her family, embarrassed by her outspokenness and vulgarity, arranges for her to be placed in a home for the elderly. Perhaps worst of all, she finds that the savings she painstakingly sent home were unneeded: her brother has banked it as a "nest egg" for her. Cass is left, as are so many Friel characters, with only her illusions to console her.

Lovers (1967) offers two perspectives on romantic love, "Winners" and "Losers." The "winners," an adolescent couple expecting their first child, are drowned shortly before their wedding. Ironically, they are winners because death spares them from what promises to be a disillusioning future. "Losers" is an often hilarious but ultimately poignant story of a middle-aged couple divided by the manipulativeness and puritanical piety of the wife's mother.

Crystal and Fox (1968), examining the self-destruction of small-time showman Fox Melarkey, to some extent presages Friel's later allegory of the artist, *Faith Healer*. In 1969, Friel produced *The Mundy Scheme*, a political satire about a scheme to transform Ireland into an international graveyard.

The Gentle Island (1971) portrays the savagery that underlies the natural beauty of the island of Inishkeen. Despite the massive emigration of islanders, Manus Sweeney attempts to keep his family together, but the appearance of two strangers causes hidden sexual frustration and violence to erupt. A darkly haunting portrait of a closed-off community, the play prefigures *Living Quarters*.

In his introduction to Friel's *Selected Plays*, Seamus Deane has noted that the cataclysmic events in Northern Ireland in the 1960s and 1970s caused Friel's writing to be infused with "the sense of a whole history of failure concentrated into a crisis over a doomed community or group" (17). Though Friel had formerly resisted making political commentary in his works, *The Freedom of the City* (1973) and *Volunteers* (1975) respond to real political events. In the former, a reaction to the killing of fourteen civil rights marchers by British paratroopers on the infamous Bloody Sunday, three civil rights marchers inadvertently take refuge in the city's Guildhall, which the authorities mistakenly interpret to be a political gesture. Through Friel's manipulation of chronology and point of view we learn the disparity between the inner lives of Lily, Skinner, and Michael and the images imposed on them by outsiders. These falsifications are deadly, for having been deemed armed and dangerous by the military authorities, the three are murdered as they attempt to leave the Guildhall.

Volunteers, in part inspired by the Dublin Wood Quay controversy, which pitted building development interests against archaeological preservationists, concerns Irish Republican Army (IRA) prisoners who, by volunteering to assist in an archaeological dig, are condemned to death as "collaborators" when they return to prison. Although both *The Freedom of the City* and *Volunteers* contain strong political overtones—the shocking mishandling of the investigation of the marchers' deaths recalls the outrage that followed the Widgery Report about Bloody Sunday, for instance—to read the plays as political propaganda, as some critics have, is surely misguided. What both plays reveal is Friel's growing preoccupation with the process of "making history," with the gulf between private experience and its public interpretation. *Living Quarters* (1977) and *Aristocrats* (1979), both set in Ballybeg, trace the disintegration of family communities. The psychological trauma occasioned by military hero Frank Butler's suicide after learning that his second wife had committed adultery with his son is innovatively dramatized. "Sir," a ledger-bearing sort of playwright-within-a-play, prompts the various family members as they agonizingly reenact the day of their father's death. *Aristocrats* concerns the fragmentation of a Catholic Big House family, the O'Donnells, also at the time of their father's death.

In the allegorical *Faith Healer* (1979), Friel explores the life of the artist through the career of Frank Hardy, whose healing gift brings him both fame and annihilation. Technically innovative, the play, a series of monologues, presents contradictory accounts of Hardy's life and art.

In *Translations* (1980), Friel's masterpiece, yet another O'Donnell family faces personal and national crisis. As part of the 1830s British Ordnance Survey, English soldiers, assisted by Owen O'Donnell, are changing Irish place-names to English as they attempt to "map" Ireland, and as Yolland, a sensitive young soldier, intuits, "It's an eviction of sorts." By the end of the play, when Yolland has disappeared under suspicious circumstances, real evictions are threatened. Hugh O'Donnell, the hedge schoolmaster rendered obsolete by the coming of the national schools, witnesses the rupture of his community, the breakdown of his family. By the end of the play, he sadly acknowledges that his community, faced with possible annihilation, must embrace the new English names—"We must make them our home."

Though *Translations* won immediate acclaim, it was initially misread as simply an elegy for Gaelic Ireland. In the "sporadic diary" he kept while writing the play, Friel expressed his desire to keep the play from being "overwhelmed by the political element . . . [b]ecause the play has to do with language and only language." Much of the play not only concerns the failure of human beings to communicate effectively but also questions the ability of language, as Hugh O'Donnell puts it, "to interpret between privacies" (446). The "tandem" play to *Translations, The Communication Cord* (1982), a farce that ridicules the sentimentalizing of the Irish past, features a linguist who can construct elaborate theories about human communication but has difficulty expressing his own feelings.

Friel's concern with social transition as well as his admiration for Chekhov and Turgenev are manifested in his Russian "translations": *Three Sisters* (1981), *Fathers and Sons* (1987), and *A Month in the Country* (1992). Not literally translations, as Friel is not proficient in Russian, these adaptations are permeated with his understanding of social flux and its attendant anomie. Another sort of "translation" is *The London Vertigo*, Friel's adaptation of Charles Macklin's *The True Born Irishman/The Irish Fine Lady*. Macklin, born Cathal MacLochlainn in 1690s Donegal, eventually abandoned the Irish language and the Catholic religion and achieved fame as a playwright and actor in London. The comedy satirizes Irish Anglophilia, both embracing and subverting the conventions of the eighteenth-century English drama.

Long concerned with the process of history making, Friel in *Making History* (1988) explores the life of Irish chieftain Hugh O'Neill. Himself a maker of history, O'Neill resists the mythologizing efforts of his biographer and in Friel's version emerges as a man deeply torn between the Irish and English cultures.

Dancing at Lughnasa (1990), an autobiographical play concerning Friel's mother's Donegal family, has become perhaps Friel's most popular work. In a device reminiscent of *The Glass Menagerie*, a now-adult Michael imaginatively reconstructs a childhood spent with his unmarried mother and her four sisters in 1930s Ballybeg, their daily routine transformed by the return of his uncle, Father Jack, from African missionary work and the visits of Michael's charming, unreliable father. This subtle play continues Friel's preoccupation with communication, but here dance is more efficacious than words in voicing the heart's mysteries. Likewise, Friel's ongoing concern with cultural conflict is manifested in the numerous clashes between pagan and Christian religions.

Friel's most recent plays, *Wonderful Tennessee* (1993) and *Molly Sweeney* (1994), though quite different in style, both evoke the potency and disappointment of dreams. In *Wonderful Tennessee*, three married couples wait on Ballybeg pier for a ferryman who will take them to their desired destination, *Oileán Draíochta*, the mysterious island. Passing the time in conversation, dance, and song, the couples reveal and learn much about themselves but never reach their destination. The play's use of allegory and symbolism recalls *Faith Healer*, as does the structure of *Molly Sweeney*, in which a series of long monologues provides differing perspectives on Molly's blindness and the operation that both restores her sight and destroys her peace. Through Molly, Friel continues to explore the nature of language, but here language is equated with the sighted Molly's having to learn to perceive the world in an entirely new fashion.

Brian Friel's plays continue to probe the ways in which human beings perceive and deceive themselves, the collision between private self and public image. Rooted in the cultural fissures of Northern Ireland, his drama reveals an intimate awareness of his native place. Yet Friel's profound understanding of humanity has enabled him to translate his world to an international audience, and though eavesdropping in Ballybeg, listeners hear the cadences of their own disparate hearts.

CRITICAL RECEPTION

Friel's status as a major international dramatist is now widely accepted, though his short stories are most frequently discussed in terms of their influence on his drama. Friel's background as a Northern Irish Catholic has sometimes led to difficulties in "translation": like many Northern writers, he has been accused of being both too political and not political enough. His long-standing exploration of the limitations of language, of the conflict between private and public selves, and of the nature of history has likewise elicited wide critical discussion.

In his 1973 study, D.E.S. Maxwell discusses Friel's development as a writer, including the influence of the political turmoil in Northern Ireland, and concludes that "Friel will continue to find the dramatic forms that generalize, with humor and compassion, on his particular and regional veracities, where art begins" (170). In his 1985 book (rev. 1988), Dantanus emphasizes Friel's use of Irish "dichotomies of place," "East-West and North-South." George O'Brien's "critical and cultural" study (1990) praises the author's "range and growth" and provides a sustained discussion of Friel's use of language, noting, "Behind every verbal construct lies a silence out of which an alternative meaning to the text emerges" (116). Richard Pine's 1990 book combines psychoanalytical, postcolonial, and linguistic approaches, placing particular emphasis on Friel's Northern Irish identity. The essays collected in Alan Peacock's *The Achievement of Brian Friel* offer a variety of literary approaches to Friel's writing.

BIBLIOGRAPHY

Works by Brian Friel

American Welcome. In *Best Short Plays 1981* ed. Stanley Richards. Radnor, PA: Chilton, 1982.

Aristocrats. Dublin: Gallery, 1980.

The Communication Cord. London: Faber and Faber, 1983.

Crystal and Fox. London: Faber and Faber, 1970.

Crystal and Fox and *The Mundy Scheme*. New York: Farrar, Straus, and Giroux, 1970.

Dancing at Lughnasa. London: Faber and Faber, 1990.

The Diviner. Dublin: O'Brien, 1983.

The Enemy Within. *Journal of Irish Literature*, 4.2 (May 1975); Dublin: Gallery, 1979.

Faith Healer. London: Faber and Faber, 1980.

Fathers and Sons. After Turgenev. London: Faber and Faber, 1987.

The Freedom of the City. London: Faber and Faber, 1974.

The Gentle Island. London: Davis-Poynter, 1973.

The Gold in the Sea. New York: Doubleday, 1966.

Living Quarters. London: Faber and Faber, 1978.

The London Vertigo. Loughcrew: Gallery, 1990.

Lovers. London: Faber and Faber, 1969.

The Loves of Cass McGuire. New York: Noonday, 1966; London: Faber and Faber, 1967.

Making History. London: Faber and Faber, 1988.

Molly Sweeney. Loughcrew: Gallery, 1994.

A Month in the Country. After Turgenev. Loughcrew: Gallery, 1992.

Philadelphia, Here I Come! London: Faber and Faber; New York: Farrar, Straus, and Giroux, 1965.

The Saucer of Larks. New York: Doubleday; London: Gollancz, 1962.

Selected Plays. Intro. Seamus Deane. London: Faber and Faber, 1984; Washington, DC: Catholic University Press, 1986.

Selected Stories. Dublin: Gallery, 1979.

Three Sisters by Anton Chekhov. Dublin: Gallery, 1981.

Translations. London: Faber and Faber, 1981.

Wonderful Tennessee. London: Faber and Faber, 1993.

Studies of Brian Friel

Dantanus, Ulf. *Brian Friel: A Study*. London: Faber and Faber, 1988. Rev. ed. of *Brian Friel: The Growth of an Irish Dramatist*. Gothenburg, Sweden: Acta Universitatis Gothburgensis, 1985; Atlantic Heights, NJ: Humanities, 1986.

Maxwell, D.E.S. *Brian Friel*. Lewisburg, PA: Bucknell University Press, 1973.

O'Brien, George. *Brian Friel*. Boston: Twayne, 1990.

Peacock, Alan, ed. *The Achievement of Brian Friel*. Gerrards Cross: Smythe, 1992.

Pine, Richard. *Brian Friel and Ireland's Drama*. London and New York: Routledge, 1990.

Oliver St. John Gogarty

(1878–1957)

John D. Conway

BIOGRAPHY

Oliver St. John Gogarty, a Roman Catholic, was born in Rutland Square, Dublin, on August 17, 1878. The Gogartys, an old Gaelic clan, could boast of three generations of doctors, highly unusual for a Catholic family at that time.

Gogarty attended the Christian Brothers School in North Richmond, after which he was enrolled in a series of boarding schools—Mungret, Stonyhurst, and Clongowes. His one year at Clongowes established him as a top player in both cricket and football and as an immensely popular, witty, and gregarious student. The Gogarty legend was beginning to take hold.

After Conglowes Gogarty enrolled in the Royal University in Dublin to study medicine in 1896. He lasted two years, during which time his chief preoccupations appear to have been cycling, drinking, carousing at night, and failing examinations. In 1898 he transferred to the medical school of Trinity College, which, with its view of ancient Greece as model, provided the aesthetic soil in which Gogarty's art would take root.

When Gogarty completed his studies at Trinity, he left behind a legend: champion cyclist, superb swimmer, Rabelaisian wit who authored outrageous limericks, aesthete who could from memory recite Virgil, Homer, and Catullus by the yard, prankster, poet, mocker, and finally, in 1907, doctor of medicine.

In 1922 Gogarty, along with W. B. Yeats, became a member of the Irish Free State Senate. Gogarty eventually moved his practice to Grosvenor Square in London but continued to attend meetings of the Senate in Dublin while Ireland slipped closer to anarchy. In 1924 *An Offering of Swans* won the Taillteann poetry medal. In 1932 he was elected as a foundation member of the Irish

Academy of Letters. He then published *As I Was Going Down Sackville Street* (1937), *I Follow St. Patrick* (1938), and *Tumbling in the Hay* (1939).

Gogarty gained his greatest notoriety as the source for Buck Mulligan in Joyce's *Ulysses* (1922). Gogarty was outraged at what he considered a gross betrayal of friendship by Joyce, but neither Joyce nor Gogarty distinguished himself in the *Ulysses* flap. Gogarty returned to Ireland after World War II for visits and died in New York City on September 22, 1957, from heart disease.

MAJOR WORKS AND THEMES

Gogarty's life, his energetic and joyous romp through the quotidian, may well have been his major work. The full extent of his contribution to Ireland cannot be measured by his writing alone. The life he lived—the friends, the foes, the battles, the politics, the Dublin intrigues, the insults, the lawsuits, the jests, the repartees, the laughter, the limericks, and the wit—often seem more engaging than the published works.

From the time Gogarty was a student he wrote and published, often indiscriminately. Hence his journalistic pieces in Dublin and America, his plays—*Blight* (1917), *A Serious Thing* (1919), *The Enchanted Trousers* (1919)—other impressionistic ramblings—*Rolling Down the Lea* (1950) and *Intimations* (1950)—and his meanderings in long fiction—*Going Native* (1940), *Mad Grandeur* (1941), and *Mr. Petunia* (1945)—do not constitute the essential Gogarty.

The Gogarty that endures is found in the autobiographical *As I Was Going Down Sackville Street, Tumbling in the Hay, I Follow St. Patrick,* and *The Collected Poems.* Of these the most celebrated is that "Phantasy in Fact" that explodes through the Dublin of Yeats, Joyce, Moore, AE, Griffith, Collins, de Valera, Trinity College, Phoenix Park, Guinness, the Kips, and Endymion (a man gone "natural") in the pages of *As I Was Going Down Sackville Street,* which takes its title from an old Dublin ballad. Its mixture is so rich, comprising anecdote, characterization, verse, limerick, libel, and more, that one Henry M. Sinclair brought forward a lawsuit. A jury awarded him £900 plus costs in a libel action. Gogarty was outraged. Dublin had high theater.

Tumbling in the Hay, a student memoir narrated by Gideon Ousley (a fictitious Gogarty), is a rollicking ride among medical students who journey from the exuberance of youth to the more sobering reality of professional responsibility. More joyous and exhilarating than *As I Was Going Down Sackville,* its characters are the stuff of Dublin, "the high place of humbug." It has rightly been called Gogarty's "comic masterpiece."

The Collected Poems, including nearly all the poems from the earlier *An Offering of Swans, Wild Apples,* and *Others to Adorn,* plus selected others, most notably the elegy on Yeats, substantiates, for many, the latter's claim that Gogarty was "one of the great lyric poets of our age." But to write of beauty and friendship, love and loss, and living and death in the classical style of the ancients, as Gogarty does, is to write for another time.

At his best there is a hint of the classics—of Virgil, Horace, Catullus, Propertius—of Swinburne and Housman and Herrick and the Connemara countryside. He is then a poet of clarity and wit, of grace and dignity, of exuberance and challenge and humanity. Throughout Gogarty's poetry and prose, Beauty is the mark. Where his trajectory is accurate, as it is in "To the Liffey with Swans" and "Golden Stockings" and elsewhere, the effect is magical. Unfortunately he sometimes misses his mark, but let it be remembered that when he sings from the mountaintop, there is a jubilant rumble in the valley below: "Dum vivimus vivamus" (While we live, let us live).

CRITICAL RECEPTION

Any discussion of Gogarty's critical reception begins with Yeats, who, in the preface to *The Oxford Book of Modern Verse* (1936), refers to Gogarty as a "great" lyric poet and includes seventeen of his poems in the volume. Yeats does not stand alone in his praise of Gogarty's verse, but since 1936 the general consensus is that his assessment was overly generous.

From the time of his death in 1957 until the present, Gogarty has received only intermittent attention from scholars and critics. His reputation is mired somewhere between his authorship of *As I Was Going Down Sackville Street* and his fictional presence as the prototype for Buck Mulligan in *Ulysses*. The time has clearly come for a major reassessment of the man and his works. There is considerably more to Gogarty than flashing wit, repartee, limericks, and legend.

Scholarly work includes Ulick O'Connor's essential biography (1990). J. B. Lyons's monograph (1976) and his subsequent biography (1980) update O'Connor's earlier work in a sympathetic appraisal that includes a valuable checklist of primary and secondary sources. James F. Carens's book contends that future readers will better understand Yeats's enthusiasm for Gogarty's verse and that *Sackville Street* and *Tumbling in the Hay* are among the major achievements of the Irish Renaissance. Mary Regan offers a recent assessment of Gogarty's use of the mock-heroic in his myth and poetry, and Ulick O'Connor explores the tortured Joyce–Gogarty relationship again in *James Joyce: The Artist and the Labyrinth*.

BIBLIOGRAPHY

Works by Oliver St. John Gogarty

Prose

As I Was Going Down Sackville Street. London: Rich and Cowan; New York: Reynal and Hitchcock, 1937.
I Follow St. Patrick. London: Rich and Cowan; New York: Reynal and Hitchcook, 1938; London: Constable, 1950.

Tumbling in the Hay. London: Constable; New York: Reynal and Hitchcock, 1939.
Going Native. New York: Duell, Sloan, and Pearce, 1940; London: Constable, 1941.
Mad Grandeur. Philadelphia and New York: Lippincott, 1941; London: Constable, 1943.
Mr. Petunia. New York: Creative Age, 1945; London: Constable, 1946.
Intimations. New York: Abelard, 1950.
Rolling Down the Lea. London: Constable, 1950.
It Isn't That Time of Year At All! London: MacGibbon and Kee; Garden City, NY: Doubleday, 1954.
Start from Somewhere Else. Garden City, NY: Doubleday, 1955.
A Weekend in the Middle of the Week and Other Essays on the Bias. Garden City, NY: Doubleday, 1955.
Mourning Became Mrs. Spendlove. New York: Creative Age, 1958.
W. B. Yeats: A Memoir. Dublin: Dolmen, 1963.

Poetry

Hyperthuleana. Dublin: Gaelic, 1916.
The Ship and Other Poems. Dublin: Talbot, 1918.
An Offering of Swans. Dublin: Cuala, 1923; London: Eyre and Spottiswoode, 1934.
An Offering of Swans and Other Poems. London: Eyre and Spottiswoode, 1924.
Wild Apples. Dublin: Cuala, 1928, 1930; New York: Cape and Smith, 1929.
Elbow Room. Dublin: Cuala, 1929; New York: Duell, Sloan, and Pearce, 1940.
Selected Poems. New York: Macmillan, 1933.
Others to Adorn. London: Rich and Cowan, 1938.
Perennial. London: Constable, 1946.
The Collected Poems. London: Constable, 1951; New York: Devin-Adair, 1954.
Unselected Poems. Baltimore: Contemporary, 1954.

Plays

Blight. Dublin: Talbot, 1917.
The Enchanted Trousers. Dublin: Privately printed, 1919.
A Serious Thing. Dublin: Privately printed, 1919.
The Plays of Oliver St. John Gogarty. James F. Carens, ed. Newark, DE: Proscenium, 1971.

Letters

Many Lines to Thee. Ed. James F. Carens. Dublin: Dolmen, 1971.

Studies of Oliver St. John Gogarty

Carens, James F. *Surpassing Wit: Oliver St. John Gogarty, His Poetry and His Prose*. New York: Columbia University Press 1979.
Hedlund, Magnus. "Tre processer: En sammanstallning." *Ord och Bild* 102.3 (1993): 85–90.
Hyde, H. Montgomery. "Yeats and Gogarty." *Yeats Annual 5* (1987): 154–60.
Jeffares, Norman A. *The Circus Animals*. London: Macmillan, 1970.
Lyons, John B. *Oliver St. John Gogarty*. Lewisburg, PA: Bucknell University Press, 1976.

————. *Oliver St. John Gogarty: The Man of Many Talents*. Dublin: Blackwater, 1980.

O'Connor, Ulick. "Joyce and Gogarty: Royal and Ancient, Two Hangers-On." In *James Joyce: The Artist and the Labyrinth*, ed. Augustine Martin. London: Ryan, 1990, 333–54.

————. *The Times I've Seen: Oliver St. John Gogarty, A Biography*. New York: Obolensky, 1963.

Regan, Mary J. "Beyond the Pale: A Wider Reading of Oliver St. John Gogarty's Mock-Heroic Poems." *Notes on Modern Irish Literature* 2 (1990): 12–18.

Riley, Mary. "Joyce, Gogarty, and the Irish Hero." *Canadian Journal of Irish Studies* 10 (1984): 45–54.

Lady Augusta Gregory

(1852–1932)

Noelle Bowles

BIOGRAPHY

Lady Isabella Augusta Gregory, as she came to be known, was born Isabella Augusta Persse on March 15, 1852. Her father was a member of the Protestant landholding class, and his estate, Roxborough House, was the setting of Augusta's childhood and young adult life.

Augusta spent her early years reading the Bible and other religious texts as well as Shakespeare, Tennyson, Malory, and books on Irish history. She taught herself French, German, and Italian with the help of translations, but she did not have an opportunity to use her knowledge until the illness of her elder brother forced her to leave Roxborough and travel to France and Italy as his companion during his convalescence. During one such visit to Cannes her Connacht neighbor and former governor of Ceylon, Sir William Gregory, began a friendship with her that led to their eventual marriage in 1880.

Through her marriage to Sir William she gained entry into international society. As Lady Gregory, she met and mingled with much of Europe's aristocracy, and she had access to many of her era's famous writers and politicians. Although she spent time in London, she felt most at home on her husband's estate, Coole Park, which was only a few miles from Roxborough House, and she resided at Coole during her widowhood. Her marriage to Sir William ended with his death in 1892, having produced one son, William Robert (1881–1918). Sir William left Coole to his son, and his wife acted as the estate's trustee until Robert reached his majority. After Robert was killed in action during World War II, his wife, Margaret, arranged to sell Coole to the Irish Land Commission on the condition that her mother-in-law could remain in residence for the rest of her life.

Lady Gregory's involvement with the Irish Literary Renaissance began in 1896, when she invited Yeats to stay at Coole. Their friendship and collaboration resulted in what is certainly the greatest single contribution to the movement, the founding of the Abbey Theatre. Opening in 1904 with Gregory, John Millington Synge, and Yeats as directors, the Abbey Theatre provided Irish playwrights with a venue that supported their creative efforts to produce plays counter to the English stereotype of the Irish as amoral, drunken buffoons. The patent for the theater specified that the only productions staged would be either classical works or creations of Irish playwrights.

In her position as a director, Gregory encouraged Sean O'Casey's development as a playwright and defended Synge's *Playboy of the Western World*, both in Dublin (1907) and during its American tour. In 1909, she supported the controversial production of G. B. Shaw's *The Shewing-Up of Blanco Posnet* and risked losing the theater's operating license as well as incurring heavy fines by permitting the production to open in spite of Dublin Castle's desire to censor the play (Coxhead 130–131). Her social position helped in her fund-raising endeavors to keep the Abbey solvent, and she continued in her directorship until her death. However, her involvement with the theater was not confined solely to administration; Gregory was in her own right a popular and productive dramatist, writing forty plays and collaborating on four with Yeats and two with Douglas Hyde.

Lady Gregory helped Hyde form a Kiltartan branch of the Gaelic League, and in 1897 she began to study Gaelic intensively. She quickly became competent enough to translate folk ballads and to compile the legends that would lead to the publications of *Cuchulain of Muirthemne* (1902), *Gods and Fighting Men* (1904), and a number of tales and ballads based on the folklore of the Kiltartan district. Her charity toward the peasants who worked the land is noted in her autobiography, *Seventy Years*, and is evident in her efforts to improve their living conditions (16). Like many other Protestant landholders she was initially wary of Parnell's Home Rule, fearing the Catholic majority might easily disenfranchise the Protestant minority. However, by 1897 she had joined Horace Plunkett's Irish Agricultural Organization Society, a coordinating organization that assisted farmers and small factories to form mutually beneficial cooperatives, and by 1900 she was backing Parnell's Home Rule efforts (366). In the early 1920s she also contributed articles to *The Nation*, detailing the atrocities committed by the Black and Tans; however, most of these were published anonymously, with the understandable fear of reprisal.

The time that she did not spend with the Abbey and its players and writers was spent in attempting to secure for Dublin the French impressionist collection of her nephew, Sir Hugh Lane, who perished with the sinking of the *Lusitania* in 1913. Murphy, editor of the *Journals*, states that they were originally begun to document her efforts to wrest the paintings from the National Gallery in London (xii). Although the death of her nephew affected her deeply, her greatest grief was the loss of her son, Robert, whose plane was shot down over Italy in

1918. She titled a chapter of her autobiography "My Grief" in commemoration of his death.

The last works to receive her attention were *Seventy Years* and her *Journals*, both of which were published posthumously. She died in May 1932 at the age of eighty after a long and painful decline. Breast cancer may have been a factor of her illness, and certainly rheumatism was involved; the final entries of her *Journals* emphasize the agony of her last days. In his afterword to her *Journals*, Smythe states that the news of her passing "brought tributes from all over the world" (639).

MAJOR WORKS AND THEMES

Lady Gregory began her literary career and political activism with the publication of a pamphlet, *Arabi and His Household* (1882), which defended the cause of Arabi Bey, an Egyptian who sought changes in the Turkish administration of his country. She later edited her husband's memoirs and published them as his autobiography (1894), and she compiled and edited his grandfather's correspondence for publication (1898). Also as an editor Lady Gregory made her initial entrance into the Irish Literary Revival. In 1901, she edited *Ideals in Ireland*, a collection of essays by AE, Douglas Hyde, George Moore, D. P. Moran, Standish O'Grady, and Yeats. The purpose of the collection was, as Gregory saw it, to reveal "a passionate love of Ireland" (*Seventy Years* 394).

Irish nationalism was the driving force behind her mythological and folkloric themes. Citing British and Trinity College denigration of Irish culture as the cause of her motivation, Gregory set out to demonstrate that Irish mythology contained a richness equivalent to that of Arthurian tales the English valued so highly (*Seventy Years* 391). *Cuchulain of Muirthemne* helped to renew popular interest in Ireland's mythological heritage, and the prose style she invented by transposing Gaelic into English served as an inspiration for Yeats, O'Casey, and others. Upon *Cuchulain*'s publication, Gregory stated, "I had done what I had wanted; something for the dignity of Ireland. The reviews showed that the enemy could no longer scoff at our literature and its 'want of idealism' " (400). Her interpretation of Irish mythology gave nationalists a hero of whom they could be proud. Indeed, so popular was her version of the Cuchulain story that Yeats later revised the original ending of "Cuchulain's Fight with the Sea" (1897), wherein the hero dies fighting the waves, to coincide with that of Gregory's book. She states that this change was made because "his death in battle is much better known through my Cuchulain than when the poem was written" (*Journals II* 603).

Kincora (1905, rev. 1909) builds upon the mythology of ancient Ireland and simultaneously comments upon Ireland's relationship with its colonizers, in this case, the Danish, whom Brian Boru defeats and exiles. Sitric's forces symbolize the British occupation of Ireland, and Brian's offer to allow them to remain in Ireland if they agree to the conditions of his leadership seeks to legitimate a position of acceptance for Protestant Unionists: Protestant interests in Ireland will be protected if they agree to put the good of the nation before self-interest. Sitric's refusal of Brian's peace is based not on the unfairness of the terms of surrender but on his desire to bow to no authority higher than himself. *Kincora* thus functions as a parable and a warning to Unionist factions whose rejection of nationalism turned solely on the issue of self-rule; the Danish are exiled only after Sitric betrays his agreement with Brian.

The Gaol Gate (1906) expresses the radical nationalist ideal in its preference of martyrdom over the betrayal of comrades. Mary Cahel, mother of an innocent man who was executed, transforms the grief of her daughter-in-law from that of a personal loss to a national triumph. Through his mother's exclamations, Denis Cahel quickly becomes a heroic figure who died for his friends rather than betray them to English justice.

Loyalty is also the theme of *The Rising of the Moon* (1907), whose title refers specifically to the ballad of the 1850s Fenian movement, but the action of the play itself was certainly relevant to the turmoil of the early twentieth century. The play centers on the conflicting loyalty of a police sergeant who must decide whether to arrest a fleeing Fenian and fulfill his duty to his employers, in this case the British-backed police force, or to let the fugitive go. The happy, nationalist ending, in which the sergeant forfeits the £100 reward and allows the Fenian to go free, attempts a reconciliation for those who, as Saddlemyer notes, "are torn between loyalty to their masters and loyalty to their country" (87).

In addition to transcribing and preserving local traditions such as those included in her *Kiltartan* series of folklore, Lady Gregory acted as a chronicler for the development and progress of the Irish Literary Renaissance. *Our Irish Theatre* (1914) details the founding of the Abbey Theatre and offers her interpretation of contributions and efforts made by those involved.

CRITICAL RECEPTION

Criticism of Lady Gregory's works has had very little middle ground even from the beginning. Either she is perceived as an opportunist whose fame and talent were really the products of her associates, or she is viewed as a woman of creative genius who was constrained from many achievements by the sexism of her era. Kopper makes note of "the false, almost slanderous, impression of Lady Gregory created by Moore, Joyce, and Gogarty earlier in the century" (9). Her harshest critics often relegate her to the position of a literary wet nurse, a woman who supported and coddled men more talented than herself through whom she could gain literary glory. Kohfeldt positions Gregory "behind" the Irish Renaissance in the same patronizing sense of there being a good woman behind a successful man. Kohfeldt's analysis defines Gregory's role in Irish literature as purely auxiliary—as the hostess of Coole.

Coxhead's text refutes assertions such as those of Gogarty, who suggested that Yeats wrote Gregory's better plays, and emphasizes the degree to which

Gregory actually authored *Cathleen Ni Houlihan, Pot of Broth,* and *The Unicorn from the Stars* (105–15). Lady Gregory herself seems to have been aware of the accusations of mediocrity that were made against her, and her documentation of her works' enthusiastic reception may have been an effort to counter such perceptions. In *Seventy Years,* she cites excerpts of the letters she received upon the publication of *Cuchulain,* including accolades from President T. Roosevelt, Mark Twain, and folklore scholar Sir John Rhys. She remarked upon Yeats's failure to credit her properly with the authorship of *Cathleen Ni Houlihan* in a 1925 publication, and as she states herself, his action was "rather hard on me not giving my name with *Cathleen Ni Houlihan* that I wrote all but all of" (*Journals* II 28).

Saddlemyer's critique of Lady Gregory's works emphasizes the nationalist aspects of her writing and counters perceptions of Gregory as a socialite with no political agenda. Indeed, Saddlemyer asserts that Gregory was more of a "rebel nationalist" (in Ronsley's *Myth and Reality in Irish Literature* 29) than was either Yeats or Synge and interprets *Cathleen Ni Houlihan* as a work of "political propaganda" (30). Interest in colonial and feminist theory has led to reexaminations of Gregory's writing as it functions within colonial and gender issues. Hawkins, for example, views *Kincora*'s Gormleith as an expression of the frustrations of Ascendancy nationalists, who occupied the awkward position of being both the colonizer and the colonized, and of women, who were marginalized by the "increasing misogyny which marked late nineteenth and early twentieth century" (in Komesu and Sekine's *Irish Writers and Politics* 94) nationalist movements, especially those of Ireland.

BIBLIOGRAPHY

Selected Works by Lady Augusta Gregory

Prose

Coole. Dublin: Cuala, 1931.
Ed. *Ideals in Ireland.* London and New York: At the Unicorn, 1901.
Lady Gregory's Journals. Ed. Daniel Murphy, Coole edition 14–15. 2 vols. New York: Oxford University Press, 1978.
Our Irish Theatre. New York and London: Putnam, 1914.
Seventy Years: Being an Autobiography of Lady Gregory. Ed. Colin Smythe. New York: 1976.

Folklore

Cuchulain of Muirthemne. London and New York: Murray, 1902.
Gods and Fighting Men. London and New York: Murray, 1904.
The Kiltartan History Book. Dublin and New York: Maunsel, 1909.
The Kiltartan Poetry Book. Dublin and London: Putnam, 1918.
Visions and Beliefs in the West of Ireland. London and New York: Putnam, 1920.

Plays

The Image and Other Plays: *The Image, Hanrahan's Oath, Shanwalla, The Wrens*. London and New York: Putnam, 1922.
Irish Folk History Plays. First series: *Kincora, Grania, Dervorgilla*. London and New York: Putnam, 1912.
Irish Folk History Plays. Second series: *The Canavans, The White Cockade, The Deliverer*. London and New York: Putnam, 1912.
Seven Short Plays: Spreading the News, Hyacinth Halvey, The Rising of the Moon, The Jackdaw, The Workhouse Ward, The Travelling Man, The Gaol Gate. Dublin and New York: Maunsel, 1909.

Plays in Collaboration

The Poorhouse (with Douglas Hyde). *Samhain*, September 1903.
The Unicorn from the Stars (with W. B. Yeats). New York: Macmillan, 1908.

Studies of Lady Augusta Gregory

Butler, George F. "The Hero's Metamorphosis in Lady Gregory's *Cuchulain of Muirthemne*: Scholarship and Popularization." *Eire-Ireland* 22.4 (Winter 1987): 36–46.
Coxhead, Elizabeth. *Lady Gregory: A Literary Portrait*. New York: Harcourt, Brace and World, 1961.
Kohfeldt, Mary Lou. *Lady Gregory: The Woman behind the Irish Renaissance*. New York: Atheneum, 1985.
Kopper, Edward A., Jr. *Lady Gregory: A Review of the Criticism*. Modern Irish Literature Monograph Series (MILMS) 2. Butler: Kopper, 1991.
McDiarmid, Lucy. "Augusta Gregory, Bernard Shaw, and the Shewing-Up of Dublin Castle." *PMLA* 109 (1994): 26–44.
Saddlemyer, Ann. *In Defense of Lady Gregory*. Dublin: Dolmen, 1966.
Scott, Romine. "Lady Gregory and the Language of Transgression." *Arkansas Quarterly* 2 (1993): 109–23.
Smythe, Colin. "Lady Gregory's Contribution to Periodicals: A Checklist." In *Lady Gregory: Fifty Years After*, ed. Ann Saddlemyer and Colin Smythe. Gerrards Cross: Smythe; Totowa, NJ: Barnes and Noble, 1987, 322–45.

Seamus Heaney

(1939–)

Rand Brandes

BIOGRAPHY

In a 1989 interview on the British Desert Island Disc radio program, Seamus Heaney says that although he grew up in South County Derry as a member of the Catholic minority in Northern Ireland, he never personally felt the physical brunt of sectarianism. Aware of the cultural differences dividing the province, he felt his home was "secure" and devoid of what he calls "sectarian energy." One source of this freedom was what he describes as the "aristocratic" demeanor of his farmer father, Patrick Heaney, who also dealt in cattle. Another source of security was the unusual attention his mother, Margaret, was able to give him and his eight younger brothers and sisters as a result of his live-in aunt Mary's help with the farm. Seamus Justin Heaney was born on April 13, 1939; he spent his first twelve years growing up on the family farm, Mossbawn, situated near the Moyola River and the town of Castledawson, approximately thirty-five miles northwest of Belfast.

As a child, Heaney loved to read and became an adept student; after attending the local Anahorish school from 1945 to 1951, Heaney entered St. Columb's College, in the town of Derry. Graduating from St. Columb's with honors, he was awarded a highly coveted scholarship to Queen's University, Belfast. During his time at Queen's from 1957 to 1961 Heaney began to test himself as a writer and published his first poem, "Nostalgia in the Afternoon" (under the pen name "Incertus," 1959) in the student publication, *Gorgon*. Other poems, articles, and even a short story soon followed. Heaney says in a 1965 interview: "The most important thing that Queen's did for me was to make writing seem real." Heaney graduated from Queen's in 1961 with first-class honors in English language and literature. Soon after this Heaney encountered the work of the writer whom he says inspired him the most at this important time—Ted Hughes.

Although Heaney was encouraged to pursue postgraduate work in England, he decided to enroll in St. Joseph's College of Education in Andersontown, Belfast, where he received his teacher's diploma. During this time Heaney published his first poems outside the university. "Tractors" and "Turkeys Observed" were published in the *Belfast Telegraph* (1962); soon after, Heaney's poems appeared in the *Irish Times* in Dublin and, perhaps most importantly in the *New Statesman* and *The Listener* in London. In the early and mid-1960s Heaney's literary life intensified. He participated regularly in informal gatherings with other writers (now referred to as "The Group") that included poets such as Michael Longley, Derek Mahon, and, later, Paul Muldoon. As a lecturer in English at St. Joseph's College in Belfast in 1963, Heaney met the short story writer Michael McLaverty, who encouraged the poet to pay attention to details and gave Heaney Patrick Kavanagh's *A Soul for Sale*. Heaney has often attested to the centrality of Kavanagh's antipastoral vision to his own work.

In 1964 Heaney submitted his book-length manuscript *Advancements of Learning* to Dolmen Press; when the Irish publisher did not show interest in the text, Heaney offered it to the British publishing house of Faber and Faber, which accepted it in 1965 in its revised form as *Death of a Naturalist*, the poet's first book. Heaney has referred to 1965 as his *annus mirabilis* not only because of the book and the respect being shown for his work in England but also because of his marriage to Marie Devlin.

After 1965 the poet's career began to accelerate with every new professional position and literary award. In 1966 he became a lecturer in English at Queen's University, Belfast, an honored appointment that anticipated his 1984 designation as the Boylston Professor of Rhetoric and Oratory at Harvard University and his election as professor of poetry at Oxford in 1990. Heaney's work has received numerous awards, including the Geoffrey Faber Prize (1966), the Gregory Award (1966), Somerset Maugham Award (1966), Denis Devlin Award (1973), American-Irish Foundation Award (1973), E. M. Forster Award (1976), Bennett Award (1982), Whitbread Book of the Year Award (1987), and the Premio Mondale (Italy, 1993). He has also received numerous honorary degrees.

Heaney's home life, including the birth of three children, has kept pace with his hectic professional and poetic movements. After spending a year in Berkeley, California, in 1970–1971, Heaney resigned his position at Queen's, and the family moved to Glanmore Cottage, County Wicklow. The reasons for the move to the republic were complex, but, as Heaney says, he "was determined to put the practice of poetry more deliberately at the centre of [his] life. It was a kind of test."

In 1975 Heaney took a teaching position at Carysfort College, Blackrock, Dublin, where he became the head of the English Department in 1976. The family moved to Dublin the same year and has resided there since. In 1981

Heaney resigned his Carysfort position to become a visiting professor at Harvard University. In 1980 he became one of six (Northern) founding directors of the Field Day Theatre Company, which has also produced *The Field Day Anthology of Irish Writing*. Heaney is a contributing editor.

The deaths of Heaney's mother in 1984 and his father in 1986 are milestones in the poet's recent life. Each death shaped the volume of poems that followed it, *The Haw Lantern* and *Seeing Things*, respectively. The poet's response to these deaths reminds us of the significance of Heaney's childhood to his work.

Heaney currently spends four months a year teaching at Harvard. Despite the end of his tenure as professor of poetry at Oxford, which required him to deliver fifteen formal lectures over five years, his time continues to be in high demand as one of the most sought-after readers or lecturers in the literary world. Heaney also gives a great deal of his time to emerging and established Irish writers (launching books, introducing readings) and to his country, while maintaining his reputation for generosity and friendship. In 1995 Heaney received the Nobel Prize in literature, the fourth Irishman thus honored.

MAJOR WORKS AND THEMES

"Digging," the first poem in Heaney's first book, *Death of a Naturalist* (1966), is a synecdoche, of sorts, for the poet's entire oeuvre: it is a poem based upon a childhood memory that is recalled in vivid detail. The memory often recalls a rite of passage, epiphany, or Wordsworthian "spot of time" that either confirms or disturbs the poet's sense of self. The poem's diction is concrete, sensual, and relatively simple and is shaped by the poet's adept use of dialect, sound devices (inspired by Hopkins, Keats, and Dylan Thomas), and iambic meter inherited from the English lyric tradition. The dominant image ("digging") functions as an analogy for the writing process—digging into past, into myth and history. The poem points to Heaney's preoccupation with origins.

Door into the Dark (1969) is a further consideration of mostly rural material covered in Heaney's first book. Traditional tradesmen such as blacksmiths, thatchers, and diviners, who work on an almost unconscious, intuitive level, come to represent not only the individual artist but also the quickly disappearing imaginative and cultural life of the rural community. The volume's final poem, "Bogland," represents an important addition to his subject matter and imagery: the Irish bog is a place Heaney associates with the Irish collective unconscious, the racial memory of the land and its people.

Heaney's third volume, *Wintering Out* (1972), is much more overtly public and political than his previous books. Heaney looks more directly at Irish history and myth in the context of colonial oppression and cultural appropriations. These forces often intersect in words themselves: language then becomes a contested territory, a place of division, or, conversely, a shared awareness, common ground. Heaney often traces the etymology of words to their Irish origins, which embody both cultural histories and personal memories and are typically associated with a particular place, as in the poems "Anahorish, "Broagh," and "Toome."

In 1968 Heaney read P. V. Glob's book, *The Bog People*, which discussed the discovery in the bogs of Denmark of several perfectly preserved bodies of what were apparently the sacrificial victims of a prehistoric cult. In *North* (1975), Heaney constructs an analogy between the archaeologist and the poet and between these victims and their violent world and the violence in Northern Ireland. The poems' lines are even more truncated than in previous volumes, adding to the tension and sense of entrapment.

Field Work (1979) is a much more personal and generous book than *North*. The subject matter is noticeably more neopastoral, and the lines are longer and more lush. The poems cover topics from the writing process (again) to the tremors and tingles of domestic life. The volume feels the weight of several elegies to victims of the violence as well as to other artists and friends of the poet. The ten "Glanmore Sonnets" are the heart of the book. Heaney examines the nature of his verse, its stoic energies and classic organizing principles.

Field Work closes with "Uglino," Heaney's translation of Dante, who becomes the guiding presence in Heaney's next book, *Station Island* (1984). Guilt informs many of the volume's poems, especially the title sequence. In the *Station Island* poems, the poet appears as a pilgrim who encounters ghosts from the past. Personal and poetic responsibility are again questioned, as well as the ability of art/poetry to represent the brutalities of the world.

The poet's inner, personal sense of guilt in *Station Island* is externalized and politicized in *The Haw Lantern* (1987), whose major achievement is Heaney's use of the parable as a way of dealing with political issues—an approach to politics Heaney discovered in the works of contemporary Eastern European writers. The sequence "Clearances," written in memory of his mother, contains several moving but unsentimental poems. Absence, as a potentially vivifying state or poetic starting point, is a dominant theme.

The death of a parent, this time the poet's father, also sets the tone for *Seeing Things* (1991), whose overall feel is much more metaphysical, even mystical, as the title suggests. The mystical dimensions of the ordinary are a dominant theme of the sequence titled "Squarings." These poems attempt to square the circle of life and to flesh out its mysterious spiritual operations. The poems meditate upon the nature of the soul, the soul of poetry, the essence of the beautiful. In this regard, Heaney is entering the imaginative world of Yeats, if not Blake.

In addition to his poetry, Heaney has published three volumes of criticism, a verse translation from the Irish, and a play. In *Preoccupations: Selected Prose 1968–1978* (1980) Heaney examines the major influences in his life as a writer. In *Government of the Tongue* (1988) he discusses the work of other, mostly contemporary, writers, often in relation to their potential function as historical witnesses. *The Redress of Poetry* (1995) is a collection of his Oxford lectures, which are more explicitly informed by Irish politics than are many of his earlier essays. Heaney's version of the ancient Irish text *Buile Suibhne, Sweeney Astray* (1984) depicts the struggles between pagan Ireland and Christianity, the painful freedom of the creative imagination, and the demands of civic responsibility. Heaney's play/translation, *The Cure at Troy* (1990), can be seen as an allegory for the strife, suffering, and fear of forgiveness crippling Northern Ireland.

CRITICAL RECEPTION

Heaney's work and life have attracted more critical attention than those of perhaps any other poet writing in English at the end of the twentieth century. A bibliography of writings about Heaney from 1965 to 1993 contains over 1,500 entries. Among these entries are over twenty books, collections of essays, and special Heaney issues of major periodicals. In addition, the bibliography documents numerous Ph.D. dissertations, hundreds of scholarly essays, and even more reviews, interviews, profiles, and notices (of awards, appointments, and other public events). The reasons behind this extensive attention are complex. Cultural, political, commercial, and pedagogical forces have helped to increase and shape the critical reception of Heaney's poetry.

In general, the response to Heaney's work has been positive. Readers are drawn to the earthy, evocative language (especially of the early poems). Critics often see the poems' typically rural or domestic subject matter both in the context of specifically Irish traditions and paradigms and in relation to more inclusive international movements/issues, such as postcolonialism and cultural identities. Heaney's work is also praised for the metaphysical spin he puts upon the simplest of objects (such as a harvest bow or pitchfork) or his ability to ritualize common experiences, such as peeling potatoes. Critics also admire Heaney's treatment of the Troubles of Northern Ireland and its devastating impact on both Protestants and Catholics. Influencing all of these critical affirmations is Heaney's control of the language and poetic form. John Carey's review of *Eleven Poems* in 1965 observed Heaney's handling of feeling, form, and language as "masterly."

Reviewers of Heaney's *Death of a Naturalist* (1966) considered it a promising first book. C. B. Cox, however, argued that it was "the best first book of poems" he had read for some time. Other reviewers responded favorably to Heaney's concrete imagery and "pungent images" ("pungent" appeared in many reviews) and, like the Northern Irish poet John Hewitt, found the book to be the work of an "authentic countryman." Christopher Ricks praised the poet's "technical fertility." For some, however, Heaney's work was too technical and too fertile. Ian Hamilton found the book to be "deeply mannered," and Giles Sadler wrote, "The entire volume suffers from oppressive sogginess."

Reviewers were quick to see Heaney's second volume, *Door into the Dark*, as a continuation of his first book and described the book as more confident, mature, and varied and "cleaner." Not surprisingly, as Heaney's reputation grew, reviewers began to compare him to other writers. Ted Hughes, Wordsworth, Frost, Roethke, and R. S. Thomas are some of the earliest poets mentioned.

Language as a central theme and issue in Heaney's verse dominated many of the discussions of Heaney's third volume, *Wintering Out*. Critics quickly noticed the increased presence of "place-names" in Heaney's new poems. Patricia Beer, for example, astutely connected Heaney's place-names with concerns relating to sound and pronunciation. Despite the overt politicalization of language in *Wintering Out*, some reviewers, like Douglas Dunn and Stephen Spender, asserted that Heaney's poetry was not political enough since it did not deal more explicitly with "the troubles of Ulster." Peter Porter was concerned that the *Wintering Out* poems would be "fatally charming to London's literary tastes."

Those critics who were waiting for a more political Heaney found him in the next volume, *North*, published coincidentally the same year as the first book-length study of Heaney in 1975 by Robert Buttel. Even though *North* was a more political book, it still approached the violence in Ulster obliquely through "myth," which is the operative term in many of the critical responses to *North*. The Northern Irish poet Ciaran Carson is representative of those who saw Heaney's use of myth as a way of glossing over the violence, even possibly exploiting the violence. In his review "Escaped from the Massacre?" Carson concludes that Heaney moves "from being a writer with the gift of precision, to becoming the laureate of violence." In contrast, Anthony Thwaite in the *Times Literary Supplement* (*TLS*) argues that the *North* poems' use of ritual and myth strengthens the sense of tragedy without mystifying or trivializing the violence. Importantly, critics were also beginning to note the interrelatedness of language, land, history, and sexuality in Heaney's vision.

While *North* appeared to be a particularly provocative volume that produced contesting critical camps, *Field Work* experienced almost universal praise. Derwent May in *The Listener* said that the elegies are more than personal tributes and are "mythical representatives of Ireland at peace." The most often-cited poem in *Field Work*, "Harvest Bow," includes the famous line, "The end of art is peace." Critics also considered the "Glanmore Sonnets" to be a particularly accomplished sequence.

Although some reviewers were put off by the "confessional," guilt-ridden tone of Heaney's next book of poems, *Station Island*, most critics, like Elizabeth Jennings and Richard Ellmann, would agree with Helen Vendler, who, in her *New Yorker* review, argues that Heaney remakes his voice in *Station Island* because "to attempt a new complexity of voice is to create future possibilities for one's past." Other critics, including Declan Kiberd and Richard Kearney, noted that in *Station Island* Heaney was still struggling with the role of the poet in society or "weighing loyalties," as Blake Morrison described it.

In the mid-1980s critical responses to Heaney's work boomed. Not only were retrospective essays being written on Heaney's career, but also essays were being collected into books. In addition, several book-length studies appeared. The most significant of these came from England. Neil Corcoran's *Seamus Hea-*

ney not only offered insightful, informed readings of Heaney's major poems but also included extremely helpful new biographical information taken from interviews with Heaney. Blake Morrison's *Seamus Heaney* was more ideologically informed than Corcoran's. Morrison was particularly interested in Heaney's role as "historical witness," especially in the context of *North*.

Heaney's most recent two collections to date, *The Haw Lantern* and *Seeing Things*, which were more experimental than previous volumes, were received with restrained praise and occasionally great skepticism. In addition to discussing the poems, critics were anxious to talk about influences and affinities. References to Beckett, Auden, and MacNeice were accompanied by allusions to Eastern European poetry and the increasing global scope of Heaney's vision. Most critics were unsure of how to respond to Heaney's use of parables in *The Haw Lantern* or the twelve-line "Squarings" poems in *Seeing Things*. There was general agreement that the writing in these two volumes is spare, more abstract, and more oblique than in previous volumes. There was also much discussion of Heaney's move into the explicitly transcendent and mystical dimensions of human experience. But as one critic has put it, after such a prolific career, Heaney's main problem is learning how not to sound like himself.

BIBLIOGRAPHY

Works by Seamus Heaney

Death of a Naturalist. London: Faber, 1966.
Door into the Dark. London: Faber, 1969.
Wintering Out. London: Faber, 1972.
North. London: Faber, 1975.
Field Work. London: Faber, 1979.
Preoccupations: Selected Prose 1968–1978. London: Faber, 1980.
Selected Poems 1975–1985. London: Faber, 1980.
The Rattle Bag: An Anthology of Poems. Selected by Seamus Heaney and Ted Hughes. London: Faber, 1982.
Station Island. London: Faber, 1984.
Sweeney Astray. London: Faber, 1984.
The Haw Lantern. London: Faber, 1987.
Government of the Tongue: Selected Prose, 1978–1987. London: Faber and Faber, 1988.
The Place of Writing. Atlanta: Scholars, 1989.
New Selected Poems 1966–1987. London: Faber, 1990.
The Cure at Troy: A Version of Sophocles' Philoctetes. London: Faber, 1990.
Seeing Things. London: Faber, 1991.
Sweeney's Flight. Trans. Seamus Heaney. Photographs by Rachel Giese Brown. London: Faber, 1992.
The Redress of Poetry. London: Faber, 1995.
Crediting Poetry. Dublin: Gallery, 1995. (Nobel Address).
The Spirit Level. London: Faber, 1996.

Limited Editions

Eleven Poems. Belfast: Festival, Queen's University, 1965.
An Open Letter. Derry: Field Day, 1983.
Midnight Verdict. Loughcrew, Ireland: Gallery, 1993.

Studies of Seamus Heaney

Andrews, Elmer. *The Poetry of Seamus Heaney: All the Realms of Whisper*. New York: St. Martin's, 1988.
———, ed. *Seamus Heaney: A Collection of Critical Essays*. London: Macmillan; New York: St. Martin's, 1992.
Beer, Patricia. "Seamus Heaney's Third Book of Poems." *Listener* 88, 2280 (December 7, 1972): 795.
Bloom, Harold, ed. *Seamus Heaney*. New Haven, CT, New York, Philadelphia: Chelsea, 1986.
Broadbridge, Edward, ed. *Seamus Heaney*. Kobenhavn: Skoleradioen, 1977.
Buttel, Robert. *Seamus Heaney*. Lewisburg, PA: Bucknell University Press, 1975.
Carey, John. "Lost and Found." *New Statesman* (Dec. 31, 1965): 1033.
Carson, Ciaran. "Escaped from the Massacre?" *Honest Ulsterman* 50 (Winter, 1975): 183–186.
Corcoran, Neil. *Seamus Heaney*. New Haven, CT: Chelsea; London: Faber, 1986.
Cox, C. B. "The Painter's Eye." *Spectator* 216, 7195 (May 20, 1966): 638.
Curtis, Tony, ed. *The Art of Seamus Heaney*. 3d ed. Chester Springs: Dufour, 1994.
Dunn, Douglas. "Moral Dandies." *Encounter* 40 (March, 1973): 70.
Durkan, Michael J. and Rand Brandes, eds. *Seamus Heaney: A Reference Guide*. New York: G.K. Hall, 1996.
Ellmann, Richard. "Heaney Agonistes." *New York Review of Books* March 4, 1985.
Hart, Henry. *Seamus Heaney: Poet of Contrary Progressions*. Syracuse: Syracuse University Press, 1992.
Jennings, Elizabeth. "The Spell-Binder." *Spectator* 253, 8159 (November 24, 1984): 30–31.
Kearney, Richard. "Annual Review '84: Literature: The year of 'The Gigli Concert'." *Irish Times*.
Kiberd, Declan. "Breech birth of a naturalist." *Sunday Tribune* (October 28, 1984): 20.
*Marsh, "Props for a Proposition." *Observer* (June 19, 1966): 12. (*This is Ian Hamilton*)
May, Derwent "Peace in Ireland?" *Listener* (November 22, 1979): 720–721.
Mcguinn, Nicholas. *Seamus Heaney: A Guide to the Selected Poems 1965–1975*. Leeds: Arnold-Wheaton, 1986.
Molino, Michael R. *Questioning Tradition, Language, and Myth: The Poetry of Seamus Heaney*. Washington, DC: Catholic University Press, 1994.
Morrison, Blake. *Seamus Heaney*. London: Methuen, 1982.
O'Donoghue, Bernard. *Seamus Heaney and the Language of Poetry*. New York: Harvester Wheatsheaf, 1994.
Parker, Michael. *Seamus Heaney: The Making of the Poet*. Iowa City: University of Iowa Press, 1993.
Porter, Peter. "Poets' places." Guardian (November 30, 1972): 12.

Ricks, Christopher. "Growing Up." *New Statesman* 71, (May 27, 1966): 778.

Sadler, Giles. "Gummidge and others." *The Review* (Oxford), 16 (October, 1966): 43–45.

Spender, Stephen. "Can Poetry Be Reviewed?" *New York Review of Books* 20, 14 (September 20, 1973): 8.

Thwaite, Anthony. "Neighbourly Murders." *The Times Literary Supplement* 3829 (August 1, 1975): 866.

Periodicals: Special Heaney Issues

Agenda 27.1 (Spring 1989).

Colby Quarterly 30.1 (March 1994).

Salmagundi 80 (Fall 1988).

F. R. Higgins

(1896–1941)

Regina M. Buccola

BIOGRAPHY

Frederick Robert Higgins—poet, editor, director of the Abbey Theatre, and close friend of W. B. Yeats in the final years of the literary luminary's life—was born in Foxford, County Mayo, on April 24, 1896.

Raised by a father who adhered strictly to the Protestant Ascendancy tradition, Higgins proved more loyal to the Catholic, Gaelic-speaking tradition that characterized his western homeland. His passion for the concerns of Irish folk manifested itself in a variety of ways throughout his short life, beginning with his entry into the workforce as a Dublin office boy at age fourteen.

During his early working days in Dublin, Higgins established himself as a pioneer in the labor movement. While working in the paint department at a large building firm, Higgins founded a Clerical Workers Union and founded/edited an array of trade journals. With funding provided by a Dublin widow, he founded the first women's magazine in Ireland, which ran for two issues. In a characteristic display of fun that friends such as Frank O'Connor would come to label "Falstaffian," Higgins titled the first issue *Welfare* and the second *Farewell*.

Beginning in the early 1920s, Higgins began serving as the editor of several equally short-lived literary publications, such as *To-morrow*. The Irish Bookshop published six of Higgins's poems in a pamphlet titled *The Salt Air* (1923). This was succeeded by *Island Blood* (1925), a work steeped in the folk traditions of Connemara, and *The Dark Breed* (1927), a body of poems characterized by a bleakness similar to that of the sea-swept land of Higgins's birth.

By 1927 Higgins had established himself in literary circles and began contributing to the *Irish Statesman* reviews of works by writers such as A. M.

Stephens and Humbert Wolfe. His own poetry began to appear in publications such as *The Dial, Spectator, Atlantic Monthly*, and *Dublin Magazine*.

The 1930s brought a fourth volume of poetry, *Arable Holdings*, which includes one of Higgins's best-known poems, "The Woman of the Red-Haired Man." Far more concerned with the musicality of his verse than its sense, Higgins here combines the sensuousness, eroticism, and controlled, vowel-based rhyme that would come to be his poetic calling cards.

In this same decade Higgins solidified his friendship with Yeats, who came to have a dramatic influence on the poet's life. The two paired up as editors of the literary journal *Broadsides* in 1935, and in 1938 Yeats was instrumental in having Higgins appointed managing director of the Abbey Theatre, a post he held until his death. Higgins made his only foray into playwriting with Yeats's encouragement: the monumentally unsuccessful play, *The Deuce of Jacks* (1935). Higgins was also named secretary to the Irish Academy of Letters due to Yeats's influence.

Higgins turned full concentration to his own poetry again in the late 1930s and produced the work that earned him the greatest critical acclaim he enjoyed while living, *The Gap of Brightness* (1940). Higgins drew on his memories of County Meath, the land where his father worked as an engineer and where Higgins visited his paternal relatives as a boy, to create verse that was softer and more delicate than that of his earlier work. This volume contains "Father and Son," a tender poem of reconciliation with his deceased father, with whom Higgins clashed repeatedly on ideological grounds.

Ironically, soon after the publication of *The Gap of Brightness*, in which Higgins seemed to find some peace for age-old demons, he sickened with his final illness. Despite its unlucky publication schedule just before the outbreak of war, Bertie Smyllie of the *Irish Times* devoted a great deal of attention to it. Higgins's wife, May, showed him the poster promoting the issue of the *Irish Times* praising it, and he promptly got out of bed for one last celebratory tour through the Dublin pubs with his friends among the Irish literati, including Donagh MacDonagh, Austin Clarke, and Padraic Colum. He died on January 8, 1941, and is buried at Laracor, where Jonathan Swift once served as vicar.

MAJOR WORKS AND THEMES

Higgins's first collection of published work, *The Salt Air*, contained a mere six poems and had a first run of 500 copies. Though only a small sampling of Higgins's work, its poetry possessed the musical qualities that Higgins would come to stress in his later, more mature poetry. Certain of the poems, however, strained a little too far in order to achieve their melodic quality.

A second characteristic of Higgins' poetry, its distinctive Irish flavor, came to the fore in his next, more substantial collection, *Island Blood* (1925), but it was left to *The Dark Breed* (1927) to bring both of these elements to complete fruition. In a note appended to the text of *The Dark Breed*, Higgins noted the effort made by both him and Austin Clarke as well as other young Irish poets to incorporate aspects of Gaelic prosody into English verse. One of the methods that both Higgins and Clarke employed to achieve what Higgins referred to as "the rhythm of gapped music" (*The Dark Breed* 66) was reliance on internal rhyme and assonance.

Higgins's fourth collection of poetry, *Arable Holdings* (1933), continued the harmonic assonance so carefully crafted in the poetry of *The Dark Breed* as well as that collection's reliance on the Irish folk tradition for poetic themes and their treatment.

The Gap of Brightness (1940) is typically treated as the culmination of Higgins's poetic efforts. Though it includes some experimental, symbolic verse such as that in the poem "Auction," which critics consider a product of Yeats's influence on Higgins, *The Gap of Brightness* also includes some of Higgins's most widely anthologized work. "Song for the Clatter Bones" is a simultaneously bitter and whimsical equation of the Old Testament figure of Queen Jezebel with Ireland itself, and "Father and Son" is disarmingly honest and evocative.

CRITICAL RECEPTION

Higgins is most commonly remembered now as the close friend of Yeats in the final years of his life and is more frequently noted for his work with the Abbey and even for work he did with trade unions before mention is made of his own poetry.

Early critical discussion of Higgins's work was usually polarized. Critics loyal to Austin Clarke and Padraic Colum in particular often bitterly censured Higgins, a response apparently prompted largely by the indignant opinion that Yeats passed over far superior poetic talents in Clarke and Colum in taking such note of Higgins. Less partisan critics acknowledged the influential role Higgins played in the Irish literary scene in its modern formative years and regretfully noted his marked absence from discussions of the period's serious poetry.

Richard Loftus, a member of the former group, asserts, "In Higgins' verse one finds two contradictory visions, the first clearly a copy of Colum's, the second a poor imitation of Yeats' " (37). He argues that the vision in Higgins's later poetry, which was the best critically received contemporaneously, is simply an inversion of his earlier vision, which Loftus characterizes as sentimental and romanticized. Furthermore, Loftus sees no creative ideology or rationale to support the change: "What was gentle in his earlier poetry is now bitter; what was soft is now hard; what was sentimental is now cynical. Nowhere, however, is his aesthetic turnabout given intellectual justification" (255).

Robert Farren is somewhat kinder to Higgins, noting that he "was unlucky in dying soon after Yeats, for his fame would have grown more quickly when the other was dead" (147). However, his 1947 assessment that Austin Clarke had been even less lucky than Higgins in developing an audience outside Ireland has not been borne out. Clarke's work figures prominently in recent anthologies such as Anthony Bradley's *Contemporary Irish Poetry* (1980), for instance, while Higgins is not even mentioned. Unfortunately, Higgins's detractors seem to have gained the upper hand, leaving his poetry to lapse out of serious consideration.

Higgins's letters are preserved in a collection at the National Library of Ireland, Dublin. The collection includes his at times combative correspondence with notable writers such as Bernard Shaw, Louis MacNeice, and T. E. Lawrence, occasioned by his appointment as secretary to the Irish Academy.

BIBLIOGRAPHY

Works by F. R. Higgins

Arable Holdings: Poems. Dublin: Cuala, 1933.
The Dark Breed: A Book of Poems. London: Macmillan, 1927.
The Gap of Brightness: Lyrical Poems. London and New York: Macmillan, 1940.
Island Blood: Poems. Foreword by AE. London: John Lane at the Bodley Head, 1925.
Salt Air. Dublin: Irish Bookshop, 1923.
"Yeats and Poetic Drama in Ireland." In *The Irish Theatre: Lectures Delivered during the Abbey Theatre Festival Held in Dublin in August 1938*, ed. Lennox Robinson. London: Macmillan, 1939, 65–88.

Studies of F. R. Higgins

Clarke, Austin. "Early Memories of F. R. Higgins." *The Dublin Magazine* 6.2 (1967): 68–73.
Farren, Robert. *The Course of Irish Verse in English*. New York: Sheed and Ward, 1947.
"F. R. Higgins." In *Irish Literary Portraits: W. B. Yeats, James Joyce, George Moore, J. M. Synge, George Bernard Shaw, Oliver St. John Gogarty, F. R. Higgins, AE (George Russell)*, ed. W. R. Rodgers. New York: Taplinger, 1973, 169–84.
Kavanagh, Patrick. "The Gallivanting Poet." *Irish Writing* 3 (November 1947): 62–70.
Loftus, Richard J. "F. R. Higgins: The Gold and Honey Land." *Nationalism in Modern Anglo-Irish Poetry*. Madison: University of Wisconsin Press, 1964.
MacManus, M. J. "A Bibliography of F. R. Higgins." *Dublin Magazine* new series 12 (1937): 61–67.

Rita Ann Higgins

(1956–)

Jane Biondi

BIOGRAPHY

Rita Ann Higgins was born in 1956 and raised in Galway. Largely self-educated, she left formal schooling at age thirteen to work in a factory and married at seventeen. She first began reading fiction and poetry after a bout with tuberculosis at age twenty-two. While in the hospital, she read *Animal Farm* and *Wuthering Heights*, texts that kindled an interest in literature that led to her writing poetry. She published her first collection, *Goddess on the Mervue Bus* (1986) four years after joining the Galway Writers' Workshop. Higgins currently lives in Galway with her husband and two daughters.

Higgins's work has been read and performed on RTE Radio 1 and 2, BBC Radio 4, "The Poet's Eye," RTE television, as well as on RTE's "Good Morning Ireland" program. Recently, she began writing plays and has seen her work dramatized by the Galway Theatre Workshop and in Belfast. She has read her work in Ireland, England, Germany, Hungary, and the United States.

MAJOR WORKS AND THEMES

The Goddess on the Mervue Bus offers a powerful, often angry look at contemporary Irish society. These poems, like much of her work, also possess a sense of humor and generosity, as her characters survive the complexities of everyday life. Many of the poems consist of character sketches and vignettes about women, family life, and those marginalized by society. The poems contain powerful indictments of class divisions, economic disfranchisement, and the government bureaucrats who maintain these inequalities.

"Tommy's Wife" summarizes some of these themes as it portrays a young woman who ages quickly under the burdens of many children and an unemployed, alcoholic husband. The wife's responsibilities tarnish her view of marriage and her future. Women's financial and emotional suffering, however, as they cope with alcoholic and perhaps violent husbands, is characterized as a common problem for women, who are then forced to support and raise their families alone.

Not only young women but also middle-aged and older women serve as symbols of strength and courage in the face of long suffering in Higgins's work. "Middle-Aged Irish Mothers" affectionately admires the women who put their faith in the Catholic Church and use that faith for the protection and well-being of friends, family, and neighbors. A sense of close-knit community, with both positive and negative connotations, haunts the collection; nosy neighbors serve as both a curse and a blessing.

This first collection, then, presents the daily lives of men and women facing the frustrations of poverty while retaining their humor and generosity. In the nostalgic "Work On," a poem that idealizes the friendships among young country girls working in a shirt factory, Higgins gives an early portrait of those middle-aged Irish mothers and old women whom she so admires. Similarly, Higgins offers a beneficent reading of the Catholic Church in "Middle-Aged Irish Mothers," where she finds a certain beauty, security, and strength in the communal nature of Irish Catholicism as practiced by these women while recognizing the irony of women's involvement in the veneration of the male trinity. "Poetry Doesn't Pay" challenges the special connection between the poet and her community that haunts the Irish literary heritage. This humorous critique of the economic realities of contemporary Ireland also slyly suggests that the poet–community relationship may be affected differently by the gender of the poet.

As in much of Higgins's work, these poems are not personal, metaphorical explorations of private themes; they are public expressions, celebrations, and condemnations of Irish society that accurately reflect contemporary life for working-class men and women in the west of Ireland. This communal quality explains Higgins's popularity on Irish radio and television.

Witch in the Bushes (1988) exhibits a far angrier tone than her first collection. These poems radiate the anger of the powerless toward those who exercise power cruelly and arbitrarily. They point to the power of words to wound. Poems such as "It's All Because We're Working Class" and "Woman's Inhumanity to Woman" express anger at a bureaucratic system that blames the poor for their poverty and exercises an unnecessary emotional power over those queuing for the dole. Although she criticizes patriarchy, both political and personal, Higgins does not aim her anger at men only. In "It Wasn't the Father's Fault," Higgins condemns the collusion of women in cycles of violence and brutality as well.

Furthermore, Higgins suggests the similarities between the working class and other oppressed groups, such as the traveling community. "The K.K.K. of Kastle Park" and "End of a Free Ride" both exemplify these similarities, while recognizing the complicity of working-class people in the discrimination directed toward the travelers and in the hierarchy of superiority that affects a community.

Higgins's most recent collection, *Philomena's Revenge* (1992), revives the tone of her first. Less angry and more intimate, *Philomena's Revenge* offers a less-institutionalized portrait of the despair that many women live through on a daily basis, while Higgins continues to use the communal spaces and domestic interiors that frequently appear in her work. She exposes domestic violence in poems such as "The Woman Who Lived Here," "Philomena's Revenge," and "Crooked Smiles." Moreover, she lays bare the hideous side of the situation that blames women and children for this violence. Ultimately, Higgins portrays women as survivors resisting the destructive nature of social violence in all its forms.

The Catholic Church remains relatively unscathed by Higgins's anger in most of her work. She acknowledges the Catholic Church as a benevolent and ironic force in the lives of women of a previous generation, but she does not detail the role of the Church in contemporary society. Nevertheless, the hypocrisy of religion is exposed in "God Dodger's Anonymous" by the angry and humorous answer given in response to the Jehovah Witness' question, "Have you a God?" The persona responds that she hasn't "a pot to spew libations in," and yet gods are "hopping up/all over the joint."

CRITICAL RECEPTION

In the decade since her first collection was released, the critical reception of her work has been minimal. She is often described as working-class and lauded for her vibrant language, the clarity of her voice, and her ability to reflect upon, and write about, complex social situations while conveying both humor and frustration.

Yet while critics comment positively on her anger, her humor, and her working-class background, they simultaneously hint that these qualities need to be discarded in future work. The poet, furthermore, is criticized for a lack of formal poetic qualities.

Very few reviews of her work exist in scholarly journals. *Cyphers*, in a review of her first collection in 1987, refers to Higgins's poetry as "well-focused photographs of the world," while simultaneously ruing the poet's inability to leave an image to stand on its own. The major Irish newspapers have also reviewed her work, but usually long after its release or on the occasion of its re-release. Carol Rumens compares her sense of humor and ear for modern culture to Paul Durcan. Mary O'Donnell, in a review of *Philomena's Revenge*, correctly suggests that Higgins views "the world from a position of female political consciousness."

Reviews of her work also suggest a widespread, nonacademic audience. A reviewer in the *Evening Herald* (Ireland) suggests that typically, nonpoetry readers are drawn to Higgins's "direct and street-wise style."

BIBLIOGRAPHY

Works by Rita Ann Higgins

Face Licker Come Home. Galway: Salmon, 1991. Staged by Punchbag Theatre Co., 1991.
God-of-the-Hatch-Man. Staged by Punchbag Theatre Co., 1992.
Goddess on the Mervue Bus. Galway: Salmon, 1986.
Goddess and Witch. Galway: Salmon, 1990.
Philomena's Revenge: Poems. Galway: Salmon, 1992.
Witch in the Bushes: Poems. Galway: Salmon, 1988.

Studies of Rita Ann Higgins

Burke, Molly MacAnailly. "The Iron Fist." *Sunday Independent* (Ireland), February 11, 1990: 20.
Hannan, Dennis, and Nancy Means Wright. "Irish Women Poets: Breaking the Silence." *Canadian Journal of Irish Studies* 26.2 (December 1990): 57–65.

Reviews

Boran, Pat. Rev. of *Goddess on the Mervue Bus. Cyphers* 28 (1987): 50–52.
O'Donnell, Mary. "Rage, Rage." Rev. of *Philomena's Revenge. Irish Times*, June 6, 1992: 9.
Rev. of *God of the Hatchman. Evening Herald* (Ireland), March 25, 1993.
Rumens, Carol. "Finding the Poet's Voice." Rev. of *Goddess on the Mervue Bus, Witch in the Bushes*, and *Philomena's Revenge. Irish Times*, January 29, 1994.

Denis Johnston

(1901–1984)

John O'Brien

BIOGRAPHY

William Denis Johnston was born on June 18, 1901, in Dublin. Educated at St. Andrew's College (Dublin) and at Merchiston Castle (Edinburgh), Johnston finished his law degree from Cambridge in 1923. The following year, he traveled to the United States as a Puglsey Scholar at Harvard University Law School. Taking in as many American "little theater" productions as he could, Johnston was introduced to, and inspired by, experimental American and European theater and decided to become a playwright—even after failing to be admitted to the George Baker Workshop. The next year he was called to the bar, and in the next few years he became active in the Irish theater scene, acting in Drama League and Abbey Theatre productions, including European dramas such as Strindberg's *The Father*.

His first play was rejected by the Abbey Theatre in 1928, the same year he married Abbey actress Shelah Richards and directed *King Lear* in the Abbey's first Shakespeare production. One year later, the Gate Theatre produced Johnston's rejected expressionistic play, titled *Rhapsody in Green* and then *Shadowdance*. Eventually it was renamed *The Old Lady Says "No!"*—supposedly a satirical reference to Lady Gregory's saying no to his first effort. His daughter, Jennifer Johnston, the contemporary novelist, was born a year later. The early 1930s were another active period for Johnston in the Irish theater. He served on the Gate Theatre's Board of Directors (1931–1935) and opened a number of his own plays, including *The Moon in the Yellow River* (1931), *A Bride for the Unicorn* (1933), *Storm Song* (1934), and his adaptation of Ernst Toller's *Die Blinde Göttin* (*Blind Man's Buff*, 1932).

In the mid-1930s, Johnston gave up his law practice. After a decade in law, he began what would become a ten-year association with the BBC, where he worked as a producer, scriptwriter, broadcaster, director, and war correspondent in the Middle East and Europe (the first war correspondent to enter Buchenwald). In 1945, Johnston divorced Shelah Richards and married Gate Theatre actress Betty Chancellor. In 1950, he came to America as a visiting professor at Amherst, spending the next ten years as a professor of English at Mt. Holyoke College, during which time he published *Nine Rivers from Jordan*, based on his experiences as a war correspondent. During his time at Mt. Holyoke and his subsequent years as chair of Smith College's theater department, Johnston completed several other plays, including *The Dreaming Dust* (1940), *Strange Occurrence on Ireland's Eye* (1956), and *The Scythe and the Sunset* (1958), and published academic studies of Swift (1959) and Synge (1965). *The Brazen Horn*, a scattered and somewhat mystical mathematical/scientific "nonbook," was published in 1968. Johnston moved to Dalkey in 1977 and died on August 8, 1984.

MAJOR WORKS AND THEMES

The enigmatic nature of Denis Johnston's artistic vision makes difficult any kind of concise statement of themes or motifs in his work as a whole. In fact, if there is any theme running through Johnston's artistic accomplishments, it is an impatience that is evident in form and theme, not to mention his biography as well, broken up as it is with episodic moves and career changes.

His first recognized artistic success is a play that is itself born of stark conflict. Though the eventual title *The Old Lady Says "No!"* reflects Johnston's mischievous sense of humor and iconoclastic disregard for authority, his earlier title, *Rhapsody in Green*, is perhaps a more suitable title for this expressionist-influenced play, which combines traditional Irish themes of revolutionary fervor, idealism, and sentimentality with trenchant and distinctly Continental critique of Stage Irishness and nationalistic true believers. Written during a period of the Irish dramatic movement, noted for melodrama and political propaganda, Johnston's play starts as a typical melodrama about Robert Emmet and then rapidly disintegrates into a blurred but nonetheless sharp criticism of Irish hypocrisy often stitched together with ironic intertextual allusions and with bits and pieces of sentimental and poetic quotes. While this theme would be impossible to miss, one can also find in Johnston's first work a methodology that reappears in his later work. In order to criticize the mythology of Irish romanticism, Johnston splits the consciousness of the Robert Emmet character. Variations of this kind of presentation of two distinctly different realities to enrich the understanding of both is a strategy familiar to the reader of Johnston's prose works, one that is pursued in different ways in other works, such as *Nine Rivers from Jordan*, with its opposite final scenes, or *The Brazen Horn*, with its ambitious and dizzying bending of time and space.

Johnston's next play, *The Moon in the Yellow River*, remains one of his best-known works, even though some initially dismissed it as an attack on Irish culture and Catholicism. While the structure and plotting of this play are traditional and even Shavian in many ways, critics did not miss Johnston's willingness at the thematic level to present a vigorous criticism of Irish nationalism and its morality. As he did in his first play, Johnston exposes all that is singularly unromantic about Irish romanticism, while ambivalently and simultaneously criticizing cold reason divorced from idealism. Ferrar notes that Johnston began writing the play as a parody of an Abbey play, much like his first drama, but as powerful themes developed, the structural parody faded.

Compared to *The Old Lady Says "No!"* Johnston's iconoclasm is here far less reckless and conclusive and consequently less satisfying, on the whole, to some. Unlike a kind of "problem play," there is no implied solution waiting in the curtains; in fact, Johnston's play presents opposing ideas (technology/tradition, modernity/nostalgia, idealism/rationality, "Germanic" efficiency/"Irish" chaos, and so on) to reveal the troubles that result from the irreconcilability of the difficult issues of the time. The play is full of parody and almost slapstick bits of "Irish" humor, in which intentions are both comically and tragically thwarted—most obviously in the accidental blowing up of the powerhouse, which is destroyed, but not because of the fervent political positions of Blake or anyone else. Just as Li Po faces the intractable reality of death in the life-enriching gesture of romantic embrace (drowning in the reflection of the moon in the river), this play ends in the dark, a shadow dance of sorts, in which lack of conviction and passionate intensity together produce a tragicomic paralysis that the play suggests is general all over Ireland.

A Bride for the Unicorn (1933) and *Storm Song* (1934), according to Hogan in *After the Irish Renaissance*, are, respectively, Johnston's own most and least favorite plays. While *A Bride* falls short in being too rigorously expressionist, *Storm Song* fails by being too pedestrian a drama, uncharacteristic of Johnston's successful work, which typically runs against the spirit of the times. Johnston's copious diaries at the time reveal a personal conviction that these two plays had already "damned" him, making it impossible to be restored to what he saw as his "brief eminence as the 'White hope of the Irish Theatre.'"

The Scythe and the Sunset (1958), a historical play dramatizing the events of Easter week, is a self-conscious companion to O'Casey's *The Plough and the Stars*. Joseph Ronsley reports that Johnston has described this play in relation to the earlier play as like "the smell following the motor car," but it is nonetheless one of the best representations of Johnston's ability and, in many ways, more successful than O'Casey's effort. Johnston sees his Easter-week play as an "antimelodrama," and in this way his dissection of Irish nationalism and romanticism in *Scythe* is a continuation of his earliest dramatic effort in *The Old Lady Says "No!"* Instead of glamorizing the proclamation of the Irish republic, Johnston's play is punctuated with the looting of a candy store and the petty incompetence of participants on both sides. As the Easter uprising begins, the nationalistic and idealistic Emer wonders why the people are not rising with the rebels: "Why can't they cheer? Don't they know they're free?"

When the people do cheer, it is inspired by looting, not patriotism, all of which underscores Johnston's skepticism of the human tendency to cheer for the wrong reasons—or worse, as the rebel leader named Tetley observes: "I was watching their faces during the reading of the proclamation, and there was nothing but derision in those eyes—derision, and that murderous Irish laughter. It was as if we were putting on a rather poor entertainment for them, and they wanted their money back." Whether it is Tetley's loss of faith in the Irish masses or Palliser's loss of faith in the military intelligence of his leaders, the play repeatedly returns to the idea that "causes always let you down." Finally, unlike O'Casey, Johnston goes out of his way to avoid, if not counter, any kind of implied or overt pacifist theme.

Johnston's two major works of prose—one a book, *Nine Rivers from Jordan*, and the other a "nonbook," *The Brazen Horn*—share an interest in exploring alternate views of reality. While in many respects *Nine Rivers* can be read as an autobiographical account of Johnston's experiences during World War II, it can also be seen as an early effort aiming toward *The Brazen Horn* in its attempts to "fold back" time and consider multiple and simultaneous happenings. Much as the first book offers two versions of events that take place at the Brenner Pass, the "nonbook" takes apart traditional understandings of time and reality, attempting to give a "composite view of more Nows than one." *The Brazen Horn*, however, is much more speculative or theoretical than artistic in its explorations at the crossroads of mysticism and the scientific breakthroughs of the twentieth century.

CRITICAL RECEPTION

Johnston himself felt at times that he never lived up to the potential he demonstrated in his first two plays and that he never became a foremost dramatist of the Irish stage, and there is evidence that his aloofness and outright assaults on "everything that is Irish" led many to share his assessment. Though his work did not provoke riots as O'Casey's plays did, Johnston's ultimate ability to become a significant force at the Abbey, for example, was undoubtedly limited by this aspect of his work. On the other hand, his formal innovations and willingness to counter traditional themes have led critics to respond favorably to his work. As late as 1977, *The Irish Times* concluded that Johnston's first play "still stands unchallenged as the most exciting play ever staged in Ireland." Though most critics acknowledge the uneven quality of Johnston's work as a whole, few would dispute that his work is at its best, exciting. Hogan's assessment that Johnston is the most intelligent and, along with Beckett, the most daring dramatist of his time is no exaggeration.

Then again, the marked contrast with the frequently performed works of Beckett underscores that for all his potential and demonstrated abilities, Johnston's work is typically more acclaimed and appreciated than it is performed. Johnston's refusal to settle down with perfecting a single dramatic form made it difficult for the theatergoing public to know exactly what to expect from one of his plays.

The two-sided nature of the critical response to Johnston's work is perhaps best documented in Joseph Ronsley's collection of essays celebrating the author's eightieth birthday, *Denis Johnston: A Retrospective*. While critical responses range from praising Johnston's indeterminacy and eclecticism to disappointment with the exact same features of his work, critics of all kinds recognize that Denis Johnston has made a significant contribution to the Irish theater.

BIBLIOGRAPHY

Works by Denis Johnston

Nine Rivers from Jordan: The Chronicle of a Journey and a Search. London: Vershoyle, 1953.
In Search of Swift. Dublin: Figgis, 1959.
John Millington Synge. New York and London: Columbia University Press, 1965.
The Brazen Horn: A Non-Book for Those Who, in Revolt Today, Could Be in Command Tomorrow. Dublin: Dolmen, 1977.
The Dramatic Works of Denis Johnston. Vol. 1. Gerrards Cross: Smythe, 1977.
The Dramatic Works of Denis Johnston. Vol. 2. Gerrards Cross: Smythe, 1979.
Orders and Desecrations: The Life of the Playwright Denis Johnston. Ed. Rory Johnson. Dublin: Lilliput, 1992. (A selection of Johnston's articles and talks from 1929–1980.)

Studies of Denis Johnston

Barnett, Gene A. *Denis Johnston*. New York: Twayne, 1978.
Ferrar, Harold. *Denis Johnston's Irish Theatre*. Dublin: Dolmen, 1973.
Ronsley, Joseph, ed. *Denis Johnston: A Retrospective*. Gerrards Cross: Smythe, 1981.

Jennifer Johnston

(1930–)

Barbara E. McLaughlin

BIOGRAPHY

Jennifer Prudence Johnston was born on January 12, 1930, in Dublin. Her mother was noted actress, director, and producer Shelah Richards, and her father, Denis Johnston, was the well-known playwright. Johnston's parents were divorced when she was eight. Educated at the Park House School in Dublin, she entered Trinity College in 1947. In 1951, she married fellow student Ian Smyth and moved to London. Johnston has since remarried, to David Gilliland, and resides in Derry, Northern Ireland.

Johnston began writing in her thirties. Her novel *The Captains and the Kings* (1972) won three awards, including the Yorkshire Post Fiction Award for the Best First Book. She has garnered several awards for her subsequent fiction. While she is better known for her novels, Johnston has written several plays that have achieved critical acclaim and been performed in Dublin, in Belfast, and on Radio Eireann.

MAJOR WORKS AND THEMES

Identifying herself as an Irish writer because her "preoccupations are [those] of an Irish person," six of Johnston's novels contain elements of the Big House, featuring aristocratic Anglo-Irish families in decline; all her novels feature Irish settings. However, Johnston is resistant to labels because "we are all diminished" by them ("Keynote Address," *Culture* 11), and she resists categorization as a Big House writer, a common critical response to her work, which she terms a "sort of backwater" (Perrick, *Interview* 3). Johnston's novels generally feature characters from privileged backgrounds; in fact, *Shadows on Our Skin* (1977) is her only novel to date to feature a working-class protagonist.

Johnston loads her prose with literary allusions: Irish, British, Russian, and German authors are included, and she quotes from nursery rhymes and popular songs. Johnston's novels are characteristically delivered from multiple points of view; usually the story is told in part by the protagonist in the first person, by an omniscient narrator, and, in some cases, through the consciousness of a third character. Time sequences are similarly distorted; several novels begin with the ending made explicit—the imminent death of the protagonists. The present is constantly interrupted by conversations, memories, and events from the past. The dead ignore temporality and rise to haunt the living. Johnston's disruption of the restrictions of narrative technique often echoes the waywardness of her protagonists' actions. Destabilizing time and voice allows Johnston to create a world without stable centers or reliable authorities.

Relationships in Johnston's Ireland are usually painful and destructive. Care-takers generally are the least worthy of trust. Many characters are orphans, and the parents who do survive are at odds with their children: in *How Many Miles to Babylon?* (1974) Alexander Moore struggles to withstand his frustrated and bitter mother's taunts and small cruelties; in *The Gates* (1973) and *The Invisible Worm* (1991), the female protagonists are the objects of incestuous advances.

Several novels are *kunstlerromans*, featuring youthful protagonists with artis-tic aspirations who struggle toward maturity against the harsh environment of their restrictive society. Minnie MacMahon in *The Gates* and Nancy Gulliver in *The Old Jest* (1979) struggle through art to achieve self-definition and inde-pendence. However, Johnston does not restrict creative actualization to the young: several of her older characters endure a painful process of enlightenment and maturation as well.

Johnston's novels tend toward bleak and grim resolutions. Happiness must be found individually, through a "private and personal internal miracle" (135), as Constance Keating puts it in *The Christmas Tree* (1981). Her characters vari-ously face financial, spiritual, educational, conventional, class, and physical re-strictions that must be overcome in order to achieve self-definition.

Despite the grinding losses her characters experience, they respond by seeking a sense of order in the face of chaos, usually through the act of authorship or similar creative expression. *The Railway Station Man* (1984) features Helen Cuffe, a middle-aged widow whose husband was a victim of the Provos in Derry. Helen finds in his death the "present of freedom" (Perrick, *Interview* 8), as Johnston herself terms it, and she turns to painting for solace and respite from the violence plaguing Ireland.

Johnston's most recent novel, *The Invisible Worm* (1991), which takes on the issue of incest, is the book she has always "wanted to write" (Woodworth 5). Once again using a Big House backdrop, Johnston's protagonist, Laura Quinlan, is the product of mismatch between her Anglo-Irish mother and Catholic father. The novel depicts Laura's struggle to achieve mental balance as the memories of years of sexual abuse by her father slowly rise to the surface of her con-sciousness.

Johnston's refusal to sentimentalize Ireland or the characters she creates forces her readers to deal with Ireland's complicated issues. Further, by creating female protagonists who themselves author texts, Johnston is revising a national literary tradition that has fictionalized women for political ends and has excluded women from active participation in public life, including literary work. She implicates the reader in the experiences she depicts through her stylistic and thematic choices: by disrupting conventional expectations brought by the reader to her texts, that reader is forced to reconsider his or her position—not only to the text but to the substance of the story as well.

CRITICAL RECEPTION

Critical responses to Johnston's work are few. There are several Big House studies, for example, Karl Lubbers's essay in Rauchbauer's *Ancestral Voices*, Mark Mortimer's article in Genet's *The Big House in Ireland*, and Bridget O'Toole's study in Dawe and Longley's *Across a Roaring Hill*. David Burleigh's 1985 study (in Sekine's *Irish Writers and Society at Large*) remains the most comprehensive study of recurrent images and themes in Johnston's fiction.

Shari Benstock's 1982 study of Johnston's first five novels resists reading Johnston as either an Irish or woman writer only, suggesting that her work "defeats facile assessment" (192) and exceeds the "historical or generic contexts" within which she is usually studied.

Christine St. Peter's 1990 essay in Cairns and Johnson's *Gender in Irish Writing* attempts "the reading that Benstock avoided—the consideration of Jennifer Johnston as both an Irish writer and a Woman writer" (113). St. Peter reads Johnston's texts from the feminist-materialist standpoint; additionally, she provides a resistant survey of the critical reception of Johnston's work.

In *Irish Women Writers*, Ann Owens Weekes studies Johnston's first seven novels as a "map of artistic and thematic progression" (193) and performs solid readings of her novels up through *The Christmas Tree*.

There is a dearth of criticism on Johnston's plays. Eileen Kearney's 1991 essay includes a paragraph describing Johnston's work; Steve Wilmer's article, also from 1991, lists Johnston as one of the "handful of women" (355) working in theater in Ireland.

BIBLIOGRAPHY

Works by Jennifer Johnston

Novels

The Captains and the Kings. London: Hamilton, 1972.
The Gates. London: Hamilton, 1973.
How Many Miles to Babylon? 1974. Garden City, NY: Doubleday, 1980.
Shadows on Our Skin. 1977. New York: Avon, 1979.

The Old Jest. 1979. Garden City, NY: Doubleday, 1980.
The Christmas Tree. 1981. New York: Morrow, 1982.
The Railway Station Man. 1984. New York: Viking, Penguin, 1985.
Fool's Sanctuary. 1987. New York: Viking, 1988.
The Invisible Worm. London: Sinclair-Stevenson, 1991.

Short stories

"The Theft." In *Irish Ghost Stories*, ed. Joseph Hone. London: Hamilton, 1977.
"Trio." In *Territories of the Voice: Contemporary Stories by Irish Women Writers*, ed. Louise DeSalvo, Kathleen Walsh D'Arcy, and Katherine Hogan. Boston: Beacon, 1989.

Plays

Indian Summer. Performed Belfast and Cork, 1983.
Triptych. Performed Peacock Theatre, Dublin.
How Many Miles to Babylon? Performed Belfast, 1993.
Desert Lullabye. Performed Belfast, 1996.

Short Plays

The Nightingale and Not the Lark. Performed in Dublin, 1980.
The Porch. Performed in Dublin, 1986.
The Invisible Man. Performed in Dublin, 1987.
O, Ananais, Azarias and Miseal. Performed in Dublin and Belfast, on BBC Radio, 1989.
Mustn't Forget High Noon. Performed on BBC Radio, Belfast, and Radio Eireann, 1989.
Twinkletoes. Performed in Dublin and Belfast, 1993.

Work in Progress

The Illusionist (working title). London: Sinclair-Stevenson, forthcoming.

Addresses by Johnston:

"Keynote Address." *Culture in Ireland—Division or Diversity: Proceedings of the Cultures in Ireland Group Conference*. Edna Longley, ed. Belfast: Institute of Irish Studies, Queen's University, 1991.

Studies of Jennifer Johnston

Benstock, Shari. "The Masculine World of Jennifer Johnston." In *Twentieth Century Women Novelists*, ed. T. F. Staley. London: Macmillan, 1982.
Connelly, Joseph. "Legend and Lyric Structure in the Selected Fiction of Jennifer Johnston." *Eire-Ireland* 21.3 (Fall 1986): 119–23.
Deane, Seamus. "Jennifer Johnston." *Ireland Today* 1015 (February 1985): 4–6.
Dunleavy, Janet Egleson, and Rachael Lynch. "Contemporary Irish Women Novelists." In *The British Novel since 1960*, ed. James Acheson. New York: St. Martin's, 1991.
Kearney, Eileen. "Current Voices in the Irish Theatre: New Dramatic Voices." *Colby Quarterly* 27.4 (December 1991): 225–32.
Wilmer, Steve. "Women's Theatre in Ireland." *New Theatre Quarterly* 7.28 (1991): 353–60.

Interviews

Perrick, Penny. "An Interview with Jennifer Johnston." *Sunday Times*, February 24, 1991: 6–7D.

Quinn, John. "Jennifer Johnston." *A Portrait of the Artist as a Young Girl*. London: Methuen in association with Radio Telefis Eireann, 1986.

Woodworth, Paddy. "Invisible Characters of the Heart." *Irish Times*, February 23, 1991: 5.

James Joyce

(1882–1941)

Paula Gillespie

BIOGRAPHY

Born the oldest of ten children to survive infancy, James Augustine Aloysius Joyce saw his family's fortune evaporate, his father fail, and his family struggle. He started out his formal schooling at Clongowes Wood College, a prestigious Jesuit school, but finances forced him first to a Christian Brothers school and then on to Belvedere College, where the Jesuits admitted him and his brothers without fees. He earned his B.A. in 1902 from University College, Dublin, where he studied languages.

His talent for writing was apparent from a very early age; when he was nine, he wrote, and his father distributed, a tribute to the dead Parnell. While still at Belvedere he wrote both verse and prose, and he developed an abiding love for the writings of Swedish playwright Henrik Ibsen. While a student at University College, he wrote a review for the *Fortnightly Review* of Ibsen's *When We Dead Awaken* and was thrilled to receive a reply from Ibsen himself.

At University College, Joyce neglected his formal studies but read copiously and pursued his study of languages. In addition to a play and a collection of poems, he began writing and collecting his epiphanies.

During this time of study and experimental writing, Joyce's family suffered a steady financial decline. They moved into increasingly squalid lodgings and sold off much of the family's furnishings but clung tenaciously to family portraits and a coat of arms.

In 1902 Joyce introduced himself to poet and mystic George Russell, who brought his attention to John Millington Synge, W. B. Yeats, and Lady Gregory. They all agreed that Joyce showed great promise, and each tried in his or her way to help. Joyce prepared to study medicine in Paris, but since his family had little money to offer him, he dropped out, continued his studies of languages and literature, and began his long tradition of letters either to his family or friends, asking for money.

In 1903 Joyce's mother, Mary, died of cancer. Joyce had been called home only to encounter her dying pleas that he resume his formal religious observance and to encounter his father's inebriated outbursts. Joyce's alternating passionate attachment to, and distance from, his family characterized this time.

In the period that followed, Joyce began to write fiction, polishing and revising over a period of months and years. He fought his remorse over his mother's death with the bawdy companionship of his Dublin friends. He attempted a number of professions, none of which provided him with the kind of income he needed, and he borrowed generously from his friends. During this time he lived with Oliver St. John Gogarty (Buck Mulligan in *Ulysses*) in a Martello Tower in Sandycove, now the Joyce Museum.

On June 16, the day on which he set *Ulysses*, he had his first date with Nora Barnacle, a simple girl from Galway. Despite their differences, almost immediately Joyce fell in love with Nora, and after a brief, intense courtship, the two left for Europe together.

Joyce did his most intense writing and completed his mature works in Paris, Trieste, and Zurich. Although he felt he had to leave Ireland to become an artist, Ireland was, and remained, the subject of his writing during his entire life.

In Trieste his children, Giorgio and Lucia, were born, and Joyce gave lessons in English. When Italy entered the war in 1915, Joyce and his family were allowed to move to Zurich. He gave private lessons in English there, but the income was not enough; his vision problems necessitated a number of surgical procedures and a great deal of medical attention. By this time his genius had become recognized, and he began to receive help. Harriet Shaw Weaver, editor of *The Egoist*, began a lifelong benefaction that included money and assistance in publishing, advancement of his works, and encouragement in the face of her occasional perplexity over his writing. Edith Rockefeller McCormick supported him generously for a time.

In 1920 the family moved to Paris, where Joyce was occupied by writing and publishing. This period of intense creativity was also marked by reverses for Joyce: his eyes continued to deteriorate so that at times he could not read, and at others he was in intense pain. But the anguish of his life was the increasingly obvious mental illness of his daughter, Lucia. Joyce seldom returned to Ireland. In 1931, in response to pressure from Lucia, Joyce and Nora married.

Joyce continued his habit of revising and rewriting his books, taking years to complete each of his major works. After the publication of *Finnegans Wake*, the critical reception to which distressed him, events of World War II caused him further stress, and as Germany closed in on France, the Joyces moved once again to Zurich. Shortly after their move, Joyce was diagnosed as having a perforated duodenal ulcer, and although Swiss doctors tried to save him with surgery, he died at age fifty-eight on January 13, 1941, and was buried in Zurich.

MAJOR WORKS AND THEMES

Joyce's essays called attention to his writing talents when he was still in school. His verse, collected and published eventually in *Pomes Pennyeach* (1927) and *Chamber Music* (1907), was his introduction to the literary elite of Dublin and Ireland. It also succeeded in winning over George Russell, John Millington Synge, W. B. Yeats, and Lady Gregory.

Joyce never truly entered into the Irish Revival, saying of it, "I distrust all enthusiasms." However, Ireland is a major theme in his great works of fiction. *Dubliners* (1914), a collection of short stories, offers a depiction of Dublin life and characters—the struggles of characters with one another and a harsh economic climate, with the church, with politics, and with the family.

The stories are roughly chronological, the first dealing with the adventures and misadventures of children, then moving into tales of young adults, and then into the world of adult responsibility and irresponsibility. The stories are stark, not sparing the reader from the painful realities of lives of hardship and struggle, but finally, in "The Dead," Joyce said in a letter to his brother Stanislaus that he had never dealt with the hospitality of Ireland (September 26, 1906, *Letters II*, 168), and he concluded his study with a haunting story of death and lost love juxtaposed with artistic expression and Irish warmth. Often seen as representations of Irish paralysis, Joyce's stories are nevertheless alive with vibrant and unforgettable characters who people his fictional Dublin.

A Portrait of the Artist as a Young Man (1916) went through several manifestations. Beginning as an essay, "A Portrait of the Artist," actually a combination of essay and story, it became *Stephen Hero* (1944), only fragments of which survive, and it finally emerged as *A Portrait of the Artist as a Young Man*, a semiautobiographical novel that chronicles the life of Stephen Dedalus from infancy to young adulthood. The young child is shaped by forces of family, history, language, religion, and nationality; he struggles with conflicting voices that compete with one another and with the whispering voices of sensuality and lust. In the course of the novel, Stephen learns to put these contradictory voices into perspective and to listen to his own voice as he emerges as an artist. To do so, Stephen finds he must leave Ireland to fly by the nets of nationality, language, and religion. The book ends with his departure for the Continent.

In *Ulysses* (1922), Stephen has returned from exile for the death of his mother; gathering his resources to go back to Paris, he spends June 16, 1904, wandering about Dublin, taking stock. But while he is the main character in *A Portrait of the Artist as a Young Man*, he is one of two main male characters in *Ulysses*. The other, more mature figure is Leopold Bloom, a Dublin Jew whose wife, a concert singer, plans and carries out an affair while Bloom, obliging but heartbroken, stays away. He, like Stephen, takes stock of his life on this Dublin day, attending a funeral, doing a bit of work, attempting to raise money for the widow of his friend, and going through the motions of a normal day. He finally encounters Stephen, follows him to nighttown and into a brothel, stands by him while Stephen becomes increasingly drunk, takes him home for chocolate, and finally reencounters his wife, Molly, who has the last word of the novel, a long, unpunctuated stream of consciousness.

The novel has many themes. *The Odyssey* of Homer forms the scaffolding of the novel. During the composition, Joyce had named the eighteen chapters after segments or elements of *The Odyssey*, and wandering, homelessness, and alienation are themes. Bloom, as a Jew, encounters hostility all day in a prejudiced Dublin. However, he treats others humanely in the face of his own mistreatment at their hands.

Stephen still struggles with nationality, religion, and language as he experiences grief and guilt over his mother's death, but he also struggles with conflicting emotions about his perceived rejection by the Dublin literary scene. While he refuses on principle to play by the rules of the Irish Literary Revival, he does create a sketch for a group of journalists and friends that could easily have fitted into *Dubliners*, an unflattering and comic but very humane tale of two Dublin women.

Throughout the day, Stephen recalls his mother and her death with remorse and guilt, and Bloom, Stephen's near-counterpart, reflects on the loss of his own children, one to death and the other to distance. Bloom's interest in Stephen has, of course, its mythical counterpart in Odysseus and Telemachus, but it is also an ironic allusion to Icarus and Dedalus, Bloom possessing a touch of the artist but having little ability to rescue Stephen from the serious problems that plague him. As the two urinate in Bloom's garden, their arcing streams of urine fit as natural phenomena into the cosmos of a magnificent night sky and into the other cosmos, illuminated by Molly's lamp, still shining in her bedroom. Stephen refuses Bloom's offer of a bed and wanders off, with dawn about to break, leaving Bloom to come to terms with Molly.

Molly's long monologue ends the book, putting Bloom into a new perspective, showing us Dublin through a female perspective, uninhibited, lewd, and ending in the ambiguous ''yes'' that has been so variously and richly interpreted.

In *Finnegans Wake* (1939), Joyce's final masterpiece, language is a major theme. Not a conventional novel, not exactly a long poem, it is a dreamscape, a dream of the characters. Neither is it written in conventional sentences, its poetic cadences comprising foreign puns, invented words, fragments of songs, quotations from all sorts of literature—from the sublime to the mundane—puns on names, catalogs, and diagrams. Beginning in midsentence as it does, *Finnegans Wake* frustrates those who want to force a linear interpretation on it. It is made up of dreamlike fragments and repeated images that weave it ultimately into an integrated whole; those who feel discouraged by it at first find that if they read it aloud, it makes a different sort of sense to them, but many of the puns are visual, so the text must be seen as well as heard. Language and its nuances, its potential to delight, become the focus.

Finnegans Wake lacks a linear plot but concerns a family of characters. Humphrey Chimpden Earwicker (HCE, or Here Comes Everybody) is accused of having done something vile in Phoenix Park. His wife is Anna Livia Plurabelle, associated with the River Liffey. Their children are Shem and Shaun, who are twins, and Isabel, or Isolde. The text winds its way through the dream consciousness of these characters, representing not only their actions but their nursery rhymes, their myths and legends, their saints, and their lessons at school. This makes a sort of timeless universality of experience that crosses languages and cultures a major theme.

The *Wake* is peopled with minor characters who come and go: old washerwomen, the ant and the grasshopper, Saint Patrick, and the four apostles, to name just a few. While it helps to know the arcane references structured into The *Wake*, it is not essential for a delightful reading. Often groups, both face-to-face and electronic, read The *Wake* together, just for the joy of discovery, to excavate the levels of meaning Joyce structured into it.

CRITICAL RECEPTION

Today the Irish revere Joyce as a hero and understand his works as the sometimes harsh but always truthful representations of Dublin life; today the Martello Tower, where Joyce lived, is a Joyce museum; today people come from all over the world to celebrate Bloomsday in Dublin, and there is a statue of the *Finnegans Wake* character Anna Livia Plurabelle erected downtown. But initially, his novels and stories met with resistance, harsh criticism, and outright censorship.

Joyce is regarded by most critics as the most brilliant prose stylist of the century, the English-language innovator of stream of consciousness or narrated discourse. The genius of his work was always acknowledged, but as a groundbreaking modernist, his early works were initially difficult to publish, partly because people were unfamiliar with his experimentation and partly because they objected to the always honest representations of human emotions and sexuality.

Now regarded as the brilliant representation of a rich range of Dublin life and character, *Dubliners* initially met with publishing difficulties and hostility from those who felt it would harm Ireland. Joyce initially arranged with Maunsel and Company for publication of the entire collection, but as the negotiations proceeded, George Roberts of Maunsel began to feel trepidations about *Dubliners* and began by asking Joyce to drop "An Encounter," a story in which two boys meet a frightening and perverted homosexual, and to change all names of businesses, for fear of libel. Joyce managed to salvage a copy of the manuscript before Maunsel ultimately destroyed it as anti-Irish.

In spite of his early difficulties with publication, his next attempt met with uneventful success, and while many initial reviews called the stories cynical or pointless, critics such as Ezra Pound saw *Dubliners* as the work of a man of genius.

Contemporary criticism often centers around how much to read symbolism into the stories, as opposed to reading them as naturalistic surface to be taken strictly on its own terms. Joyce had a love for realism, and when pressured by Roberts to change the names of establishments, he refused, even in the face of possible libel suits. Yet while the stories are not as symbolic as *A Portrait of the Artist as a Young Man, Ulysses,* and *Finnegans Wake,* symbolic elements certainly add to the readings of the stories, particularly those written later in Joyce's career.

Similarly, Joyce's letters show that the stories are rich with autobiographical detail. But how to interpret these details and with what significance to invest them are crucial questions. Two critical essays on "The Dead," for example, take different critical approaches. Joyce's biographer, Richard Ellmann, in "The Backgrounds of 'The Dead' " in *Dubliners* discusses the biographical and autobiographical material Joyce uses in its composition, and therefore he focuses on authorial intentionality to an extent. Florence Walzl, probably the most thoroughgoing and scholarly critic of *Dubliners,* focuses on the ways Joyce tied the stories together through repeated motifs in "The Dead." In "Gabriel and Michael: The Conclusion of 'The Dead' " in *Dubliners* she fleshes out, for example, the repeated images of light and dark, and she points out the symbolism of the names of main characters in the story. Both these essays can be found in the Viking Critical Edition of *Dubliners.* There would be little critical disagreement, however, in A. Walton Litz and Robert Scholes's statement in the introduction to that text that "the real hero of the stories is not an individual but the city itself, a city whose geography and history and inhabitants are all part of a coherent vision" (1).

Like *Dubliners, A Portrait of the Artist* also encountered publication problems, but they stemmed as much from the difficulty of carrying on normal transactions during wartime as they did from publishers who refused to print the book. Ezra Pound, however, enthusiastic about *Portrait,* brought it to the attention of the editors of *The Egoist,* which serialized it. B. W. Huebsch, who had brought out the American edition of *Dubliners,* published *Portrait* in 1916.

Upon its publication, H. G. Wells praised it highly for its reality but commented on Stephen Dedalus's representation of the limitations placed on the Irish. Fellow Irishman and writer George Moore disparaged Joyce's work, comparing *Portrait* quite unfairly to his own book, *Confessions of a Young Man* (1888). Ezra Pound, in a review in *The Egoist,* which bound a run of 750 copies using sheets from Huebsch, compared Joyce favorably with Flaubert and commented on the reaction he was likely to get when he praised Joyce: "I am . . . fairly safe in reasserting Joyce's ability as a writer. It will cost me no more than a few violent attacks from several sheltered, and therefore courageous, anonymities. When you tell the Irish that they are slow in recognizing their own men of genius they reply with street riots and politics" (February 1917, 323). Pound, like generations of scholars, went on to praise the writing and Joyce's style, for which he was becoming famous.

Critics today look at *Portrait* as a forerunner of *Ulysses,* finding characters, styles, and motifs that would appear later, with a sort of incremental repetition. Critics analyze Joyce's use of interior monologue and epiphanies, of free indirect discourse, as innovations in modernist fiction. They place *Portrait* in the tradition of the bildungsroman. They look to Stephen's aesthetic theory, sometimes taking it to be Joyce's, and they measure Joyce's canon according to its standards. They analyze the movements from joy to despair that mark the sections of *Portrait* and that lead into *Ulysses*.

The publishing history of *Ulysses* was even more adventuresome than that of his previous books. It was first published serially in the American *Little Review*; copies of that periodical were censored, seized by the U.S. Postal Service, and burned because they contained chapters of *Ulysses*. Harriet Shaw Weaver attempted to find a European printer for the book and approached Virginia and Leonard Woolf, but they refused, and in her diary, Virginia Woolf claimed that the book "reeled with indecency." Even Ezra Pound appealed to Joyce to censor Bloom's flatulence at the end of the "Sirens" episode. But T. S. Eliot justified and defended the use of crudity in the book. Publishers, fearing a public outcry over vulgarity, refused to publish it in book form.

However, Sylvia Beach, proprietor of Shakespeare and Co., a bookstore in Paris, agreed to bring out a limited first edition, published by a Paris printer. She solicited names of buyers who would agree to pay 150 francs apiece for a first edition and received a tart refusal from George Bernard Shaw.

Ulysses met with contradictory first reviews. Condemned by some as obscene, it was lauded by others as brilliant. Like *Portrait*, it was passionately defended by T. S. Eliot against the criticisms of Virginia Woolf. Joyce loved the critical controversies *Ulysses* engendered, and the publicity the book received made it much in demand. Bennet Cerf wanted to publish an American edition but waited until the 1933 decision whereby Judge John M. Woolsey ruled that it was not obscene and could be published in the United States.

Much of the early history of the criticism of *Ulysses* is based on the solving of the many riddles and the fleshing out of buried allusions in the book. Some of it actually answers the occasionally difficult question, "What is happening here?" Some of it fleshes out the Homeric allusions. Some of it traces the chapters to their actual Dublin locales and is published complete with maps. Some early criticism focuses on Joyce's use of the antihero.

Much contemporary criticism looks at Joyce's narrative innovations and experimentation and his use of free indirect discourse and narrated monologue. Some critics look at *Ulysses* as a postmodernist work that ultimately questions the nature of language. Some feminist critics look at Joyce's treatment of women characters and debate Bloom's androgyny. Some look at Joyce's use of Irish popular culture. The nature of the narrative has been much discussed.

The most recent critical controversy has surrounded the 1986 publication of Hans Walter Gabler's text of *Ulysses*, in which he corrected a number of longstanding errors and included textual material not previously printed in copies of the novel. But many of the corrections sparked disavowals and criticisms from textual scholars, and although the Gabler edition is now the standard text, the debate is far from resolved.

The initial critical response to *Finnegans Wake* was harsh and negative. Some allowed that in time it would emerge as a work of genius, but many dismissed it as unreadable. The criticism, along with his ill health and the onset of another war, made Joyce dejected and dispirited. Ironically, the Irish author Samuel Beckett saw the worth of the book when even stalwart supporters such as Ezra Pound criticized it, and Flann O'Brien imitated it in *At Swim-Two-Birds* (1939).

Too late to lift Joyce's spirits, critics began to take delight in the allusive richness of *Finnegans Wake*, seeing in its dream state the story of civilization, lampooned and yet told lovingly in Joyce's polyglot language. Much of the criticism today focuses on close readings of the text and upon its history: Joyce's sources, notebooks, and early drafts. *Finnegans Wake* is now rightly recognized by many scholars as the enduring masterstroke of Joyce the genius.

BIBLIOGRAPHY

Works by James Joyce

Collected Poems. New York: Viking, 1957.
The Critical Writings of James Joyce. Ed. Ellsworth Mason and Richard Ellmann. New York: Viking, 1959.
Dubliners: Text, Criticism and Notes. Ed. Robert Scholes and A. Walton Litz. New York: Viking, 1967.
Exiles. New York: Penguin, 1973.
Finnegans Wake. New York: Viking, 1939.
Giacomo Joyce. Ed. Richard Ellmann. New York: Viking, 1968.
Letters of James Joyce. Vol. 1, ed. Stuart Gilbert. New York: Viking, 1957; reissued with corrections 1966. Vols. 2 and 3, ed. Richard Ellmann. New York: Viking, 1966.
A Portrait of the Artist as a Young Man: Text, Criticism, and Notes. Ed. Chester G. Anderson. New York: Viking, 1964.
Selected Letters of James Joyce. Ed. Richard Ellmann. New York: Viking, 1975.
Stephen Hero. Ed. John J. Slocum and Herbert Cahoon. New York: New Directions, 1944, 1963.
Ulysses. Ed. Hans Walter Gabler et al. New York: Garland, 1984, 1986.

Studies of James Joyce

Attridge, Derek, ed. *The Cambridge Companion to James Joyce*. Cambridge: Cambridge University Press, 1990.
Benstock, Bernard. *James Joyce: The Undiscover'd Country*. New York: Barnes and Noble, 1977.
Byrne, John Francis. *Silent Years: An Autobiography, with Memoirs of James Joyce and Our Ireland*. New York: Farrar, Strauss, and Young, 1953.
Ellmann, Richard. *The Consciousness of Joyce*. London: Faber and Faber, 1977.

————. *James Joyce*. New York: Oxford University Press, 1982.

————. *James Joyce's Tower*. Dun Laoighaire: Eastern Regional Tourism Organisation, 1969.

Fargnoli, A. Nicholas, and Michael Patrick Gillespie. *James Joyce A to Z*. New York: Facts on File, 1995.

Gogarty, Oliver St. John. *As I Was Going Down Sackville Street*. London: Rich and Cowan, 1937.

Groden, Michael, ed. *The James Joyce Archive*. 63 vols. New York: Garland, 1977.

Joyce, Stanislaus. *The Complete Dublin Diary of Stanislaus Joyce*. Ithaca, NY: Cornell University Press, 1971.

————. "The Joyces." *The Listener* 41 (May 26, 1949): 896.

————. *My Brother's Keeper: James Joyce's Early Years*. Ed. with an introduction and notes by Richard Ellmann. Preface T. S. Eliot. New York: Viking, 1958.

————. *Recollections of James Joyce*. Trans. from the Italian by Ellsworth Mason. New York: James Joyce Society, 1950.

Kenner, Hugh. *Dublin's Joyce*. London: Chatto and Windus, 1956.

Manganiello, Dominic. *Joyce's Politics*. London: Routledge and Kegan Paul, 1980.

Pierce, David, *James Joyce's Ireland* New Haven, CT: Yale University Press, 1992.

Ryan, John, ed. *A Bash in the Tunnel: James Joyce by the Irish*. London and Brighton: Clifton, 1970.

Scott, Bonnie Kime. *Joyce and Feminism*. Bloomington: Indiana University Press, 1984.

Sullivan, Kevin. *Joyce among the Jesuits*. New York: Columbia University Press, 1958.

Patrick Kavanagh

(1904–1967)

Shawn Holliday

BIOGRAPHY

Patrick Joseph Gregory Kavanagh was born in the townland of Mucker in Inniskeen Parish, County Monaghan, on October 21, 1904, the fourth of ten children and the eldest son born to James and Bridget Kavanagh. As their son grew
up, both parents hoped that he would spend most of his adult life helping to
supplement the family's income by taking up his father's occupations of cobbling and subsistence farming. Subsequently, they encouraged Patrick to leave
Kednaminsha primary school at the age of thirteen to earn a living. Although
his formal education had come to an end, his parents could not quench their
son's early love for literature and poetry. The youth would spend most of his
teenage years memorizing stanzas from poems in any book or journal that he
could find. However, very few books were allowed to adorn the Kavanagh
household, for his mother believed that reading promoted idleness, keeping men
from properly supporting their families, and his father confined his literary interests to the local newspaper. As a result, Kavanagh's early influences range
from the popular writers found in such volumes as *Old Moore's Almanac* to the
canonized Romantic and Victorian poets gathered in the preponderance of local
schoolbooks. For most of his early career, Kavanagh's verse would be plagued
by sporadic development caused by his continual floundering between the high
art of his schoolbooks and the dross he found in popular magazines geared
toward the lower classes.

In 1925, Kavanagh stumbled upon *The Irish Statesman*, a journal edited by
AE (George Russell). For the first time, he was introduced to modern literature
by reading experimental works by such contributing artists as James Joyce,
Gertrude Stein, and Thomas McGreevy. From September 1, 1928, to June 8,

1929, Kavanagh published his first series of poems in *The Irish Weekly Independent*. At this time, his verse emulated the same "archaic imagery and outmoded poetic diction" of earlier Romantic and Victorian models (Quinn 8). However, after avidly studying *The Irish Statesman* for four years, Kavanagh learned the idealistic, dreamy formula of AE's poetry. In February 1930, the editor published "The Intangible," "Dreamer," and "Ploughman" in the journal, three of Kavanagh's more experimental poems.

Encouraged by this early success, Kavanagh briefly left Monaghan for Dublin in December 1931. The poet's purpose in making the sixty-mile trek was to meet with AE for further literary advice and patronage. Although *The Irish Statesman* had folded, AE took it upon himself to handle Kavanagh's further reading and education. The poet returned to the farm with borrowed volumes by Dostoevski, Emerson, Melville, Whitman, and others. Subsequently, he spent most of the 1930s at home cobbling, farming, and writing poetry. After several more trips to Dublin, he began to build a minor reputation as a "peasant poet." Besides becoming friendly with Frank O'Connor and Sean O'Faolain, both of whom also took active roles in Kavanagh's education, the poet met with Seumas O'Sullivan, the editor of *The Dublin Magazine*. These friendships proved beneficial to Kavanagh. All three helped to introduce him to Irish literary culture, and he submitted much of his early poetry to O'Sullivan's journal. In April 1936, Macmillan published Kavanagh's first book of verse, *Ploughman and Other Poems*, in its Contemporary Poets Series. He further attempted to establish himself in Dublin by writing articles for *The Irish Times* newspaper and by publishing his first autobiographical novel, *The Green Fool* (1938).

To further cement his place in the Irish literary world, Kavanagh permanently left his Monaghan farm for Dublin in 1939. He earned much of his living during the 1940s by working as a journalist. Besides writing book and film reviews for *The Standard*, Kavanagh also published a diary column for *Envoy* and maintained a gossip column in another local paper. Much of this journalistic work, however, had adverse effects on the poet's literary career. His running feuds with fellow writers concerning their opportunism and mediocrity made him more enemies than friends, and his opposition to the Revival's "stage-Irish lie" ran counter to the philosophy of many of his contemporaries. To express his honest critical views, the poet took up residence at Dublin's Palace Bar, where he achieved local fame by being known as either a foul-mouthed buffoon or the peasant poet. Even the publication of his poetic masterpiece, "The Great Hunger" (1942), could not stop the sudden deterioration of his personal relationships.

In 1947, Kavanagh published his second volume of poetry, *A Soul for Sale* and, one year later, his second semiautobiographical novel, *Tarry Flynn*. After these small critical successes, however, the author's career ran into more trouble: he failed to find journalistic work in London, the Irish Cultural Committee refused to sponsor his proposed lecture tour of America, and Macmillan would no longer publish his work. Being unhappy without a steady public forum from which to expound his views, the author and his younger brother, Peter, started their own eight-page newspaper, *Kavanagh's Weekly*, but this venture proved unsuccessful as well. The publication lasted for only three months and folded when Peter ran out of money. Later, in 1952, Kavanagh stumbled upon an unflattering profile of himself in *The Leader* and sued the newspaper for libel. The trial lasted for a week, and Kavanagh spent thirteen hours testifying. Unfortunately, the jury found in favor of the defendant and ordered the author to pay all court costs. Kavanagh immediately appealed, and the new trial ended in his favor.

For the most part, the author spent the last ten years of his life drowning his sorrows in alcohol and nursing his bad health. In 1955, he had a cancerous lung removed. Although the operation proved a success, the illness left him permanently weakened. During this time, the author completely stopped writing fiction and turned most of his attention to writing poetry and various biographical accounts of his literary career. Many critics agree that Kavanagh wrote many of his finest poems late in life. They cite his sonnets as being particularly effective, especially the posthumously published "Lough Derg." In April 1967, the author finally achieved personal happiness by marrying his longtime friend Katherine Barry Maloney. Five months later, however, his highly troubled life and literary career ended with his death from pneumonia.

MAJOR WORKS AND THEMES

By the time Kavanagh reached the age of fifty, he no longer approved of much of his early poetic output. Many of the thirty-one poems appearing in *Ploughman and Other Poems* are either weak imitations of the pastoral verse written by earlier Georgian poets or pale attempts at employing AE's mystical aestheticism. Almost all of the poems Kavanagh wrote in the 1930s are meditative lyrics, and his apparent lack of sophistication at this time surely caused him later to view these pieces as mere juvenilia. Although AE criticized the poems in *Ploughman* as being "fake," the poet does write with some sense of originality in his early work. Unlike Yeats, Kavanagh never employed a poetic mask. He wrote straightforwardly about his own experiences with the land. While most other Irish writers at the time bought into the "Stage-Irish lie," Kavanagh's self-limitation helped the poet to revolt against the clichéd writings of the Irish Literary Revival.

Six years later, Kavanagh published "The Great Hunger," his first major work. The author's main purpose in writing this long poem was to depict the harsh realities of rural life by showing how one man's will is suffocated by unending labor and religious confinement. With the poem's protagonist, Patrick Maguire, Kavanagh created a rural Everyman figure who is tyrannized by the land and sexually repressed by his domineering mother. The poet's main accomplishment with this piece, however, lies in his use of the omniscient narrator. Kavanagh creates great dramatic irony by employing a narrative voice that is both angry and ironic. While Kavanagh uses the technique to warn us of the dangers of Maguire's behalf, he cannot fail to see the humor in a peasant who longingly yearns for a more fulfilling life and love—a theme and attitude extensively explored in the fiction of his contemporary Brinsley MacNamara. Like all of the poet's best work, "The Great Hunger" treats the tragedies of our existence without reverting to the sentimentality and didacticism that plague so much Irish writing at this time.

Kavanagh's most objective work, however, comes with his two finished novels, *The Green Fool* and *Tarry Flynn*. For the most part, *The Green Fool* is a semiautobiographical work that treats the poet's first thirty years of life. In the book, Kavanagh intentionally places many fabricated events against the authentic background of Inniskeen Parish in an attempt to highlight the romantic and realist components of his personality. Likewise, *Tarry Flynn* deals with Kavanagh's life shortly before he chose to leave his Monaghan farm for Dublin. Here, the writer further explores his development by showing how Monaghan's restrictive community alienated him from his family and farm life. Like many typical bildungsroman, the author uses each chapter to show how his main character grows from being a simple naif into a somewhat sophisticated poet and seer. The main strength of this book remains Kavanagh's realistic portrayal of peasant life. Through his use of documentary realism, he offers us the only legitimate depiction of the daily activities and rough language of the Irish peasantry that exists in modern Irish literature.

CRITICAL RECEPTION

One of the first book-length studies to appear on Kavanagh was Alan Warner's *Clay Is the Word: Patrick Kavanagh 1904–1967* (1973). The author's main purpose is to bring Kavanagh's work "to the notice of a wider reading public and to reveal something of the background that may make it more intelligible to readers outside of Ireland" (7). Since Warner was aware of Kavanagh's distrust for academics, he drops any clear theoretical perspective that may deepen our understanding of the poet's work. Instead, Warner opts to let Kavanagh lead most of the book's discussion by providing material taken from his vast amount of journalism. Although the author gives us an opportunity to glimpse much previously inaccessible material taken from such sources as *The Irish Farmers' Journal* and *The Dundalk Democrat*, the study never fully recovers from the poet's smothering of Warner's own voice and point of view. *Clay Is the Word* simply remains too friendly for its own good.

A much more balanced, objective, and recent work is Antoinette Quinn's *Patrick Kavanagh: A Critical Study* (1991). Quinn devotes at least a chapter to each of Kavanagh's novels and collections of verse in an attempt to provide the necessary biographical and cultural contexts in which the poet produced his work. Especially insightful are the author's discussions of Kavanagh's early influences and his deliberate imitation of them in his early verse. Although she acknowledges that she views Kavanagh as a "born-again Romantic," Quinn also realizes that she may have "straight-jacketed" him in her critical discussion (459). To alleviate this problem, Quinn balances her own perspective with quotations taken from a wide range of Kavanagh's work so that readers are able to reach their own theoretical conclusions.

An especially groundbreaking discussion of Kavanagh appears in Terry Gifford's *Green Voices: Understanding Contemporary Nature Poetry* (1995). By placing Kavanagh's long poem "The Great Hunger" in an environmental context, Gifford shows how many of the poet's concerns "echo those found in eighteenth-century anti-pastoral poetry" (55). Gifford claims that by countering the traditional, pastoral view of landscape, Kavanagh shows how the land can be "both a joy and a trap" to an individual (59–60). The author maintains that the poem's success is a result of the tension created by Kavanagh's harsh, realistic knowledge of rural culture and his romantic notions about the function of poetry.

In all, there remain two opposing notions about Kavanagh's body of work. While some regard him as one of the most important poets writing in the generation after Yeats, others consider him a provincial poet whose only accomplishment was to infuse the exhausted Irish Literary Revival with a genuine voice from the rural peasantry. However, Darcy O'Brien maintains that Kavanagh "tried to be parochial without being provincial" and that the writer's best work captures "the poetry of ordinary life as he knew it," making him a poet of universal significance (13, 17). Likewise, Brendan Kennelly cites the tension between the author's "comic vision" and his "insatiable hunger for reality" as giving Kavanagh a final poetic dignity and a definite place in modern Irish literature (182).

BIBLIOGRAPHY

Works by Patrick Kavanagh

Letters

Lapped Furrows: Correspondence 1933–1967 between Patrick and Peter Kavanagh. Ed. Peter Kavanagh. New York: Peter Kavanagh Hand Press, 1969.
Love's Tortured Headland: A Sequel to Lapped Furrows. Ed. Peter Kavanagh. New York: Peter Kavanagh Hand Press, 1978.

Novels

By Night Unstarred. Ed. Peter Kavanagh. Curragh: Goldsmith, 1977; New York: Peter Kavanagh Hand Press, 1978.
The Green Fool. London: M. Joseph, 1938; New York: Harper, 1939.
Tarry Flynn. London: Pilot, 1948; New York: Devin-Adair, 1949.

Poetry

Collected Poems. New York: Devin-Adair, 1964: London: MacGibbon and Kee, 1967.
Come Dance with Kitty Stobling and Other Poems. London: Longmans, Green, 1960;
    Philadelphia: Dufour, 1964.
Complete Poems. Ed. Peter Kavanagh. New York: Peter Kavanagh Hand Press, 1972.
The Great Hunger. Dublin: Cuala, 1942; London: MacGibbon and Kee, 1966.
Ploughman and Other Poems. London: Macmillan, 1936.
Recent Poems. Ed. Peter Kavanagh. New York: Peter Kavanagh Hand Press, 1958.
A Soul for Sale. London: Macmillan, 1947.

Prose

Collected Prose. London: MacGibbon and Kee, 1967.
November Haggard, Uncollected Prose and Verse of Patrick Kavanagh. Ed. Peter Ka-
    vanagh. New York: Peter Kavanagh Hand, 1971.
Self-Portrait. Dublin: Dolmen, 1964.

Recording

Almost Everything: Written and Spoken by Patrick Kavanagh. Dublin: Claddagh Records,
    1964.

Studies of Patrick Kavanagh

Duffy, Patrick J. "Patrick Kavanagh's Landscape." *Eire-Ireland* 21.3 (1986): 105–18.
Garrat, Robert F. "Patrick Kavanagh and the Killing of the Irish Revival." *Colby Quar-
    terly* 17.3 (1981): 170–83.
Grennan, Eamon. "Pastoral Design in the Poetry of Patrick Kavanagh." *Renascence* 34.1
    (1981): 3–16.
Holliday, Shawn. "Sex and Comedy in Patrick Kavanagh's 'The Great Hunger.' " *Notes
    on Modern Irish Literature* 7.1 (1995): 34–40.
Kavanagh, Peter, *Sacred Keeper: A Biography*. Curragh: Goldsmith, 1980.
———. ed. *The Garden of the Golden Apples: A Bibliography*. New York: Peter Ka-
    vanagh Hand Press, 1972.
———. ed. *Patrick Kavanagh: Man and Poet*. Orono: University of Maine Press, 1986.
Kennelly, Brendan. "Patrick Kavanagh." *Ariel* 1 (1970): 7–28.
Kiberd, Declan. "Beckett and Kavanagh: Comparatively Absurd?" *Hermathena* 141
    (1986): 45–55.
Klejs, Lene. "Seed like Stars: Kavanagh's Nature." *Eire-Ireland* 18.1 (1983): 98–108.
Muri, Allison. "Paganism and Christianity in Kavanagh's 'The Great Hunger.' " *Ca-
    nadian Journal of Irish Studies* 16.2 (1990): 66–78.
Nemo, John. *Patrick Kavanagh*. Boston: Twayne, 1979.
O'Brien, Darcy. *Patrick Kavanagh*. Lewisburg, PA: Bucknell University Press, 1975.
O'Loughlin, Michael. *After Kavanagh*. Dublin: Raven Arts, 1985.
Popowich, Barry. "Patrick Kavanagh's Space beyond Time." *Canadian Journal of Irish
    Studies* 17.2 (1991): 31–38.
Quinn, Antoinette. *Patrick Kavanagh: A Critical Study*. Syracuse: Syracuse University
    Press, 1991.
Warner, Alan. *Clay Is the Word: Patrick Kavanagh 1904–1967*. Dublin: Dolmen, 1973.

John B. Keane

(1928–)

Patricia Kane O'Connor

John Keane was born on July 21, 1928, in Listowel, County Kerry. From child-hood, Keane was aware of the existence of regional wisdom and traditions, and he recognized the uniqueness of the language and customs of the area. As a boy he spent summers in the Stacks Mountains, where he enjoyed traditional sto-rytelling and music and experienced a manner of life even less altered by the modern world than Listowel itself.

Following a two-year stint working in England, he and Mary O'Connor pur-chased a public house/grocery shop in Listowel and were married. After attend-ing a performance of Joseph Tomelty's *All Soul's Night* in 1958, the young poet was inspired to write a play. Late at night in the back room of his new pub he poured his heart into *Sive*. His first play's victory at the All-Ireland Drama Festival gained him instant recognition, and the playwright was born. His many plays have appeared on stages across Ireland—including several performances at the Abbey—and the world, and *The Field* was produced as a major motion picture. John B. Keane continues to live and write in Listowel.

MAJOR WORKS AND THEMES

As well as being an active columnist, Keane has published poems; autobi-ography; collections of short fiction, essays, and quotations; novels; and many books in his *Letters* series; but his greatest literary achievement both in publi-cation and in stage production has been his plays. The common thread that binds Keane's prolific work in various genres is the honest and consistent portrayal of the ways and concerns of Ireland—particularly rural Ireland. The issues, values, and traditions of the people of Kerry pervade all of his works and give them an authentic regional flavor.

Thematically, Keane's plays grow out of the Abbey tradition and that of the Irish peasant plays, focusing on issues of land greed, emigration, and the challenges of love, sexuality, and personal fulfillment in the rural, religious, and political environment of Ireland. He reaches beyond the boundaries of the dramatic tradition, though, as his focus on individuals allows him to engage in social commentary—a practice that the Abbey mold lacked. Keane disdains stereotypes of the Irish but is truly nostalgic about his country's vanishing traditions. He goes some way toward preserving them in the costumes, dialects, settings, and characters in his dramas. The struggle between inherited traditions and the influences of the modern world is a central motif.

His first play, *Sive*, tackles the issue of "made marriage," a country tradition ultimately condemned by the tragic work. The play so accurately captured the language and the manner of life of his region that his community saw itself exposed as never before. Conceived and told like a storyteller's tale, *Sive* reflects the influence of the *seanchaí* on Keane—an influence recognizable in all of his work.

In *Many Young Men of Twenty* (1962) and *Hut 42* (1967), Keane addresses a more immediate theme and indeed one of more national concern: emigration. Both capture the painful predicaments—such as bittersweet holidays at home—of his young countrymen who were compelled to live far away and who yearned ceaselessly for their homeland. Their experiences were realistically depicted by Keane, who had lived as an emigrant in England, the setting of *Hut 42*; it portrays the frustrating and lonely lives of Irishmen abroad and tackles the relationship between emigration and economics.

The Field (1966) reveals the Irish preoccupation with land, the unique predicament of the outsider in the rural setting, and the "law of community" that is often independent of the legal system. *Big Maggie* (1969) gives evidence of Keane's skill at depicting the Irish woman, in this case one whose struggles with issues of sex, religion, and the role of mother reflect challenges to the national consciousness. Like Maggie, Keane's Ireland wrestles under the "chains" of pride, ignorance, and religion.

CRITICAL RECEPTION

If the Irish public—those who people Keane's plays and fiction— is considered the most important and astute of critics, then this Kerry playwright has from the start been a great critical success, as he has always been a popular success. More conventional critical appreciation was somewhat more elusive at first, however, and remained less reliable than the general public's appreciation of his talents.

The theater establishment of Ireland—namely, the Abbey—disappointed Keane in its rejection of his early plays. *Sive*'s victory in Athlone at the All-Ireland Drama Festival after its rejection by the Abbey seemed a rebuttal to the national theater's decision. Still, other Abbey rejections would follow, though the popularity of his plays across the nation never waned. With the acceptance of *Hut 42* in 1962—and other plays after it—Keane deservedly entered the ranks of the Abbey playwrights.

Newspaper and other media critics consistently disagree about the overall merits of Keane's dramas in performance, though they tend to concur on the brilliance of his use of language and his skill in the traditional art of storytelling. Smith and Hickey carefully chronicle the critical reactions to many of the plays' productions in Ireland. In her *Kerry Playwright*, Kealy competently studies both the regional and national aspects of the dramas.

Keane's overall body of work deserves, indeed demands, more substantial consideration by literary critics. Despite that shortage, however, Keane's contribution to the Irish theater is unquestionable.

BIBLIOGRAPHY

Works by John B. Keane

Plays

Big Maggie. Dublin: Mercier, 1969.
The Buds of Ballybunion. Dublin: Mercier, 1976.
The Change in Mame Fadden. Cork: Mercier, 1972.
The Chastitute. Dublin: Mercier, 1981.
The Crazy Wall. Dublin: Mercier, 1974.
The Field. Cork: Mercier, 1966.
The Good Thing. Proscenium, 1975.
The Highest House on the Mountain. Dublin: Progress House, 1961.
Hut 42. Proscenium, 1967.
The Man from Clare. Cork: Mercier, 1962.
Many Young Men of Twenty. Dublin: Progress House, 1962.
Moll. Dublin: Mercier, 1971.
No More in Dust. Dublin: Progress House, 1962.
The One-Way Ticket. Proscenium, 1972.
The Rain at the End of Summer. Dublin: Progress House, 1967.
Sharon's Grave. Dublin: Progress House, 1960.
Sive. Dublin: Progress House, 1959.
Values. Dublin: Mercier, 1973.
The Year of the Hiker. Cork: Mercier, 1963.

Poems

The Street. Dublin: Progress House, 1961.

Short Fiction

Death Be Not Proud. Dublin: Mercier, 1976.
Innocent Bystanders. Cork: Mercier, 1994.

Irish Short Stories. Dublin: Mercier, 1976.
More Irish Short Stories. Dublin: Mercier, 1981

Novels

The Bodhran Makers. Dingle: Brandon, 1986.
The Contractors. Cork: Mercier, 1993.
Durango. Cork: Mercier, 1992.
A High Meadow. Dublin: Mercier, 1994.

Nonfiction

Dan Pheaidí Aindí. Baile Átha Cliath: Cló Mercier, 1977.
Man of the Triple Name. Dingle: Brandon, 1984.
Self-Portrait. Dublin: Mercier, 1964.

Collection of Quotations

The Power of the Word. Dingle: Brandon, 1989.

Collections of Essays

The Gentle Art of Matchmaking. Cork: Mercier, 1973.
Is the Holy Ghost Really a Kerryman? Dublin: Mercier, 1976.
Love Bites. Cork: Mercier, 1991.
Owl Sandwiches. Dingle: Brandon, 1985.
The Ram of God. Dublin: Mercier, 1992.
Stories from a Kerry Fireside. Cork: Mercier, 1980.
Strong Tea. Cork: Mercier, 1963.
Unlawful Sex. Dublin: Mercier, 1978.
Unusual Irish Careers. Dublin: Mercier, 1982.

Letters Series

The Celebrated Letters of John B. Keane. Dublin: Mercier, 1991.
Letters of a Civic Guard. Cork: Mercier, 1976.
Letters of a Country Postman. Dublin: Mercier, 1977.
Letters of an Irish Minister of State. Dublin: Mercier, 1978.
Letters of an Irish Parish Priest. Cork: Mercier, 1972.
Letters of an Irish Publican. Dublin: Mercier, 1973.
Letters of a Love-Hungry Farmer. Dublin: Mercier, 1974.
Letters of a Matchmaker. Cork: Mercier, 1975.
Letters of a Successful T. D. Cork: Mercier, 1967.
Letters to the Brain. Dingle: Brandon, 1993.

Studies of John B. Keane

Feelian, John M., ed. *Fifty Years Young*. Cork: Mercier, 1979.
Kealy, Marie Hubert. *Kerry Playwright: Sense of Place in the Plays of John B. Keane*. Selinsgrove: Susquehanna University Press, 1993.
———. "The Wall and the Wanderer: Unresolved Domestic Conflict in the Plays of John B. Keane." *Notes on Modern Irish Literature* 2 (1990): 74–78.

Rush, Desmond. "Keane to Begin." *Eire-Ireland* 15 (1980): 112–15.

Smith, Gus, and Des Hickey. *John B: The Real Keane*. Dublin: Mercier, 1992.

Winkler, Elizabeth Hale. "Eejitin About: Adolescence in Friel and Keane." *Eire-Ireland* 16.3 (Fall 1981): 138–44.

Molly Keane

(1904–)

Ann Owens Weekes

BIOGRAPHY

Molly Keane was born to the Skrine family in County Kildare, where she lived for five years before the family moved to County Wexford. While her mother was religious and concerned about her children's modesty and good behavior, her father, an excellent horseman, taught the children that hunting mattered more than anything, a lesson revealed in all Keane novels.

The larger world of European tensions and Irish political struggles infringed but little on the Skrine household until the family home, an ascendancy Big House, was burned in retaliation for Black-and-Tan atrocities. Sent to boarding school in Bray during this time, Molly was disliked by her classmates, found academics uninteresting, but eventually came to enjoy English literature. Getting a job was never an option—girls stayed home until they married—but Molly was introduced to a wider world when she encountered the wealthy, sophisticated Perry family, which welcomed her into their home for many months of hunting each year, and John Perry would later assist her to write plays.

The legend of Molly Keane's becoming a writer is well known, though indeed she tells several versions. In one she avers that at seventeen she wrote her first novel, *The Knight of the Cheerful Countenance* (1926), to supplement her dress allowance, using the pseudonym M. J. Farrell to hide the embarrassing activity from her hunting friends. A productive writing career followed; she published ten novels between 1928 and 1952, plus a book of Irish sporting scenes, *Red Letter Days* (1933), and had three plays produced in London, all directed by John Gielgud. Although she wrote one more play, Molly Keane retreated from the literature scene when her beloved husband, Robert Keane, died, and she struggled to care for her two young daughters. To many readers' delight, she broke her silence in 1981 with *Good Behaviour*, a novel immediately acclaimed a classic. This has been followed by two more novels, a cookbook, and a book of Irish reminiscences. Molly Keane now lives in Ardmore, County Waterford.

MAJOR WORKS AND THEMES

Forgotten in the British Library since 1926, *The Knight of the Cheerful Countenance* was reissued in 1993. A beginner's novel, it introduces, nevertheless, the familiar Keane themes: the hunt, the upstairs-downstairs society of the Big House, and the beautiful, plucky, unconventional girls whom the author admires more than the good, sensible, dull ones. The romantic plot is predictable, serving only as rationale for the enthusiastic detailing of one rare, healthy, exciting hunt scene after another. The twilight of the Anglo-Irish ascendancy is the world Keane inhabits and records: affection for this society characterizes the early novels, with few insights into the cruelties of the system. *Young Entry* (1928) tells the story of Prudence Lingfield-Turrett's alienation from her adolescent girlfriend "Peter" as the latter becomes involved in romance. The suicide of the dismissed cook haunts Prudence but receives less attention throughout than the small dogs to whom Prudence and Peter devote themselves. In *Taking Chances* (1929), the last of this trio of novice novels, Keane moves from the successful romantic formula to near tragedy. Mary Fuller, a typical Keane woman—beautiful, sensuous, and dangerous—wrecks the marriage of her friend, as love becomes less like a game and more like the compulsive sport of hunting.

Sense of place, a constant in Keane's fiction, emerges fully in *Mad Puppetstown* (1931). The novel's first part depicts the golden childhood of Easter Chivington and her cousins, Basil and Evelyn, in an idyllic Ireland of devoted servants, mysterious mountains, and glorious hunts before the Great War and the Irish Troubles. British distrust of Irish servants is treated ironically, the distrust leading a British soldier into an ambush and sending the Chivingtons scurrying for safety to England. Discovering their mutual love of place, Easter and Basil return as adults to a neglected Puppetstown, jealously guarded by an elderly aunt and longtime retainer. Love of place, not romance, enables cousins, aunt, and retainer to share and restore Puppetstown.

Lady Honour, in *Conversation Piece* (1932), is the first of Keane's awful mothers, a series of vicious, elderly women who prey on, or dominate, the young. The lesbian relationship of Jessica and Jane drives the plot of the following novel, *Devoted Ladies* (1934). Opening in fashionable London, a suitable setting for the brittle heroines, the novel quickly moves to the hunting scenes of Big House Ireland. Piggy, who effects the dramatic conclusion and "saves" the day for heterosexual love, is a marvelous portrait of Keane's unattractive innocents: greedy, selfish, lacking self-knowledge, madly desiring love, Piggy will be perfected in the Aroon of *Good Behaviour*.

In *Full House* (1935), *The Rising Tide* (1937), and *Loving without Tears*

(1951) Keane continues to develop superb portraits of cruel mothers: women whose gift it is to charm and bind the very people they destroy. Lady Olivia Bird (*Full House*), adored by her silly husband, dominates her children so completely that even when they see through her strategies, they are unable to leave her. Lady Charlotte (*The Rising Tide*) is the evil genius who, like most of these Keane women, refuses to see the changes taking place in Ireland at the beginning of the century and bullies her children into submission. Angel (*Loving without Tears*) is as manipulative as the other two mothers, but Keane wraps this novel up in comic harmony.

Two Days in Aragon (1941) focuses on the threat to Anglo-Irish life, as Grania, the daughter of the Big House, has a secret affair with her nurse's son, Foley O'Neill, a member of an illegal Irish military unit. *Treasure Hunt* (1952), the last of the early novels, features a Big House after the Troubles, where the mad hilarity continues despite the family's being forced to take English paying guests.

Three very good novels appeared since 1981, *Good Behaviour* (1981), *Time after Time* (1983), and *Loving and Giving* (1988). While the earlier works depicted both the charming and useless lives of the ascendancy, frantically involved with horses, dogs, and lovers to keep boredom at bay, the three recent novels reveal a savagery never fully concealed by the code of good behavior, a savagery bred from that very code, the only remaining proof of a dying, impoverished class's mistaken sense of superiority. Ignorance and utter lack of self-knowledge bolster this mistaken sense, turning would-be models of good behavior into examples of stupidity and cruelty. In a brilliant stroke, Keane allows Aroon to narrate *Good Behaviour*, revealing, as she attempts to hide, her ignorance, greed, and ugly personality. Aroon's murder of the Mummie she professes to love in the opening pages sets the stage for the funniest, blackest of Keane's comedies. All three novels look back from a present in the 1970s or 1940s to the time of the characters' and Keane's own youth. All three jolt the reader with their mix of the mundane and the shocking, the comic and the tragic. Always characters in their own right, the beautiful houses of the earlier novels decay in these later years, revealing the hostile, dangerous face that money and confidence disguised in their youth. While horses and dogs remain an obsession, the beautiful, plucky girls of the past have been replaced by elderly, ugly, barren women. The last novels toll a death knell, not a lament, for Anglo-Ireland.

CRITICAL RECEPTION

Reviewers were generally appreciative of Molly Keane's novels from the publication of *Young Entry*; American critics found the fox-hunting life foreign but delighted in the antics of the ascendancy, while British and Irish reviewers saw Keane as worthy successor to Somerville and Ross. The cruel acuity of her perception was noted, and her mixture of comic wit and poetic sensibility was called delightful. Some reviewers, however, recoiled at the "indecent" subject of *Devoted Ladies*; others found the "doggie" talk tedious. Reviewers of the three recent novels and of Virago's reissue of the first eleven continue the praise but also take Keane's work more seriously. *Good Behaviour*, "with its mixture of the macabre and the mundane, the terrifying and the ridiculous," may well become a "classic among English novels," the *New York Times Book Review* proclaimed (August 9, 1991). Caroline Blackwood applauds Keane's portraits of the "profoundly philistine" life of the Anglo-Irish, singling out "maternal cruelty" as a recurring theme (Afterword, *Full House*). Polly Devlin sums up Anglo-Ireland in the early novels: "The 'real' Irish (the peasant Catholic Irish) seem only to enter this world—and thus Molly Keane/Farrell's faithful rendering—as a sub-species, good for opening gates and giving amusing, barely subservient lip service" (Introduction, *The Rising Tide*). Fuller studies are available in Imhof's *Ancestral Voices* and Weekes's *Irish Women Writers*.

BIBLIOGRAPHY

Works by Molly Keane

The Knight of the Cheerful Countenance. 1926. Reprinted, London: Virago, 1993.
Young Entry. (In United States, *Point-to-Point*.) 1928. Reprinted, London: Virago, 1989.
Taking Chances. 1929. Reprinted, London: Virago, 1987.
Mad Puppetstown. 1931. Reprinted, London: Virago, 1986.
Conversation Piece. 1932. Reprinted, London: Virago, 1991.
Red Letter Days. 1933. Reprinted, London: Deutsch, 1987.
Devoted Ladies. 1934. Reprinted, London: Virago, 1984.
Full House. 1935. Reprinted, London: Virago, 1986.
The Rising Tide. 1937. Reprinted, London: Virago, 1984.
Two Days in Aragon. 1941. Reprinted, London: Virago, 1985.
Loving without Tears. (In United States, *Enchanting Witch*.) 1951. Reprinted, London: Virago, 1988.
Treasure Hunt. 1952. Reprinted, London: Virago, 1990.
Good Behaviour. London: Deutsch, 1981.
Time after Time. London: Deutsch, 1983.
Molly Keane's Nursery Cooking. London: Macdonald, 1985.
Loving and Giving. (In United States, *Queen Lear*.) London: Deutsch, 1988.
Molly Keane's Ireland. London: HarperCollins, 1994. (An anthology compiled by Molly Keane and Sally Phipps [Keane's daughter.])

Studies of Molly Keane

Boylan, Clare. *Sex, Snobbery and the Strategies of Molly Keane*. New York: St. Martin's, 1993.

Benedict Kiely

(1919–)

Andrew J. Haggerty

BIOGRAPHY

Born on August 15, 1919, Benedict Kiely spent his childhood in Omagh, County Tyrone, receiving his early education from the local Christian Brothers. Feeling a call to the clerical life, he entered the Jesuit novitiate at Emo Paric in 1937. April 1938, however, saw him confined by a tubercular spinal illness to a hospital in Finglas, County Dublin, for a year and a half. He devoted his convalescence to reading and to study, making use of the excellent library resources of the Jesuits then available to him.

Unfortunately for his benefactors, the society of attractive young nurses left a more lasting impact upon the young writer than did the Society of Jesus—at least according to Kiely's later fond recollection. Upon his recovery, instead of returning to the novitiate he enrolled in University College, Dublin, taking B.A.s in history, English, and Latin in 1943. He then embarked upon his literary career, beginning with journalism and progressing into fiction. After several years at *The Irish Independent*, he became literary editor for *The Irish Press* in 1950. In 1964 Kiely accepted an offer to teach creative writing at Hollins College in Virginia. He spent four more years in the States, teaching in Oregon and in Georgia and writing for *The New York Times Book Review*, the *Kenyon Review*, and many other periodicals. Since his return to Ireland he has concentrated chiefly upon his art, but he has also done occasional pieces for the *Irish Times*, broadcasts for radio and television, and a good deal of travel writing. The high regard in which Kiely and his work are held in his native land was confirmed in 1980, when he received the Irish Academy of Letters Award for Literature.

MAJOR WORKS AND THEMES

Kiely relies to a great extent upon the reworking of his personal history for his literary enterprise. The landscape of Omagh is, for example, recognizable as that of the unnamed ''town'' at the center of his sprawling second novel, *In a Harbour Green* (1949). In a larger sense, Kiely's writing always deals with the complicated realities of Irish culture and history. His fiction is driven by an engaging, distinctive narrative voice: Kiely is often seen as a modern-day Irish storyteller, in the tradition of William Carleton, about whom Kiely published a critical study, *Poor Scholar: A Study of William Carleton (1794–1869)*, in 1947. Kiely's critical acumen is also demonstrated in his valuable *Modern Irish Fiction* (1950).

After his first two novels, *Land without Stars* (1946) and *In a Harbour Green*, Kiely's fiction gradually increases in complexity, as he begins to experiment with his storytelling technique. The interplay of narrative perspectives in *Call for a Miracle* (1951) elevates the novel's chronicle of sin and suicide in a Dublin family to almost the level of fable; *Honey Seems Bitter* (1952) is even darker, an intense tale of murder and betrayal. In *The Cards of the Gambler* (1953), the modern world interacts with the ancient, and the real mingles strangely with the legendary. Kiely's experiences as a Jesuit-in-training serve as the backdrop to *There Was an Ancient House* (1955), an account of one year in the strangely timeless, spiritual world of a novitiate. The sometimes lighthearted, sometimes hypnotic first-person narration of Kiely's Owen Rodgers in *The Captain with the Whiskers* (1961) subtly brings to life the monstrosity of the Captain, the novel's domineering patriarch. As dissimilar as these novels may appear, they are yet united in their examination of disturbing or profound psychic realities that lie beneath an apparently untroubled veneer—an examination of obvious significance in a society determined to preserve propriety at all costs. *In a Harbour Green*, *Honey Seems Bitter*, and *There Was an Ancient House* all fell victim to censorship.

After the publication of *The Captain with the Whiskers*, Kiely's work has largely been devoted to the short story rather than the novel, with the notable exceptions of *Dogs Enjoy the Morning* (1968), the novella *Proxopera* (1977), and *Nothing Happens in Carmincross* (1985). Kiely's mastery of short fiction is apparent even in his first collection, *A Journey to the Seven Streams* (1963), despite its somewhat diluting sentimentality. In *A Ball of Malt and Madame Butterfly* (1973), Kiely achieves a kind of perfection, handling with humor and compassion such familiar themes as love lost and regained, the sorrows of death and sickness, and the persistence of memory. *Dogs Enjoy the Morning*, the story of three days of roisterous sexual byplay in a rural town, exhibits a similar generosity of spirit.

The unquiet forces of Irish history, however, were to awaken once again, having an unsettling impact upon Kiely's work. The stories collected in *A Cow in the House* (1978) play upon the seemingly irreparable, violent divides in

Ulster society. *Proxopera* constitutes a deeply felt condemnation of political violence as the life of a middle-class family is interrupted by a Republican assassination plot. *Nothing Happens in Carmincross* is even more bleak. Mervyn Kavanagh, a middle-aged historian, returns from America to his Ulster home-town for a wedding, which is torn apart by an Irish Republican Army (IRA) bomb. If Kiely's early work focuses upon the disturbing currents that flow beneath a seemingly placid surface, in the later fiction not even the semblance of normality can be maintained any longer. The elegiac tone of Kiely's most recent published collection of stories, *A Letter to Peachtree* (1988), however, reveals his deep sympathy and affection for the land he has passionately chronicled for so long.

CRITICAL RECEPTION

Kiely's narrative style has often been compared with that of the *seanachaí*, the ancient Irish storyteller and keeper of local history and wisdom: Kiely's critics have generally been at pains to describe Kiely as, primarily, a storyteller. Grace Eckley tells us that in writing the first critical study of Kiely's work she has primarily "attempted to prove that Kiely tells a good story well" (8). This thesis resonates with that of Daniel J. Casey, who sees Kiely's relationship with Irish culture as so deep as to be almost unconscious: "To a greater degree than even he would perhaps admit, the content and technique of Kiely's fiction are dictated by a voice out of the past" (24). Casey feels also that despite Kiely's ability as a writer of short stories, "it is in the novel that Benedict Kiely excels and in the novel that he will be best remembered" (103). A useful evaluation of Kiely from a Northern perspective can be found in John Wilson Foster's *Forces and Themes in Ulster Fiction* (1974).

Despite the favorable reception to both *Proxopera* and *Nothing Happens in Carmincross*, sufficiently focused and extensive critical examinations of Kiely's recent, political fiction are lacking. However, Margaret Scanlan's 1985 article provides valuable contextualization of the tangled issues involved.

BIBLIOGRAPHY

Works by Benedict Kiely

Counties of Contention: A Study of the Origins and Implications of the Partition of Ireland. Cork: Mercier, 1945.

Land without Stars. London: Christopher Johnson, 1946.

Poor Scholar: A Study of the Works and Days of William Carleton. London: Sheed and Ward, 1947.

In a Harbour Green. London: Cape, 1949. New York: Dutton, 1950.

Call for a Miracle. London: Cape, 1950. New York: Dutton, 1951.

Modern Irish Fiction: A Critique. Dublin: Golden Eagle, 1950.

Honey Seems Bitter. London: Methuen, 1952. New York: Dutton, 1952. Republished as
    The Evil Men Do. New York: Dell, 1954.
The Cards of the Gambler. London: Methuen, 1953.
There Was an Ancient House. London: Methuen, 1955.
The Captain with the Whiskers. London: Methuen, 1960. New York: Criterion, 1961.
A Journey to the Seven Streams: Seventeen Stories. London: Methuen, 1962. Republished
    as *A Journey to the Seven Streams and Other Stories*. Dublin: Poolbeg, 1977.
Dogs Enjoy the Morning. London: Gollancz, 1968.
A Ball of Malt and Madame Butterfly: A Dozen Stories. London: Gollancz, 1973.
Proxopera. London: Gollancz, 1977.
All the Way to Bantry Bay, and Other Irish Journeys. London: Gollancz, 1978.
A Cow in the House. London: Gollancz, 1978.
The State of Ireland: A Novella and Seventeen Stories. New York: Penguin, 1980.
Dublin. Oxford: Oxford University Press, 1984.
Ireland from the Air. New York: Crown, 1985.
Nothing Happens in Carmincross. Boston: Godine, 1985.
A Letter to Peachtree. Boston: Godine, 1988.
Yeats's Ireland: An Enchanted Vision. New York: Potter, 1989.
Drink to the Bird. London: Methuen, 1991.

Studies of Benedict Kiely

Casey, Daniel J. *Benedict Kiely*. Lewisburg, PA: Bucknell University Press, 1974.
Eckley, Grace. *Benedict Kiely*. New York: Twayne, 1972.
Kersnowski, Frank. "Ben Kiely and His Ball of Malt." *Journal of the Short Story in
    English* 7 (Autumn 1986): 17–27.
Scanlan, Margaret. "The Unbearable Present: Northern Ireland in Four Contemporary
    Novels." *Etudes-Irlandaises* 10 (December 1985): 145–61.

Thomas Kinsella

(1928–)

Shawn Holliday

BIOGRAPHY

Thomas Kinsella was born on May 4, 1928, in Dublin. The childhood event that had the most profound effect on Kinsella's later poetic outlook was living through the Second World War as a teenager and viewing its disastrous effect upon the world. As a youth, he came to believe that humankind was inherently wicked, and he decided that "the human mind was an abyss, and that the will, just as much as the imagination, was capable of every evil" (quoted in Harmon 11). Subsequently, much of Kinsella's poetry functions as a direct response to the Cold War era by focusing on the poet's need to construct some sort of existential order out of personal misery and societal chaos.

Kinsella received a series of grants and scholarships that enabled him to obtain a degree in public administration from University College, Dublin. In 1946, he gained employment with Ireland's civil service, where he worked for the next nineteen years. Also during this time, Kinsella formed relationships with two people who would help to soften his cynical outlook on life. Having started writing seriously in the late 1940s, Kinsella met Liam Miller in 1952 and began a publishing relationship with the Dolmen Press that still exists today. Ultimately, Kinsella became the director of the press. Also, in 1955 Kinsella married Eleanor Walsh, whose "vitality and brilliance" suggested that there was "a possibility of order" and "a (barely) positive dream" in store for the poet's future life (quoted in Harmon 120).

In 1965, Southern Illinois University invited Kinsella to join its faculty as artist in residence and professor of English. Having become a member of the Irish Academy of Letters in 1958 and winning such literary prizes as the Irish Arts Council Triennial Book Award for *Poems and Translations* (1961) and the

Denis Devlin Memorial Award for *Wormwood* (1966) gave Kinsella the courage to leave his post at the Department of Finance to take up full-time teaching and writing at Carbondale in 1967. Three years later, he moved to Philadelphia to teach one semester per year at Temple University, where he both founded and directed the School of Irish Tradition. In 1972, Kinsella established the Peppercanister Press, which operated out of his own home in Dublin and provided an outlet for the poet's many diverse works in progress.

Despite recurring health problems, Kinsella remained active in both writing and publishing throughout the 1970s and 1980s. Besides editing the *Selected Poems of Austin Clarke* (1976) and translating Seán Ó Tuama's *An Duanaire, an Irish Anthology* (1981), he has prepared the *New Oxford Book of Irish Verse* (1989) and has written several recent volumes of poetry, all notable for their increased interest in Irish themes filtered through the poet's consciousness. Although his sojourn in the United States has given him a distanced perspective from which to view Irish society, Kinsella remains preoccupied with his notion that personal survival depends upon the exploration of one's imagination.

MAJOR WORKS AND THEMES

Thomas Kinsella's work can be best described as a search for meaning and order through the poet's psychoanalytic exploration of his own consciousness. Deeply personal, his poetry shows a distinct break from the literary tradition established by the two earlier generations of Irish poets. Notably absent are such characteristics as Yeats's intentional "Irishness," Austin Clarke's Catholic guilt, and Patrick Kavanagh's parochialism. What the public received from Kinsella's first major collection, *Another September* (1958), was a will to obscurity caused by the poet's early collegiate interest in chemistry, physics, and natural science. A miscellany of different types of poems, this volume focuses on the human being's lifelong process of dying. In *Downstream* (1962), the poet finds the creed that will control much of his later poetic output. Kinsella realizes that only by taking the journey to the underworld of one's own psyche can an individual receive the insight that makes existence bearable and that only through creativity can a person's soul survive. Also in this volume, Kinsella becomes more politically charged by writing a poem about U.S. president Truman; "Old Harry" focuses on Truman's military decision to drop the atomic bomb on Hiroshima and Nagasaki as well as on the presumed guilt or innocence of the weapon's Japanese victims. Also, in the long, meditative poem, "A Country Walk," the poet concentrates on the moral decay that greed and materialism have brought to postrevolutionary Ireland.

A change occurs in Kinsella's work with his move to the United States in 1965. Besides starting to read Carl Jung, an event that further darkens his poetry, Kinsella begins to deal directly with more specifically Irish themes. In "Baggot Street Deserta," from *Nightwalker and Other Poems* (1968), the poet uses Jung's idea of the creative union of opposites to fuse his anima and animus.

The narrator and his muse become one as the poet recalls making love with a woman in his Baggot Street room. Here, Kinsella no longer remains alone as an isolated individual in a destructive society. Being more politically conscious, Kinsella uses "Nightwalker" to yearn for the national ideals set forth by Kathleen Ni Houlihan while concurrently viewing, with disdain, the loss of cultural values by an Irish government becoming less isolationist in order to attract the wealth of foreign investment.

In the 1970s, Kinsella's preoccupation with Irish concerns increased. Not only is his translation of the Irish epic *Táin Bó Cuailnge* (1969) considered by many to be a major achievement, but also *A Selected Life* (1972), an elegy concerning the death of Irish musician and composer Seán O Riada, remains a touching tribute to one of the country's most important modern artistic figures. This sparse poem gently illustrates how the premature death of an artist and his catalog of unfinished work can detrimentally affect a country's culture and the continuing lives of both family and friends. The work from this period that expresses the most outrage is surely *Butcher's Dozen* (1972), Kinsella's response to British paratroopers opening fire upon a crowd of civil rights protesters on January 30, 1972, in the Northern Ireland city of Londonderry. This event, now known as Sunday Bloody Sunday, helped move Kinsella away from strictly private matters and convinced him to write a satiric, public poem full of extreme bitterness and compassion for his compatriots.

Most recently, Kinsella has spent his time attempting to fill the gap in Irish poetry between the virtual death of the Irish language and the appearance of William Butler Yeats. Kinsella feels that this gap represents his place in a broken literary tradition. His English translation of Sean O Tuama's *An Duaniare, an Irish Anthology* (1981) covers a wide array of poetry written in Irish from 1600 to 1900, while his own *New Oxford Book of Irish Verse* (1989) attempts to find a wider audience for Irish poetry on both sides of the Atlantic.

CRITICAL RECEPTION

Although now more than twenty years old, the most friendly critical work on Kinsella remains Maurice Harmon's *The Poetry of Thomas Kinsella: 'With Darkness for a Nest'* (1974). A personal friend of the poet, Harmon offers a balanced new-critical discussion of the author's early work highlighted by several excerpts from previously unpublished interviews. This book's weaknesses, however, remain what they were upon publication. The author provides very little biographical information on Kinsella, and his discussion of the poet's translation of *The Táin* (1969) is limited to four pages, most of which is taken up by lengthy quotations from the work.

Even though Kinsella claims that he wrote his first poem at eighteen "out of curiosity" and his second, at twenty, "as a joke" (Harmon 7), many contemporary critics regret the poet's willful obscurity, which they find to be a result of his overseriousness and his obsessive concern for personal troubles. Although

Richard Tobias claims that Kinsella is "the best poet speaking from the Republic of Ireland today" (633), Calvin Bedient believes that the poet's best days are past. While noting that Kinsella can "hardly write a worthless poem" (7), Bedient believes that in *Notes from the Land of the Dead* (1972) Kinsella has finally "brooded himself to pieces" (7). Likewise, Seamus Deane criticizes Kinsella's decision to use Peppercanister Press as an outlet only for the poet's works in progress, claiming that Kinsella prefers "to write poetry rather than to make poems" (200). He finds the poet's later verse to be "at times rhythmically cumbersome."

BIBLIOGRAPHY

Selected Works by Thomas Kinsella

Poetry

An Duanaire, an Irish Anthology. Trans. Thomas Kinsella. Ed. Sean O Tuama. Dublin: Dolmen, 1981; Philadelphia: University of Pennsylvania Press, 1981.
Another September. Dublin: Dolmen, 1958; Philadelphia: Dufour, 1958.
Butcher's Dozen: A Lesson for the Octave of Widgery. Dublin: Peppercanister, 1972.
Downstream. Dublin: Dolmen, 1962.
Fifteen Dead. Dublin: Dolmen and Peppercanister, 1979.
From Centre City. Oxford and New York: Oxford University Press, 1994.
The Good Fight. Dublin: Peppercanister, 1973.
New Oxford Book of Irish Verse. Ed. Thomas Kinsella. Oxford and New York: Oxford University Press, 1989.
Nightwalker and Other Poems. Dublin: Dolmen, 1968; London: Oxford University Press, 1968; New York: Knopf, 1969.
Notes from the Land of the Dead and Other Poems. New York: Knopf, 1973.
One and Other Poems. Dublin: Dolmen, 1979; London: Oxford University Press, 1979.
Peppercanister Poems, 1972–1978. Dublin: Dolmen, 1979; Winston-Salem, NC: Wake Forest University Press, 1979.
Poems 1956–1973. Winston-Salem, NC: Wake Forest University Press, 1979.
A Selected Life. Dublin: Peppercanister, 1972.
Selected Poems: 1956–1968. Dublin: Dolmen, 1973; London: Oxford University Press, 1973.
A Technical Supplement. Dublin: Peppercanister, 1976.
The Táin. Dublin: Dolmen, 1969; London and New York: Oxford University Press, 1970.
Vertical Man: A Sequel to "A Selected Life." Dublin: Peppercanister, 1973.
Wormwood. Dolmen, 1966.

Studies of Thomas Kinsella

Bedient, Calvin. Rev. of *Notes from the Land of the Dead. The New York Times Book Review*, June 16, 1974: 7.
Deane, Seamus. "The Appetites of Gravity: Contemporary Irish Poetry." *The Sewanee Review* 84 (1976): 199–208.

Garrat, Robert F. "Fragilities and Structures: Poetic Strategy in Thomas Kinsella's 'Nightwalker' and 'Phoenix Park.' " *Irish University Review* 13.1 (1983): 88–102.

Harmon, Maurice. *The Poetry of Thomas Kinsella: "With Darkness for a Nest."* Atlantic Highlands, NJ: Humanities, 1975.

Johnston, Dillon. "A Response to Hugh Kenner: Kinsella's Magnanimity and Mean Reading." *Genre* 13.4 (1980): 531–37.

Kenner, Hugh. "Thomas Kinsella: An Anecdote and Some Reflections." *Genre* 12 (1979): 591–99.

McGuinness, Arthur E. "Fragments of Identity: Thomas Kinsella's Modernist Imperative." *Colby Quarterly* 23.4 (1987): 186–205.

O'Hara, Daniel. "An Interview with Thomas Kinsella." *Contemporary Poetry* 4.1 (1981): 1–18.

Skloot, Floyd. "Muck, Matter, and an Enclosing Heart: The Newer Poetry of Thomas Kinsella." *Commonweal* 107 (1980): 337–39.

Tattersall, Carol. "Thomas Kinsella's Exploration in *Notes from the Land of the Dead* of His Sense of Alienation from Women." *Canadian Journal of Irish Studies* 16.2 (1990): 79–91.

Tobias, Richard. "English: *Poems 1956–1973.*" *World Literature Today* 54.4 (1980): 633–34.

Mary Lavin

(1912–1996)

Mary E. Donnelly

BIOGRAPHY

Mary Lavin was born June 11, 1912, in Walpole, Massachusetts, the only daughter of Irish immigrants. When Mary was nine, she returned with her mother, who ''loathed and detested'' the United States (Bowen 17), to her home in Athenry, County Galway. In less than a year, the family purchased a house in Dublin and were reunited for several years. In 1926, they were separated again when her father moved to Meath.

Mary attended the Loreto Convent School and University College, Dublin (UCD), where she pursued both a master's degree (writing her thesis on Jane Austen) and a doctorate in English. One famous anecdote, promulgated by Lavin herself, says that she was in the middle of writing her dissertation on Virginia Woolf when she began writing a story on the back of her draft and abandoned scholarship for creative writing without looking back. (She received an honorary doctorate in literature from UCD in 1968.) She taught French at her old convent school for two years before marrying William Walsh, an old school friend and Dublin lawyer, in 1942. When her father died in 1945, the Walshes used her inheritance to purchase the farm he had managed. Walsh died in 1954, leaving Lavin a widow with three small children. Much of her time, then and for years afterward, was spent in trying to make a living from the farm while continuing to write and raise a family. In 1969, she married again, this time to Michael MacDonald Scott, an old friend and ex-Jesuit. She continued writing, though less prolifically, until her death in 1996.

MAJOR WORKS AND THEMES

Lavin's first short story, "Miss Holland," was published in 1938, and her first complete volume of short stories, with an introduction by her friend and mentor Lord Dunsany, in 1942. Though she has written two novels and some poetry, she is primarily committed to the genre of the short story, saying that "it is in the short story that a writer distills the essence of his thought" (Preface, *Selected Stories* vii). Her later work, breaking from traditional forms, tends toward longer stories or novellas.

Lavin's stories are centered in personal experience: the life of the heart takes precedence over the life of the mind. Her vision is profoundly personal, her style introspective. She writes compellingly of domestic situations in which passions are contained by religion, social mores, or just the sheer bulk of shared pain that separates couples or families instead of bringing them together. As Zack Bowen has written, "[T]here is more Ethan Frome than Heathcliff in most of the seemingly tractable types who inhabit the writer's small Irish villages" (29). This is not to imply, however, that her characters are in any radical way disconnected from society. Indeed, they suffer from external constraints as much as internal ones. The themes for her stories are taken from quotidian reality: marriages good and bad, the struggles of children, loneliness, poverty, and the all-pervasive topic of social-class order. These situations, particularly the last, lead to the theme of freedom and escape that runs through much of her work.

Another theme she often considers is death and mourning. Death is sometimes a punishment for illicit passion, as in her novel *The House in Clewe Street* (1945), in which the servant girl Onny Soraghan is killed by a botched abortion. But it can also be a consummation devoutly to be wished, by the dying if not the survivors, as is Robert's death in "A Happy Death." Escape is occasionally a possibility, but most of her characters stoically suffer and survive.

Some critical debate surrounds the issue of whether her vision is more tragic than comic or vice versa, but that very debate points up the fine ambiguity of her writing. Her awareness of the always doubled meaning of events, no matter how mundane, gives her often deceptively simple stories a depth and resonance unusual in modern fiction. Though less pyrotechnic than that of her compatriots, her writing has an intensity.

One of the distinguishing characteristics of Lavin's fiction that marks it as distinctly female fiction is the concentration on relationships between and among women. Some of her most widely known stories are focused on this theme, including "The Becker Wives," "Lilacs," and "The Small Bequest." These relationships are as often marked by dedication and love as pettiness and snobbery; for the bleakness of every "Small Bequest" there is the richness of a "Happiness." In this, as in her treatment of comedy and tragedy, Lavin takes an admirably parallactic view.

Some of her most interesting stories deal intensely with the issues of widowhood that she faced in her own life, including "In a Café," "The Cuckoo-

Spit,'' and ''Happiness.'' The last of these, especially, is a gracefully drawn vignette of a woman at once mourning her loss and rejoicing in her life. Lavin's best work is driven more by character than plot.

Lavin is not a self-consciously Irish author. She came to her form from outside the tradition of the Irish short story: ''I did not read Irish writers until I had already dedicated myself to the short story'' (Peterson 16). Though much of her work is infused with a sense of the land that is common among Irish writers, one senses that this is merely a result of Ireland, especially Athenry, as the site of her own experience, rather than a calculated use of the land itself as a symbol, à la Corkery. Janet Egleson Dunleavy suggests that Lavin's American birth gives her an ambivalent sense of national identification and may be why ''nationality is not a significant identifying factor in her characterizations'' (in Kilroy's *The Irish Short Story: A Critical History* 146). Few are anxious to reclaim her characters and situations as essentially Irish. For Seamus Deane, Lavin ''wears her Irish rue with a difference'' (in Brown and Rafroidi's *The Irish Short Story* 245), the difference being her sex, which makes her ''highly skeptical of the importance of the 'male' worlds of politics and work'' (245). Thus, Lavin's reticence on so-called ''national'' subjects does not negate Deane's characterization of her as an Irish author; the personal constraints her characters negotiate, both internal and external, are specifically Irish constraints for Deane.

CRITICAL RECEPTION

Early critical reception of Lavin's work tends to compare her with the male writers of her generation, next to whom she is routinely found wanting. Her work simply does not fit into comfortable categories. A common criticism seems to be the lack of directly political or historical material in her stories. A prime example of this is the debate surrounding her story ''The Patriot Son.'' Frank O'Connor, in his *A Short History of Irish Literature*, identifies her primarily as a writer of personal stories, a common critical attitude toward her work. But O'Connor goes on to say that ''only once has she written about Irish nationalism . . . in a story called '[The] Patriot Son,' and from my point of view it was once too often'' (229). Roger Garfitt also distinguishes ''The Patriot Son'' from the rest of Lavin's work; for him it is ''the outstanding exception'' to a corpus that presents ''an Ireland in which the War of Independence and the Civil War might simply not have occurred'' (in Dunn's *Two Decades of Irish Writing* 233). For Bowen, the story is not political at all but ''is really about matriarchy and personal liberation'' (23). Few seem to realize, with Alan Warner, that she ''belongs to a world rather different from that of O'Faolain and O'Connor. . . . Mary was not caught up in the early years of the national struggle in the way that [they] were'' (*A Guide to Anglo-Irish Literature* 216). Each of these critics, however, seems to ascribe a fairly narrow definition to what could be construed as "political." Deane considers her more a social, than a personal, writer and has written that her work "articulates communal values in terms of individual experiences" (*A Short History of Irish Literature* 218–19).

Much critical effort has been spent comparing her to other writers, from Dunsany, who said in his introduction to *Tales from Bective Bridge* (1942) that it "seems reminiscent of the Russians more than any other school of writers" (ix), through Frank O'Connor, who calls "The Becker Wives" "a Henry James fable without the excuse of James' sexual peculiarities" (*The Lonely Voice* 211), to Dunleavy, who compares Lavin in short order to Virginia Woolf, Henry James, Gertrude Stein, and the French naturalists.

Lavin received a brief flurry of critical attention from the mid-1970s until around 1980, causing Richard Peterson to project hopefully that "Mary Lavin's admirers will soon be complaining less about her critical neglect and more about their conflicting opinions and interpretations of her work" ("Review" 150). Since then, however, little has been written on her work. The notable exception to this is a fine chapter in Ann Owens Weekes's *Irish Women Writers: An Uncharted Tradition.*

BIBLIOGRAPHY

Works by Mary Lavin

Tales from Bective Bridge. Boston: Little, Brown, 1942; London: Joseph, 1943. Reprinted Dublin: Poolbeg, 1978.
The Long Ago and Other Stories. London: Joseph, 1944.
The House in Clewe Street. Boston: Little, Brown; London: Joseph, 1945.
The Becker Wives and Other Stories. London: Joseph, 1946. Reprinted, New York: New American Library, 1971.
At Sallygap and Other Stories. Boston: Little, Brown, 1947.
Mary O'Grady. Boston: Little, Brown; London: Joseph, 1950.
A Single Lady and Other Stories. London: Joseph, 1951.
The Patriot Son and Other Stories. London: Joseph, 1956.
A Likely Story. New York: Macmillan; Dublin: Dolmen, 1957.
Selected Stories. New York: Macmillan, 1959.
The Great Wave and Other Stories. London and New York: Macmillan, 1961.
Stories of Mary Lavin. Vol. 1, London: Constable, 1964; vol. 2, 1974; vol. 3, 1981.
In the Middle of the Fields and Other Stories. London: Constable, 1967; New York: Macmillan, 1969.
Happiness and Other Stories. London: Constable, 1969.
Collected Stories. Boston: Houghton Mifflin, 1971.
The Second Best Children in the World. Boston: Houghton Mifflin, 1972.
A Memory and Other Stories. Boston: Houghton Mifflin, 1973.
The Shrine and Other Stories. London: Constable, 1977.
A Family Likeness and Other Stories. London: Constable, 1985.

Studies of Mary Lavin

Critical Sources

Collections of some of Lavin's papers and letters are located at the Glenn G. Bartle Library, State University of New York at Binghamton; the Mugar Memorial Library, Boston University; and the Morris Library at Southern Illinois University.

Bowen, Zack. *Mary Lavin*. Lewisburg, OH: Bucknell University Press, 1975.

Dunleavy, Janet E. "The Fiction of Mary Lavin: Universal Sensibility in a Particular Milieu." *Irish University Review* 7 (Autumn 1977): 222–23.

Harmon, Maurice, ed. *Irish University Review* 9 (Autumn 1979). (A Lavin issue.)

Kelly, A. A. *Mary Lavin: Quiet Rebel*. New York: Barnes and Noble, 1980.

Krawschak, Ruth, and Regina Mahlke. *Mary Lavin: A Checklist*. Berlin: Hildebrand 1979.

Mahlke, Regina. *Die Erzahlkunst Mary Lavin: Unter suchungen zur kunstlerischen Gestaltung der Kurzgeschichten*. Bern: Frankfurt am Main, 1980.

Peterson, Richard. *Mary Lavin*. Boston: Twayne, 1978.

———. Review of three books on Lavin. *Eire-Ireland* 16.3 (Fall 1981): 150–52.

Michael Longley

(1939–)

Alan I. Rea, Jr.

BIOGRAPHY

Michael Longley was born on July 27, 1939, in Belfast, Northern Ireland. He attended the Malone Primary School from 1946 to 1951 and the Royal Belfast Academical Institution from 1951 to 1958. In 1958 he left for Dublin, where he attended Trinity College.

While at Trinity Longley studied the classics, but he maintained, in his words, "amateur status." To this day, he still enjoys the classics, although he considers himself a lapsed classicist. He has retained very little Latin and Greek, but he attributes his study of the languages with his awareness of syntax in his poetry.

During his stay at Trinity in the early 1960s—which he considered quite an exciting time for himself—he met Derek Mahon, a fellow Ulsterman, and the two began discussing each other's poems. After receiving his B.A. with honors in 1963, Longley returned to Belfast, where he attended the now-famous writers' workshop run by the poet and critic Philip Hobsbaum. Here he met his close friend, Seamus Heaney. Longley credits his literary friendships with much of his growth as a poet as he struggles with ideas of the public and private, the urban and the rural.

Longley has worked as an assistant master of school in Blackrock, Northern Ireland (1962–1963), high schools in Belfast and Erith, Northern Ireland (1963–1964), and the Royal Belfast Academical Institution (1964–1969). From 1970 until recently, Longley has served in various positions in the Arts Council of Northern Ireland, whose purpose is to promote and support cultural life.

In 1964, he married the critic and scholar Edna Longley, who is now a professor of English at Queen's University, Belfast. The couple live in Belfast with their three children. Currently, Longley is writing, publishing, and giving poetry readings.

MAJOR WORKS AND THEMES

Michael Longley's first major collection of poetry, *No Continuing City* (1969), contains many of his poems from previous pamphlets. Its poems range in subject from Greek mythology, to Jazz, to the intimate and domestic, but Longley does not specifically address issues pertaining to the Irish political situation. Rather, he is concerned more with the various forms and techniques of poetry itself as his consistent and sometimes forced rhymes attest. In a BBC radio interview with Clive Wilmer, Longley admits that he does find form to be "one of the mysteries" and "enjoy[s] taking advantage of all the things that words do." With *No Continuing City*, Longley demonstrates a command of these areas.

In his next collection, *An Exploded View* (1973), Longley's command of form is still prominent, but his poems are less literary and more focused on the world around him and his reaction to it. His series of poems, "Letters," aptly illustrates his concern for the position that the Northern Irish poets James Simmons, Derek Mahon, Seamus Heaney, and himself occupy in the Irish struggle. References to colonialism, squatter's rights, bloodshed, and death reverberate throughout this sequence of poems and the collection itself, as Longley deals with his place in Irish society as a Northern Protestant and British citizen during the Troubles of the 1970s. This discord is further emphasized in "Wounds." Here Longley juxtaposes his father's heroism in the Ulster Division at the Somme with the fighting going on in present-day Belfast. What was once a patriotic death for "King and Country" and proof that Protestants are superior to Catholics (" 'Fuck the Pope' ") now becomes an image of dead-drunken boys who have indiscriminately killed with no more than a quick apology to the remaining loved ones. Longley's commentary seems to be that all of these soldiers are finally relegated to the same Irish soil.

Longley's next collection, *Man Lying on a Wall* (1976), retreats from the intense political and religious atmosphere of Northern Ireland he explored in *An Exploded View*. On the back cover Longley argues that this collection is not "in reaction to the political and more public utterances of its predecessor": a charge leveled by many critics. As with all of Longley's poetry, there is still a great artistic command of form and words, but this collection focuses more on the poet's personal experiences. These are nature and love poems, and Longley may be faulted by some critics for his light verse, but his artistry acts to negate these accusations. The title poem best describes the collection. Here is a man suspended between life and death, in a world free from the Troubles, and able to enjoy whatever pleases him the most. In Longley's case this seems to be nature, love, and his family.

The Echo Gate (1979) resounds with many of Longley's previous themes.

Nature is still at the forefront, but now it reflects Irish cultural and political instability. An underlying motif is mutability, but one gets the sense that Longley is working for a sense of permanence in this collection, much as he works toward a stability between people in his love poems. "The Echo Gate" demonstrates how Longley reconstructs Irish culture and history as he attempts to link the Celtic culture—represented by the Aran Islands—with contemporary Ireland.

Longley's next two collections of poetry, *Selected Poems: 1963–1980* (1981) and *Poems: 1963–1983* (1987), are most important because they illustrate his poetic development over twenty years. These selections reflect a structural and thematic unity that attest to his artistic care and craftsmanship.

Gorse Fires (1991) is Longley's first new collection in twelve years. He admits that, during these years, the silence was painful for him, and he thought he was done writing poetry. This collection says otherwise. Combining Greek myth, historical references, and the circumstances in contemporary Ireland, he brings new commentary to a volatile political situation. Although he has explored the idea of culture and creating a home, a stasis for oneself in previous works, this collection intensively explores Ireland's and the poet's struggle to find a place to call home. The parallel with the journey of Odysseus is particularly telling, especially as Longley chooses to end the collection with the violent poem "The Butchers," instead of with Odysseus's final meeting with Penelope and Laertes. We are left with images of the dead and ghosts trapped within the bog that is Irish history. *Gorse Fires* leads one to believe that Longley is still searching for that home, that place of definition for himself and Ireland. We must wonder if he has come any closer with his new collection, *The Ghost Orchid* (1995).

CRITICAL RECEPTION

Longley has received only limited attention from critics. Most early reviewers tend to focus on two areas: his attention to the forms and techniques of poetry; and the close comparison to, and his being overshadowed by, Seamus Heaney. John Mole highlights both points quite effectively, noting that what seems important to both of the poets is their "emphasis on learning the craft—on *honing* a voice, *shaping* a method." Longley agrees that his relationship with Heaney began as a friendly competition at Philip Hobsbaum's Belfast workshop in the 1960s and asserts that both he and Heaney are formalists, although he has "carried it to greater extremes in the past" (Wilmer 114). Ultimately, Longley does not view himself as working in Heaney's shadow. He has benefited from his relationship with Heaney but does not need Heaney to make him a good poet.

More recently, we see studies primarily focused on Longley. Peter McDonald's relatively recent article in Corcoran's *The Chosen Ground* is a fascinating study that traces Longley's search in his poetry for a true "home." McDonald points out that, for Longley, "home" invokes two definitions:

" 'Home' means a place of origin, or the concrete site in which a poetic voice is located, and in this sense is as intimate a word as poetry can use. But 'home' is also a statement arising from intimacy: to say a place is 'home' is to imprint the place with a personal meaning" (65). While it could be argued that all poets and artists battle with the issue of public versus private art, Longley approaches this dilemma from an interesting position. He is a Northern Protestant with an English father who tries to find a sense of self and nation in a country that traditionally associates this connection with a Celtic and a Catholic heritage. Longley has not found his answers, but he seems to move closer with each of his collections.

BIBLIOGRAPHY

Works by Michael Longley

Poetry

Ten Poems. Belfast: Festival, 1967.
Room to Rhyme. Belfast: Arts Council of Northern Ireland, 1968. (Poems by Longley and Seamus Heaney; songs and ballads collected by David Hammond.)
Secret Marriages: Nine Short Poems. Manchester: Phoenix Pamphlet Poets, 1968.
Three Regional Voices. London: Poet and Printer, 1968. (Poetry by Longley, Iain Crichton Smith, and Barry Tebb.)
No Continuing City: Poems 1963–1968. Chester Springs, PA: Dufour, 1969.
Lares: Poems. Woodford Green:Poet and Printer, 1972.
An Exploded View: Poems 1968–1972. London: Gollancz, 1973.
Fishing in the Sky: Love Poems. Pinner: Poet and Printer, 1975.
Penguin Modern Poets: 26. London: Cox and Wyman, 1975. (Poems by Longley, Dannie Abse, and D. J. Enright.)
Man Lying on a Wall: Poems 1972–1975. London: Gollancz, 1976.
The Echo Gate: Poems 1975–1979. London: Secker and Warburg, 1979.
Patchwork. Dublin: Gallery, 1981.
Selected Poems: 1963–1980. Winston-Salem, NC: Wake Forest University Press, 1981.
The Linen Workers. Winston-Salem, NC: Wake Forest University Press, 1986.
Poems: 1963–1983. Winston-Salem, NC: Wake Forest University Press, 1987.
Gorse Fires. Winston-Salem, NC: Wake Forest University Press, 1991.
River and Fountain. Dublin: Trinity College, 1992.
Birds and Flowers: Poems. Edinburgh: Morning Star, 1994.
The Ghost Orchid. London: Cape Poetry, 1995.

Prose

"A Misrepresented Poet." *The Dublin Magazine* 6.1 (1967): 68–74.
Introduction. "The Neolithic Night: A Note on the Irishness of Louis MacNeice." In *Two Decades of Irish Writing: A Critical Survey*, ed. Douglass Dunn. Chester Springs, PA: Dufour, 1975, 98–104.
"Tu'penny Stung." *Poetry-Review* (London) 74.4 (1985): 5–11.

"The Empty Holes of Spring: Some Reminiscences of Trinity and Two Poems Addressed to Derek Mahon." *Irish University Review* 24.1 (1994): 51–57.

Tuppenny Stung: Autobiographical Chapters. Belfast: Lagan, 1994.

Studies of Michael Longley

Allen, Michael. "Options: The Poetry of Michael Longley." *Eire-Ireland* 10.4 (1975): 129–36.

DeShazer, Mary. "Michael Longley and Paul Muldoon." *Concerning Poetry* 14.2 (1981): 125–31. (Rev. of Longley's *Selected Poems: 1963–1980* and Muldoon's *Why Brownlee Left*.)

Marten, Harry. " 'Singing the Darkness into the Light': Reflections on Recent Irish Poetry." *New England Review* 3.1 (1980): 141–49.

McIlroy, Brian. "Poetry Imagery as Political Fetishism: The Example of Michael Longley." *Canadian Journal of Irish Studies* 16.1 (1990): 59–64.

Mole, John. "A Question of Balance." *The Times Literary Supplement* (London), February 8, 1980: 133.

O'Neill, Charles. "Three Irish Voices." *Spirit: A Magazine of Poetry* (Fall–Winter 1989): 31–35.

Robben, Bernhard. "Vom Erfinden der Geschichte: Vier nordirische Lyriker." *Merkur: Deutsche Zeitschrift fur Europaisches Denken* 41.4 (1987): 297–318.

Wilmer, Clive. "Michael Longley." *Poets Talking: The "Poet of the Month" Interviews from BBC Radio 3*. Manchester: Carcanet, 1994, 113–19.

John McGahern

(1934–)

Margaret Lasch Mahoney

BIOGRAPHY

John McGahern was born on November 12, 1934, in Ballinamore, County Leitrim. The son of Francis McGahern, a police sergeant, and Susan McManus, a teacher, the author and his siblings spent their early years with their mother, whose junior status as a national school Teacher kept the family moving almost yearly from town to town in Counties Roscommon and Leitrim. When McGahern was nine, his mother died of cancer, so the children went to live with their temperamental father in the Cootehall Police Barracks amid the bogs and rivers of County Roscommon. The emotional instability of his home life was matched by the humorless sense of national and moral mission that characterized the early isolationist and church-dominated years of the Irish Free State.

Scholarships propelled McGahern through the highly regarded Presentation Brothers College in Carrick-on-Shannon, but two Protestant neighbors, survivors of a once-prominent landed family, initiated him into the world of books by giving him free rein of their extensive private library. In retrospect, McGahern recognizes this opportunity as the seminal point of his life as a writer. He read Shakespeare, Milton, Dickens, and the cowboy writer Zane Grey with equal abandon and embarked on a literary path.

Following the example of his mother, McGahern graduated from St. Patrick's Teacher Training College in Drumcondra, Dublin, and qualified as a teacher at the age of twenty. He spent his first year as a national school teacher in the market town of Drogheda, County Louth, and began working on a B.A, which he finished in 1957, at University College, Dublin. In 1955, he secured a coveted position closer to Dublin at St. John the Baptist Boys National School in Clontarf and began to rub elbows with the Dublin literati such as Patrick Kavanagh, Brendan Behan, and Flann O'Brien and to submit pieces to literary magazines.

In 1963 he published his first novel, *The Barracks*, to great acclaim at home, winning both the AE Memorial Award from the Irish Arts Council and the generous Macauley Fellowship. The latter allowed the author to take a year's sabbatical and live abroad—primarily in London, though he also traveled to Spain, France, and Germany—where he finished his second novel, worked odd jobs as a barman and laborer, and married Finnish theater director Anniki Laaski. Fame became notoriety, however, with the publication in 1965 of this next novel, *The Dark*. He was dismissed in disgrace from his job at St. John the Baptist's after the book was banned as pornographic, and it was discovered that he had married a non-Catholic in a civil ceremony. McGahern later learned that the order to dismiss him came from the bishop of Dublin himself, meaning he could not teach anywhere in the diocese of Dublin. Refusing to return to rural teaching, the thirty-one-year-old McGahern left Ireland.

The controversial Leitrim man then spent nearly ten years living in England, Spain, France, and the United States, producing, after a long creative drought, a collection of short stories, *Nightlines* (1970), and his third novel, *The Leave-taking* (1974, rev. 1984). At last in 1974, McGahern and his second wife, Madeline Green (whom he married in 1973), moved to a secluded farm in County Leitrim, only seventeen miles from Cootehall, where his father was a guard, prefiguring the circular journeys of his protagonists, and produced two more collections of short stories, *Getting Through* (1978) and *High Ground* (1985), numerous reviews and dramatic scripts, and two more novels, *The Pornographer* (1979) and *Amongst Women* (1990). The latter, rightly acclaimed his masterpiece by many critics, won the Aer Lingus/*Irish Times* award for fiction in 1990 and was short-listed for the Booker Prize the same year.

In 1991, this prodigal son, who says he now spends his time divided between his farm work and his written work—and only two hours a day at each—had his first stage play, *The Power of Darkness*, produced at the Abbey and, in 1992, gathered all his short fiction, plus a handsome new novella, *The Country Funeral*, into *The Collected Stories*.

MAJOR WORKS AND THEMES

The search for fulfillment under the shadow of death propels all of McGahern's work. For this reason, he has been labeled the foremost existential writer in English today. The author realizes his thematic vision, with various protagonists embarking on quests for meaning and then counterpointing the temporality of their situations with a backdrop of the eternal elements of life found in the rhythmic cycles of nature, the repeating patterns of human behavior, and the permanence of art. His fiction searches for points of connection to the eternal as an answer to the finality of death.

While all of his writing works toward illuminating the darkness and solving life's mystery, his five novels form one developing analysis of the universal and timeless journey of human life by chronicling its various passages in progressively maturing protagonists. The development begins as a growing sense of confinement in the family environment as the child becomes an adolescent, followed by a move away where the maturing individual identity can emerge. A growing sense of despair at the unconnected life, then, gives way to the return to the ancestral home as an adult where the context of family gives meaning to the individual identity. McGahern's thematic goal, thus, involves finding the way back home. Each step is fraught with the angst of the post–World War I Western world, where God, country, and communication are called into question, and the individual remains doubtful and afraid. Despite the despair so pervasive in his work, though, McGahern is not a despairing writer. In each novel the disillusioned protagonist works his way to an affirmation of life that drives him on to life's next passage and, for McGahern, the next novel. The journey of the central consciousness in each novel in turn mirrors the development of the artistic sensibility and the social evolution of Ireland itself.

The shorter fiction published at significant intervals between the novels features a developmental pause where the author recasts his motifs of the life cycle from different angles. What emerges in his short stories are fuller treatments of the generational conflicts, male–female relationships, and coming-of-age disillusionments that have transpired in the novels.

Novels

The journey home is presented microcosmically in *The Barracks*. Though focusing on the last year of a middle-aged woman dying of cancer, through flashbacks the novel re-creates Elizabeth Reegan's earlier life. She was born on a farm in the west, moved to London, where she worked as a nurse, and then came home to marry not far from where she was born. As she is dying, this early character acknowledges the joy she has found and continues to find in being a part of life, despite never penetrating its mystery. Her ability both to reach this realization and continually to love and support those around her casts Elizabeth as a model for succeeding protagonists.

In this first novel, it is a minor character, young Willie Reegan, whose life emerges as the one we follow in the next three novels. *The Dark* dramatizes a rural boy's adolescent rage against his violently domineering father and the boy's attempts to escape this farm life through first the priesthood and then a university education. *The Leavetaking* follows an older protagonist, a schoolteacher, who prepares to leave the restricting environmental forces of Ireland itself. *The Pornographer* finds an even older central character who, having freed himself of all social, religious, and familial restrictions, lives a life as sterile and pointless as the pornography he writes. At this stage McGahern reclaims his hero. In these first four novels, the author carefully studies and poignantly renders the difficulties of a determined young man breaking from the adolescent stage and the subsequent experiences of leave-taking and homecoming. Only through removal, McGahern demonstrates, can an individual discover an internal sense of authority and identity; yet there remains, for the author, an acceptance of a further step, back toward communal traditions, for the life process to become complete. McGahern's active premise in these novels emerges as a modern rendering of the New Testament parable of the Prodigal Son. The allegory enacts the story of returning, but with the return having meaning only in relation to the journey.

What follows in *Amongst Women* emerges as a picture of family life on a rural farm. Michael Moran, the central character of McGahern's most recent novel, reenacts the monstrous patriarchal domination of a family first dramatized in *The Dark*. However, though there is not an assurance of stable interpersonal relationships, for Moran's children, there is a connection with their source and a means of support in a society of weak institutions. The Moran children, despite their father, intuit the greater value of family. The family unit, flawed as the human relations within it may be, becomes a connection to the eternal.

McGahern reviews the development of his maturing protagonists in considering the older children of Michael Moran in *Amongst Women*, who take that consciousness in directions that both compare and contrast to the Prodigal Son motif. The elder son, Luke, leaves his father but never returns, thus sentencing himself to a repetition of his father's inability to connect with anything larger than himself. The Moran daughters and younger son, however, leave and return. In this novel, it is through them that McGahern concludes the journey of his central consciousness. They follow the pattern of leaving home for urban environs where they marry and embark on careers, but they are able to stake out individual lives without breaking with their home at Great Meadow. They traverse the divide between city and country effortlessly and are empowered by the blending of both worlds. In considering the women, in particular, Mona, Maggie, and Sheila Moran achieve in fact what Elizabeth Reegan of *The Barracks* did in spirit, bringing McGahern's fiction full circle. The children are home and they are free. It has been a contest for this Irish novelist to bring them to this desired end point.

Alongside the human development, McGahern charts the maturation of Ireland. The infant independent nation depends on an agrarian way of life, as did the generations before it came into being. In *The Barracks* the police guard, Reegan, is essentially a farmer, disdainful of his police uniform and uncomfortable in cities. He yearns to buy a farm and live "like his people always did." *The Dark* symbolizes the story of Ireland's adolescence as an independent nation, moving away from the agrarian life, briefly testing the saints-and-scholars stereotype, and moving toward urban middle-class materialism with its petty bourgeois shopkeepers and civil servants. The change causes great social upheaval, reflected in the fierce conflict between Mahoney, the farmer, and his son, who wants to be anything but a farmer. McGahern uses such archetypal generational tension as a metaphor for traditional lifestyles being replaced by new ones.

Capturing the tenor of middle-class Ireland with the narrow-minded and priest-riddled attitudes of the teachers at the hero's school, *The Leavetaking* follows the social evolution of the country toward internationalization as its determined protagonist chooses work in England with his American wife. *The Pornographer* could be said to expose the result of shallow imitation of foreign cultures at the expense of a native tradition, to which McGahern will eventually find a way to return in the fourth novel.

The picture of Ireland in *Amongst Women* reveals contemporary society, mobile and progressive, where the farm, in a metaphoric sense, is part of an urban-oriented country. The agrarian life is dying along with Michael Moran, and there is literally no one to inherit it, but as McGahern intimates, by way of intertextures blended into the novel, though the farmers are dying, their strength and loyalty and the memory and spirit of their way of life do have successors regardless of where they live. Ireland has changed, but the "indomitable Irishry" continue. That character, initially imbued in the male figures with their prodigal efforts, lends "story" to the resilience of the Irish; and then it becomes that other character, embraced by Moran's daughters in their surly father, that finally liberates the Irish, even the historically most disfranchised, harking back to Elizabeth, the women.

A third thematic strand concerns the making of the artist. With Elizabeth Reegan, we see the artistic sensibility learning to draw on the resources of imagination to transform her physical reality into symbols of profound significance and striving to find permanence in this changing life. In *The Dark*, the young hero grows to discover that true vision comes from within. *The Leavetaking* and *The Pornographer* examine the conscious emergence of the artist through experiences with loss and death, and McGahern makes the first-person novels themselves the evidence of his protagonists' commitments. *Amongst Women* finds the author, in the words of Stephen Dedalus, "refined out of existence" (Joyce, *Portrait*), and as the Moran daughters liberate themselves from their father, this novel emerges as the true by-product of the artist we have seen developing in the preceding novels. It seems safe to say that McGahern's body of work presents the author's own development as an artist. McGahern uses the journeyman stages of his own expanding artistic sensibility as the subject of his novels until he emerges as a confident master craftsman. With *Amongst Women*, life truly and purely becomes the subject of the book, the artist, again to quote Stephen, "within or behind or above or beyond his handiwork, invisible" (Joyce, *Portrait*).

Readers quickly notice in McGahern's work a pattern of recurring images, family types, events, settings, experiences, and even names, acting, as McGahern himself has said, like refrains in a song or poem. The device effectively connects all of the author's major fiction as one story and enriches each new tale with what has been gleaned from the one before. The echoes thus serve as touchstones of meaning. The name "Moran" is chosen for different protagonists in two separate novels and a handful of short stories and crops up in minor characters in several other pieces. Sheila and Mona Moran remember a boat ride with their father as it happened to characters earlier in *The Dark*; the children in both *The Barracks* and *The Leavetaking* ask local fishermen to take them out on the lake the day of their mothers' funerals; and old Mahoney's abuse of his young son mirrors Moran's of Luke, his eldest prodigal, in *Amongst Women*. Stepmothers who have lived in Britain marry widowers with children, the blue and white presbyteries stand prominently in local towns, Cootehall always figures as hometown or next town, and the River Shannon flows through each novel.

Short Stories

During the writing of his five novels, McGahern published four collections of short stories: *Nightlines, Getting Through, High Ground*, and, collecting all of these stories plus "The Country Funeral," *The Collected Stories* (1992). Where the novels mark decided passages in a journey, the short stories appear to be thematic replays of motifs of the previous novel or thematic digressions to play out a situation in a direction other than that dramatized in a novel. What emerges, then, are fuller treatments—by virtue of their variety—of McGahern's themes.

The twelve stories of *Nightlines*, for example, primarily concern loss of youthful innocence expressed in terms of sexual knowledge and generational conflicts. Both the novels that precede and succeed this collection, *The Dark* and *The Leavetaking*, focus on youthful jolts into maturity. The tension of *Nightlines* results from shocking sexual discoveries that force the hero into the next psychic phase—"Coming into His Kingdom" is one example—a developmental leap that threatens McGahern's patriarchs by nudging them closer to death. "Korea" is perhaps the most dramatic exploration of the tenuous relationship between generations: in this story of understated horror, a son discovers his father's wish that he be conscripted into the American army so the father can collect the wages and, in the case of death, the insurance settlement. In the first two stories of this collection, McGahern offers his thematic blueprints for his fictional world. "Wheels" establishes the circle as the controlling image of the author's vision, which charts the movements of individual lives and reveals the interdependent relationships between generations affixed to different cogs on the wheel. "Why We're Here" illuminates the human environment—cruel, lonely, and confusing—in which all the fiction unfolds.

Getting Through has a similar function in McGahern's middle phase. *The Leavetaking* ends with Moran departing Ireland with his new American wife. This collection, highlighting McGahern's more refined use of the single controlling image as symbol, explores life abroad with protagonists eager to find better lives in stories that unanimously point to the better life at home. McGahern portrays the exiled world here as dangerous and the success rate of relationships as bleak. The collection is populated by young men left bewildered by women who intuit their inability to commit. The wheel has turned from childhood to adulthood in this collection, the author illuminating the next segment as the psychic jolt from sexual maturity to death. Stories such as "The Stoat" and "All Sorts of Impossible Things" examine reactions to mortality.

With *High Ground*, appearing after *The Pornographer*, McGahern looks again at the empty urban lives of jaded pornographer types in some stories, "Parachutes," for example, and anticipates the broader social panorama of *Amongst Women* with other stories, such as "Old Fashioned," sweeping across generations of dramatize social changes.

The Country Funeral, the last piece of fiction McGahern has published to date, finds a resolution in the central issues that have developed in McGahern's fiction for nearly thirty years. The novella hosts the return of Philly Ryan from the isolated oil wells of the Middle East to the brash and hostile Dublin of previous fiction and on again to his ancestral home in the rural west of Ireland. There he recognizes at last the solemn and timeless beauty of country customs and traditions as a bulwark against the abyss of uncertainty before which each human stands alone.

CRITICAL RECEPTION

John McGahern has been a published writer since the early 1960s, and, like the shape of the wheel that informs his thematic structure, his critical reputation has come full circle during that time. *The Barracks* met with such instant critical praise in Ireland that the young author won both the AE Memorial Award and the generous McAuley Fellowship, and he was catapulted at the age of twenty-nine to national fame.

When *The Dark* emerged two years later, it, too, met with artistic praise both in Ireland and abroad. Terence de Vere White said in his review in the *Irish Times* that "the story has a wholeness of artistic integrity" while Vivian Mercier wrote in the *New York Times Book Review* that "no work since Joyce has presented an Irish adolescence with such freshness and objectivity." Within a month of publication, however, discussions of the spare bildungsroman's artistic achievement were halted abruptly when the book was banned by the Irish Censorship Board as "obscene" because of scenes enacting masturbation and suggesting sexual abuse and homosexuality.

In the fifteen years in which he wrote *Nightlines, The Leavetaking, Getting Through, The Pornographer*, and *High Ground* (1970–1985), McGahern received quiet critical attention ranging from praise of his "lyrical touch" (about *The Leavetaking* in the *New York Times Book Review*) and "creative and recreative energy" (about *The Pornographer* in the *Irish Times*), to negative remarks of being stylistically "slipshod" and thematically redundant.

During these years, however, the author won numerous literary awards in Ireland, England, and France, and he was invited as guest lecturer at universities on both sides of the Atlantic. Consideration of McGahern's oeuvre was simultaneously finding its way into scholarly journals, and his vision and craftsmanship were prompting serious critical discussion. Full chapters on McGahern appeared during this time in book-length studies of Irish literature such as Brophy and Grennan's *New Irish Writing*, Brophy and Porter's *Contemporary Irish Writing*, Dunn's *Two Decades of Irish Writing*, and Cahalan's *The Irish Novel*. With the rare exception, the consensus of these scholars emerged as an overwhelming recognition of John McGahern as one of the most significant writers of fiction in English in the world today. Denis Sampson wrote in 1991: "McGahern's oeuvre reflects a deeply reflective and comprehensive vision of life. . . . He has managed to write in a plain style and in a somewhat traditional manner which allows a large audience access to his fiction, and yet there is a quality of austere inner order and stylistic precision which indicate there is an original and powerful imagination at work" (2–3).

With the 1990 publication of *Amongst Women*, McGahern's public appeal caught up with his scholarly reputation. As winner of the *Irish Times*/Aer Lingus Award and runner-up for the Booker Prize, *Amongst Women* has been lauded by such important Irish literary figures as John Banville as a "masterpiece," by Thomas Kilroy as "one of the most significant achievements in Irish fiction," and by Colm Toibin as having "captured the particular isolation of rural post-independent Ireland and wrought it into a universal treatment of solitary humanity." Reviews in England and the United States were equally appreciative.

The 1990s have seen McGahern emerge as a more visible man of letters in Ireland. *Amongst Women* invited a host of newspaper interviews, radio and television appearances, and international reading tours. Scholarly studies too have increased, most notably with the *Canadian Journal of Irish Studies'* special issue on McGahern in July 1991 and the 1993 appearance of Denis Sampson's *Outstaring Nature's Eye*, the first full-length volume on the author's fiction. Sampson sheds floodlights on McGahern's analysis of the making of the artist and the concomitant parallel of art with spirituality, love, and the moral life, all of which defend us against the destructive encroachment of time.

BIBLIOGRAPHY

Works by John McGahern

The Barracks. London: Faber and Faber, 1963.
The Dark. London: Faber and Faber, 1965.
Nightlines. London: Faber and Faber, 1970.
The Leavetaking. London: Faber and Faber, 1974; rev. with preface.
Getting Through. London: Faber and Faber, 1978.
The Pornographer. London: Faber and Faber, 1979.
High Ground. London: Faber and Faber, 1985.
Amongst Women. London: Faber and Faber, 1990.

The Power of Darkness. London: Faber and Faber, 1991. (Play.)
The Collected Stories. London: Faber and Faber, 1992.

Studies of John McGahern

Banville, John. "To Have Is to Hold, and Hate." Rev. of *Amongst Women. Sunday Observer* (London) 7 May 1990: 41.

Cook, Bruce. "Irish Censorship: The Case of John McGahern." *Catholic World* 206 (January 1968): 176–79.

Cronin, John. "*The Dark* Is Not Light Enough: The Fiction of John McGahern." *Studies* 58 (Winter 1969): 427–32.

———. John McGahern's *Amongst Women*: Retrenchment and Renewal." *Irish University Review* 22.1 (Spring/Summer 1992): 168–76.

Devine, Paul. "Style and Structure in John McGahern's *The Dark.*" *Critique* 21.1 (1979): 49–57.

Fournier, Suzanne. "Structure and Theme in McGahern's *Pornographer.*" *Eire-Ireland* 22.1 (Spring 1987). 139–50.

Freyer, Grattan. "Change Naturally: The Fiction of O'Flaherty, O'Faolain, and McGahern." *Eire-Ireland* 18.1 (Spring 1983): 138–44.

Gitzen, Julian. "Wheels along the Shannon." *Journal of Irish Literature* 22.3 (September 91): 36–49.

Kilroy, Thomas. "The Steady Pulse of the World." Rev. of *Amongst Women. Irish Times* 12 May 1990: Weekend 9.

Lloyd, Richard. "Memory Becoming Imagination: Novels of John McGahern." *Journal of Irish Literature* 18.3 (September 1989): 5–23.

———. "The Symbolic Mass: Thematic Resolution in the Irish Novels of John McGahern." *Emporia State Research Studies* 36.2 (Autumn 1987): 5–23.

Mercier, Vivian. "Growing up in Ireland." Rev. of *The Dark. New York Times Book Review* 6 Mar. 1966: 50.

Molloy, F. C. "The Novels of John McGahern." *Critique* 19.1 (1977): 5–27.

O'Connell, Shaun. "Door into the Light: John McGahern's Ireland." *Massachusetts Review* 25 (Summer 1984): 255–68.

Quinn, Antoinette. "Varieties of Disenchantment: Narrative Technique in John McGahern's Short Stories." *Journal of the Short Story in English* 13 (Autumn 1989): 77–89.

Sampson, Denis. "Introducing John McGahern." *Canadian Journal of Irish Studies: Special Issue on John McGahern* 17.1 (July 1991): 1–9.

———. "A Note of John McGahern and John McGahern's *Leavetaking.*" *Canadian Journal of Irish Studies* 2.2 (1976): 61–65.

———. *Outstaring Nature's Eye: The Fiction of John McGahern.* Washington, D.C.: Catholic University Press, 1993.

———. ed. *Canadian Journal of Irish Studies: Special Issue on John McGahern* 17.1 (July 1991).

Schwartz, Karlheinz. "John McGahern's Point of View." *Eire-Ireland* 19.3 (Autumn 1984): 92–110.

Skeffington, Owen Sheehy. "The McGahern Affair." *Censorship* 2 (Spring 1966): 27–30.

Toibin, Colm. "Out of the Dark." *In Dublin* (5 Sept. 1985): 10–13.
Toolan, Michael. "John McGahern: The Historian and the Pornographer." *Canadian Journal of Irish Studies* 7.2 (December 1981): 39–55.
Wallace, Arminta. "Out of the Dark." *Irish Times*, April 28, 1990. (Interview.)
White, Terence de Vere. "Five to One." Rev. of *The Dark. Irish Times* 8 May 1965: 8.

Medbh McGuckian

(1950–)

Mary O'Connor

BIOGRAPHY

Medbh McGuckian was born on August 12, 1950, in Belfast, Northern Ireland, a third child to Hugh and Margaret (Fergus) McCaughan. Her father (d. 1992) figured large in her emotional and creative life and is the oblique or direct subject of many poems. Another important mentor for McGuckian was Seamus Heaney, who taught her at Queen's University, Belfast, and invited her to become part of the poetry group he was moderating—a group that, out of diffidence, she never joined. She completed her B.A. at Queen's 1972 and her M.A. and Dip. Ed. in 1974. She taught at Dominican Convent, Fortwilliam Park, at St. Patrick's College, at St. Mary's College of Education, and at the University of California, Berkeley, where she held a visiting lectureship. She was the first woman to hold the position of Writer in Residence at Queen's University, Belfast; in 1995 she was appointed Writer in Residence at the University of Ulster, Coleraine.

McGuckian began her writing career proper in 1977, after her marriage to John McGuckian and in the three-year space before the first of their four children arrived. In 1979 she won Britain's National Poetry Competition and in 1980 an Eric Gregory Award. Between 1982 and 1995 she published five important collections: *The Flower Master*, *Venus and the Rain*, *On Ballycastle Beach*, *Marconi's Cottage*, and *Captain Lavender*. She has received the Rooney Prize and the Irish Arts Council Award (1982), the Poetry Society's Alice Hunt-Bartlett Award (1983), the Cheltenham Award (1989), the Bass Ireland Award (1991), and the Helen Waddell Award (1992). She is, so far, the only woman among Northern Ireland writers to be widely published and anthologized.

MAJOR WORKS AND THEMES

Medbh McGuckian's unique voice, characterized by lyrical complexity, sensuous imagery, and semantic disorientation, sets her apart from other Irish authors of her generation. On the margin in Belfast as a woman and a Catholic, she seems well positioned to question oppressive structures. Apart, however, from instances in her most recent collection, *Captain Lavender*, her poetry does not refer directly to the social and political realities of Northern Ireland. Neither does McGuckian identify in any conventional way with feminist projects. Her challenge to the patriarchy, whether in its colonial, clerical, or nationalist guise, lies in her transgression of borders, destabilizing linguistic, gendered, and cultural points of reference in a subtle but deliberate rejection of the status quo.

Cryptic, fragmented, and diffuse, the poetry in its constant movement from one image to the next produces a cumulative effect of anxiety, delight, or surprise. All is ambiguity and flux: a day, a novel, a house, a speaker turn into each other, so that one finds no contrast between setting and action, no background or foreground: all are part of the same complex surface. Successive collections repeat themes and images with fugal insistence. Already in *The Flower Master* (1982) the poet begins a complex interweaving of key images, introducing the house, flower, sun, blue, river, and garden/gardener metaphors. Emblems of fruition and generativity especially characterize this collection. The revised version of this book (1993) includes several early poems omitted from the 1982 edition.

McGuckian's second collection, *Venus and the Rain* (1984), shows the poet even less limited by the fixed and ruled universe. In the last poem of the collection, the speaker's "absolute address" hints, among other things, at absolution from such controlled areas. Houses here become structures of a certain provisionality and openness: the speaker says, "I have jilted all the foursquare houses" ("Prie-Dieu"); some have a "boat-shaped/Spirit" ("Dovecote"); some float above the ground ("Sky-House"). Despite an essentializing of male–female roles in the title characters, binary oppositions—as between mind and body, houses and ships, seas and shores—are more likely to refer to the split self than to Aristotelian dualities. The terms are always somehow in danger of being swept away by their attraction to their opposites: the house turns into a boat, the writer into a painter, the speaker incorporates her dream-sister. Many poems seem to comment on the poetic process: the idea of language as seed to be scattered is echoed by lines about escape, release, beginnings; movement is always preferable to a frozen stasis; a womblike darkness in introduced as the site of greatest creativity.

Themes of impermanence and loss begin to emerge more definitively in *On Ballycastle Beach* (1988). Perhaps one-third of the poems react to, or anticipate, the death of a father figure: the title poem and "My Brown Guest" are especially affecting as meditations on mortality. A different kind of father figure is described in the poem "Coleridge," which foregrounds both the poet's gratitude for her inheritance from the Romantics, and the sense that she has left that relationship. As in *Venus and the Rain*, McGuckian's portraits of women are characterized by an erotic sensuality. The poet, newly inspired by the spirituality, passion, and revolutionary opposition of poet Anna Akhmatova, sets several poems within her geographical and historical range. In this collection, Mc-Guckian's love of language and her fluid, ecstatic, disseminative use of it reach their height.

In *Marconi's Cottage* (1992) the climactic event is not death but birth, as McGuckian meditates on the gestation and birth of her fourth child and first daughter, Emer Mary Charlotte Rose. Though faced with the impending loss of her father, the poet strives "to distract death's attention back to love." Many poems show the poet returning to the near-narrative style of her early work, in which verbs seem to move the actors through time. McGuckian has begun to write longer poems and, less felicitously, longer words: a new Latinate vocabulary at times infuses the diction with the seriousness of scholastic philosophy. A number of poems seem to repeat themes in the manner of a Philip Glass score, though her music is unfailingly intelligent and complex. But the poems that describe a mother's evolving relationship to her first daughter give this collection its "flying-heartedness," so fresh, complex, and newly inevitable are the reactions and interactions they imagine.

McGuckian's grief or anxiety at societal violence in Northern Ireland breaks forth in indirect ways in each of her first four collections. But in *Captain Lavender* (1995) she refers directly to the struggle. In 1994 she spent some time teaching creative writing in the Maze Prison, where suspected and actual members of paramilitary groups have been incarcerated. The poem "Flirting with Saviours" seems to describe these men and their conditions directly, often through the distancing tools of passive verbs and abstract nouns, certainly from a stance critical of those forces "that made the criminal fit the crime" (15). Other surprisingly unguarded references to McGuckian's political world flicker through the entire collection. Poems such as "The Albert Chain" play off the experience of World War II veteran (an imagined version of McGuckian's father, whose middle name was Albert) but contain, unmistakably, a Belfast cityscape, and "the betrayed North of my soul." Mixed with them are interesting variations on old themes: the separation from a mentor figure, now played by Dante; unsettling reversals of gender and gender roles; erotic duets and games.

The speaker in "Field Heart" seems to address and mock the "attentively incomprehending" reader seduced by McGuckian's elusive yet charged intensity. The poet has spoken in interviews of her need to protect the creative core: "[T]he imagination is so very vulnerable . . . if anyone did actually deconstruct the whole poem, the poem is dead" (*Southern Review* 31.3 (1995): 606). Thus, she has seemed almost extravagantly reticent and guarded, particularly about the North. But in an interview published in the Belfast magazine *Causeway* in the summer of 1994, she was responsive to the suggestion that her poetry is less obscure than it used to be: "I may be getting more accessible because things here are changing so rapidly on a political level and on the 'war front' that it's become easier for me to say what I mean."

CRITICAL RECEPTION

Overall critical regard for McGuckian has from the beginning been accompanied by a certain frustration with her seemingly deliberate obscurity. David Mason complains about "the painful opacity of so much of the writing" (227). A more moderate Dillon Johnston speaks of savoring "the poems in which we sense coherence" (*Irish Poetry after Joyce* 261). Other critics endeavor to rescue by odd rationalizations the ordinary objects that furnish the poems: R. J. C. Watt says that "her domestic subjects are saved from coziness by placing them near bold images of desire and sexuality" (557). Gerald Dawe speaks of "the miniaturized world of Medbh McGuckian's domestic interiors" (quoted in Porter 93). Clair Wills objects: "To read this as autobiographical poetry, obscurely concerned with domestic life, mistakes the extent to which the home, the family, the mother tongue and the nation are each torn away from their traditional representations" ("Making Waves" 23). But even critics such as Wills who praise McGuckian's subversive and unsettling poetics seem pleased to be able to identify a real-life event or urtext in dialogue with the "dream language."

Critical reservations about aspects of the poet's work are, however, overwhelmed by praise for her achievement. Here, what is remarkable is the protean quality of McGuckian's attractiveness, the variety of ways in which she is contextualized by individual critics. An early reviewer, Anne Stevenson, sees her as a "contemporary . . . Emily Dickinson." Stephen Yenser traces the "steadfastly provisional" quality of her poetry to a lineage that includes John Ashbery, Wallace Stevens, and Baudelaire. Though McGuckian does not pretend to a feminist stance—she recently confessed, "I can't think of a poem where I have a woman being independent or assertive" (interview with Kimberly Bohman, *Irish Review* 17–18 (1995): 95–108)—feminist critics find her poetry eminently usable: Molly Bendall sees in McGuckian "the struggle to subvert what some feminist theorists have named as characteristics of phallocentric discourse: a strict linearity and an affirmation of authority." Thomas Docherty (in Corcoran's *The Chosen Ground*) links her with the surrealists. Calvin Bedient declares her to be the heir of the English Romantics.

Overall, the critical response to the poet has affirmed McGuckian's gift for sounds and rhythms, the fascination of her shifting kaleidoscope of words, the richness of her synesthetic imagery, and her startling metonymic revelations.

BIBLIOGRAPHY

Works by Medbh McGuckian

"Birds and Their Masters." *Irish University Review* 23.1 (1993): 29–33.

Captain Lavender. Loughcrew, Ireland: Gallery, 1994; Winston-Salem, NC: Wake Forest University Press, 1995.

"Don't Talk to Me about Dance." Rev. of *Philomena's Revenge*, by Rita Ann Higgins. *Poetry Ireland Review* 35 (1992): 98–100.

The Flower Master. Oxford and New York: Oxford University Press, 1982.

The Flower Master and Other Poems. Loughcrew, Ireland: Gallery, 1993.

Marconi's Cottage. Loughcrew, Ireland: Gallery, 1991; Winston-Salem, NC: Wake Forest University Press, 1992.

On Ballycastle Beach. Oxford and New York: Oxford University Press 1988; Winston-Salem, NC: Wake Forest University Press, 1988.

Portrait of Joanna. Belfast: Ulsterman, 1980.

Single Ladies: Sixteen Poems. Budleigh Salterton: Interim, 1980.

Trio Poetry 2. Belfast: Blackstaff, 1981. (McGuckian, Damian Gorman, and Douglas Marshall.)

Two Women, Two Shores. Baltimore: New Poets; Galway: Salmon, 1989. (McGuckian and Nuala Archer.)

Venus and the Rain. Oxford and New York: Oxford University Press, 1984.

Studies of Medbh McGuckian

Bedient, Calvin. "The Crabbed Genius of Belfast." *Parnassus* 16.1 (1990): 198–216.

Beer, Anne. "Medbh McGuckian's Poetry: Maternal Thinking and a Politics of Peace." *Canadian Journal of Irish Studies* 18.1 (1992): 192–203.

Bendall, Molly. "Flower Logic: The Poems of Medbh McGuckian." *Antioch Review* 48.3 (1990): 367–71.

Cahill, Eileen. " 'Because I Never Garden': Medbh McGuckian's Solitary Way." *Irish University Review* 24.2 (1994): 264–71.

Drexel, John. "Threaders of Double-Stranded Words: News from the North of Ireland." *New England Review and Bread-Loaf Quarterly* 12.2 (1989): 179–92.

Gray, Cecile. "Medbh McGuckian: Imagery Wrought to Its Uttermost." In *Learning the Trade: Essays on W. B. Yeats and Contemporary Poetry*, ed. Deborah Fleming. West Cornwall, CT: Locust Hill, 1993, 165–77.

Mason, David. Rev. of *Marconi's Cottage*, by Medbh McGuckian. *The Hudson Review* 46.1 (1993): 227–28.

Melander, Ingrid. "Two Poems of Medbh McGuckian: Symbol and Interpretation." In *Anglo-Irish and Irish Literature: Aspects of Language and Culture: Proceedings of the Ninth International Congress of the International Association for the Study of Anglo-Irish Literature, Uppsala University, 4–7 August, 1986*, ed. Birgit Bramsback (and foreword) and Martin Croghan. Uppsala: Uppsala University, 1988, 237–41.

———. "The Use of Traditional Symbol in Three Poems by Medbh McGuckian." *Moderna Spraak* (Sweden) 83.4 (1989): 298–303.

O'Brien, Peggy. "Reading Medbh McGuckian: Admiring What We Cannot Under-
    stand." *Colby Quarterly* 28.4 (1992): 239–50.
Porter, Susan. "The 'Imaginative Space' of Medbh McGuckian." *Canadian Journal of
    Irish Studies* 15.2 (1989): 93–104.
Sirr, Peter. " 'How Things Begin to Happen': Notes on Eiléan Ní Chuilleanáin and
    Medbh McGuckian." *Southern Review* 31.3 (1995): 450–67.
Stevenson, Anne. Review of McGuckian's early work. *Times Literary Supplement* August
    21, 1981: 952.
Watt, R. J. C. "Medbh McGuckian." In *Contemporary Poets*, 4th ed, ed. James Vinson
    and D. L. Kirkpatrick. New York: St. Martin's, 1985.
Wills, Clair. "Making Waves." *Times Literary Supplement*, July 10, 1992: 23.
———. "The Perfect Mother: Authority in the Poetry of Medbh McGuckian." *Text and
    Context* 3 (1988): 91–111.
Yenser, Stephen. Rev. of *On Ballycastle Beach*, by Medbh McGuckian. *Poetry* 158.4
    (1991): 228–33.

Michael McLaverty

(1907–1992)

Bernard McKenna

BIOGRAPHY

Michael McLaverty was born on July 6, 1907, in Carrickmacross, County Monaghan, part of the old nine counties of the Ulster province. He spent the better part of his childhood on Rathlin Island in the North Channel in County Antrim, was educated at Saint Malachy's College and Queen's University in Belfast, taking a M.Sc. in 1933, and worked as a mathematics teacher and headmaster of Saint Thomas's Secondary School. In 1933, he married Mary Conroy. They had four children. McLaverty died in Ardglass, County Down, in 1992 and is buried in Stranford.

MAJOR WORKS AND THEMES

McLaverty's early life corresponds with many of the formative political and historical events that shape the modern profile of Northern Ireland—the growing industrialization of Belfast, the debates over Home Rule and partition, the independence of the twenty-six counties, British involvement in both world wars, the dissolution of the British Empire, and the reemergence of the Troubles. These events and the associated polarization of the Protestant and Catholic communities into Unionist and nationalist camps, find expression in McLaverty's writings. However, his major themes encompass the not unrelated social developments of the industrialized and postindustrialized North. Significantly, McLaverty's approach to these themes distinguishes him from his immediate literary predecessors, most probably because of his Catholic ancestry and birth. As in much of Ireland at the turn of the century, the Anglo-Irish aristocracy in Ulster and many, though most certainly not all, in Ulster's Presbyterian community began earnestly to explore Ireland's rich cultural past in a movement known as the Gaelic Revival. These Ulster Protestants, Anglican and Presbyterian alike, began to construct an imagined Irish heritage linked inexorably to a fecund, bucolic paradise populated by spirits of the dead and dead traditions, faeries and bean sidhes, and a peasant-Catholic community as unreal as the other legends. As appealing as these myths and traditions are and for as much good as these Protestant writers accomplished in preserving and perpetuating the literary and cultural legacy of ancient Ireland, their poetry and stories also tend to demean the reality of the poor Catholic experience, especially when exploited by less well intentioned practitioners. Considered within this literary and cultural tradition, McLaverty's writings speak to the reality of the Catholic experience, the pain of the decline of the rural culture and customs in the industrialized twentieth century, and the humanity behind the myths of an imagined past.

Novels

McLaverty's first and, by most critical estimates, his best novel was *Call My Brother Back* (1939), which explores the themes of contrasting rural and urban identities in the lives and experiences of the McNeill family, specifically in the person of Colm McNeill. At the novel's outset, Colm is thirteen and is quite contented and fulfilled by his life on Rathlin Island. He is very much reminiscent of the heroes of the poetry and stories of the Gaelic Revival; he is at one with nature, knows the wind and tides, is familiar with the island's wildlife. However, the island cannot financially support its inhabitants, and, shortly after the novel begins, Colm leaves Rathlin for Belfast and for life in boarding school, an education sponsored by the local priest. Sadly, Colm loses all confidence when faced with the difficulties of disciplined study and its endemic failures and when confronted by the political and economic realities of life in 1920s Belfast. In time, Colm's family joins him in Belfast, where their poverty and their identity as Catholics begin to expose their lives to the circumstances of sectarian and cultural upheaval. The novel details political assassinations, economically based migration, and urban angst and its consequent isolation.

Lost Fields (1941) addresses many of the same themes as *Call My Brother Back*. However, in McLaverty's second novel, economic rather than political hardship serves to push the narrative toward its climax. The Griffin family is forced to sell the fields of their rural ancestral heritage and move the thirty miles to Belfast. The matriarchal grandmother remains in the old family cottage while the rest of her children and grandchildren take up the lives of industrial labor. Eventually, the grandmother too comes to Belfast and is appalled by its urban landscape, calling it a "wasteland." The young people mend handkerchiefs, attend industrial schools, and lose all sense of the contentment and belonging they found in their rural home. In the end, the grandmother dies after a horrible accident, and the children are faced with the dreary desolation of urban life, which will most certainly kill them, or a return to poverty in their former rural home.

In *In This Thy Day* (1945) McLaverty explores the effects of the famine on the consciousness of the Irish rural poor after the passage of the Wyndham Land Act (1903) enabled them to possess land. For them, it symbolized autonomy, social respectability, and the ability to resist the disasters and starvation of the past. McLaverty has his character, Mrs. Mason, become possessed by the idea of the land at the expense of relations with her family. McLaverty consciously parallels this emotional and spiritual lack to the physical famine of the 1840s.

The Three Brothers (1948) and *Truth in the Night* (1951) explore the pressures and expectations of modern life on urban and rural communities. In each, the values of the agrarian past are supplanted by the selfishness and greed of modern industrialization. In the first novel, one brother owns a fairly successful business in Belfast but is consumed by a vicarious need for his children's success, an obsession that destroys their family. A second brother becomes obsessed with money and material gain and emotionally and physically abuses those around him. The third brother withdraws from society into drunkenness and depression. The second novel explores life on Rathlin Island and the decline in the island's values as it increasingly falls under the influence of the mainland and, by connection, the twentieth century. A woman from the mainland marries an island man and, subsequently, rejects all the values of rural Ireland—community, family, social responsibility—in favor of the values of the urban world—self-aggrandizement and cruelty.

The Choice (1958) represents a transition for McLaverty. Rather than representing urban values corrupting the individuals of rural Ireland, he represents an individual, born in a rural village, as able to preserve the rural values of his childhood not only in the urban world but in the rural world that has lost its values and ability to distinguish itself from the city.

Two of McLaverty's three final novels, *Schools for Hope* (1954) and *Brightening Day* (1965), detail the struggle of individuals to overcome stigmas associated with their past. In the city, they are able to conceal what they see as irrevocable stains on their character—the stains of disease and violence. In each, the characters confront their fears and come to terms with their own self-hatred in a way that would not have been possible in the rural world. There, the close-knit community would not have allowed the characters to grow beyond their past.

Short Stories

Best known as a short story writer, McLaverty published four volumes: *The White Mare and Other Stories* (1943), *The Game Cock and Other Stories* (1947), *The Road to the Shore* (1976), and *Collected Short Stories* (1978). These works explore many of the same themes as his longer writings—the rural and urban landscapes of the North of Ireland, the interaction of individuals and their environment, the corruption of the urban, industrialized world, economic and political violence, and the humanity of the individual behind stereotypes. In this short form, where McLaverty seems most comfortable, his love of language and almost poetic preoccupation with detail find their clearest voice.

Other Writings

In addition to his novels and short stories, McLaverty has published a children's book, *Billy Boogles and the Brown Cow*, and also a collection of a portion of his lectures, journals, and letters, *In Quiet Places* (1989).

CRITICAL RECEPTION

Literary critics consider McLaverty very much a regional writer in the best sense of the word, representing the circumstance of life in the North of Ireland with careful detail and attention to the unique qualities of life under British colonial and industrial rule. They commend his stories and his first novel, although many of them regret that the quality of these works does not extend to his other writings. Specifically, Seamus Heaney praises McLaverty for his attention to detail and his precise language. J. W. Foster agrees with Heaney's assessment, suggests that McLaverty's true gift is for the short story, and observes that his writing accurately reflects the lives of the Catholic urban and rural poor in the North of Ireland. Sean McMahon says that McLaverty "writes of the unheroic lives of ordinary people: city children with golden memories of the country . . . [and] the quiet lives of fishermen and farmers where the only violence and passion is [*sic*] that of the wind and sea." McMahon goes on to say that McLaverty is "aware of evil—greed, slander, even lust—but his vision of life is one in which good is stronger than evil and resignation and renunciation are the supreme virtues. At times his simplicity makes the writing seem limp. He is occasionally pedantic" (70). The most extensive assessment of McLaverty's life and career belongs to Sophia Hillan King, who has edited his letters and journals and published a book-length appraisal of McLaverty's career, *The Silken Twine*. King sets out "to show the gradual movement" in his writing toward a "point of renunciation and dedication . . . and to examine the consequences throughout his career of his decision to become a moral novelist" (24).

BIBLIOGRAPHY

The Poolbeg Press in Swords and Dublin has reissued all of McLaverty's novels and other writings.

Works by Michael McLaverty

Call My Brother Back. London: Longmans, Green, 1939.
Lost Fields. New York: Longmans, Green, 1941.

The White Mare and Other Stories. Newcastle, County Down: Mourne, 1943.
In This Thy Day. London: Cape, 1945.
The Game Cock and Other Stories. New York: Devin-Adair, 1947.
The Three Brothers. London: Cape, 1948.
Truth in the Night. New York: Macmillan, 1951.
School for Hope. London: Cape, 1954.
The Choice. London: Cape, 1958.
The Brightening Day. New York: Macmillan, 1965.
The Road to the Shore and Other Stories. Swords, County Dublin: Poolbeg, 1976.
Collected Short Stories. Swords, County Dublin: Poolbeg, 1978.
Billy Boogles and the Brown Cow. Dublin: Poolbeg, 1982.
*In Quiet Places: The Uncollected Stories, Letters and Critical Prose of Michael Mc-
    Laverty.* Ed. S. Hillan King. Swords, County Dublin: Poolbeg, 1989.

Studies of Michael McLaverty

Boyd, John. "Ulster Prose." In *The Arts in Ulster,* ed. Sam Hanna Bell, Nesca Robb,
    and John Hewitt. London: George G. Harrap, 1951, 99–130.
Foster, J. W. "McLaverty's People." *Eire-Ireland* 6.3 (Fall 1971): 92–105.
Heaney, Seamus. "Introduction." *Collected Short Stories.* Dublin: Poolbeg, 1978, 7–9.
King, Sophia Hillan. "Conscience and the Novelist: Michael McLaverty's Journals and
    Critical Writings of the Forties." *Studies* 78.309 (Spring 1989): 58–71.
———. "Quiet Desperation: Variations on a Theme in the Writings of Daniel Corkery,
    Michael McLaverty, and John McGahern." In *Aspects of Irish Studies,* ed. Myrtle
    Hill and Sarah Barber. Belfast: Institute of Irish Studies at Queen's University,
    1990, 39–46.
———. *The Silken Twine: A Study of the Works of Michael McLaverty.* Swords, County
    Dublin: Poolbeg, 1992. (Complete bibliography.)
Lubbers, Klaus. "Irish Fiction: A Mirror for Specifics." *Eire-Ireland* 20.2 (Summer
    1985): 90–104.
———. "Michael McLaverty: Pigeons." *Die Englische und Amerikanische Kurzges-
    chichte.* Darmstadt: Buchgesellschaft, 1990, 315–28.
McMahon, Sean. "The Black North: Prose Writers and the North of Ireland." *Threshold*
    21 (Summer 1967): 158–74. (Originally appeared in *Eire-Ireland* 1.2 [Summer
    1966]: 63–74.)

Bryan MacMahon

(1909–)

Madeleine Marchaterre

BIOGRAPHY

It would be difficult to say whether writing or teaching was MacMahon's primary career; the two are inextricably combined. Educated at St. Patrick's College in Drumcondra, MacMahon taught for a year in Dublin before returning to his native Listowel, County Kerry. There he taught at a national parochial school from 1931 to 1975, when he retired as a principal teacher. During his tenure as a teacher, MacMahon raised five sons, ran a bookshop with his wife, Kitty (née Ryan), and began his long and prolific career publishing poems, essays, plays, children's books, short stories, and novels.

MacMahon's interest in theater led him to start the Listowel Drama Group, for which he cowrote several plays; his playwriting talents, however, extend beyond the local. MacMahon has written historical pageants for various commemorative events, and four of his plays have been performed at the Abbey and the Peacock Theatres in Dublin. MacMahon also began the Radio Eireann Series "The Balladmaker's Saturday Night," a program that helped to renew the ballad as an art form in Ireland. A member of the Irish Academy of Letters, MacMahon is also the recipient of an honorary LL.D. from the National University of Ireland.

MacMahon has been recognized both internationally and nationally. In 1963 he was a representative for Ireland at the Harvard International Seminar, and he returned to the United States in 1965 to teach at the University of Iowa Writers' Workshop. This experience led him to help found the annual Writer's Week in Listowel, where he leads the Irish Short Story Workshop. In 1993, MacMahon was the recipient of the American Ireland Fund Literary Award.

MAJOR WORKS AND THEMES

MacMahon's short stories—like those of his predecessors Frank O'Connor and Sean O'Faolain—describe small-town and rural Irish life in the first half of the century, but they are not marked by the disillusionment that characterizes the work of those earlier writers. Instead, MacMahon's stories are distinctive for the kind eye they cast on post-independence Ireland. Thematically, Mac-Mahon emphasizes reconciliation and acceptance. In *The Red Petticoat* (1955), the protagonist of "Exile's Return" comes home from abroad intending to "swing for" (risk being hanged for murdering) his unfaithful wife, but he is instead reconciled with her and the child she has had by another man.

Evident in all his collections is a belief in the transforming power of love. In *The End of the World* (1976) this love lends his characters mythic qualities. Unwilling to be parted by death, the elderly couple in "The Gap of Life" become momentarily the Orpheus and Eurydice of Greek mythology. In this same collection, MacMahon demonstrates his ability to examine the same subject from different perspectives. "The Crab Tree," "Evening in Ireland," and "The Bull Buyers" all revolve around the business of Irish matchmaking. While the stories' minutiae reveal the disparate motives of each character, the themes they illustrate are universal: the relationships and rivalries between men and women, old and young, clergy and laity.

The themes and techniques of MacMahon's stories spill over into his novels. Set in a fictionalized Listowel, called Cloone, in the early years of the Irish Free State, MacMahon's first novel, *Children of the Rainbow* (1952), recounts the adventures of its narrator, Chestnut MacNamara, and his close friend, Finn Dillon. Sometimes with a comic touch, sometimes with deadly intensity, Mac-Mahon presents Chestnut's growing awareness of the intricacies of human relationships and his struggle to find his proper place in Cloone. The novel is at its best when it details the vanishing folk customs of the community, particularly the festivities of the Wren Boys at Christmas and the keening of the dead at Irish wakes.

MacMahon's second novel, *The Honey Spike* (1967), was first produced as a play at Dublin's Abbey Theatre in 1961. The work is notable for its inside perspective on Irish travelers. MacMahon once posed as a traveler in order to learn their language, Shelta; his experiences led him to publish an article on travelers in *Natural History*. *The Honey Spike* charts the day-to-day lives and the family allegiances and internecine feuds that structure the traveling community as well as the distrust and abuse (and only intermittent acts of kindness) dealt out to them by the non-traveling Irish. MacMahon's cinematic crosscutting between plots, his use of flashbacks, and his interlacing of multiple points of view work brilliantly to disclose the history of the novel's protagonists, Breeda and Martin Claffey, and to generate the tension that surrounds the final and tragic meeting between Breeda and her rival for Martin's affection.

CRITICAL RECEPTION

MacMahon's work has been widely reviewed and is most often praised for its vivid, if sometimes overly romanticized, portraits of rural Irish life. Critical studies of MacMahon are few; a comprehensive study of his work is overdue. The most complete study of MacMahon's short stories is Kristin Malloy's dissertation, "The Short Stories of Bryan MacMahon: Theme and Craft." Malloy contends that MacMahon's profound sense of the history and traditions of Kerry distinguishes the themes and language of his stories from those of other Irish writers. She further argues that the comic and compassionate tone of his stories stems from his respect for the human condition in all its infinite manifestations. Her work is supplemented by Earl Ingersoll, author of two articles on Mac-Mahon, both of which concern "Exile's Return." In "Irish Jokes" Ingersoll argues that with its "scrupulously engineered structure of expectations" (237), MacMahon's "An Exile's Return" can be read as an "elaborated joke." Lacan's reading of Freud's theory of the joke and its relationship to the unconscious and sexual desire informs his interpretation of the story's surprise ending: "MacMahon has offered us the happy ending of the Oedipal triangle when the son recognizes that the story he tells is ultimately also the discourse of the Other's desire" (245).

Robert Hogan has written a short analysis of MacMahon's major plays in his *After the Irish Renaissance*, giving a good account of their plots along with incisive critical commentary. MacMahon's first major play, *The Bugle in the Blood*, was produced at the Abbey Theater in 1949. Hogan notes that in plot and style it relies heavily on O'Casey's *Juno and the Paycock*, saying that "the play is imitative, but it imitates quality" (71). Admiring *The Song of the Anvil* for its blend of fantasy and romance and satire, Hogan calls it "as theatrical a play as the Abbey has staged in the last forty years" (73). Hogan reserves his highest praise for *The Honey Spike* because of its "real observation and intimate knowledge" of travelers (74) and MacMahon's ability to transform a picaresque story into stage action.

BIBLIOGRAPHY

Works by Bryan MacMahon

The Lion-Tamer and Other Stories. London and Toronto: Macmillan, 1948; New York: Dutton, 1949.

The Bugle in the Blood. Abbey Theatre, Dublin, 1949.

Jack O'Moora, and the King of Ireland's Son. Toronto: Smithers, 1950; New York: Dutton, 1950. (Children's book.)

Children of the Rainbow. London and Toronto: Macmillan, 1952; New York: Dutton, 1952.

The Red Petticoat, and Other Stories. London: Macmillan, 1955; New York: Dutton, 1955.

The Honey Spike. Abbey Theatre, Dublin, 1961.
Brendan of Ireland. Photographs by Wolfgang Suschitzky. London: Methuen, 1965; New York: Hastings House, 1967. (Children's book.)
The Honey Spike. London: Bodley Head, 1967; New York: Dutton, 1967.
Song of the Anvil. In *Seven Irish Plays, 1946–1964,* ed. Robert Hogan. Minneapolis: University of Minnesota Press, 1967.
Patsy-O and His Wonderful Pets. New York: Dutton, 1970. (Children's book.)
Here's Ireland. London: Batsford, 1971; New York: Dutton, 1971.
"Portrait of Tinkers." *Natural History* 80 (1971): 24–35.
The Death of Biddy Early. The Journal of Irish Literature 1.2 (1971): 30–44.
The Gap of Life. Dublin: Peacock Theatre, 1972.
Jack Furey. The Journal of Irish Literature 1.2 (1972): 45–62.
Peig. Trans. Peig Sayers. New York: Syracuse University Press, 1974.
The End of the World and Other Stories. Dublin: Poolbeg, 1976.
The Sound of Hooves and Other Stories. London: Bodley Head, 1985.
Patsy-O. Dublin: Children's Poolbeg, 1989. (Children's book.)
The Master. Dublin: Poolbeg, 1992.
The Storyman. Dublin: Poolbeg, 1994.
The Tallystick and Other Stories. Dublin: Poolbeg, 1994.
The Cobweb's Glory (with Michael Kenneally and Patrick O'Connor under the pseudonym Bryan Michael O'Connor). Listowel, Ireland: Bookshop, n.d.
———. *Fledged and Flown.* Listowel, Ireland: Bookshop, n.d.

Studies of Bryan MacMahon

Henderson, Gordon. "An Interview with Bryan MacMahon." *Journal of Irish Literature* 3.3 (September 1974): 3–23.
Henderson, Joanne L. "Checklist of Four Kerry Writers: George Fitzmaurice, Maurice Walch, Bryan MacMahon, and John B. Keane." *Journal of Irish Literature* 1.2 (1972): 101–19.
Ingersoll, Earl G. "Irish Jokes: A Lacanian Reading of Short Stories by James Joyce, Flann O'Brien, and Bryan MacMahon." *Studies in Short Fiction* 27 (1990): 237–45.
———. "Metaphor and Metonymy in James Joyce's 'A Little Cloud' and Bryan MacMahon's 'Exile's Return.' " *Canadian Journal of Irish Studies* 16.2 (1990): 27–35.
Malloy, Kristin. "The Short Stories of Bryan MacMahon: Theme and Craft." Diss., University of Minnesota, 1988.

Brinsley MacNamara

(1890–1963)

Maureen McLaughlin

BIOGRAPHY

Brinsley MacNamara, the actor, novelist, and playwright known for his realistic portrayal of regional life in Ireland, was born September 6, 1890, in Hinskenstown, Westmeath, Ireland. Known as John Weldon before adopting his pseudonym, MacNamara was the oldest of seven children born to James Weldon, a national schoolteacher, and Fanny Duncan.

After early success as an actor, MacNamara left his village of Delvin and briefly toured the United States in 1912 with the Abbey's first U.S. tour. However, he soon ended his acting career so that he could concentrate on writing. After returning to Delvin in 1913, MacNamara wrote prolifically, publishing articles and poems in national newspapers and magazines. During 1916, MacNamara wrote *The Valley of the Squinting Windows*, a controversial book that became his best known, although not the best written, of his seven novels.

In 1920, MacNamara married Helena (Lena) Degidon in Quin, County Clare. Their only child, Oliver Weldon, was born in 1921. In 1922, MacNamara became the registrar in the National Gallery. However, he depended on playwriting for much of his income and had nine plays produced at the Abbey between 1919 and 1945.

In 1932, he became a founding member of the Irish Academy of Letters. In 1935, he served briefly as director of the Abbey Theatre, resigning after O'Casey's *The Silver Tassie* was performed against his wishes. From 1939 until 1945, MacNamara was drama critic for *The Irish Times*. He resigned from the National Gallery in 1960. MacNamara died on February 4, 1963.

MAJOR WORKS AND THEMES

MacNamara gained credit for originating the "squinting windows" school of Irish realistic fiction after the publication of his first novel. His work was an obvious rebellion against conventional Irish novels because he presented unsentimental aspects of the Irish people. While he was sharp and precise as he wrote in painstaking detail, MacNamara's descriptions of villagers were one-sided caricatures, focusing on drunkenness and backbiting, and he was often criticized for not seeing any good that might also have existed. The somber tone of his work may have lessened its popular appeal and led to neglect of his later work. As Michael McDonnell has written about MacNamara in Hogan's *The Dictionary of Irish Literature*, "His novels and stories describe a people whose only traditions were the traditions of orthodoxy, greed and ignorance—and always the antagonist is the Church and its clergy" (418).

When *The Valley of the Squinting Windows* appeared (1918), a furor erupted in MacNamara's hometown. Many villagers saw mocking similarities between themselves and the book's characters. The novel was burned, his father's school was boycotted, and MacNamara was driven into exile in Dublin. As a result of the scandal, MacNamara only strengthened his determination to write critically and realistically about rural life.

While MacNamara wrote about what he detested in his village, he made the midlands his setting in numerous works. He also wrote about pseudointellectual society in Dublin, and his writing on this topic has been compared with Joyce's in *A Portrait of the Artist as a Young Man* and *Ulysses*. However, MacNamara's satire is considered by some to be superficial, and his technique for creating humor and serious impressions was surely not as effective as Joyce's. However, like Joyce, MacNamara's life was one of distance from the area of Ireland that he most loved and hated.

MacNamara was remembered for the rest of his life for his controversial first novel, but his second, *The Clanking of Chains* (1920), should have created more of a stir because of its satirical stance toward Irish politics. Shunning the popular romantic approach to nationalism, MacNamara emphasized the disillusionment, jealousies, and cowardice behind the drive for independence. By studying the narcissism that can grow out of patriotism, MacNamara marked his own loss of idealism and, as a result, created an examination of a great movement that reflects Ibsen's view in *An Enemy of the People*. However, *The Clanking of Chains* also has been called MacNamara's worst novel because its characters are two-dimensional caricatures—types rather than individuals.

Due to its autobiographical nature, *In Clay and in Bronze* (1920), first published as *The Irishman* under the pseudonym "Oliver Blyth," essentially explains how *The Valley of the Squinting Windows* came to be written. It focuses on a young farmer who leaves the country to pursue his literary and theatrical ambitions, which gave MacNamara ample opportunity to satirize the Irish Literary Renaissance. MacNamara's anger is muted somewhat in this third novel, and his characters are better developed than in his previous work. His fourth novel, *The Mirror in the Dusk* (1921), is a hauntingly beautiful and tragic novel in which MacNamara strongly develops the theme of land-ownership in a mature manner. In service of his theme, he makes use of time shifts and stories that are peripheral to the main plot, while developing a complex and nuanced story.

While MacNamara's literary output was strong from 1916 to 1922, he produced only three more novels in the following forty years, and the first two were almost finished during his early period. *The Various Lives of Marcus Igoe* (1929), a tragicomic fantasy, is a neglected work that shows MacNamara's comic sense and poetic writing. Again the setting is Garradrimna, the village of the squinting windows, in which Igoe's various lives have been a series of personal conflicts. The plot is a study of human nature, as it explores the character's past, present, and future. This most experimental novel of MacNamara's canon creates a subjective reality where the reader can sometimes hardly distinguish between what is real and what is imagined. The sometimes confusing effect is ultimately delightful—both touching and hilarious. The novel is often compared to Flann O'Brien's *At Swim-Two-Birds*.

Return to Ebontheever (1930) is a novel whose theme is based loosely on Shakespeare's *Othello*. Filled with dramatic irony, it denounces compliance with orthodoxy and shows MacNamara becoming a more mature and controlled writer. *Michael Caravan* (1941) is a comedy of rural manners, focusing on conflicts between romance and reality, that is a tour de force in its cultivation of dramatic irony as the reader watches two naive sisters conned out of their life savings by an actress-trickster.

MacNamara's later efforts were various. *Some Curious People* (1945) is a book of sad, ironic, and humorous stories, some of which received high praise. *Abbey Plays 1899–1948* is a nonfiction compilation (1949) that has been criticized for its inaccuracy. *The Whole Story of the X, Y, Z* (1951), a novella about a man's absorption with fantasy, is not one of MacNamara's better works. Rather, it appears to be evidence of the decline of his skills with age. A posthumous reminiscence, ''Growing Up in the Midlands'' (1964) was published in *The Capuchin Annual*.

Some of MacNamara's plays also reject the idealistic view of Irish peasant life. His first play, *The Rebellion at Ballycullen*, a three-act work set in the midlands, was performed at the Abbey in 1919. A series of successful plays followed, but by the 1920s he had begun writing comedies of romantic intrigue. Alone with George Shiels and Sean O'Casey, MacNamara was counted as one of the playwrights who helped the Abbey gain financial success in the early years after the revolution. MacNamara was a popular success from 1923, when his first comedy, *The Glorious Uncertainty*, was introduced. The plot occurs in a bar and revolves around a horse race that is to be held in Ballymacoyle. This play and *Look at the Heffernans!* (1926), a comedy about the developments involving four separate marriages, would indicate that MacNamara compromised himself as an artist to produce commercially successful Abbey formula plays.

MacNamara's most memorable play, *Margaret Gillan* (1933), a powerful tragedy that is a study of a woman's frustrated love, repressed passion, jealousy, and revenge, is usually accepted as his greatest achievement in drama. It won the Casement Prize as the best Irish play of the year, as well as the Harmsworth Literary Award. His other plays were *The Land for the People* (1920); *The Master* (1928); *The Grand House in the City* (1936); *The Three Thimbles* (1941); and *Marks and Mabel* (1945).

CRITICAL RECEPTION

Several scholars have hailed MacNamara as the pioneer of a new school of Irish realism because his plays and novels cast a satirical, critical, whimsical, and often ironic eye on rural Irish life and mentality. He is credited as the first Irish writer to use his own experience as the basis for writing a novel about provincial society. As a forerunner of writers such as O'Flaherty and Peadar O'Donnell, MacNamara contributed to the picture of Ireland that eschewed the romantic version of the Island of Saints and Scholars. While his work from 1918 until 1921 exhibited great anger, MacNamara's final three novels are more daring, mature, and controlled in the use of form and technique. As a result of his later work, MacNamara is noted for being, along with Joyce and Flann O'Brien, an Irish writer who in the 1920s was introducing innovative techniques in fiction.

MacNamara does not receive his fair share of attention in contemporary histories of Irish literature. Indeed, Benedict Kiely is the only literary historian to discuss MacNamara's later work at any great length (in *Modern Irish Fiction*). When MacNamara's work is acknowledged, it is generally for *The Valley of the Squinting Windows*. Padraic O'Farrell's monograph tells of the real-life drama surrounding the uproar that the book caused in Delvin. Using original research, O'Farrell provides detailed background information about MacNamara and his family, as well as the story behind the book and how the sins of the son were visited upon the father.

When MacNamara's controversial book was first published, O'Farrell notes, it was given an unfavorable review in *The Irish Times* for its unflattering portrayal of rural life: "There is not a good man or decent woman on the closely-crowded canvas or one gay and happy scene in the book" (79). Reviews in other papers, ranging from *The Irish Independent* to *The New York Globe*, were much more complimentary toward the writing and the story. In a more recent critique, Ruth Fleischmann has called the work an "unpalatable novel" that contains "penny-dreadful stereotypes" (63–60). In *A Short History of Anglo-Irish Literature*, Roger McHugh and Maurice Harmon called *The Valley of the Squinting Windows* "a success de scandale" that would be regarded today as "rather tame and not particularly well-written" (273).

Of *The Clanking of Chains* Richard Fallis has said in *The Irish Renaissance* that it is a "thin novel with cliched characters and too much flat prose" (205). Alexander G. Gonzalez has noted in *Irish University Review* that "no one in this novel—not even the idealistic protagonist—is in any way an interesting or appealing character'' (273).

McHugh and Harmon have cited *The Mirror in the Dusk* and *The Various Lives of Marcus Igoe* as worthy novels. In contrast, Seamus Deane, in *A Short History of Irish Literature*, has called *The Valley of the Squinting Windows* ''one of the most effective exposures of the narrowness of village life'' and criticizes *Marcus Igoe* for its ''fey and whimsical style'' (200). However, Kiely has called *Igoe* MacNamara's best book, noting its daring and original structure and calling it a ''delicate, vague, confused fantasy'' (15). Gonzalez ranks *The Mirror in the Dusk* among MacNamara's finest works (''Theme and Structure'').

In *The Dictionary of Irish Literature*, McDonnell maintains that MacNamara's turn to whimsy may have resulted from the financial burdens of marriage, his failure at being a prophet in his native land, or his drive to succeed: ''Whatever the reasons, in thus retreating into himself and away from reality in his work, he discovered the milieu which best suited his peculiar talents, and in *The Various Lives of Marcus Igoe* he produced what must eventually be his most acclaimed work and the assurance of his real place in twentieth-century Irish literature. MacNamara had determined, at excessive personal sacrifice and with the heroism essential to the truly dedicated artist, not to succumb to the bleak anomaly of this life, but to become its master, its historian, and its savior. Always though, there is a sense of the tragicomic, the presence of what he called 'the long, low chuckle of the mind' '' (420).

The first time that MacNamara does not mention Garradrimna as his setting is in *Return to Ebontheever*. With a strong sense of balance, MacNamara filled the novel with thorough detail and made good use of shifts in time and narrative focus. The experimentation in structure deepened the complexity of the novel, which addressed the theme of jealousy.

MacNamara continued his experimentation with structure in *Michael Caravan*. By continuing to explore the nature of reality, as he had started to do in *Marcus Igoe*, MacNamara sharpened his use of dramatic irony and in new ways continued to develop his reputation as a literary maverick.

Gonzalez concludes that ''MacNamara's work becomes impressive once he ceases trying to be impressive. Where in his earlier work it would appear that he wanted to overwhelm his readers, in his later period he seems instead intent on expressing his idiosyncratic vision to the best of his ability'' (*Irish University Review* 274). His later novels are characterized ''by a carefully balanced structure, strong presentation of the marriage theme, and masterful cultivation of dramatic irony through painstakingly developed foreshadowing'' (272).

MacNamara also gained a place in Irish drama for *Margaret Gillan*. As T. C. Murray wrote in *The Irish Theatre*, ''The writing is so deliberately controlled as to seem almost bare but it is a dramatic medium which focuses the mind on the fateful play of forces underneath and thus intensifies the appeal of the drama . . . this play, I think, comes nearer to Ibsen than any that I can recall in the repertory of the Abbey'' (145–46).

In *Ireland's Literary Renaissance*, Ernest Boyd makes the connection between MacNamara's novels and plays and the influence of realism in drama and literature: "MacNamara has an unrivalled faculty of seeing certain aspects of Irish life as they are. The peasantry, as he sees them, are neither the buffoons of Lover nor the visionaries of Yeats and Lady Gregory. They are the eternal peasant as Maupassant and others have described him, brutalized only too often by the intolerable conditions of existence in an agricultural slum" (401).

Throughout his work, MacNamara strove to break down conventions in Irish fiction. He is remembered not only for describing rural Ireland with unvarnished realism but for experimenting with dramatic irony and structure.

BIBLIOGRAPHY

Works by Brinsley MacNamara

Books

The Valley of the Squinting Windows. London: Sampson Low, Marston, 1918.
The Clanking of Chains. Dublin: Maunsel, 1920.
In Clay and in Bronze (New York, 1920).
The Irishman (pseudonym Oliver Blyth). London: Nash, 1920.
The Mirror in the Dusk. Dublin and London: Maunsel and Roberts, 1921.
The Smiling Faces. London: Mandrake, 1929. (Short stories.)
The Various Lives of Marcus Igoe. London: Sampson Low, Marston, 1929.
Return to Ebontheever. London: Cape, 1930/reissued in 1942 as *Othello's Daughter*.
Some Curious People. Dublin: Talbot, 1945. (Short Stories.)
Michael Caravan. Dublin: Talbot, 1946.
Abbey Plays 1899–1948. Dublin: At the Sign of the Three Candles, 1949. (Pamphlet.)
The Whole Story of the X.Y.Z. Belfast: Carter, 1951. (Novella.)
"Growing up in the Midlands." *The Capuchin Annual* (1964). (Biographical sketch.)

Plays

Look at the Heffernans! Dublin and Cork: Talbot, n.d.
Margaret Gillan. London: Allen and Unwin, 1934.
Marks and Mabel. Dublin: Duffy, 1945.
The Glorious Uncertainty. Dublin: Bourke, 1957.

Studies of Brinsley MacNamara

Fleischmann, Ruth. "Brinsley MacNamara's Penny Dreadful." *Eire-Ireland* 18.2 (Summer 1983): 52–74.
Gonzalez, Alexander G. "Brinsley MacNamara's Short Stories." *The Canadian Journal of Irish Studies* 21.1 (July 1995): 77–87.
———. "The Novels of Brinsley MacNamara's Later Period."
Irish University Review 19.2 (Autumn 1989): 272–86.

———. "Theme and Structure in Brinsley MacNamara's *The Mirror in the Dusk.*" *South Atlantic Review* 61.4 (Fall 1996): 53–65.

McDonnell, Michael. "Brinsley MacNamara: A Checklist." *Journal of Irish Literature* 4.2 (1975): 79–88.

———. "Stereotypes and Caricatures of the Abbey Theatre (1910) as Described in *The Irishman* by Brinsley MacNamara." *Eire-Ireland* 24.3 (Fall 1989): 53–64.

McMahon, Sean. "A Reappraisal: *The Valley of the Squinting Windows.*" *Eire-Ireland* 3.1 (Spring 1968): 106–17.

O'Farrell, Padraic. *The Burning of Brinsley MacNamara.* Dublin: Lilliput, 1990.

Louis MacNeice

(1907–1963)

Bernard McKenna

BIOGRAPHY

On September 12, 1907 in Belfast, the poet Frederick Louis MacNeice was born into an Ireland and a way of life undergoing irrevocable change. MacNeice's work as a poet would bear witness to the implications of these changes—the political and labor upheavals of the early to mid-twentieth century and the irretrievable loss of a way of life that had dominated Ireland for centuries. Specifically, MacNeice was born into the Anglo-Irish community, and, although his inheritance did not include a literal Big House, it included much that shaped the conception of Ireland's landed gentry. Indeed, MacNeice identified himself as an Irishman, even though his education took him to England and the world of the British public school—Sherborne Preparatory School and Marlborough—and later Merton College, Oxford. MacNeice's father was a Church of Ireland minister and bishop who supported Home Rule and spoke out passionately for the rights of Catholics and movingly against the horrors of war. His mother and her family nurtured in the young man a love for her native Connaught. The influences of his father's religion and politics, his mother's early death and her love for the Irish west and the countryside in Ulster, and the civil unrest in the North and in the world consumed the poet's life and writings. In them, a reader discovers the characteristic Anglo-Irish sense of detachment. His communion with Ireland and its people, then, was largely imaginative or in direct relation to nature. His identification with the English in his work is equally distant, as an objective but not disinterested observer of their behavior and way of life.

MAJOR WORKS AND THEMES

Poetry

MacNeice's early published poetry, *Oxford Poetry 1929* (1929) and *Blind Fireworks* (1929), is considered by some critics juvenilia filled with the characteristic ennui of boys from "public school." However, a careful review of these poems reveals that, although some are affected and spotted with occasional classical allusions designed more to impress than to advance understanding, more of the poetry of these early collections warrants careful consideration than critics have previously allowed. Specifically, many of the poems shed light on MacNeice's imaginative relationship with his mother, a relationship rhetorically fused into a relationship with the Irish landscapes of his youth. He details a cyclical pattern of growing adult awareness that begins in the childhood of an idyllic garden, proceeds to a growing understanding of transience, and ends with images of relentlessly passing time.

MacNeice's next collection, *Poems* (1935), marked him as an emerging poetical talent and marked the beginnings of his relationship with Faber and Faber's T. S. Eliot, who took a special interest in MacNeice. *Poems* details the changing urban and political landscapes of the 1930s. He seems a distant observer of the communist or revolutionary or the cities he describes, most especially Belfast.

Autumn Journal (1939) is clearly MacNeice's masterpiece. Comprising twenty-four occasionally rhyming cantos, it is a diary of the closing months of 1938 that chronicles issues ranging from the personal experience of a lost love, to the effects of war and revolution in Ireland and Spain, to the threat of a cataclysmic, all-consuming war. Throughout, the poem carries with it a sense of irrevocable loss and rates as one of the best-written accounts of the anxiety of the period "between the wars." It also contains MacNeice's most extended treatment of the violence in Ireland. Significantly, he speaks not only as an Irishman but as an Anglo-Irishman from Ulster writing of Irish figures and circumstance as well as of Belfast and its factories and slums and of the poet's personal sense of Irish identity separate from England. Simultaneously, he seems removed from the people of Belfast or Dublin.

The Earth Compels (1938), *The Last Ditch* (1940), *Plant and Phantom* (1941), *Springboard* (1944), and *Holes in the Sky* (1948) mark the final effort of MacNeice's most impressive period of poetic achievement. Each continues the themes established in the 1930s. However, they contain some of his most notable smaller poems, including "Bagpipe Music," "Carrickfergus," and two impressive sequences of poems titled "The Kingdom" and "The Closing Album"; the latter includes poetry devoted to the landscapes of Connaught; the former examines the poet's reaction to his father's death.

MacNeice's poetry of the 1950s and 1960s published in *Ten Burnt Offerings* (1952), *Autumn Sequel* (1954), *Visitations* (1957), *Solstices* (1961), and *The*

Burning Perch (1963) is sometimes considered the work of a poet declining in his talents and abilities. Indeed, the poems are not as strong as his earlier work. However, they address issues associated with more religious and spiritual topics and include works contemplating death and transience in a more personal way.

Radio Plays and Other Works

MacNeice spent most of his adult life as a writer and editor for the BBC. Significantly, after the outbreak of the Second World War, MacNeice, unlike Auden, returned to England to help with the war effort as a writer for radio. He produced several works that represent minor masterpieces of radio drama. At Oxford and as a lecturer, MacNeice developed his skills as a critic and translator, publishing highly respected studies of W. B. Yeats and modernism, *The Agamemnon of Aeschylus*, travel journals, and the autobiographical *These Strings Are False*, which speaks movingly of the poet's life and experiences.

CRITICAL RECEPTION

Early critical assessment of MacNeice's poetical achievement rates him as a minor member of Auden's circle. However, after the posthumous publication of *Collected Poems* (1966), his reputation began to rise over the next thirty years with articles and longer works that contributed to MacNeice's growing critical reception, culminating in Jon Stallworthy's 1995 biography. However, MacNeice's writings should properly be considered in the framework of Irish literary tradition. Terence Brown, Derek Mahon, William McKinnon, and Christopher Fauske (in Westendorp and Mallinson's *Politics and the Rhetoric of Poetry*) explore the poet within this context and are, consequently, able to appreciate the subtleties and nuances of MacNeice's work, thereby further increasing his poetic reputation not only as an Irish writer but also as a major twentieth-century literary figure. Currently, as an Irish poet, he is generally ranked along with Patrick Kavanagh and Seamus Heaney as the best since Yeats.

BIBLIOGRAPHY

Works by Louis MacNeice

Blind Fireworks. London: Gollancz, 1929.
Oxford Poetry 1929. London: Oxford University Press, 1929.
Roundabout Way. London: Putnam, 1932.
Poems. London: Faber and Faber, 1935.
The Agamemnon of Aeschylus. London: Faber and Faber, 1936.
Letters from Iceland. London: Faber and Faber, 1937.
Out of the Picture. London: Faber and Faber, 1937.
Poems. New York: Random House, 1937.

The Earth Compels. London: Faber and Faber, 1938.
I Crossed the Minch. London: Longmans, Green, 1938.
Modern Poetry: A Personal Essay. Oxford: Oxford University Press, 1938.
Zoo. Plymouth: M. Joseph, 1938.
Autumn Journal. London: Faber and Faber, 1939.
The Last Ditch. Dublin: Cuala, 1940.
Selected Poems. London: Faber and Faber, 1940.
Collected Poems 1925–1940. New York: Random House, 1941.
Plant and Phantom. London: Faber and Faber, 1941.
The Poetry of W. B. Yeats. London: Oxford University Press, 1941.
Meet the U.S. Army. London: His Majesty's Stationery Office, 1943.
Christopher Columbus. London: Faber and Faber, 1944.
Springboard. London: Faber and Faber, 1944.
Poet's Choice. Surrey: Council, 1945.
The Dark Tower and Other Radio Scripts. London: Faber and Faber, 1947.
Holes in the Sky. London: Faber and Faber, 1948.
Collected Poems 1925–1948. London: Faber and Faber, 1949.
Goethe's Faust. London: Faber and Faber, 1951.
Ten Burnt Offerings. London: Faber and Faber, 1952.
Autumn Sequel: A Rhetorical Poem in XXVI Cantos. London: Faber and Faber, 1954.
The Penny That Rolled Away. New York: Putnam, 1954.
Visitations. London: Faber and Faber, 1957.
Eighty-Five Poems. London: Faber and Faber, 1959.
Writers against Apartheid. London: Villiers, 1960.
Solstices. London: Faber and Faber, 1961.
The Burning Perch. London: Faber and Faber, 1963.
Round the Corner. London: Faber and Faber, 1963.
Astrology. London: Faber and Faber, 1964.
The Mad Islands and The Administrator. London: Faber and Faber, 1964.
Selected Poems. London: Faber and Faber, 1964.
The Strings Are False: An Unfinished Autobiography. Ed. E. R. Dodds. London: Faber
        and Faber, 1965.
Varieties of Parable. Cambridge: Cambridge University Press, 1965.
Collected Poems of Louis MacNeice. Ed. E. R. Dodds. London: Faber and Faber, 1966.
One for the Grace: A Modern Morality Play. London: Faber and Faber, 1968.
Persons from the Porlock and Other Plays for Radio. London: British Broadcasting,
        1969.
The Revenant: A Song Cycle. Dublin: Cuala, 1975.
Selected Literary Criticism of Louis MacNeice. Ed. A. Heuser. Oxford: Clarendon, 1987.
Louis MacNeice: Selected Poems. Ed. M. Longley. London: Faber and Faber, 1988.
Selected Prose of Louis MacNeice. Ed. A. Heuser. Oxford: Clarendon, 1990.
Selected Plays of Louis MacNeice. Ed. A. Heuser and P. McDonald. Oxford: Clarendon,
        1993.

Studies of Louis MacNeice

Brown, Terence. *Louis MacNeice: Sceptical Vision*. Dublin: Gill and Macmillan, 1975.
Coulton, Barbara. *Louis MacNeice and the BBC*. London: Faber and Faber, 1980.

Longley, Edna. *Louis MacNeice*. London: Faber and Faber, 1988.

McDonald, Peter. *Louis MacNeice: The Poet in His Contexts*. London: Oxford University Press, 1990.

McKinnon, William. *Apollo's Blended Dream*. London: Oxford University Press, 1971.

Marsack, Robyn. *The Cave of Making: The Poetry of Louis MacNeice*. London: Oxford University Press, 1982.

Stallworthy, Jon. *Louis MacNeice*. Boston: Faber and Faber, 1995.

Derek Mahon

(1941–)

Kevin Murphy

BIOGRAPHY

Derek Mahon was born in Belfast, Northern Ireland, and raised in the northern section of the city, an area of mixed economic status populated by both Catholics and Protestants. Mahon was raised Church of Ireland and was a chorister at St. Peter's Church on the Antrim Road. He attended the Royal Belfast Academical Institution and Trinity College, Dublin, where he majored in French. Upon graduation, Mahon spent two years working odd jobs in Canada and the United States. Returning to Ireland, he worked as a teacher in Belfast and Dublin. In 1970 he settled in London for a period of fifteen years and began a career as a freelance journalist and a writer in residence at British, American, and Irish universities. In 1972 he married Doreen Douglas, with whom he has had two children. For most of the past decade, he has been writer in residence at various American universities and is currently living in New York City.

MAJOR WORKS AND THEMES

In his initial volume of poems, *Night-Crossing* (1968), Mahon establishes both a voice and a stance that would carry in various refinements and transformations throughout his subsequent poetry. "In Carrowdore Churchyard," an elegy at the grave of Louis MacNeice, links Mahon's vision to that of the earlier Belfast Protestant poet, embracing both the ironic ambiguity and enduring humanism at the core of MacNeice's vision. Exactly what shape this ironic ambiguity would take in Mahon's own experience, though, becomes clearer in "Glengormley," a meditation on the area north of Belfast where Mahon was raised that combines his attraction and resistance to his origins. In several other poems, "Grandfather," "My Wicked Uncle," and "In Belfast" (later titled "The Spring Vacation"), Mahon explores his familial and psychological origins, caught between his fascination with liberated family characters and the staid, Northern reserve of Belfast. In "The Forger," Mahon also introduces a complex, ironic view of the artist/forger as humanistic fraud, a con man so close to aspirations of real artists that it becomes morally and aesthetically difficult to distinguish one from the other. This portrait of the artist, which both asserts and undermines the sensibility and morality of art, is a theme to which Mahon returns in some of his best-known and most widely anthologized poems.

Mahon's second major volume of poems, *Lives* (1972), develops, with some prompting from Samuel Beckett and Edvard Munch, earlier issues of specific origin into much broader meditations. Poems such as "Homecoming" and "Ecclesiastes" again explore Mahon's conflicted and ambiguous attachments to his Northern Irish roots. On the one hand, there is a world-weariness in the recognition of his culture's stasis; on the other, a compulsive need to acknowledge his natal, and perhaps fatal, point of view. Once again, too, Mahon ironically questions the capacity of art to come to terms with the obdurate and complex intractability of human history. In "Lives," Mahon presents a series of imagined objects, each illustrative of the culture that produced it but each also powerless to prevent that culture's extinction. Like Seamus Heaney in his bog poems, Mahon takes on an archaeological/anthropological point of view, but, unlike Heaney, who finds in the excavated corpses of ancient bogs morality lessons for the current political turmoil of Ireland, Mahon wryly repudiates such moral certainties by transforming the speaker into a comically overequipped social scientist and finishes with a deft reprimand for any who believe that such historical or moral interpolation is possible.

The Snow Party (1975) opens with "Afterlives," a poem dedicated to James Simmons that, as the title suggests, reconsiders the secure irony of "Lives." Mahon, in the initial section of this two-part poem, sardonically exposes the void at the center of the nonsectarian, rational principles that guide (or blind) the London culture in which he lives. The second part records once again a reluctant voyage back to Belfast, now torn by five years' war. In many ways, the poem's conclusion with its telling "bomb/home" offrhyme illustrates succinctly the sense of metaphysical displacement at the core of Mahon's complex, conflicted vision. "A Disused Shed in Co. Wexford," perhaps Mahon's most celebrated poem, also situates the violence of history against the claims and necessities of art. Coming upon a shed of mushrooms growing in the dark "since civil war days," the speaker of the poem allows the mushrooms' vegetative silence and tenuous connection to the world that has forgotten them to expand into a meditation on the traces of neglected or unrecorded human suffering in the progress of civilization. The poem ends with these lost souls pleading directly with the speaker (and reader) to acknowledge somehow in the rarified detachment of art their enduring presence, their very being. The masterful counterbalancing of ironic detachment and urgent compassion at the core of this poem is Mahon at his best.

The Hunt by Night (1982), Mahon's most impressive volume of poems, uses paintings as points of departure for his continued exploration of poetic origins and aspirations. "Courtyards in Delft" is a meditation on de Hooch's 1659 painting. The detailed depiction of the bourgeois courtyard scene evokes an ambivalent admiration and dismay, a scene described as much by what is missing as by what is present. As with his earlier explorations of his poetic origin, Mahon reluctantly accepts this seventeenth-century Dutch scene, even as he is aware of the suppressive political entities this repressive Protestant culture will generate (the contemporaries of de Hooch, Mahon has pointed out, founded the Cape colony and took the Williamite Wars to Ireland). Mahon acknowledges his ambivalent allegiance to this culture and sees his own poetic formation simultaneous with the violence inherent in such repression. As in earlier volumes, Mahon juxtaposes images of calm with intimations of violence, both historical and aesthetic. "The Hunt by Night" is a response to Uccello's 1465 painting. The poem, whose complex stanzaic form parallels the highly stylized figures of the painting, considers the discrepancy between the detached, aesthetic pageantry of the hunt as depicted in Uccello's painting and the urgent, primordial necessity that compelled the first Neolithic hunters and cave artists. As with Mahon's other considerations of the purposes of art, the poem both embraces and ironically undercuts the aesthetic enterprise.

Several poems in *Antarctica* (1985) imply a stasis and an aesthetic stalemate. The title poem seems a kind of willed, aesthetic death wish, with the speaker of the villanelle abandoning his Antarctic companions to search out in a blurred, self-destructive gesture amid the ice some romantic clarification. The strongest poem in the collection, however, remains the most bleakly philosophical. "Death and the Sun," which begins as an elegy to Albert Camus, quickly becomes a detailed portrait of a Northern Irish generation afflicted by sectarian hatred. Concluding with the image of the dweller in Plato's cave suddenly being exposed to the blinding sun (the parallel antithesis of the Antarctica ice quester), the poem recognizes, in its "rich despair," the limits of human ability to wrest meaning or morality from history.

Mahon's *Selected Poems* (1991) contains selections from all five of his earlier volumes, as well as "Dawn at St. Patrick's," an aubade of sorts recording Mahon's stay in a Dublin sanatarium for alcoholism. The poem alludes to Robert Lowell's "Waking in the Blue," and in many ways Mahon's personal sense of disaffection and displacement, like Lowell's, has analogy to, and provides insight into, his culture at large. Mahon, as a Protestant Irish poet, can never be fully at home in an Ireland divided along sectarian lines, and yet there is nowhere else he can be centered. His most recent collection, *The Hudson Letter* (1995), carries this stance of disaffection and exile to lower Manhattan. The title piece is an eighteen-poem sequence which, in its deft interlace of formal elegance and streetwise savvy, interrogates Mahon's elegiac sense of homelessness across a range of perspectives: familial, national, artistic, spiritual.

Despite the fact that Mahon has, like Joyce and Beckett, spent most of his adult life away from Ireland, his poetry continually records his being drawn back toward that center, even as he ironically acknowledges the impossibility of such an orientation. Appropriately enough, when he was asked at a 1991 interview in Philadelphia if he still considered Belfast his home, he responded no. But then he added, "This is very close to the bone: where is home now? Where do you want to be buried? They've widened the bridge, they've destroyed the beach, but I suppose home for me would be a little place in County Antrim called Cushendun, where both my children were baptized."

CRITICAL RECEPTION

In Ireland, the critical response to Derek Mahon's poetry has taken two distinct forms, both of which have to do with his Northern Protestant origins. Even though Mahon has described himself as "lapsed" in terms of any specific religious affiliation with the Church of Ireland, it is clear that most Irish commentators see him culturally and intellectually shaped, both positively and negatively, by the group in which and by which he was raised. The first is summed up by Seamus Deane's opening remark in the chapter devoted to Mahon in *Celtic Revivals*: "Derek Mahon's poetry expresses a longing to be free from history." Deane sees the urbane, cosmopolitan elements of Mahon's poetry to be an attempt "to fend off the forces of atavism, ignorance and oppression which are part of his Northern Protestant heritage" (156). For Deane, Mahon's irony and ambiguity are in essence a deflection of the historical realities of contemporary Northern Ireland, even though Deane recognizes that the city of Belfast is the locus of much of Mahon's urbanity.

Approaching this issue from a very different direction, Brendan Kennelly sees Mahon's Protestantism as being at the core of his humanistic vision. Defining humanism as "a form of intelligent loneliness," Kennelly contrasts the "absolving paternalism" of Catholicism with the highly individual morality he associates with Protestant humanism, at least as it manifests itself in Irish culture: "One cannot avoid the term 'Protestant' in describing this humanism because it involves the habitual workings of a conscience and/or of a consciousness which seem interchangeable" (143). Seeing Mahon as a direct descendant of Louis MacNeice, Kennelly understands Mahon's ironic and ambiguous style as the essence of a humane perspective: "And this too is the painful language of the Protestant humanist; words at war within themselves, or at least in argument with each other, ironical, loving, wild, reticent, fragile, solving. This idiomatic argument, this warring in words is evidence of conscience in action" (in Brown and Grene's) *Tradition and Influence in Anglo-Irish Poetry* 143).

Seamus Heaney also sees Mahon as a direct descendant of Louis MacNeice. He captures the complexity of Mahon's position, at least in terms of his affiliation with the Northern Protestant community, in this comment about one of Mahon's poems: "This poem, let it be said, is the work of another poet sprung from the Protestant community in Northern Ireland, although Derek Mahon would be as grateful for being described as a Northern Protestant as James Joyce would have been for being called a Southern Catholic. Mahon is, in fact, the Stephen Dedalus of Belfast'' (48).

Edna Longley, while acknowledging Mahon's Ulster Protestant origins, sees the long-term perspectives in his poems as reaching a more universal level. Taking a position somewhat antithetical to Deane's, she says, ''Mahon's dreams of human absence, his ironical long-term perspectives, have been attacked as denying history and politics. But there are more ways than one of internalizing the pathologies of Northern Ireland. Mahon's poetry partly originates in a deep recoil from Ulster Protestant society, perceived as antithetical to art and 'karma.' The fine poem ''Courtyards in Delft,'' based on de Hooch's genre-paintings, traces the connection between Calvinistic repressions and political oppressions, between virtuous materialism and spiritual lack'' (7). Even so, Longley sees this critique of European Protestantism and the progressivist ideologies it has promoted as ''itself informed by a religious sense of values.'' In a range of his poems, Longley finds that ''millenarian traces adhere to his deeply spiritual sense of the aesthetic'' and concludes on a universal rather than sectarian religious note: ''The scope of Mahon's poetry, its easy leaps from the mundane to the cosmic, the strength and yearning of its rhythms, its aesthetic conviction: all this owes something to residual links with a religiously significant universe'' (8).

As recently as 1991 in his introductory paragraph to Mahon's poetry in the *Field Day Anthology*, Declan Kiberd notes that Derek Mahon remains the ''most underrated Irish poet of the century'' (Vol. 3, 1380). Since then, however, Mahon has gained considerable critical recognition. In 1994 the *Irish University Review* devoted its entire spring/summer issue to Mahon's work, and with that publication Mahon has moved to the forefront of both Irish and international critical attention.

BIBLIOGRAPHY

Works by Derek Mahon

Poetry

Twelve Poems. Belfast: Festival, 1965.
Design for a Grecian Urn. Cambridge, MA: Erato, 1966.
Night-Crossing. London: Oxford University Press, 1968.
Beyond Howth Head. Dublin: Dolmen, 1970.
Ecclesiastes. Manchester: Phoenix Pamphlet Poets, 1970.
Lives. London: Oxford University Press, 1972.
The Man Who Built His City in Snow: London: Poem-of-the-Month Club, 1972.
The Snow Party. London: Oxford University Press, 1972.
In Their Element: A Selection of Poems (with Seamus Heaney). Belfast: Ulsterman, 1977.
Light Music. Belfast: Ulsterman, 1977.
Poems, 1962–1978. London: Oxford University Press, 1979.

The Sea in Winter. Dublin: Gallery, 1979.
Courtyards in Delft. Dublin: Gallery, 1981.
The Hunt by Night. London: Oxford University Press, 1982.
A Kensington Notebook. London: Anvil, 1984.
Antarctica. Dublin: Gallery, 1986.
Selected Poems. New York: Viking Penguin, 1991.
The Yaddo Letter. Oldcastle: Gallery, 1991.
Selected Poems. New York: Penguin/Gallery in association with Oxford University Press;
     1993. (New version removes "A Lighthouse in Maine" and adds "The Yaddo
     Letter.")
The Hudson Letter. Oldcastle: Gallery, 1995; Winston-Salem, NC: Wake Forest Univer-
     sity Press, 1996.

Drama

High Time. Dublin: Gallery, 1985. (After Molière.)
The School for Wives. Gallery, 1986. (After Molière.)
The Bacchae. Oldcastle: Gallery, 1991. (After Euripides.)

Translations

The Chimeras. A version of *Les Chimères* by Gérard de Nerval. Dublin: Gallery, 1986.
Selected Poems by Philippe Jaccottet. London: Viking, 1987.

Studies of Derek Mahon

Allen-Randolph, Jody. "Derek Mahon: Bibliography." In Christopher Murray, *Irish Uni-
     versity Review* 24.1 (Spring/Summer 1994): 131–56.
Heaney, Seamus. "The Pre-Natal Mountain: Vision and Irony in Recent Irish Poetry."
     In *The Place of Writing.* Atlanta: Scholars, 1989, 36–53.
Longley, Edna. "Where a Thought Might Grow." *Poetry Review* 81.2 (Summer 1991):
     7–9.
Murray, Christopher, ed. *Irish University Review* 24.1 (Spring/Summer 1994). (A special
     Mahon issue.)

Edward Martyn

(1859–1923)

Rebecca Creasy Simcoe

BIOGRAPHY

Edward Joseph Martyn was born on January 30, 1859, in County Galway, to a wealthy landowning Catholic family whose roots in Ireland dated back to the eleventh century. Tulira, four miles from Lady Gregory's estate, Coole Park, was Martyn's ancestral home where, even after renovations were made to the centuries-old castle, he chose to live in rather austere conditions. Refusing to marry, he lived with his mother until her death in 1898 and thereafter alone. Martyn's piety and asceticism many of his literary associates considered eccentricities but were reflections of his lifelong devotion to the Catholic faith.

In 1897 Martyn, Lady Gregory, and W. B. Yeats cofounded the Irish Literary Theatre, an endeavor to which he contributed financially and through which he found success with his first two plays. A third play was, however, sharply criticized by the group, and afterward Martyn resigned from the theater, claiming artistic differences. While Yeats and Lady Gregory continued to promote the peasant drama that would characterize the Abbey Theatre, Martyn was under the influence of Continental dramatists and their experiments, particularly those of Ibsen. In 1906 he founded the Theatre of Ireland for the performance of realist drama, and in 1914, with the partnership of Thomas MacDonagh and Joseph Plunkett, he created the Irish Theatre Company.

A loyal Unionist until the turn of the century, Martyn's politics took an about-face as he embraced Home Rule and was elected president of Sinn Fein, serving from 1904 to 1908. His nationalist views, unpopular with the landowning class he once championed, are clearly articulated in his plays. Before he died on December 5, 1923, Edward Martyn promised his art collection to the National Gallery of Ireland, endowed the Gaelic League with a generous sum for the training of Irish teachers and bequeathed his extensive library and much of his family's financial legacy to the Catholic Church.

MAJOR WORKS AND THEMES

Morgante the Lesser: His Notorious Life and Wonderful Deeds (1890) was his first published work and his only novel. Authorship of this satiric look at nineteenth-century values and philosophy was attributed to "Sirius." Morgante's experience in the utopian island-state Agathopolis reveals the young writer's idealism, a condition frequently explored in the plays to come.

Martyn's two earliest plays, *The Heather Field* (1899) and *Maeve* (1899), were produced by the Irish Literary Theatre, which he founded with Yeats and Lady Gregory. The two pieces are markedly different in theme and tone. The former, a realistic drama, was staged with Yeats's controversial play *The Countess Cathleen*; the latter, a romantic piece, appeared in the theater's second season.

The Heather Field—an immediate success for Martyn and considered by most critics to be his greatest work—presents a clash of temperaments: the idealistic earnestness of Carden Tyrrell, a landowner in the west of Ireland, is set against the pragmatic calculations of his wife, Grace. Carden's battles against a disintegrating marriage and a diminishing grasp of his circumstances, which result in his complete mental and financial collapse, are mirrored by his battle against an unconquerable field of heather. The psychological realism and naturalistic setting reflect Martyn's devotion to the work of Ibsen.

In *Maeve*, an example of the Celtic Twilight literature popular within the nationalist movement, the Irish heroine, Maeve O'Heyne, is promised in marriage to a young Englishman, Hugh Fitz Walter. Maeve, like Carden Tyrrell, refuses to accommodate the financially motivated plans of her family, preferring instead to occupy a dreamworld where she pines for a lover she has never met, the prince of the fairy kingdom of Tir nan Ogue. *Maeve* is a highly symbolic piece, and the dramatic conflict is easily identified as the struggle of the pure-hearted Irish against domination by the materialist-minded English.

Martyn's *The Tale of a Town*, a play that satirized both English authority and Irish political corruption, was rejected by his cousin, George Moore (who had joined the Irish Literary Theatre), Yeats, and Lady Gregory. Moore, with Yeats's assistance, rewrote the play as *The Bending of the Bough*. Although Martyn refused to acknowledge the revised piece as his own or even to consider it as a collaboration with Moore, it was produced in 1900 with *Maeve*. After his departure from the company, the original was published with another play, *An Enchanted Sea* (1902).

Martyn wrote two plays that satirized his experience with the Irish Literary Theatre: *Romulus and Remus or the Makers of Delights* (1907) and *The Dream Physician* (1914). The latter was the first play produced by the Irish Theatre Company, which Martyn cofounded with Thomas MacDonagh and Joseph Plunkett, Irish nationalists who were both executed after the 1916 Rising.

CRITICAL RECEPTION

Numerous studies have been written about the Irish Literary Renaissance, and, as a founding member of the Irish Literary Theatre, Martyn's participation is noted. A particularly evenhanded account of Martyn's work for the company is found in Ernest Boyd's early study, *Ireland's Literary Renaissance*, which describes all of the writer's published works and focuses on their context, Irish or otherwise. More recent accounts of Martyn's role in the Irish Literary Theatre, however, tend to reduce him to the kind of caricature found in George Moore's reminiscences of the Irish Literary Revival, *Hail and Farewell*, where Martyn's personal habits and deeply felt principles are characterized as refreshingly bizarre.

Two biographies have been published on Edward Martyn, one by Denis Gwynn and the other by Marie-Thérèse Courtney. Gwynn pays particular attention to separating Martyn's comic reflection, appearing in Moore's account, from the man who was, according to Gwynn, "one of the most original and vigorous characters of his generation" (37). Courtney's biography is a study of Martyn's artistic and intellectual development, and connections are made between the man's life and his writing. Within her in-depth and thoughtful analysis of all of Martyn's published works is, again, an attempt to remove Martyn from the impression left by his cousin.

Ann Saddlemyer investigates the dynamic crosscurrent created by the trio of Yeats, Martyn, and Moore. While particular attention is given to the works that were truly collaborative efforts for the Irish Literary Theatre, Saddlemyer asserts not only that Martyn and Moore found great material in each other but that the phenomenon known as the Irish Literary Renaissance was largely the result of the "chaotic collaboration" of the three diverse temperaments.

The conflicted relationship between Edward Martyn and George Moore has been further explored by the Irish cultural historian F.S.L. Lyons. Patricia McFate's essay is a comparison of Moore's revision of *The Tale of a Town* and Martyn's *The Heather Field*. McFate pays particular attention to the biographical and autobiographical details involved, concluding that the two plays are "samples of a number of Moore and Martyn's portraits of themselves and their contemporaries" (61).

William J. Feeney's *Drama in Hardwicke Street: A History of the Irish Theatre Company* presents a comprehensive and compelling account of Martyn's last theatrical endeavor.

BIBLIOGRAPHY

Works by Edward Martyn

Morgante the Lesser: His Notorious Life and Wonderful Deeds. By "Sirius." London: Swan Sonnenschein, 1890.
The Heather Field and *Maeve*. London: Duckworth, 1899.

The Place-Hunters. The Leader 26 (July 1902).
The Tale of a Town and *An Enchanted Sea*. Kilkenny: O'Grady, 1902; London: Unwin, 1902.
Romulus and Remus or the Makers of Delights. Irish People (December, 21 1907).
Grangecolman. Dublin: Maunsel, 1912.
The Dream Physician. Dublin: Talbot, 1914; London: Unwin, 1914.

Studies of Edward Martyn

Courtney, Marie-Thérèse. *Edward Martyn and the Irish Theatre*. New York: Vantage, 1956.
Feeney, William J., ed. *Irish Drama Series*. Chicago: DePaul University, 1966, 1967, 1972. (Reprints *The Heather Field, Maeve*, and *The Dream Physician*.)
Gwynn, Denis. *Edward Martyn and the Irish Revival*. London: Cape, 1930.
Hall, Wayne. "Edward Martyn (1859–1923): Politics and Drama of Ice." *Eire-Ireland* 15. (Summer 1980): 113–22.
Lyons, F.S.L. "George Moore and Edward Martyn." *Hermathena* 98 (1964): 9–32.
McFate, Patricia. "*The Bending of the Bough* and *The Heather Field*." *Eire-Ireland* 8.1 (Spring 1973): 532–61.
Saddlemyer, Ann. " 'All Art Is a Collaboration'? George Moore and Edward Martyn." In *The World of W. B. Yeats: A Symposium and Catalogue*, ed. Robin Skelton and Ann Saddlemyer. Seattle: University of Washington Press, 1965.
Setterquist, Jan. *Ibsen and the Beginnings of Anglo-Irish Drama*. Vol. 2, *Edward Martyn*. Uppsala: Lundquist, 1960.

Paula Meehan

(1955–)

Lauren Onkey

BIOGRAPHY

Paula Meehan was born to a working-class Dublin family. Her grandfather taught her to read before she went to school, turning her into a "print junkie," as she recently put it (Dorgan 265). She describes school as the first place where she became aware of her social class and its limitations. Meehan began to write poetry and song lyrics at age thirteen, and the first contemporary poets she recalls being interested in were the American Beat poets Lawrence Ferlinghetti, Allen Ginsberg, and Gary Snyder. She attended Trinity College, Dublin, and received an M.F.A. from Eastern Washington University in Spokane. In college, she was greatly influenced by Brendan Kennelly, who was one of her lecturers; she says he left her "with the sense that behind every text there was a human life" (Dorgan 267). Also at college, she was a member of a street-theater group, which she credits with teaching her how to reach an audience. She published her first book of poetry, *Return and No Blame*, in 1984, although she had published very little poetry before that. While working as a community activist, she published her second collection, *Reading the Sky* (1986). Meehan's work was featured in two important anthologies of Irish women's writing, *Pillars of the House* (1988) and *Wildish Things* (1989), which helped to make her reputation as one of the most noteworthy of young Irish women poets. In 1991, she published her third collection, *The Man Who Was Marked by Winter* and, most recently, *Pillow Talk* (1994). She has been Writer Fellow of the Trinity English Department and has received Arts Council bursaries in literature. She continues to teach creative writing in schools, community groups, and prisons, and she disseminates her poetry in a wide variety of formats such as television, radio, broadsheets, and small publications by women's writing groups. Meehan's mother and grandmother still serve as major inspirations for her; as she says, "they won't let me stop" (Dorgan 269).

MAJOR WORKS AND THEMES

Meehan has said, "I still have trouble thinking of poetry as a career. A poet's training is the life," and her poetry reflects the importance of personal expression and experience, often set in opposition to an isolated academic voice. An "I" is prominent everywhere in her poems about her family's past, raising children, and relationships with lovers; she uses open, colloquial language throughout all of her poetry. Her form ranges from short, one-verse poems, to multipart longer works, to pieces of narrative prose. Meehan values accessibility and connection to a community; as she writes in "The Standing Army" from *Pillow Talk*, she sees herself part of "the people," especially working people, who take to the streets. The poem suggests that her ability to take to the streets comes from her connection to her mother, a maternal lineage of inspiration that transforms her into a "warrior"—a word that comes up frequently throughout her work.

Much of Meehan's poetry is taken up with reminiscences of her childhood, such as "Buying Winkles" from *The Man Who Was Marked by Winter*, a poem that tries to re-create the streets and people of her past. In "A Child's Map of Dublin" she reveals that the Dublin of her childhood is gone: "not a brick remains" of the tenement in which she came of age.

Meehan's father appears occasionally in her work, especially in the reconciliation poem "Return and No Blame," but her mother appears repeatedly as a source of inspiration for living and writing in an Ireland she could have hardly imagined. The street life Meehan joins in "The Standing Army" is possible only because she carries her "mother's spear." She seems to recognize her mother's importance first in "The Pattern" from *The Man Who Was Marked by Winter*, emphasizing what they share rather than their differences. She recognizes the roles into which her mother was trapped but asserts that there was some essential, powerful womanhood underneath: a warrior woman. Meehan has discussed the way the women in her family talked and understood life; she recognizes in them a kind of poetic voice: "The central fact about poetry is that it talks about one thing in terms of another thing, and the women in my family lived totally in a world of signs, symbols, portents—where nothing was ever what it seemed, people's dreams were as important as the news, and so talking about one thing in terms of another was a familiar way to operate in the world" (Dorgan 266). The voices of the women from her past give her a strength for her own personal behavior. In "The Ghost of My Mother Comforts Me," the speaker turns to her mother when faced with public ridicule and receives reassurance that she will not be harmed, even by "the lightning bolts of a Catholic god." The mother figure is powerful enough to resist even the Church.

As "The Standing Army" reveals, Meehan's mother is also the source of her desire to speak out for all women. Meehan has come of age as a writer in a time of resurgent feminism in Ireland; as she has said, "The single greatest adventure of my lifetime has been watching and participating in the reassertion of the female power on the planet" (Dorgan 268). Many of her poems attempt to assert that female power, again with an emphasis on the woman as warrior. She has often reached out into the public arena with such poems as "She-Who-Walks-among-the-People," a poem commissioned by Combat Poverty Agency to honor Mary Robinson and presented to her in April 1993. The poem, collected in *Pillow Talk*, is written in the form of a story from "Granny" to the speaker of the poem. Granny tells the story of the oppression of her people and its land, a nightmarish vision. A woman appears from the northwest, whose heart responds "with pity for the people and pity for the women in special." The woman learns law, as Robinson did, and fights for the women of her country. The girl asks if the people lived happily ever after, to which Granny responds that although scattered, they will endure. The poem functions as both a tribute to Robinson and an inspiration to all the young women of Ireland.

Meehan enters into public debate over Irish womanhood in "The Statue of the Virgin at Granard Speaks," a poem that comments on the case of Ann Lovett, who, in 1984, gave birth and then died in secret in front of a statue of the Virgin in Granard. The case exemplified for feminists the disastrous results of Ireland's silencing of women, especially about matters of sexuality and the body. The poem is written in the voice of the statue itself. The Virgin (and therefore the voice of the Church itself) is represented as ignoring Ann in her time of deepest need. The poem forces the audience to question its own and the Church's responsibility to girls like Lovett. By remembering and giving voice to Lovett's tragedy, Meehan connects the story to women's struggle to find a voice. Similarly, in "The Wounded Child," the speaker tells the woman to open up the wounded child inside her, wounded by rape, and let her out. This will allow the woman to be ready for battle. In the spirit of Meehan's belief in poetry as a public performance, the poem was originally conceived as a text for a dance by Rubato, choreographed by Fiona Quilligan, Dublin Theater Festival. As Meehan says, "My poems, though they're autobiographical in one way, are public speech. And the way they're made, what is crafty about them, is to give them battle dress to survive" (Dorgan 269). Ultimately, her work suggests that poetry must function to inspire and protect those who do not have a public voice.

CRITICAL RECEPTION

In a recent article assessing contemporary Irish women poets, Katie Donovan asserts that "Irish women are finding a voice that is unafraid to broach heretofore taboo subjects like desire and the female body," and she cites Meehan as an example of such a voice (505). Meehan is most often written about in the context of the emergence of a new female presence in Irish literature generally and in poetry in particular. Meehan describes the surge of Irish women writers as "a flood tide, and it can't be stopped or turned back" (Dorgan 268). She has most often been anthologized as a woman poet (most recently in Donovan's anthology, *Ireland's Women: Writings Past and Present*). Critics like Donovan and Antoinette Quinn praise Meehan for powerfully rendering contemporary female experience, as well as giving voice to, in Donovan's words, an "urban, working-class perspective" not often seen among women poets. "The Statue of the Virgin at Granard Speaks" is probably the most frequently quoted poem of Meehan's, representative of her perspective on contemporary Irish feminism. Critics praise her frank, personal language and her use of the maternal connection of family in the context of sexually open and urban subject matter. Bill Tinley is representative of the opposite view, which criticizes Meehan for those very same things. He criticized *Pillow Talk* for its "facile version of feminism and the workshop/confessional voice that so beatifies the 'I' " (33).

BIBLIOGRAPHY

Works by Paula Meehan

The Man Who Was Marked by Winter. Loughcrew: Gallery, 1991.
Pillow Talk. Loughcrew: Gallery, 1994.
Reading the Sky. Dublin: Beaver Row, 1986.
Return and No Blame. Dublin: Beaver Row, 1984.

Anthologies

Donovan, Katie. *Ireland's Women: Writings Past and Present.* Dublin: Gill and Macmillan, 1994.
Kelly, A. A., ed. *Pillars of the House: An Anthology of Verse by Irish Women from 1690 to the Present.* Dublin: Wolfhound, 1988.
Smyth, Ailbhe. *Wildish Things: An Anthology of New Irish Women's Writing.* Dublin: Attic, 1989.

Studies of Paula Meehan

Donovan, Katie. "Hag Mothers and New Horizons." *Southern Review* 31.3 (July 1995): 503–14.
Dorgan, Theo. "An Interview with Paula Meehan." *Colby Quarterly* 28.4 (December 1992): 265–69.
Quinn, Antoinette. "Pilgrim Soul." Rev. of *The Man Who Was Marked by Winter. Irish Literary Supplement* 11.2 (Fall 1992): 20.
Tinley, Bill. "The Limitations of the Self as a Poetic Subject." Rev. of *Pillow Talk. Irish Literary Supplement* 14.1 (Spring 1995): 33.

Máire Mhac an tSaoi

(1922–)

Cóilín D. Owens

BIOGRAPHY

Máire Mhac an tSaoi (pronounced Maurya WOK an Tee) was born in Dublin in 1922 into a prominent Catholic, Gaelic, and nationalist family. Her father was Seán MacEntee of the Belfast Old Irish Republican Army (IRA), a longtime Fianna Fáil TD, a cabinet member, and Táiniste. Her mother, Margaret Browne, had three brothers, two of them distinguished clerics: Monsignor Pádraig de Brún, president of University College, Galway, and Michael Cardinal Browne, superior general of the Dominican Order. Both of her Browne grandparents were native speakers of Irish, and the family connection with the living language was maintained when "Father Paddy" (as Máire's spiritual father was affectionately known) built a summer house for the family at Dunquin, Dingle, County Kerry. Máire was educated at the local national school in Dunquin, where she acquired her passion for the language and culture of the Gaeltacht. Her education continued at Alexandra College, Beaufort High School Rathfarnham, and University College, Dublin, where she acquired a double degree in modern languages and Celtic studies in 1941. Until the end of the war she was a scholar at the Dublin Institute for Advanced Studies, which published her *Two Irish Arthurian Romances* (1946). She subsequently attended the Sorbonne on a scholarship (1945–1947) and won an Oireachtas prize for her early Irish poetry. On her return, she qualified as a barrister and then joined the Department of External (now Foreign) Affairs, serving in Paris and Madrid as third secretary. She was soon promoted to first secretary and became part of the new United Nations section in New York from 1957 to 1960 and, during the following two years, to the European Community posting at Strasbourg. She resigned the service in 1962 and married Conor Cruise O'Brien. While pursuing her diplomatic career she was writing and translating: *Margadh na Saoire* appeared in 1956, and *A Heartful of Thought* in 1959. During the United Nations intervention in Katanga, she visited the Congo and lived in Ghana (1962–1965) and New York (1965–1969). The O'Briens adopted two African children, Sean Patrick and Margaret, and have lived in Howth, County Dublin, and Dún Chaoin, since 1969.

MAJOR WORKS AND THEMES

Margadh na Saoire (1956) was an impressive debut for an Irish-language poet. Comprising some forty poems, personal lyrics, experiments in traditional forms, and translations from English, Spanish, and French, it established her as the leading lyricist writing in Irish. The poems conjoin the personal with the classical in the Irish formal tradition while expressing romantic themes in fresh and striking imagery. The poems are most eloquent when articulating the sense of loss, whether personal, of the people of the Gaeltacht, or of the Gaelic past. Thus, the most pleasing poems in this volume express the themes of lost or hopeless love (''Finit,'' ''Labhrann Deirdre''), the passing of traditional life (''Ba Chuimhin Leis an Seanduine . . .''), or colonial exploitation (''Inquisitio 1584'').

Her second book, *Miserere* (1971), is an English translation of Monsignor Pádraig de Brún's reflections on a series of pictures by Georges Rouault. An exercise of familial *pietas*, its citation of the Rouault legend, ''Nous devons mourir, nous et tout ce qui est notre'' (we are fated to die, we and all that is ours), seems also applicable to Mhac an tSaoi's own view of Irish language and culture.

In her second and third collections, *Codladh an Ghaiscígh* (1973) and *An Galar Dubhach* (1980), she abandons the formal experiments of her earlier poetry in favor of a more personal and maternal expression. In their thirty lyrics, many are dedicated to her adopted children, recording their growth into adolescence.

An Cion go dtí Seo (1987) is a cumulative collection of these volumes, to which is added a futher score of lyrics. It embraces a variety of subjects and forms—religious meditations, eulogies for deceased friends and scholars, blessings for children, dedications to the younger Irish-language poets—and registers culture shock in the age of the worldwide media explosion.

Besides the poetry represented in these collections, she has published many other poems, some short stories, and a range of scholarly essays and lectures on Celtic studies and modern and contemporary writing in Irish. She has contributed to various radio series and numerous symposia on Irish culture and history and is a leading critic and patron of younger Irish writers.

Her critical stance favors cautious experiment, respect for canonical standards of expression, and the integrity of the language, valuing its unique role as preserver of the national soul. She has subsequently modified this classicist position, becoming less the critic than the patron of the younger generation of urban writers influenced by modernist and postmodernist trends. Thus, whereas she was inclined to chastise the untraditional use of language in the work of Seán Ó Ríordáin, she admits to a resigned acceptance or even an admiring enthusiasm for later writers such as Alan Titley, Nuala Ní Dhomhnaill, or the group associated with the Irish-language journal *Innti*. For their part, especially for the women writing since 1980, she is the singular voice writing in the bleak years of Ireland's previous political and cultural isolation.

In all of her work, the same themes and ideals persist: affectionate respect for family and intellectual mentors, the love for the people and landscapes of Corca Dhuibhne, and a deep loyalty to the traditions of classic Irish literature. Against these standards she views her own output as well as that of others. Thus, in her estimation, only three Irish writers of the present age reach the highest standards—Tomás Ó Criomthain, Máirtín Ó Cadhain, and Nuala Ní Dhomhnaill.

CRITICAL RECEPTION

Margadh na Saoire (Market of Freedom) was universally praised for its sense of craft, its command of Munster Irish, and its erudition. Like the best examples of lyrical poetry from the Early Irish, Mhac an tSaoi's poetry is disciplined and understated. Her reviewers praise her controlled energy, her passion for the values in Gaeltacht culture rooted in pre-Christian Ireland, and her emulation of Old Irish metrics. Although the volume contains some juvenilia, its many fine lyrics show a disciplined shaping of inherited forms to modern subjects without dissolution into confessionalism. For all its emotional energy, the persona retains a tribal timbre. Subsequently, many of the poems from *Margadh*—such as "Caoineadh," "Do Shíle," "An Chéad Bhróg," "Oíche Nollag," and "Jack"—have become standard selections in Irish-language and school anthologies. Some of her critics wish for more extravagance, but all admire the manner in which she crafts the emotionally intense poems of love and family feeling.

At its periphery, her later work reflects images from the public sphere. Yet her personal universe takes its shape in highly refined phrases drawn from the pure idiom of authentic native speech. Her best poems, so full of personal intensity, are informed by the traditional love song and, behind that, the direct emotion of medieval Gaelic literature. The blend produces a classic elegance, unique in modern Irish poetry. Deeply committed to the language and cultural revival in Ireland, her work exhibits a fidelity to the ideals and discipline of that movement. To the next generation of Irish writers facing even more rapid and fundamental change than she encountered during her formative years, her criticism, counsel, and example are all reminders of the cultural stakes in the potential loss of the national language.

For their part, the next generation of Irish writers, especially the women, appreciate the complex, even paradoxical, example she sets: brought up among passionate cultural nationalists, trained by eminent Celticists to appreciate the impersonality of that tradition, she is the only one of her generation writing with a voice that is emotional, personal, and unambiguously feminine.

BIBLIOGRAPHY

Works by Máire Mhac an tSaoi

Margadh na Saoire. Dublin: Sáirséal agus Dill, 1956, 1971.
A Heart Full of Thought. Dublin: Dolmen, 1959. (Translations from the Irish.)
Miserere. Dublin: Gill and Macmillan 1971. (Translations from the Irish of poems of
    Monsignor Pádraig deBrún.)
A Concise History of Ireland (with Conor Cruise O'Brien). London: Thames and Hudson,
    1972.
Codladh an Ghaiscígh. Dublin: Sáirséal agus Dill, 1973.
"An t-Oileánach." In *The Pleasures of Gaelic Literature*, ed. John Jordan. Dublin: Mer-
    cier, 1977, 25–38.
An Galar Dubhach. Dublin: Sáirséal agus Dill, 1980.
(As Maire Cruise O'Brien). "The Role of the Poet in Gaelic Society." In *The Celtic
    Consciousness*, ed. Robert O'Driscoll. New York: Braziller, 1981, 243–54.
An Cion Go Dtí Seo. Dublin: Sáirséal agus Ó Marcaigh, 1987.
(As Máire Cruise O'Brien). "The Female Principle in Gaelic Poetry." In *Woman in Irish
    Legend, Life and Literature*, ed. S. F. Gallagher. Totowa, NJ: Barnes and Noble,
    1983, 26–37.
"Writing in Modern Irish—A Benign Anachronism?" and "In Celebration of the Irish
    Language." *Southern Review* 31.3 (1995): 424–31, 772–85.

Studies of and Interviews with Máire Mhac an tSaoi

Davitt, Michael. "Cómhrá le Máire Mhac an tSaoi." *Innti* 8 (1984): 37–59.
Henry, P. L. *Dánta Ban: Poems of Irish Women Early and Modern*. Cork: Mercier, 1991.
O'Brien, Frank. *Filíocht Ghaeilge na Linne Seo*. Dublin: An Clóchomhar, 1968, 163–
    201.

Susan L. Mitchell

(1866–1926)

Laurie Champion

BIOGRAPHY

Susan Langstaff Mitchell was born in Carrick-on-Shannon on December 5, 1866. Her father, manager of a bank, died in 1872, and her mother moved to Sligo with the four youngest children, while Susan moved to Dublin to live with her aunts, with whom she eventually returned to Birr, the hometown of the Mitchell family. After her aunts died, she stayed for a while in Sligo to help her sisters manage a school.

In 1899 Mitchell suffered an illness that required treatment in London, where she stayed with the Yeats family until 1900. Later she lived with her mother and sister and various family members. In 1901 she began coediting *The Irish Homestead*, first with H. F. Norman, then with AE. Between 1902 and 1907 her poems appeared in various literary magazines, and in 1908 her poetry collections *Aids to the Immortality of Certain Persons in Ireland, Charitably Administered* and *The Living Chalice and Other Poems* were published. Her third collection, *Frankincense and Myrrh* (1912), was followed by *George Moore* (1916), a biography written for the "Irishmen of To-Day" series.

In 1923 she became assistant editor of AE's *The Irish Statesman*, second series, to which she also contributed reviews and fillers. In her contributions she employed the same lighthearted, satirical approach she used in much of her poetry.

Mitchell was also politically active. She joined Sinn Fein and was well known for mocking members of the Parliamentary Party and other political groups. In her works, she often parodies political issues and both local and national Irish politicians. On March 4, 1926, Mitchell died in Dublin.

MAJOR WORKS AND THEMES

In her humorous writings, Mitchell satirizes herself, the literary figures involved in modern Irish literature, and Irish politics. On the other hand, her serious writings are filled with nostalgia, sentiment, and religious mysticism.

Aids to the Immortality of Certain Persons in Ireland, Charitably Administered is her most celebrated collection of satirical poetry, in which she caricatures literary figures such as Yeats and AE. However, as the subtitle suggests, she writes more as a tribute to these writers than as a means to ridicule their works. The disputes among literary figures that she illustrates represent typical arguments of the time, debates over issues such as the Municipal Gallery in Dublin and the revival of the Irish language.

With the possible exception of her sarcastic portrayal of George Moore, her approach in *Aids to the Immortality of Certain Persons in Ireland* is intended to be taken blithely. The opening ballad, ''Crosses to Ireland,'' and two additional ballads parody George Moore. Another poem, ''The Voice of One,'' satirizes Yeats's position as a dominating figure in the Irish theater. Representative of a subject that recurs throughout the collection, ''The Ballad of Shawe Taylor and Hugh Lane'' refers to the controversies over the establishment of the Municipal Gallery. Irish politics is another motif that recurs in this collection. ''The Irish Council Bill, 1907,'' for example, refers to a proposal that would initiate an administrative council of 106 members, with only 82 elected. The poem commemorates an Irish convention's defeat of the proposal, recognizing it as a compromise of England's promise of Home Rule.

Aids to the Immortality of Certain Persons in Ireland exemplifies some self-reflexive techniques, for it is impossible to understand the poems without recognizing the literary allusions. Not only does Mitchell allude to many other works of art and artists, but she also includes a parody of announcements for future volumes to be published, including a sequel to Yeats's *Ideas of Good and Evil*, entitled *No Ideas Good or Bad*. She also includes a mocking ''Author Review,'' where she reviews the collection of poems, overtly referring to the text itself. In this way, the collection of poems is doubly a work of art that is concerned with art. Moreover, the second edition of *Aids to the Immortality of Certain Persons in Ireland* (1913) is expanded and includes an extended ''Author Review.'' In her self-review, Mitchell says, ''There is too much George Moore in it'' and quotes from her review of his autobiography, *Ave*.

Mitchell also demonstrated her sense of humor in her scholarly endeavors. Her biography of Moore contains many humorous anecdotes and digressions, some about her own life, including incidents involving the time she spent living with the Yeats family. She also comments on other titles in the ''Irishmen of To-Day'' series, a technique similar to the self-reflexive device she employs in *Aids to the Immortality of Certain Persons in Ireland*. When considering Moore, she focuses primarily on his role as novelist, noting issues such as his portrayal of ''pleasant women.'' Although at times her biography parodies Moore, she seriously and analytically looks at his novels. For example, she provides a favorable assessment of the Christian religious story in his novel *The Brook Kerith*.

In addition to her satirical writings, Mitchell wrote serious poetry. Many of her poems are collected in *The Living Chalice* and *Frankincense and Myrrh*. *Frankincense and Myrrh* contains eleven poems, four of which are reprinted from the 1908 edition of *The Living Chalice*. In the 1913 edition of *The Living Chalice*, Mitchell included six poems from *Frankincense and Myrrh*, making the revised and expanded edition of *The Living Chalice* most representative of her serious poetry.

The poems collected in *The Living Chalice* and *Frankincense and Myrrh* are written in the Celtic Twilight tradition, with traditional religious motifs recurring throughout the collections. The poems tend to be confessional, reflective of one who is called to perform a religious duty. The title poem of *The Living Chalice* provides an abstract for the themes the collection conveys, portraying the speaker as a holy chalice ready to walk in communion with the Lord. Other poems in the collection reflect idyllic, pastoral descriptions of nature. For example, in "Carrick" and "The Greenlands," the speaker describes the Irish landscape and the desire to return to her youth. As Richard Kain points out, the collection is filled with contrasting images and subtle tones that describe metaphors for human versus spiritual conditions (68–69).

CRITICAL RECEPTION

Susan Mitchell is considered a minor figure in the Irish Literary Revival, as her work is not considered to be among that of the top literary figures of the movement and has received minimal contemporary critical attention. She did editorial work with AE and often wrote satirical poems alluding to him. He frequently evaluated her work as well. Commenting on her work in general, he says that she portrays "a delightful wit, sentences shaped with a rare grace, and a humanity so kindly and tolerant and understanding that it seemed the consummation of womanly wisdom." He also says Mitchell represents "one of the best Irish women of her time, capable of following the profoundest thinking and of illuminating it by some flash of her own intuition" ("Notes" 1).

Commenting on *Aids to the Immortality of Certain Persons in Ireland*, Kain notes that the second edition lacks the unity of the first, among other distractions, breaking up the "Ballad History" of Moore. He notes, "The magnificent finale of the first volume is almost lost between these satires of Moore" (52). Considering *Aids to the Immortality of Certain Persons in Ireland*, Robin Skelton says she is a "lampoonist rather than a satirist; her best jokes are both local and ephemeral, but on occasion she can wield the weapon of parody with some force" (201). Kain notes that the political poems in the collection "are less successful, because the author relies heavily on contemporary allusions to such now-forgotten names as Dermody, Hynes, or John Cotton. In Miss Mitchell's verse they often remain merely names, because their own characters are not developed'' (55). Concerning ''Anti-Recruiting Song'' in particular, Kain observes that it is less successful than other poems because her portrayal of the ''recruit who becomes a pathetic gull of the military'' is unoriginal. He also notes that perhaps because Mitchell tries ''to avoid sentimentality, or possibly because of her facility in the meter, an unfortunate jingling effect is achieved'' (57).

The Living Chalice initially received generally favorable reviews, including comments about the Celtic spirit, tenderness, mystery, and sincerity portrayed in the poems (Kain 76). Remarking on these poems, AE says, ''Susan Mitchell was more than a witty writer: she was a woman with a true spirituality which lit up the lyrics in her beautiful book of verse, *The Living Chalice*.'' He notes that some of the poems take ''their place in the golden procession of Irish poetry'' (''Notes'' 1). In a more recent assessment of this collection, Kain says that ''in a manner suggestive of Emily Dickinson, spiritual crises are given homely, domestic metaphors'' (71). Commenting on the 1913 edition, where Mitchell adds nearly twice as many poems to those published in the first edition, Kain observes that ''it became apparent that the work represented a personal *via crucis*, a suite expressing the sometimes despairing path of a believer toward a firmer faith'' (64).

Although most of the writers Mitchell portrayed appreciated her comical approach to their lives and works, George Moore was offended by Mitchell's biography of him. He found her too facetious in her satirical approach and thought she attacked his philosophical and religious ideas, misrepresenting his character. Because AE defended Mitchell's book, Moore suspected that AE ''instigated many of the offending passages'' (Hone, *The Life of George Moore* 331). In a more recent evaluation of *George Moore*, Kain notes that Mitchell ''remains unprejudiced in evaluating [his] novels'' (81).

As the sparse contemporary critical attention given to Susan Mitchell demonstrates, she remains a minor figure in the Irish Literary Revival. The few studies of Mitchell's work often discuss the artists she portrayed as much as they discuss her. Rather than considered a poet in her own right, her artistic merit seems to be evaluated in terms of her relation to, and depiction of, major writers such as Yeats, AE, and Moore. Additionally, as Skelton points out, ''Mitchell intended her lampoons to act with maximum efficiency in a particular situation, and did not expect them to interest posterity. As a consequence her work is now largely forgotten, but, when rediscovered, brings back the feel of her times more strongly than the work of many of her more distinguished contemporaries'' (202–3). As future critics review the traditional canon, they may discover that Mitchell is worthy of more scholarly attention, and her works may be reevaluated in light of contemporary literary criticism that could identify her as a more important Irish satirist and humorist than she is presently considered.

BIBLIOGRAPHY

Works by Susan L. Mitchell

Aids to the Immortality of Certain Persons in Ireland, Charitably Administered. Dublin:
New Nation, 1908. (Poetry, rev. and expanded, Dublin: Maunsel, 1913.)
The Living Chalice and Other Poems. Dublin: Maunsel, 1908. (Rev. and expanded,
Dublin: Maunsel, 1913.)
Frankincense and Myrrh. Dublin: Cuala, 1912. (Poetry.)
George Moore. Dublin: Maunsel, 1916. (Biography.)
Preface. *Secret Springs of Dublin Song*. Dublin: Talbot, 1918. (Poetry.)

Studies of Susan L. Mitchell

AE. "Notes and Comments." *Irish Statesman*, March 13, 1926: 3.
————. "The Poetry of Susan Mitchell." *Irish Statesman*, March 27, 1926: 71–74.
Hone, Joseph. *The Life of George Moore*. New York: Macmillan, 1936.
Kain, Richard M. *Susan L. Mitchell*. Lewisburg, PA: Bucknell University Press, 1972.
Skelton, Robin. "Aide to Immortality: The Satirical Writings of Susan L. Mitchell." In
The World of W. B. Yeats, ed. Robin Skelton and Ann Saddlemyer, rev. ed. Se-
attle: University of Washington Press, 1967, 199–206.

John Montague

(1929–)

Ann Marie Adams

BIOGRAPHY

John Montague was born on February 28, 1929, in Brooklyn, New York. He was the third son of James Montague and Mary ('Molly') Carney. His father, who had been involved in Republican activities in County Tyrone, emigrated to New York in 1925. His mother, Mary Carney, didn't follow until 1928, when she brought her two small sons with her. The couple's third son was conceived and born in the new country.

In 1933, the unsuccessful and unemployed James sent his children back to Ireland to live with relatives. John's two older brothers lived with his mother's relations at the Carney home in Fintona, County Tyrone, while John was sent to the Montague home in Garvaghey (also in Tyrone) to live with his paternal aunts.

Although Mary returned to Ireland in 1936, the family was never fully reunited. James remained in Brooklyn, and Mary chose to live with her mother at the Carney family home. John remained at his aunts', seeing his mother only during infrequent visits and holidays. Although he saw his mother more as he grew older, he never overcame his sense of being "abandoned."

Despite this maternal "loss," Montague grew up healthy and intelligent. In Garvaghey Primary School (which he entered in 1935), John was considered an excellent student. His transferral to Glencull Primary School in 1938 gave him a chance to learn Gaelic. According to his own admission, Montague never became a great scholar of the tongue, but he considered his training invaluable to his education.

In 1946 Montague won a County Tyrone scholarship to attend University College, Dublin. While there, he published poems for the first time in a student magazine. He also won a poetry competition. He graduated in 1949 with a B.A. in history and in English, only to stay at University College to begin an M.A. in English.

Montague stayed on in Dublin, working on his M.A. and receiving various prizes for poetry and for scholarly work, until he received a government-sponsored scholarship to study in the United States. Shortly after he received this scholarship, his father returned to County Tyrone. Father and son were able to spend some time together before Montague left for the States in 1953.

Montague's return to America was definitely eventful. He attended graduate school at Yale, Indiana, and Iowa, finally receiving an M.F.A. from Iowa in 1955. Montague then traveled to Mexico and the Pacific Coast, eventually settling in Berkeley, where he intended to undertake a Ph.D. at the University of California. But shortly after his marriage to Madeleine de Brauer in 1956, he returned to Ireland to work at Bord Failte Eireann. For three years, Montague proofread, arranged publications, and wrote speeches for officials. When his wife began work in the French Embassy in 1959, Montague quit his job at Bord in order to write full-time.

Although Montague received much praise for his work, he found it necessary to join the ranks of the employed again, so he served as the Paris correspondent for *The Irish Times*, then as an instructor at Berkeley. During these years (1961–1967), his art flourished, but his marriage did not. He eventually returned to Ireland in 1967. Shortly afterward, he married again and gained the prestigious post as the editor of the *Faber Book of Irish Poetry*.

In 1972, Montague took a teaching position at University College, Cork, where he stayed until 1988. While there, Montague published the majority of his major collections and received a Guggenheim Fellowship (1980). In 1985, he founded *Poetry Ireland* and took time out from Cork to be poet in residence at SUNY-Albany and at Berkeley. Also during these years Montague twice became a father.

In 1988, Montague resigned from University College, Cork, to become a full-time writer again, but he eventually returned to academe, becoming Distinguished Professor in the Writers Institute at SUNY-Albany, a post that he holds to this day.

MAJOR WORKS AND THEMES

Although Montague published *Forms of Exile* in 1958, *Poisoned Lands* (1961) is considered his first major collection of poetry. Filled with reissued poems and new revisions, this work, like its predecessor, is haunted by the specter of "old Ireland"—whether that Ireland be manifest in the figure of priests, in legendary Celtic heroes ("Old Mythologies"), or in ancient women ("Sean Bhean Vocht"). As the title of the collection suggests, this "haunting" is not unproblematic. In many ways, the "lingering" of the past has "poisoned" the land, making it uninhabitable, especially for the young. Yet while the young poet may seek to slough off the ossifying characteristics of tradition, he refuses to renounce his native land in its entirety. Whether it is the "purifying waters" that spurt at the close of "A Footnote on Monasticism" or the "purging lament" in "The Mummer Speaks," Montague displays a small glimmer of possible redemption for Ireland.

Montague's next major work was a collection of short stories entitled *Death of the Chieftain* (1964), a collection that was eventually revised and reissued as *An Occasion of Sin* (1992). The most celebrated story is the eponymous "Death of a Chieftain." Set in Central America (most likely a tribute to the author's own travels in that area), it concerns Bernard Corunna Coote, a reticent and silent explorer of jungles. Ostensibly concerned with Aztec artifacts, the story (and Coote himself) is clearly more concerned with Coote's Irish past. Descended from one of Cromwell's slaughtering men, Coote represents the "colonization of the colonizer"—a settler entranced and overtaken by the splendor of the "conquered" culture. In this way, the darkly comic story retains thematic cohesion with the rest of the collection, which is set in Ulster and southern Ireland. The stories, more "political" in nature than his verse, revolve around Irish culture, Catholicism, and the "problems" of the North.

With *A Chosen Light* (1967), Montague again resumed his poetic career. Although segmented into three distinct sections ("All Legendary Obstacles," "The Country Fiddler," and "The Cage"), concerns about the harsh nature of modern life suffuse and cohere the entire (rather pessimistic) text. Montague termed this particular collection his only "complete flop" ("Figure in Cave" 10).

The pessimism of *A Chosen Light* is slightly (but only slightly) ameliorated by *Tides* (1971), in which Montague explores the process of death and decay, manipulating the imagery of the tide to symbolize the cycle of death and rebirth. Moving away from the "rustic" cast of *Chosen Light*, Montague attempts to insert more of his own experiences in this exploration of Ireland.

The Rough Field (1972), Montague's most celebrated work, is also his most political. A poetic reconstruction of Northern Ireland's troubled history, this extended sequence attempts to chart life in the North since the expulsion of the O'Neills. Admixing contemporary events with historical ones, Montague displays a continuity in Ulster's plight. In "The Bread God," he explores the persecution Catholics suffered under the penal laws. In "A Severed Head," Montague takes historical account and common Irish symbology to explore the linguistic erasure the Celts have suffered. Montague also delves into the destruction that the Irish have brought upon themselves (the building of new roads, the persistence of censorship). Although the work is obsessed with what has been lost, it is not a completely bleak account of Irish history. In "The Wild Dog Rose," Montague metaphorizes Ireland as an old woman (a much-used trope in his oeuvre). Although the "rose" has suffered rape at the hands of brutal betrayers (whether English or Irish), the fragile flower has survived.

A Slow Dance (1975) picks up the theme begun in *Poisoned Lands* (and

Tides) and attempts to render the precarious balance of life and death, the successive turns of life and decay. Using the figure of the dance to metaphorize the cycle of death and regeneration, Montague fleshes out his collection with works suffused by Celtic imagery. These works explore the "double edge/of birth and grave" (37). This collection is often seen as a dark parallel to the work that followed it, *The Great Cloak* (1978), which is considered by many to be some of the finest love lyrics to be written in recent poetry and is meant to narrate the decay of one marriage and the birth of a more lasting relationship. Void of the direct Irish referents of its predecessor, this work focuses on the "universal" nature of love and is thus not secured to any national identity.

With *The Dead Kingdom* (1984), Montague returned to a specifically Irish locale. Relying upon the old theme of *Dinneseanchas*, or the lore of place, Montague constructs this collection as a poetic journey across Ireland. Although this sequence contains some of the historical character of the earlier *Rough Field*, the impetus for this "exploration" of Ireland is entirely personal. The poet is charting his own journey from Cork to Ulster—where his mother's funeral is being held. Throughout the journey, Montague relates poems from his mother's vantage point, attempting to understand the hardships that would drive a mother to abandon her son. Although the incredibly personal nature of this sequence cannot be denied, Montague attempts to use this autobiographical information to broach larger themes. He is still very much concerned with "writing" Ireland, and this extended sequence does act as poetic cartography.

In 1987, Montague issued *The Lost Notebook*, a collection of drawings and narratives that chronicle his early youth in Paris. This "notebook," which charts the sexual and emotional awakening of an Irishman abroad, has been much celebrated.

Montague's latest works were released in 1988–1989. In those years, his collection of essays, *Figure in the Cave and Other Essays* (1989), and *Mount Eagle* (1988) were released. Although selections of his verse have been reissued or rereleased (*Selected Poems* and *About Love*), *Mount Eagle* represents his most recent "new" verse. Still concerned with Irish themes and imagery, *Mount Eagle* nonetheless marks a departure for Montague, as he has let American images and themes play in his verse. His invocation of the eagle and its bestial perspectives demonstrates an awareness and an exploration of Native American legend. Montague may still shudder in front of his construction of the terrible Mother Goddess ("Sheela na Gig"), but this collection offers him a new locale to explore.

CRITICAL RECEPTION

Considered one of the premier poets of his generation, Montague has been the object of a fair amount of scholarship. In fact *Irish University Review* devoted an entire issue (1989) to the poet to celebrate his sixtieth birthday. Most of this critical attention attempts to position the poet within historical Irish "tradition.'' While it may seem natural when discussing a particular nation's or culture's poetry to place a poet within that context, it cannot be denied that Montague's own poetry begs such comparisons and positioning. As many critics have noted, Montague's work is obsessed with the idea of history and place. An exile himself (an Irishman who was born in Brooklyn), Montague's work reflects on his own sense of cultural separation and loss.

Yet while Montague may search for a ''collective past'' into which he can insert himself, he refuses to embrace unproblematically all of Ireland (its myths, history, and symbols). As the critics who have studied his ''exile'' have noted, the separation that Montague feels is more than just a crisis of identity, an accident of birth—it is, in part, a rejection of Romantic ideals and images. While Montague may be entranced by ''Old Mythologies'' or awed by the old people who cluster around him ''like dolmens,'' he cannot return to Yeats's Romantic Ireland. For this reason, his poetry is, according to Robin Skelton, ''divided'' and typified by ''succession and disinheritance'' (John, *Medieval and Modern Ireland* 51). Montague feels the pull of the past and refers to numerous predecessors (such as Yeats and Joyce), but he must demonstrate how he is not, or cannot be, a full part of that legacy.

Most scholars tend to agree upon Montague's themes and messages, as well as his (tenuous) position within the Irish ''tradition.'' While they laud his romantic (love) poetry, they usually circle back to his more ''political'' verse, undoubtably centering upon *The Rough Field*, his most widely studied collection. A few critics, though, have begun to branch out and do more deconstructive readings of Montague's oeuvre. While they acknowledge the message Montague's work is supposed to embody, and while they highlight his ambivalent relationship to Romantic Ireland, scholars, such as Patricia Coughlan (in *Gender and Irish Writing*), have begun to investigate Montague's tropes, such as his use of ''Mother'' Ireland or his Jungian biases. Much has already been written about the poet, but there is plenty of room for new scholarship.

BIBLIOGRAPHY

Selected Works of John Montague

Poisoned Lands and Other Poems. London: MacGibbon and Kee, 1961.
Death of a Chieftain. London: MacGibbon and Kee, 1964. (Reprinted as *An Occasion of Sin*. New York: White Pine, 1992.)
A Chosen Light. London: MacGibbon and Kee, 1967.
Tides. Dublin: Dolmen, 1970.
The Rough Field. Dublin: Dolmen, 1972.
Faber Book of Irish Verse. London: Faber and Faber, 1974.
A Slow Dance. Dublin: Dolmen, 1975.
The Great Cloak. Dublin: Dolmen, 1978.
Selected Poems. 1982. Winston-Salem, NC: Wake Forest University Press, 1989.
The Dead Kingdom. Mountrath: Dolmen, 1984.

The Lost Notebook. Cork and Dublin: Mercier, 1987.

Mount Eagle. Loughcrew: Gallery, 1988.

Bitter Harvest. New York: Scribner's, 1989.

Figure in the Cave and Other Essays. Syracuse: Syracuse University Press, 1989.

Studies of John Montague

Bradley, Anthony G. "Pastoral in Modern Irish Poetry." *Concerning Poetry* 14.2 (1981): 79–96.

Frazier, Adrian. "John Montague's Language of the Tribe." *Canadian Journal of Irish Studies* 9.2 (1983): 57–75.

Grubgeld, Elizabeth. "Topography, Memory and John Montague's *The Rough Field*." *Canadian Journal of Irish Studies* 14.2 (1989): 25–36.

John, Brian. "Contemporary Irish Poetry and the Matter of Ireland: Thomas Kinsella, John Montague and Seamus Heaney." In *Medieval and Modern Ireland*, ed. Richard Wall. Totowa, NJ: Barnes and Noble, 1988, 34–59.

———. " 'A Slow Exactness': The Poetry of John Montague." *The Anglo-Welsh Review* 72 (1982): 46–57.

Johnson, Conor. "Poetry and Politics: Response to the Northern Ireland Crisis in the Poetry of John Montague, Derek Mahon, and Seamus Heaney." *Poesis: A Journal of Criticism* 5.4 (1984): 12–35.

Kernowski, Frank. *John Montague*. Lewisburg, PA: Bucknell University Press, 1975.

———. "Politics and Other Affirmations in John Montague's Narratives." *Journal of the Short Story in English* 8 (1987): 103–112.

Marten, Harry. "Memory Defying Cruelty: The Poetry of John Montague." *New England Review and Bread Loaf Quarterly* 5.1–2 (1982): 214–41.

Murray, Christopher, ed. *Irish University Review* 19.1 (1989). (John Montague issue.)

Poger, Sidney B. "Crane and Montague: 'The Pattern History Weaves.' " *Eire-Ireland* 16.4 (1981): 114–24.

Redshaw, Thomas Dillon. "Montague's Revision: 'The Water Carrier' (1961) and The Rough Field." *Concerning Poetry* 14.2 (1981): 59–75.

———. "That Surviving Sign: John Montague's The Bread God (1968)." *Eire-Ireland* 17.2 (1982): 56–91.

Weatherhead, A. K. "John Montague: Exiled from Order." *Concerning Poetry* 14.2 (1981): 97–113.

Brian Moore

(1921–)

Robert Sullivan

BIOGRAPHY

Brian Moore was born in Belfast on August 25, 1921, into a middle-class Catholic family that had been originally Protestant until Moore's grandfather converted to Catholicism. Moore's father was a confirmed nationalist and, from all accounts, very similar in disposition to Professor O'Neill in the *The Lonely Passion of Judith Hearne* and Gavin Burke's father in *The Emperor of Ice-Cream*. Despite the younger Moore's reaction against his father's ideology and his mother's dogmatized way of life, the mature man is on record as saying that he came to admire their adherence to a faith and a set of firm values. Such a stance finds its way into several novels of Moore's middle period, especially *An Answer From Limbo* and *Fergus*.

Moore left his school, St. Malachy's College, in 1940 with insufficient qualifications for university entrance, and, much like Gavin Burke in *The Emperor of Ice-Cream*, he joined an Air Raid Precaution unit in Belfast. Eventually, Moore enlisted in the British Ministry of War Transport, serving in North Africa, Italy, and France. After the war he was recruited to go with the United Nations to Poland, an experience he called upon some forty years later for his novel *The Color of Blood* (1987). After traveling extensively in Europe, Moore emigrated to Canada in 1948. There he became involved in the newspaper business, at first as a proofreader (like his character Ginger Coffey) and then as a reporter with the Montreal *Gazette*. During this period Moore turned his hand to writing fiction, and while supporting himself on income earned from pulp fiction, he embarked upon the more weighty project of writing *Judith Hearne*, which eventually won him international recognition. He then went on to complete *The*

Feast of Lupercal before leaving for New York to finish *The Luck of Ginger Coffey*.

Moore wrote his next novel, *An Answer From Limbo*, in New York and then moved to California, partly at the request of Alfred Hitchcock, who was interested in filming *The Lonely Passion of Judith Hearne*. Instead, Moore wrote the script for Hitchcock's *Torn Curtain*, a financial and creative disaster, and before long Moore withdrew from the movie business. However, he still lives in Malibu, California, with his second wife, Jean, and has written all his novels subsequent to *An Answer From Limbo* there.

MAJOR WORKS AND THEMES

Despite the fact that some of Moore's novels have international settings—Montreal, New York, California—there has been, even in the most American of his fictions, a continuous investigation into the consequences of an Irish childhood or ancestry on the characters' position in the ''now'' of the narrative. The theme of the fragility of identity recurs when the protagonists ponder their roots and their present rootlessness. This concern with an exilic crisis of identity is a subtext in *The Luck of Ginger Coffey* (1960) and gains momentum in the novels *An Answer From Limbo* (1962), *I Am Mary Dunne* (1968), *Fergus* (1970), and, with an ironic twist, *The Mangan Inheritance* (1979). Essentially, these books depict the struggle to construct and maintain a secure sense of self in a fictional world rife with flux and agnosticism. In these books of Moore's middle period, there is a desire on the part of the protagonists to debate with the past in the hope that the process will result in a securer sense of self in the present. This thematic concern is given paradigmatic utterance in *I Am Mary Dunne*, and Mary's motto—*momento ergo sum* (I remember therefore I am)—underscores the crucial role of memory in these novels.

The importance of memory and the continual desire on the part of these protagonists to help forge a fruitful connection with their past are an ironic counterpoint to the thematic interests of the earlier Belfast books. In these books, atavistic habits are a major factor in the denial of desire. The wholly negative perspective that marked *Judith Hearne* and *The Feast of Lupercal* can be seen, retrospectively, as undergoing a form of transformation. The cruel insularity that permeates the lives of Judy Hearne and Diarmud Devine can also be seen (in relation to these American characters) as providing a bulwark against fragmentation and despair. Nevertheless, as a group, the ''Belfast novels''—from *Judith Hearne* (1955) to *Lies of Silence* (1990)—depict a social space that acts as a site of denial. In the earlier Belfast novels, Judith Hearne, Diarmud Devine, and, to a lesser extent, Gavin Burke in *The Emperor of Ice-Cream* are all ''subject'' to the representatives, or representations (pictures and icons are very important in these books), of abrasive social forces. In the three early novels, the main characters police themselves, whereas in the later *The Doctor's Wife* (1976) and

Lies of Silence Sheila Redden and Michael Dillon, respectively, are strong enough to fly over those nets of insularity and sectarian strife, only to have Belfast's representatives track them down and "kill" any hopes they might have had of happiness. After *Lies of Silence*, which has the air of a summation about it, it remains to be seen whether or not Moore has concluded his protracted, fictional dialogue with his native city.

The Temptation of Eileen Hughes (1981), Moore's other novel set in Northern Ireland, has a different agenda from that of the other Belfast books. It marks a shift in his ouevre toward a number of books that are concerned with spiritual quest and that, generically, move away from a psychosocial realism toward allegory or fable. Moore had experimented with this type of fiction in *The Great Victorian Collection* (1976)—a multilayered fable about creation and its consequences—and he returns to such a method in this set of books from the 1980s. *The Temptation of Eileen Hughes, Cold Heaven* (1983), *Black Robe* (1985), and *The Color of Blood* (1987) are all concerned with the search for certitude in a universe whose God is not fully present as unambiguous meaning, but rather as a text to be read, its author absent. In the absence of such immanent meaning, these characters put their *faith* in the redemptive power of love, which, in its various forms, turns out to be self-sacrificial. Thus, prototypically, Bernard in *The Temptation of Eileen Hughes* realizes before the end of his "passion" and his suicide that "love is a religion whose God is fallible."

Black Robe and *The Color of Blood* return to a concern that Moore had taken up as early as 1972 in his novella, *Catholics*. A fictional world in which *realpolitik* is as important as the meaning of the Sacrament, it is also a world that can no longer be read as God's book, but rather as one rife with all the ambiguities inherent in text. Like Marie Davenport in *Cold Heaven*, the three clerics in these novels confront a host of ambiguous signifiers ("signs") that may or may not signify God's will. This concern with the nature of belief and the mystery of faith (and the various signs that would give them credence) goes back to Moore's first novel, but these books foreground a kind of sacramental or supranatural semiotics. Moore's recent novel, *No Other Life* (1993), continues this exploration of the spiritual and the political. The cleric/redeemer in this novel, Jean Cantave (the initials suggesting the parallels with Jesus Christ), gives his people both spiritual and political hope through his personal sacrifice and his possible return, which can be "read" as a second coming.

CRITICAL RECEPTION

Hallvard Dahlie's 1969 monograph offered not only the fullest account of Moore's work to that date but also the first outline of the author's life. Dahlie's book, which dealt with Moore's work novel by novel up to *I Am Mary Dunne*, was also the first to remark on the parallels with the Joyce of *Dubliners* in Moore's early fiction and the shift in perspective in Moore's work from the harsh realism of the early novels to the "broader vision" inaugurated by *The*

Luck of Ginger Coffey. Dahlie updated his work on Moore by publishing another study in 1981, this time accounting for the novels up to *The Mangan Inheritance* (1979), adding a discussion of the nonfiction as well as a valuable account of the short stories and their relation to the later novels.

The pattern of Moore's fiction—in which the early Belfast books depict characters caught in a world of stasis whereas the books set in North America tend to have characters caught in a world of flux and uncertain identity—was documented in John Wilson Foster's *Forces and Themes in Ulster Fiction* (1974). Foster's treatment of Moore relies heavily on an ethnological, or socioanthropological, approach and is based on van Gennep's theories as outlined in his book *The Rites of Passage*.

In her 1974 monograph and in subsequent articles, Jeanne Flood argues that all Moore's fiction can be reduced to a disguised psychobiography, a family romance in which the son (Moore) plays out (sublimates) the fear of oedipal punishment by inventing characters who are necessarily castrated. This includes his female characters, who ''represent, as well, the artist as castrated man.'' Latent in her monograph, Flood's contention of how Moore's themes affect the form of his fictions reaches a summary position in her article ''Brian Moore and the Failure of Realism'' (1983). Essentially, Flood argues that as the repressed oedipal stuff of Moore's unconscious clamors for more and more expression, the censor of his reportorial realism steps in, as it were, to disguise it.

Michael Paul Gallagher suggests that it is a ''modern aloneness that forms the core of Brian Moore's first book'' and unites this with the ''still more fundamental loneliness of disbelief'' (Gallagher, 1971). In a later essay (see p. 435 Murray 1988), Gallagher traces the meanings of ''faith'' in Moore's work, both religious and metaphysical, and suggests that Moore has ''developed an acute sense for the collapse of any secure meanings as *the* crisis of today'' (52). In the *Irish University Review* ''Special Issue'' (1988), Terence Brown and Brian Cosgrove demonstrate the modernity, indeed the postmodernity, of some of Moore's central concerns; how his characters seek both epistemological and ontological certitudes in a world of ''immanent meaninglessness.''

Moore's ambiguous relationship to faith and belief forms a kind of structuring premise to Jo O'Donoghue's study (1991). In the context of her discussion of *The Color of Blood*, O'Donoghue suggests that Moore ''has come full circle from his earlier anti-clericalism and hostility to belief'' (225). Despite the healthy growth in recognition that Moore has always deserved, very few commentators have engaged the nuances of Moore's stylistic and narratological choices: the craft of his fiction. To O'Donoghue's credit, she deals with this aspect of Moore's fiction in the most intelligent and comprehensive way to date.

BIBLIOGRAPHY

Works by Brian Moore

Novels

The Lonely Passion of Judith Hearne. Boston and Toronto: Little, Brown, 1956. First
    published as *Judith Hearne.* London: Deutsch, 1955.
The Feast of Lupercal. Boston and Toronto: Little, Brown, 1957.
The Luck of Ginger Coffey. Boston and Toronto: Little, Brown, 1960.
An Answer From Limbo. Boston and Toronto: Little, Brown, 1962.
The Emperor of Ice-Cream. New York: Viking, 1965.
I Am Mary Dunne. New York: Viking, 1968.
Fergus. New York, Chicago, and San Francisco: Holt, Rinehart, and Winston, 1970.
Catholics. London: Cape, 1972.
The Revolution Script. London: Cape, 1972.
The Great Victorian Collection. New York: Farrar, Straus, and Giroux, 1975.
The Doctor's Wife. New York: Farrar, Straus, and Giroux, 1976.
The Mangan Inheritance. New York: Farrar, Straus, and Giroux, 1979.
The Temptation of Eileen Hughes. New York: Farrar, Straus, and Giroux, 1981.
Cold Heaven. New York: Holt, Rinehart, and Winston, 1983.
Black Robe. New York: Dutton, 1985.
The Color of Blood. New York: Dutton, 1987.
Lies of Silence. New York: Doubleday, 1990.
No Other Life. London: Bloomsbury, 1993.
The Statement. London: Bloomsbury, 1995.

Nonfiction

"The People of Belfast." *Holiday,* February 1964: 58–63.
"The Expatriate Writer." *Antigonish Review* 17 (1974): 27–30.
"The Writer as Exile." *Canadian Journal of Irish Studies* 2.2 (1976): 5–17.
"Old Father, Old Artificer." *Irish University Review* 12.1 (1982): 13–16.

Studies of Brian Moore

Bibliographies

*The Brian Moore Papers: First Accession and Second Accession. An Inventory of the
    Archive at the University of Calgary Libraries.* Comp. Marlys Chevrefils. Ed.
    Jean F. Tener and Appollonia Steele. Biocritical essay by Hallvard Dahlie. Cal-
    gary: University of Calgary Press, 1987.
"A Brian Moore Bibliography 1974–1987" McIlroy, Brian. *Irish University Review,*
    18.1 (Spring 1988): 106–33.
Studing, Richard. *Eire-Ireland* 10.3 "A *Brian Moore* [sic] Bibliography" (1975): 89–
    105.

Books

Dahlie, Hallvard. *Brian Moore.* Toronto: Copp Clark, 1969.
———. *Brian Moore.* Boston: Twayne, 1981.

Flood, Jeanne. *Brian Moore*. Lewisburg, PA: Bucknell University Press, 1974.

Murray, Christopher, ed. *Irish University Review* 18.1 (Spring 1988). (A Brian Moore special issue.)

O'Donoghue, Jo. *Brian Moore: A Critical Study*. Montreal and Kingston: McGill-Queen's University Press, 1991.

Sullivan, Robert. *A Matter of Faith: The Fiction of Brian Moore*. Westport CT: Greenwood, 1996.

Articles and Interviews

Flood, Jeanne. "*The Doctor's Wife*: Brian Moore and the Failure of Realism." *Eire-Ireland* 18.2 (Summer 1983): 80–102.

———. "*Black Robe*: Brian Moore's Appropriation of History." *Eire-Ireland* 25.4 (Winter 1990): 40–55.

Foster, John Wilson. "Crisis and Ritual in Brian Moore's Belfast Novels." *Eire-Ireland* (Autumn 1968): 86–91.

———. "Passage through Limbo: Brian Moore's North American Novels." *Critique: Studies in Modern Fiction* 13 (1971): 5–18.

Gallagher, Michael Paul. "The Novels of Brian Moore." *Studies* (1971): 180–94.

McSweeney, Kerry. "Brian Moore's Grammars of the Emotions." In *Four Contemporary Novelists: Angus Wilson, Brian Moore, John Fowles, V. S. Naipaul*. Kingston and Montreal: McGill-Queen's University Press, 1983, 56–99.

Mahon, Derek. "Webs of Artifice: On the Novels of Brian Moore." *New Review* 3.32 (1976): 43–46.

Sullivan, Robert. "Brian Moore: A Clinging Climate." *London Magazine*, December 1976/January 1977: 63–71.

George Moore

(1852–1933)

Elizabeth Grubgeld

BIOGRAPHY

George Augustus Moore was born the eldest son of a Catholic landholding family who at the time of his birth held extensive properties near Westport, County Mayo. Moore Hall, the large Georgian house overlooking Lough Carra, was built in 1795, although the family had previously resided in Ireland for several generations. The family became Catholic through intermarriage in the late eighteenth century, and, despite their landholding interests, the Moores were continually associated with causes advocating Catholic and tenant rights, as well as with Irish nationalism.

George Moore's father was a formidable figure in Irish politics. Tempestuous and energetic, he threw himself into a parliamentary career with the same enthusiasm with which he raced horses. Profits from the latter occupation put a new roof on Moore Hall and sent his sons to Oscott (where they were classmates with Oscar Wilde), and the world of the stable yards is lovingly re-created within an English setting in Moore's best-known novel, *Esther Waters* (1894). Moore regarded less affectionately the legacy of his father's involvement in Irish politics. G. H. Moore's participation in liberal causes alienated him from his landholding neighbors and, in his son's view, led to little but his having "wasted his life in the desert of national politics" (*Hail and Farewell*).

Freed from the dreaded fate of an army career by both his incapacity to pass school examinations and his father's early death during a rent strike at Moore Hall, George Moore left Mayo in 1873 for Paris, where he hoped to study painting. Quickly realizing his lack of genuine talent as a painter, he turned instead to literature, beginning in earnest his work as a novelist when financial pressures resulting from the land agitation in Mayo forced him to settle in London during the early 1880s. As his reputation developed, Moore moved into the upper echelons of Mayfair society, despite his sometimes outrageous social behavior and iconoclastic views. He never married but enjoyed love affairs, both real and imagined, with a number of fashionable and artistic women.

At the turn of the century, Moore felt himself at an artistic standstill and much in need of new material and approaches. Encounters with W. B. Yeats, Edward Martyn, and other emerging Irish writers led him to reconsider his earlier repudiation of Ireland as a suitable place for either life or art. Curious about new possibilities in Ireland, he moved to Dublin in the spring of 1901. He brought practical assistance to the fledgling theater, promoted the Gaelic movement, and investigated the literary potential of the nation he had hitherto rejected as hopelessly provincial. Although what are arguably his finest works came out of this period, Moore departed after slightly less than a decade in Dublin, leaving behind him a few friends, more enemies, and a country that had ceased to interest him in its contemporary condition. In 1923, the burning of his ancestral house by Republican forces sealed his permanent estrangement from Ireland.

For the remainder of his life, Moore resided in Ebury Street, London, where he wrote, entertained visitors, and held forth to the admirers who came to see him in his later years. Despite physical deterioration and chronic pain, he continued to write for publication until the last week of his life. In accordance with the spirit of his wish that his ashes be scattered on Lough Carra, they were placed in a replica of a Celtic urn and buried on Castle Island, in the middle of the lake and within sight of the charred shell of Moore Hall.

MAJOR WORKS AND THEMES

Although a number of Moore's novels, short stories, and essays have English characters and settings, they echo the same preoccupations as his overtly Irish works. For the duration of his long career, Moore was concerned with the necessity for individual freedom, be it in artistic expression, religious dissent, sexual difference, or the economic and educational opportunities that make freedom of choice most possible.

Having already published two novels, in 1885 Moore completed a third novel, having as its subject the struggle of an earnest Irish debutante to maintain integrity and independence of mind amid the cupidity, conformity, and sheer boredom of Irish landlord society during the time of the Land League. *A Drama in Muslin* (1886) was based upon firsthand observations of the Dublin social season and drew much of its naturalistic detail from the Mayo community in which Moore came of age. Through literary techniques borrowed from Flaubert, Moore draws close correlations between the restrictions placed upon young women and the economic stultification of the Irish tenant farmers whose labors support a class he represents as entirely idle. ''While the girls are crying for white dresses,'' he wrote in a letter describing his novel to the Dutch naturalist Frans

Netscher, "the peasants are crying for the soil." Moore also returns to the question of his first novel, the obligations of the artist. Through the character of the novelist John Harding, Moore scrutinizes Harding's—and by inference, his own—incapacity to form attachments to the communities that his artistic integrity compels him to analyze.

Immediately following *A Drama in Muslin*, Moore contracted with a French periodical for a series of essays depicting contemporary Ireland; they were revised and later published in English as *Parnell and His Island* (1887). Moore himself despised the book and forbade its reprinting, and while it is awkward and unpolished in style, the vehemence of its repudiation of Ireland makes it an important text for the study of Moore and his period. All representatives of Irish life—the landlord, the tenant, the reformer, the priest, the politician, and the artist—are condemned for their ignorance and self-serving motivations.

The following year, Moore offered the first of seven distinct versions of *Confessions of a Young Man*. In this first work of autobiography, Moore celebrates his rebirth as a cosmopolitan artist. His years in France, he writes, were spent "not as an indifferent spectator but as an enthusiast, striving heart and soul to identify himself with his environment, to shake himself free from race and language and to recreate himself as it were in the womb of a new nationality, assuming its ideas, its morals, and its modes of thought." The work is as iconoclastic in its structure as in its ideas. Alternately absurd and earnest, Moore blends essay, anecdote, conversation, and fantasy into a composite of multiple genres, tenses, topics, and rhetorical positions.

After *Confessions*, Moore had difficulty finding a successful subject or mode of writing. After three failed novels and two books of art criticism and essays, he finally triumphed with *Esther Waters*, which has been issued in more than twenty-five printings and translated into four languages. Although the locale is English, this tale of an impoverished servant's struggle to raise her illegitimate child develops many of the same concerns with which Moore addressed his Irish subjects. He explores the power of religion and poverty in shaping personality, the exploitation of women and children by the upper classes and by men of all classes, the compulsion toward self-development despite environmental constraints, and perhaps of greatest relevance to his Irish works, the duty owed—or not owed—to the community by its individual members.

After producing two novels specifically concerned with the relationship of sexuality and Catholicism, again with an English setting yet recalling his Irish preoccupations, Moore moved to Dublin and set immediately to writing on Irish subjects. His three major Irish works, all completed during this period, not only represent significant refinements in his own skill as a writer but stand as major innovations in the development of the short story, novel, and autobiography in English. *The Untilled Field* (1903) contained six stories that had appeared the prior year in Gaelic as Moore's contribution to the language movement. Modeled after Turgenev's stories of Russian peasant life, these subtle and empathic stories constitute his attempt to delineate the national consciousness. As an integrated portrait of an entire world, the volume influenced Joyce's *Dubliners* and bears comparison with other early twentieth-century English and American experiments with the short story cycle. Some of the best stories are a sequence involving the efforts of a sympathetic priest to bring literary culture to his parish and another concerning the thwarted love of impoverished young people forced by economic and religious constraints to suppress their individual yearnings. Three other stories (and a later conflation appearing in the 1931 edition) relate the frustrations of artists in a nation they discover to be bound by religious bigotry, sexual repression, and a devastating narrowness of viewpoint.

The Lake, originally conceived as part of *The Untilled Field*, grew beyond the confines of the short story to require a separate publication in 1905. Moore revised the novel in 1921, deleting long digressions on Wagner, biblical history, and the Catholic Church, as well as numerous facetious or extraneous passages. He also tightened plot elements and effected seamless transitions between narrative and speech and between different temporal planes. The story of a Mayo priest's awakening to the call of self-realization is accomplished by means of a technically complex indirect discourse, epistolary exchanges between the priest and two correspondents, and the highly unusual technique of representing the subconscious through the depiction of landscape as reflected through the senses of the protagonist. As might be expected, Father Oliver leaves the Catholic Church, his parish, and Ireland itself, but Moore's depiction of all involved is empathic and powerfully felt.

The remainder of Moore's residence in Dublin was devoted to another book of autobiographical reminiscences, a play, and what may well be his masterpiece, the three-volume autobiography *Hail and Farewell* (1911–1914). Much more than a slanderous history of the Irish Renaissance, *Hail and Farewell* presents a tour de force of comic autobiography, as well as a profound meditation on what it means to know and describe the self. Engaging the arts of caricature and parody, Moore explores the origins of self in the language of others, the difficulty of transcending one's origins (and even the shape of one's physical body), and the dangerous temptations of idealism in the search for a pattern by which to see one's life. These explorations regarding the self are, through inference and sometimes through direct analogy, relevant to a nation's own quest for its fundamental narratives of identity. Throughout the text, Moore reveals the power that the world of his father—the Mayo landlord and his retainers—continues to hold upon his imagination, and only with great regret does his autobiographical narrator leave behind the claims of home.

Before *Hail and Farewell* was finished, Moore settled in London, where he continued steadily to write. He revised some of his earlier works, composed a play, edited a volume of imagist poetry, and published more volumes of essays differing from their predecessors in that the exposition of ideas occurs through imaginary dialogues between Moore and various acquaintances. He also developed another version of his short story sequence on the subject of sexual frustration, this time entitled *Celibate Lives* (1927). These restrained psychological studies are technically astute in their condensation and use of indirect discourse, irony, and narrative frames. Two of the newer additions, "Sarah Gwynn" and "Albert Nobbs," are set, respectively, in Belfast and Dublin. While the Irish setting is not integral to their plots, by incorporating autobiographical references within "Albert Nobbs," Moore complicates the frame tale to underscore his thematic inquiry into the evidence by which we decide what is true.

As in his other twentieth-century works, he continued in the efforts of his last decade to bring into prose an oral style with few distinctions between narrative planes. Additionally, the majority of Moore's late years were spent in reading and retelling ancient and medieval literature in translation. Of the works of this last stage, *A Story-Teller's Holiday* (1918) is of greatest Irish interest. Modeled after Boccaccio's *Decameron*, the volume presents a tale-telling contest between Moore and a local Mayo storyteller. The stories range from the comically bawdy to the tragic, and while most derive from the early Christian period, some, like "Albert Nobbs" (later inserted in *Celibate Lives*) are set in mid-nineteenth-century Dublin. Nearly all involve the struggle between clerical authority, on the one hand, and sexual expression and intellectual freedom, on the other. In the book's overtly autobiographical passages, Moore recounts his final farewell to Ireland and makes clear that living in the present requires, for him, a decisive distance from the past, even if so distancing himself results in the same ethical judgments to which he subjected John Harding in his very first work on Ireland, *A Drama in Muslin*, written more than thirty years before.

CRITICAL RECEPTION

Much of the early criticism of George Moore's work—both that found in periodical reviews and in the analysis of literary scholars—tended to view his writings as indicative of his personal morality or his discipleship in various literary movements. Many newspapers and magazines of his own period saw his books as signs of his immersion in the morally suspect waters of French naturalism (or the equally suspect "cesspool" of English decadence). Yet other reviewers found such novels as *A Drama in Muslin* or *Esther Waters* to be the crusading works of a social reformer.

Similarly, early critical studies of Moore tended either to pass ethical judgments upon his life or to trace the correspondences between his works and those of Flaubert, Zola, or Pater. Despite the complexity and variation of his literary output, he became known as a realist, a naturalist, or an aesthete—all depending upon the preferences of the critic. Despite the wide readership he had enjoyed until the mid-1920s, near the end of his life Moore's popularity as a writer suffered a decline. Until the 1950s, no substantial study of his work existed. Several factors may have accounted for this failure of critical attention. His well-publicized antagonism toward contemporary society, his repeated denunciations of Ireland, and his often supercilious manner served to alienate him from many other writers and a younger generation of readers. The naturalism on which his reputation rested during the nineteenth century fell into critical disrepute among many academics, and the autobiographies that perhaps constitute his highest accomplishments were, like most other autobiographies, regarded as sources of biographical data rather than as works of art. Although his well-crafted short stories earned excellent reviews, their explorations of sexual psychology did not find a wide audience among conservative Irish readers, and he was perhaps too old and too Irish to be truly integrated into the circles of younger English writers and critics.

Two fundamental steps in the resurgence of George Moore's reputation have been the publication of Malcolm Brown's *George Moore: A Reconsideration* (1955) and the establishment of the journal *English Literature in Transition* (*ELT*), founded by Helmut E. Gerber. Although Brown's treatment of French influences is sketchy, and he fails to recognize the modernism of Moore's later writing, his analysis is refreshingly unburdened of the heavy-handed treatments of influence or the moral posturing of many earlier critics. Most important, Brown brilliantly explores the pervasive impact of Moore's origins as an Irish landlord. Perhaps stimulated by Brown's book, other critics began to produce a steady flow of critical and bibliographical studies for which *ELT* and other journals provided a forum. Over the years these articles have included investigations of Moore's influence upon James Joyce; his relations with writers like George Russell (AE), W. B. Yeats, D. H. Lawrence, and Olive Schreiner; his interest in Wagner, Shelley, and Turgenev; his interpretations of early Irish history and folklore; and numerous thematic studies of his fiction, particularly in light of its criticism of sexual and intellectual repression in both England and Ireland.

Several collections of essays on Moore followed, edited by Owens (1968), Hughes (1970), Welch (1982), and Dunleavy (1983). The diverse essays that appear in these four volumes cover a wide range of subjects, including biographical reminiscence, stylistic analysis, influence studies, and examinations of Moore's interpretations of Irish life and religious questions.

Moore scholars were greatly aided in 1968 by the publication of Gerber's *George Moore in Transition: Letters to T. Fisher Unwin and Lena Milman, 1894–1910*, as well as Gerber's later collection, *George Moore on Parnassus* (1988). While compilations of Moore's letters had previously appeared, Gerber's editions presented accurate transcriptions, full annotations, and, through their extensive editorial apparatus, a narrative of Moore's development over selected periods. Gerber, like Brown, presents a strong case against the formerly prevailing tendency to see Moore as—to use his own term—"a literary magpie" (*Hail and Farewell*): one whose derivative, if skillful, productions appeared as a long series of disconnected experimentations. Instead, Gerber highlights the questions and preoccupations that appear consistently throughout Moore's work.

In the last decades, five other works have appeared that merit fuller discussion. Richard Cave's 1978 study provides very detailed thematic readings of all of Moore's major novels, with some attention to the historical context in which the works were written. In *George Moore and German Pessimism* (1988), Patrick Bridgewater follows in the tradition of source studies, but with greater specificity and accuracy than many of his predecessors by offering invaluable identifications of those precise passages in the works of the German philosophers that were adapted, quoted, and sometimes plagiarized by Moore. Wayne Hall's *Shadowy Heroes* (1980) is devoted only in part to Moore but is important nevertheless. Hall develops the direction initiated by Brown in looking at Moore's writing as the expression of a disaffected yet guilt-ridden Irish landlord. With a bold reading of *Esther Waters* through the lens of *Parnell and His Island*, Hall discovers a consistent pattern of thought in keeping with what he believes to be the fatalistic withdrawal from action evident in the Irish Renaissance artists as a group. John Wilson Foster's *Fictions of the Irish Literary Revival* (1987) also contains only sections on George Moore but places Moore within a fully developed Irish context. Elizabeth Grubgeld's *George Moore and the Autogenous Self: The Autobiographies and Fiction* (1994) examines Moore's complete corpus as the expression of a lifelong struggle between his attraction toward determinist explanations of human behavior and his need to create himself apart from such influences. Examining the autobiographies, the letters, novels, and many previously neglected short stories, Grubgeld, like Brown and Hall, finds the root of Moore's life's work in his ambivalent attitude toward his homeland and his status as an Irish landlord.

With the development of autobiographical theory in the mid-1970s, more critics began to read Moore's autobiographies and to read them as works of art. Several groundbreaking essays on *Confessions of a Young Man* and *Hail and Farewell* appear during this period, followed by essays on *Memoirs of My Dead Life* (1906) in the 1980s and Grubgeld's focus on the autobiographies in her book. Liberated, in part, by the assertions of theorists as diverse as James Olney and Paul de Man that autobiography is more figure than fact, more metaphor than facsimile, critics have been able to put aside previous qualms regarding the fictive nature of those texts Moore offered to the public as representations of his life and instead to concentrate upon them as literature.

Almost all reviews and critical studies of Moore's work have been listed and, in most cases, described and evaluated in Langenfeld's *George Moore: An Annotated Secondary Bibliography of Writings about Him* (1987). Any serious critical work on Moore must begin with Langenfeld's bibliography and the exhaustive primary bibliography compiled by Edwin Gilcher, *A Bibliography of George Moore* (1970), as well as Gilcher's *Supplement* (1988).

BIBILOGRAPHY

Works by George Moore

Celibate Lives. 1927. London: Heinemann, 1938.
Confessions of a Young Man. 1888. Montreal: McGill-Queens University Press, 1972.

A Drama in Muslin. 1886. Gerrards Cross: Smythe, 1981.
Esther Waters. 1894. New York: Oxford University Press, 1983.
Hail and Farewell. 1911–1914. Gerrards Cross: Smythe, 1976.
The Lake. 1905. Gerrards Cross: Smythe, 1980.
Memoirs of My Dead Life. 1906. London: Heinemann, 1937.
Parnell and His Island. London: Swan Sonnenschein, Lowrey, 1887.
A Story-Teller's Holiday. 1918. London: Heinemann, 1937.
The Untilled Field. 1903. Gerrards Cross: Smythe, 1976.

Studies of George Moore

Bridgewater, Patrick. *George Moore and German Pessimism*. Durham, England: University of Durham Press, 1988.
Brown, Malcolm. *George Moore: A Reconsideration*. Seattle: University of Washington Press, 1955.
Cave, Richard Allen. *A Study of the Novels of George Moore*. Gerrards Cross: Smythe, 1978.
Dunleavy, Janet Egleson, ed. *George Moore in Perspective*. Totowa, NJ: Barnes and Noble, 1983.
Gerber, Helmut, ed. *George Moore in Transition: Letters to T. Fisher Unwin and Lena Milman, 1894–1910*. Detroit: Wayne State University Press, 1968.
———. *George Moore on Parnassus*. Newark: University of Delaware Press, 1988.
Gilcher, Edwin, ed. *A Bibliography of George Moore*. DeKalb: Northern Illinois University Press, 1970.
———. *Supplement to a Bibliography of George Moore*. Westport, CT: Meckler, 1988.
Grubgeld, Elizabeth. *George Moore and the Autogenous Self: The Autobiographies and Fiction*. Syracuse: Syracuse University Press, 1994.
Hughes, Douglas, ed. *The Man of Wax: Critical Essays on George Moore*. New York: New York University Press, 1970.
Langenfeld, Robert, ed. *George Moore: An Annotated Secondary Bibliography of Writings about Him*. New York: AMS, 1987.
Owens, Graham, ed. *George Moore's Mind and Art*. New York: Barnes and Noble, 1968.
Welch, Robert. *The Way Back: George Moore's The Untilled Field and The Lake*. Totowa, NJ: Barnes and Noble, 1982.

Paul Muldoon

(1951–)

Michael F. Hart

BIOGRAPHY

Paul Muldoon was born in Portadown, County Armagh, on June 20, 1951. His parents, Patrick Muldoon and Brigid Regan, came from poor families. Muldoon's youth was spent in the small rural community of Collegelands, where he was raised a Roman Catholic. During the 1950s, when Muldoon was growing up, Collegelands was an enclave of Roman Catholics in the predominantly Protestant parish of Loughgall, a village in which the Orange Order was founded in 1795.

He attended the local primary school and then St. Patrick's College, Armagh, from 1962 to 1969. During this time, partly due to the influence of teachers such as Sean O'Boyle, who taught him Irish, and John McCarter, who encouraged him to write poetry, he began to write seriously. In April 1968, he met the Irish poets Michael Longley and Seamus Heaney at a poetry reading in the Armagh Museum. Both poets influenced his early work and Heaney arranged to publish his first two poems, "Thrush" and "Behold the Lamb," in an issue of *Threshold*. Heaney also brought Muldoon's early poetry to the attention of Charles Monteith, poetry editor at Faber and Faber, where much of his poetry has been published.

In 1969 he enrolled at Queen's University, Belfast, during a time of extreme social tension and political unrest. It was also a time of poetic ferment, especially among a group of poets who met at Seamus Heaney's house and later became known as the "Belfast Group." During his years at Queen's University he befriended a number of writers and critics, among them Edna Longley, Michael Allen, Frank Ormsby, Ciaran Carson, and Medbh McGuckian.

New Weather (1973), his first collection of poetry to be published by Faber and Faber, won an Eric Gregory Award. He also graduated that year from Queen's University with a B.A. in English language and literature, with minors in Celtic and Scholastic philosophy. At the same time he began working as a radio producer for the BBC, a job he held for the next thirteen years. In 1974 he married Anne-Marie Conway, from whom he was later divorced.

Muldoon continued to write poetry while employed at BBC. However, in 1985, after his father's death, he resigned his position and sold the family property in Collegelands. During a nine-month hiatus he lived in Dingle on a stipend from the Irish government-funded Aosadana scheme, where he completed *Meeting the British* (1987), his fifth collection of poetry. After spending the academic year 1986–1987 at Cambridge and the University of East Anglia, he moved to the United States. Brief teaching stints at Columbia, Berkeley, and the University of Massachusetts were followed by a move to Princeton in 1990, where he is currently director of the Creative Writing Program. Muldoon lives near Princeton with his wife, Jean Hanff Korelitz, and their daughter, Dorothy.

MAJOR WORKS AND THEMES

In addition to eight volumes of poetry, Muldoon has published an opera libretto, *Shining Brow* (1993), based on the life of architect Frank Lloyd Wright, published translations from the Irish of the poetry of Nuala Ní Dhomnaill, and edited several collections of Irish poetry, including *The Faber Book of Contemporary Irish Verse*. His recent work includes *The Annals of Chile*, awarded the T. S. Eliot Prize for poetry in 1994, and *The Prince of the Quotidian*, a poetic journal recounting a month in his life during his move to Princeton. He has also written several children's books and a handful of plays, including a one-act play, *Six Honest Serving Men* (1995).

His first two collections of poetry, *New Weather* (1973) and *Mules* (1977), received wide critical praise. They contain finely crafted lyrics announcing a distinctive new voice in contemporary Northern Irish poetry. In poems such as "Dancers at the Moy," "Lunch with Pancho Villa," and "Armageddon, Armageddon" Muldoon combines an ability to create graphic images with a comical sense of the absurd. Many of these early poems are set in the Moy, an Irish village with a rich sense of history and folklore that Muldoon compares with Hardy's Wessex and Faulkner's Yoknapatawpha.

In *Why Brownlee Left* (1980), Muldoon's third volume, he extends the range of his poetic materials to include the medieval Irish voyage tale, *Immram Mael Duin*. In his ironic retelling of this traditional tale he juxtaposes a Byronic sense of poetic form with the language of Raymond Chandler to create an elusive quest narrative. The next two volumes, *Quoof* (1983) and *Meeting the British*, continue his exploration of narrative structure by creating stories composed of fragments of history and cultural memory. In *Quoof* this cultural memory includes his own childhood seen through the prism of hallucination and trance filtered through the effluvia of American popular culture. In the poem "The

More a Man Has the More a Man Wants,'' we are given a bizarre narrative of a picaresque antihero, whose name—which appears in various manifestations—remains somewhat of a mystery. In a series of misadventures this elusive figure travels from Belfast to Florida to Boston, following an itinerary that includes terrorism, drugs, and the recipes of Alice B. Toklas. *Meeting the British*, Muldoon's next collection of poetry, includes the poem ''7, Middagh Street,'' a deftly arranged collage composed of bits of popular culture collected from the history of Brooklyn in the 1940s. In a series of formally inventive vignettes, Muldoon re-creates brief episodes from the lives of several famous inhabitants of this address, including the poets W. H. Auden and Louis MacNeice, the composer Benjamin Britten, and the stripper Gypsy Rose Lee. With references to Boethius, Marx, and Luis Bunuel, Muldoon creates a poetic cultural archive where the sublime is preserved alongside the surreal.

Madoc: A Mystery (1991) is Muldoon's longest and most complex narrative so far. Based loosely on the poem *Madoc* by the English Romantic poet Robert Southey, it recounts the fictional adventures of Southey and Samuel Taylor Coleridge as they travel to the banks of the Susquehanna in search of utopia and the ideals of pantisocracy. The poem is organized in 233 sections, each identified with the name of a thinker in the Western tradition, from the Greek philosopher Thales, to the contemporary physicist Stephen Hawking. Along the way, Muldoon incorporates a Joycean display of allusions to the Welsh Indian myth of Prince Madoc, the Lewis and Clark expedition, American painter George Catlin, Thomas Jefferson, and Aaron Burr, along with literary sources that include Byron and Coleridge in addition to Southey. As in his early poetry, *Madoc* includes references to Irish history, Native American culture, and the history of colonialism.

In *The Annals of Chile* (1994), Muldoon creates a phantasmagoric vision of culture, history, and memory in the poem ''Yarrow,'' which includes cable television, Maud Gonne, Michael Jackson, Davy Crockett, and the drug culture of the 1960s. ''Yarrow'' is also a lyrical evocation of the past-as-present moment of vision, a vision that attempts to dig out Muldoon's own past from the trash heap of the postmodern present. Muldoon's capacity for lyricism is further demonstrated in the deeply evocative elegy ''Incantata,'' written in memory of the Irish artist Mary Farl Powers.

From his earliest poems to *The Annals of Chile* Muldoon explores the possibilities of language through a series of experiments in poetic form and narrative structure. Through his use of puns, wordplay, and the visual hallucination of the poetic image, Muldoon creates a poetic world where the postmodern meets the pastoral, and history vanishes into vision.

CRITICAL RECEPTION

When Seamus Heaney referred to Muldoon as ''one of the best'' poets of his generation writing in Ireland in the late 1970s, he paved the way for widespread critical interest in Muldoon's early poetry. However, despite the enthusiastic early reviews, Muldoon's work has not received the detailed scholarly attention it deserves. Most of the scattered articles, essays, and reviews treat one or two poems in isolation from the corpus of his writing. No one seems to have studied the development of his writing as a whole from the early poetry to the mature works. Although many critics group Muldoon with other Northern Irish poets, such as Tom Paulin, Ciaran Carson, and Derek Mahon, very few have paid attention to Muldoon's work in the comparative, international context that his work evokes and incorporates.

The most extensive critical study of his poetry to date can be found in Clair Wills's book *Improprieties: Politics and Sexuality in Northern Irish Poetry*. In a chapter on Muldoon she writes, "Whatever its extensive subject-matter, Paul Muldoon's poetry is fundamentally bound up with an investigation of the nature of origins, whether biological, familial, 'tribal,' or national" (194). Wills traces Muldoon's transgressive defiance of fixed origins and boundaries to "the fragmented nature of Irish historical experience." Other critics, such as Neil Corcoran (in Hyland and Samuels's *Irish Writing: Exile and Subversion*) and Richard Brown (in Terence Brown's *Ireland's Literature*) emphasize Muldoon's postmodern sense of textuality and narrative dispersal. Dillon Johnston (in *Irish Poetry after Joyce*) and Terence Brown, on the other hand, situate Muldoon's work within the political and cultural contexts of Northern Ireland during the troubled history of its recent past.

Muldoon's relations with his poetic predecessors, including his relation to Yeats, Kavanagh, and MacNeice, are the subject of essays by Jonathan Allison (in Deborah Fleming's *Learning the Trade*) and William A. Wilson. Muldoon's anthology, *The Faber Book of Contemporary Irish Verse* (1986), has been the subject of a lively discussion, especially since Muldoon's anthology selects poets predominantly from Northern Ireland. Douglas Dunn's review in *The Irish Review* and Edna Longley's historically informed essay in Brown and Grene's *Tradition and Influence in Anglo-Irish Poetry* both discuss the importance of this anthology for contemporary Irish poetry in some detail.

Although Muldoon has discounted his own views on politics in the interview with Michael Donaghy published in the *Chicago Review* (1987), much of the recent criticism of his work centers around political questions and themes. Clair Wills's book deals with the question of politics and sexuality, as does Wilson's essay "Paul Muldoon and the Politics of Sexual Difference." Dillon Johnston provides an illuminating social and political history of the poetry of Northern Ireland in the decades following the death of Joyce while Wills's "The Lie of the Land: Language, Imperialism and Trade in Paul Muldoon's *Meeting the British*" (in Corcoran's *The Chosen Ground*) approaches this work from a postcolonial perspective.

All of the critics who have written on Muldoon's work have commented on his hermetic interest in obscure knowledge and his tendency to explore the limits of language and narrative form. Corcoran's essay in Hyland and Samuels's

Irish Writing compares this interest in language to Derrida's critique of logo-centrism and to poststructuralist criticism in general. Richard Brown (in Corcoran's *The Chosen Ground*) finds a mixture of postmodernism and myth that recalls the Irish novelist Flann O'Brien, while Barbara Buchanan, in her essay in Elmer Andrews's *Contemporary Irish Poetry*, relates his interest in the limitations of language to the philosophical tradition of skepticism. In her commentary on *Madoc* she writes, "Allusively and elusively, Muldoon, himself a voyager westward, reflects on all voyagers, legendary, literary or philosophical, treating our attempted excursions 'beyond ourselves' with skeptical zest, the skepticism and the celebration accomplished by his release of the subversive vitality of language itself" (326).

Buchanan's phrase "subversive vitality" aptly describes Muldoon's poetic journey into the bewildering complexities of postmodern histories. Like Joyce, Muldoon has laced his works with enough material to keep the professors busy for a long time. Although many critics, such as Wilson, have drawn attention to the richly diverse sources of Muldoon's poetry, it remains for the next generation of scholars to unearth the unlikely origins of Muldoon's skepticism without murdering his infectious vitality in order to dissect it.

BIBLIOGRAPHY

Works by Paul Muldoon

Knowing My Place. Portrush: Ulsterman, 1971.
New Weather. London: Faber and Faber, 1973.
Spirit of Dawn. Portrush: Ulsterman, 1975.
Mules. London: Faber and Faber, 1977.
Names and Addresses. Belfast: Ulsterman, 1978.
Ed. *The Scrake of the Dawn*. Belfast: Blackstaff, 1979.
Immram. Dublin: Gallery, 1980.
Why Brownlee Left. Wake Forest University Press, 1980.
The O-O's Party: New Year's Eve. Dublin: Gallery, 1981.
Out of Siberia. Dublin: Gallery, 1982.
Quoof. London: Faber and Faber, 1983.
"Five Poems" ["Bears," "Tibet," "Toxophilus," "Pandas," and "Wolves"]. *Times Literary Supplement*, February 10, 1984, 137.
The Wishbone. Dublin: Gallery, 1984.
Selected Poems, 1968–1986. London: Faber and Faber, 1986.
Ed. *The Faber Book of Contemporary Irish Verse*. London: Faber and Faber, 1986.
Meeting the British. London: Faber and Faber, 1987.
Ed. *The Essential Byron*. New York: Ecco, 1989.
Madoc: A Mystery. New York: Farrar, Straus, and Giroux, 1991.
Ed. *The Astrakhan Cloak, Poems in Irish by Nuala Ní Dhomnaill, Translations by Paul Muldoon*. Winston-Salem, NC: Wake Forest University Press, 1992.
Shining Brow. London: Faber and Faber, 1993.
The Annals of Chile. New York: Farrar, Straus, and Giroux, 1994.

The Prince of the Quotidian. Winston-Salem, NC: Wake Forest University Press, 1994.
The Last Thesaurus. London: Faber and Faber, 1995.
Six Honest Serving Men. Dublin: Gallery, 1995.

Studies of Paul Muldoon

Donaghy, Michael. "A Conversation with Paul Muldoon." *Chicago Review* 35.1 (Autumn 1987): 317–31.
Dunn, Douglas. Rev. of *The Faber Book of Contemporary Irish Verse*. *The Irish Review*, November 1986: 84–90.
Frazier, Adrian. "Juniper, Otherwise Known: Poems by Paulin and Muldoon." *Eire-Ireland* 19.1, (Spring, 1984): 123–33.
Heaney, Seamus. *Preoccupations, Selected Prose 1968–1978*. London and Boston: Faber and Faber, 1980.
Jenkins, Alan, "The Art of Gentleness." Rev. of *Why Brownlee Left*. *Times Literary Supplement*, November 14, 1980: 1287.
Keller, Lynn, "An Interview with Paul Muldoon." *Contemporary Literature* 35.1 (Spring 1994): 1–29.
McCracken, Kathleen. "A Northern Perspective: Dual Vision in the Poetry of Paul Muldoon." *The Canadian Journal of Irish Studies* 16.2 (December 1990): 92–103.
O'Neill, Charles L. "Paul Muldoon's *Madoc: A Mystery* and the Romantic Poets." *The Wordsworth Circle* 24.1 (Winter 1993): 54–56.
Wilson, William A. "The Grotesqeuries of Paul Muldoon, 'Immram' to *Madoc*." *Eire-Ireland* 28.4 (Winter 1993): 115–32.
———. "Paul Muldoon and the Poetics of Sexual Difference." *Contemporary Literature* 28.3 (Autumn 1985): 76–85.

Richard Murphy

(1927–)

Kellie Donovan Wixson

BIOGRAPHY

Richard Murphy was born at Milford House, his family's estate in County Galway, on August 6, 1927. His father, William Lindsay Murphy, was mayor of Colombo, Ceylon, and Murphy spent several years there as a young boy.

Murphy was educated in the English public school system. In 1937, he studied music as a member of the Canterbury Cathedral choir. The onset of World War II forced Murphy to return to Milford House, where he discovered the "pleasure ground" of his grandparents' garden. He soon returned to school, winning a scholarship to King's School, Canterbury, and continuing on to Wellington College. Despite the military traditions of both his family and the school, Murphy rejected a career in the military in favor of pacifism and began writing poetry. Another scholarship enabled Murphy to attend Magdalen College, Oxford, in 1944. In 1946, he left Oxford to rent a cottage in Connemara, but he eventually returned and finished his B.A. in 1948, earning his M.A. in 1955. While studying at the University of Paris in 1954, Murphy met Patricia Avis. They were married the next year, and their daughter Emily was born in 1956. The couple divorced in 1959.

Before publishing his first collection of poems, *The Archaeology of Love* (1955), Murphy held a variety of jobs, including insurance broker at Lloyd's of London, and night guard on the river Erriff. During this time he wrote reviews for *The Times Literary Supplement* and *The Spectator* and was director of the English School in Canea, Crete, in the mid-1950s.

In 1959, seeking to simplify his life and to become familiar with the country of his birth, Murphy bought an Irish hooker, the *Ave Maria*, and ran a fishing and tourism business in Cleggan. Murphy's long narrative poems of the sea,

"Sailing to an Island," "The Cleggan Disaster," and "The Last Galway Hooker," took shape during this period, incorporating his firsthand knowledge of sailing.

Murphy's commitment to Cleggan deepened throughout the 1960s and early 1970s. He bought a second hooker, *The Truelight*, in 1961, and his business revitalized Cleggan's fishing industry, which had been dormant since the 1927 storm described in "The Cleggan Disaster." He built his first house in Cleggan in 1966 and purchased High Island in 1969, occasionally staying on the island to work in solitude. He then built a second retreat on nearby Omey Island in 1974.

Murphy moved to Dublin in 1980 to be closer to his friends and peers in the poetry-writing community. Two underlying reasons for this relocation were a sense that he, as well as Cleggan, had changed significantly in the two decades since he had moved there and the unexpected death of his close friend, Tony White, in 1976. Murphy's son, William, was born in Dublin in 1982, and the poet continues to live in his Dublin house, Knockbrack.

Murphy has won several awards throughout his career, including the AE Memorial Award for Poetry (1951), the Guinness Award (1962), two Arts Council of Great Britain Awards (1967, 1975), and the 1983 Literary Award from the American Irish Foundation. He has also taught at numerous English and American universities, including the University of Hull, England; Morley College, London; Colgate University, New York; Bard College, New York; Princeton University; the University of Iowa; and the University of Virginia.

MAJOR WORKS AND THEMES

The primary theme of Richard Murphy's first collection, *The Archaeology of Love*, is his love for Patricia Avis, whom he had met the summer before the collection's publication. This early set of short lyrics previews some of Murphy's poetic interests: his use of traditional forms and meters (e.g., "Auction"), his careful evocation of, and rootedness in, a particular place ("Letter from Babylone"), and the theme of re-creation and renovation ("The Archaeology of Love").

Sailing to an Island (1963) marks several developments in Murphy's poetry. "Sailing to an Island," "The Last Galway Hooker," and "The Cleggan Disaster" establish Murphy's talent for descriptive narrative and precise diction. These three poems, which initiate Murphy's recurring images of islands and the sea, explore the personal and communal legacies of history, as does the poem about his grandmother, "The Woman of the House." *Sailing to an Island* reveals Murphy's attempts to reconcile his Anglo-Irish background and education with his boyhood desire to be, in his words, "truly Irish."

Bridging Ireland's two cultures is the central theme of *The Battle of Aughrim* (1968). The title poem is a long narrative about the final Protestant victory over Catholic forces in 1961, which established the Protestant Ascendancy. Claiming that his ancestors fought on both sides, Murphy blends his personal history with Ireland's national history and shows that the past is still shaping the present. The narrative was originally written as a radio script for the BBC, with four separate sections of varying numbers of shorter poems, in several different voices. The theme of clashing cultures continues in the other poem in this volume, "The God Who Eats Corn," a long piece about Murphy's father's retirement in Rhodesia after a career in the British Foreign Service.

Murphy returns to the Connemara coast in *High Island* (1974), with a greater emphasis on a personal exploration of the self. The language is tighter; the metaphors and images, more layered. Murphy's voice is internal, isolated from the communities that populated his earlier works. Loyalty to the inherent truth of place continues to be significant in this collection. Murphy's desire to unite the disparate cultures in his life is highlighted by the poems reflecting his childhood fears in the exotic culture of Ceylon and by the poems about the Irish itinerants, who are forced to live on the margins of society because they have no land.

Selected Poems (1979) contains some new pieces in addition to revisions of older pieces. Murphy's next major volume of new material, however, was *The Price of Stone* (1985). The collection is divided into two sections: twenty-one poems of various lengths and forms, followed by the title sequence of fifty sonnets. This volume deepens the personal exploration begun in *High Island*, including the sonnet sequence's device of personifying buildings in Murphy's life so that they may address him directly. Because Murphy had moved from Cleggan to Dublin in 1980, the image of the poet moves from sailor to builder; the prices of stone are both private ("Stone Mania") and public ("Folly"), past ("Birth Place") and present ("Wattle Tent"). *The Price of Stone* has a cyclical feel in the way poems from each section balance each other and ends with the joyous birth of Murphy's son.

Murphy's two volumes published in 1989 complement each other across the different cultures of his background. *New Selected Poems* collects the majority of Murphy's earlier works, including most of *Sailing to an Island* and *High Island*, all but eight lines of "The Battle of Aughrim," and all of *The Price of Stone*. This volume exhibits Murphy's development in form and language and traces his concerns with history, culture, and finding a place for the self. Ancient frescoes of dancing women at the site of a fifth-century palace in Sri Lanka are the backdrop for *The Mirror Wall*, a collection of poems inspired by a translation of the songs inscribed at the base of the frescoes in the eighth, ninth, and tenth centuries. These short lyrics are in freer forms and meters than Murphy's previous work but display his interest in language and communication between cultures. No longer distanced from the Ceylon of his childhood, Murphy engages this aspect of Sri Lankan culture in a variety of voices and themes. Like "The Battle of Aughrim," *The Mirror Wall* bridges two cultures through history.

CRITICAL RECEPTION

Richard Murphy's work has received a broad range of critical responses. In his essay in *Richard Murphy: Poet of Two Traditions*, Maurice Harmon acknowledges Murphy's effort to bridge his two cultures, stating that "the dichotomies that are visible in his work . . . should not encourage us to see it merely as a stereotype of the Ascendancy–peasant relationship" (8). Other critics, including Seamus Heaney in his essay from the same volume and James Lafferty in his essay "Perceptions of Roots . . ." (in Kosok's *Studies in Anglo-Irish Literature*), have noted what Edna Longley identifies as "Murphy's excessive consciousness of being an outsider, of needing to work his passage and establish credentials for naturalization" (Dunn's *Two Decades of Irish Writing* 131).

Critics frequently comment on Murphy's emphasis on form and diction. Reviewing *The Price of Stone*, Peter Denman notes that "Murphy quarries some challengingly unusual words. . . . He also has a trick of shifting a word or phrase between its figurative and literal senses" ("Allusive and Aloof, Quizzical and Detached," excerpted in *Contemporary Literary Criticism* [*CLC*], vol. 41 [1987] 319). Elsewhere in the *Poet of Two Traditions* essay, Heaney describes some of Murphy's early narratives as "severely formal," in which "the finish of the verse, the eccentric stress of the metric, the conscious wording" result in "clinker-built poetry" (22).

Murphy's shift to more personal explorations of self in *High Island* and *The Price of Stone* has been widely noted. In Denman's essay cited earlier, he calls *The Price of Stone* "more forthcoming than *High Island*" (319). Denis Donohue disagrees, stating that Murphy "leaves a good deal unsaid. The price of stone is high, apparently, but he hasn't computed it in detail" ("Ten Poets," excerpted in *CLC*, Vol. 41 [1987] 319).

The Mirror Wall has been well received for its own merits, with additional attention to its connections to Murphy's previous work. In "Archaeologies of Love," Denman notes that "[i]n their relationship to antecedent discourse—text, folklore, history—[these poems] are equivalent to 'The Battle of Aughrim' " (58). Antoinette Quinn also comments on this link, asserting that in "[h]istorical site, cultural shrine, mythological locus, Sigiriya is a Sri Lankan Aughrim" (20).

BIBLIOGRAPHY

Works by Richard Murphy

The Archaeology of Love. Dublin: Dolmen, 1955.
Sailing to an Island. London: Faber and Faber, 1963.
The Battle of Aughrim. London: Faber and Faber; New York: Knopf, 1968.

High Island. London: Faber and Faber, 1974.
High Island: New and Selected Poems. New York and London: Harper, 1974.
Selected Poems. London: Faber and Faber, 1979.
The Price of Stone. London: Faber and Faber, 1985.
The Price of Stone and Earlier Poems. Winston-Salem, NC: Wake Forest University Press, 1985.
The Mirror Wall. Winston-Salem, NC: Wake Forest University Press; Dublin: Wolfhound; Newcastle upon Tyne: Bloodaxe, 1989.
New Selected Poems. London: Faber and Faber, 1989.

Studies of Richard Murphy

Bowers, Neal. "Richard Murphy: The Landscape of the Mind." *Journal of Irish Literature* 11.3 (1982): 33–42.
Denman, Peter. "Archaeologies of Love." *Poetry Ireland* 26 (1989): 55–59.
Harmon, Maurice. "By Memory Inspired: Themes and Forces in Recent Irish Writing." *Eire-Ireland* 8.2 (Summer 1973): 3–19.
————, ed. *Richard Murphy: Poet of Two Traditions*. Dublin: Wolfhound, 1978.
Kilroy, Mark. "Richard Murphy's Connemara Locale." *Eire-Ireland* 15.3 (Fall 1980): 127–34.
Kinsella, Thomas. "Murphy, Richard." In *Contemporary Poets*, 2d ed., ed. James Vinson and D. L. Kirkpatrick. London: St. James; New York: St. Martin's, 1975, 1094–95.
"Murphy, Richard." In *Contemporary Literary Criticism*, Vol. 41, ed. Daniel G. Marowski and Roger Matuz. Detroit: Gale Research, 1987. 87 vols. to date, 1973–.
Quinn, Antoinette. "Aughrim in Sri Lanka." *The New Nation* 7 (1989): 20.

Thomas Murphy

(1935–)

Claire Gleitman

BIOGRAPHY

Thomas Bernard Murphy was born in Tuam, County Galway, and attended the Christian Brothers school from age seven. The casual brutality practiced by his instructors left an indelible impression upon Murphy's imagination. The Brothers taught Murphy to distrust religion, which he could not easily detach from the image of a stupid man brandishing a leather strap. He went on to technical school and, in 1955, received a scholarship to attend vocational school.

At the same time, he began to perform in amateur productions at the Tuam Little Theatre Guild, acquainting himself with the works of Synge, O'Casey, and Lorca. He wrote his first dramatic piece on a whim in 1959, when his friend Noel O'Donoghue proposed that they collaborate on a play. The result was a one-act, *On the Outside*, which takes place outside a dance hall that the primary characters cannot afford to enter. Murphy's work as a factory apprentice provided him with intimate knowledge of the frustrations suffered by such men, whose outsider status at the dance hall is an image for their larger sense of exclusion from a world of privilege they cannot fathom or penetrate.

Shortly before composing his first solo effort, *A Whistle in the Dark*, Murphy read *A Streetcar Named Desire*, which (in a 1991 conversation with Claire Gleitman) he called "a punctuation mark in my life." His encounter with Stanley Kowalski, in particular, was revelatory: "I didn't even see Blanche in it; and of course the play is about Blanche. . . . But . . . I had never come across a male character the likes of [Stanley]: plates thrown against the wall, and 'I've got a lawyer acquaintance.' " The result was a blistering tragedy originally entitled *The Iron Men*, which won two amateur playwriting prizes before Mur-

phy submitted it to the Abbey Theatre, which rejected it with the pious observation that Irish people do not behave that way. Hence, Murphy took his play
to London, where it premiered in 1961 as *A Whistle in the Dark.*

Murphy's next work, *The Fooleen* (later retitled *A Crucial Week in the Life
of a Grocer's Assistant*), was also rejected by the Abbey in 1962, prompting
his decision to become an exile in London, where he remained for eight years,
marrying Mary Hamilton-Hippisley in 1966 and writing three plays. From this
distance he found the objectivity to confront Ireland's most wrenching trauma,
the potato blight of 1845–1849, which he dramatized with remarkable emotional
control and Brechtian scope in *Famine.*

But Murphy could not stay away from Ireland, and in 1970 he brought his
family home. The next play to appear, *The White House* (later revised as *Conversations on a Homecoming*), concerns an exile who returns to Ireland in search
of some solidity against which to bolster his fractured self. He finds instead a
culture suffering from a crisis of identity as acute as his own. Still, Murphy has
remained in Ireland ever since and speaks enthusiastically about a changed artistic climate that allows the Irish writer to address Irish experience without
fearing that it is unworthy of dramatic expression.

In recent years, Murphy's explorations have been nurtured by his position as
writer in association first with the Druid Theatre in Galway (from 1983 to 1985)
and then with the Abbey (from 1986 to 1989). The fruit of the Druid years was
the highly acclaimed *Bailegangaire.* But succeeding years brought disappoint-
ments, including lukewarm reviews for *Too Late for Logic* and a revival of *The
Patriot Game.* Prompted in part by this fallow period, Murphy wrote a novel,
The Seduction of Morality (1994). Yet Murphy's reputation continues to rest
upon his plays, whose portrayal of Ireland's lowlife is marked by his own bruis-
ing experiences.

MAJOR WORKS AND THEMES

Tom Murphy is a difficult dramatist to pigeonhole. He has experimented with
various forms, and his dramatic territory extends from dingy hovels in contemporary Dublin to remote villages ravaged by famine in the nineteenth century.
Murphy's subject is the underclass, and his intention is to make the inarticulate
speak. Like Sean O'Casey before him, Murphy is preoccupied with characters
who are economically and linguistically impoverished but who turn their tongue-
tied stammerings into a kind of poetry that is sometimes almost baroque. The atmosphere of his work is electric, poised somewhere between hilarity and despair.

That despair stems in part from the social and cultural upheaval that overtook
Ireland in the late 1950s and 1960s, as a result of government initiatives designed to open the country to foreign investment and hurl it into the modern
age. The result was economic betterment for some and massive shock for many,
as Ireland became, more conspicuously than before, a nation of the haves and
have-nots; the professionals and the working classes; the ''clever blokes'' and

the "thick lads." Thus, in *On the Outside*, the characters' dim awareness of a selective social mobility that excludes them elicits their hopelessness and rage. *A Whistle* goes further, suggesting that the Carney brothers suffer not only from economic disadvantage but from their absorption of a mythology of Irish identity that is no longer operative in the world that they inhabit. Part of the pathos of the play arises from its implicit contrast between the present circumstances of the characters and the absent, putative grandeur of Irish legend. While the Carneys proclaim themselves latter-day Cuchulains fighting for the glory of Eire and their own dear Mama, in truth their mother scrubs floors in Ireland while they subsist as petty criminals in the English suburb to which they have emigrated. Meanwhile, the adversary in their nightly street rumbles is another gang of Irish brothers. It is to this, *A Whistle* suggests, that Irish self-mythologizing has sunk: to a hopeless battle with oneself on foreign ground.

A Crucial Week stages a struggle between an infantilizing woman and the son who longs to escape her shackles. Like Patrick Maguire in *The Great Hunger*, John Joe Moran feels that life has "slipped between the bars" because of a mother to whom he is tied inextricably. The play is enriched by Murphy's textured portrait of Mother, whose castrating tendencies are rendered understandable by the historical legacy that she has absorbed. As Murphy's stage directions remark wryly, there is "something great about her—one could say 'heroic' if it were the nineteenth century we were dealing with." She thus becomes not merely Shan Van Vocht as gossip and nag but an emblem for the damaged, postfamine generations.

Murphy's latest work leaves the midcentury for the century's end. *Bailegangaire*, for example, is set in the 1980s, in a post-DeValera, postmodern Ireland. The play takes place in a decidedly modern 1984, as references to motorcycles and linoleum make clear. But by setting *Bailegangaire* in the west of Ireland in a thatched cottage, Murphy inevitably calls to mind the rural Irish paradise revered by countless Abbey plays and tourist brochures. Yet *Bailegangaire* inhabits that landscape in order to explode its fictions. The peasant Eden of Irish legend, it suggests, is an invention that has spawned an obsessive and crippling preoccupation with the past. The centerpiece of the play is a fragmentary story that the senile Mommo alternately tries, and tries not, to tell. Mommo is driven to tell her story repeatedly, while refusing to relinquish the third-person pronoun that would allow her to acknowledge it as her personal tragedy. Though her granddaughters know large portions of the tale by heart, they have never heard its conclusion, which Mommo doggedly evades until Mary urges her to "finish it, move on to a place where, perhaps, we could make some kind of new start." Gradually, the effort to complete the tale blossoms into a dynamic theatrical exercise in which both Mary and Mommo take part. At last, the past-tense narrative of the embedded story merges with the present tense of the play itself, putting to rest Mommo's tortured obsession with her past, reconciling Mary with her past and present, and resolving the dilemma of Dolly's unwanted pregnancy.

But the culminating litany of the dead and destitute toward which Mommo's story builds has relevance beyond the immediate struggles of the women in the drama. Mommo and her granddaughters are suggestive of a people hobbled by a past that they cannot fully face except through fragments of mythologized narrative. By remaining frozen in time in the moment preceding the catastrophe, incapable of articulating it or moving beyond it, Mommo crystallizes the condition that plagues her culture. Only by gaining access to the past in all its troubled complexity can the women imagine the future as something other than an endless repetition of the past.

Bailegangaire, then, represents a culmination of many impulses in Murphy's drama. From plays of entrapment, he moves toward plays of transcendence, in which the incantatory power of performance works miracles of personal and communal healing. From plays in which women are chased from the stage, Murphy gradually grants them top billing. This movement, in turn, replicates the movement from a fatal patriarchial preoccupation with tribal abstractions to the need to establish community in the present. That community, as it struggles into existence in *Bailegangaire*, encompasses the generations, comprehends the mythic past by incorporating it and passing beyond it, and joyfully embraces the future.

CRITICAL RECEPTION

Although Tom Murphy has won less international recognition than he deserves, his work has not failed to spark its share of discord. When *A Whistle* premiered in 1961, it was reviled in English newspapers with a vehemence usually reserved for criminals and politicians. In Ireland, Murphy's stature was bolstered when *Famine* was staged by the Peacock Theatre in 1968. But several subsequent plays received mixed reviews, and the anticlerical sentiment in *The Sanctuary Lamp* prompted a hostile audience walkout. Not until the late 1980s did Murphy's reputation soar. Both *Gigli* and *Bailegangaire* were universally hailed, and several early plays received triumphant revivals. By the time *A Whistle* was revived by the Abbey in 1987, Murphy was widely regarded as one of the two or three most important Irish playwrights of his generation.

In the gradually amassing critical corpus, certain preoccupations can be identified. Early on, Murphy was viewed as something of an angry young man, in contrast to his more lyrical contemporary Brian Friel. Christopher Murray refined this characterization when he adopted Peter Brook's terminology to describe Murphy's drama as ''rough'' and ''holy.'' These adjectives capture Murphy's immediacy, his Artaudian ability to reach directly for the audience's viscera and disturb (in Artaud's words) ''the sense's repose.'' Murphy's success in doing so stems in part from the unflinching honesty with which he portrays Ireland. In Kenneally's *Cultural Contexts*, Fintan O'Toole has assailed some of his contemporaries for taking refuge in an aestheticized realm; Murphy, by contrast, deals directly ''with the contemporary reality of the country'' (26). Shaun Richards agrees, noting that Murphy's late plays confront the urgent need for

Ireland to transcend both "the old lie of a peasant paradise . . . and the new lie of an economic progress arrested by the helicopter-borne Japanese business-men" who soar over Mommo's cottage in *Bailegangaire* (97).

A further issue is the interplay between language and gesture that critics have detected in Murphy's work. T. Gerald FitzGibbon identifies as a "striking re-current motif . . . the crucial failure of language to deliver its burden of feeling, insight and meaning" (Murray 42). Endowed with a remarkable ear for collo-quial speech, Murphy nevertheless often resorts to nonverbal signs to articulate what words cannot express. Examples of his "pure theatre symbols" include the choreographed movement in *A Whistle* that underscores tribal realignments; the characters dozing in an upturned confessional box at the close of *Sanctuary Lamp*; and *Bailegangaire*'s climactic image of three women together in one bed.

Much recent discussion has focused upon the stylistic innovations in Mur-phy's later work. Nicholas Grene has argued for a progression in Murphy's drama, from the highly representational, "tell it like it is" early plays, to a more postmodern style of playwriting. Despite Murphy's insistence that he cannot abide Beckett, much recent commentary has sought to show the affinities be-tween the two. Yet while Murphy certainly has elaborated his technique, it is worth noting that he was never a textbook realist. As early as *A Crucial Week*, he made use of surrealistic dream sequences; in *A Whistle*, the Carneys are bent upon smashing up the naturalistic mise-en-scène that surrounds them, as if in rebellion against the form itself. In his dialogue, as FitzGibbon has shown, Murphy regularly strays from naturalism's boundaries, adopting instead a flam-boyant opulence that might be described as Synge in an antic mood.

Clearly, though, Murphy's latest work exhibits an increased emphasis upon performance and experimentation. No longer willing to accept the cyclical rep-etition of tragedy as the only paradigm for human (or Irish) experience, Murphy has begun to offer "images of transformation," in O'Toole's words, "rather than mere reflections of reality." The result is a drama of greater scope and feeling that seems likely to widen the playwright's appeal. Indeed, it seems certain that Murphy will receive increasing attention in the coming years, as his drama is persistently occupied with issues of great moment, not only in Ireland but in the rest of the postmodern world.

BIBLIOGRAPHY

Works by Thomas Murphy

After Tragedy. London: Methuen, 1988. (Includes *The Gigli Concert, Bailegangaire, Conversations on a Homecoming*.)

Murphy: Plays One: Famine, The Patriot Game, The Blue Macushla. London: Methuen, 1992.

Murphy: Plays Two: Conversations on a Homecoming, Bailegangaire, A Thief of Christ-mas. London: Methuen, 1993.

The Sanctuary Lamp. Dublin: Gallery, 1984.
The Seduction of Morality. London: Little, Brown, 1994.
Tom Murphy: A Whistle in the Dark. London: Methuen, 1989. (Also includes *A Crucial Week in the Life of a Grocer's Assistant, On the Outside, On the Inside*.)
Too Late for Logic. London: Methuen, 1990.

Studies of Thomas Murphy

Grene, Nicholas. "Talking, Singing, Storytelling: Tom Murphy's *After Tragedy*." *Colby Quarterly* 27.4 (December 1991): 216–20.

Lane, Mark. "Theatrical Space and National Space in Four Plays by Thomas Murphy." *Irish University Review* 21.2 (1991): 219–28.

Maxwell, Desmond. "New Lamps for Old: The Theatre of Tom Murphy." *Theatre Research International* 15.1 (1990): 57–66.

Murray, Christopher, ed. *Irish University Review* 17.1 (1987). (This special Murphy issue contains essays by FitzGibbon, Murray, and Roche, among others.)

O'Toole, Fintan. *The Politics of Magic: The Work and Times of Thomas Murphy*. Dublin: Raven Arts, 1987.

Richards, Shaun. "Refiguring Lost Narratives—Prefiguring New Ones: The Theatre of Tom Murphy." *Canadian Journal of Irish Studies* 15.1 (July 1989): 80–100.

T. C. *Murray*

(1873–1959)

Albert J. DeGiacomo

BIOGRAPHY

T. C. Murray was born in Macroom, County Cork. From his youth Murray desired to be a writer, as evidenced by the character of Stephen Mangan in *Spring Horizon* (1937), Murray's autobiographical novel. In 1893, when he became a national teacher in County Cork, Murray began publishing poems and essays on educational topics to relieve what he called the "oppressive background of officialdom."

Stagestruck, he witnessed performances of Sir Frank Benson's acting company at the Cork Opera House. Urged by Daniel Corkery, Murray wrote a one-act comedy, *The Wheel of Fortune* (1909), for the Cork Dramatic Society, of which Corkery was a founder. The clerical subject matter of *Maurice Harte* (1912) caused so much conflict with the priest manager of his school that in 1915 Murray accepted a headmaster's post at the Inchicore Model Schools, Dublin. The devoted father of five children, Murray persevered in this position until his early retirement in 1932. After the deaths of his wife and his only son, Murray became an admitted recluse, calling his Ballsbridge home "a hermitage."

During Murray's distinguished career, he was chosen a member of the Irish Academy of Letters in 1932 and assumed its presidency in 1952. In 1949, the National University of Ireland awarded him an honorary doctor of literature degree. In addition, he was a director of the Authors' Guild of Ireland, president of the Irish Playwrights' Association, and a member of the Film Censorship Appeal Board. His plays, essays, and book reviews appeared in various important Irish literary magazines.

Standards in the Abbey repertoire from 1910 to the early 1950s, Murray's

plays were regular features on Abbey Theatre tours of America from 1911 to
1935. Translated into German, Spanish, Welsh, Breton, and Japanese and printed
in braille, they are occasionally broadcast by Radio Éireann and appear in Ireland's amateur drama festivals.

MAJOR WORKS AND THEMES

Murray produced a body of seventeen plays in one, two, and three acts, which,
in their dramaturgical structure, show the influence of the well-made-play tradition. In theme and subject matter, they reveal the influence of Ibsen's social-
problem plays. In characterization and environmental climate, they recall the
psychological constriction found in Racine's dramatic world.

The 1909 Cork visit of the Abbey company proved revelatory for Murray as
he saw the possibilities for a "warts-and-all" Cork realism in Lennox Robinson's *The Clancy Name* (1908). In authentic rural speech, Murray's characters
manifest an intense Catholicism that both shapes and represses them. Freedom
from priests and parents is the iterative theme of his peasant tragedy. Oppressed
young males fill his early work, though his later plays show a progressive growth
toward their autonomy.

Murray attracted notice in Dublin with *Birthright* (1910), his debut piece for
the Abbey. A two-act melodrama, it dramatizes a Jacob-and-Esau conflict over
the inheritance of a family farm. At the finale the younger Shane leaps upon
the older, disenfranchised Hugh, striking him a fatal blow. The onstage fratricide
created a sensation at the Abbey Theatre. When *Birthright* appeared—with
Synge's *In the Shadow of the Glen*—on the inaugural bill of "the Irish Players"
in America, it stirred controversy among Irish-American audiences, accustomed
to nostalgic treatments of Ireland in Boucicault-like melodramas.

Maurice Harte (1912), a play in two acts, depicts a young man pressured into
seeking priestly ordination for the prestige and economic security it will bring
to his family. During the rigors of seminary study, Maurice comes to realize
that he has no vocation. Despite his protest and the intercession of a kindly yet
ineffectual priest, his desperate family, led by his mother, forces Maurice to
return to Maynooth. Suffering a conflicted conscience, Maurice suffers a psychological collapse just short of his ordination. The play was viewed as a bitter
critique of the stranglehold of priests and parents upon the younger generation.

The Briery Gap (1914) concerns the effect of a country priest's fiery sermons
on Joan, an unmarried, pregnant woman. When Father Coyne castigates her
lover, Morgan, the young man deserts Joan, who, in the original version, goes
off to drown herself. Although Murray excised the suicide for the play's 1926
republication, the one-act tragedy was considered so potentially controversial
that it was not performed publicly at the Abbey until 1948. In the one-act tragedy
Spring (1918), Murray examines rural poverty and old age prior to the 1909
Pension Act. In the unpublished *The Serf* (1920), Murray questions the clerical

control of schools. Afraid of ecclesiastical reprisals, Murray offered the melo-dramatic two-act play to the Abbey under the pseudonym "Stephen Morgan."

Aftermath (1922), a play in three acts, continues the themes of land hunger, parental oppression, and self-realization. Poet/teacher Myles O'Regan falls in love with a city-bred colleague, yet Mrs. O'Regan badgers Myles into marrying a wealthy farmer's daughter so that the lost O'Regan farm, now owned by the woman's father, may be regained. When life in this loveless marriage proves intolerable, Myles leaves to seek a new existence. The scene shows the obvious influence of Ibsen's *A Doll's House* and marks a new movement in Murray's characters as Myles achieves a hard-won, bitter freedom from family oppression.

Autumn Fire (1924) is considered Murray's masterpiece. A September–May romance, this three-act peasant tragedy depicts middle-aged widower Owen Kee-gan marrying the lovely young Nance Desmond against the wishes of his son and daughter. In this most Racinian of Murray's plays, the claustrophobic en-vironment overwhelms all four characters in the farmhouse as son and wife fall in love under the shattered farmer's gaze.

Influenced by Yeats's and Robinson's interest in Continental drama, Murray attempted to incorporate expressionistic elements, through music and dance, in *The Pipe in the Fields* (1927), a one-act play that dramatizes the artistic awak-ening of young Peter Keville through the inspirational effect of a flute's music. Exploring religious experience, Murray creates the ideal priest, who, as a wis-dom figure, promotes the course of greater personal freedom in Peter's life. Peter's parents are amazed as the priest links artistic expression with the divine, calling it "holy."

The unpublished two-act *Illumination* (1939) treats religious experience and the spiritual life most fully. Murray's last play produced at the Abbey, it dram-atizes a young solicitor's decision to leave his father's country-town law firm in order to become a Trappist monk. With confidence derived from his religious conviction, Brian Egan withstands his father's protest unassisted and liberates himself.

CRITICAL RECEPTION

In *The Irish Renaissance* Fallis claims that Murray, in his strongest contri-butions to the Abbey repertoire, "helped define the norms of modern Irish drama"(112). Hogan, Burnham, and Poteet in *The Rise of the Realists* acknowl-edge Murray's carefully constructed plots (46). Thomas Hogan praises Murray's knowledge of Irish peasant life, asserting that Murray "wrote from within the people" (42). In *The Irish Drama* Malone notes the "deep religious feeling, which forms the undercurrent in all his plays" (186). Though Murray called himself "a bloody realist," Fitzgibbon argues that Murray's awareness of the human spirit, "pushing towards growth, knowledge, achievement, emotional completion, could equally suggest that he is, in some sense, a romantic" (65). Among Murray's deficiencies, critics note his reliance on coincidence to work out his plots, his inability to treat life beyond rural Cork convincingly, and his occasional alteration of play endings, sacrificing truthfulness to avoid offending Catholic Dublin audiences.

Though critics generally regard *Birthright, Maurice Harte*, and *Autumn Fire* as Murray's finest dramas, they also debate the enduring merit of these works. Theater historians Hogan and Burnham claim that "*Birthright* and *Maurice Harte* were sound products of their own era [1910–1912], but do not really transcend it" (*Years* 204). Yet in *Theatre in Ireland*, Micheál ÓhAodha asserts, "In at least six of his fifteen published plays, Murray has left us not only an authentic expression of country ways, but a profound criticism of a way of life that is fast disappearing" (76). Murray's plays also influenced subsequent playwrights Eugene O'Neill, Paul Vincent Carroll, Michael J. Molloy, and John B. Keane.

BIBLIOGRAPHY

Selected works by T. C. Murray

Aftermath. 1922. London: Allen and Unwin, 1926.
Autumn Fire. 1925. London: Allen and Unwin, 1927.
Birthright. 1911. (*The Pipe in the Fields* and *Birthright.*) London: Allen and Unwin, 1928.
A Flutter of Wings. The *[Dublin] Daily Express*, October 13–23, 1930.
The Green Branch. The *Dublin Magazine* 18.3 (July–September 1943): 15–34.
Maurice Harte. 1912. (*Maurice Harte* and *A Stag at Bay.*) London: Allen and Unwin, 1934.
A Spot in the Sun. The *Dublin Magazine* 13.2 (April–June 1938): 14–36.
Spring and Other Plays. (*Sovereign Love* and *The Briery Gap.*) 1917. London: Allen and Unwin, 1926.
Michaelmas Eve. London: Allen and Unwin, 1932.
Spring Horizon. London: Nelson, 1937.

Studies of T. C. Murray

Conlin, Matthew T. "Ireland on the Stage." *Renasence* 13 (1961): 125–31.
———. "The Tragic Effect in *Autumn Fire* and *Desire under the Elms*." *Modern Drama* 1 (February 1959): 228–35.
Connolly, Terence L. "T. C. Murray: The Quiet Man." *The Catholic World* 190 (March 1960): 364–69.
———. "T. C. Murray, 1873–1959." *America*, April 25, 1959 : 245–50.
DeGiacomo, Albert J. " 'Gloom without Sunshine': The Popular and Critical Reception of T. C. Murray in America, 1911–1935." *Eire-Ireland* 30.3 (Fall 1995): 151–64.
———. "Remembering T. C. Murray: The Man and His Plays." *Irish University Review* 25.1 (Fall 1995): 298–307.

Fitzgibbon, T. Gerald. ''The Elements of Conflict in the Plays of T. C. Murray.'' *Studies* 64 (Spring 1975): 59–65.

Hogan, J. J. ''Thomas Cornelius Murray.'' *Studies* 38 (1949): 194–96.

Hogan, Thomas. ''T. C. Murray.'' *Envoy* 3 (November 1950): 38–48.

MacManus, Francis. ''Three First Meetings'' (Daniel Corkery, T. C. Murray, and Padraic Colum). *The Capuchin Annual* (Dublin, 1959): 53–59.

ÓhAodha, Micheál. ''T. C. Murray and Some Critics.'' *Studies* 47 (Summer 1958): 185–91.

Eiléan Ní Chuilleanáin

(1942–)

Jane Biondi

BIOGRAPHY

Eiléan Ní Chuilleanáin, who was born in Cork City in 1942, has been writing and publishing since 1966. The daughter of the late Cormac Ó Cuilleanáin, a professor of Irish, and the writer Eilís Dillon, Ní Chuilleanáin was educated at University College, Cork, and Oxford. She currently teaches English at Trinity College, Dublin, specializing in medieval literature, and coedits the poetry journal *Cyphers*. She is married to the poet Macdara Woods, and they have one son. Winner of the Irish Times Award for poetry in 1966, the Patrick Kavanagh Award for Poetry for her first collection, *Acts and Monuments*, and the Books Ireland Publishers Award for *Site of Ambush*, Ní Chuilleanáin won the O'Shaughnessy Award from the Irish-American Cultural Institute in 1992.

MAJOR WORKS AND THEMES

Acts and Monuments (1972) abounds with nature imagery, but in a decidedly unpastoral manner. Nature here is a powerful, cyclical force that entangles and rewrites lives, memories, and histories. Much like a zoom lens, Ní Chuilleanáin calls our attention to minute details of nature and domestic spaces and then moves to encompass much larger views of historical space and time. History becomes a layer of time in a particular space, a technique that blurs the line between past and present.

Ní Chuilleanáin focuses on the history of structures, monuments, houses, and convents and their relationship to time, history, and nature. These structures exist as memory while simultaneously returning to nature—becoming overgrown in a restructuring and reclaiming of a space. The collection ultimately questions the basis of single historical interpretations.

Site of Ambush (1975) contains remarkably fine work, from the opening poem, "The Lady's Tower," to Ní Chuilleanáin's treatment of war in the title poem. "The Lady's Tower" challenges the masculine trope of the phallic tower by feminizing this image. The tower becomes a domestic and eroticized space. The reinvesting of tropes, symbols, or mythologies is central to the collection as a whole, forcing a reinterpretation of cultural and historical events and symbols. In "Site of Ambush," the Anglo-Irish and civil wars are complicated by the ambiguity of identity. Questions such as who is the enemy and who is guilty refuse clear-cut answers in this lengthy poem. Death becomes an equalizer, and historical time becomes encapsulated in a historical space that contains the bones of generations of men and women, not simply those who died in ambush. Once again nature reclaims and renews that space in an inescapable pattern. Ní Chuilleanáin's concern with the unwritten histories of place and of people unfolds further in "Odysseus Meets the Ghosts of the Women." Odysseus's experiences are rewritten here to emphasize the suffering and anger of the women whom he meets in the underworld and who send him, afraid of the power of their collective voices, fleeing.

The Second Voyage, Ní Chuilleanáin's first effort to reach an American audience, focuses further on the voyage of Odysseus. His universality as mythic origin and, by extension, Homer's as poetic origin become problematic. This collection offers only four new poems in addition to selections from her first two books. As in much of Ní Chuilleanáin's work, images of water and of bones suggesting birth and death, and the continuous recycling of the earth are prevalent. The physical give-and-take between water and human bodies, bones and soil, adds to Ní Chuilleanáin's theme of regeneration, of histories intertwined on one spot.

The Rose-Geranium (1981) consists mainly of two poetic sequences, "Cork," which was published in 1977 along with drawings of the city by Brian Lalor, and "The Rose-Geranium." The two sequences explore issues of perspective and structure. Ní Chuilleanáin compares and contrasts the large, silent cityscapes of the "Cork" section with the minute metaphoric structures of an egg, of grammar, and of "spirals of dust" found in "The Rose-Geranium" section. Both sequences point to language, poetic and prosaic, and its intricate structures, which allow for flexibility, hidden reflections, and inflections—surfaces that belie depth and rely on perspective. The language in this text, imitating her thematic concerns, contains richly textured meanings; her surface language belies depth and explores the power of the veiled phrase. Additionally, Ní Chuilleanáin addresses the body as a structure, with its own complex and entangled history, irreducible to single determinants, as in "Like One Borne Away in a Dance and Veiled." The history of the body, as in much of Ní Chuilleanáin's writing, emerges as the "history of shapes transformed" (41) and transforming, as much through memory as through the poet's reconstruction.

"Pygmalion's Image" opens *The Magdalene Sermon* (1989). This reinterpretation of the myth centralizes the role of women in the creative act.

Pygmalion comes to life on her own with the dangerous and powerful ability to speak. Women's bodies again emerge as central images in the text, specifically in the poem "History," which exchanges the political definition of wars and great events as history for the physical record of women's bodies. Such poems as "In Rome," "J'ai Mal á nos Dents," and "A Voice" similarly recognize women's physical, emotional, and sexual labor in everyday life.

In *The Brazen Head* (1994), the poet assumes the role of storyteller in poems that resemble narratives, many of which, written in the past tense, relate stories and memories from the past. Many of these narratives reexamine how history, both personal and political, becomes recorded and codified. Ní Chuilleanáin tells the unrecorded stories about the hard work and many hands that go into creating art or history, as in the exquisite "Fireman's Lift." Ní Chuilleanáin readjusts our perspective by taking us into the lives of ordinary people who literally and physically make history. *The Brazen Serpent* highlights family and women as those makers of history. Ní Chuilleanáin hints at the untold, through her use of silences, secrets, and witnesses. These secret witnesses, like the poet herself, reconstruct silent histories of family secrets, of unease and discontent. As in much of her work, Ní Chuilleanáin uses female religious imagery, such as nuns and convents, to express what is silenced; however, she reinvests these women with power, as in "The Real Thing," where the masculine image of the brazen serpent, charged with saving the inflicted, remains in the care of a nun.

CRITICAL RECEPTION

Much of the critical reception of her work tends to focus on the historical and mythological aspects of her work and on the complexities of her language. John Wilson Foster has suggested that her "treatment of Irish history is oblique and problematic"; Ciaran Carson has called her work "willfully obscure." The sense that Ní Chuilleanáin's complexity stems from childlike (or womanly) perversity haunts much of the criticism of her work. She is more often blamed, rather than commended, for her intricately layered, indeterminate meanings and complicated symbol structure.

Furthermore, she is censured for being too "Continental" and avoiding Irish subject matter. Robert Henigan observes that "[a]lthough her poems are highly regarded in Ireland, American critics have been, at best, condescending" (106). Readings of reviews by Irish and American critics, however, suggest similar condescension by both groups.

Recently, however, critics such as Deborah Sarbin and Sheila Conboy have reevaluated the Irishness of these poems, finding in her work complex metaphors and allusions that acknowledge unique Irish cultural phenomena. Sarbin notes Ní Chuilleanáin's connection to specifically Irish places in "Old Roads" and "Site of Ambush." In fact Sarbin stresses Ní Chuilleanáin's connections to Yeats's work as strongly as she notes similarities to contemporary women poets.

Conboy writes about the poet's expressions of the female consciousness in her work and her portrayal of women's lives both inside and outside Ireland, myth, and history. Ní Chuilleanáin's work demands fuller attention to her representations of women and her reinterpretation of history and the value of historical events as monuments of time.

BIBLIOGRAPHY

Works by Eiléan Ní Chuilleanáin

Acts and Monuments. Dublin: Gallery, 1972
The Brazen Serpent. Dublin: Gallery, 1994.
Cork (with Brian Lalor). Dublin: Gallery, 1977.
Ed. *Irish Women: Images and Achievement*. Dublin: Arlen House, 1985.
"Love and Friendship." In *The Pleasures of Gaelic Poetry*, ed. Seán Mac Reamoinn.
    London: Allen Land (Penguin),1982.
The Magdalene Sermon. Dublin: Gallery, 1989.
The Rose-Geranium. Dublin: Gallery, 1989.
The Second Voyage. Dublin: Gallery, 1977, 1986.
Site of Ambush. Dublin: Gallery, 1975.
"Woman as Writer: The Social Matrix." *Cranebag* 4.1 (1980).
"Women as Writers: Danta Gra to Maria Edgeworth." In *Irish Women: Images and
    Achievement*, ed. Eiléan Ní Chuilleanáin. Dublin: Arlen House, 1985.

Studies of Eiléan Ní Chuilleanáin

Carson, Ciaran. Review of *Site of Ambush*. *The Honest Ulsterman* Jan/April (1976): 90–
    91.
Conboy, Sheila C. " 'What You Have Seen Is Beyond Speech': Female Journeys in the
    Poetry of Eavan Boland and Eiléan Ní Chuilleanáin." *Canadian Journal of Irish
    Studies* 16.1 (July 1990): 65–72.
Consalvo, Deborah McWilliams. "An Interview with Eiléan Ní Chuilleanáin." *Irish
    Literary Supplement* 12.1 (Spring 1992): 15–17.
Foster, John Wilson. Review of *The Second Voyage*. *Eire-Ireland* 13.4 (1978): 147–51.
Hannan, Dennis, and Nancy Means Wright. "Irish Women Poets: Breaking the Silence."
    Canadian Journal of Irish Studies 26.2 (December 1990): 57–65.
Henigan, Robert. "Contemporary Women Poets In Ireland." *Concerning Poetry* 18.1–2
    (1985): 103–15.
Sarbin, Deborah. " 'Out of Myth into History': The Poetry of Eavan Boland and Eiléan
    Ní Chuilleanáin." *Canadian Journal of Irish Studies* 19.1 (July 1993): 86–96.

Nuala Ní Dhomhnaill

(1952–)

Deborah H. McWilliams

BIOGRAPHY

Nuala Ní Dhomhnaill was born on February 16, 1952, in St. Helens, Lancashire, England. Although raised in both England and Ireland, she locates her familial roots at the westernmost tip of Ireland in Ventry parish, one of several districts in the Dingle Gaeltacht, County Kerry. Ní Dhomhnaill unearths here the premodern origins of Irish expression, an enclave of the idioms, vernaculars, dialects, and locutions of ancient Munster. Within this setting of local custom, nomenclature, topography, and geography she discovers correlations between the history of human existence and the subtext of lingual survival.

Ní Dhomhnaill received a bachelor of arts (with honors) in Irish and English from University College, Cork, in 1972, where she also earned a higher diploma in education the following year. From 1975 to 1980, Ní Dhomhnaill taught at the Middle East Technical University (METU), Ankara, Turkey, as an instructor in English. While living in Turkey she met her husband, and they have had four children.

Among the influences contributing to her literary development are the language patterns and dialectal etymology manifest in ancient Irish manuscripts. Ní Dhomhnaill is especially indebted to those whose skills in preserving fragments of ancient Irish literary works have ensured that the anomalous nature of Irish utterance endures. Furthermore, these literary texts are an invaluable repository of lingual devices: cadences, rhythms, metrical patterns, and idioms.

MAJOR WORKS AND THEMES

A cursory review of Ní Dhomhnaill's writings supports her admission that her task as a writer is one of adaptations and transformations, as well as cultivation of reciprocations. This tenet of writer-as-translator is fundamental to understanding the poet's reliance upon linguistic forms.

Ní Dhomhnaill disdains any homogeneous ideal of a national literary canon, inasmuch as the superscription of cultural identity in Ireland persists. Her poetry depicts themes, images, and motifs of human sexuality, abundant with all the sensual passions and erotic desires of primordial humanity, as a symbol of the de-evolution of the national ideal. We find evidence of this in *Selected Poems/ Rogha Dánta* (1988), in which a majority of the poems addresses the matter of corporeal transgressions.

Through her use of metaphor, imagery, and description, Ní Dhomhnaill renders poetic portrayals of trauma sustained by the human psyche in the wake of a physical assault of insular penetration. For example, the motif of copulation in "Féar Suaithinseach" propagates a potent ethos of unity between church and state, namely, the body politic. The poet's use of liturgical tropes and allusions to clerical impunity introduces the possibility that the meaning of her text resides in the sacrosanct ideal of human physicality. Descriptives and images of ritual in this poem do not represent sanctification alone. They also depict the probability of psychological trauma as an aftermath of the unwilling copulation. Moreover, what the poet describes are clearly her own observations of the violence and terror of unwilling transgression: the physical penetration of a rape.

In another poem, "Táimid Damanta, a Dheirféaracha," the feminine persona of the narrator voices anger at the restrictions of church and state orthodoxies. Religion as a social organization renders a political metaphor to the images of physical insularity abundant throughout Ní Dhomhnaill's texts.

Subthemes of penetration and deposition also illustrate the vulnerability of any cultural form in unprotective environs. Ní Dhomhnaill's desire is, without doubt, to disabuse her audience of any real evidence of cultural homogeneity in Ireland and debunk any existing myths regarding the liberality of today's mainstream Establishment. She achieves this goal in *Pharaoh's Daughter* (1990, rev. 1993) by adopting the journey motif and so breaches the restrictions of worldly structures by probing into otherworldly possibilities.

In such poems as "An Bóithrin Coal," "Hag," and "Ag Tiomáint Siar," Ní Dhomhnaill concedes that she herself is a subtext for regional expression. Her use of nomenclature to describe the geographical and topographical surroundings gives us a sense of local orientation. In addition, the poet's propensity for native inscriptions confirms the role of the writer as that of cultural transliteration. For Ní Dhomhnaill, at least, the Irish language is a kind of political tool, a medium having the capacity to transform the meanings of the invisible into the visible and to render signification to the unconscious, or otherwise repressed, forms of expression.

Ní Dhomhnaill pushes the creative and philosophical experiences of the literary imagination beyond the boundaries of orthodoxy and convention by insisting that the Irish language offers us an expressive mode uncensored and unrestricted by historic indoctrination. The lack of fixities and intonations evident in the idioms and interpretations of the Irish past discloses the possibilities of other modes of being. To change the key of language is to disallow the composition of any literary canon that retains ordinary conventions but negates individual articulations.

The poet's tone in "Ceist na Teangan" is optimistic, advocating a need to ensure the continuity of Irish oral and written traditions. Ní Dhomhnaill insists that we do not mistake the significance of language in bringing about a healing within the modern Irish consciousness and in effecting a reconciliation of a once-variegated and unfractured oral and literary tradition. As she declared in "Why I Choose to Write in Irish," "Irish is a language of enormous elasticity and emotional sensitivity. . . . it is an instrument of imaginative depth and scope."

In her most recent collection of poems, *The Astrakhan Cloak* (1992, rev. 1993), the poet develops her notions about the Irish-language issue into a full-blown treatise that criticizes the use of a predominantly univocal architecture to profile the works of *all* Irish writers. The poet opposes a monoglot form of expression. Her commitment is to Ireland's dual-language tradition and to the formation of a national canon based upon a foundation of literary bilingualism. She maintains in her essay in *Unfinished Revolutions* that a univocal canon germinates more than an anxiety about cultural extinction: "We suppress this discontent into the abyss of the subconscious where it multiplies and increases in conjunction with every other personal shortcoming" (28). It is Ní Dhomhnaill's perception that a writer who denies her own idiomatic inheritance may also endanger her capacity for self-expression.

CRITICAL RECEPTION

In *Changing States* Robert Welch asserts that Irish writers such as Ní Dhomhnaill *must* rely upon the accents and icons of the indigenous culture, if for no other reason than that language by itself denotes a distinct tradition, or cultural identity. Accordingly, Ní Dhomhnaill and others compose in Irish because, as Welch argues, "no other language will do; no other language will convey, for them, those interior states of being. . . . They experience the trauma of the fracturing of Irish culture and attempt the healing process in their own work and language" (3). This linguistic mode of composition has not, however, altogether erased the marks of "trauma" that the poet recalls for us as she speaks out against the extinction of language and resists further loss of Irish expression.

Ní Dhomhnaill's insistence on linguistic variations and literary bilingualism opposes critics who argue instead that Irish society is pluralistic. Discussing with Deborah McWilliams Consalvo (in *Studies* interview) the issue of a homogeneous island populace, the poet alleges that "one of the few, genuinely alternative cultural stances now would be the Irish language tradition, albeit a marginal one" (316). Moreover, in Somerville-Arjat and Wilson's *Sleeping with Monsters*, Rebecca E. Wilson notes that those who choose the Irish language as a literary medium, particularly women writers, embrace a mode of creative expression that is "relevant in relation to the concepts of nationality and cultural identity. . . . [but they] are faced with a literary structure that lends them little entry" (xiii).

Consalvo argues that one of the poet's fundamental objectives is to "cultivate a contemporary arena for the Gaelic tradition" (*Eire-Ireland* 159). The critical focus of Consalvo's essay, however, is on commentary regarding the technical achievements of the poet, particularly her use of such literary devices as idiomatic variations, to create an expression of Irish cultural identity that is able to transcend the antithetical modes of human history, namely, religious, political, social, and linguistic forms of domination. Consequently, Ní Dhomhnaill's commitment to debunking the myth of the Irish language as a defunct form of cultural expression persists.

BIBLIOGRAPHY

Works by Nuala Ní Dhomhnaill

Poetry in Irish

An Dealg Droighin. Corcaigh: Cló Mercier, 1981.
Féar Suaithinseach. Maigh Nuad: An Sagart, 1984.
Feis. Maigh Nuad: An Sagart, 1991.

Poetry in Irish with Translations in English

Selected Poems. Trans. Michael Harnett. Dublin: Raven Arts, 1986.
Selected Poems/Rogha Dánta. Trans. Michael Harnett. Dublin: Raven Arts, 1988.
Pharaoh's Daughter. Ireland: Gallery, 1990.
The Astrakhan Cloak. Trans. Paul Muldoon. Ireland: Gallery, 1992.
The Astrakhan Cloak. Trans. Paul Muldoon. Winston-Salem NC: Wake Forest University Press, 1993.
Pharaoh's Daughter. Rev. ed. Winston-Salem NC: Wake Forest University Press, 1993.

Other Writings

"An Ghaeilge Mar Uirlis Fheiminfeach." *Unfinished Revolutions: Essays on the Irish Women's Movement*. Belfast: Meadbh, 1989.
Jumping Off Shadows: Selected Modern Irish Poets 1946–1994. Coedited by Greg Delanty. Cork, Ireland: University College Cork Press, 1995.
"Survival of the Irish." *Los Angeles Times Magazine* (March 5, 1995): 25–26, 36.
"Why I Choose to Write in Irish: The Corpse That Sits Up and Talks Back." *New York Times Book Review* (January 8, 1995): 3, 27–28.

Studies of Nuala Ní Dhomhnaill

Cannon, M. Louise. "The Extraordinary within the Ordinary: The Poetry of Eavan Boland and Nuala Ní Dhomhnaill." *South Atlantic Review* 60.2 (May 1995): 31–46.

Consalvo, Deborah McWilliams. " 'Adaptations and Transformations': An Interview with Nuala Ní Dhomhnaill." *Studies* 83.331 (Autumn 1994): 313–20.

———. "The Lingual Ideal in the Poetry of Nuala Ní Dhomhnaill." *Eire-Ireland* 30.2 (Summer 1995): 148–61.

McDiarmid, Lucy, and Michael Durkan. "Questions and Answers: Nuala Ní Dhomhnaill." *Irish Literary Supplement* 6.2 (Fall 1987): 41–43.

O'Connor, Mary. "Sex, Lies and Sovereignty: Nuala Ní Dhomhnaill's Re-vision of *The Tain.*" *Working Papers in Irish Studies* 4 (1992).

Edna O'Brien

(1930–)

Allison T. Hild

BIOGRAPHY

Edna O'Brien was born on December 15, 1930, in County Clare. She grew up on a farm with few books but received a national school education, during which a teacher supported her interest in writing. In 1941, she traveled to County Galway to attend school at the Convent of Mercy. In 1946 she began studies at the Pharmaceutical College of Ireland in Dublin. Dublin brought greater experience to O'Brien, including her first reading of James Joyce. By 1948 she had begun sending small contributions to the *Irish Press*. O'Brien's writing was encouraged by Peadar O'Donnell, novelist, an editor at *The Bell*, and mentor to many young Irish writers. In 1951 O'Brien married Ernest Gebler, also a novelist, with whom she had two sons. She and her family moved to London in 1959. Since O'Brien and Gebler's divorce in 1964, she has continued to live in London.

As an author, O'Brien feels it was imperative for her to leave Ireland in order to be able to write about it, "[b]ecause one needs the formality and the perspective that distance gives in order to write calmly about a place. Ireland is a wonderful incubator" (quoted in Eckley 26). Thus, Edna O'Brien added her name to the flow of other Irish writers into self-exile. In a later interview she was more vehement about her homeland's influence on her writing, contending that "Ireland is the most rich, unescapable land . . . a brand that's put on a beast" (quoted in Woodward 51). O'Brien's reaction to the banning of her books in Ireland for their frank treatment of sexuality has been to defend the importance of truth in art, stressing the authenticity of her portrayal of rural Ireland and its impact on all facets of her characters (Eckley 24).

MAJOR WORKS AND THEMES

In all her works, O'Brien is chiefly concerned with giving a voice to women, exploring their most personal pains and joys, their pleas for love, and their emotional, psychological, maternal, and sexual needs. She thus grants speech to those who have been denied independent voices. O'Brien has called these characters her "strange, throttled, sacrificial women" (quoted in Woodward 42), and in them she explores the notion of loneliness and the search for romance, the impossibility of ever attaining a lasting and fulfilling union with anyone: parent, lover, or child. O'Brien often employs a first-person narrator, sometimes a child, whose search for security is painfully exposed through the intimacy of the narration. Her books explore female sexuality, and recent fiction (specifically *The High Road*) investigates the nature of women's friendships and sexual relationships with each other.

Although not all of O'Brien's works take place in Ireland, in many the presence of Ireland is felt, whether as childhood memories, homesickness, elation at escape, or remnant of Irish Catholic guilt. This entry focuses on her works that are most directly Irish.

O'Brien's first novel, *The Country Girls* (1960), set in a characteristic Irish village, explores the life of a child growing up with, and trying to escape from, the restraints of family life defined by Irish Catholicism, poverty, and village morality. The first-person child narrator reveals a bond with her mother (even after the mother's death in the book's beginning) and a fear of her father, which is a theme replicated in much of O'Brien's work. The child Caithleen's removal to the Brennan household following her mother's death highlights her continual fear of her father's drinking and subsequent violence; O'Brien replicates the figure of the brutal yet weak father figure in various guises throughout her fiction. Caithleen and Baba discover greater discipline at the convent school to which they are sent and manage to have themselves evicted from it through a ruse of Baba's. O'Brien provides in the character of Mr. Gentleman, with whom Caithleen becomes infatuated, the first example of an older man who seems to be the true romantic ideal but who fails her miserably. The novel leaves Kate and Baba more independent and more alone in rented rooms following their flight to Dublin.

The Lonely Girl (1962), the second novel in the famous trilogy, finds Kate working in a Dublin grocery as she and Baba gain a more realistic view of a woman's means of survival—each date becomes a battle for gaining necessary food and drink without relinquishing control of virtue. In her relationship with the older Eugene Gaillard, Kate gets caught between the censure of her family and provincial background and the snobbery of her lover, who educates her about art and culture but mocks her remaining links to her Irish childhood as expressed in her Catholicism, her love for nature, and her social and sexual inexperience. Kate is brought away from Eugene's house, escapes back to him, and eventually flees to London, hoping he will pursue her and fulfill her romantic dreams of love. He does not.

Girls in Their Married Bliss (1964), with its highly ironic title, gives Baba her first opportunity to narrate (for much but not all of the book). She reveals much more vigor, a greater spirit of defiance, and far more irreverence for childhood and village morality than Kate can muster. Married to a rich but impotent builder who beats her when he is drunk, Baba sees the hypocrisy of societal standards that regulate women and their sexuality and targets the need to survive and enjoy herself as much as possible in a woman's world. Kate survives a painful divorce from Eugene, who, like most men in O'Brien's fictions, proves to be cold, spiteful, and calculating. Eventually, Kate wins custody of her son and continues in her impossible search for love and cessation of personal loneliness. The novel ends with Kate's voluntary sterilization, a clear commentary on the sterile nature of human relationships. The *Epilogue* to the trilogy, a 1986 addition, continues this theme of an empty, unfulfilled life that seems to be woman's lot. In Baba's voice, the epilogue recounts her memories and realizations as she waits at the train station for the arrival of Kate's body, from a drowning death that Baba suspects was suicide.

Written in the second person, *A Pagan Place* (1970) continues the theme of a child's seeking closeness to her mother and fearing her father's drunken bouts of violence and the inevitable separation from both parents. The child and mother are allies, caring for each other as the child recognizes her mother's lack of romantic fulfillment with her husband. The narrator's older sister, Emma, returns home pregnant and unrepentant and provides for the younger narrator an introduction to both female sexuality and its subsequent punishment, a theme reinforced when the narrator herself is beaten after a young priest attempts to seduce her and fails. The novel leaves us with the narrator's flight from home to a convent school in Belgium, continuing the need to create a self-imposed exile to escape simple replication of her parents' relationship and the impossibility of attaining the romantic fulfillment she seeks. The child narrator's flight also signals an attempt to avoid the sexual repression she has witnessed being inflicted on women in provincial Ireland.

Night (1972) is Mary Hooligan's night reverie. A middle-aged woman from "County Coose," Mary has long ago left Ireland for England, but her memories swirl through her present reality and help her maintain her fierce independence through many and varied emotional troubles and sexual explorations. Like most O'Brien men, those Mary has known are abusive and undependable, and she is repeatedly disappointed in her search to find emotional intimacy and sexual fulfillment. But O'Brien creates in Mary Hooligan a more independent, successful narrator than in earlier books, since Mary manages not merely to survive but partially to triumph through maintaining her own independence and sense of humor.

In a nonfiction piece, O'Brien completes in *Mother Ireland* (1976) a journalistic journey through Ireland (with photographs). In her tour of the birthplace from which she fled, O'Brien specifically links the land with the maternal and so yokes together the themes of childhood, repression, escape and self-exile that dominate her works of fiction.

Returning (1982) is a collection of stories depicting childhood in Ireland, often from a first-person narrator much like Caithleen in *The Country Girls*. O'Brien continues to explore themes of children seeking security within relationships to their parents, the strictures of village life with all its gossip and small-town censure, and growing awareness of young female sexuality. Stories like "Savages" and "Courtship" involve specific conflicts between young girls developing psychologically and sexually and the community of adults around them. *Lantern Slides* (1990) contains deftly wrought stories of small-town Irish life. O'Brien adeptly depicts the private yearnings of her often idiosyncratic characters with humor and with sympathy, as she exposes their loneliness and their dreams.

Time and Tide (1992) is a novel that reexamines the maternal bond but this time concentrates on the mother's attempt to deal with her growing children's need for independence, their rebelliousness, and one son's premature death. Nell is much like Kate Brady of the *Country Girls Trilogy*, divorced by a hateful man, bringing up two children whom she desperately loves and who have quickly become the focal point of her life. O'Brien focuses on the maternal, exploring a mother's fears of loving her children too much. Through Nell's somewhat overwhelming suffering, O'Brien explores a woman's capacity to survive as she ages, unsupported by men who fail her in romance and by children who interpret maternal love as stifling dependence.

House of Splendid Isolation (1994) shows a turn to a more political consciousness in a novel that directly addresses the war between political and religious factions in Ireland and the Irish citizens caught in the middle. In addition, this is O'Brien's first foray into an intimate representation of the mind of a man. McGreevy, an Irish Republican Army (IRA) soldier, is not the abusive, cold, and cruel male found in other works by Edna O'Brien. Interestingly, in this portrayal of a trained killer O'Brien presents her first sympathetic, emotional man. Josie O'Meara, an older woman completely isolated in her run-down manse, has her own emotional scars from a failed marriage with a husband turned drunken and abusive and a disastrous emotional attachment to a local priest. But Josie exhibits an independence and defiance of spirit that few women in O'Brien's fiction develop through their experiences with men and the world. Originally held captive in her own house by McGreevy, Josie grows to care about him and to understand more about his cause and his motivations. Josie's death in the successful attempt to recapture McGreevy and the soldier's eloquent, silent endurance of his fate underline the novel's preoccupation with the recurring violence of human passions and relationships.

CRITICAL RECEPTION

Critics have acclaimed O'Brien for granting a voice to those who previously have been denied speech, recognizing O'Brien's skill in portraying anguished women in search of love, whether they be Catholic girls desperate to experience romance and their own sexuality or grown women involved with married lovers and emotional loneliness. Woodward calls her "a poet of heartbreak, [who] writes most tellingly about the hopeless, angry passion that courts self-ruin" (42). Philip Roth has named her the Irish Collette, one of the most fascinating writers in today's fiction. Critics also draw attention to O'Brien's painfully accurate depictions of female frustrations and personal loss; indeed, some feel that in her works "the main theme is always concerned with loss and with how heterosexual relations and, more specifically, sexual relations may be used to replace the loss of the self" (Hargreaves 292, in Michael Kenneally's *Cultural Contexts*). Others focus on the emphasis in O'Brien's novels on "breaking away—from home, family, marriage or love affair—and yet each is also testimony to the impossibility of the clean or permanent break" (Darcy O'Brien 179). Important also is the attention given to O'Brien's beautiful, well-crafted prose (what Louise Doughty calls O'Brien's "precision" and "consummate skill"), which creates sensitively drawn and extremely sensuous pictures.

Some critics have also noted that Edna O'Brien at times retravels familiar territory of loneliness and emotional pain. According to Hugh Kenner, "[L]ike a lot of talented people, she has a performance that she repeats" (Woodward). However, O'Brien in her latest novel reaches into new areas of political and social consciousness. Critics have previously cited the lack of an external, public world that might be expected to affect O'Brien's characters, but in *House of Splendid Isolation* that public world directly confronts the private lives of Josie and McGreevy. This novel has won high praise for the careful interweaving of intimate histories with the larger public story of Ireland—both victims of unceasing violence and pain.

BIBLIOGRAPHY

Works by Edna O'Brien

The Country Girls. New York: Knopf, 1960.
The Lonely Girl. New York: Random House, 1962. (Repub. as *Girl With Green Eyes*, 1964.)
A Cheap Bunch of Nice Flowers. Plays of the Year. Ed. J. C. Trewin. New York: Ungar, 1963.
Girls in Their Married Bliss. London: Cape, 1964. (Rev. ed. London: Penguin, 1967.)
August Is a Wicked Month. New York: Simon and Schuster, 1965.
Casualties of Peace. London: Cape, 1966.
The Love Object and Other Stories. London: Cape, 1968.
A Pagan Place. New York: Knopf, 1970.

X, Y and Zee. New York: Lancer, 1971. [Pub. as *Zee and Co*. London: Weidenfeld and
    Nicolson, 1971.]
Night. London: Weidenfeld and Nicolson, 1972.
A Scandalous Woman. London: Weidenfeld and Nicolson, 1974.
Mother Ireland. New York: Harcourt Brace Jovanovich, 1976.
I Hardly Knew You. New York: Avon, 1977.
Mrs. Reinhardt and Other Stories. London: Weidenfeld and Nicolson, 1978.
A Rose in the Heart. New York: Avon, 1978.
Some Irish Loving: A Selection. New York: Harper and Row, 1979.
James and Nora: Portrait of Joyce's Marriage. Northridge, CA: Lord John, 1981.
Virginia. New York: Harcourt Brace Jovanovich, 1981.
Returning. New York: Penguin, 1982.
A Fanatic Heart: Selected Stories. New York: New American Library, 1984.
The Country Girls Trilogy and Epilogue. New York: Farrar, Straus, and Giroux, 1986.
The High Road. New York: Farrar, Straus, and Giroux, 1988.
On the Bone. Warwick, England: Greville, 1989. (Poems.)
Lantern Slides. New York: Farrar, Straus, and Giroux, 1990.
Time and Tide. New York: Farrar, Straus, and Giroux, 1992.
An Edna O'Brien Reader. New York: Warner, 1994.
The House of Splendid Isolation. New York: Farrar, Straus, and Giroux, 1994.

Studies of Edna O'Brien

Doughty, Louise. "Restless Dreaming Souls." *Times Literary Supplement* (June 8,
    1990): 616.
Eckley, Grace. *Edna O'Brien*. Lewisburg, PA: Bucknell University Press, 1974.
Haule, James. "Tough Luck: The Unfortunate Birth of Edna O'Brien." *Colby Quarterly*
    23.4 (1987): 216–24.
L'Heureux, John. "The Terrorist and the Lady."*New York Times Book Review* 99 (June
    26, 1994): 7.
O'Brien, Darcy. "Edna O'Brien: A Kind of Irish Childhood." In *Twentieth-Century
    Women Novelists*, ed. Thomas Staley. Totowa, NJ: Barnes and Noble, 1982. 179–
    90.
Roth, Philip. Foreword. *A Fanatic Heart* by Edna O'Brien. New York: New American
    Library, 1984.
Woodward, Richard B. "Edna O'Brien: Reveling in Heartbreak." *New York Times*,
    March 12, 1989, 42+, 51+.

Flann O'Brien

(1911–1966)

Andrew J. Shipe

BIOGRAPHY

Flann O'Brien was one of several pen names used by Brian O'Nolan, one of the most irreverent writers of his time. O'Nolan also wrote under other pseudonyms, such as Myles na gCopaleen, for newspaper columns in both English and Irish, but Flann O'Brien was used for O'Nolan's literary effort, including four novels in English and one in Irish.

Various "autobiographies" of the personae behind O'Nolan's pseudonyms include details such as birth in Paris in 1691, a claim to being an illegitimate son of Henry VIII, and an informal victory over contemporary chess champion Alexander Alekhine. The "real" Brian O'Nolan was a respectfully married and faithfully Catholic civil servant, a fervent horse-race bettor, and a loud patron of many Dublin pubs. O'Nolan was born in County Tyrone on October 5, 1911, the third of twelve children, and moved to Dublin with his family permanently in 1923, after several moves throughout Ireland. Irish and English were both spoken in the household, and O'Nolan grew up completely bilingual and interested in the complexities of each language.

O'Nolan attended University College, Dublin (UCD), in the years immediately following the civil war, as the identity the new nation would take was a topic often debated. While his intelligence was clear as a young man, his attitude toward his studies was at best ambivalent; O'Nolan clearly preferred billiards, drink, and extracurricular debate to more formal pursuits. Yet during this time O'Nolan first began to gain notoriety (rather than fame) as a writer with his first work, a bawdy Dublin version of the *Decameron* written in Old Irish, published in the students' magazine *Comhthrom Féinne*. Part of the reason for writing in Old Irish was to evade censorship, an only partially successful ruse. Niall Sheridan, editor of the magazine and friend of O'Nolan, was summoned before the president of the college and accused of printing obscene material, even though neither Sheridan nor the president could read Old Irish. Later, O'Nolan began editing a literary magazine called *Blather*, in which his comic potential showed under the pseudonym of Count O'Blather.

Although O'Nolan claimed to spend little time studying, he did an extensive amount of reading while at UCD, with Eliot, Proust, Kafka, and Kierkegaard among his favorites. Yeats and Joyce were by that time virtually required reading among the student body, even though the luster of the Revival had faded, and O'Nolan expressed an immense dislike for Synge's apotheosis of the Irish peasant.

Upon graduation from UCD, O'Nolan entered the civil service and worked there from 1935 to 1953. But O'Nolan was unenthusiastic toward his job, focusing his attention on a project he began while working on his M.A. thesis at UCD, a novel based on a college student's revision of the Sweeney myth that was to become *At Swim-Two-Birds*.

The title, which O'Nolan did not like, comes from Snámh-dá-én, where Sweeney recited one of his most famous lays, which ironically is not included in the novel. To reinforce the centrality of the Sweeney myth, O'Nolan wanted to rename the book *Sweeney in the Trees*, but the publisher was already set on the original, which gives virtually no clue about the focus of the novel and is mentioned only parenthetically (95). The pseudonym had already been established by a series of letters O'Nolan and some friends had sent to the *Irish Times*, and O'Nolan requested that the publisher not use his "real" name but "John Hackett." The publisher refused, and Flann O'Brien became the name associated with O'Nolan's literary work.

At Swim-Two-Birds was popular in Dublin for a short period and even received praise from James Joyce. However, few copies sold after the first weeks of activity, as the book was supplanted in bookstores by *Gone with the Wind* and Joyce's *Finnegans Wake*.

After interest waned in *At Swim-Two-Birds*, and publishers rejected *The Third Policeman*—O'Nolan claimed that the manuscript was blown page by page out of the backseat of his car while he drove from Donegal to Dublin—O'Nolan retired from writing fiction in English for nearly twenty years. His novel in Irish, *An Béal Bocht* (1940), was one of the most acclaimed works in Irish of the year. However, O'Nolan refused to permit the work to be translated into English during his lifetime, claiming that much of the humor would be lost in the translation.

Accidents, illnesses, arguments with editors, and heavy drinking hampered O'Nolan's literary production during the next twenty years. In the early 1940s, O'Nolan dabbled in drama, but only *Thirst*, a short sketch, was revived after a short run, and *Faustus Kelly* was a mild success. In 1953, O'Nolan contemptuously resigned after eighteen years of civil service and took to writing full-time in order to supplement his pension. However, most of O'Nolan's writing of the late 1950s consists of hack journalism, advertising, and minor columns for provincial newspapers.

Abruptly, this low period in O'Nolan's life ended in May 1959, when MacGibbon and Kee suggested a republication of *At Swim-Two-Birds*. The new edition brought about a fresh interest in Flann O'Brien, and O'Nolan responded with two novels in English during the 1960s, *The Hard Life* and *The Dalkey Archive* (the latter borrowing substantially from the posthumously published *The Third Policeman*).

However, O'Nolan's enthusiasm for future works, such as a farce on Irish-American politics, tentatively titled *Slattery's Sago Saga*, was in stark contrast to the daily bouts of vomiting and other physical pain of his final years. He died on April Fool's Day 1966 after a long bout with skin cancer.

MAJOR WORKS AND THEMES

Underlying O'Nolan's various authorial personae are a comic undermining of convention and the intellectual's demand that reality somehow conform to these conventions. One unfinished college project demonstrated O'Nolan's early fascination with cliché, the "all-purpose opening speech," consisting of one 850-word incomplete sentence, designed to be spoken fluently in any language without communicating anything. Later during his tenure at UCD, O'Nolan proposed to a few friends that they undertake the composition of the Great Irish Novel by writing (mostly stealing) passages independently and then pasting the separate passages together into a whole. While this plan never came to fruition, it can be seen as a basis for some of the themes of *At Swim-Two-Birds*, usually considered his finest work.

The novel, which begins with "Chapter 1" but contains no other chapter, revolves around a complex metafictional gyre: the narrator, a lazy university student, lives with his uncle and describes the process of writing a great novel. The student's novel focuses on a pub keeper named Dermot Trellis, who hopes to compose a novel that will counter the decline in Irish morals—although Trellis gladly plans for "plenty of smut" to lure readers to his book. Through "aestho-autogamy," Trellis brings to life his characters, most of whom are taken from Irish myth, except for Furriskey and Sheila Lamont, who are supposed to represent the extremes of moral purity and corruption. The characters must stay at Trellis's pub, the Red Swan Hotel, and follow Trellis's orders while he is awake. But the walls between the author and narrative collapse as the characters rebel against the unrealistic modes their author sets for them. For example, the "villain" Furriskey declines to rape Sheila Lamont and instead marries Peggy, a domestic servant, and resolves to settle down in the suburbs. Overwhelmed by Sheila Lamont's beauty, Trellis rapes her himself—fathering a son, Orlick, who has inherited his father's gift for language. The Pooka and the Good Fairy fight over Orlick's soul at a game of cards, which the Pooka wins after catching the Good Fairy cheating. Orlick then returns to the Red Swan Hotel and composes a novel in which his father suffers incredible torment at the hands of his own characters. Trellis is saved only when his servant inadvertently throws his manuscript in the fire. *At Swim-Two-Birds* concludes with the narrator passing his exams and reconciling with his uncle.

Adding to the complexity and confusion of O'Brien's novel are the scraps of other texts used in the various narratives, from the Christian Brothers' *Literary Readers* to a tip on a horse race. Styles range from the popular western to the overly grandiose English translations of Irish myth. The structure of the novel is based on ten "biographical reminiscences," which correspond to various parts of the student's novel. But to speak of traditional plot in *At Swim-Two-Birds* is frustrating, made no easier by the inclusion of "Synopsis, being a summary of what has gone before, FOR THE BENEFIT OF NEW READERS" (85).

At Swim-Two-Birds lampoons the concept of the artist as God and father of his creation, social realism, the modernist aesthetic, and literary scholarship. The structure of the novel is often compared to the guidelines Aldous Huxley set forth in *Point Counter Point*. Huxley suggests a novel with a series of narrators and narratives melded within each other like the infinite regression of figures on a box of Quaker Oats. But the comparison most often made is to Joyce, with the themes of artistic creation, literary allusion, and contemporary relationship to ancient myth. O'Nolan, infuriated rather than honored by comparisons to Joyce, came to view *At Swim-Two-Birds* as his worst book, seeing the dense allusion and complex narrative structure as pretentious. However, the novel's reputation within the discussion of modern and postmodern literature remains strong.

As O'Brien's career continued, his novels became more linear, while no less fantastic and comic. His second novel in English, *The Third Policeman* (1967), was written in 1940, yet was not published until after his death. Longman's, which published *At Swim-Two-Birds*, found this novel, another satiric portrayal of the representation of reality within the conventions of science and philosophy, too fantastic. The unnamed narrator and an accomplice connive to rob Mathers in order to publish a definitive edition of the work of de Selby, an eccentric thinker who believes life is a hallucination and who claims to have used a series of mirrors to view an image of himself at the age of five. De Selby's insights are so profoundly inscrutable that scholars analyze his feces in order to gain insight into the workings of his mind. After the crime, the narrator finds himself in a world where the theories of de Selby seem to be dominant, and the "law" is enforced by Sergeants Pluck and MacCruiskeen. During his life, O'Nolan thought this book would never be published and borrowed some of its scenes and characters when composing *The Dalkey Archive* some twenty years later.

As he wrote *The Third Policeman*, O'Nolan also worked on *An Béal Bocht*, which satirized the Gaelic Revival movement and the outlandish romanticization of the Irish peasant in literature and art. The novel is an extended satire of Gaeligores, literal translations of modern and Old Irish, and the conventional image of the Irish peasant, made popular by autobiographies such as Tomás Ó

Criomhthain's *An tOileánach* (The Islandman). The title, translated as "The Poor Mouth," refers to an Irish idiom for grumbling or pitifully pretending to be poorer than one is. The narrator, Bonaparte O'Coonassa, describes his home of Corkadoragha as filled with illiterate yet conniving peasants who speak sweetly and have no grasp of reality—which makes them truly Gaelic, from the narrator's perspective. A variety of animals live in O'Coonassa's house, including a pig that grows so large it cannot get out the door and eventually dies of its own stench. Another pig's grunts are recorded by a linguist doing field research, believing the pig's snarls to be the profoundly poetic and inscrutable sounds of the pure Gaelic language. However, the peasants of Corkadoragha eventually fail to live up to the image the Gaeligores had expected of them.

The Hard Life, completed quickly and accepted immediately for publication, marked the return of Flann O'Brien to fiction in English after an absence of over twenty years. The older O'Nolan clearly had a much harder edge, resulting in the much darker comedy of a novel that begins with a death and ends with a "tidal surge of vomit." Set in turn-of-the-century Dublin with an atmosphere that makes Joyce's *Dubliners* seem a series of uplifting fables, *The Hard Life* joins The Brother (from Myles's *Cruiskeen Lawn* columns) and the sophomorically named Father Kurt Fahrt, S. J., to provide a satire on the authority of the Church and a description of the squalid in Irish life; the novel is subtitled "An Exegesis of Squalor." In typical O'Brien fashion, the disclaimer lampoons the habit of the Irish literati to find references to themselves in new novels: "All persons in this book are real and none is fictitious even in part."

O'Brien's final completed novel, *The Dalkey Archive*, combines the satire on scientific discourse with the godlike reputation of James Joyce, who becomes a character in the novel along with De Selby (with a new spelling) from *The Third Policeman*. The protagonist, the simple Mick Shaughnessy, tries to make sense of an irrational universe and the eccentric minds of De Selby and Joyce, as he enjoys strong drink with his friend Hackett—who seems to be battling Mick for the attention of his girlfriend, Mary. Joyce, according to the novel, did not die in Zurich but survived the war and lives as a pub keeper north of Dublin, hoping to become a Jesuit priest. He drinks little, attends mass daily, and calls *Ulysses* a work of "smut" written by "ruffians" who attached his name to the novel to avoid persecution. His only literary contribution is *Dubliners* (cowritten with Gogarty), and his only writing since then has consisted of pamphlets for the Catholic Truth Society. In spite of Joyce's obvious piety, his visit to the Jesuits results only in his employment repairing their undergarments. Meanwhile, De Selby, looking to verify the story of Jonah and the whale, has discovered a material he calls D.M.P. (storing it in containers left over from the Dublin Metropolitan Police), which can remove all oxygen from a sealed space and revokes the sequential nature of time, allowing De Selby to speak with John the Baptist and St. Augustine. De Selby believes that D.M.P. is such a purifying force that he promises to use it to exterminate the world in order to save it in the name of God. The fire that consumes De Selby's house seems like a miracle, an element from the fantastic, an aspect of the novel reinforced by Mary's confession at the end of the novel that she is pregnant. Nowhere in the novel do Mick and Mary have sex, and the ambiguous relationship Mary has with Hackett leaves the identity of the father unclear to the reader.

O'Brien's focus on the fantastic and the inexplicable has continued to intrigue readers interested in the literature of the last years of modernism and the first years of post–civil war Ireland. Few writers match O'Brien's ability to portray the comedy of the conventional mind in an unconventional world.

CRITICAL RECEPTION

While *At Swim-Two-Birds* and O'Brien's other works are enjoyed by scholars today, writing long critical studies of his work has proved daunting. A significant obstacle may be the recognition that a prospective author is spouting the type of clichés that provide the target for much of O'Brien's wit.

Nonetheless, since the revival of *At Swim-Two-Birds* in 1960, several critical studies have appeared, moving critical debate over O'Brien beyond the simple thesis that his wit and humor were typical of all that is best in Irish life (from the Myles na gCopaleen Catechism of Cliché: "Of what was any deceased citizen you like to mention typical? Of all that is best in Irish life" [*The Best of Myles* 203]).

Clissman sees the chaotic structure as representative of the aesthete's mind, thinking in the clichés of literary tradition. Under this view, *At Swim-Two-Birds* complicates the traditional form of the novel and its assumptions about art's goal of representing reality. This reading is reinforced by the portrayal of the author as very unlike God, with an omnipotent control over his or her work while seeming absent. The inadequacies of authorial control are on full display in *At Swim-Two-Birds*.

Yet the novel can also be seen as an anti-anti-novel, parodying the "self-evident sham" that the narrator espouses to be the ultimate goal of any novel and calling imagination into question as well as reality. The attempt at subjective reality is no more fulfilling than the attempt at objectivism. Mackenzie reads O'Brien as criticizing the self-reflexive nature of high modernism and argues that O'Brien is at least as *anti*modern as *post*modern. Mackenzie also claims that O'Brien's later focus on religion can be seen as a criticism of science and rationalism, rather than as parodies of religious faith.

Much has been made of the influence of James Joyce on O'Brien's work. Similarities can be drawn—the fascination with language, daily life in Ireland, and the use of the Ossianic cycle, with its focus on Finn and Sweeney's poetry, rather than of the Ulster cycle, with its emphasis on nobility that attracted Yeats. Robert Martin Adams claims in *AfterJoyce: Studies in Fiction after Ulysses* that O'Brien is "a *post*-Joyce if not wholly *propter*-Joyce writer" (190), but Joseph Browne takes Adams to task for the "kind of sweeping and often unquestioning pronouncement that infuriated O'Brien during his career and that has negatively influenced readers and critics to the present day'' (150). Mackenzie's argument that O'Brien is anti-Joyce and antimodern must be mentioned here as well. O'Brien's later contempt for Joyce's work, particularly *Finnegans Wake*, can be seen in the description of de Selby's *Codex* in *The Third Policeman*: 2,000 pages of unintelligible scribble, of which four copies exist, with intense disagreement among scholars as to which is the original.

But to discuss critically O'Brien's relationship to Joyce is ultimately reductive, and the opportunity for further work is substantial. O'Brien's use of popular historical romance and contemporary writing styles seems ripe for investigation under current cultural theory, and his interest in the Irish language—coupled with his satire of the Gaelic Revival—may yet produce an interesting postcolonial study.

Among the shortcomings of O'Brien's work is the lack of complete female characters, which has frustrated feminist critics and reduced his appeal to a larger critical audience.

BIBLIOGRAPHY

Works by Flann O'Brien

At Swim-Two-Birds. New York: Walker, 1966.
The Dalkey Archive. Normal, IL: Dalkey Archive, 1993.
The Hard Life: An Exegesis of Squalor. Normal, IL.: Dalkey Archive, 1994.
The Poor Mouth. (An Béal Bocht) Trans. Patrick Power. London: Hart-Davis MacGibbon, 1973.
Stories and Plays. London: Hart-Davis MacGibbon, 1973.
The Third Policeman. New York: Walker, 1967.
na Gopaleen, Myles (pseudonym). *The Best of Myles*. New York: Walker, 1968.

Studies of Flann O'Brien

Asbee, Sue, *Flann O'Brien*. Boston: Twayne, 1991.
Browne, Joseph. ''Flann O'Brien: *Post* Joyce or *Propter* Joyce.'' *Eire-Ireland* 19.4 (Winter 1984): 148–57.
Clissman, Anne. *Flann O'Brien: A Critical Introduction to His Writings*. New York: Barnes, 1975.
Cronin, Anthony. *No Laughing Matter: The Life and Times of Flann O'Brien*. London: Grafton, 1989.
Imhof, Rudiger, ed. *Alive Alive O!: Flann O'Brien's At Swim-Two-Birds*. New York: Barnes, 1985.
Mackenzie, Ian. ''Who's Afraid of James Joyce? Or, Flann O'Brien's Retreat from Modernism.'' *Études des Lettres* 1 (1983): 55.
O'Keefe, Timothy, ed. *Myles: Portraits of Brian O'Nolan*. London: Brian, 1973.

Kate O'Brien

(1897–1974)

Patricia J. Ferreira

BIOGRAPHY

As Ireland recovered from the devastation that plagued the nineteenth century, a growing middle class emerged, gaining a foothold in the national economy as business entrepreneurs and professionals. Members of the new population differed from previous generations of Irish society in at least two important ways. Although largely Catholic, they were unlike those of the same religion from the working classes in that they were less concerned with national politics. Likewise, they could be distinguished from the Protestant elite because they carried little of the exploitative baggage from the nineteenth-century Big House, though they were gaining monetary parity. Kate O'Brien was born into a household of the rising Irish gentry, and her contributions to Irish literature are largely made up of her portrait and critique of that world.

The daughter of Thomas and Catherine ("Katty" Thornhill) O'Brien, Kate and her four sisters and five brothers were brought up in a Limerick manor called "Boru House," with plenty of material comforts. Her father earned his living by breeding thoroughbred horses, which enabled the O'Brien children to be educated at the best neighborhood schools and to enjoy vacations at the seashore. They also had fashionable wardrobes and were taken care of by a crew of servants. In 1902, however, Catherine O'Brien died, and Kate was sent to board at Laurel Hill, a convent school where she stayed throughout most of her childhood and adolescence until she entered University College, Dublin (UCD), in 1916 to study for the B.A. Her acceptance to UCD, like her admittance to Laurel Hill, was marred by the death of a parent, this time her father, forcing Kate to finance her own education by winning a County Council scholarship.

After graduation, O'Brien moved to England and supported herself by working as a freelance journalist and part-time teacher. She also worked as an au pair in Spain, before returning to England to marry Gustaaf Renier, a Dutch journalist, only to leave him after less than a year.

MAJOR WORKS AND THEMES

Although she began her creative writing career as a playwright with the successful British production of *Distinguished Villa* (1926), O'Brien made her literary mark with the publication of her first novel, *Without My Cloak* (1931). In the text she moves the action from the London neighborhood of Brixton, where *Distinguished Villa* is set, to the town of Mellick, Ireland, which serves as the backdrop to much of her subsequent fiction. *Without My Cloak* is similar to O'Brien's first play, however, in that the novel also ridicules the importance that the middle class placed on social status and material wealth, as well as their preoccupation with conventional social roles found in relationships between men and women. Although at the end of the novel the world of the Considines, her main characters, remains intact, O'Brien's later fiction begins to dismantle the bourgeois ways of life that allow an existence insulated from the social and political concerns troubling both Ireland and the world at large.

In works such as *The Ante-Room* (1934) and *Mary Lavelle* (1936), O'Brien more forcefully explores the limitations of parochial lifestyles and attitudes. In *The Ante-Room*, such investigation takes shape when her main character, Agnes Mulqueen, struggles with her orthodox religious convictions, questioning whether her faith is the result of blind adherence or sincere belief. Because Agnes's doubt stems from her secret love for her sister's husband, Vincent O'Regan, it too provides O'Brien with an opportunity further to critique convention. Agnes's behavior totters between the values and mores of the society in which she lives and her dreams to act in accordance with her own desires.

In *Mary Lavelle*, O'Brien again invokes the tension that evolves when society's rules contradict an individual's longings; however, the heroine's relocation to Spain from Ireland, rather than a relationship with a man, awakens her to a greater knowledge of her true self. The story revolves around Mary, who, like O'Brien in real life, leaves Ireland to work as a child-care worker abroad. No longer confined to the narrow views of Mellick, she discovers a world that is more connected to social issues rather than social standing. She also learns Spanish and reads newspapers, bringing her closer to the community in which she resides. With *Mary Lavelle*, O'Brien's ultimate belief in individual freedom is upheld as an ideal that is no longer detached from worldly concerns. In her subsequent fiction, she continues to honor decisions that are based upon one's own sense of right and wrong. Spain also figures as a metaphor for individuality while Ireland symbolizes a world of social restriction and conformity.

CRITICAL RECEPTION

Nearly every scholar who has approached Kate O'Brien's work laments the fact that she has received so little critical attention, especially considering her prolific writing career. In 1990, Adele Dalsimer provided the first substantial study, claiming O'Brien as one of Ireland's first writers to deal with the concerns of female autonomy, self-definition, and sexual freedom. In a chronological examination of O'Brien's fiction, Dalsimer also situates the author within the artistic milieu of the era, demonstrating the influences of other writers such as George Eliot, who equally examined the ways that moral dilemmas and constraints have impact upon individuals. Dalsimer's work is particularly useful, however, in revealing the ways that O'Brien helped to illustrate Ireland through a twentieth-century perspective.

Given the neglect of her work, a collection of essays edited by Eibhear Walshe marks another important scholarly contribution, demonstrating the diversity of O'Brien's writing interests with pieces that focus on her journalism and travel writing, as well as on her fiction. Essays in this collection by Ailbhe Smyth and Emma Donoghue also explicitly connect O'Brien to feminist and lesbian themes.

BIBLIOGRAPHY

Works by Kate O'Brien

Novels

Without My Cloak. London: Heinemann, 1931; London: Virago, 1986.
The Ante-Room. London: Heinemann, 1934; Dublin: Arlen House, 1980.
Mary Lavelle. London: Heinemann, 1936; London, Virago, 1984.
Pray for the Wanderer. London: Heinemann, 1938.
The Land of Spices. London: Heinemann, 1941; London, Virago, 1988.
The Last of Summer. London: Heinemann, 1943; Dublin: Arlen House, 1982.
That Lady. London: Heinemann, 1946; London: Virago, 1985.
Teresa of Avila. London: Parrish, 1951.
The Flower of May. London: Heinemann, 1953.
As Music and Splendour. London: Heinemann, 1958.
Presentation Parlour. London: Heinemann, 1963.

Play

Distinguished Villa. London: Benn, 1926.

Travel Writing

Farewell Spain. London: Heinemann, 1937.
My Ireland. London: Batsford, 1962.

Studies of Kate O'Brien

Dalsimer, Adele M. *Kate O'Brien: A Critical Study*. Dublin: Gill and Macmillan, 1990.
————. "A Not So Simple Saga: Kate O'Brien's *Without My Cloak*." *Eire-Ireland* 21.3 (Fall 1986): 55–72.
Hildebidle, John. *Five Irish Writers: The Errand of Keeping Alive*. Cambridge: Harvard University Press, 1989.
Kiely, Benedict. "Love and Pain and Parting: The Novels of Kate O'Brien." *The Hollins Critic* 29.2 (April 1992): 1–11.
Quiello, Rose. " 'Disturbed Desires': The Hysteric in Kate O'Brien's *Mary Lavelle*." *Eire-Ireland* 25.3 (Fall 1990): 46–57.
Reynolds, Lorna. *Kate O'Brien: A Literary Portrait*. Gerrards Cross, UK: Smythe, 1987.
Walshe, Eibhear, ed. *Ordinary People Dancing: Essays on Kate O'Brien*. Cork, Ireland: Cork University Press, 1993.

Sean O'Casey

(1880–1964)

Claire Gleitman

BIOGRAPHY

John Casey was born on March 30, 1880. He eventually Gaelicized his name to Sean O'Cathasaigh when he learned the Irish language and reinvented himself as Sean O'Casey when the Abbey accepted his first play. Dublin's slums into which he was born—teeming with overcrowded, rat-infested, and typhoid-ridden tenement houses—became the seeding ground for O'Casey's finest plays. This urban squalor fired his imagination with a lifelong sympathy for the plight of the working poor and a fervent disgust for the various orthodoxies that he regarded as distractions from the pursuit of any remedy.

As a boy, O'Casey suffered from trachoma, a painful eye disease that contributed to an anxious and isolated childhood. Because of his frequent need for medical attention, he attended a local Protestant church school sporadically and owed much of his education to his mother's diligence and his own intellectual zeal. Meanwhile, his involvement in local theatrical activities introduced him to Shakespeare and Boucicault, both of whom proved to be crucial influences upon his own drama. In his teens O'Casey expanded his repertoire, avidly reading English and European literature in spite of the half-blindness that rendered the task laborious.

After a brief romance with the church (where he taught Sunday school and promoted the inclusion of Irish-speaking pastors), O'Casey became drawn to Irish nationalism and found himself engrossed by all things Irish. In 1902 he joined the Gaelic League and the Irish Republican Brotherhood (IRB); he also taught himself Irish, performed in Irish bands, and took up hurling. But O'Casey was never one who could play the role of the refined esthete, shrouding himself in a sublime Irishness while standing at a distance from the unscrubbed masses.

In fact, O'Casey identified closely with those unscrubbed masses in whose company he had always lived and worked. When Michael Casey died in 1886, the family descended into poverty, and Sean began work as an unskilled laborer at the age of fourteen. O'Casey continued to support himself as a laborer for the next thirty years.

The figure who proved most inspirational for O'Casey in his young manhood was Jim Larkin, the Irish labor leader who organized unskilled workers under the rubric of the Irish Transport and General Workers' Union. O'Casey joined the union in 1911 and became secretary of the Irish Citizen Army (ICA) three years later. In the interim, he resigned from the Gaelic League and the IRB, as they seemed to him to lack any real commitment to labor. But the ICA soon roused O'Casey's blistering disapproval as well, when it drifted toward an affiliation with the more militant Irish Volunteers. After an unsuccessful move to block members from joining both organizations simultaneously, O'Casey resigned from the ICA.

Thus, when the ICA united with the Volunteers in the Easter Rising of 1916, O'Casey was not in their company. His retrospective views upon the event are encapsulated in a letter that he wrote to an imprisoned Rising rebel, to whom he reported that Dublin was little changed: "The pubs are doing their best to satisfy their patrons; the children in the slums still run around naked and hungry; the hospitals and the theatres are always full; and the sneering moon looks down and laughs quietly at us all" (Margulies 71). This mood—both amused and horror-stricken, absurdist and incensed—found its way into O'Casey's Dublin plays.

O'Casey's life as a writer really began when in 1907 he helped form the St. Laurence O'Toole Pipers Band, for which he wrote a series of songs that made their way into print in 1918. When the O'Toole club refused to stage his first play because it satirized one of the club's founding members, he submitted the work to the Abbey, which also rejected it and three more of O'Casey's plays before accepting *On the Run*, later retitled *The Shadow of a Gunman* (1923). This drama proved to be the first in O'Casey's Dublin trilogy and the start of a brief but fruitful partnership with Yeats's theater, which went on to stage *Juno and the Paycock* (1925) and *The Plough and the Stars* (1926).

The turbulence that accompanied the *Plough*'s opening week is well known. While *Juno* provoked some objections from audiences discomfited by pungent dialogue and out-of-wedlock pregnancies, in general the dramatist's first two plays were warmly received. But the Abbey stage had seen nothing to compare to the uproar provoked by *Plough* since the word "shift" created pandemonium at the premiere of Synge's *Playboy of the Western World* (1907). The appearance of the prostitute Rosie Redmond, who laments the fact that Republican activities have interfered with business, was bound to unsettle a culture accustomed to exalting the purity and patriotism of Irish womanhood; and *Plough*'s irreverent treatment of the revered Rising rebels was a provocative deflation of cherished assumptions. However, the sight of the sacred Republican flag being dragged into a pub full of drunken brawlers was the real catalyst for mayhem.

In the ensuing tumult—during which chairs were hoisted from the floor, vegetables were hurled at the actors, and not a word of the performance could be heard—Yeats assumed the same role that he had played with great dignity at the time of the *Playboy* riots. He chided the rioters for their disgraceful behavior and lauded O'Casey as an Irish genius whom he proclaimed born like a phoenix from the fiery rubble of their disfavor. But Yeats's praise, O'Casey soon found, was not without boundaries. When O'Casey submitted his fourth work, *The Silver Tassie* (1928), to the Abbey, he was astonished to learn of its rejection. In *The Silver Tassie* O'Casey broke new ground thematically and structurally, and Yeats frowned upon both developments. He criticized O'Casey for venturing away from the Dublin slums to write about a subject that he had not traversed in the flesh, that is, the Great War. Yeats also disliked O'Casey's fusion of naturalism and expressionism in one, sprawling, stirring antiwar play. When Yeats misguidedly suggested that the author might save himself embarrassment by simply withdrawing his play, O'Casey's rage deepened, and he promptly gave all of the letters touching upon the dispute to London and Irish newspapers to publish—without Yeats's permission. The two men remained estranged for nearly a decade.

But O'Casey's growing disenchantment with Ireland was not merely the product of his clash with Yeats. O'Casey reacted to the *Plough* furor with disappointment and revulsion. Kathleen ni Houlihan, the old woman symbolic of Irish rebellion, now struck him as an "untidy termagant, brawling out her prayers"; and when he set sail for London in 1926, he imagined Ireland "spitting a last, venomous, contemptuous farewell" (O'Casey, *Inishfallen* 393, 396). The newly independent country, presided over by businessmen in alliance with the Catholic Church, was not at all the Irish Workers' Republic of his dreams. Hence, O'Casey sought permanent exile in England, where he married the Irish-born Eileen Carey in 1927, raised three children, and wrote eight plays, numerous essays, and a six-volume autobiography.

O'Casey's later dramas found mixed success. *The Silver Tassie* had a short run in London in 1929, *Within the Gates* (1933) received both London and New York productions, and many of his subsequent dramas received English premieres. Meanwhile, O'Casey continued to ruffle feathers in Ireland, where the first two volumes of his autobiography and *Windfalls* (1934), a collection of short writings, were banned for several years. "In Ireland," O'Casey wrote in disgust, "they wear the fig leaf on the mouth" (Krause, 1989, 80). His didactic "prophetic plays," as he called them, did not see performances in Ireland during his lifetime; his late Rabelasian comedies, which mock Irish religiosity and repression, were hardly likely to prompt a warm welcome. The greatest storm was provoked by *The Drums of Father Ned*, which was scheduled for performance as part of Dublin's Tostal celebration in 1958. A dramatization of *Ulysses* was also planned. But the archbishop of Dublin objected to both *Father Ned* and *Bloomsday*, and the Theatre Festival dropped the plays. O'Casey, never one to suffer a slight mildly, rejoined by banning all professional productions of his work in Ireland during his lifetime, a ban he lifted shortly before his death in 1964.

Such battles were ingrained in O'Casey's temperament. He could no more keep his hackles down in the presence of what he perceived as stupidity or tyranny than he could resist celebrating the beauty of goodness and health and human love. Old age brought a worsening of the eye condition from which he had always suffered, as well as the heartbreaking loss of his youngest son, Niall, to leukemia. Yet, in spite of his life's struggles, worsening illnesses, and failing sight, O'Casey sustained an energetic and compassionate optimism, coupled with a shrewd sense of humor. He predicted his own future in the Ireland that had often shunned him when he remarked to a friend in his later years: "They'll get me in the end. They'll make me a part of Ireland's Litherary [*sic*] Glory, God help me!" (Fay 168).

And so they did.

MAJOR WORKS AND THEMES

O'Casey's reputation rests predominantly upon the Dublin trilogy, whose action stems from the cataclysmic events in the years just before and after Ireland achieved partial independence. Hence, all three dramas can be described as historical plays, though of an unconventional sort. *The Shadow of a Gunman* takes place in 1920 during the War of Independence that preceded the signing of the Anglo-Irish Treaty. *Juno and the Paycock* stages the aftermath of the treaty, when supporters of the new Irish Free State came into conflict with diehard Republicans who opposed partition. Finally, *The Plough and the Stars* enacts the Easter Rising of 1916. However, in some important respects O'Casey places himself in the tradition of Bertolt Brecht rather than Shakespeare by opting to enact history not from the center but from the margins. His strategy is to displace dramatic interest away from history's leading characters, shifting the focus instead to those disempowered men and women whom traditional historical accounts efface. When more prominent players do appear, as Patrick Pearse does in *Plough*, they are consigned to the shadows and dramatized through the perspective of the slum dwellers around whom the dramas center.

By focusing upon the margins, O'Casey displays the irrelevance of Ireland's epic struggles to the actual problems that plague these lives. Though swaggering braggarts like Captain Boyle and his leech, Joxer, might ape the rhetoric of their Republican heroes, this rhetoric becomes not a means by which to improve their lot but a hollow evasion of their life's squalor. Throughout the trilogy, O'Casey insistently registers his sense that political movements in Ireland and the rhetoric that undergirds them are abstracted from the real lives and concerns of ordinary Irish people. As nationalists go off to march in political parades, and Unionists depart for the European War, *Plough*'s Act I curtain rings down upon the re-

marks of a child dying of consumption. "Is there anybody goin'," she asks,
". . . with a titther of sense?" Mollser and the multitudes of Dublin children for
whom she stands suffer from a disease of poverty that remains unaltered by the
feuds that so mesmerize their elders.

Further, the Dublin plays deplore the glorification of violence that O'Casey
finds endemic to Irish culture, the rush toward self-immolation that Pearse exalts
in his soliloquies. Many of O'Casey's characters accept early and violent death
as an omnipresent fact of life; they may even thrill in its ubiquity, as Mrs. Gogan
does in *Plough*, or they may regard self-sacrifice as their duty, as Johnny Boyle
pretends to do in *Juno*. But this attitude is self-defeating, as it engenders the
view that horror and destitution are inexorable, rather than the analytical mood
that might enable change.

The one positive value to emerge consistently in the trilogy is fellow-feeling,
a value most prominently revealed by women. Yet it is a value that is perpetually
on the verge of defeat. In *The Shadow of a Gunman*, in the form of Minnie
Powell, it is shot. *Plough*'s Nora Clitheroe collapses into insanity, and the humane Bessie Burgess dies with a curse as well as a prayer on her lips. *Juno*'s
title character comes triumphantly into her own when she recognizes her connection to other suffering mothers, and she leaves the stage dedicated to the
code of domesticity and love that O'Casey clearly reveres. Yet the salient fact
about Juno's final stand is that she leaves: for all her goodness, she is powerless
to save her home, and the stage is given over to a pair of drunken braggarts
who ensure the continuation of the circumstances that have defeated Juno's
family.

From such drunken braggarts O'Casey achieves some of his most exuberant
comedy. Like Beckett, he specializes in the construction of clownish pairs who
prattle merrily as their pants fall down, or the world around them disintegrates
into "chassis." Yet the tendency to bury oneself in illusion and dream is more
forgivable in Beckett's world, where an assertion of self is a futile whimper in
the wilderness. In the Dublin trilogy, which is vehemently historical, the possibility of change is ever-present; hence, a capitulation to circumstances as they
are is not a recognition of the inevitable (as it is in Beckett) but a tragic abdi-
cation of personal responsibility. Thus, when Juno leaves the stage to Joxer and
Boyle, who burble on about their imaginary contributions to Ireland's struggle,
we can be confident that the "terr . . . ible state o' . . . chassis" into which the
world has descended is not unrelated to these men's habit of mind. A fundamental problem is their tendency, shared by many characters in the Dublin plays,
to commit themselves without thought to the twin pieties of nationalism and
religion, which assist them in evading the facts of their existence. Boyle and
Joxer's adulation for their bloated selves is hilarious, even captivating. But as
their society is on the brink of devastation, O'Casey compels us to regard them
critically.

While the trilogy is oblique on the subject of solutions, O'Casey's later drama
is more overtly didactic, offering a visionary Marxism as a positive antidote to

social disintegration. As his writing grew more polemical, O'Casey also began to explore new forms, adopting Strindberg and Toller as models and experimenting with dramas no longer driven by plot and character in the traditional sense. The results are mixed. The expressionistic second act of *The Silver Tassie* is a remarkable evocation of the hellishness of warfare, and the play offers its message of pacifism with breathtaking dramatic power. But O'Casey strained for poetry throughout his career, and the problem worsens in the prophetic works. In *Red Roses for Me* (1943), for instance, a young woman explains to her lover why she cannot join him at a meeting in preparation for a railroad strike: "My mother . . . chatters red-lined warnings and black-bordered appeals into my ears night and day, and when they dwindle for lack of breath, my father shakes them out of their drowsiness and sends them dancing round more lively still, dressed richly up in deadly black and gleaming scarlet." Romantic interludes were never O'Casey's strongest suit (one recalls the rather grating repetitions of "little, little, red-lipped Nora" in *Plough*); the awkward poeticisms seem all the more conspicuous in the prophetic plays, as they are no longer grounded in textured characters defined by their own, linguistic idiosyncracies.

A more sustained vibrancy returns in the late comedies, which belong to a tradition of satiric writing that O'Casey might have learned from Jonson, Swift, or even Aristophanes. The target of his satire remains recognizable: he continues to indict Ireland for its piety, its rigidity, and particularly its suppression of sexual joy. Now, though, it is a pastoral rather than an urban Ireland that he evokes, which allows him to reach back to an older form of festive drama in which ritual, magic, and ecstatic experience are venerated. These plays are paeans to the Dionysian forces in human nature that O'Casey embodies in supernatural Cocks with crimson plumage, in bottles of enchanted whiskey, in bewitching young maidens with lovely legs. But because modern Ireland is figured as a negation of such impulses, the comedies eventually darken into melodrama, as the more vivacious characters are propelled into exile or killed off by forces hostile to their vitality.

Indeed, at times the exile's view of his home country seems more uncompromising than ever: it is a joyless land, according to Marion in *Cock-a-Doodle Dandy* (1949), in which "a whisper of love . . . bites away some of th' soul!" Yet O'Casey's belief in the potential vigor of Irish culture never evaporates entirely. In his last play, *The Drums of Father Ned*, he places his hopes for the regeneration of such a culture in a young couple whose merriment and love are unbounded. Ironically, this work, perhaps the merriest O'Casey ever wrote, was censured by the Tostal Council, as if in malevolent confirmation of the playwright's darker vision of his native land.

CRITICAL RECEPTION

While the reception granted to O'Casey by Irish audiences was sufficient to drive him into exile, he did receive some appreciative reviews to offset the denunciations of his work as "dirt for dirt's sake." James Agate and Denis Johnston wrote admiringly about *Plough and the Stars*, and Shaw was an enthusiastic champion of *The Silver Tassie*. But not until the 1960s did full-length studies of O'Casey's drama begin to accumulate. The first important such works are David Krause's intellectual biography, *Sean O'Casey: The Man and His Work*, and Robert Hogan's *The Experiments of Sean O'Casey*. Meanwhile, broader studies of the drama tended to relegate O'Casey to the margins of modern playwriting. In *Drama from Ibsen to Eliot*, Raymond Williams banishes O'Casey to a footnote appended to a chapter on Synge, remarking that O'Casey's linguistic idiosyncracies are "very irritating" (169). Tom Driver's history of the modern theater, *Romantic Quest*, praises O'Casey's "winsome" personality yet laments that his drama "never quite escaped Irish provincialism" (342).

But a reassessment of O'Casey's work appeared in *Sean O'Casey: Modern Judgements* (1969), edited by Ronald Aylin. The volume contains a thorough selection of essays and offers an overview of critical issues that continue to generate debate today. One such issue was first articulated by Joseph W. Krutch, who in *Modernism in Modern Drama* was moved to complain: "To this day, I do not know just where the author's sympathies lie. . . . O'Casey offers no solution; he proposes no remedy; he suggests no hope" (99). The issue is one of tone as well as "message": how is the trilogy intended to be staged (is it tragicomedy, or something darker?), and what, if anything, is it hoping to convey to us? Is O'Casey a social critic, a comic, or merely a confused and confusing nihilist? David Krause counters Krutch's exasperation with readings that emphasize the dramatist's antiheroic comedy. Such readings allow him to universalize the works (Fluther is Don Quixote, Boyle is Falstaff, Joxer is the Roman parasite) and to find in the characters a redeeming comic spirit that transcends the bleak political crisis in which they are enmeshed.

But other critics insist that the plays' prevailing spirit is not so benign. Though O'Casey disavowed any affinity to Beckett's despairing worldview, D.E.S. Maxwell, in *A Critical History of Modern Irish Drama*, maintains that "absurdist" is nevertheless the best label for the tenement dramas. While it is a commonplace to argue that O'Casey's women function as a humane and pragmatic counterpart to his ineffectual males, Maxwell maintains that female characters are often deeply compromised as well. This is so, Maxwell concludes, because *all* institutions, whether they be political, religious, or familial, are regarded as untrustworthy in a world "whose nature is to fall apart" (100).

O'Casey's representation of politics has drawn special attention from critics, many of whom are perplexed by the apparent contradiction between his avowed Marxism and his failure to create a single serious political thinker in his trilogy. Pointing to his tendency to contrast dehumanizing politics with a more fundamental human decency, Seamus Deane, in *Celtic Revivals*, has pronounced O'Casey a rather simple-minded political thinker in comparison to his sometimes-nemesis Yeats. But Bernice Schrank argues that the Dublin plays underscore not the failure of politics by definition but the characters' inability to construct an alternative to the blood-curdling ideologies that surround them, a failure begotten by their impoverished circumstances as well as by the psychological handicaps exacerbated by such circumstances. One might add that O'Casey's cynicism about political movements was fueled by the deep frustration he felt when he watched Ireland first riven by violence and later risen from the ashes of revolution in essence (or so it seemed to O'Casey) unchanged. The plays reflect their author's enraged disenchantment, and they are a magnificent chronicle of a particular moment in Irish history as seen through scaleless eyes.

By contrast, the later work strikes some analysts as a sad falling off. Maxwell states the dominant position: "The popular view is right. . . . O'Casey's first three plays are his best" (105). Yet the opposing view—that the late work is not the floundering of an author who foolishly bade farewell to his tenement constituency but rather the riveting result of ingenious exploration—has been offered by such critics as Robert Hogan, Carol Kleiman, and John O'Riordan. Irrespective of one's position on this matter, there is widespread agreement that the rupture of O'Casey's fertile collaboration with the Abbey was a grave misfortune for both sides. While O'Casey lost his connection to a theater that might have nurtured and focused his experiments, the Abbey never again was fruitfully connected to an important Irish dramatist for any length of time. Instead, it earned a reputation as a naysayer to such innovators as not only O'Casey but also Denis Johnston and Brendan Behan.

When *The Plough and the Stars* received a revival at the Abbey in 1991, one might argue that O'Casey's encounters with Irish audiences came full circle. The play was performed under the direction of Garry Hynes, known for her provocative approach to Irish classics. In interpreting *Plough*, she inflected the play through a postmodern perspective, stripping O'Casey's naturalistic stage nearly bare and shaving the heads of the women. The Easter Rising was introduced to "punk," and many Dubliners raised their eyebrows. One taxi driver nicely encapsulated the debate when he piously denounced the irreverent production, which he had not seen, as "sacrilege."

The playwright himself might have predicted it.

BIBLIOGRAPHY

Selected Works by Sean O'Casey

Plays

The Complete Plays of Sean O'Casey. 5 vols. London: Macmillan, 1951. Includes (vol. 1) *The Shadow of a Gunman, Juno and the Paycock, The Plough and the Stars*; (vol. 2) *The Silver Tassie, Within the Gates, The Star Turns Red*; (vol. 3) *Purple Dust, Red Roses for Me, Hall of Healing*; (vol. 4) *Oak Leaves and Lavender, Cock-a-Doodle Dandy, Bedtime Story, Time to Go*; (vol. 5) *The Bishop's Bonfire, The Drums of Father Ned, Behind the Green Curtain, Figuro in the Night, The*

Moon Shines on Kylenamoe, The Harvest Festival, Kathleen Listens In, Nannie's Night Out.

Autobiography

Within the Gates. London: Macmillan, 1933.
I Knock at the Door. London: Macmillan, 1939.
Pictures in the Hallway. London: Macmillan, 1942.
Drums Under the Windows. London: Macmillan, 1945.
Inishfallen, Fare Thee Well. London: Macmillan, 1949.
Rose and Crown. London: Macmillan, 1952.
Sunset and Evening Star. London: Macmillan, 1954.

Essays and short fiction

The Green Crow: Selected Writings. London: Allen, 1987.
(Includes *The Flying Wasp*; *Windfalls*; diverse essays.)

Studies of Sean O'Casey

Ayling, Ronald, ed. *Sean O'Casey: Modern Judgements.* London: Macmillan, 1969.
Fay, Gerard. "Sean O'Casey, Saint and Devil." *In The Sting and the Twinkle: Conversations with Sean O'Casey*, ed. E. K. Mikhail and John O'Riordan. London: Macmillan, 1974.
Hogan, Robert. *The Experiments of Sean O'Casey.* New York: St. Martin's, 1960.
Kilroy, Thomas, ed. *Sean O'Casey: A Collection of Critical Essays.* Englewood Cliffs, NJ: Prentice-Hall, 1975.
Kleiman, Carol. *Sean O'Casey's Bridge of Vision: Four Essays on Structure and Perspective.* Toronto: Toronto University Press, 1982.
Krause, David. *Sean O'Casey: The Man and His Work.* New York: Macmillan, 1960.
———. *Sean O'Casey and His World.* New York: Scribner's, 1989.
Margulies, Martin B. *The Early Life of Sean O'Casey.* Dublin: Dolmen, 1970.
O'Casey, Eileen. *Sean.* London: Macmillan, 1971.
O'Connor, Gary. *Sean O'Casey: A Life.* New York: Atheneum, 1988.
O'Riordan, John. *A Guide to O'Casey's Plays.* London: Macmillan, 1984.
Schrank, Bernice. "Anatomizing an Insurrection: Sean O'Casey's *The Plough and the Stars.*" *Modern Drama* 24.2 (June 1986): 216–28.

Pádraig Ó Conaire

(1883–1928)

Cóilín D. Owens

BIOGRAPHY

Pádraig Ó Conaire was born in Galway in March 1883. Eleven when both his parents died, he was raised by his grandparents in the Connemara Gaeltacht. After finishing secondary school, he spent some time at sea and joined the British civil service in London. Under the auspices of the London branch of the Gaelic League, he met many of the new generation of political and cultural nationalists and began his writing career. He soon established himself as the leading new figure in Irish writing. His wide reading in European fiction and drama, especially the Russians, Scandinavians, de Maupassant, Balzac, Hardy, and Meredith, shaped his attitudes toward writing in Irish.

Undertaking a purely literary career was a high-risk venture, especially for a man with a weakness for alcohol and a commitment to writing in Irish only. But in this pioneering venture Ó Conaire persevered, living precariously as a nomad mainly in the Galway and Wicklow regions, with occasional walking tours to the Continent. He supported himself mainly by journalism and the writing of schoolbooks, supplemented in his later years by part-time teaching of Irish. A complete bibliography of his writing includes a dozen books, 400 short stories, four dramas, a novel, and more than 200 essays and occasional pieces (see Ní Chionnaith). His legend survives his premature death (October 6, 1928) in F. R. Higgins's fond and admiring poem and in Albert Power's leprechaun-like statue in Eyre Square, Galway. (Ó Conaire is not to be confused with Pádraig Óg Ó Conaire, 1893–1971.)

MAJOR WORKS AND THEMES

With *Nóra Mharcuis Bhig* (1909), Ó Conaire introduced a number of themes and attitudes into Irish-language fiction. His subjects were the loneliness and vices of rural, especially Gaeltacht, society, the victimization of women, the specters of mental illness and emigration, and the debasement of human values in the modern city. In this and subsequent volumes of short stories, he laid bare the sufferings of the rural poor, their hunger for land, and the prospect of the poorhouse waiting for those lacking the courage to emigrate. Yet, for all their degradation, Ó Conaire's country people retain a dignity and imaginative energy not found in city dwellers. The title story, for instance, skillfully manages shifting points of view to expose the competition between these two social orders for control of the character's identity.

"An Bhean a Ciapadh" (The Woman Made to Suffer) is an exposé of the old *cleamhnas* system (the arranged marriage) and of marital rape. This dour, realistic story, unrelieved by any humor, brings some of the techniques of the naturalistic Continental short story to bear on such abuses in rural life. For the first time, such stories present a critique in Irish more associated with his renowned English-language contemporaries, George Moore, James Joyce, and J. M. Synge.

Deoraídheacht (1910) is a picaresque novel set in London. A young Irishman, suffering a physical debility, goes through a series of grotesque adventures in the seamy sections of town inhabited by poor immigrants like himself. It is the first novel of urban life in Irish, and for all its deficiencies of style and form, it showed how such a subject could be managed in native dialect. On the other hand, *An Chéad Chloch* (1914) enlarged the scope of modern fiction in Irish by its evocations of an imaginary biblical Palestine.

His *Seacht mBuaidh an Éirighe Amach* (1918) comprises seven stories of Dublin life linked by the Easter Rising. The "seven victories" celebrate instances of courage and compassion among the ordinary citizens of Dublin. The best is "Beirt Bhan Misniúil," a cleverly constructed story in the manner of Chekhov. In these disciplined short stories, Ó Conaire is at his best. He is most popularly known, however, for his many stories for children, stories reflecting the oral tradition, about animals and the happiness of life in the open air. The most famous of these is the title story from his posthumous collection *M'Asal Beag Dubh agus Scéalta Eile* (1944), a charming little tale of country life.

CRITICAL RECEPTION

In 1903 in the pages of the Gaelic League weekly, *An Claidheamh Soluis*, Patrick Pearse called for a contemporary literature in Irish. He wanted, as he put it, "to cut the rope of traditionalism which was strangling our writers." They should aspire to more than the simple reproduction of peasant life and speech, the recitation of folklore or Celtic myth. He wanted a realistic portrayal of Irish life following European models, but employing native idiom, to represent the social realities of loveless marriages, poverty, and land conflicts, which would have the effect of exposing the depredations of colonialism. Ó Conaire was the first to realize these issues in fiction.

The appearance of his name among prizewinners in Gaelic League literary competitions and the rapid adoption of his short stories and *Deoraídheacht* into school and university curricula are an indication of his early recognition. Contemporary reviews remark his fresh and original talent. Yet there were protests from nationalists (such as William P. Ryan) who regarded his work as an insult to Ireland, and from clerics (such as An tAthair Peadar Ó Laoghaire) who thought him immoral and irreligious. Knowing the power of these orthodoxies, it took extraordinary courage for a writer committed to the Irish language to write so searing a story as "Nóra Mharcuis Bhig" when he did.

Nevertheless, most published reviews of *Deoraídheacht* praised its concentrated honesty in representing the anomie of the emigrant in London. The publication of *Seacht mBua* (1918) consolidated his position as the preeminent writer in modern Irish and the only one of international stature. Subsequent writers in Irish and English on urban subjects attested to his influence. Among them were Sean O Casey, Seosamh Mac Grianna, Máirtín Ó Cadhain, Liam O' Flaherty, and Austin Clarke (see de Bhaldraithe, Denvir, 1983, and Jordan). These writers record their appreciation of his powers of observation, his love of Connacht, his critique of shallowness brought about by urbanization, his lonely dedication to his craft, and his good humor and patriotism. Jordan praises the deliberate artistry and modernity of *Deoraíocht*, its nightmarish adventures constituting "the objective correlative of a great spiritual wound."

As Ó Conaire progressed in his literary career, the oral tale tended to dominate over the more writerly models with which he had begun. This helps account for the popularity of many of his later stories, "M'Asal Beag Dubh" in particular, with Irish schoolchildren. But his claim to permanence rests on his early short stories of the lonely outsider. In the only full-length study of Ó Conaire's work, Pádraigín Riggs argues that both literal exile and metaphorical exile are his sustaining themes.

In his magisterial study of the Gaelic Revival, Philip O'Leary concludes that Ó Conaire was a true pioneer in that movement, in showing that "the language possessed the flexibility to treat entirely new [subjects] in a natural and artistic manner," while remaining "as suspicious as any Gaeltacht nativist of the 'false civilization of the age' (sibhéaltacht bréige na haoise)" (430).

BIBLIOGRAPHY

Works by Pádraig Ó Conaire

An Crann Géagach: Aistí agus Scéilíní. Dublin: Educational, 1900, 1919.
Nóra Mharcuis Bhig agus Sgéalta Eile. Dublin: Gaelic League, 1909.
Deoraídheacht: Uirsgéal ar an Aimsir Seo i Láthair. Dublin: Gaelic League, 1910, 1916; Educational, 1920; Talbot, 1973; Helicon, 1980.
An Chéad Chloch. Ed. Pádraigín Riggs. Dublin: Gaelic League, 1914; Dublin: Mercier, 1978.

Seacht mBuaidh an Éirighe Amach. Ed. Tomás de Bhaldraithe. Dublin: Maunsel, 1918;
    Dublin: Sairséal and Dill, 1967.

Béal an Uaignis. Dublin: Mártan Lester, 1921.

M'Asal Beag Dubh agus Scéalta Eile. Dublin: Educational, 1944.

Scothscéalta. Ed. Tomás de Bhaldraithe. Intro. Seosamh Mac Grianna. Dublin: Sáirséal
    and Dill, 1956, 1957, 1978; Sáirséal, Ó Marcaigh, 1981. Trans. *The Finest Stories
    of Pádraic Ó Conaire including the Complete Translation of Scothscéalta.*
    Swords, County Dublin: Poolbeg, 1982, 1986.

Aistí Phádraic Uí Chonaire. Ed. Gearóid Denvir. Inverin, County Galway: Cló Chois
    Fharraige, 1978.

Bairbre Rua agus Drámaí Eile. Ed. Pádraig Ó Siadhail. Béal an Daingin: Cló Iar-
    Chonnachta, 1989.

Iriseoireacht Uí Chonaire. Ed. An tSr. Eibhlín Ní Chionnaith. Béal an Daingin: Cló Iar-
    Chonnachta, 1989.

Studies of Pádraig Ó Conaire

de Bhaldraithe, Tomás, ed. *Pádraig Ó Conaire: Clocha ar a Charn.* Dublin: An Cló-
    chomhar, 1982.

Denvir, Gearóid, ed.; *Aistí Phádraic Uí Chonaire.* Inverin, County Galway: Cló Chois
    Fharraige, 1978.

Denvir, Gearóid, ed. *Pádraig Ó Conaire: Léachtaí Cuimhneacháin.* Inverin, County Gal-
    way: Raidio na Gaeltachta, 1983.

Higgins, F. R. "Padraic O'Conaire, Gaelic Storyteller." In *Arable Holdings.* Dublin:
    Cuala, 1933. (Poem.)

Jordan, John. "*Deoraíocht,*" *The Pleasures of Gaelic Literature.* Cork: Mercier, 1972.

Mac Grianna, Seosamh. *Pádraic Ó Conaire agus Aistí Eile.* Dublin: Government
    Publications Office, 1936, 1969.

Murphy, Maureen. "The Short Story in Irish." *Mosaic* 12.3 (Spring 1979): 81–89.

Ní Chionnaith, An tSr. Eibhlín. "Pádraic Ó Conaire: Liosta Saothair." *Pádraic Ó Con-
    aire: Léachtaí Cuimhneacháin.* Inverin, County Galway: Cló Chonamara, 1983,
    65–83.

Ó Broin, Tomás. *Saoirse Anama Uí Chonaire: Campánach d'Urscéal Fiontrach "Deo-
    raíocht".* Gaillimh: Officina Typographica, 1984.

Ó Háinle, Cathal. *Promhadh Pinn.* Maynooth, County Kildare: An Sagart, 1978.

O'Leary, Philip. *The Prose Literature of the Gaelic Revival: 1881–1921.* University Park,
    PA: Penn State University Press, 1994.

Riggs, Pádraigín. *Pádraic Ó Conaire: Deoraí.* Dublin: An Clóchomhar, 1994.

Frank O'Connor
(Michael O'Donovan)

(1903–1966)

Michael Steinman

BIOGRAPHY

An only child, Michael O'Donovan was born into poverty in Cork on September 17, 1903. His father, an ex-soldier, was intermittently employed as a laborer, and his beloved mother worked as a domestic to keep them from starving. Except for the brief period when Daniel Corkery was his teacher, his formal education was unrewarding and ended before his teens. During the Troubles, he joined the Republicans, was captured by Free State soldiers, and was imprisoned. On his release, he became a librarian, heading the Cork County Library, then organizing the Pembroke Library in Dublin. The security these positions provided enabled him to write, and he worked as a librarian for a decade. Being a civil servant, however, restricted free expression, so he took the pseudonym Frank O'Connor, combining his middle name and his mother's maiden name. In his twenties, he found a mentor and friend in AE, who published his first fiction, translations, and essays in the *Irish Statesman* and praised him in 1928, saying, ''There will be a biographer for Frank O'Connor.'' On a ''youthful pilgrimage'' to Paris, he met Joyce and came away with the anecdote of Joyce's picture of Cork in a cork frame. Although fascinated by Joyce's innovations, O'Connor took as his literary models nineteenth-century realists Chekhov, Flaubert, and Turgenev. He also began a gratifying relationship with Yeats, who published his work in Cuala editions and, in 1935, made him a director of the strife-torn Abbey Theatre. For his part, Yeats was inspired by O'Connor's translations of Irish poetry, such as ''Kilcash,'' and buoyed by the younger man's affection. Those who would see Yeats plain will find him in O'Connor's portraits, simultaneously loving and irreverent. After Yeats's death, O'Connor made writing his profession for the rest of his life, except for intervals of teaching and lecturing.

O'Connor's life to 1939 is marvelously presented in his autobiographies, *An Only Child* and *My Father's Son*. The 1983 biography, *Voices*, offers new information but is consistently unsympathetic; Maurice Sheehy's memorial collection of essays, *Michael/Frank*, is an invaluable counterbalance. In the late 1930s O'Connor's work was praised beyond Ireland; he was an often controversial public figure at the Abbey and a founding member of *The Bell*; he broadcast regularly on the BBC and Radio Eireann. The 1940s were less hospitable times, beginning with the Irish government's severe disapproval of his 1942 *Horizon* article "The Future of Irish Literature," which attacked the censorship, the "emptiness and horror of Irish life." In March 1952, having endured a decade's official hostility, he left for America to teach Irish literature, the modern novel, and fiction writing at Northwestern and Harvard. After returning permanently to Ireland in 1961, he also taught at Trinity, the only institution to grant him an honorary degree. When he died of a heart attack on March 10, 1966, his reputation as a masterful writer of short stories, a magnificent translator, and an assured literary critic had been secure for more than thirty years.

MAJOR WORKS AND THEMES

O'Connor's stories and novels show him as an enthralled student of human behavior who viewed his subjects realistically yet entirely without cynicism. Lyrical and detailed, his fiction looks closely at a middle-class Irish Catholic world with amusement, sorrow, puzzlement, and occasionally, anger. He concentrated on those moments of stress that reveal essential character, whether the stress was the Irish Troubles, a morally censorious community, an ungratifying marriage, or an unsympathetic family. The irreversible changes intense stress produced, which O'Connor said were inspired by Gogol's "The Overcoat," defined the short story for him, a transfiguring experience with lasting repercussions. In his stories, individuals define themselves in relation to overlapping communities—nation, township, parish, extended family, spouse, and children—and confront loss, loneliness, and estrangement. In the grip of yearnings they cannot verbalize, they often die unfulfilled. Although O'Connor's settings are domestic, his ordinary kitchens and bedrooms are built on emotional abysses. Much of his work focuses on conflicts (within the family and between families) over marriage, religion, personal ethics, and work. The difficulties of love were a predominant theme; indeed, a favorite working title for many stories was "First Love," although he always avoided romantic formulas. The struggle between personal morality and a depersonalized law reverberates in many stories, as in "Guests of the Nation," "The Majesty of the Law," and "In the Train." The surface of his fiction is exceedingly deceptive in its apparent simplicity, yet his moral vision is complex, his characters entangled in conflicting desires.

Because O'Connor was rarely satisfied with his own work, he revised it even after publication, so his output is remarkably large. He believed in his own creative method, which began with a four-line "theme" in which the "kernel" of the story was presented in algebraic plainness. He described the theme of "Michael's Wife," for instance, as "X marries Y abroad. After Y's death, X returns to home of Y's parents, but does not tell them Y is dead." Rewriting diligently, he created multiple versions, experimenting with point of view, language, narration and dramatization, and expansion and compression. A particularly difficult and ambitious story, "The Little Mother," survives in seventeen separate versions, over 500 pages in all, the results of a decade's work. Many stories began with an anecdote, heard or remembered, but comparing a finished story with the unembellished incident shows that he consistently re-created his first inspirations.

His first volume of stories, *Guests of the Nation* (1931), and his first novel, *The Saint and Mary Kate* (1932), were works he later assessed with unjustified severity, although the novel and its 1940 successor, *Dutch Interior*, are memorable primarily for the stories that might have been formed from the same material. His first book, collecting 1924–1930 stories primarily about the Irish civil war, bears the title of the widely anthologized "Guests of the Nation," which drew on his experiences as a young rebel. A story many writers envied (and some "borrowed"), "Guests of the Nation" easily overshadows the volume's other stories, except "Procession of Life."

His second collection, *Bones of Contention* (1936), explores familiar provincial territory: the lane, the group around the gas lamp, the tram, the church, the brass band, the pub. Its stories display his skill at capturing the nuances of the spoken voice, which he modestly ascribed to a weak visual imagination. "In the Train" portrays the opposition of traditional codes of honor and new, urbanized law in the tensions between Helena Maguire, who has poisoned her elderly husband, and the people of provincial Farranchreesht, who perjure themselves at her trial. "The Majesty of the Law" again dramatizes the struggle between tradition and modernity as old Dan Bride, who has cracked his neighbor's skull in argument, refuses to pay the fine but chooses to uphold his honor in jail. *Bones of Contention* is also distinguished by a mournful comedy of a Cork brass band devoted equally to music and liquor, "Orpheus and His Lute," and a satire on the endless talk about national problems offered as a substitute for action, "What's Wrong with the Country?" "Michael's Wife," richer than its theme, is an early example of O'Connor's exploration of the heart-mysteries of affection.

The stories of *Crab Apple Jelly* (1944) transfigured the incidents of his childhood. In "Old Fellows," the child-narrator must accompany his easily intoxicated father on a weekend outing; "The Long Road to Ummera" recalls his grandmother's insistence on being buried in her village cemetery. The most affecting tales are "The Bridal Night" and "The Luceys." The first depicts love's power to create and destroy human loneliness; the latter focuses on the pride that divides brothers and their families in a small town where secrets are impossible. Because of his struggle to write the latter, O'Connor called it his favorite story.

In 1945, he published "News for the Church" in the *New Yorker* and began a twenty-year relationship with the magazine, which brought his work its widest audience. It also allowed him to work with editor William Maxwell, a gifted writer and his devoted friend. *The Common Chord* (1947) is characterized by a sexual openness that shocked some reviewers. It was not O'Connor's intention to seem "modern" or to pander to an audience but instead to write freely about the crises of adult life. In "The Holy Door," a respected tradesman is miserable because he and his wife are childless, the situation complicated by his extra-marital affair. All is enacted against the backdrop of a proudly moral town, hungry for every detail. In reality, that censorious Irish community surrounded O'Connor as he wrote: his translation of Brian Merriman's *The Midnight Court* was banned as indecent in 1946, *The Common Chord* in 1947, *Traveller's Samples* in 1951.

Traveller's Samples displays four famous and psychologically unerring examples of a boy's-eye view of the universe, where the narrator and his affectionate mother often form an alliance against an unsympathetic father—"First Confession," "The Man of the House," "The Drunkard," "The Thief." His precocious young boys are cheerfully self-confident, although their innocence, ignorance, and inexperience result in bittersweet comedies. Yet O'Connor refused to condescend to them, even when they were most foolish; in laughter, we recognize ourselves.

In 1952, he assembled his first retrospective collection, *The Stories of Frank O'Connor*, which Horace Reynolds called "a new landmark in Anglo-Irish fiction." It was followed by *More Stories* (1954), equally well received. His second retrospective collection was notable for "The Mad Lomasneys" and "Lonely Rock," atypical love stories. The first, resembling "The Little Mother" in scope, celebrates our propensity for making wrong choices with (or perhaps because of) the best intentions, as the couple meant for each other since childhood marry others for foolish but irreversible reasons. "Lonely Rock" is a moving story of an unorthodox extended household under one roof in wartime England—a philandering husband, his knowing yet loyal wife, his elderly mother, his latest love, and her child.

Domestic Relations, a 1957 collection, reminded Denis Johnston of *Dubliners*, although Johnston said that O'Connor's "sense of form and discipline" surpassed Joyce's. It returned to the thematic format of earlier collections: O'Connor had envisioned a companion volume, *Public Relations*; one devoted to priests, *The Collar*; one about children, with the punning title *Small Ones*; and *The Little Town: Scenes of Provincial Life*. Beginning with six stories about "Larry Delaney," it follows his growth from a mother's boy of five to a seventeen-year-old brigade quartermaster in the Volunteers. Of these, "The Man of the World" is a memorable exploration of voyeurism and shame.

When O'Connor lectured at Stanford University, Wallace Stegner urged him to publish his theories about the short story and his observations about the masters of the form; the resulting book, *The Lonely Voice: A Study of the Short Story*, says as much of O'Connor as of his subjects. To him, the short story had, instead of a hero, "a submerged population group" made up of "tramps, artists, lonely idealists, dreamers, and spoiled priests." His literary criticism was always vividly, even audaciously, personal, but his experience gave him undeniable credibility, and his prose challenges readers' preconceptions. *The Lonely Voice* was no anomaly, as shown by forty years of essays and articles on Irish history, politics, archaeology, culture, fiction, theater, and dream interpretation.

Collection Two (1964), the British version of *More Stories*, was the last volume he assembled; to understand his creative process, readers should compare the 1931 and 1963 versions of "Procession of Life," about a teenage boy whose father locks him out of the house. His later work is more deeply melancholy, exploring complicated relations. It is neither gloomy nor bleak, but the solutions once accessible are now unattainable or won only through loss. *Collection Three* (published in America, slightly revised, as *A Set of Variations*) contains remarkable and little-known stories. "Music When Soft Voices Die" is technically striking, apparently a plotless series of conversations about romance, love, sexuality, and morals among three women, as if they were string instruments in a chamber trio. A darker story, "The Cheat," depicts Dick Gordon, an atheist who is born Catholic and who marries a Protestant; when she [his wife] begins taking instruction secretly, he is heartbroken at what he perceives as a betrayal. Similarly, the conventions of parenthood are rewritten in "A Set of Variations on a Borrowed Theme," where the foster children Kate Mahoney takes in at sixty become a family more real than her own children. In 1981, his widow, Harriet Sheehy, assembled *The Cornet Player Who Betrayed Ireland* from uncollected and unpublished stories; in 1993, she collected his stories of Irish priests in *The Collar*. The 1982 *Collected Stories*, introduced by his friend Richard Ellmann, assembled one-third of his 200 published stories. Given the immensity of O'Connor's canon, even ignoring multiple published versions, a truly "collected" single volume is inconceivable. *A Frank O'Connor Reader* (1994) emphasized previously unavailable material: translations of poetry, essays, and interviews, as well as fiction.

His bibliography, thirty-two pages in *Michael/Frank*, shows that O'Connor was prolific and versatile. His plays—several produced at the Abbey, several published after his death—are often set against tumultuous events in Irish history, such as the Phoenix Park murders and Parnell's fall. Even more memorable are his translations of early Irish poetry, not only for his scholarship but also for the animation he brought to the originals, especially his *The Midnight Court* and the *Lament for Art O'Leary*, which are fully realized, satisfying poetry on their own. Yeats called his translations "beautiful and moving"; the *Times Literary Supplement* ranked them with the work of Rosseti, Pound, or Waley.

CRITICAL RECEPTION

O'Connor's reputation over the past sixty-five years rests on paradoxes. Although his short fiction is highly regarded, only a few stories are well known and widely reprinted (to the exclusion of others, equally memorable)—"Guests of the Nation," "My Oedipus Complex," and "First Confession." Too, he is often misread as limited to affectionate vignettes of children, where no dilemma is irreparable. During his lifetime an international audience agreed with Yeats's tribute that "O'Connor is doing for Ireland what Chekhov did for Russia"; he was published before he was thirty, translated widely, appreciated early: L.A.G. Strong said that "*Guests of the Nation* puts its author at once among the finest living writers of the short story." Otis Ferguson praised *Bones of Contention* in *The New Republic*: "Whatever the setting and whoever the people . . . O'Connor belongs to literature by virtue of having the seasoned heart and mind (by which we mean a good man) together with the certain craft of hand and eye, by which we mean a fine writer." Indeed, reviewers criticized his work only when they felt it fell short of the high standards set by his last book. When, after his death, his fiction and reminiscences no longer appeared in *The New Yorker*, his literary criticism in the *New York Times Book Review* or the *Spectator*, he seemed to fade from view, and some readers wrongly saw his moral sense as that of an older generation.

O'Connor has, as well, received less critical attention than his work deserves, perhaps because critics cannot chart "development" from early to mature work, as his best writing, whether from 1930 or 1965, stands assuredly on its own, and he belonged to no particular modernist school or movement. Ironically, however, he has been no more badly neglected than his contemporaries O'Faoláin and O'Flaherty. Yet his influence is pervasive, primarily on writers who transform the textures of experience in their fiction. Although more "contemporary" authors might deny his influence as somehow unfashionable, his fiction made theirs possible. His is a tangible presence behind the work of William Trevor, Ita Daly, Edna O'Brien, John McGahern, and Roddy Doyle, who offer their own, sometimes bleaker, sometimes wilder variations on cherished themes. To casual readers, he may at first seem too direct, too traditional, his faith in individuals anachronistic. He may appear old-fashioned to those who require their fiction be explicitly sexual, narrow to those who expect it to be nakedly political. Yet his loving scrutiny of the strife between individual yearning and inescapable social constructs is undiminished by cultural changes; his lovers, couples, families are timeless, their voices resonant. We recognize their elation and frustrations, the continual battles for allegiance and affection that enliven his writing. At the end of "Guests of the Nation," the young soldier Bonaparte says, "And anything that ever happened me after I never felt the same about again"; O'Connor's best writing retains an equal power to startle, enlighten, delight, and transform its readers.

BIBLIOGRAPHY

Works by Frank O'Connor

Short stories

Guests of the Nation. New York and London: Macmillan, 1931.
Bones of Contention. New York: Macmillan, 1936.
Three Tales. Dublin: Cuala, 1941.
Crab Apple Jelly. New York: Knopf, 1944.
Selected Stories. Dublin: Fridberg, 1946.
The Common Chord. London: Macmillan, 1947.
Traveller's Samples. New York: Knopf, 1951.
The Stories of Frank O'Connor. New York: Knopf, 1952.
More Stories by Frank O'Connor. New York: Knopf, 1954.
Stories by Frank O'Connor. New York: Vintage, 1956.
Domestic Relations. New York: Knopf, 1957.
Collection Two. London: Macmillan, 1964.
Collection Three. London: Macmillan, 1969.
A Set of Variations. New York: Knopf, 1969.
Collected Stories. Ed. Richard Ellmann. New York: Knopf, 1981.
The Cornet Player Who Betrayed Ireland. Ed. Harriet Sheehy. Dublin: Poolbeg, 1981.
The Collar: Stories of Irish Priests. Selected and intro. Harriet Sheehy. Belfast: Blackstaff, 1993.

Novels

The Saint and Mary Kate. New York and London: Macmillan, 1932.
Dutch Interior. New York and London: Macmillan, 1940.

Autobiography and biography

The Big Fellow: A Life of Michael Collins. London: Nelson, 1937.
An Only Child. New York: Knopf, 1961.
My Father's Son. New York: Knopf, 1969.

Literary, historical, and cultural studies

A Picture Book, Illustrated by Elisabeth Rivers. Dublin: Cuala, 1943.
Irish Miles. London: Macmillan, 1947.
Leinster, Munster, and Connaught. London: Hale, 1950.
The Lonely Voice: A Study of the Short Story. Cleveland: World, 1962.
A Short History of Irish Literature: A Backward Look. New York: Putnam's, 1967.

Original poetry and translations from the Irish

The Wild Bird's Nest: Poems from the Irish by Frank O'Connor with an Essay on the Character in Irish Literature by A.E. Dublin: Cuala, 1932.
Three Old Brothers and Other Poems. New York and London: Centaur Poets, Nelson, 1936.
Lords and Commons. Dublin: Cuala, 1938.

The Fountain of Magic. London: Macmillan, 1939.
A Lament for Art O'Leary. Dublin: Cuala, 1940.
The Midnight Court. London and Dublin: Fridberg, 1945.
Kings, Lords and Commons. New York: Knopf, 1959.
The Little Monasteries. Dublin: Dolmen, 1963.
A Golden Treasury of Irish Poetry, A.D. *600–1200*. Ed. trans., and intro. Frank O'Connor
        and David Greene. London: Macmillan, 1967.

Other collections

Matthews, James, ed. "A Frank O'Connor Number." *The Journal of Irish Literature*
        4.1 (January 1975).
Steinman, Michael, ed. "Frank O'Connor Issue." *Twentieth Century Literature* 35.3 (Fall
        1990).
————. *A Frank O'Connor Reader*. Syracuse: Syracuse University Press, 1994.

Selected Articles

"Joyce—The Third Period." *Irish Statesman*, April 12, 1930: 114–16.
"A Boy in Prison." *Life and Letters*, August 1934: 525–35.
"Two Friends—Yeats and A. E." *Yale Review* 29.1 (September 1939): 60–88.
"An Irishman Looks at England." *The Listener*, January 2, 1941: 20–21.
"At the Microphone." *The Bell* 2.6 (March 1942): 415–19.
"The Future of Irish Literature." *Horizon* 5.25 (January 1942): 55–63.
"James Joyce: A Post-Mortem." *The Bell* 5.5 (February 5, 1942): 363–75.
"W. B. Yeats." *Sunday Independent* (Dublin), September 12, 1948: 4.
"Ireland." *Holiday*, December 1949: 34–65.
"And It's a Lonely, Personal Art." *New York Times Book Review*, April 12, 1953: 1+.
"A Good Short Story Must Be News." *New York Times Book Review*, June 10, 1956:
        1+.
"Writing a Story—One Man's Way." *The Listener*, July 23, 1959.
"Adventures in Translation." *The Listener*, January 25, 1962: 175+.
"Introduction." In *A Portrait of the Artist as a Young Man*, by James Joyce. New York:
        Time Reading Program, 1964, xv–xxi.
"Quarrelling with Yeats: A Friendly Recollection." *Esquire*, December 1964: 157+.
" 'Willie [Yeats] Is So Silly.' " *Vogue*, March 1, 1965: 122+.

Interviews

Breit, Harvey. "Talk with Frank O'Connor." *New York Times Book Review*, June 24,
        1951: 14.
————. *The Writer Observed*. Cleveland: World, 1956, 259–61.
"Meet Frank O'Connor." *The Bell* 16.6 (March 6, 1951): 41–46.
Cowley, Malcolm, ed. *Writers at Work: The Paris Review Interviews*. New York: Viking,
        1959, 161–82.
"Talk with the Author." *Newsweek*, March 13, 1961: 98.

Studies of Frank O'Connor

Bibliographies

Brenner, Gerry. "Frank O'Connor, 1903–1966: A Bibliography." *West Coast Review* 2
        (Fall 1967): 55–64.

Sheehy, Maurice, ed. *Michael/Frank: Studies on Frank O'Connor*. New York: Knopf, 1969. ("Toward A Bibliography of Frank O'Connor's Writing," 168–99.)

Biography

Matthews, James. *Voices*. New York: Atheneum, 1983.

Studies of Frank O'Connor

Ferguson, Otis. Review of *Bones of Contention*. *New Republic* June 2, 1936: 87.

Hildebidle, John. *Five Irish Writers: The Errand of Keeping Alive*. Cambridge: Harvard University Press, 1989.

Johnston, Denis. Review of *Domestic Relations*. *Saturday Review* September 21, 1957: 40.

Kavanagh, Patrick. "Coloured Balloons: A Study of Frank O'Connor." *The Bell* 15.3 (December 1947): 11–21.

O'Connor, Harriet. "Listening to Frank O'Connor." *Nation*, August 28, 1967: 150–51.

O'Faoláin, Sean. *The Short Story*. New York: Devin-Adair, 1951.

———. "A World of Fitzies." *Times Literary Supplement*, April 29, 1977: 502–3.

Sheehy, Maurice, ed. *Michael/Frank: Studies on Frank O'Connor*. New York: Knopf, 1969.

Steinman, Michael. *Frank O'Connor at Work*. Syracuse: Syracuse University Press, 1990.

———. "A Frank O'Connor Theme-Book." *Irish University Review* 22.2 (Autumn–Winter 1992): 242–60.

Steinman, Michael, ed. *The Happiness of Getting It Down Right: Letters of Frank O'Connor and William Maxwell, 1945–1966*. New York: Knopf, 1996.

Strong, L.A.G. Review of *Guests of the Nation*. *Spectator*, October 3, 1931: 147.

Tomás Ó Crohan

(1856–1937)

Cóilín D. Owens

BIOGRAPHY

Tomás Ó Crohan was the most famous son of the Great Blasket, the largest of a group of small islands at the western extremity of the Dingle Peninsula, County Kerry. He and his wife reared ten children on a few rocky fields inherited from his father. He supported his large household by fishing, beachcombing, turf-cutting, and working his small holding. In addition to these normal hardships, he endured personal suffering with remarkable dignity. The loss of his family through emigration and death would have left him entirely alone in his latter years, were it not for his renown as a master of his native language.

Karl Marstrander, the Norwegian linguist, was the first to discover Tomás's gifts when, on a visit to the Blaskets in 1907, he asked for a vocabulary list of local fauna and flora. Marstrander directed Robin Flower, deputy keeper of manuscripts at British Museum, to the island in 1910. He continued to visit the island each summer, where he conducted lengthy daily interviews, subsequently carrying on a lifelong correspondence until Tomás's death in 1937. But it fell to a local schoolteacher and Gaelic League enthusiast, Brian O Kelly, who spent the year 1917 on the island, to encourage Tomás in the writing of his autobiography. From then on, Tomás kept a diary (published as *Allagar na hInise/ Island Cross Talk*) and wrote periodic letters to Brian, which eventually, under the editorship of Pádraig Ó Siochfhradha (''An Seabhac''), appeared as *An t-Oileánach* (1929). Robin Flower's English translation was published as *The Islandman* (1934). In the meantime, Ó Crohan was collaborating with other scholars, including George Clune and George Thompson, and dictating stories to Robin Flower, which appeared in Dublin under the title *Seanchas ón Oileáin Tiar* (1956).

Tomás Ó Crohan is the outstanding figure in a remarkable island population. While limited to a subsistence economy, living on the margins of statute law, and suffering extraordinary hardship, these people exhibited a high degree of intelligence, resource, and cultural complexity. As a repository of archaic Gaelic culture, the island community was discovered by language scholars and cultural enthusiasts, resulting in a small library, the centerpiece of which is *An t-Oileánach*. The life and work of Tomás represent the last phase of that community, from its high point of about 170 persons in 1917 to its slow depopulation and eventual abandonment in 1953.

MAJOR WORKS AND THEMES

An t-Oileánach is the first book of its kind, a genuine peasant autobiography. But it has great ethnographic interest too. It describes in absorbed detail the daily life of the people of the Blaskets: Tomás's childhood, his family, schoolteachers, neighbors; their daily and seasonal chores of fishing for mackerel and lobsters, hunting for seals and rabbits, and foraging for flotsam; their arranged marriages and dependency on the mainland for supplies and markets; their closeness to America through the bonds of emigration; the hazards and joys of their lives through storms, festivals, conversation, industry, and wit. It embraces its author's own life story within that of his people, falling into three periods: primitive life on the island before the 1850s, his childhood and youth (1856–1875), and his own and the island community's fading years (1875–1929).

It is the classic expression of vernacular Irish, showing an unequaled mastery of dialectal idiom, lean and pithy diction, and sharp and spare expression. Scholars of historical Irish are unanimous in their admiration that these qualities of clear-cutting and polishing of phrases, so much admired in the literary style of the verse and prose of the Old Irish period, should have survived in the everyday speech of ordinary members of the Gaeltacht, such as Tomás. The narrative is, moreover, interwoven with quotations from the Finn saga, scraps of legend and folklore, traditional songs, and proverbs: all the signs of traditional learning.

An t-Oileánach, then, is the still-living voice of medieval Ireland, speaking the language of its living descendants. Devoid of any latter-day politicized consciousness, its vision is parochial, its inner spirit stoic and Christian. Its character is dignified, restrained, and free of self-pity. It ushered in the vogue of autobiography from the Blaskets (such as those by Peig Sayers and Muiris Ó Suilleabháin) and other Gaeltacht dialect areas.

Allagar na h-Inse (1928), the first of Ó Crohan's books, was written 1919–1922. It captured the moment of transition from speech to writing and is thus the urtext of the flowering of the truly native literature of the western Irish seaboard. In these vivid sketches, Tomás writes from the immediacy of his experience: the delight and perils of island and sea, the struggle for subsistence, but also the consolations of community life, its humor and energy.

Seanchas ón Oilean Tiar is a fine collection of Blasket tradition, legend, and history in Ó Crohan's classic style. The result of his collaboration with Robin Flower from his first visits to the island in 1910, it was edited by Séamus Ó Duilearga and appeared in 1956.

CRITICAL RECEPTION

"The voice of the Gaeltacht itself!" was Brian O Kelly's excited comment on reading the first installments of *An t-Oileánach*. Upon its publication in 1929, it was universally and instantly recognized as a classic: for its documentary value, its style, and its moral dignity.

Daniel A. Binchy praised the spare and sinewy hardness of Ó Crohan's Irish. Rooted in regional dialect, it nevertheless has many qualities that distinguish it from ordinary conversation: mastery of idiom, effortless vocabulary, a wealth of literary allusion, and, in Flower's words, "his own informal genius for speech." Binchy found some inconsistencies and interferences in An Seabhac's editing of Ó Crohan's text. But he reserved his highest accolade for the portrait of the Gaeltacht community that emerges: the quick intelligence of the people, their ready wit, their innate good breeding and perfect manners, their hospitality and friendliness to strangers, their fortitude in adversity, their generosity, but also their contentiousness, their wild bouts of drinking, and exasperating improvidence. From the whole there emerges the epic of great and lovable people, illiterate in the modern sense but steeped in the traditional culture. He found significant differences between Tomás and the peasant of the Celtic Revival or the Gaelic nationalist, concluding poignantly that Tomás is a stranger in his own land, the spokesman for "the only survivors of the historic Irish nation."

Binchy considered Flower's translation, for its scholarly and poetic sensitivities, the ideal interpretation of Tomás's narrative. This estimation was not shared, however, by many others, including Flann O'Brien, whose *An Béal Bocht* (1941) is a pungent satire on the vogue of Gaeltacht reminiscence.

In *The Western Island*, Robin Flower saw in Tomás a symbol of a fundamental shift in the development of civilization: the representative of the stable oral tradition that had remained alive for centuries, now poisoned by the fatal drip of the printer's ink.

Classicists J. V. Luce and George Thompson found analogies between life and literature on the Great Blasket as between the early Ionian way of life and the Homeric epics. Each culture embodied communal self-reliance, a simple and virile humanism, the virtue of *mórchroí* (greatness of heart), a heroic way of life, and a precapitalist economy in which poverty was no discredit. Similarly, Tomás' style exhibits elements equivalent to those that can be found in the ancient narratives.

Seán Ó Tuama (in Rafroidi and Harmon's *The Irish Novel in Our Time*) regarded Ó Crohan as lacking in the imaginativeness, humor, inventiveness, and natural storytelling ability of either Peig Sayers or Muiris Ó Súilleabháin. Yet, paradoxically, his book rightly remains the masterpiece of Gaeltacht literature:

"more the biography of an island community than of a single islander . . . a majestic sociological document."

To John Wilson Foster, Ó Crohan "comes as close to unequipped genius as it is reasonable to expect," a primeval man awakening in a remote pocket of existence from archaism into selfhood. Thus, *An t-Oileánach* reenacts the early development of the novel almost two centuries after it occurred. Foster saw in Ó Crohan's vigilant, moral, detached circumspection a potential model for Irish writing as against the romantic pastoralism of the Revival (see *Fictions of the Irish Literary Revival* 323–40).

BIBLIOGRAPHY

Works by Tomás Ó Crohan

Réiltíní Óir. 2 vols. Ed. Seoirse MacClúin. Dublin: Educational, 1922.

Allagar na hInise. Dublin: Government Publications Office, 1928; Ed. Pádraig Ua Maoleoin, Dublin: Government Publications Office, 1977. *Island Cross-Talk: Pages from a Diary*. Trans. Tim Enright. New York: Oxford University Press, 1986.

An t-Oileánach. Ed. An Seabhac (Pádraig Ó Siochfhradha). Dublin: Fallon, 1929. Ed. Pádraig Ua Maoileoin, Dublin: Talbot, 1973. *The Islandman*. Trans. Robin Flower. Dublin: Talbot, 1937. London: Oxford University Press, 1951.

Dinnsheanchas na mBlascaodaí. Dublin: Government Publications Office, 1928.

Seanchas ón Oileán Tiar. Ed. Séamus Ó Duilearga. Dublin: Educational, 1956.

Studies of Tomás Ó Crohan

Binchy, Daniel A. "Two Blasket Autobiographies." Rev. of *The Islandman* by Tomás Ó Crohan and *Twenty Years A-Growing* by Maurice O'Sullivan. *Studies* 23 (1934): 544–60.

Flower, Robin. *The Western Island or The Great Blasket*. New York: Oxford University Press, 1944.

Luce, J. V. "Homeric Qualities in the Life and Literature of the Great Blasket Island." *Greece and Rome* 2d ser. 16 (1969): 151–68.

Mac Conghail, Muris. *Oileán Eile: Another Island*. Dublin: Radio Telefís Éireann, 1988.

O'Brien, Maire Cruise. "*An t- Oileánach*: Tomás Ó Criomhthain (1856–1937)." In *The Pleasures of Gaelic Literature*, ed. John Jordan. Dublin and Cork: RTÉ/Mercier, 1977.

Ó Lúing, Seán. "Robin Flower (1881–1946)." *Studies* 70 (1981): 121–34.

Thompson, George. *Island Home: The Blasket Heritage*. Dingle: Brandon, 1988.

Peadar O'Donnell

(1893–1986)

Bernard McKenna

BIOGRAPHY

Peadar O'Donnell was born in Meenmore, County Donegal on February 22, 1893, and attended Saint Patrick's Teacher Training College in Dublin. Even though he worked for some years as a teacher in Innisfree (1913–1916) and as principal of a school on Arranmore Island (1916–1918), O'Donnell's life work was with various social and political causes, including the Irish Transport and General Workers Union, which he joined as an organizer in 1918. In 1919 he joined the Irish Republican Army (IRA) and fought in the Anglo-Irish War. After 1922, he fought with the Republican irregulars against the treaty and was jailed for two years under sentence of death. After his escape from prison, he began a career in letters that was dedicated to social justice and a revived sense of nationhood. As part of his work, he edited two Republican newspapers: *An tOglach* (1924–1926) and *An Phoblacht* (1926–1934). In 1931 he founded Saor Eire as an organization within the IRA. However, its policies so enraged the leadership of the IRA that O'Donnell was expelled from the organization in 1934 and subsequently founded the Irish Republican Congress. In addition, he was business manager and later editor, after Sean O'Faolain, of the literary journal *The Bell* and became a founding member of the Irish Academy of Letters. Throughout his life, O'Donnell played an active role in the literary and theatrical life of the Thirty-Two Countries, participating in a variety of cultural and political causes. He died on May 13, 1986, in Dublin.

MAJOR WORKS AND THEMES

O'Donnell's novels and other creative writings tend to be political and semiautobiographical. At their worst, they read like propaganda. At their best, they bring into conflict the forces and values of rural, precolonial Ireland and the colonial culture of the naturalistic, industrialized world. The latter strips the former of its virulence and forces the inhabitants to succumb to despair and poverty, to despise the land, or to leave the land for America or an itinerant life void of family and community. The imaginative geography of O'Donnell's world vests in the ancient island communities of the Irish northwest the power to resist the oppressive forces of nature and vests in those communities the powers of solidarity, heroism, and vitality.

Novels

Storm: A Story of the Irish War (1925), O'Donnell's first novel, shows in rudimentary form its author's strengths and weaknesses as a writer. Written, in part, while O'Donnell was imprisoned by the Free State government, *Storm* contains scenes and images of landscapes and the forces of nature that serve as allegory, defining character and conflict. However, political propaganda and, at times, inappropriate political didacticism punctuate the narrative and unavoidably detract from the novel's strengths.

O'Donnell's second novel, *Islanders* (1928), was also written—or at least conceived—while the author was imprisoned, and critics consider it one of O'Donnell's best works. The book tells stories of the courage and self-sacrifice of individuals for the good of their family and community. The novel's characterization is complex and quite moving. A mother starves herself so her children might eat. A young man works himself to exhaustion fishing for his family and struggles in a curragh to reach a doctor. The use of the lone figure caught in a storm, by his own intention, in what is literally in Irish an "unstable craft" also illustrates O'Donnell's use of nature as allegory. Critics are wont to describe O'Donnell's work, particularly this novel, as naturalistic. However, the naturalistic sense of desperation does not really enter into O'Donnell's work in a sustained way. Rather, individual character and the strength of community seem able to counter the forces of blind circumstance in just the way a skilled seaman can manipulate the "unstable craft" with great skill and to his advantage precisely because it is unstable. In addition, there are subtle references to a living Irish mythic past that further reinforce the power and vitality present in these islanders' lives.

O'Donnell's next four novels move away from island life in Donegal onto the mainland and, in moving, focus in more traditionally naturalistic terms on the lives of desperation of residents of various communities. The first of these novels, *Adrigoole* (1929), is considered an uneven work. Written in Dublin, its first half is brilliantly executed. However, the second half seems rushed and at times ill conceived and contrived. Early in the novel, the main character leaves his home to seek work; his absence of eight years steals from him the sense of family and community that sustain the families in *Islanders*. Upon his return, he forms a family, builds a home, and begins a farm. However, the forces of the natural world and poverty destroy his family and destroy any remnant of a connection he may have had in his youth with a spiritual or mythic past that could have sustained him.

Critics consider O'Donnell's next work, *The Knife: A Tale of Irish Troubles* (1930), his weakest, condemn its oftentimes melodramatic plot twists and dialogue, criticize its sometimes shallow characterization, and find fault with its incoherent plot. However, it does have value insofar as the intelligible portions of plot lend insights into the subtleties of shifting allegiances and loyalties during the War of Independence and the civil war. Also, the novel's setting moves further away from the rural agrarian communities of the Irish northwest, and, as it does so, the naturalistic tone of despair gains dominance.

On the Edge of the Stream (1934) returns thematically to *Islanders*, and critics consider it one of O'Donnell's best works. Its tone is frequently humorous, and its theme is the strength of individuals and communities against the forces of the colonial and the industrialized world. Set in a town in Donegal, the novel examines, on a community level, the efforts of the church and the wealthy to destroy a cooperative. However, this plot serves largely as comic relief and as a means to clarify the novel's central conflict—the struggle of a woman to escape the emotional and physical abuse of her husband. The dialogue and imagery tie the husband to the powers that attempt to destroy the cooperative. The woman, like the community of farmers, attempts to cling to her humanity and individual spirituality despite her condition.

O'Donnell's next novel, *The Big Windows* (1955), is considered the best of O'Donnell's work, and, indeed, it clarifies many of the themes of his early career. Brigid, a woman from a coastal island, moves, as a consequence of marriage, into a mainland town that, isolated from its Irish rural heritage and somewhat insulated from the effects of capitalism and industrialization, grotesquely serves as a setting for bizarre and dehumanizing customs and traditions. Brigid, however, with her island heritage, is able to reinvigorate the town.

O'Donnell's last novel, *Proud Island* (1975), is considerably weaker than his previous work. However, it does carry forward many of his themes and, significantly, returns O'Donnell's creative setting to an island. Set in contemporary (1970s) times, the novel explores the efforts of a single family to cling to the ideals of island life. However, the spiritual and economic blight that had spread throughout Ireland in his earlier works comes to the island's inhabitants. They demonstrate a possessiveness and a propriety over the land absent from islanders of earlier O'Donnell writings, and they lack the sense of family and community. Interestingly, O'Donnell gives the old traditions an ally in Dublin students who come to the island from the city as the inheritors of the old traditions.

Drama and Short Stories

O'Donnell's only play, *Wrack*, premiered on November 21, 1932. Contemporary critics compare it favorably to Synge's *Riders to the Sea*. A play in six scenes, it is set in a Donegal fishing village and explores many of O'Donnell's familiar communal themes. In addition, O'Donnell published three short stories in *The Bell*. "Remembering Kitty" is a humorous first-person reminiscence of a town gossip. "Why Blame the Sea Gulls" is about the salvage of a war supply ship off a remote portion of the Donegal coast. The story's characters initially rejoice and embrace their "good fortune" at finding the abandoned vessel. However, the reality of war haunts them when they discover the gouged eyes and pale face of a body floating in the sea. "War" studies the attitudes of a community toward those who fought in Ireland's conflicts. The story begins with a discussion of the war between Russia and Japan but soon broadens into a study of the psychological nuances of the community, which tries to put distance between itself and the conflict. Subsequently, they are haunted by memories of Irish wars that have had a direct impact on their lives.

Autobiographical Books, Reminiscences, and Political Writings

Of O'Donnell's other writings, the major work involves three "autobiographical" tracts and a short memoir. The earliest, *The Gates Flew Open* (1932), reads as a type of jail diary detailing O'Donnell's thoughts and experiences while in prison. It not only contains reflections on contemporary politics but reveals the sources of many of O'Donnell's creative works. *Salud!* (1936) details O'Donnell's experiences in Spain at the outbreak of the Spanish civil war and contains interesting observations and reflections not only on the situation in Spain but also on the Irish community's response. *There Will Be Another Day* (1963) details the events surrounding the late 1920s annuity crisis from the perspective of farming communities in Donegal. *Monkeys in the Superstructure* (1986), O'Donnell's last published work, is a short reminiscence of his career as a political activist. O'Donnell also published numerous editorials and pamphlets on Irish politics, world events, and the Irish-language question.

CRITICAL RECEPTION

Literary critics observe that the quality of O'Donnell's writings varies considerably and agree that he produced three very good novels, three excellent short stories, and a high-quality drama. Specific criticism ranges from articles on specialized aspects of O'Donnell's career to longer, book-length studies. Recently, critics in journals ranging from *Eire-Ireland* and *Cranebag*, to Irish-language periodicals such as *Comhar* and *An tUltach* have explored O'Donnell's representations of rural Ireland and an Irish heritage linked to a precolonial, pre-Christian Ireland. In 1974 Michael McInerney published a collection of newspaper biographic stories on O'Donnell's political life and work. Grattan Freyer published a specialized literary biography that coherently articulates O'Donnell's place in Ireland's literary heritage. In general terms, Freyer notes that O'Donnell has an "ear for the subtle and vivid phrase [and] . . . firsthand knowledge of the unsentimental shrewdness" of rural life (*Peadar O'Donnell* 15). Alexander G. Gonzalez has produced the first sustained critical assessment of O'Donnell's life and career, placing his work in the context of Irish literary history and giving a careful review of each of O'Donnell's literary works (*Peadar O'Donnell: A Reader's Guide*).

BIBLIOGRAPHY

Works by Peadar O'Donnell

Storm. Dublin: Talbot, 1925.
Islanders. London: Cape, 1928. (Also published under the title *The Way It Was with Them*.)
Adrigoole. London: Cape, 1929.
The Knife. London: Cape, 1930. (Also published under the title *There Will Be Fighting*.)
The Gates Flew Open. London: Cape, 1932.
Wrack. London: Cape, 1933.
On the Edge of the Stream. London: Cape, 1934.
Salud! An Irishman in Spain. London: Methuen, 1937.
"Remembering Kitty." *The Bell* 1. 1 (1940): 60–62.
"Why Blame the Seagulls." *The Bell* 1. 3 (1940): 7–9.
"War." *The Bell* 15. 3 (1954): 3–10.
The Big Windows. London: Cape, 1955.
There Will Be Another Day. Dublin: Dolmen, 1963.
Proud Island. Dublin: O'Brien, 1975.
Monkeys in the Superstructure. Galway: Salmon, 1986.

Studies of Peadar O'Donnell

Doyle, Paul. "Peadar O'Donnell: A Checklist." *Bulletin of Bibliography* 28 (January–March 1971): 3–4. (Complete list of political writings.)
Freyer, Grattan. "*Big Windows*: The Writings of Peadar O'Donnell." *Eire-Ireland* 11. 1 (Spring 1976): 106–14.
———. *Peadar O'Donnell*. Lewisburg, PA: Bucknell University Press, 1973.
Gonzalez, Alexander G. "Intricacies of Glen Life at the Turn of the Century: The Broad Appeal of Peadar O'Donnell's *The Big Windows*." *Journal of Irish Literature* 20.3 (September 1991): 19–26.
———. *Peadar O'Donnell: A Reader's Guide*. Chester Springs, PA: Dufour, 1997.
———. "Peadar O'Donnell's Short Stories." *Journal of Irish Literature* 17.1 (January 1988): 54–56.
Higgins, Michael. "Liam O'Flaherty and Peadar O'Donnell—Images of Rural Community." *Cranebag* 9. 1 (1985): 41–45.
Mac Caba, Anton. "An Brat ar Foluain i gCionn Aird, Co Thir Eoghain." *An tUltach* 68.6 (June 1991): 13.
McInerney, Michael. *Peadar O'Donnell, Irish Social Rebel*. Dublin: O'Brien, 1974.
Ni Ghruagain, Maire. "Peadar O'Donnell: Udar agus Soisialai." *Comhar* 46.7 (July 1987): 10–12.

O'Leary, Philip. "The Donegal of Seamus O Grianna and Peadar O'Donnell."*Eire-Ireland* 23.2 (Summer 1988): 135–49.

O Ruairc, Maolmhaodhog. "Seosamh Mac Grianna: Aistriheoir." *Comhar* 47.1 (January 1988): 30–35.

Zemlyanoy, O. "Heroic Spain in the Works of Peadar O'Donnell." *Studies in Roman and German Philology* (1977): 172–77.

Julia O'Faolain

(1932–)

Ann Owens Weekes

BIOGRAPHY

Julia O'Faolain was born into a family of writers and romantics; her mother, Eileen Gould O'Faolain, wrote children's stories; her father, Sean O'Faolain, was a distinguished writer and editor of the fine literary journal, *The Bell*. Disillusioned by the protectionist, isolationist Ireland of the 1940s, Sean became a voice of dissent against the pruderies and pretensions of this Ireland, a voice that his daughter would echo. Eileen also shaped her daughter's perspectives by keeping her home until she was eight, audience for her own stories of fairies, pookas, and leprechauns. When she finally went to school, Julia incautiously revealed her knowledge and belief in the fairy world. The mockery of her skeptical peers determined her never to be caught out again, and from this time, she turned a "cold eye" on all the myths of church and state and, we should add, class. Her parents, she says, bequeathed her a fascination with magic and an inability to believe in it; the conjurer's art attracts, but she is alert to the sleight of hand rather than the pleasure of mystery.

MAJOR WORKS AND THEMES

Many of the stories in O'Faolain's first collection, *We Might See Sights!* (1968), were reprinted in *Melancholy Baby* (1978). The stories range through several levels and age groups in Irish society and introduce a distinctive narratorial voice with an acute delight in penetrating pretention and an ability to paint a vivid picture with a few, apt, original, and witty words. The title story is a haunting tale about the irrational nature of desire and the link between sexuality and violence. It is an accomplished, brief story whose theme O'Faolain explores in more detail in later work, particularly in novels. The pettiness of social distinctions, urged on children by their protective parents and teachers, another familiar O'Faolain theme, also appears here. A self-conscious young Catholic woman, struggling to realize an identity through sexuality, is the narrator in "A Pot of Soothing Herbs." Alluding to the hero of Irish myths, Cuchulain, and to the heroes of the Irish war against England, the author invites us to see the young woman's situation as both a continuation and a consequence of the Irish love of talk, of story, over action. "The Knight" delights in revealing the narcissistic qualities of the Knight of Christ, bedecked in all his medieval grandeur. Fine social comedy and devastating powers of observation mark this first collection.

The next three books, *Godded and Codded* (1970), *Women in the Wall* (1975), and *Man in the Cellar* (1974), continue the social comedy and the focus on women's struggle for identity through passion, religious or secular. Sally, the protagonist of *Godded and Codded*, moves to Paris in search of sexual education and freedom from her dominating, repressive father. Godded and codded, the beautiful young woman finds lovers in plenty but discovers that lovers leave when confronted with the tedium of pregnancy or age. *Women in the Wall*, a more substantial novel, mixes fact and fiction in the story of religious and secular passion in the war-torn world of sixth-century Gaul. The title story of *Man in the Cellar* is a remarkable fable of a woman's escape from an Italian bourgeois family that expects a wife, particularly an English Protestant one, to nourish her husband's machismo. O'Faolain's comedy succeeds, despite the drastic conclusions for many of the characters, because she distances her readers, refusing to allow identification with the objects of ridicule. In 1973, O'Faolain and her husband published *Not in God's Image: Women in History from the Greeks to the Victorians*, selections from documents relating to the legal status of women. This done, she says, she can now write of women without being bound by their political concerns.

In *No Country for Young Men* (1980), the finest novel to date and short-listed for the Booker Prize, O'Faolain links the Troubles of the 1920s with those of the 1970s, as she weaves a pattern of gender and political intrigue rooted in Irish literature, history, and myth. The title and the plot undo Yeats and question both the historical and mythic record. Much of the complicated plot is embedded in the bog of Judith Clancy's mind. When her convent closes in the 1970s, Sister Judith, who was a young woman during the 1920s Troubles, is forced to live with her niece and nephew. The Diarmuid and Grainne story is replayed with the same tragic conclusion in the 1970s story of Grainne and Michael O'Malley and the American filmmaker James Duffy. The comedy here is largely restricted to the peripheral characters, and O'Faolain paints a sympathetic picture of both Grainne and Michael as one struggles for passion and identity, and the other for security. Repressed or distorted sexuality, the novel implies, in Irish myth, history, and fiction, erupts in physical violence.

Several short stories in *Daughters of Passion* (1982) also focus on sexual relations and marriage, the title story again linking violence and sexual denial. The past flashes through Maggie's mind as she endures a hunger strike for political status in Brixton Prison. Involved in the Irish Republican Army (IRA) almost by accident, Maggie, motivated by a mixture of jealousy and betrayal, kills a Special Branch investigator.

The Obedient Wife (1982) can be seen as an anatomy of a marriage, so detailed and penetrating is the analysis. Carla Verdi wishes to be a model mother and housewife as she attempts to bring up her son in a traditional Italian manner despite the chaos of her Los Angeles surroundings. Feeling rejected by her macho husband, Carla turns to Leo, a priest, who, sensitive to her every need, is the antithesis of her husband. Carla weighs the ties of marriage: the mutual responsibilities, the good and bad memories, the defining duties, against the excitement of a love affair and decides for marriage. Marco, Carla's husband, plays every card to persuade her to return to the life they have built in Italy, whereas Leo never makes demands. Carla sees Leo's restraint as evidence of an autonomy fatal to human relationships: needing only God, Leo cannot participate in a relationship built in large part from mutual need.

The Irish Signorina (1984) turns to the lover's side, as Anne Ryan visits the Italian family with whom her mother lived twenty-five years previously. Befriended by the family, Anne almost becomes her mother, her passion for her mother's ex-lover transcending even the natural concerns of incestuous marriage. This exploration into forbidden love was followed by *The Judas Cloth* (1992). Covering the reign of Pius IX, 1846–1878, this panoramic novel moves from Italy to France and introduces a wide cast of historic and fictional characters, including Nicola Santi, the pope's son. O'Faolain describes Machiavellian intrigue skillfully and wittily, re-creating historical scenes vividly, with detailed, authentic, and bloody descriptions of atrocities and betrayals. Characters in this too-large cast are not fully developed, however, and hence their behaviors are often unbelievable.

CRITICAL RECEPTION

Julia O'Faolain's original and apt description, insight into the complexities of human motivation and action, and acid sense of humor won attention and usually acclaim from the earliest stories. John Mellors finds *Man in the Cellar* "brilliantly disturbing" and notes the writer's manipulation of perspective, "so that you finally sympathize with the harpy, cancel your admiration of the sophisticated daughter of stuffy parents, wonder whether the hero is not far sicker than the villain" (*The Listener*, September 26, 1974: 416). Janet Egleson Dunleavy notes O'Faolain's "ability to draw a repulsive character with a few cruel strokes," but she laments that the writer uses satire for ridicule rather than forcing her readers to relate the characters to their own lives (*Irish University Review* 4.2 [Autumn 1974]: 299–300). Other critics complain of "superfatted" descriptions or wallowing in violence. On the other hand, Maurice Harmon finds

O'Faolain's vision "harshly realistic," for "she sees the fury and the mire of human blood in an era when the supernatural was closer to human perception than it is now, when mystics apprehended the divine in terms of startling reality" (*Irish University Review* 5.2 [Autumn 1975]: 324). "Skillfully spun and splendidly readable," William Trevor says of *No Country for Young Men*, "illuminated by a seriousness that is refreshing to encounter; though entertaining and rich in comedy, it eschews the trivial and is actually *about* something" (*Hibernia*, June 5, 1980).

BIBLIOGRAPHY

Works by Julia O'Faolain

We Might See Sights. London: Faber and Faber, 1968.
Godded and Codded. (In United States, *Three Lovers*.) New York: Coward, McCann and Geoghegan, 1970.
Not in God's Image: Women in History from the Greeks to the Victorians. Ed. with Lauro Martines. 1973. Reprinted, London: Virago, 1979.
Man in the Cellar. London: Faber and Faber, 1974.
Women in the Wall. 1975. Reprinted, London: Virago, 1985.
No Country for Young Men. Middlesex: Penguin, 1980.
Daughters of Passion. Middlesex: Penguin, 1982.
The Obedient Wife. 1982. Reprinted, Middlesex: Penguin, 1983.
The Irish Signorina. Middlesex: Penguin, 1984.
The Judas Cloth. 1992. Reprinted, London: Minerva, 1993.

Studies of Julia O'Faolain

Mastin, Antoinette. "Stephen Dedalus in Paris: Joycean Elements in Julia O'Faolain's *Three Lovers*." *Colby Quarterly* 30.4 (December 1994): 244–51.
Moore, Thomas. "Triangles and Entrapment: Julia O'Faolain's *No Country for Young Men*." *Colby Quarterly* 27.1 (March 1991): 9–16.
Weekes, Ann Owens. "Diarmuid and Grainne Again: Julia O'Faolain's *No Country for Young Men*." *Eire-Ireland* 21.1 (Spring 1986): 89–102.

Sean O'Faolain

(1900–1991)

Richard Bonaccorso

BIOGRAPHY

Much of Sean O'Faolain's writing reflects upon his youthful rebellions against familial and cultural constraints. The son of transplanted country folk, John Whelan was born in Cork, Ireland, on February 22, 1900. With patriotic ardor, he would adopt the Irish version of his name two years after the 1916 Easter Rising. His father, Denis, a member of the Royal Irish Constabulary, was a devoted servant of the British imperial system. Religious duty toward the family's Catholic faith obsessed his mother, Bridget. Poor, morally conservative, and yet desperately ambitious, Denis and Bridget required their three sons to keep aloof from their less-pretentious schoolmates.

O'Faolain's inclination to break from his parents' narrow lives partly accounts for his embracing of the underdog fellowship of Irish political rebellion. While at University College, Cork (UCC), he joined the revolutionary movement as a twenty-year-old Irish Volunteer. Within two years, as an Irish Republican Army (IRA) man in the civil war, he would be a defeated and religiously excommunicated rebel on the run. These times were alternately inspiring and traumatizing, but with the establishment of what for him was an unsatisfactory peace, O'Faolain began to react against the unproductive sentimentality of his heretofore unquestioning patriotism.

Literary friendships with two fellow Corkonians, Daniel Corkery and Michael O'Donovan (Frank O'Connor), were of early and long-lasting significance. In the case of the older, Irish Irelander Corkery, inspiration would turn into intellectual and political antagonism. The relationship with O'Connor was close and mutually productive for many years, but their temperamental differences caused them to be intensely combative with each other.

In 1926, three years after returning to UCC as an M.A. student, O'Faolain received a Commonwealth Fund Fellowship that allowed him to study abroad; he chose Harvard. At about the same time, his early Cork story, "Lilliput," appeared in *The Irish Statesman*, edited by George Russell (AE). With introductions from Liam O'Flaherty, he also made contact with the publisher's reader, Edward Garnett, who would nurture his early career as a fiction writer. In Boston in 1928, he married Eileen Gould, also from Cork. He had known her since he was eighteen, and the marriage lasted until her death in 1988. They had two children: Julia, the future writer, born in 1932, and Stephen, born in 1938. The young family returned to live in Ireland in 1933, where his precarious economic existence made O'Faolain's general man-of-letters role a necessity.

From his early maturity as a thinking man, O'Faolain was inclined to challenge the zealotry of right-wing nationalism and conservative religion. After two of his earliest works, *Midsummer Night Madness* (1932) and *Bird Alone* (1936), were banned by the Irish Censorship Board, O'Faolain began a lifelong intellectual confrontation with Little Irelander provincialism. To him, the Irish censorship mentality was a betrayal of the sacrifices of the revolutionary generation and a threat to the intellectual future of his country. Considerations of the relationship between nationality and personality, his biographies of Constance Markievicz (1934) and Daniel O'Connell (1938) were ambitious efforts to liberate and modernize the Irish conscience. Between 1941 and 1945, in the period of Irish neutrality and, in effect, cultural isolation, he labored as the dynamic editor of *The Bell*. He almost single-handedly created the cultural journal, midwifing the fledgling efforts of a generation of Irish writers and articulating his opposition to the socially conservative Establishment.

This intense involvement with Irish affairs sometimes left him exhausted and depressed, but in the 1950s he again found stimulation by going abroad. Graham Greene helped arrange terms with publishers of O'Faolain's two Italian travel books, works that reflect the optimistic, expansive sides of his nature. He also conducted, at Princeton, the first of several academic lecture tours in the United States in 1953. He became an admired literary figure in America, where his wit was less combative and more amiable. *The Vanishing Hero*, his book on the antihero in modern fiction, was one fruit of this first tour. The 1960s were as productive a period as he ever had as a story writer, yet the deaths of friends and loved ones haunted him. In 1966 O'Connor died. Three years later Alene Erlanger—an American woman he had loved since meeting her in the early 1950s—also died. Yet he continued being a workhorse into his seventies and even early eighties. Robie Macauley, fiction editor for *Playboy* from 1966 to 1974, published a great number of his later tales, which were among his best.

Though tending to be reclusive, he was a vital, engaging old man, but after Eileen died in 1988, he finally seemed to lose his drive and focus. He died in Dublin on April 20, 1991.

MAJOR WORKS AND THEMES

O'Faolain's vision and style grow in sophistication throughout his long career, but the essential romantic irony that is at the heart of his particular appeal is there from the beginning. His first collection of stories, *Midsummer Night Madness* (1932), and his first novel, *A Nest of Simple Folk* (1934), are enormously nostalgic and almost mystical evocations of Irish times and places, qualities he would mute but never abandon in his later work. There is also an uncompromising, intellectually detached strain in this early fiction, a tough-mindedness that would emerge as his signature prose quality. This ability at once to be and not be seduced by one's own emotions is a natural element of O'Faolain's personality, and he found a model for its expression in Chekhov and in the story writing of the nineteenth-century Europeans. O'Faolain was as capable as his mentor, Corkery, of being an idealistic nationalist and of admiring revolutionary heroes, but he was much quicker to have second thoughts and to question his own enthusiasms. This tendency often made his life unsettling in absolutist Ireland, but as a complexity projected into his writing, it made him a special kind of artist, particularly in the story form.

"Fugue," a story in *Midsummer Night Madness*, serves as an example of that collection's merging of nationalistic and personal obsessions. The revolutionary experience is defined in romantic terms, yet the story rests upon a predominating irony. A young Irish rebel is fleeing through the West Cork mountains from advancing Black and Tans. Distant perspectives of the hills and valleys are set against the cringing claustrophobia that a hunted man feels. While the wind and rainy fog alternately brace and oppress him, this young man runs for his life in actual and figurative terms. In a brief, amorous meeting with a young woman in a farmhouse where he hides, one glimpses his intense loneliness and life-longing, which seem to correlate with the romantic but barren landscape itself. The great outer world of Ireland feeds a sublime but seemingly insatiable hunger for an all but impossible union of national and personal life, freedom and love. The story and the whole collection deal with inspiring but unfulfilling Irish idealism, imaged in "Fugue" when the hunted and haunted protagonist sees, from the hills, a small farmhouse light in a vast, dark valley.

O'Faolain's second novel, *Bird Alone* (1936), also deals with the exaltation and the despair of the rebellious. It shows a correspondence between national insurrection against the political oppressor and personal rebellion against a homebred moral repression. Set in the city of Cork in the years following the death of Parnell, the work is narrated as a tragic reminiscence by the protagonist, Corney Crone, who, in his intellectually proud youth, defied the sexual mores of his community. Learning anticlericalism from his old Fenian grandfather, Corney attempts to indoctrinate his morally conservative girlfriend, Elsie Sherlock, in his freethinking ways. She becomes pregnant and, unable to defy the placid rectitude of her family, destroys herself. Corney is left to grieve for her, to regret his vain gesture, and to live as a moral pariah in his native city.

Difficult, though successful, revolution, wherein intellectual and practical ends ultimately unite, might be considered the theme of O'Faolain's great biography of Daniel O'Connell, *King of the Beggars* (1938). Here again, the historical manifests the personal. In *Sean O'Faolain: A Life* (1994), Maurice Harmon points to this work as a challenge to its author's life vision: "O'Connell's wavering, ambiguous personality seemed to resemble his own day-to-day uncertainties as he tried to cope with the new Ireland and to accommodate his own moral dilemmas" (112). Knowing the habits of subservience that history had inculcated in his people, O'Connell, O'Faolain argues, freed the Irish mind from the paralysis of sentimental, Gaelicized nostalgia and gave it an idea of a viable future as a modern European nation. In *King of the Beggars* O'Faolain makes his strongest case against the Irish Ireland mentality represented, for example, in Corkery's *The Hidden Ireland*.

The Man Who Invented Sin (1948) contains several masterful tales, including the title story and "The Silence of the Valley"—both set in the West Cork environs of Gougane Barra—and "Up the Bare Stairs," a semiautobiographical work set in Cork. These stories are elegiac comedies, gently satiric considerations of how the Irish past disturbs the Irish present. In "Up the Bare Stairs," Francis Nugent, a successful man of the world, tells the story of his escape from the shabby-genteel lives of his parents. They are modeled on O'Faolain's own parents, and the bare stairs of the title refer to his childhood home on Half Moon Street. O'Faolain hints that to some extent both he and Nugent remain troubled by old family self-afflictions, that one can rise above, but never forget, the compromising pity of such a childhood.

To seek an escape from the limitations of the past and yet to be ever conscious of its unsettling power is more than a fictional motif in his writing. It is part of a paradoxical vision of the whole Irish experience. In his cultural study, *The Irish*, O'Faolain evokes a nation struggling to complete its identity out of its fragmented history. He also prescribes a fusionist, rather than an exclusivist, approach to this national task, arguing that Ireland's uniqueness is best found by embracing its cultural variousness, not by retreating into xenophobic racialism.

The struggle for integrity amid the ruins of the past is one of the main concerns of *I Remember! I Remember!* (1959), a story collection that marks a change in O'Faolain's fictional tone. From this time onward, his stories tend to be less romantically combative and more humorously contemplative in the way they confront Irish life and personal obsessions. Yet these are deeply felt works. A spiritual coming-of-age and an acceptance of the unresolved legacy of memory prove to be lifelong challenges for his characters. Even the most ordinary and unreflective must eventually confront themselves in this way. For example, late in his life, Daniel Cashen, a hardheaded country businessman, finds himself touched by a penetrating reverie of young love in "A Touch of Autumn in the Air." He, like many of O'Faolain's aging characters, stumbles over his past and kicks up a long-dormant part of himself, "that part of memory," as O'Faolain states in the collection's title story, "where desire lies dozing, awaiting the call to arms" (3). "The Sugawn Chair," a brief, brilliant story from the same collection, is almost straight autobiography—a recollection of boyhood in Cork and of O'Faolain's parents warming themselves in sentimental recollections of their agrarian roots. Here again the writer evokes the seductions of old affections while being ironically precise about the self-delusions involved.

The creative use of the past is the main preoccupation of his autobiography, *Vive Moi!* (1964). In this essential expression of his personality, O'Faolain carries on a dialogue with the remembered boy and young man within, realizing that all creativity is an attempt to unify, by means of imaginative form, the illuminations of memory with the energies of the present.

O'Faolain's characters generally age with him, tangentially referring to his personal obsessions. Even as he projects his evolving identity into his work, the characters of *The Heat of the Sun* (1966), for example, try to take imaginative possession of their lives by bringing their unresolved desires to bear upon present relationships and actions. In "Dividends," the narrator, Sean, takes a train from his present home in Dublin back to his native Cork, a journey he likens to Orpheus's descent. Contemporary Cork is represented by his old friend Mel Meldrum, a sporting bachelor who runs a successful brokerage and who pursues, with some success, an attractive young woman. But all this is superimposed upon ghostly, antique Cork, mainly represented by Sean's old Aunt Anna Whelan, a retired housekeeper living in a tenement along the quays. Sean has come to attend to her confused economic affairs, for, after having withdrawn her shares from one of Meldrum's stocks, she still troubles him for her monthly "divvies." Indeed, all of the characters in the story would like emotional dividends without the necessary debts to pay to age, poverty, loneliness, or uncertainty. Anna's absurdly romantic notion of a grand old age reminds Sean and Mel of their own long-standing compulsions, old desires that alternately stagnate and stimulate their present lives. Imaginative improvisation, both wise and foolish, reflects the life-urge in all of this collection's tales.

Memories of Cork figure prominently in O'Faolain's *The Talking Trees* (1971), one of his best story collections. The title story, about childhood, and "The Kitchen," about old age, are exceptional works. In the first of these, a fast schoolgirl undresses for a group of young boys who are desperate to know the so-called facts of life. Puritan Cork has kept them so uninformed about sex that they conspire to pay her for her revelations. The event is a great success. The boys, who up to this moment have only imagined what they are seeing, are awakened from their imposed ignorance. But Gong Gong, the youngest, the most artistic of the gang, is sent into a new and inspiring reverie by the merest glimpse of the naked girl. She is beautiful to him, and he feels no lechery even when it is intended. The artist type, O'Faolain ironically suggests, does not merely reject the imposed myths of his community; he replaces them with those of his own invention, trading inherited enthrallment for a created one.

"The Kitchen," originally conceived as a piece of autobiography, recalls Half

Moon Street and his mother's widowhood and old age. Her peasant background causes her to fear and distrust her landlord, and when he encroaches upon her home (he wishes to expand his boot-making business into another room—her kitchen), she defends her miserable, red-tiled kitchen as if it were the "ark of the covenant that she had kept through forty years of sweat and struggle for her lost husband and her scattered children." Her son, revisiting the scene after her death to clean up her paltry possessions, considers that she was entirely right. There is nothing of value in life except that to which one gives oneself.

Foreign Affairs (1976) is O'Faolain's last original collection of tales. In them, Irish characters, caught in a limited and culturally conservative environment, search for imaginative escape routes to a more fulfilling life-mode. Their foreign affairs do not involve literal travel, but rather the daring to think the unusual in order to liberate or fulfill themselves. In "An Inside Outside Complex," for example, an antique dealer named Bertie Bolger engages in voyeuristic and narcissistic indulgences in order to come to terms with his life. A middle-aged bachelor, he spies into the living room of a widowed dressmaker named Maisie, falls in love with her domestic image, weds her, walks out, returns, and reconciles himself to his life with her. This acceptance occurs in a moment when he, standing in her living room, looks out her window and sees himself reflected in a mirror that has been left outside. Maisie is to Bertie what Ireland is to O'Faolain, an alluring but sometimes confining familiarity, a base of operations from which to see the world and to see oneself as insider and outsider at once.

The desire for the fullness of life, to live it in all of its manifestations, is the comically treated theme of *And Again?* (1979), O'Faolain's last novel and last important work. Aptly named, Robert Younger proves life to be worth living by doing so a second time, in reverse. He makes several of the same mistakes despite his countermaturation, and yet he finds lost loves, missing memories, and himself by merely living out his humanity as the gods have decreed, beginning at age sixty-five and younging through middle-age, youth, childhood, and infancy. Though the entire world is aging in the standard way around him, he finds a compatible love-mate, a woman who as lover, wife, and, ultimately, mother, helps him to unite his beginnings, two lives back, with his ending. The novel is a paradoxical parable of the creative life, imaginatively seeking out the past in order to take passionate possession of the present.

CRITICAL RECEPTION

Maurice Harmon, who knew O'Faolain well, places his work in the context of modern Irish history and culture in his *Sean O'Faolain: A Critical Introduction* (1966, 1984). Typical of his approach is his discussion of "The Silence of the Valley," pointing out the story's implicit presentation of the "disintegration of the old way of life" of peasant Ireland (101). Harmon sees the story's ancestral quality as part of a fictional vision wherein "the present and the past combine in a complex relationship" (105).

Paul Doyle's *Sean O'Faolain* (1968) also makes much of O'Faolain's Irishness. Doyle connects the writer's lover's quarrel with his country with his priorities as an artist: his poetic aspect checked by his realism, his lyric exuberance by his objective intelligence.

Joseph Rippier's *The Short Stories of Sean O'Faolain: A Study in Descriptive Techniques* (1976) emphasizes the unique features of O'Faolain's language—down to specific figures of speech—in its consideration of the writer's technical development in the story form.

A main interest of Richard Bonaccorso's *Sean O'Faolain's Irish Vision* (1987) is the writer's use of time and place as a way of exploring human identity. It considers O'Faolain's paradoxical way of winding himself into old attachments, acknowledging them in order to transcend them.

In *Sean O'Faolain: A Study of the Short Fiction* (1993), Pierce Butler considers the characters as projections of O'Faolain's own situation: eccentric, exceptional individuals at odds with their environments, people who "regard the past with a mixture of fear and longing" (92). The O'Faolain story, Butler asserts, poises upon "moments of awareness."

Harmon's *Sean O'Faolain: A Life* gives a thorough account of the contentious and difficult years of O'Faolain's struggles in becoming a writer and public figure. Harmon gives a balanced assessment of the toughness and the vulnerability of the man and the achievement and the frustration of the artist.

BIBLIOGRAPHY

Works by Sean O'Faolain

Midsummer Night Madness and Other Stories. London: Cape, 1932.
The Life Story of Eamon DeValera. Dublin: Talbot, 1933
A Nest of Simple Folk. London: Cape, 1933.
Constance Markievicz, or the Average Revolutionary. London: Cape, 1934.
Bird Alone. London: Cape, 1936.
A Purse of Coppers. London: Cape, 1937.
King of the Beggars, a Life of Daniel O'Connell. London: Nelson, 1938.
She Had to Do Something: A Comedy in Three Acts. London: Cape, 1938.
DeValera. Harmondsworth: Penguin, 1939.
Come Back to Erin. London: Cape, 1940.
The Great O'Neill, a Biography of Hugh O'Neill, Earl of Tyrone, 1550–1616. London: Longmans, Green, 1942.
An Irish Journey. London: Longmans, Green, 1942.
The Story of Ireland. London: Collins, 1943.
The Irish. West Drayton: Penguin, 1947.
The Man Who Invented Sin and Other Stories. New York: Devin-Adair, 1948.
The Short Story. London: Collins, 1948.
A Summer in Italy. London: Eyre and Spottiswoode, 1949.
Newman's Way, the Odyssey of John Henry Newman. London: Longmans, Green, 1952.

South to Sicily. London: Collins, 1953.
The Vanishing Hero. London: Eyre and Spottiswoode, 1956.
The Finest Stories of Sean O'Faolain. Boston: Little, Brown, 1957.
I Remember! I Remember! Boston: Little, Brown, 1961.
Vive Moi! Boston: Little, Brown, 1964.
The Heat of the Sun, Stories and Tales. Boston: Little, Brown, 1966.
The Talking Trees and Other Stories. London: Cape, 1971.
Foreign Affairs and Other Stories. Boston: Little, Brown, 1976.
And Again? London: Constable, 1979.
The Collected Stories of Sean O'Faolain. London: Constable, 1982.

Studies of Sean O'Faolain

Bonaccorso, Richard. *Sean O'Faolain's Irish Vision*. Albany: State University of New
        York Press, 1987.
Butler, Pierce. *Sean O'Faolain: A Study of the Short Fiction*. New York: Twayne, 1993.
Doyle, Paul. *Sean O'Faolain*. New York: Twayne, 1968.
Harmon, Maurice, ed. *Irish University Review* 6 (Spring 1976). (An O'Faolain issue.)
———. *Sean O'Faolain: A Critical Introduction*. Notre Dame; IN: University of Notre
        Dame Press, 1966; rev. 1984.
———. *Sean O'Faolain: A Life*. London: Constable, 1994.
Rippier, Joseph. *The Short Stories of Sean O'Faolain: A Study in Descriptive Technique*.
        Gerrards Cross: Smythe, 1976.

Liam O'Flaherty

(1896–1984)

James M. Cahalan

BIOGRAPHY

No full-length biography of O'Flaherty has appeared to date, in contrast to the other two Irish short story masters in the triumvirate of "Big O's," Frank O'Connor and Seán O'Faoláin, even though O'Faoláin died much more recently than O'Flaherty; both published fascinating reviews of O'Flaherty. The absence of a biography is no doubt partly due to O'Flaherty's own hard-bitten opposition to the genre. He declared that his two autobiographical books, *Two Years* (1930) and *Shame the Devil* (1934), were written deliberately to preempt any would-be biographer. They appeared a half-century before his death and must be considered works of fiction as much as of fact. During the last thirty years of his life, during which he published very little, O'Flaherty changed the subject whenever anyone asked about his life. When he himself wrote a biography, *The Life of Tim Healy* (1927), O'Flaherty frequently digressed from his subject into his own ironically expressed views, reflecting his own attitude to biography by reporting that when Healy heard that he was working on his biography, Healy "threatened to write my life in revenge." Clearly, O'Flaherty cared little for biography.

Sooner or later, though, a biography will appear, given O'Flaherty's status as a major Irish author of short stories and novels. The basic facts are clear enough. Born on Inis Mór, the largest of the Aran Islands, on August 28, 1896, O'Flaherty grew up speaking both Irish and English within a large family and a close-knit community. He was a talented schoolboy who others hoped would become a priest, and he won scholarships that took him to Rockwell College in Country Tipperary in 1908 and University College, Dublin, in 1914–1915. O'Flaherty later claimed that he decided to leave the university after reading

Karl Marx for a week in the National Library in Dublin. He subsequently attacked O'Casey's *The Plough and the Stars* (1926) for its irreverence about the Easter Rising rebels, but in 1916 O'Flaherty was out of the country, serving in the British army. He fought in World War I from 1915 until he was injured in 1917, often later complaining about remaining shell-shocked, a theme also reflected in his fiction. The "two years" of his first autobiographical book were spent wandering and working in London, South America, Turkey, Canada, and the United States, between 1918 and 1921. After a return visit to Inis Mór, O'Flaherty led a brief workers' occupation of the government building, the Rotunda, in early 1922. Soon thereafter he left for London, determined to become a writer.

A turning point was meeting the London editor Edward Garnett, who became a key mentor to O'Flaherty, much as Garnett was also for Joseph Conrad, D. H. Lawrence, and several other important modernists. Garnett's advice was always to keep it short and tell the truth. He sent O'Flaherty back to Inis Mór to write about what he knew most intimately: the animals and people there. In 1923 O'Flaherty began writing the short stories that made his reputation, often translating himself from Irish to English and vice versa. As reflected in his many letters to Garnett during the 1920s, however, he also maintained an ambition to write the great Irish novel.

O'Flaherty married the writer Margaret Barrington in 1926, but they separated in 1932. He lived in a variety of locations in Ireland and England during the 1920s, spent several years in Connecticut beginning in the early 1930s, and then returned to Dublin in 1946, soon settling there for the rest of his life.

MAJOR WORKS AND THEMES

O'Flaherty published nearly thirty books—mostly during his extremely prolific period of 1923–1935—including a study of Conrad and a half-dozen other nonfictional works such as the satiric *A Tourist's Guide to Ireland* (1929) and *A Cure for Unemployment* (1931). His main achievement, though, consists of the best of his more than 150 stories collected in ten different volumes and the best three of his ten novels: *The Informer* (1925), *Skerrett* (1932), and *Famine* (1937). O'Flaherty wrote perhaps the most celebrated animal stories in this century after those of his fellow socialist wanderer Jack London; as a native of Inis Mór O'Flaherty had even more intimate knowledge of animals than London, whom he admired, and he stripped his narratives down to a spare, objective style much closer to Hemingway's. "The Cow's Death," for example, unforgettably describes a cow pursuing the discarded corpse of her stillborn calf over a cliff. In "The Wounded Cormorant," O'Flaherty closely observes birds mercilessly attacking and killing an injured member of their flock; in "The Hawk," the bird's predators are men. His visually oriented naturalism is even purer in stories describing basic natural forces, such as "The Wave," "The Flood," and "The Tide." These stories contain no dialogue, only photographic descriptions.

The people of O'Flaherty's best stories inhabit the same naturalistic universe inhabited by animals and rocks. In "Spring Sowing," a young island couple take pride in their work and their love; in "Poor People," a father comes home to discover his dead son. O'Flaherty, who more than once expressed misogynist views, was capable of writing a story such as "The Mirror," with its maudlin concluding description of a young girl "naked in the sunlight on silken moss and no longer afraid in the least of love's awe-inspiring fruit, the labour of pregnancy." But he also wrote some good stories about women, such as "The Touch" and "The Old Woman." There is also an underappreciated comic vein of O'Flaherty stories, with "The Post Office" as only the best-known example. He is also a fascinating author because of his bilingualism—often rewriting stories from one language to the other early in his career, then swearing off writing in Irish because of a lack of remuneration, finally returning to stories in Irish after he moved back to Dublin from Connecticut, and publishing the volume *Dúil* (Desire) in 1953.

Like his stories—many of which are superb, but a few quite awful— O'Flaherty's novels, which are divided into rural versus Dublin settings, are strikingly varied in quality. *The Informer*, his Dublin thriller about the doomed Gypo Nolan, is certainly his best-known novel, due to John Ford's famous, classic film version; perhaps as a result, *Land* (1940) reads like a film script and is therefore a cardboard failure. O'Flaherty's best novel, *Famine*, is the predecessor of *Land* in a trilogy of historical novels that also includes *Insurrection* (1950). Here O'Flaherty drew on his own intimate knowledge, from his earliest years on Inis Mór, of starvation and peasant families, transposing what he himself had known to the horrific period of 1845–1851, in his gripping narrative of the Kilmartin family. *Skerrett* exposes the difficult social fabric of island life through the account of a defiant schoolteacher modeled on O'Flaherty's own early teacher. *The Black Soul* (1924), also set on Inis Mór and O'Flaherty's most autobiographical novel, and *Mr. Gilhooley* (1926) and *The Puritan* (1931), two portraits of unbalanced Dublin protagonists, are also worthy of study.

CRITICAL RECEPTION

For the most part, criticism on O'Flaherty has followed two narrow tracks: naturalism in his short stories and politics in his novels. My own book, *Liam O'Flaherty: A Study of the Short Fiction*, takes up these topics but also seeks to open up critical discussion beyond them, particularly in chapters on bilingualism, gender, and satire and comedy. It also includes reprinted selections from critics on O'Flaherty from 1924 to 1988, from the first reviews to the most recent criticism.

The introductions to O'Flaherty by Paul Doyle and James O'Brien are both good starting points, though Doyle's is fuller than O'Brien's. John Zneimer's book is an excellent close reading of O'Flaherty that takes an existentialist approach, while Angeline A. Kelly's is a thorough, though pedestrian, thematic analysis of his stories. Patrick Sheeran's book is filled with good insights and valuable information about O'Flaherty's life and politics. My own two books, *Great Hatred, Little Room* and *The Irish Novel*, contain chapters assessing O'Flaherty's historical novels and his novels in general.

Among critical articles, the pioneering one was George Brandon Saul's in 1963. A rich strand of articles focusing on O'Flaherty's bilingualism can be found in those by (in chronological order) Vivian Mercier, Tomás de Bhaldraithe, Maureen Murphy, and William Daniels. The articles by Helene O'Connor (on ecology) and Alexander G. Gonzalez (on O'Flaherty's urban stories) are noteworthy for their fresh critical perspectives.

BIBLIOGRAPHY

Works by Liam O'Flaherty

Short Fiction

Dúil. Baile Atha Cliath (Dublin): Sáirséal agus Dill, 1953.
The Ecstasy of Angus. 1931. Reprinted, Dublin: Wolfhound, 1978.
The Mountain Tavern and Other Stories. New York: Harcourt, 1929.
Short Stories. Dublin: Wolfhound, 1986. Originally published by Wolfhound in 1976 as *The Pedlar's Revenge and Other Stories*.
The Short Stories of Liam O'Flaherty. 1937. Reprinted, Kent, England: New English Library, 1986.
Spring Sowing. London: Cape, 1924.
The Stories of Liam O'Flaherty. New York: Devin-Adair, 1956.
Two Lovely Beasts. 1948. Reprinted, New York: Devin-Adair, 1950.
The Wounded Cormorant and Other Stories. New York: Norton, 1973.

Novels

The Assassin. London: Cape, 1928.
The Black Soul. 1924. Reprinted, Dublin: Wolfhound, 1981.
Famine. 1937. Boston: Godine, 1982.
The Informer. 1925. Reprinted, New York: Harcourt, 1980.
Insurrection. London: Gollancz, 1950.
Land. New York: Random, 1946.
Mr. Gilhooley. London: Cape, 1926.
The Puritan. New York: Harcourt, 1931.
Skerrett. 1932. Reprinted, Dublin: Wolfhound, 1982.
Thy Neighbour's Wife. London: Cape, 1923.

Nonfiction

A Cure for Unemployment. London: E. Lahr, 1931.
I Went to Russia. New York: Harcourt, 1931.
Joseph Conrad: An Appreciation. London: Lahr, 1930.
The Life of Tim Healy. London: Cape, 1927.
Shame the Devil. 1934. Reprinted, Dublin: Wolfhound, 1981.

A Tourist's Guide to Ireland. London: Mandrake, 1929.
Two Years. London: Cape, 1930.

Studies of Liam O'Flaherty

Cahalan, James M. *Liam O'Flaherty: A Study of the Short Fiction.* New York: Macmillan, 1991.

Daniels, William. "Introduction to the Present State of Criticism of Liam O'Flaherty's Collection of short Stories: *Dúil.*" *Éire-Ireland* 23.2 (Summer 1988): 124–32.

De Bhaldraithe, Tomás. "Liam O'Flaherty—Translator (?)." *Éire-Ireland* 3.2 (Summer 1968): 149–53.

Doyle, Paul A. *Liam O'Flaherty.* New York: Twayne, 1971.

Gonzalez, Alexander G. "Liam O'Flaherty's Urban Short Stories." *Études Irlandaises* 12.1 (1987): 85–91.

Kelly, Angeline A. *Liam O'Flaherty the Storyteller.* London: Macmillan, 1976.

Mercier, Vivian. "The Irish Short Story and Oral Tradition." In *The Celtic Cross*, ed. Ray B. Brown, William John Rocelli, and John Loftus. West Lafayette, IN: Purdue University Press, 1964, 98–116.

———. "Man against Nature: The Novels of Liam O'Flaherty." *Wascana Review* 1.2 (1966): 37–46.

Murphy, Maureen O'Rourke. "The Double Vision of Liam O'Flaherty." *Éire-Ireland* 8.3 (1973): 20–25.

———. " 'The Salted Goat': Devil's Bargain or Fable of Faithfulness." *Canadian Journal of Irish Studies* 5.2 (1979): 60–61.

O'Brien, James H. *Liam O'Flaherty.* Lewisburg, PA: Bucknell University Press, 1973.

O'Connor, Frank. "A Good Short Story Must Be News." Rev. of *The Short Stories of Liam O'Flaherty. The New York Times Book Review* (June 10, 1956): 1, 20.

O'Connor, Helene. "Liam O'Flaherty: Literary Ecologist." *Éire-Ireland* 7.2 (1972): 47–54.

O'Faoláin, Seán. "Don Quixote O'Flaherty." *The London Mercury* 37 (December 1937): 170–75. Rev. ed. in *The Bell* 2 (June 1941): 28–36.

Saul, George Brandon. "A Wild Sowing: The Short Stories of Liam O'Flaherty." *Review of English Literature* 4 (July 1963): 108–13.

Sheeran, Patrick F. *The Novels of Liam O'Flaherty: A Study in Romantic Realism.* Atlantic Highlands, NJ: Humanities, 1976.

Zneimer, John. *The Literary Vision of Liam O'Flaherty.* Syracuse: Syracuse University Press, 1971.

Seumas O'Kelly

([c. 1875–1878]–1918)

John D. Conway

BIOGRAPHY

Seumas O'Kelly was born at Mobhill, Loughrea, County Galway, sometime between 1875 and 1878. What little formal education he received was taken at Fury's "hedge-school" and St. Brendan's College, Loughrea, and he learned Irish by listening to his elders. His childhood was spent in the pastoral isolation of a region of rugged beauty dominated by a lake—influences visible throughout his fiction.

In addition to early journalistic work, O'Kelly began writing plays, three of which were produced at the Abbey Theatre. The most significant was *The Shuiler's Child* (1909), written for a beautiful Irish revolutionary—Mary Walker—and well received. Although he authored twelve plays, he has been largely dismissed as a dramatist, in spite of the fine qualities of *The Shuiler's Child* and *The Bribe* (1914).

His enduring claim to distinction, however, comes from his short fiction, which places him among the most distinguished short story writers identified with the Irish Literary Renaissance. *By the Stream of Killmeen* (1906) is the work of an apprentice, but *Waysiders* (1917) and two posthumous volumes, *The Golden Barque and The Weaver's Grave* (1919) and *Hillsiders* (1921), generally reflect the hand of a mature craftsman. O'Kelly also wrote two novels—*The Lady of Deer Park* (1917) and *Wet Clay* (1922), a volume of verse—*Ranns and Ballads* (1918)—and miscellaneous pamphlets. "The Weaver's Grave," however, is his masterpiece.

After ill health forced him to leave Dublin in 1915, he returned to his brother's home in Galway. In spite of a weakened heart, he returned to Dublin to assume editorship of *Nationality*, the Sinn Fein publication, after Arthur Griffith's arrest by the British. He died in Dublin in Jervis Street Hospital on November 14, 1918, after the armistice, the direct result of a break-in on the Sinn Fein premises by drunken soldiers and others. A much beloved, good-natured, and gentle man, O'Kelly was given the funeral of a national hero and buried in Glasnevin.

MAJOR WORKS AND THEMES

Although the body of his published work is considerable and varied, his major work is his prose fiction, particularly his short stories and novella. The rhythms, contour, and people of Galway are in his fiction—peasants, tinkers, and merchants. He writes of their isolation and loneliness, of their bond with the land, of their timeless traditions, and of their daily struggles amid a landscape of hills and green fields, of boreens and beech-trees, of crops and the big lake, of sod and stars. He is a storyteller, a *shanachie*.

"The Weaver's Grave" is so clearly a masterpiece that it alone would have assured O'Kelly a lasting place in Ireland's literature. The story is simple: Mortimer Hehir, the weaver, has died. His widow must find him a burying place. Into Cloon na Morav, the Meadow of the Dead, she goes, accompanied by two ancients, a nail-maker and a stone-breaker, as guides, followed by two young gravediggers (twins). So many generations have been laid to rest in Cloon na Morav that in O'Kelly's description, "[t]he mind could only swoon away into mythology, paddle about in the dotage of paganism, the toothless infancy of Christianity."

Within and without this mapless, pathless region two stories emerge: the principal one, of both comic and tragic dimension, concerns the final and definitive locating of the weaver's grave site; the second culminates in the widow's (the weaver's fourth wife and considerably his junior) romance with the more attractive of the two gravediggers. At the end of the story, she speaks with the accents of a young girl transformed and says simply, "I'm satisfied." The epitaph for Cloon na Morav, the ancient burial ground, is not chiseled in stone but found in the living voice.

No other work of O'Kelly's and few in the fiction identified with the Irish Renaissance will so handsomely reward the effort of subsequent readings. The stubbornness of the old men, the widow's extraordinary visit with Malachi Roohan and his daughter to locate the local precise spot of the weaver's grave, the widow's determination, the impatience of the young gravediggers, the reminiscences, the family histories, the humor, the dialogue, the awakening romance, and the setting all create an atmosphere of rich antiquity and even richer humanity. What counts most in the telling is the sound of the human voice echoing in a region of rounded stones and swollen monuments.

In *Waysiders*, a collection of ten stories, the range of O'Kelly's identification with the Irish short story suggests a commonality with George Moore, James Stephens, and Frank O'Connor, but, to be sure, O'Kelly is his own man, his stories fresh from the land and its people. His characters share with Moore's and O'Connor's, however, a pervasive sense of isolation and loneliness. Although *Waysiders* is an uneven mixture, four stories can be included among O'Kelly's finest. "The Can with the Diamond Notch," about the tribulations of the area's leading merchant, Festus Clasby, with a group of clever tinkers, is a combination of wit, invention, and unerring characterization. For all his business acumen, Festus Clasby is no match for Mac-an-Ward and his wife when it comes to bartering on the road for the Can with the Diamond Notch. Throughout this story and "The Shoemaker"—with his tales of swallows wearing shoes, a Chinese cat, and Gobstown, his town, lost because of landlords with perfect hearts—O'Kelly reveals his affection for a people of imagination, pluck, and humor. The two concluding stories, "The Gray Lake" and "The Building," each build to a dramatic conclusion in the rendering of a drowning town, in the former story, and in a final recognition that no building on a hill can ever be placed above the "companionship of the fields," in the latter.

The Golden Barque and The Weaver's Grave enjoys a greater structural unity than does *Waysiders*. The *Golden Barque* stories concern life on the barge of the same name and along the Midland Canal. The principals in these six stories include the Boss, Hike, and Calcutta. There are less humor here than in *Waysiders* and a more impassioned bitterness in the portrayal of the feuding title characters in "Hike and Calcutta" and in "The Haven." Life along the canal is grim, and there is no enchanted countryside for aesthetic and imaginative relief. Even the story of betrayed love in "Michael and Mary" offers little solace to Mary as Michael responds to the call of the wide ocean. These stories are different in tone, atmosphere, characterization, and overall achievement from "The Weaver's Grave," which dominates the volume.

The six stories in *Hillsiders* are more consistently developed than those in either *Waysiders* or the *Golden Barque* section of *The Golden Barque and The Weaver's Grave*. The community of Kilbeg provides O'Kelly with a center from which his interrelated stories can evolve. The sense of the people with their rising and falling rhythms is palpable in the characterization of Hannah from Boherlahan, Winnie O'Carroll, Nan Hogan, Sara Finnessy, Fardy Lalor, Fergus Keaveney, and others, who provide gossip, family histories, and unflinching judgment concerning life in Kilbeg. At the conclusion of *Waysiders* O'Kelly emphasizes "the companionship of the fields," but here it is the "companionship" of a people who know, from household to household, the whispers, the secrets, the dreams, the joys, the hardships, and the fears that bind them together.

Throughout *Hillsiders* the women are often portrayed as possessing great strength of character and even greater resilience. In the opening story, "Hannah," for example, the community looks upon the charwoman not simply as a sweeper of the church but as a moralist who moves about Kilbeg with the swagger of a cat and the authority of an archbishop. In "Nan Hogan's House" three women dominate the tale: Nan Hogan, suffering from the "weakness" but with character sufficient to leave the Poorhouse and reclaim her own cabin; Sara Finnessy, Nan's adversary of long standing; and Maura Casey, an opportunist with whom Nan is finally reconciled. Even Winnie O'Carroll, "born under an unlucky star," in "The Miracle of the Tea" has the last laugh concerning a packet of tea that causes a bit of a tempest in Kilbeg. The most memorable male in the entire collection is Fardy Lalor, whose heroic rescue of a romantic adversary amid a roaring sea gives "The Elks" a special poignancy. O'Kelly's rustics in *Hillsiders* are a convincing lot, the happy result of firsthand observation and genuine affection on the part of the author. The theme of isolation so prevalent elsewhere is muted here by the extraordinary sense of community.

Despite the enthusiasms of Stephen Gwynn (*Irish Literature and Drama*), Seumas O'Sullivan, and others, neither of O'Kelly's novels can be considered major. Clearly, *The Lady of Deerpark* is much better than *Wet Clay* because of its characterization of Mary Heffernan, the Big House, and the conniving racehorse breeder "Kish," whom Mary ultimately and tragically marries. Despite the hold that her entangled and tragic story has on the reader, O'Kelly's pace, development of tale, and denouement are more clearly rendered in "The Weaver's Grave."

CRITICAL RECEPTION

Forrest Reid was not the first to refer to O'Kelly's "genius" and the beauty of "tenderness and understanding" in his best stories (181). Of the more extended treatments of the author, however, George Brandon Saul's *Seumas O'Kelly* remains preeminent. In addition to his telling commentary about the life and works within the context of the Ireland of O'Kelly's time, Saul includes an annotated and definitive bibliography of primary sources.

In more recent scholarship of note, Anne Clune's essay in Rafroidi and Brown's *The Irish Short Story*, among the most perceptive of its kind, reveals how O'Kelly's involvement with Sinn Fein colored everything that he wrote afterward, including "The Weaver's Grave." Elizabeth Colley discusses at length and with insight the role of the widow in the story and her final transformation. Deborah Averill (in *The Irish Short Story from George Moore to Frank O'Connor*) places O'Kelly within the context of the Irish short story. Brendan O'Grady compares the O'Kelly use of fantasy and Celtic myth with that of James Stephens in Ben-Merre and Murphy's *James Joyce and His Contemporaries*. In a Joycean comparison Alexander G. Gonzalez suggests that a coming to awareness among O'Kelly's characters may be likened to certain epiphanies in Joyce's fiction and notes O'Kelly's early use of interior monologue.

BIBLIOGRAPHY

Works by Seumas O'Kelly

Prose

By the Stream of Killmeen. Dublin: Sealy, Bryers, and Walker, n.d. [1906].
The Lady of Deerpark. London: Methuen, 1917.

Waysiders. Dublin: Talbot, 1917; New York: Stokes, 1919.
The Golden Barque and The Weaver's Grave. Dublin: Talbot, 1919.
The Leprechaun of Killmeen. Dublin: Martin Lester, 1920.
Hillsiders. Dublin: Talbot, 1921.
Wet Clay. Dublin: Talbot, 1922.

Plays

The Shuiler's Child. Dublin: Maunsel, 1909; DePaul University Press, 1971.
The Bribe. London: Maunsel, 1914: Dublin: James Duffy, 1952.
The Matchmakers. Dublin: Talbot, 1925.
Meadowsweeet. Dublin: Talbot, 1925.
The Weaver's Grave. Dublin: Talbot, 1925.

Poetry

Ranns and Ballads. Dublin: Candle, 1918.

Studies of Seumas O'Kelly

Brennan. R. *Allegiance*. Dublin: Browne and Nolan, 1950.
Colley, Elizabeth. "Seumas O'Kelly's 'The Weavers Grave': 'What Lies beneath a Story
    of Old Men.' *Studies in Short Fiction* 26.4 (1989): 453–62.
Gonzalez, Alexander G. "Seumas O'Kelly and James Joyce." *Eire-Ireland* 21.2 (1986):
    85–94.
Grennan, Eamon. "Introduction." *The Land of Loneliness, and Other Stories*. Dublin:
    Gill and Macmillan, 1969.
Nic Shiubhlaig, Marie. *The Splendid Years*. Dublin: Duffy, 1955.
O'Hegarty, P. S. A *Bibliography of Books by Seumas O'Kelly*. Dublin: Printed for the
    author by Alex Thom, 1934.
O'Sullivan, Seumas (James Starkey). *Essays and Recollections*. Dublin and Cork: Talbot,
    1944.
————. The *Rose and Bottle and Other Essays*. Dublin: Talbot, 1946.
————. "Seumas O'Kelly. His Work and Personality." Sunday *Independent* (Dublin),
    November 17, 1918.
Reid, Forrest. *Retrospective Adventures*. London: Faber and Faber, 1942.
Saul, George Brandon. *Rushlight Heritage*. Philadelphia: Walton, 1969.
————. *Seumas O'Kelly*. Lewisburg, PA: Bucknell University Press, 1971.

James Plunkett

(1920–)

James M. Cahalan

BIOGRAPHY

James Plunkett Kelly was born on May 21, 1920, in the Sandymount area of Dublin; he later dropped the "Kelly" from his publications in order to have a more distinctive pen name. When he was four, his family moved to a flat in Upper Pembroke Street, where he grew up "in the shadow," as he put it, "of those tall houses" of Georgian Dublin. As with Joyce, Dublin permeated everything that Plunkett would write, but unlike Joyce, Plunkett felt no need to escape it, for he found that "Dublin was a good city to grow up in" (*Gems* 37) in the 1920s and 1930s. He later expressed the belief that "nothing much happens to a writer after the age of twenty or so that will affect his work; the small store of material which informs the imagination for the rest of life is made up of the remembered experiences of childhood and youth" (*Gems* 112–13).

Young Jim Kelly soon developed abiding interests in literature, music, and trade unionism. He attended the Christian Brothers School on Synge Street, where he began writing stories and little satirical verses and also studied violin and viola at the College of Music from age eight to age twenty-three. His father, whom he greatly admired, fought in World War I and was a member of James Larkin and James Connolly's Irish Transport and General Workers' Union (ITGWU).

Plunkett left school at seventeen to work as a clerk in the Gas Company for seven years, becoming increasingly active in the Workers' Union of Ireland. He worked closely under James Larkin as a Workers' Union staff member beginning in 1946 and continued as branch and staff secretary after Larkin's death in 1947. He also began publishing what he later described as "deplorable little verses" in magazines such as *Passing Variety* and his earliest short stories, such as "Working Class." He sent his first stories to Seán O'Faoláin at *The Bell*; O'Faoláin wrote back with the influential advice "to cut it down and speak plainly and if you didn't have anything to say not to say it." Plunkett's stories "The Mother" and "Working Class" appeared in *The Bell* in 1942–1943, and his career as a fiction writer was launched, though it would remain a part-time occupation for much of his life.

In January 1955, Plunkett visited the Soviet Union as part of a delegation invited by the Soviet secretary of the arts. As a result he was attacked by Irish McCarthyites such as the editor of the *Catholic Standard*, who urged that Plunkett be forced to resign his position in the Workers' Union. But the union refused to bow to pressure. Plunkett left quite voluntarily in August 1955 in order to become drama assistant at Radio Éireann. He then became one of Radio Telefis Éireann's (RTE) first two television producers in 1960, continuing at RTE until his retirement in the 1980s. His RTE work kept him busy but soon became dwarfed by his career as a novelist, and he moved out of Dublin into a home in the Wicklow mountains south of Enniskerry. Following the death of his wife, Valerie, in 1986, he moved to Bray in 1992, where he now lives in proximity to his four children in the Dublin area.

MAJOR WORKS AND THEMES

The dozen short stories of *The Trusting and the Maimed* (1955) make it still the best collection of Dublin stories since Joyce's *Dubliners*. There are a striking range and depth to this volume, moving from the slapstick comedy of "The Scoop" to the political broadside of "The Wearin' of the Green," to the pathos of "Janey Mary," "Mercy," and "Weep for Our Pride," to the penetrating lyricism of "The Trusting and the Maimed" and "The Eagles and the Trumpets." This very well balanced collection contains four stories about childhood and adolescence, four about young manhood, and four about old age. The best stories are "A Walk through the Summer," "The Trusting and the Maimed," and "The Eagles and the Trumpets." The main characters of these stories are presented in isolation from each other in time and space, in separate sections fused together at the end of each story. They end up, respectively, lying half-asleep in a car, resting under the flight of a maimed pigeon, or staring up at the moon as if it were "a big bloody aspirin."

Radio Éireann broadcast four of Plunkett's radio plays: "Dublin Fusilier" (1952), "Mercy" (1953), "Homecoming" (1954), and "Big Jim" (1954). Plunkett rewrote "Big Jim" into *The Risen People*, which was successfully produced at the Abbey Theatre in 1958 and which shows O'Casey's influence. His lifelong admiration for his old boss, Larkin, eventually also resulted in the novel that made Plunkett a massively popular author, *Strumpet City* (1969). In this long work, however, Plunkett followed the conventions of the best historical novels by withdrawing Larkin to the background. Instead he developed his work through separate sections focused on representative, unforgettable characters who come into increasing contact with each other. They are all affected in various ways by the epochal 1913 lockout of the ITGWU by the reactionary Dublin stopped Employers' Federation, which resulted in the employers' short-term victory but the union movement's long-term apotheosis and growth. Plunkett's large ensemble cast includes Rashers Tierney, the proletarian everyman; Fitz, the striking foreman; his wife, Mary; Fitz's O'Caseyesque friends Hennessey and Mulhall; Keever, the employers' stool pigeon; Yearling, the upper-class ITGWU sympathizer; Father O'Connor, the puritanical priest; and Father Giffley, the alcoholic priest who has seen more than he can handle. The popularity of *Strumpet City* was further extended in the 1980s by a seven-part RTE adaptation starring Cyril Cusack, Peter O'Toole, and Peter Ustinov.

Farewell Companions (1977) took up chronologically where *Strumpet City* left off, focusing on the period of the author's own youth in the 1920s and 1930s. There is much of Jim Plunkett Kelly in his protagonist, Tim McDonagh, and his friends, but Plunkett left the Workers' Union out of Tim's life and surprised his readers with a very un-Joycean ending. He also began experimenting more, particularly with his seriocomic character O'Sheehan, who has visions of himself as the mythical Oisín, expressed in lyrical streams of consciousness. Such playfulness is also evident in "Ferris Moore and the Earwig," a story included in his *Collected Short Stories* (1977).

Plunkett showed his talent for nonfiction in *The Gems She Wore, a Book of Irish Places* (1972), written rather in the style of Frank O'Connor's earlier travelogue/memoir, *Irish Miles*. *The Boy on the Back Wall and Other Essays* (1987) collected twenty-seven of Plunkett's most stimulating prose works written over a quarter-century and divided into several categories: memoirs of youth and experiences, essays on mentors such as O'Faoláin and Frank O'Connor, essays about Larkin, essays about fellow writer/activists such as O'Casey and Peadar O'Donnell, and discussions of writing techniques.

Plunkett's most recent book is *The Circus Animals* (1991), which continues the story of *Farewell Companions* by focusing on Plunkett's young manhood in the 1950s, dealing directly with the 1955 Soviet debacle, for example. This novel alternates between two main interrelated characters: Frank McDonagh, Plunkett's autobiographical journalist, and Lemuel Cox, an older man who becomes a kind of father figure to Frank and who has inherited from his own father a peculiar obsession with Jonathan Swift. Plunkett also presents in this novel a critical view of conservative Irish social practices during this period, such as those of the Catholic Church concerning birth control.

CRITICAL RECEPTION

John Jordan published an admiring review of *The Trusting and the Maimed* in 1955 that set the tone for appreciative responses to Plunkett's writing, also reflected in reviews of *Strumpet City* (such as Anne O'Neill-Barna's in the *New York Times Book Review*) and his later books. Eavan Boland published an interview with Plunkett in 1972, as did Jim Hawkins in 1981, myself in 1986, and Rosa Gonzalez in 1992.

Many critics have expressed admiration for Plunkett's work, and several have discussed it in passing, but few have dealt with it in depth. Brian Cleeve and Thomas MacIntyre each published a brief article on *The Trusting and the Maimed* in *Studies* in 1958, the first two journal articles on Plunkett. *Strumpet City* has attracted more critical attention, including articles by Godeleine Carpentier in 1976 and myself in 1978. Like Hanna Behrend's 1979 examination of "James Plunkett's Contribution to Democratic and Socialist Culture," these later articles concentrated largely on Plunkett's politics.

In *Great Hatred, Little Room: The Irish Historical Novel* (1983), I devoted much of a chapter to assessing *Strumpet City* within this particular subgenre and discussed his place among contemporary Irish novelists in *The Irish Novel: A Critical History* (1988). In somewhat parallel fashion, John Newsinger focused on "The Priest in the Irish Novel: James Plunkett's *Strumpet City*" (1989).

BIBLIOGRAPHY

Works by James Plunkett

Big Jim. Dublin: Martin O'Donnell, 1955.
The Boy on the Back Wall and Other Essays. Dublin: Poolbeg, 1987.
The Circus Animals. London: Arrow, 1991.
Collected Short Stories. Dublin: Poolbeg, 1977.
The Eagles and the Trumpets, and Other Stories. The Bell 20.9 (August 1954). (Special issue.)
Farewell Companions. London: Hutchinson, 1977.
The Gems She Wore, a Book of Irish Places. London: Hutchinson, 1972.
The Risen People. 1958. Dublin: Irish Writers's Co-operative, 1978. Reprinted as a special issue of *The Journal of Irish Literature* 21.1 (January 1992).
Strumpet City. London: Hutchinson, 1969.
The Trusting and the Maimed, and Other Irish Stories. New York: Devin-Adair, 1955.

Studies of James Plunkett

Behrend, Hanna. "James Plunkett's Contribution to Democratic and Socialist Culture." *Zeitschrift für Anglistik und Amerikanistik* 27.4 (1979): 307–26.
Boland, Eavan. "Dublin's Advocate." *This Week* 12 October 12, 1972: 40–44. (Interview.)
Cahalan, James M. "James Plunkett: An Interview." *The Irish Literary Supplement* 5.1 (Spring 1986): 9–11.
———. "The Making of *Strumpet City*: James Plunkett's Historical Vision." *Eire-Ireland* 13.4 (Winter 1978): 81–100.
———. Rev. of *The Boy on the Back Wall and Other Essays*. *Éire-Ireland* 23.3 (Fall 1988): 153–54.
———. Rev. of *Farewell Companions*. *Éire-Ireland* 13.2 (Summer 1978): 147–30.

Carpentier, Godeleine. "Dublin and the Drama of Larkinism: James Plunkett's *Strumpet City.*" *Cahiers Irlandaises* 4–5 (1976): 209–19.

Cleeve, Brian. "The Worm as Hero." With Replies by Seán O'Faoláin, Peadar O'Donnell, John C. Kelly, and Plunkett. *Studies* 47 (Spring 1958): 21–31.

Gonzalez, Rosa. " 'Writing out of One's Own Experience': An Interview with James Plunkett." *Revista Alicantina de Estudios Ingleses* 5 (1992): 185–94.

Hawkins, Jim. "A Visit with Jim Plunkett." *Aisi-Éiri, The Magazine of Irish-America* Spring 1981: 4–8. (Interview.)

Jordan, John. Rev. of *The Trusting and the Maimed, and Other Irish Stories. Irish Writing* 32 (Autumn 1955): 56–57.

MacIntyre, Thomas. "Some Notes on the Stories of James Plunkett." *Studies* 47 (Autumn 1958): 323–27.

Newsinger, John. "The Priest in the Irish Novel: James Plunkett's *Strumpet City.*" *Études Irlandaises* 14.2 (1989): 65–76.

O'Neil-Barna, Anne. Rev. of *Strumpet City. New York Times Book Review*, November 9, 1969: 69.

Lennox Robinson

(1886–1958)

Thomas Akstens

BIOGRAPHY

Esmé Stuart Lennox Robinson was born in Douglas, County Cork, on October 4, 1886. His family was Protestant and staunchly Unionist. In 1907 he saw the Abbey company perform Yeats's *Cathleen ni Houlihan* at the Cork Opera House, an experience he described as a "revelation" that transformed him into an ardent nationalist and provided him with the motivation to become a dramatist (*Curtain Up* 18).

Robinson's career was launched in 1908, when the Abbey staged his first play, *The Clancy Name*. Within a year, Yeats had chosen the inexperienced Robinson to manage the Abbey. In 1910, Yeats sent Robinson to London to study stagecraft with Shaw and Harley Granville-Barker. Shortly after his return, Robinson precipitated a serious rift between the Abbey directors and Annie Horniman, the theater's antinationalist patron, when he failed to cancel performances on the death of Edward VII. Robinson survived the resulting furor, and over the next four years he matured as a director and proved to be an energetic manager. Faced with Lady Gregory's increasing antagonism, Robinson resigned in 1914; he was reappointed in 1919.

The five-year hiatus in Robinson's involvement with the Abbey was important to his development as a writer. His 1916 comedy, *The Whiteheaded Boy*, marked a departure from the grim realism of his earlier plays. Robinson's autobiographical novel, *A Young Man from the South* (1917), and his 1918 play, *The Lost Leader*, evidence his intensified concern during this period with issues of Irish nationalism and patriotism.

Prior to his return to the Abbey, Robinson helped establish the Dublin Drama League, which from 1919 to 1929 produced expressionist and other experimental drama by writers such as Strindberg, Pirandello, and Benavente. Robinson himself wrote a number of brooding, experimental plays in the 1920s and 1930s. Most were failures; the metatheatrical *Church Street* (1934) fared better and has subsequently been anthologized. During this same period he rediscovered his talent for comedy in *The Far-Off Hills* (1928) and *Drama at Inish* (1933) and wrote two serious plays that explore the effect of political and social upheaval on the Ascendancy: *The Big House* (1926) and the Chekhovian *Killycreggs in Twilight* (1937).

In 1938 Robinson organized the Abbey Theatre Festival, editing the lectures from the festival for publication as *The Irish Theatre*. From this point on, he wrote less for the theater. Among his later prose works are his autobiography, *Curtain Up* (1942), *Towards an Appreciation of the Theatre* (1945), and his edition of *Lady Gregory's Journals* (1946). His *Ireland's Abbey Theatre: A History, 1899–1951* appeared just months after the original theater was destroyed by fire. Robinson died in Dublin on October 14, 1958.

MAJOR WORKS AND THEMES

Robinson declared in *Curtain Up* that "the first thing a dramatist needs is a good subject" (46). He appears to have chosen his subjects primarily to allow for the exploration of what he called "this strange Irish thing" (*Curtain Up* 225). This awkward phrase hints at the discomfort inherent in Robinson's position as an Anglo-Irish writer with strong Republican sympathies, but it barely begins to suggest the sociopolitical earnestness of many of Robinson's plays.

Robinson's early realist plays, *The Clancy Name, The Cross Roads* (1909), and *Harvest* (1910), are melodramas of Irish peasant life. Ibsen's influence is apparent in these dark and didactic plays. Robinson admitted in *Curtain Up* that the characters in *Harvest* were "mere pegs on which to hang my ideas" (33). Unfortunately, Robinson's social ideas themselves sometimes seem muddled in these early works.

Patriots (1912) and *The Lost Leader* are concerned with the inevitable discrepancies between political ideals and political reality. Robinson attempted in these plays to treat the Republican cause in a way that would allow for ethical and social complexity. The unfortunate result is that both plays seem strangely inconclusive. A similar inconclusiveness is evident in *The Big House* and *Killycreggs in Twilight*, which examine the crisis of the Ascendancy and the dislocations inherent in wholesale social and political change.

In these serious plays, Robinson's characters lack dimension to the degree that they appear to be determined by the circumstances of their social and cultural environment—Kate Alcock in *The Big House* providing a notable exception. But the predictability of characterization that serves to limit Robinson's serious drama proved to be an asset to his comedies of Irish manners, in which the gentle satire is directed at cultural behavior. Robinson's most notable comedies include *The Whiteheaded Boy, Crabbed Youth and Age* (1922), *The Far-Off Hills,* and *Drama at Inish.*

Among Robinson's several experimental plays, *Church Street* most successfully exploits the technical innovations of European theater. As with the Pirandello plays that it imitates, *Church Street* explores the self-reflexive quality of drama and the problematic nature of the relationship between the theater and reality.

CRITICAL RECEPTION

Much of the criticism that has appeared since Michael O'Neill's *Lennox Robinson* (1964) has been primarily concerned with what Richard Peterson called "the problem of reputation"—Robinson's position in the history of the Abbey and the Irish Literary Renaissance (70). What little criticism has been devoted to the plays themselves has been uninformed by either postcolonial theory or recent drama theory.

O'Neill established the pattern for much of what has subsequently been written on Robinson, characterizing him as a competent and versatile dramatic technician with an unfortunate taste for melodrama. O'Neill defined Robinson's central theme as "the dreamer and idealist attempting to cope with the realities of existence" (164).

Writing in 1966, Ida Everson attempted to rescue Robinson from the long shadow of Yeats, insisting that Robinson himself was a pivotal figure in the Irish Literary Renaissance—primarily because he advocated naturalism, in a conscious departure from the poetic idealism of Yeats. Everson's assessment is more persuasive than an unconvincing 1980 article in which Richard Peterson attempted to refute Robinson's reputation as Yeats's toady on the basis of an evident mutual respect between the two writers.

In their 1979 monograph on the Dublin Drama League (DDL), Brenna Katz Clarke and Harold Ferrar portray a less benign Robinson, who "manipulated his influential position as Yeats' protege with great skill, striving constantly and successfully for a world perspective in Irish theatre" (11). Robinson's involvement in the DDL has been further documented by Gary Phillips, who saw the league as a strong antidote to the "provinciality" of the Dublin stage (75).

While yielding technical competence to Robinson, David Krause's *The Profane Book of Irish Comedy* saw his work suspended uncomfortably between satire and comedy of manners. Krause asserted that Robinson trivialized social problems by sentimentalizing them; he compared Robinson's sentimentality to "a thick syrup that will not pour" (197). A scarcely more favorable assessment was offered by D.E.S. Maxwell, who saw in the plays "indications of craftsmanship, though Robinson puts this skill to evading the issues he raises" (*A Critical History of Modern Irish Drama 1891–1980,* 73).

D. J. Smith, writing in 1983, offered a persuasive argument for Constance Markievicz as the model for Isabel Moore in Robinson's *A Young Man from the South*. Smith suggested that Robinson's interest in "this well-meaning, fascinating and impossible woman" (22) was complicated by his inability to cope with her political radicalism.

The most substantial recent work on Robinson has come from Christopher Murray, whose 1982 edition of *Selected Plays* might have been expected to stimulate more critical and scholarly interest than has proven to be the case. Murray has characterized Robinson as "a walking question mark"—an odd amalgam of talent and incompetence (Sekine's *Irish Writers* 114). At the same time, he offered a revisionist view of Robinson as a legitimate creative force in the Irish theater, based on the "strong theatricality" of his plays and his considerable influence on other playwrights as a director and reader of scripts (125). Most recently, Murray has argued for a vision of "the possibility of an imaginative transcendence of history" in Robinson's treatment of the Big House theme (Rauchbauer's *Ancestral Voices* 118).

BIBLIOGRAPHY

Selected Works by Lennox Robinson

Patriots. Dublin: Maunsel, 1912.
A Young Man from the South. Dublin: Maunsel, 1917.
The Whiteheaded Boy. London: Unwin, 1920.
The Big House. London: Macmillan, 1928.
Drama at Inish. London: Macmillan, 1933.
Church Street. London: Macmillan, 1935.
Killycreggs in Twilight. London: Macmillan, 1939.
Curtain Up: An Autobiography. London: Joseph, 1942.
Ireland's Abbey Theatre. London: Sidgwick and Jackson, 1951.
Selected Plays. Ed. Christopher Murray. Gerrards Cross, Bucks: Smythe; Washington, DC: Catholic University Press, 1982.

Studies of Lennox Robinson

Clarke, Brenna Katz, and Harold Ferrar. *The Dublin Drama League*. Dublin: Dolmen; Atlantic Highlands, NJ: Humanities, 1979.
Everson, Ida G. "Young Lennox Robinson and the Abbey Theatre's First American Tour." *Modern Drama* 9.1 (1966): 74–89.
O'Neill, Michael J. *Lennox Robinson*. New York: Twayne, 1964.
Peterson, Richard F. "The Crane and the Swan: Lennox Robinson and W. B. Yeats." *Journal of Irish Literature* 9.1 (1980): 69–76.
Phillips, Gary. "Lennox Robinson on the Dublin Drama League: A Letter to Gabriel Fallon." *ICarbS* 4.2 (1981): 75–82.
Smith, D. J. "The Countess and the Poets: Constance Gore-Booth Markievicz in the Work of Irish Writers." *Journal of Irish Literature* 12.1 (1983): 3–63.

W. R. *Rodgers*

(1909–1969)

Bernard McKenna

BIOGRAPHY

William Robert Rodgers was born in Belfast on August 1, 1909, to Robert Rodgers, an insurance company representative, and Jane McCarey Rodgers. W. R. Rodgers took an honors degree in English from Queen's University and later studied at the Presbyterian Theological Seminary in Belfast. He was ordained in January 1935 and served at Loughgall in County Armagh. Initially overwhelmed by the authority his congregation vested in his office, he began to grow in an understanding of the vocation and ultimately discovered a sense of reverence for his work and for his community, a spirituality that found a voice in his writing. Further, his life in Armagh was far removed from a puritan devotion. His friends and parishioners knew him as "Bertie." He was also known to drink and entertain frequently, to enjoy reading widely, and to smoke his pipe almost constantly. In 1936 he married Marie Harden Waddell, a relation to Rutherford Mayne, the playwright, and to Helen Waddell, the playwright and scholar. Marie and W. R. had two daughters; a son was stillborn. His wife, however, suffered bouts of depression. In 1946 he resigned his ministry to begin work for the BBC's Third Programme Features Department. In 1951, he was elected to the Irish Academy of Letters, taking the place left open after the death of George Bernard Shaw. In 1953 Marie committed suicide, and, subsequently, Rodgers married Marianne Helweg, the former wife of his BBC producer, Laurence Gilliam; a year before, she had left Gilliam for Rodgers, an incident that led to Rodgers's resignation from the BBC. Marianne and he had a daughter, Lucy, who was born in 1956. In 1966, he began work as a teacher and writer in residence at Pitzer College in Claremont, California. He was a success as a teacher, achieving great popularity among his students and organizing a week-long Irish Writers' Festival. With a year left on his visa and with no permanent position available at Pitzer, he took a part-time position at California State Poly-technic College despite suffering from colonic cancer. He died on February 1, 1969, at the County General Hospital in Los Angeles and is buried in Loughgall. At the memorial service, in the First Ballymacarrett Presbyterian Church, Seamus Heaney read selections from Rodgers's verse.

MAJOR WORKS AND THEMES

Rodgers was born into two influences of Ulster Presbyterianism that would profoundly affect his writing. The first was a strong puritan upbringing that required sharp discipline and fierce dedication to fundamentalist principles of Christianity. Rodgers acknowledged the deleterious possibilities of such devotion. However, critics suggest that precisely such a devotion contributes to Rodgers' unique voice. In his life and work, Rodgers doubtlessly rebelled against his upbringing, but his poetry bears witness to the battle within himself between early authority and later instincts. The second major influence on Rodgers involves the identification of religious devotion with an Ulster Unionism championed by Edward Carson's determination to use force rather than submit to "Rome Rule." In his alignment away from this influence, Rodgers found himself more closely affiliated with Ulster clergy from the Church of Ireland, most notably, Louis MacNeice's father, John Frederick MacNeice, bishop of Down and Connor and Dromore.

Poetry

Rodgers's first collection, *Awake! and Other Poems*, was published in 1941; an earlier edition was destroyed by the German blitz. An observer could rightly express curiosity over Rodgers's first collection coming out when he was over thirty. Indeed, Rodgers came late to composition, finding inspiration from a gift by John Hewitt of the works of Auden, Spender, and MacNeice. Certainly, Rodgers's work shows the influence of these and other poets, including Hopkins and Yeats. In "Words" Rodgers explores poetic inspiration through a metaphor of wind coming from the Atlantic and pouring over the countryside of Armagh, clearly reminiscent of "A Prayer for My Daughter." In addition, phrases such as "brain-land" and "sea-scalded" recall the invented language of Hopkins's works. Rodgers's first collection is very much a collage of works that celebrates the landscapes of Northern Ireland, particularly Armagh and the Mournes, and that carries the clear accents of war. "An Irish Lake" describes in careful detail the life surrounding a lake in Armagh. However, even here, there is the rumor of war. A modern reader, coming to Rodgers only through his poetic descendants, finds in these works a possible genesis for some of the images from Heaney and Derek Mahon. The Irish landscape serves as refuge and then reminder of the inevitability and, later the horrors of conflicts distant and near.

There are references to boundaries, both real and fanciful. The landscapes of Ulster, then, function as both a literal and an imaginative geography. Closest to his experiences, Rodgers explores a personal conflict between the responsibilities, the limits, of his office and received faith and an exuberance for experience, for the possibilities of escaping those boundaries.

Rodgers's second collection, *Europa and the Bull and Other Poems* (1952), rewrites Christian and classical mythology, redraws the boundaries of these received traditions, and finds in the act sexuality and sensual pleasure as a reward. "The Net" and "Lent" are the two most widely read of Rodgers's works. The former explores physical intimacy through graphic metaphor that includes references to fish straining a tightening net. The latter engenders Christ in the womb of Mary Magdalene after she abandons Lenten self-sacrifice, clearly alluding to Rodgers's own puritanical upbringing and the new life consequent from seeing the meaning in religious devotion without the cumbersome trappings of restrictive convention. Rodgers's political sensibilities can be discerned in "Armagh," in which he discloses the truth of the city, as he sees it, as home to ancient memories and conflicts, but precisely these memories and the associated turmoil give the city its distinctive character and grandeur. A metaphor is established between the tombs of various cultures and rulers who fought in their lifetime but now find harmony in death connected directly and a bit ironically to the then-sleeping conflict in the Six Counties that lies dormant in death, the only possible peace. However, the poem also offers the memories as inheritance, as proof of the city's heritage, as symbol of the community's progenitors.

Subsequent editions of Rodgers's collected work include a number of poems written after the publication of *Europa*, but there are surprisingly few works. In large measure, Rodgers abandoned composition after the death of his first wife and his subsequent remarriage, often telling friends that he was too happy to write. One of these later works, though, merits attention not only for its craft but for its theme, which focuses on the destructive rhetoric of another Presbyterian minister, Ian Paisley. Rodgers does speak with admiration for Paisley's "guts" but represents him as the personification of a puritanical devotion that the poet so needed to escape. As in his prose works, Rodgers demonstrates a remarkable foresight into the patterns of the soon-to-come resurgence of sectarian violence.

British Broadcasting Company and Other Work

Before working for the BBC full-time, Rodgers went to London in November 1945 to arrange for the production of his first script, "City Set on a Hill"—a program about Armagh. Before his work for the BBC ended in 1952, Rodgers contributed numerous scripts and story ideas, including a collaboration with Louis MacNeice, *The Character of Ireland*, which featured contributions from Frank O'Connor, Elizabeth Bowen, John Hewitt, and Sam Hanna Bell. However, Rodgers's most significant contribution to radio work involved a method of production that included interspacing commentary with selections from interviews and parts of creative works, a process now common in documentaries. Working for the BBC, far removed from his life in Northern Ireland and from its associated pressures and political and religious resonance, enabled Rodgers to come to terms with his Irish identity more clearly than would have been possible if he had stayed in Armagh.

In addition to his work for the BBC and some introductions to a variety of publications, Rodgers wrote a series of articles studying the political and social situation in Northern Ireland in the 1950s. Articles such as "An Ulster Protestant" and "The Black North" provide striking insights into the conditions that gave rise to the civil rights protests and the resurgence of violence in the late 1960s.

CRITICAL RECEPTION

Contemporary critics of Rodgers's poetry received his first volume enthusiastically, hailing him as another Auden. Subsequent critics take a less sympathetic view, speaking of him as "not a profound thinker, but a contemporaneous and candid spirit" (Bogan 218). Louise Bogan's comments take on another character when she adds that his writing is characterized by a "primitive speech" and that the origins of his distinctive rhetoric lie in the "rugged" parts of "Ulster" (218). However, not all of Bogan's criticism carries with it elements of stereotype and biased sentiment. She suggests, "What is best about this poet is his glance into the future and his realisation that more than a casual peace must be demanded" (218). Other critics observe that "most of Rodgers's poetry is buoyantly rhythmical, and as it reflects a keen eye for the form, texture, and movement of the external world and shows an exquisite sensibility for words, we get a combination of qualities likely to delight" (Stevenson 71). However, Rodgers is most properly considered within the context of his Ulster Presbyterian heritage. John Wilson Foster (in Dawe and Longley's *Across a Roaring Hill*) writes that Rodgers's "liberties, abandonments and superfluous energies might be laid at the door of transposed evangelical fervour" (140). Terence Brown (in *Northern Voices*) sees Rodgers's poetic accomplishment as "the work of a personality at war with itself, torn between the Calvinist's sense of duty and responsibility, and a romantic's need for a rich diversity and profusion of experience" (114). Finally, Michael Longley writes that he "revered" Rodgers "along with Louis MacNeice, John Hewitt, [and] Patrick Kavanagh" (21). Longley goes on to suggest that "Rodgers is a latter day metaphysical who apprehends the divine through the senses, The Word through words" (21). Considered within this context, Rodgers becomes a witness to the creative and social influences that informed a Northern Irish consciousness in the years after partition and before the resurgence of sectarian violence in the late 1960s. In his introduction to *Poets from the North of Ireland*, Frank Ormsby considers Rodgers within this framework and places his writing in the context of writers like Mac-

Neice, George Buchanan, and Robert Greacen, all of whom wrote as Protestants in the North of Ireland defining and redefining their heritage.

BIBLIOGRAPHY

Works by W. R. Rodgers

Awake! and Other Poems. London: Secker and Warburg, 1941.
The Ulstermen and Their Country. London: Longmans, Green, 1947.
Europa and the Bull. London: Secker and Warburg, 1952.
Ireland in Colour. London: Batsford, 1957.
Essex Roundabout. Colchester: Benham, 1963.
Collected Poems. London: Oxford University Press, 1971.
Irish Literary Portraits. London: British Broadcasting Corporation, 1972.
Poems: W. R. Rodgers. Loughcrew, County Meath: Gallery, 1993.

Studies of W. R. Rodgers

Amis, Kingsley. "Ulster Bull: The Case of W. R. Rodgers." *Essays in Criticism*. 3.4 (October 1953): 470–75.
Bogan, Louise. *Selected Criticism: Poetry and Prose*. New York: Noonday, 1955.
Davin, Dan. *Closing Times*. London: Oxford University Press, 1975.
Longley, Michael. "Introduction." *Poems: W. R. Rodgers*. Loughcrew, County Meath: Gallery, 1993, 11–22.
McDonald, Peter. "The Fate of 'Identity': John Hewitt, W. R. Rodgers and Louis Mac-Neice." *The Irish Review* 12 (Spring/Summer 1952): 72–86.
O'Brien, Darcy. *W. R. Rodgers*. Lewisburg, PA: Bucknell University Press, 1970.
Ormsby, Frank. "Introduction." *Poets from the North of Ireland*. Belfast: Blackstaff, 1990.
Orr, Peter. *The Poet Speaks: Interviews with Contemporary Poets*. London: Routledge and Kegan Paul, 1966, 207–12.
Stevenson, Patrick. "Volcanic Poet." *Phoenix* (July 1973): 71–76.

Peig Sayers

(1873–1958)

Cóilín D. Owens

BIOGRAPHY

Peig Sayers was born at Vicarstown, Dunquin, County Kerry, in 1873. Nine of her twelve siblings died in childhood. At the age of fourteen, she went as a servant girl to the house of a large shopkeeper in Dingle, where she was treated with kindness and affection. After some time there, she had to return home, due to ill health. Upon her recovery, she went into service in another house in Dingle, where this time she found poor living conditions and a cruel mistress. The opportunity to emigrate to America arose, but she could not afford the fare. Some years later, she learned that a match was arranged for her with Pádraig Ó Gaoithín, "Pats Flint," from the Great Blasket Island. She subsequently lived on the island for over forty years, bearing ten children, six of whom survived into adulthood. One of her sons, Tomás, was killed when he fell down a cliff, and her husband died in his middle years. When all her grown children emigrated to Springfield, Massachusetts, she was left alone. In her later years on the island, her sole companion in her household was her blind brother-in-law. She was among the last inhabitants of the island, evacuated in 1953. She finally returned to Vicarstown and died in Dingle Hospital on December 8, 1958.

MAJOR WORKS AND THEMES

Peig Sayers was the last of the three narrators from the Great Blasket. Her autobiography, *Peig*, ranks with those of Tomás Ó Crohan (*An t-Oileánach*, 1929; trans. *The Islandman*, 1934) and Muiris Ó Súilleabháin (*Fiche Bliain ag Fás*, 1933; trans. *Twenty Years A-Growing*, 1933) as the classics of their kind in modern Irish literature. *Peig* was taken down from her dictation by her son,

Mícheál Ó Gaoithín ("An File"), edited by Máire Ní Chinnéide, and published in 1936. A translation by Bryan MacMahon appeared in 1973. *Machtnamh Seana-Mhná* (1939) was translated by Seamus Ennis in 1962 as *An Old Woman's Reflections*. *Beatha Pheig Sayers*, a further installment of her autobiography, also dictated to her son, appeared in 1970.

The oral equivalent of Ó Crohan's work, her autobiographies are spontaneous, simple, and anecdotal. They are more emotional and personal than Ó Crohan's but contain a higher proportion of traditional tales. Known among the islanders and abroad as the "Queen of the Storytellers," Peig was visited by many writers who went to the Blaskets for her knowledge of oral tradition. Among them was Máire Ní Chinnéide, who edited *Peig* and also *Machtnamh Seana-Mhná* (1939; trans. *An Old Woman's Reflections*, 1962). Seósamh O Dála of the Irish Folklore Commission collected 375 tales from her—from forty long stories of the Fenian cycle (*scéalta*), to odd, whimsical pieces of common lore (*seanchas*). Of these, 325 were written down from her dictation, the remainder being recorded on 140 Ediphone records. Throughout her lifetime, she provided a succession of collectors with a large body of sociohistorical material, impeccably delivered and illustrated by lively anecdotes. She also performed forty folk songs. Most of this collection is preserved in the archives of the Folklore Department, University College, Dublin.

Her remarkable memory and natural eloquence impressed student and scholar visitors to the island. She received all with an unaffected country dignity. W. R. Rodgers, for example, recalls her receiving the gift of a mushroom: she accepted it as if she had been presented with a gold cup. Readers of the transcript of her oral style can infer that such a ceremonial pattern in her personal bearing redeemed the material conditions of her life above the subsistence level. Visitors attest to sessions with Peig that lasted from supper to midnight. After the saying of the rosary and prayers for the living and dead, she and her guests would share the day's news of the weather, the crops, and the fishing. Then she would entertain her company with recitations of the stories of the fairies, her own tragedies, and doings and sayings of the neighbors living and dead, all richly illustrated from her repertoire of verse, proverb, and prayer. She evidently had remarkable histrionic skills: being able, in an instant, to switch from gravity to gaiety, working her hands in concert with the narration, clapping to emphasize a turn of phrase, flashing her thumb over her shoulder to indicate a mystery or holding her hand over her mouth to indicate mischief or surprise.

Her accounts draw a multicolored picture of life in the Kerry Gaeltacht. They celebrate the big occasions in the life of the community: Ventry Races, saints' feast days, and pilgrimages. In pathetic stories of storms at sea, drownings, American wakes, and incidents from the Land War and the Black and Tan War, they recall communal traumas. They contain many passages—evidently the fruits of long, meditative silences—drawing mystical solace from the sublime scenery of mountain, sea, and sky. Set among the accounts of the tragedies of her life, such passages give the impression of a deeply reflected existence, possessed of great inner strength, born of spiritual discipline, Christian humility, and pride in the craft of eloquence. They break into intermittent song and make regular digressions into Fenian lore, and with vividly recalled dialogues, they recount love stories and matchmaking, the burdens of servitude, and the joys of motherhood. In general, with shrewd humor, they provide a unique account of a woman's life within the inherited patriarchal social order. The ideological content is not feminist, but Catholic nationalist. The sincerity of her piety permeates the text, as does her sympathy with the Irish Republican cause. It is no wonder that of all her children, she awards the place of favor to Muiris on account of his loyalties to Ireland, its language, and its religious traditions.

CRITICAL RECEPTION

To two generations of Irish schoolchildren, Peig Sayers is the representative Gaeltacht voice. Her Catholic nationalism, no less than the accessibility of her texts, helps account for the institutionalization of *Peig* in the Irish educational curriculum. An identification of Irish-language culture with hard times on the rainy margins was a natural, though uncomfortable, inference in the popular mind. Thus, *Peig*, along with *An t-Oileánach* and Séamus Ó Grianna's account of life in the Donegal Gaeltacht, *Thiar i dTír Chonaill* (1940), collectively received the inverted compliment of Flann O'Brien's satire in *An Béal Bocht* (1941).

Among her auditors, Robin Flower (*The Western Island*, 1944) confirms the impression one gets from listening to her recorded voice that "her words could be written down as they leave her lips, and they would have the effect of literature with no savour of the artificiality of composition." Her seemingly effortless style, her poise and delivery, make even her most casual statements into the clean and finished speech of a natural orator. His elegant portrait of her is full of personal feeling and affection and is a tribute to the oral tradition about to be obliterated by the culture of print.

In his classic essay, "The Gaelic Story-Teller" (1945), J. H. Delargy provides an invaluable account of the cultural significance of Peig Sayers's art: the place of the *scéalaí* (storyteller) and *seanchaí* (bearer of lore) in the traditional community and the repertoire and techniques of her (normally his) art.

In addition, the reports of scholars and folklorists such as Kenneth Jackson, George Thompson, Seosamh Ó Dála (in *Oileán Eile*), and Bryan MacMahon all testify to the deep impression Peig made upon them as a personality and as a representative of a vanishing culture. In her humorous and dignified demeanor and articulate Irish, she exemplified the civilized virtues of the Gaelic past. Thompson sketches the social and economic underpinnings of this culture. In his admiring introduction to the MacMahon translation (1974), Eoin McKiernan makes an interesting transatlantic comparison with Henry Conklin's account of a hardscrabble Adirondack childhood, *Through "Poverty's Vale."*

BIBLIOGRAPHY

Works by Peig Sayers

Peig: A Scéal Féin. Ed. Máire Ní Chinnéide. Dublin: Talbot, 1936. *Peig: The Autobiography of Peig Sayers*. Trans. Bryan MacMahon. Dublin: Talbot, 1973; intro. Eoin McKiernan. Syracuse: Syracuse University Press, 1974.

Machtnamh Seana-Mhná. Ed. Máire Ní Chinnéide. Dublin: Stationery Office, 1939. Ed. Pádraig Ua Maoileoin. Dublin: Stationery Office, 1980. *An Old Woman's Reflections*. Trans. Seamus Ennis, and intro. W. R. Rodgers. London: Oxford University Press, 1962.

Scéalta Ón mBlascaod. Ed. Kenneth Jackson. Dublin: Irish Folklore Commission, 1939.

Studies of Peig Sayers

Delargy, J. H. "The Gaelic Story-Teller: With Some Notes on Gaelic Folk-Tales." *Proceedings of the British Academy*. London: Oxford University Press, 1945. Reprinted, Chicago: American Committee for Irish Studies, 1969.

Flower, Robin. *The Western Island or The Great Blasket*. New York: Oxford University Press, 1944.

Mac Conghail, Muris. *Oileán Eile: Another Island*. Dublin: Radio Telifís Éireann, 1988.

MacMahon, Bryan. "Peig Sayers and the Vernacular of the Storyteller." In *Literature and Folk Culture: Ireland and Newfoundland*, ed. Alison Feder and Bernice Schrank. St. John's, Newfoundland: Memorial University, 1977.

Ó Gaoithín, Micheál. *Beatha Pheig Sayers*. Dublin: Government Printing Office, 1970.

Thompson, George. *Island Home: The Blasket Heritage*. Dingle: Brandon, 1988.

James Simmons

(1933–)

Bernard McKenna

BIOGRAPHY

James Simmons was born in Derry City, Northern Ireland, on February 14, 1933. Studying at Foyle College in Derry, Campbell College in Belfast, and Leeds University, he received his degree in 1958 and subsequently took a series of teaching positions beginning in Lisburn (County Antrim) at the Quaker School (1958–1963) and in Nigeria at Ahmadu Bello University (1963–1966). Subsequently, in 1967, he returned to Northern Ireland and a position as lecturer in drama and Anglo-Irish literature at the New University of Ulster (1968–1986), and he has served as poet in residence at Queen's University, Belfast. Additionally, in 1968 he helped to found and edited the first nineteen issues of the *Honest Ulsterman*. Currently, Simmons lives in Islandmagee, County Antrim, and runs, with his wife, Janice Fitzpatrick Simmons, Poet's House.

MAJOR WORKS AND THEMES

Simmons is one of a group of poets who developed under the tutelage of Philip Hobsbaum, then a lecturer at Queen's University, Belfast, in the decade before the resurgence of sectarian violence in 1968. Hobsbaum founded a writers' group that included Seamus Heaney, Derek Mahon, Seamus Deane, Michael Longley, and James Simmons, who published their initial work as part of the Queen's University Festival proceedings. Even at this time Simmons showed much of the promise and unique quality that characterize his poetic achievement. Like the other writers of this school, Simmons numbers among his influences traditional masters such as Yeats, Kavanagh, Shakespeare, and Marvell but also Frank Sinatra and the artists of the folk music revival of the 1960s. This rather eclectic mix of traditional lyric poets with popular entertainers manifests itself in much of Simmons's writing and has attracted the negative attention of some critics who find it difficult to separate Simmons's more serious poetic efforts from poems that function as entertainments and diversions. Consequently, he is often considered the "least accomplished" of the group of young writers to emerge from Queen's University Festival. Such an assessment, however, does grave injustice to Simmons's work. Each of his books is structured very much like an entertainment that includes moments of pathos, moments of commentary on the ills of society, and moments of laughter and joy. Within each volume there are demonstrations of significant lyrical accomplishment, of important poetic achievement, and of self-mockery, almost self-parody.

Poetry

Simmons's poetry, often regarded as "lightweight" and "undistinguished," received a significant boost in reputation in 1978 with the publication of *The Selected James Simmons*, a volume later updated and expanded in 1986 with the publication of *Poems 1956–1986*. Both of these selections, edited and introduced by Edna Longley, take the most accomplished poetry from Simmons's earlier volumes and arrange it in a more traditional manner, divesting the author's songs and entertainments from his more "literary" works. The result is an impressive volume of writing that explores in subtle and sometimes moving detail the poet's relationship to love and marriage, myth and tradition, children and family, sensuality and music. Typical of these works is "Ballad of a Marriage," a poem taken from Simmons's earliest collection, which details, the evolution of a couple's relationship from lust and romantic love through jealousy and rage, complacency and parenthood, until each partner is surprised by deep, meaningful love after they grow to understand each other in a more mature way. The structure of the poem is deceptively simple. It begins with a basic, almost too basic, rhyme and structural pattern. However, as the poem's characters grow in their understanding of each other and in their understanding of the complexity of marriage, the poem's structure grows in intricacy and subtlety.

Volumes published subsequent to the 1986 *Poems* follow the same structural pattern of Simmons's earlier work; they contain some "literary" works but also songs and light entertainments. Many have fallen victim to the same misunderstanding that plagued the critical reception of Simmons's early publications. However, most reviewers are able to distinguish his poetry from his songs and praise the accomplishment of both within each one's individual genre. Most significantly, Maurice Harmon, writing in *The Linen Hall Review*, observes that *Mainstream*, Simmons's most recent volume, contains the author's characteristic "irreverent persona" and a "comic voice." But behind the screen of comedy he deals with serious matters—life's sorrows, broken marriages, sick children, love, loneliness, violence, song, the ability to endure and keep one's love of living" (30).

Among Simmons's most accomplished poetic achievements is his writing
about the Troubles in Northern Ireland; the best of this work is contained in an
anthology of poetry about the Troubles, *A Rage for Order*, edited by Frank
Ormsby. Simmons's work in this volume marks his identity as a Protestant
writing about sectarian violence in the Six Counties. In these poems, Simmons
claims, in traditionally Anglo-Protestant ways, a connection with an Irish past
and comes to terms with the supposed sins of his community and with the
wrongs committed against his community by Catholic Republicans who claim
exclusive access to an Irish heritage. In "Lament for a Dead Policeman," Simmons, modeling his work on the ancient "The Lament for Art O'Leary," writes
that a member of the Royal Ulster Constabulary is worthy to be numbered
among Irish martyrs and heroes.

Critical Works

As editor of *The Honest Ulsterman* Simmons made his most enduring contribution to Northern Irish literature. He encouraged young poets coming of age
in the late 1960s and early 1970s, gave them a forum for their views, and
provided them a place to showcase their burgeoning talents in a time that was
particularly hostile to creative achievement. In addition, Simmons has published
an important critical work, *Sean O'Casey*, edited several anthologies of Irish
writing—such as *Ten Irish Poets* and *Soundings 3*—and done editorial work for
The Linen Hall Review.

CRITICAL RECEPTION

The critical reception of James Simmons's work follows a sharp divide. Some
critics, like Robert Hogan, find that Simmons "has been one of the most prolific
Northern poets and, . . . one of the worst. Perhaps, because of his interest in
composing popular ballads and song lyrics, the form of most of his poetry has
remained so casual as to be simply slovenly." Hogan goes on to write that
Simmons's "images are frequently incongruous," "mawkishly personal," and
"pedestrian" (*The Dictionary of Irish Literature* 615). Some critics have followed Hogan's lead and have continued to condemn Simmons's work. However,
even Hogan concedes that Simmons's talent began to grow in the late 1970s,
and Hogan and most other critics agree with Edna Longley's current assessment
of Simmons's poetic accomplishment: that he has "an air of very immediately
addressing the reader out of the immediacy of experience" in "effortlessly natural tones . . . at once source and focus of . . . persuasive vitality" (*Poems 1956–
1986*, 11).

BIBLIOGRAPHY

Works by James Simmons

Aiken Mata: The Lysistrata of Aristophanes. Ibadan: Oxford University Press, 1966.
Ballad of a Marriage. Belfast: Festival, 1966.
Late but in Earnest. London: Bodley Head, 1967.
In the Wilderness and Other Poems. London: Bodley Head, 1969.
Songs for Derry. Portrush: Ulsterman, 1969.
No Ties. Portrush: Ulsterman, 1970.
Energy to Burn. London: Bodley Head, 1971.
No Land Is Waste, Dr. Eliot. Belfast: Keepsake, 1972.
The Long Summer Still to Come. Belfast: Blackstaff, 1973.
Ten Irish Poets. Cheadle, Cheshire: Carcanet, 1974.
West Strand Visions. Belfast: Blackstaff, 1974.
Judy Garland and the Cold War. Belfast: Blackstaff, 1976.
The Selected James Simmons. Ed. and intro. Edna Longley. Belfast: Blackstaff, 1978.
Constantly Singing. Belfast: Blackstaff, 1980.
Sean O'Casey. Dublin: Gill and Macmillan, 1983.
Work in Progress. Boston: Northeastern University, 1984.
From the Irish. Belfast: Blackstaff Press, 1985.
Poems 1956–1986. Intro. Edna Longley. Loughcrew, County Meath: Gallery, 1986.
Cattle Rustling. Belfast: Fortnight Educational Trust, 1991.
Outing to Port a Doris. London: Turret Bookshop, 1993. (Individual poem.)
Sex, Rectitude, Loneliness. Belfast: Lapwing, 1993.
Mainstream. Galway: Salmon, 1995.

Studies of James Simmons

At Six O'Clock in the Silence of Things—a Festschrift for James Simmons. Belfast: Lapwing, 1993.
Chapman, Robert T. "More than an Entertainer." *Honest Ulsterman* 46/47 (1975): 71–74.
———. "Talking to James Simmons." *Confrontation* 10 (Spring 1975): 70–79.
Dalmas, Victor. "James Simmons." *Pembroke Magazine* 19 (1987): 57–105.
Harmon, Maurice. "Poetry." *The Linen Hall Review* 12.1 (Spring 1995): 28–30.
Kelly, John. "Down Seamus Avenue up Carson Street." *Fortnight* 291 (December 1991): 29–30.
Longley, Edna. "Introduction." *The Selected James Simmons*. Belfast: Blackstaff, 1978.
———. "Introduction." *Poems 1956–1986*. Loughcrew, County Meath: Gallery, 1986.
McEneaney, Kevin. "James Simmons: Poetry, Bards and Broadway, a Conversation." *An Gael* 3.1 (Summer 1985): 14–15.
Mooney, Martin. "Still Burning: James Simmons in Conversation with Martin Mooney." *Rhinoceros* 2: 101–22.

Somerville and Ross

(E.OE. Somerville, 1858–1949, and Violet Martin, 1862–1915)

Ann Owens Weekes

Somerville and Ross was the name by which the cousins and literary collaborators, Edith Oenone Somerville and Violet Martin, published their fiction. The Somerville family came to Ireland in 1690 and established themselves in Castletownshend, County Cork, where they eventually built Drishane House. Edith was educated by governesses at home, spent a term at Alexandra College, Dublin, and another at South Kensington School of Art, London. A keen artist, she overrode her family's protests to follow a cousin to Düsseldorf in 1881 and later studied art in Paris. The Martin family, which came to Ireland with Strongbow, built and lived in Ross House, County Galway, where Violet was educated by an aunt and a former hedge schoolmaster. The cousins met for the first time in January 1886 and thus began an extraordinary literary collaboration. The possibility and nature of such a collaboration were a source of critical curiosity from the beginning, but the cousins treated this collaboration as a natural outcome of the friendship of intellectual, artistic women. Edith recalled the conversational nature of their work, how frequently they hit upon a proposition simultaneously, discussed, debated, and qualified it, and finally how the purely fortuitous holder of the pen committed their ideas to paper. Violet loved to spend time in Castletownshend with the extended network of Somerville cousins, but the women were frequently requested to forgo their "nonsense" and attend to their "real" duties of entertaining.

Both Anglo-Irish scendancy families were devoted to hunting, dogs, gardens, and beautiful houses, and both women, in their lives and novels, were intensely—even defensively—loyal to their class and opposed to the forces that threatened it. But loyalty did not blind them to the class's gender injustices, which they—active in the suffragette movement—resented bitterly. Both were Unionists, Violet more so than Edith, who signed a clemency petition for the

1916 leaders of the Rising. After the initial meeting, the women traveled extensively together, often commissioned to gather material for publication in London magazines; their most famous collection, *Some Experiences of an Irish R.M.*, was originally requested by, and written for, the *Badminton Magazine*. Unfortunately, the success of the short stories led to their neglect of the serious novel: although *The Real Charlotte*, their masterpiece, won them acclaim in 1894, their pressing financial needs and lack of time made short stories more feasible than novels. Edith became mistress of Drishane when her mother died in 1895 and thereafter was engaged in multifarious activities, including horse dealing, cattle breeding, and art shows, and from 1903 to 1908 and again from 1912 to 1919, she was master of hounds to the West Carbery Fox-Hounds, a time-consuming, expensive responsibility but one very close to her heart. Violet died of a brain tumor in 1915, possibly caused by a fall from a horse in 1898, and Edith was bereft. Resorting to a medium in 1916, she believed that she made contact with Violet, who proclaimed their partnership to be merely interrupted, not ended; when she began to write again, Edith continued to publish under Somerville and Ross, insisting that Violet was a party to the creation. Edith was recognized as a woman of letters in 1932 with Trinity College's award of D.Litt. and invited by Yeats to join the Irish Academy of Letters.

MAJOR WORKS AND THEMES

The decline of the Ascendancy and the uneasy interaction between the Big House and tenants haunted Somerville and Ross's work from the start. *An Irish Cousin* (1889), their first novel, pictures the isolation and darkness of the west coast of Ireland, where the Sarsfield family's decay parallels that of their Big House, Durrus. Theo Sarsfield, a foreign innocent and frequent device, arrives from Canada to the family home, where her Uncle Dominick has an irregular relationship with the servant, Moll. Attraction between the offspring of such a relationship and the legitimate offspring of the Big House is here and elsewhere a source of conflict. Dominick rails against marriage between his son and Moll's daughter (perhaps also Dominick's) as an offense against class. Exposing his hypocrisy and his neglect of the very structures upon which class is built, the authors nevertheless usually conclude romances by pairing appropriate couples, those of the same class and creed. Supernatural or gothic elements appear in this first work, but also vivid descriptions of house and country and excellent accounts of that Somerville and Ross delight, the Irish hunt.

Naboth's Vineyard (1891) features Irish village life, about which the authors knew little; hence, the characters are often stereotypes. Exploration of Irish hunger for land, a timely topic and one they knew well, begins here. A strong woman character is also introduced: Harriet, a mixture of good and evil, whose passionate desire for another man leads her to participate by omission in the murder of her husband. Harriet's actions—her vulgarity—are explained, as are the actions of other Somerville and Ross characters, as products of an inferior social class. Their first travel book, *Through Connemara in a Governess Cart* (1892), betrays the same tendency: despite some good descriptions, the authors invent stock scenes as representations of the hilarious and ridiculous in Irish life. An 1891 tour of Bordeaux produced *In the Vine Country* (1893); once again the authors often observe from a height, but here the comic scenes are saved by self-mockery. Two more tours were made in 1893; *Beggars on Horseback* (1895) chronicles their visit to Wales, where Edith as the artist Miss O'Flannigan is often the source of comedy. A tour of Denmark led to *Stray-Aways* (1920). The books appeared months or years after magazine publication. A recurring feature is the authors' insistence on their difference from English women.

The Real Charlotte (1894), begun in 1889, was not completed until 1893, fortunately, for, as Edith notes, once the novel was conceived, the characters were rarely out of their creators' minds. This long simmering contributed to the finely developed characters and the complex, ironic plot that make *The Real Charlotte* a masterpiece. Here, for the first time, the dialect is perfect, the accents and expressions throughout authentic and hilariously funny, the harvest of many hours of collecting phrases, words, and accents of family, servants, and local people. Charlotte Mullen, the title character, is a superb mixture of intelligence, greed, and passion, a plain and unlikable woman on the periphery of polite Anglo-Irish society. The novel spans a large spectrum of Anglo-Irish society: Sir Benjamin Dysart, owner of the Big House of Bruff, is senile and bullied by his attendant, the mad James Canavan; Christopher, the heir, is uninterested in the estate and in the complex land laws that ultimately transfer land from land-lords to tenants; the English Lady Dysart, unaware of Irish dialectical nuances and behavioral patterns, fails to understand the many levels of society. Below the Dysarts is a chorus of country gentlemen, retired army officers, land agents, soldiers, and impoverished widows. Too many wives and daughters throng the parties, too few sons. All, with the exception of the Dysarts, struggle for land. All are beautifully individualized by accent and expression. Beyond the pale, Charlotte's repressed and filthy Ferry Row tenants, ignored by all but their ruthless landlady, are an ominous sign of change to come. The entrance of pretty Francie Fitzpatrick initiates the usual attraction between inappropriate couples, but Charlotte's role moves this novel from romance to tragedy. Motivated by hunger for land and an arid passion for a worthless man, Charlotte is frighten-ingly mundane as she moves from callousness, to cheating, stealing, and murder. Nothing is spared in the depiction of Charlotte's character, but finally the nar-rators express a generous understanding of the torture a plain, intelligent woman suffers in a society that values women's appearance and ignores their intelli-gence.

Unfortunately, the cousins never again wrote such a panoramic, penetrating novel, though they planned to do so. *The Silver Fox* (1898) first appeared in a newspaper, which, according to Edith, required weekly concluding sensations and thus lacks coherence. An unlikely romance dominated by superstition and legend, the novel runs true to the authors' habit of introducing English characters to the ways of Irish people but finally matches characters with appropriate partners of the same class and nationality.

In 1898, when the cousins were holidaying in France, *Badminton Magazine* requested a series of short stories similar to the hunting/country stories published through the years. Thus were born the Irish Resident Magistrate and a comic series that would win the women huge popularity, particularly with the English, for whom the stories were written. The comedy results from the encounters of Major Yeates, the Resident Magistrate, an English gentleman, with Flurry Knox, his Irish landlord, with Flurry's extended family, which ranges from Lady Knox to Larry the Liar, a Knox auctioneer, and with the local people. The joke is often at the Major's expense, but usually reader and Major are at one, surprised and amused at the extraordinary antics of the Irish. Yeates develops from the innocent in *Some Experiences of an Irish R.M.* (1899) to become temporary master of hounds in *Further Experiences of an Irish R.M.* (1908), a real indicator of acceptance in this hunting society. The final series, completed the year of Martin's death, *In Mr. Knox's Country* (1915), reveals an aging Yeates and a dispossessed Ascendancy in a post-land acts Ireland.

Pressed by their agent for the popular hunt stories, the cousins collected previously published stories into *All on the Irish Shore* (1903) and *Some Irish Yesterdays* (1906). A novel, *Dan Russel the Fox* (1911), is noteworthy only for its enthusiastic descriptions of the hunt. After Violet's death, Edith published *Irish Memories* (1917), a collection of family reminiscences begun and largely written by Violet. Edith published five more novels under both partners' names. *Mount Music* (1919) explores the relationship between Catholics and Protestants during the final years of the land transfer, 1894–1907. Although they have little sympathy with the land acts, the authors also delineate here, as in *The Real Charlotte*, the ineptness of the Ascendancy. *An Enthusiast* (1921) features an idealistic Anglo-Irishman, Dan Palliser, who attempts to heal divisions during the time of the Black-and-Tan/Irish war. *The Big House of Inver* (1925) is the novel Violet Martin dreamed of writing, the novel of the decline of the Ascendancy through debauchery, indifference, quarrels, and intermarriage with village girls. Shibby Pindy, whose name identifies her as a "side-shoot" of the Big House Prendeville family, is the last memorable Somerville and Ross character. Mistaken but, for all that, more worthy of respect than those around her, Shibby fights to restore house and family to their former grandeur—inevitably, a losing battle. *Inver* comes closest to *The Real Charlotte* in its penetration into character and grasp of history. *French Leave* (1928) is a lighthearted romance that calls on Edith's student time in Paris, and *Sarah's Youth* (1938), written as Edith neared eighty, features a tomboy heroine who succumbs not to the romantic hero but to the lure of the hounds. Writing to the last, Edith also published an account of her trip to the United States, a biography of Charles Kendal Bushe— lord chief justice of Ireland and Somerville ancestor—and several collections of essays and memoirs.

CRITICAL RECEPTION

Somerville and Ross's work received mixed reviews. The first novel was greeted as too gloomy, and *The Real Charlotte* was accorded an unsympathetic response initially, one paper finding it the most disagreeable of novels. Favorable reviews soon followed, however, and by the time the R.M. stories were published, English reviewers were loud in their praise. The Irish audience—limited during the writers' lifetimes—declined almost totally during the 1940s and 1950s, and the work went out of print. The names and work of Somerville and Ross, however, continued to be essential in academic collections of Irish or Anglo-Irish writers. With the 1960s came a renewal of interest in Ascendancy Ireland, and *The Real Charlotte* was recognized in both Ireland and England as a classic: V. S. Pritchett called it the best Irish novel of any period (*New Statesman*, May 24, 1968). Interest was fostered on both sides of the Atlantic by the very popular British Television R.M. series. Some contemporary critics remark about the Big House versus "cabins" nature of Somerville and Ross's work, but most agree that their best work, *The Real Charlotte*, the *R.M.* series, and *The Big House of Inver*, deserve their high ranking in the canon of Irish literature. Two more recent studies, in Imhof's *Ancestral Voices* and Weekes's *Irish Women Writers*, continue the trend of critical interest.

BIBLIOGRAPHY

Works by Somerville and Ross

An Irish Cousin. London: Bentley, 1889.
Naboth's Vineyard. London: Blackett, 1891.
Through Connemara in a Governess Cart. London: Allen, 1892.
In the Vine Country. London: Allen, 1893.
The Real Charlotte. London: Ward and Downey, 1894.
Beggars on Horseback. Edinburgh and London: Blackwood, 1895.
The Silver Fox. London: Lawrence and Bullen, 1898.
Some Experiences of an Irish R.M. London: Longmans, Green, 1899.
A Patrick's Day Hunt. London: Constable, 1902.
All on the Irish Shore. London: Longmans, Green, 1903.
Slipper's ABC of Fox Hunting London: Longmans, Green, 1903.
Some Irish Yesterdays. London: Longmans, Green, 1906.
Further Experiences of an Irish R.M. London: Longmans, Green, 1908.
Dan Russel the Fox. London: Methuen, 1911.
In Mr. Knox's Country. London: Longmans, Green, 1915.
Irish Memories. London: Longmans, Green, 1917.
Mount Music. London: Longmans, Green, 1919.
Stray-Aways. London: Longmans, Green, 1920.
An Enthusiast. London: Longmans, Green, 1921.
Wheel-Tracks. London: Longmans, Green, 1923.

The Big House of Inver. London: Heinemann, 1925.
French Leave. London: Heinemann, 1928.
The States through Irish Eyes. Boston and New York: Houghton Mifflin, 1930.
An Incorruptible Irishman. London: Nicholson and Watson, 1932.
The Smile and the Tear. London: Methuen, 1933.
The Sweet Cry of Hounds. London: Methuen, 1936.
Sarah's Youth. London: Longmans, Green, 1938.
Notions in Garrison. London: Methuen, 1941.
Happy Days. London: Longmans, Green, 1946.
Maria and Some Other Dogs. London: Methuen, 1949.

Studies of Somerville and Ross

Collis, Maurice. *Somerville and Ross: A Biography.* London: Faber and Faber, 1968.
Cronin, John. " 'An Ideal of Art': The Assertion of Realities in the Fiction of Somerville and Ross." *Canadian Journal of Irish Studies* 11.1 (June 1985): 3–19.
———. *Somerville and Ross.* Lewisburg: Bucknell University Press, 1972.
Flanagan, Thomas. "The Big House of Ross-Drishane." *The Kenyon Review* 28 (January 1966): 54–78.
McMahon, Sean. "John Bull's Other Ireland: A Consideration of *The Real Charlotte* by Somerville and Ross." *Eire-Ireland* 3.4 (Winter 1968): 119–35.
Martin, David. "The 'Castle Rackrent' of Somerville and Ross: A Tragic 'Colonial' Tale?" *Etudes-Irlandaises* 7.2 (December 1982): 43–53.
Mooney, Shawn. " 'Colliding Stars': Heterosexism in Biographical Representations of Somerville and Ross." *Canadian Journal of Irish Studies* 18.1 (July 1992): 157–75.
Powell, Violet. *The Books and Background of Somerville and Ross.* London: Heinemann, 1970.
Power, Ann. "The Big House of Somerville and Ross." *The Dubliner* (Spring 1942): 43–53.
Pritchett, V. S. "The Irish R.M." In *The Living Novel and Later Appreciations.* New York: Vintage, 1947.

James Stephens

(1882–1950)

Barton R. Friedman

BIOGRAPHY

In August 1915, Yeats wrote Edmund Gosse, naming Joyce and James Stephens as "the most prominent people we have in Ireland." In May 1927 Joyce wrote Harriet Shaw Weaver, proposing what Richard Ellmann calls "one of the strangest ideas in literary history," that Stephens take over *Finnegans Wake* should Joyce himself die or break down.

Who was this man, whom Yeats judged worthy to be ranked with Joyce, whom Joyce thought capable of finishing the *Wake*, and who, perhaps even more implausibly, agreed that he could and would do it? This question turns out to pose delicate biographical problems, for Stephens hid his past behind a stitchwork of tall tales, some contributed by friends, more woven out of his own fancies, most discredited by Hilary Pyle's biography. He was apparently not, as he claimed, born on Joyce's birthday, February 2, 1882; nor was he, as he once hinted, descended from gypsies; nor did he spend part of his childhood wandering the west of Ireland. He was instead the son of working-class parents; attended the Meath Protestant Industrial School for Boys, where he learned clerking; and spent his young manhood giving various Dublin firms the benefit of his education.

It was behind a typewriter at one of these firms that, in 1908, AE (George Russell), having sampled Stephens's verse in *Sinn Féin*, found him. Forty-odd years later Stephens was to relate his beginnings as a poet to Kees Van Hoek of *The Irish Times*: happening one day on a bookstall and having spare tanners in his pocket, he bought copies of Blake and Browning: "I started reading in bed and my mind suddenly said to me: 'You can do that,' and that night I wrote 25 poems." Despite suspicion that he had been visited by the puckish demon who changes artists into tricksters when answering the queries of journalists and (often, alas!) scholars, at least some truth resides in this tale. Among the most impressive of Stephens's early achievements are dramatic monologues modeled on Browning's and songs of innocence and experience modeled on Blake's.

As AE appears to have intuited, however, Stephens's talent was chiefly to realize itself in prose; and in 1912 he announced his arrival to Dublin's vibrant literary community with not one important novel but two, *The Charwoman's Daughter* and *The Crock of Gold*. Stephens's turn to fiction seems to have happened as spontaneously as his try at poetry. "I had," he was later to recall, "picked up, idly enough *The House of Pomegranates* by Oscar Wilde. After reading about twenty pages . . . I closed the book because an illuminating idea came to me, not from its pages, but from, as it were, between the lines."

When his illuminating idea came to him, Stephens had already published a volume of poems, *Insurrections* (1909). What followed was a rush of work, both prose and poetry, that slowed only after 1920. The extraordinary year 1912 saw another volume of poems, *The Hill of Vision*, and 1913 his first volume of short stories, *Here Are Ladies*. In 1914 Stephens published his third novel, *The Demi-Gods*, and in 1915 two more volumes of poems, *Songs from the Clay* and *The Adventures of Seumas Beg/The Rocky Road to Dublin*. In 1916 he responded to the Easter Rising with an elegy for the Volunteers, *Green Branches*, and a personal memoir that deserves to be included among the histories of Easter Week, *The Insurrection in Dublin*. In 1918 he embarked on a new venture, a collection of lyrics translated from Gaelic, *Reincarnations*, which was followed in 1920 by *Irish Fairy Tales*.

Irish Fairy Tales adumbrates the major project Stephens set himself for the 1920s, a five-volume redaction of the *Táin Bó Cuálnge* (*Cattle Raid of Cooley*). Of this project, only two parts materialized, *Deirdre* (1923) and *In the Land of Youth* (1924), both of which seem to have been finished by 1920. Thereafter in the 1920s, Stephens produced two chapbooks, *Little Things* (1924) and *A Poetry Recital* (1925); a second collection of short stories, *Etched in Moonlight* (1928); and a long poem, *Theme and Variations* (1929); and in the 1930s, two last volumes of poems, *Strict Joy* (1931) and *Kings and the Moon* (1938). By the final decade of his life, his creative energy had run out.

What happened can only be guessed at. He had suffered from ill health most of his adult years. His abandonment of the *Tain* seems, moreover, to have stemmed from growing disillusion with the Ireland emergent from the wreckage of Easter Week and the bitter revolutionary struggle that followed, for in 1925 he left Dublin to live the rest of his life an exile in England.

Crossing the Irish Sea entailed leaving his cultural heritage, turning from Celtic tradition to Eastern mysticism. Stephens had, from the outset, incorporated occult ideas into his art. After 1925, he passed beyond Blake and Madame Blavatsky to Buddhism itself. Especially in Zen, with its denial of utility to words, he found a deeply troubling contradiction to the prophetic role Blake had granted the poet. This contradiction he never resolved. Much of the verse in *Strict Joy* and *Kings and the Moon* seems less inspired utterance than labored rhetoric. Finally, therefore, he discarded all metaphysical schemes to seek values where he had sought them at first, within himself: he embarked on an autobiography. But the task exceeded his strength. He managed only a few isolated episodes before he died, on December 26, 1950.

MAJOR WORKS AND THEMES

Summing up Stephens's achievement in a few pages requires making unhappy choices. His corpus divides into three broad categories: verse, where he probably had least (though hardly negligible) success; prose romances, especially *The Crock of Gold*, on which his reputation mainly rests, and short stories, often better than the neglect into which they have fallen would imply.

Ruth Pitter once remarked of the stories Stephens had fashioned from his own youth that they used to strike her "as sounding as though they had been translated from some Balkan language; their roots were elsewhere, though the themes were so universal" (Pyle, 118). She had in mind his focus on the struggle of the poor and the outcast to survive by their wits, recurrent in the memories in his autobiographical fragments, persisting as an undercurrent, even in the wishfulfillment Ireland of his romances, and surfacing as the inexorable current to overwhelm the desperate couple in the wartime world of his powerful short story "Hunger."

The protagonists of "Hunger" differ little from the Makebelieves and Mrs. Cafferty's young lodger in *The Charwoman's Daughter*, the Philosopher's cellmates in *The Crock of Gold*, or the MacCanns in *The Demi-Gods*. They must all wrest livings from a society inured to human misery. But in the magical environs Stephens posits for his romances, something always intervenes to save his heroes from their ordeals, whether, as in *The Charwoman's Daughter*, Brady's bequest, announced by the letter from Platitude and Glambe and fulfilling Mrs. Makebelieve's daydreams that her brother in America will whisk Mary and herself out of their poverty; or, as in *The Crock of Gold*, the "Happy March" of the Shee, which rescues the Philosopher from the police, who would try to hang him for a murder that was never committed; or, as in *The Demi-Gods*, the descent of the angels Finaun, Caeltia, and Art, who bring wisdom and love to Patsy and Mary MacCann.

These narratives are all psychic allegories. In a note inscribed in George Keating's copy of *The Crock of Gold*, Stephens had explained, "There is only one character—Man—Pan is his sensual nature, the Philosopher his intellect at play, Angus Óg his intellect spiritualized, the policemen his conventions and his logics, the leprecauns [*sic*] his elemental side, the children his innocence." As the name he chooses for his heroines in *The Charwoman's Daughter* declares, the model to which he shapes his one character is his creative self. The policeman in *The Charwoman's Daughter*, who conjoins convention and logic with brute force, may inform Mary Makebelieve that the phoenix of Phoenix

Park is a make-believe bird, but so is Mary a "Makebelieve" girl. In the realm of Stephens's imagination, she and the phoenix are more real than he is.

That the agents of oppression, the police, bumble into comic impotence in both *The Charwoman's Daughter* and *The Crock of Gold* asserts Stephens's Blakean faith in the potential of imagination to transform society. The lodger embodies the revolutionary in Stephens. He cannot be intimidated by the policeman's superior bulk because he is "a man predestined to bruises"; the half-closed eye he displays as a badge of courage will "always be half-closed by the decent buffet of misfortune." When he is hungry or pacing by Mary's side, he believes anything possible.

In the Ireland of *The Crock of Gold* anything is possible. The Shee dancing the Philosopher away to Tir-na-nOg enact his apotheosis as surely as God transporting Elijah into heaven. Their dance symbolizes the same unity of being for Stephens as, in "Among School Children," dance symbolizes for Yeats. Identifiable as individuals, the Shee yet merge into an organic whole: "They moved freely each in his personal whim and they moved also with the unity of one being: for when they shouted to the Mother of the gods they shouted with one voice, and they bowed to her as one man bows" (308).

They are Blake's universal family, gathered in the Council of God as one man, but now in Celtic dress. As in *The Four Zoas*, they look toward a millennial future. MacCushin, chosen poet of Angus Óg, the Divine Imagination, will celebrate the son to be born to Angus and Caitilin, the Scaler of the Wall between the Tree of Knowledge and the Tree of Life.

The Crock of Gold projects a scale to history suggestive of Blake's 6,000 years, in which the millennium is almost upon us. By the publication of *The Demi-Gods* in the first year of the Great War, however, Stephens has begun to view history more through Eastern (or at least theosophical) than through Blakean eyes: the time before the end has stretched to eons. In *The Demi-Gods*, indeed, history is cyclical, without promise of end. When the MacCanns and the angels bury the degraded black magician Brien O'Brien (whose name is precisely circular), Patsy stuffs a threepenny-bit into his fist, ensuring that the quarrel between Brien and Cuchulain over the lost coin will recur, that Rhadamanthus will again banish them for destroying the peace of heaven, that Brien will again slouch toward Ireland to be reborn.

Yet the angels do not leave the MacCanns as they found them. Patsy is united to his old love, Eileen Ni Cooley. Art has torn up his wings for love of Mary. Mary (like Mary Makebelieve and Caitilin Ni Murrachu) has grown into experience. In their state of nature, the MacCanns harbor whatever capacity humankind has to redeem itself—which is why the angels gravitate to them rather than to civilized folk who could receive them in a style commensurate with their rank.

Such folk enter *The Demi-Gods* in the estranged couple of Ard-Martin, to whom Patsy has sold, and from whom he steals back, the angels' celestial finery.

Their malignancy toward each other is palpable in the conversation Patsy over-
hears:

> Said he:
> "I will leave here in the morning."
> "You will let me see the boy," she murmured.
> "If," said he, "I ever learn that you have spoken to the boy I will kill you, and I will
> kill the boy."

The effect of their malignancy on society is similarly palpable in the Darwinian
struggle of the MacCanns' daily lives. As Patsy himself says, after finding a
sumptuous breakfast for his guests in a house whose occupants have been
clubbed unconscious, "If the world wasn't full of trouble there'd be no life at
all for the poor. It's the only chance we get is when people are full of woe,
God help them! And isn't that a queer thing?"

The queerness of the thing is underscored by Finaun's remark that he would
have thought hunger the easiest problem for an organized society to solve. That
it turns out to be the hardest is reflected in the indefinite, if not infinite, length
to which Stephens expands history. Blake's Universal Brotherhood of Eden,
apparently imminent at the end of *The Crock of Gold*, becomes in *The Demi-
Gods* increasingly remote. While the angels manifest the spiritual selves of
Eileen, Patsy, and Mary, the couple of Ard-Martin and Brien O'Brien seem
without spiritual selves.

In *The Demi-Gods*, then, we can detect the stirrings of the disillusion that
gradually pushed Stephens toward silence. Intensified by the carnage of the
Great War and Ireland's own little war, the constricting effect of this disillusion
on his art can be suggested by glancing at a few poems, early and late. "The
Goat Paths" (1915) posits three poles of consciousness: the speaker, the goats
themselves, and the reader ("you") to whom the utterance is addressed. Speaker
and reader, human and therefore alien, are cut off from the goats living their
pastoral idyll:

> If you approach they run away,
>   They leap and stare, away they bound,
>   With a sudden angry sound,
> To the sunny quietude;
>   Crouching down where nothing stirs
>   In the silence of the furze,
> Crouching down again to brood
> In the sunny solitude.

While "you" presumably implies man in general, the speaker separates himself,
in sensibility, from his fellows:

> If I were as wise as they
>   I would stray apart and brood,
> I would beat a hidden way
> Through the quiet heather spray
>   To a sunny solitude;
>
> And should you come I'd run away,
>   I would make an angry sound,
>   I would stare and turn and bound
> To the deeper quietude . . .

Goathood entails instinctive wisdom, from which, as the speaker discerns, civilization has excluded him. But he at least acknowledges the existence of such wisdom. Unlike "you"—rationalists, materialists, hypercultivated patrons of the arts—he would be goatlike if he could. If nature in "The Goat Paths" still beckons as a haven from the vicissitudes of a culture in the throes of destroying itself, nature in *Theme and Variations*, a decade and a half later, is seen as incorporating ultimate self-destruction.

Having discredited Western religion and harnessed those forces in nature to produce the holocaust of 1914–1918, Western science has betrayed the culture that spawned it. For Stephens, both the science and religion of the West must be abandoned. Among the poems by which he announces their abandonment is "Nachiketas and Death" ("Thy Soul" in *Collected Poems*), rooted in the *Katha Upanishad* and written in 1922. Granted three boons by Death, Nachiketas asks to have the afterlife revealed to him. In the language of the poem, "He bargained with the Monarch grim/For Knowledge."

The knowledge Nachiketas seeks has nothing to do with empirical or intellectual inquiry. It comes instead from that special sort of meditation Stephens describes, in *On Prose and Verse*, as "looking at it without thinking about it." Or, as Death warns Nachiketas, the One is accessible neither to eye nor ear nor mind nor speech. The poem sums up communion with the One as "naught":

> Thou shalt be naught, and thou shalt be
> Thyself and thine own mystery,
> Knowledge, Bliss, Eternity
>   For Thou Art That.

Therein lies the rub. The quest for "Knowledge, Bliss, Eternity" is solipsistic—and, as such, incommunicable. What Stephens learned from the *Katha* was, as D. T. Suzuki was later to formulate it for him, the rule of "no dependence on words and letter" (*Essays in Zen Buddhism*). Literature itself had become naught.

CRITICAL RECEPTION

Stephens was neither Yeats nor Joyce. But his art earned him the (sometimes grudging) respect of his contemporaries, as the attitudes of Yeats and Joyce attest. The award of the Edmund de Polignac Prize to *The Crock of Gold* solidified his reputation as an important voice in the Irish Revival. Though his aborted attempt at the *Táin* seems to mark the waning of his creative energy, *Deirdre* was the book Joyce was reading when it came to him that Stephens might be enlisted to complete *Finnegans Wake*. *The Charwoman's Daughter* even appeared, in 1917, in a Modern Library edition. And one of Stephens's poems, "The Main Deep," was included as an example of imagism in the grandfather of all teaching texts for literature, Cleanth Brooks and Robert Penn Warren's *Understanding Poetry* (1960).

But the slow decline in his productivity and the last decade of silence depleted Stephens's literary currency, until today he is likely to be known, if at all, as the author of *The Crock of Gold*; and what continued interest may persist in *The Crock of Gold* partly derives from its claim to be the inspiration for *Finian's Rainbow*. By his death, Stephens had become what Kees Van Hoek stamped him, "the man who invented Glocca Mora." Any serious reader of his work will recognize that he deserves better.

BIBLIOGRAPHY

Works by James Stephens

Insurrections. Dublin: Maunsel, 1909.
The Charwoman's Daughter. London: Macmillan, 1912. (Published in the United States As *Mary, Mary*. Boston: Small, Maynard, 1912.)
The Crock of Gold. London: Macmillan, 1912.
The Hill of Vision. Dublin: Maunsel, 1912.
Here Are Ladies. London: Macmillan, 1913.
The Demi-Gods. London: Macmillan, 1914.
The Adventures of Seumas Beg/The Rocky Road to Dublin. London: Macmillan, 1915.
Songs from the Clay. London: Macmillan, 1915.
Green Branches. Dublin: Maunsel, 1916.
The Insurrection in Dublin. Dublin: Maunsel, 1916.
Reincarnations. London: Macmillan, 1918.
Irish Fairy Tales. London: Macmillan, 1920.
Deirdre. London: Macmillan, 1923.
Arthur Griffith, Journalist and Statesman. Dublin: Wilson, Hartnel, 1924.
In the Land of Youth. London: Macmillan, 1924.
Little Things and Other Poems. Freelands, KY: Privately printed, 1924.
A Poetry Recital. London: Macmillan, 1925.
Collected Poems. London: Macmillan, 1926; rev. and enlarged ed. 1954.
Dublin Letters. Gaylordsville, CT: Slide Mountain, 1928.

Etched in Moonlight. London: Macmillan, 1928.
On Prose and Verse. New York: Bowling Green Press, 1928.
Theme and Variations. New York: Fountain, 1929.
Strict Joy. London: Macmillan, 1931.
Kings and the Moon. London: Macmillan, 1938.
James, Seumas and Jacques. Ed. Lloyd Frankenberg. London: Macmillan, 1964.
Letters of James Stephens. Ed. Richard Finneran. New York: Macmillan, 1974.
Uncollected Prose of James Stephens. Ed. Patricia McFate. 2 vols. New York: St. Martin's, 1983.

Studies of James Stephens

Bramsback, Birgit. *James Stephens: A Literary and Bibliographical Study*. Uppsala: A. B. Lundequistaka Bokhandeln, 1959.
Finneran, Richard J. *The Olympian and the Leprechaun: W. B. Yeats and James Stephens*. Dublin: Dolmen, 1978.
Frankenberg, Lloyd. *Pleasure Dome*. Boston: Houghton Mifflin, 1949.
Friedman, Barton R. "Returning to Irland's Fountains: Nationalism and James Stephens." *Arizona Quarterly* 22 (1966): 232–52.
———. "William Blake to James Stephens: The Crooked Road." *Eire-Ireland* 1 (1966): 29–57.
McFate, Patricia. *The Writings of James Stephens*. New York: St. Martin's, 1979.
Martin, Augustine. *James Stephens: A Critical Study*. Totowa, NJ: Rowman and Littlefield, 1977.
Pyle, Hilary. *James Stephens: His Works and an Account of His Life*. London: Routledge and Kegan Paul, 1965.
Van Hoek, Kees. "The Man Who Invented Glocca Mora." *The Irish Digest* (November 1950): 50–52.

Eithne Strong

(1923–)

Deborah H. McWilliams

BIOGRAPHY

Eithne Strong was born on February 28, 1923, in the Glensharrold district of West County Limerick. Provincial allusions in the guise of regional nomenclature, religious bigotry, and church injunctions permeate her expressions of her experiences in youth. Her earliest impressions of life are interwoven with the issue of language preservation, and survival of lingual forms has remained an important issue for her. Both her parents were teachers. She herself attended schools where lessons were taught in Irish.

Strong's interest in language and writing advanced when, in 1942, she relocated to Dublin and became active in the Irish language movement. In 1943, Eithne (née O'Connell) Strong married Rupert Strong, a psychoanalyst and poet, and together they raised nine children. Three decades later, Strong received a bachelor of arts in Irish and English from Trinity College, Dublin, where she also earned an education diploma in 1975.

Among those influential in her life were the writer's late husband and the late Jonathan Hanaghan, renowned Dublin-based psychoanalyst. Strong herself has remarked that both men had a ''profound impact'' on her (conversation with Deborah McWilliams Consalvo, July 3, 1995). From them Strong developed a keen sensitivity toward—and insight into—the contradictions and distortions manifest in the patternings of human relations. Her writings ruminate upon the meaning of such psychoanalytic tenets as self-development and the ego. Evolution of the individual psyche amplifies the ideological milieu. It renders an enhanced and, ultimately, an inclusive form of human expression.

MAJOR WORKS AND THEMES

Strong's literary achievements are exceptional. She exhibits rare insight into the subconscious impulses of self-survival and the soul's tenacious pursuit of self-discovery. To a great extent, Strong's poetry is itself an exegesis of egoism. The denial of primeval urgings, ancient habits, native vernacular, and so forth provides cogent evidence of the social origins of self-abandonment; the self-betrayal of human relations; the infancy and maturity of self-discovery; and, finally, the capacity of love to render an ethos of self-awareness and, thereby, enlighten the underdeveloped *weltanschauung* of humanity.

From *Songs of Living* (1961) the poet in "To My Father" bids us to self-preservation and to lay our ideas, our thoughts, "upon the soil from which we came." Her literary project makes use of the cadences and rhythms of language to articulate the loss of alternate idiomatic and dialectic expressions and, thereby, to oppose the confines of literary orthodoxy. Besides, by her own admission, an "advocacy of inclusion" has become an issue of personal concern (letter to Consalvo, March 23, 1995).

In *Sarah in Passing* (1974), *Flesh—The Greatest Sin* (1980, rev. 1993), and, subsequently, *My Darling Neighbour* (1985), Strong further develops this theme of doctrinal resistance when she ruminates on the boon of nonpreordained associations. In "Credo," for instance, she maintains that the greatest strength humans possess is the transformative force of "interpersonal procedures." A focal subject for Strong is therefore that of the labyrinth of intimacy: the theme of love. It is a terrain that sustains the oftentimes contrary forces of the "human composition," as the poet/narrator asserts. In this poem, Strong draws our attention to the fact that there is no escape because "life demands encounters." The poet's writings examine love as a radical pattern for transcendence *and* transformation. Moreover, the emphasis she places upon the ideas of self-discovery and self-maturity abides throughout her later works as well. Her enduring focus on the interior development of the individual psyche is evident in Strong's most recent collection of poems, *Let Live* (1990), in which the poet devotes considerable attention to the topic of human evolution and reconciliation.

By her own admission, Strong's thoughts are greatly influenced by psychoanalytical inquiry into the processes of human evolution. In particular, the pioneering work of Jonathan Hanaghan impressed upon her a triadic form of selfdom as a composite of physical (organic), metaphysical (spiritual), and psychological (subliminal) attributes. Words such as "sojourn," "spaces," "travelling," "journey," "landscape," "earth," and so forth compose the theme of alteration and transitions resultant from human encounters. The passage motif also lends a structural design to the poem to demonstrate further the intricacies of human relations.

The patterning of movement and change is manifest again in "The Giant's Causeway." Descriptions of geographical, topographical, and physical elements within nature signify the temporality of organic life and symbolize the essential form of humanity. Furthermore, the theme of human evolution that underlies so much of Strong's writings is discernible again in "However Long That Dark," in which the concept of Time ("by this I am marked") adds a further dimension to the complexities of maturation. Temporality limits the physical form but not before Strong has acknowledged the possibility that "the tunnel" will become "a flow of discovery."

Within the thematic context of evolution there is the problem of social de-evolution, or ethic incivility. The tenet of maturation is *not* analogous to morality. Our physical body grows despite the state of being of our psyche and soul. By examining the processes of living, Strong must also explore the ruin of de-evolution, or the ethos of social incivility.

In her most recent novel, *The Love Riddle* (1993), the treatment of cultural relations is fundamentally developed through the character of Una Normile. Like the author herself, Una relocates to Dublin from Limerick in 1942. Soon she meets Nelson Forterre, a student at Trinity College and an Englishman. In the opening paragraphs of the narrative, we are introduced to Nelson's mother, Mrs. Paul Forterre, who is, we are told, "alone, geographically removed from kith and kin" (7). Furthermore, we are informed that "there had been times when she'd felt it necessary to veil aspects of her origins" (8). Through Mrs. Forterre Nelson inherits a legacy of impressions and observations about love. Also through the narrative disclosures regarding Mrs. Forterre's lack of understanding and insight, we become privy to the novel's thematic substructure, a subtext of familial estrangement, geographical isolation, psychological exile, and social bankruptcy.

Paramount to plot development is the theme of individual growth and social evolution, illustrated in the portraiture of the love riddle, the conjoining of Una Normile, and Nelson Forterre. For that reason, Mrs. Forterre's dismissal of Nelson represents an antithesis to Una Normile's embrace of him. Furthermore, by the novel's end, Una expresses an appreciation for self-development and enlightenment: "Thoughts, ideas forbidden were from now to have the right of utterance, the right to be examined." As Una grows in self-awareness, so too evolves within her a keener insight into the constraints of orthodoxy: "Innate curiosity had been a strong force in bringing her this far, curiosity without courage was idle."

CRITICAL RECEPTION

In a recent conversation with Consalvo, Strong shared that from an early age she felt a longing deep inside her to "keep a little notebook and [write] . . . little paragraphs." Furthermore, while she conceded a kind of pride and vulnerability as a writer, she also made the following declaration: "I must not protect vulnerability too much and there's no point in false pride. So that it's really when I've made those decisions that I go and risk myself."

In her preface to Strong's *Spatial Nosing* (1993), Mary O'Donnell suggests that Strong's writings bear witness to "human cruelty, and ignorance, the annihilation of a dream that is inevitable *only* when truth is avoided or when indifference sets in" (i–ii). Strong's poetic endeavors demonstrate a subtle prying, or "spatial nosing," into the frailties and deficiencies of humanity. Her textual commentary is cogent. Resignation will not effect a reversal of cruelty. Nor will succumbing to orthodoxy ensure anyone a form of protection or survival. Instead, to endure the lack of man-made inhibitions one must demonstrate a courage to unearth the primal (infant) and civil (mature) nature of prehistory and to uncloak the fallow and abandoned terrain of individuality. Surprisingly, no detailed study of Strong's work has yet appeared in journal or book form.

BIBLIOGRAPHY

Works by Eithne Strong

Poetry in Irish

Cirt Oibre. Baile Atha Cliath: Coisceim, 1980.
Fuil agus Fallai. Baile Atha Cliath: Coisceim, 1983.
An Sagart Pinc. Baile Atha Cliath: Coisceim, 1990.
Aoife faoi Ghlas. Baile Atha Cliath: Coisceim, 1990.

Poetry in English

Poetry Quartos. Dublin: Runa, 1942–1945.
Songs of Living. Dublin: Runa, 1961.
Sarah in Passing. Dublin: Dolmen, 1974.
Flesh—The Greatest Sin. Dublin: Runa, 1980.
My Darling Neighbour. Dublin: Beaver Row, 1985.
Let Live. Galway: Salmon, 1990.
Flesh—The Greatest Sin. New ed. Dublin: Attic, 1993.
Spatial Nosing: New and Selected Poems. Ireland: Salmon-Poolbeg, 1993.

Novels and Short Stories (selected)

Degrees of Kindred. Dublin: Tansy, 1979.
Patterns, and other stories. Ireland: Poolbeg, 1981.
The Love Riddle. Dublin: Attic, 1993.

Other Writings (selected)

"Mullaghareirk: Aspects in Perspective." *Eire-Ireland* 28.4 (Winter 1993): 7–15.

Studies of Eithne Strong

Consalvo, Deborah McWilliams. " 'To Have the Right of Utterance': An Interview with Eithne Strong." *The Celtic Pen* 2.2 (Autumn 1995): 17–20.
Holmquist, Kathryn. "An Interview with Eithne Strong." *Irish Times*, November 3, 1993: 13.
Wright, Nancy Means, and Dennis Hannan. "An Interview with Eithne Strong." *Irish Literary Supplement* 13.1 (Spring 1994): 13–15.

Francis Stuart

(1902–)

Nicole Pepinster Greene

BIOGRAPHY

Francis Stuart has lived a long and difficult life that has always kept him outside the mainstream of society. He was born in Australia of County Antrim parents and educated in Ireland and Rugby. At the age of seventeen, he met Iseult Gonne, Maud Gonne's daughter, in Dublin. After they had eloped to London in January 1920, they were married the following April, on the insistence of Maud, although both Francis and Iseult knew they were totally unsuited for each other. Stuart vividly records their relationship in his major autobiographical novel, *Black List, Section H*.

Stuart's twenty years of marriage provided a rich foundation for his development as a major Irish writer. He and Iseult had two children and led a secluded life in County Wicklow, where he became a moderately successful poultry farmer. In 1922, Stuart became involved in the Irish civil war, smuggled arms for the Irish Republican Army (IRA), and was later imprisoned in the Curragh. He converted to Roman Catholicism, became deeply interested in the lives of the mystics, and visited Lourdes. He traveled alone frequently to Dublin and London, where he engaged in several love affairs. In the early 1930s, Stuart published some critically well accepted novels, but after 1934 the quality of his work began to decline.

The year 1939 marked a major turning point in Stuart's life and his career as a writer. He accepted an invitation to lecture in Germany, and, although he knew that war was imminent, he left Ireland in April. In Germany, he was offered the position of lecturer in modern English and Irish literature at the University of Berlin. Returning to Ireland in July, he took up his post in January 1940. Shortly thereafter he was asked to write propaganda for broadcast to

England by William Joyce (Lord Haw-Haw). In July 1942, Stuart himself broadcast to Ireland, urging neutrality. In 1943, he was asked to discuss the Russian threat; he refused.

Soon after Stuart arrived in Berlin, he met Gertrud Meissner (Madeline). They lived in Germany throughout the war and its aftermath, enduring homelessness and near starvation as two displaced persons in a defeated country. In August 1945, hoping that Madeline could emigrate to Ireland, they joined a group of French refugees and traveled to Paris. Madeline was refused entry to Ireland, so they returned together to Austria, where they were soon arrested and imprisoned by the French until July 1946. Stuart, however, was not a fascist; he always sided with the losers and the outcasts.

For the next twelve years Francis and Madeline lived in Europe. They were married in 1954, after the death of Iseult, and returned to Ireland in 1958. Stuart published eight novels between 1948 and 1959; then, after a long silence, in 1971, *Black List, Section H* was published. Earlier novels and poetry were reissued; he continued publishing and was awarded grants by the Irish Arts Council and Cnuas. In his nineties, Francis Stuart continues to write and to play an active role in the Irish literary world.

MAJOR WORKS AND THEMES

Francis Stuart has been a prolific author, publishing over twenty-five novels, several books of poetry, short stories, essays, and plays. Almost all of his writing is autobiographical and marked by controversy and paradox.

The themes that predominate include the artist as the outcast; the nature of love; the relationship between the erotic and the religious; the teachings of Christ; the value of evil, suffering, and sacrifice; the paradoxes that evil leads to goodness, and violence to peace and that there is victory in defeat; and, finally, the necessity for moral change that is neither social nor political.

Stuart's first novel, *Women and God*, based on his life with Iseult, appeared in 1931. This was quickly followed in 1932 by two of his best novels of this early period, *Pigeon Irish*, a pessimistic portrait of modern Ireland, and *The Coloured Dome*, which probes the mystery of human relationships. Between 1933 and 1939 he published nine more novels, some of which attacked modern society generally and Ireland in particular.

The Pillar of Cloud (1948), Stuart's best postwar novel of this next period, is set amid the devastation of a defeated Germany. In this world all values are questioned. "Does anyone know what is guilt and what is innocence anymore?" (41) asks Halka, who believes only in "the miracle of pain" (105). The main protagonist, Dominic Malone, falls in love with the young Polish woman, Halka, who persuades him to marry her dying sister, Lisette. Dominic achieves this supreme sacrifice, finding peace as his love for Halka is transformed: "This, he knew was true love, that was patient, that was long-suffering, not puffed up, that did not seek itself'' (166). Paradoxically, through the two sisters, prostitutes and outcasts, Dominic reaches an understanding of true Christian love.

This novel is set in Germany, but Ireland is represented in Dominic's memory and in his Uncle Egan, who comes "from a little world untouched by the cataclysm and its aftermath" (208). *Redemption* (1949), however, a novel of brooding violence, is set in provincial Ireland. War-torn Europe is resurrected in the character of Ezra Arrigho and his foreign lover, Margareta, crippled in an air raid. Again, guilt and innocence are explored, as is the ability of a select few, whose values differ fundamentally from those of society, to create a community founded on Christian love.

Stuart wrote several more novels up to 1959 but was silent until the publication of his best-known novel, *Black List, Section H* (1971), a vast, panoramic novel unique in its integration of the Irish and European experience between 1920 and 1950. In it, he analyzes his life and destiny as a writer, a destiny that demanded that he live beyond the pale of established morality. The first two-thirds of the novel takes place in Ireland and traces his youth and marriage; the remainder is set in Germany, and the novel ends with him and his lover being freed from jail.

After this success, Stuart began writing experimental novels while still exploring his familiar themes. *Memorial* (1973) and *A Hole in the Head* (1977) are set in Northern Ireland, and *Faillandia* (1985) is a fictionalized critique of Ireland, the protagonist's "beloved and hated land" (11).

CRITICAL RECEPTION

Francis Stuart's first publication, a volume of poems, *We Have Kept the Faith* (1923), was praised by W. B. Yeats and won a prize from the Royal Irish Academy, while his second novel, *Pigeon Irish*, was acclaimed and made the front page of the *New York Times Book Review*. All of his novels of the 1930s were reviewed in England, Ireland, and the United States, and many were translated. After the war, however, Stuart received little critical attention. More recently, his novels have been reappraised by scholars. Maurice Harmon considers *The Pillar of Cloud* to be a novel of "great tenderness" (in Imhof's *Contemporary Irish Novelists*) and a "most successful integration of social reality with mystical vision" (10).

The reviews of *Black List, Section H* by such writers as Lawrence Durrell, Frank Kermode, and Vivian Mercier seemed to be unanimously favorable. It has been described as "massive" and as his "masterpiece." In 1973, *Memorial* topped the best-seller list in Ireland. While W. J. McCormack argues that "Stuart's reputation is never likely to be permanent and assured" (182), Seamus Deane in his *Short History of Irish Literature* writes that Stuart gives "a fully serious treatment to the action of violence in society, something which, remarkably, no other Irish writer has done" (216). Several critics have compared elements in his writing to Beckett, and Maurice Harmon considers his "radical individual vision" to be the "outstanding exception" in the fiction of post-revolutionary Ireland.

BIBLIOGRAPHY

Selected Works by Francis Stuart

Women and God. London: Cape, 1931.
The Coloured Dome. London: Gollancz, 1932.
Pigeon Irish. London: Gollancz, 1932.
Glory. London: Gollancz, 1933.
Try the Sky. London: Gollancz, 1933.
The White Hare. London: Collins, 1936.
The Pillar of Cloud. London: Gollancz, 1948.
Redemption. London: Gollancz, 1949.
The Flowering Cross. London: Gollancz, 1950.
Victors and Vanquished. London: Gollancz, 1958.
Black List, Section H. Carbondale: Southern Illinois University Press, 1971.
Memorial. London: Martin Brian and O'Keefe, 1973.
A Hole in the Head. London: Martin Brian and O'Keefe, 1977.
The High Consistory. London: Martin Brian and O'Keefe, 1981.
We Have Kept the Faith: New and Selected Poems. Dublin: Raven Arts, 1982.
Faillandia. Dublin: Raven Arts, 1985.
Night Pilot. Dublin: Raven Arts, 1988.
A Compendium of Lovers. Dublin: Raven Arts, 1990.

Studies of Francis Stuart

Elborn, Geoffrey. *Francis Stuart: A Life*. Dublin: Raven Arts, 1990.
McCormack, W. J., ed. *A Festschrift for Francis Stuart on His Seventieth Birthday, 28 April 1972*. Dublin: Dolmen, 1972.
Molloy, Francis C. "Autobiography and Fiction: Francis Stuart's *Black List, Section H*." *Critique: Studies in Modern Fiction* 25.2 (Winter 1984): 115–24.
———. "A Life Reshaped: Francis Stuart's *Black List, Section H*." *Canadian Journal of Irish Studies* 14.2 (January 1989): 37–47.
Natterstad, J. H. *Francis Stuart*. London: Associated University Presses, 1974.
———. ed. *Journal of Irish Literature: Francis Stuart Number*. 5.1 (January 1976).

J. M. Synge

(1871–1909)

Edward A. Kopper, Jr.

BIOGRAPHY

Edmund John Millington Synge was born on April 16 in Rathfarnham, a suburb of Dublin. His father died a year later, and the future playwright was left to the mercies of his religious zealot mother, Kathleen, the daughter of a Protestant rector, Robert Traill, who was refused advancement by his church because of his public and frequent anti-Catholic diatribes. Even in an age of religious extremists, Traill stood apart with his insistence upon taming the savagery of the Roman Catholics of Cork and correcting what he considered to be their abominable beliefs. Later, Synge excoriated the debilitating nature of constant hellfire and damnation preaching (such as his mother's) upon persons of a nervous and sensitive disposition.

Indeed, the Synges were thoroughly rooted in the Protestant Ascendancy, sharing without question the assumed monolithic structure of values that this conqueror class imposed upon a conquered people. The Synges' arrival in Ireland dates back to the seventeenth century, and the family produced five bishops for their adopted country. Marriage with the Hatch family provided vast landholdings and anchored their spiritual Ascendancy in material wealth. Synge's siblings—and his relatives outside the immediate family—were unquestioning loyalists: brother Samuel, for example, became a medical missionary to China, and brother Edward, land agent for the family estates, a ruthless defender of the hated practice of evicting impoverished peasants.

Synge as a boy was a silent rebel, pursuing nature studies, investigating ancient Celtic artifacts in rural areas outside Dublin, and for a time belonging to the Dublin Naturalists' Field Club. Such activities led naturally into a reading of Darwin and occasioned his first major crisis of doubt concerning orthodox religious beliefs. When he was about fourteen, he was struck by one of Darwin's evidences of his theory of evolution: the resemblance between a man's hand and the wings of a bird or bat. His world seemed to shatter, and he felt acute shame at the possibility of his becoming one of the mythic villains that he had heard about only in whispers: an abominable heretic, or worse, an atheist. His attempts to counter his doubt by telling himself that he was not yet equipped to handle what must surely be specious reasoning on Darwin's part and then by reading several works defending Christian orthodoxy were to no avail. Although Synge was to remain a man deeply interested in religion all of his life, he renounced most of the trappings of conventional Christianity by the age of eighteen.

Another wedge was driven between Synge's and his family's values in 1885 by Edward's notorious eviction of Hugh Carey from his meager farm in County Wicklow. That Carey was the sole support of two elderly sisters did not matter to Edward Synge, and following the practice of the times, Carey's hovel was burned to the ground shortly after the family was turned out. In arguing with John, Mrs. Synge maintained that eviction was God's will, a necessary way of ensuring social stability—and questioned, in a more practical manner, how the Synges would survive without rents from tenants. More egregious is the fact that, starting in 1892, Kathleen Synge and her family spent several summers living in a boycotted house in the townland of Castle Kevin. Although in later years Synge became more tolerant of rent collecting, possibly realizing that his family merely typified Establishment households during the landlord–tenant "Land Wars," Synge at fourteen was horrified by Edward's doings.

In February 1889, Synge entered Trinity College—or Dublin University as it was called until recent times—a Protestant enclave founded in the sixteenth century that has reciprocity with Oxford and Cambridge. He graduated with a gentleman's or pass degree on December 15, 1892. Despite his lackluster achievements in formal scholarship and his lack of involvement with the affairs of the university—Synge was a commuter—his years at Trinity widened the gap between him and his family. Synge continued his study of Irish antiquities and finished first in exams in Hebrew and Irish. He discovered much to his chagrin that Irish teaching at Trinity was mainly linguistic, with its overall purpose being to proselytize, to wean Gaelic-speaking Irish Catholics in western Ireland from their superstitious beliefs. Any study of the mythological Celtic past was frowned upon by Trinity's authorities, and the saga materials (resurrected by Lady Gregory and others) that sparked the Irish Revival and that Synge was to use to such advantage in *Deirdre* (1910) were considered by Trinity officials to be immoral or, at the least, barbaric and unfit for cultivated literary tastes. Synge circumvented such repression by reading on his own, in Irish, materials such as those concerning the Fate of the Daughters of Lir and the destiny of the ill-stared lovers Diarmuid and Grania. Recent commentary on Synge's writing shows that his delving into the saga materials both at Trinity

and later at the Sorbonne (where he studied sporadically for several years starting in 1895) was deep indeed and his knowledge of Celtic legends extensive.
At Trinity, Synge was also captivated by the nationalistic poetry of mid-
nineteenth-century Ireland encapsulated in *The Spirit of the Nation* (1843). Although he later came to realize that this poetry was not of great literary
importance, the patriotic utterances left their mark on his consciousness.

While attending Trinity, Synge was enrolled at the Royal Academy of Music,
where he studied violin. By 1892, he had appeared in two concerts, and he spent
almost a year in Germany, from July 29, 1893, to June 1, 1894, continuing his
studies. Synge decided not to pursue a musical career because his interests had
changed to literature and because he felt himself too nervous to continue to
appear before an audience.

On December 21, 1896, in Paris, with Synge studying at the Sorbonne, the
famous first meeting between him and W. B. Yeats occurred outside their student
lodging, the Hôtel Corneille. Yeats saw that Sygne was drifting, attempting
somewhat redundantly to become a critic of French literature and writing poetry
in pallid and morbid tones. He advised the twenty-five-year-old to go to the
Aran Islands, from which Yeats had just returned, and to forge for himself a
new destiny. Synge's five visits to the Aran Islands (from the spring of 1898 to
the fall of 1902) did indeed see a startling transformation in him; but whether,
as Yeats maintained in later years, it was mainly his advice that sent Synge to
Aran is debatable, especially in light of the fact that Synge did not leave for the
islands until seventeenth months after Yeats's admonition.

Synge had many reasons for going to Aran: his studies of Old Irish under H.
d'Arbois de Jubainville at the Sorbonne; excavations in Breton folklore by An-
atole Le Braz; his search for a transcendence to replace his lost beliefs in conventional Christianity; his interest in comparative linguistics; and a desire to be
as far away as possible (at least for brief respites) from his family's Establishment traditions.

The Aran Islanders' seamless blending of religious and pagan beliefs, of cruelty and kindness proved to be a culture shock for Synge, providing him with
a permanent two-layer, noncyclopean view of existence that forever blurred
simplistic distinctions between genres. The three desolate limestone formations
thirty miles out into the Atlantic Ocean due west from Galway City also provided him with the verisimilitude and subject matter of his plays. On the Aran
Islands he learned of the man who killed his father but was exonerated by the
natives, of prisoners who were helped to escape from the authorities, of the
remains of a drowned man identified by his clothing, of the husband who feigned
death to entrap an unfaithful wide, and of the constant battle of Aran fishermen
against the sea, memorialized in *Riders to the Sea* (1904). Above all, on Aran
Synge mastered that strange, beautiful, melodious mixture of Gaelic and English
dialect, alternately blamed and damned by his critics throughout his playwriting
career, that was to become the dialogue of his characters. Synge's *The Aran
Islands*, though composed about five years earlier, was finally published in 1907.

A tale told to Synge by Pat Dirane, Synge's *shanachie* (storyteller) on Inishmaan, the second largest of the three islands, forms the basis of *The Shadow of the Glen*, Synge's first play to be performed (though the third he composed), which was produced by the Irish National Theatre Society at Molesworth Hall (Dublin) on October 8–10, 1903. In Dirane's version, violent, while Synge's has comic elements, the cuckolded husband, who plays dead to catch his wife in the bedroom with her lover, severely beats the suitor, perhaps killing him. In *The Shadow*, Nora Burke, whose infidelity is never spelled out by Synge, is forced by her husband, Dan, to leave their dreary Wicklow cottage and exits with a visiting tramp.

Riders to the Sea, a heavily anthologized play and a universally acclaimed classic of modern drama, was written before *The Shadow* but performed after it, on February 25–27, 1904, again at Molesworth Hall. Yeats, upon hearing Synge read *Riders* in manuscript form, declared it to be classic tragedy in the mode of Aeschylus, and even Synge's critics were more temperate in their negative reactions, possibly because *Riders* was not as offensive as *The Shadow*. They did, however, point to the play's morbid nature—so many drownings are recounted, and a corpse stays on the stage for too long a period of time—and to what they felt to be Synge's ignorance (again) of the religious nature of the Catholic peasant: Maurya, who has lost all the male members of her family to the sea, should not have been so resigned to fate. These same critics, while nibbling at the edge, did not intuit Synge's major imagery in the play, the blend of paganism and Christianity that informs the aged Maurya's prayers. These she conducts in the middle of the night, while invoking the Celtic festival of Samhain, and her Holy Well is not one blessed by Christianity.

The merits of Synge's *The Well of the Saints*, performed at the Abbey Theatre on February 4–11, 1905, and of *The Tinker's Wedding*, published in 1907 but, because of the tinkers' physical abuse of a priest, not performed at the Abbey until 1971, have been defined through poststructuralist criticism, which emphasizes anti-Establishment, Rabelaisian elements in the two plays. In *The Well*, two beggars, Mary and Martin Doul ("blind" in Irish), choose final sightlessness over clear physical vision, kicking healing water from the cup of a transient holy man, so that they can live in their previous illusions, liminally seated by a "gap" in the wall on a crossroads. *The Tinker's Wedding* exalts the lives of vagrant marginality over the conventional existence of a bloated and purportedly lecherous clergyman.

Considered by many the most enigmatic—and perhaps the greatest—play in English in the twentieth century, Synge's *The Playboy of the Western World* opened to a week of rioting at the Abbey on January 26, 1907, during which time the work was never heard from beginning to end by an audience. To secure a hearing for *Playboy*, Yeats and Lady Gregory brought the play to America in 1911–1912, where it was greeted in New York, Chicago, and Philadelphia with even more tumultuous disturbances. In Philadelphia, the players were arrested on the charge of immorality. In Chicago, playgoers waited outside a theater with a noose to hang Synge, who had been dead for over two years. Lady Gregory was threatened with death should she produce "The 'Cowboy' of the Western World." In Boston, nationalists railed against Synge's portrayal of a "parasite" (read *parricide*). True, in Dublin the riots were precipitated by a relatively few drunken men in cheap seats, and in the United States, extreme nationalist groups, ignorant of the play's content, fueled the protests; yet there were deeper reasons for Irish rejection of a play whose blend of primitive beauty and violence, of humor and pathos, of love and rejection, and of vast, hovering mythic images combined through wild poetry with the commonplaces of life in Mayo makes it a deeply compelling masterpiece.

Things went downhill for Synge after the *Playboy* debacle. He served indefatigably with Lady Gregory and Yeats as one of the three directors of the Abbey, but his health declined, and Hodgkin's disease, which was first diagnosed in 1897, took his life on March 24, 1909. Molly Allgood, the Roman Catholic actress and his fiancée, with whom Synge had engaged in a bittersweet romance for three years, played the title role in Synge's unfinished *Deirdre*, which was performed at the Abbey on January 13, 1910. At Synge's funeral two lines formed: one consisted of the Catholic Abbey actors; the other, of his Protestant remaining family. Synge's mother had died on October 6, 1908, and Molly did not attend: she had told her fiancé she would not do so because of her rage at the contempt his family held for him.

Ironically, by his brilliant satire of his countrymen's foibles, expressed through an unparalleled magic of lyricism, Synge, as did Joyce, neither of whom was appreciated in his lifetime by his countrymen, helped to make Ireland an even greater nation.

MAJOR WORKS AND THEMES

The Shadow was vilified by Irish nationalists: it reflected Synge's decadent European background; it was simply a weak adaptation of the story of the Widow of Ephesus, who makes love to a Roman soldier almost in the shadow of her crucified husband; in more hushed tones, it was seen as a calumny upon the Irish Catholic peasant by the Establishment Protestant Synge (an ironic charge, given his attitudes toward his class!); the play was an attack on marriage in the manner of Ibsen (about whose plays Synge had very mixed feelings); and it questioned the purity of Irish women, whom the nationalist editor of the *United Irishman*, Arthur Griffith (later, president of the Irish Free State), called the "most virtuous women in the world"—the same Arthur Griffith who refused to allot Synge space in the pages of his newspaper to print his Aran source. Typical of the confusion in Dublin over the play is the account of the *Irish Times* reviewer who wrote that when Nora left with her lover, Micheal Dara, so startled was this critic that he forgot that the play ends with Dan and Micheal's sharing a drink.

Of course, *The Shadow* is an attack upon loveless Irish marriages, January–

May relationships perpetuated in part by Roman Catholic prohibition of birth control that resulted in many men marrying late in life: Dan enjoins Nora not to touch his body should he die suddenly, and because Dan was so cold in life, Nora cannot be sure that he is now dead (see Dorothy Parker on Coolidge). But more important is the play's depiction of Nora, a most atypical colleen, a woman trapped in an environment of rain and loneliness, where dissidents, like the shepherd Patch Darcy, go insane in the wilderness and where Peggy Cavanagh, upon whose fate Nora broods, wastes away in the passage of time. Much more complex than Ibsen's vapid heroine of *A Doll's House*, Nora Helmer, Synge's Nora has no illusions about her departure. Life with the tramp is better than the poorhouse, and like Brecht's later Anna Fierling, she faces the future with subdued courage and the hope that nature, described in Synge's brilliantly lyrical terms, will provide some assuagement from her misery.

Riders contains many levels of meaning, from biblical resonances of the Four Horsemen of Revelation, to Synge's consummate awareness of Aran Islands folkloric superstitions, such as the curse that follows an uncompleted blessing—which here leads to Bartley's death as he is knocked into the sea by a horse that he is bringing to a ship bound for mainland Galway after Maurya's "God bless you" sticks in her throat.

All of Synge's symbolism is rooted in actual details of Aran life. He insisted that Maurya's funeral keen (*caoine*) be chanted by an old woman actually raised on Aran, that the spinning wheel in the opening scene be authentic, and that the pampooties, the cowskin slippers worn by Aran Islanders, be shipped from the islands. Much to Lady Gregory's olfactory relief he was not successful in this last request.

At a time when Ireland was struggling for national sovereignty, *The Playboy* seemed to revive the image of the apelike Irishman caricatured in British tabloids of the late nineteenth century. Worse still, the play attacked the supposed purity of the western Ireland peasant at a time when the Irish looked for renewal to a pastoral west that never really existed. Additionally, *The Playboy* seemed to dismiss concepts of hospitality and decency that average Irishmen in 1907, just nine years before the Easter Rising of 1916, needed to believe were their chief capital in the struggle against crude England.

When Christy Mahon tells the Mayo villagers that he has killed his father, they venerate him, so meager is the excitement in this small Mayo hamlet, where folks hang dogs for sport and stone lunatics until they run into the sea and drown. When his father appears alive, they turn against Christy and his deception. When Christy proceeds to attack his pa in front of them, and the villagers think that he has truly killed him this time, through cowardice they decide to turn Christy over to the peelers. Christy resists this betrayal to the hated authorities by wrapping his legs around a table, and they burn him to make him relinquish his hold. The father revives, and son and dad leave town, threatening to tell tales of the "fools" that are in Mayo.

So many illusions shattered in so short a period of time!

CRITICAL RECEPTION

David H. Greene and Edward M. Stephens's *J. M. Synge, 1871–1909*, the standard biography, is well researched and in the main reliable. The authors, however, tend to minimize Synge's religious tendencies and to emphasize the morbidity that they feel overshadowed the playwright's life. Daniel Corkery's *Synge and Anglo-Irish Literature: A Study*, though limited by Corkery's severe nationalism, which led him to undervalue *Playboy*, includes cogent comments on other Synge works. Nicholas Grene's *Synge: A Critical Study of the Plays* treats effectively the specifically Irish background of Synge's works, although Grene tends to underestimate the depth and subtlety of Synge's symbolism. Declan Kiberd's *Synge and the Irish Language* brings to bear Kiberd's vast knowledge of Gaelic language and myth upon Synge's works to show that Synge's awareness of both areas is much greater than previously thought. Weldon Thornton's splendidly reasoned *J. M. Synge and the Western Mind* forever lays to rest the Yeats-proclaimed view that Synge was unsuited to entertain a political (or religious) thought. Toni O'Brien Johnson's convincing *Synge: The Medieval and the Grotesque* limns Synge's knowledge of much medieval writing, such as versions of the Ulster cycle and the Deirdre legend. Edward A. Kopper, Jr.'s, *A J. M. Synge Literary Companion* is a collection of fourteen original essays dealing with subjects ranging from traditional source criticism to poststructuralist modes; it also contains a stage history of productions of his plays in several countries. And, finally, Gonzalez's *Assessing the Achievement of J. M. Synge* addresses the issue of the continued relevance of Synge's plays to contemporary audiences.

In general, then, critics no longer debate how Irish Synge is; now they are concerned with elucidating the depth of his works and of his own complex personality.

BIBLIOGRAPHY

Works by J. M. Synge

Synge, J. M. *J. M. Synge: Collected Works*. Gen. ed. Robin Skelton. 4 vols. London: Oxford University Press, 1962–1968. Reprinted, Gerrards Cross: Smythe; Washington, DC: Catholic University of America Press, 1982.

Studies of J. M. Synge

Corkery, Daniel. *Synge and Anglo-Irish Literature: A Study*. Dublin and Cork: Cork University Press; London: Longmans, Green, 1931. Reprinted, New York: Russell and Russell, 1965.

Gonzalez, Alexander G. ed. *Assessing the Achievement of J. M. Synge*. Westport, CT: Greenwood, 1996.

Greene, David H., and Edward M. Stephens. *J. M. Synge, 1871–1909*. New York: Macmillan, 1959. Rev. ed. New York University Press, 1989.

Grene, Nicholas. *Synge: A Critical Study of the Plays*. Totowa, NJ: Rowman and Littlefield; London: Macmillan, 1975.

Johnson, Toni O'Brien. *Synge: The Medieval and the Grotesque*. Gerrards Cross: Smythe; Totowa, NJ: Barnes and Noble, 1982.

Kiberd, Declan. *Synge and the Irish Language*. Totowa, NJ: Rowman and Littlefield, 1979.

Kopper, Edward A., Jr., ed. *A J. M. Synge Literary Companion*. New York: Greenwood, 1988.

———. *Synge: A Review of the Criticism*. Lyndora, PA: Kopper, 1990.

Thornton, Weldon. *J. M. Synge and the Western Mind*. New York: Barnes and Noble, 1979.

William Trevor

(1928–)

Mary Fitzgerald-Hoyt

BIOGRAPHY

William Trevor was born William Trevor Cox on May 24, 1928, in Mitchelstown, County Cork. His father's banking business necessitated frequent moves, so Trevor's childhood was spent in a variety of provincial Irish locales. He notes in his memoirs that his heritage put him "on the edge of things": he was Protestant but not Ascendancy at a time when Catholic Ireland was coming into power under de Valera's leadership. Trevor's fiction, replete as it is with sympathetic portraits of outsiders, including both Catholics and Protestants stultified by life in provincial Ireland, bears the impress of his early experiences. After attending St. Columba's College near Dublin, Trevor received a degree in history from Trinity College. In 1952 he married Jane Ryan, and the couple has two sons.

In the early 1950s Trevor taught in Northern Ireland, but economic necessity provoked a reluctant emigration to England, where he continued to teach for several years. At that time his artistic life centered around his sculpture, and for seven years he worked—like Jude the Obscure, as he has observed—as a church sculptor. But although his work gained favorable recognition, he found it difficult to make a living and accepted a job as an advertising copywriter in London. Though he disliked the job, it allowed him a great deal of free time, and he began to write stories. Disappointed with his sculpture, he abandoned it for writing, and in this new artistic pursuit adopted the pseudonym William Trevor.

Since the publication of his first novel, *A Standard of Behaviour* (1958), Trevor has written novels, short stories, plays, television and radio scripts, and nonfiction. Although he has not lived in Ireland for over forty years, spending much of his time in either England or Italy, since the 1970s Ireland has increasingly engaged his imagination. His subtle, brilliantly written fictions about lonely lives trapped in inescapable circumstances have earned him international acclaim, including numerous literary prizes.

MAJOR WORKS AND THEMES

Trevor's first novels, *The Old Boys* (1964), *The Boarding-House* (1965), and *The Love Department* (1966), reflect the author's now-famous ability to elicit both sympathy and humor for the plight of eccentric, isolated people. (Trevor's first novel, *A Standard of Behaviour*, has since been repudiated by the author, who asserts that he wrote it to relieve his straitened financial situation.) Although deeply unhappy about his emigration—Trevor once admitted to a *New York Times* interviewer that he finds the English "rather strange people"—he has also acknowledged that he finds distance useful: he is a Protestant who writes convincingly about Catholics and a man who creates credible women characters. His early fiction attests to his acute powers of observation and empathy, for at this time he was writing primarily about English characters. He has now come to believe that, like many Irish writers, expatriation was a prerequisite for writing about Ireland.

Trevor's first collection of short stories, *The Day We Got Drunk on Cake* (1967), contained several Irish stories, and the novel that followed, *Mrs. Eckdorf in O'Neill's Hotel* (1969), is a poignant, wildly humorous account of a bizarre English photographer's attempt to mythologize the denizens of a down-at-heels Dublin hotel. The novel's tracing of the peregrinations and discordant points of view of characters trapped in futile dreams reveals a strong Joycean influence. As with most of Trevor's fiction, English and Irish alike, *Mrs. Eckdorf*'s characters are thwarted in their quests for love and community.

Trevor's two subsequent novels, *Miss Gomez and the Brethren* (1971) and *Elizabeth Alone* (1973), return to an English setting to limn sympathetic portraits of isolated women. In the title story of the intervening collection, *The Ballroom of Romance* (1972), Trevor provides one of his most memorable studies of a woman's isolation in provincial Ireland. The ironically named Bridie, weathered and aged by grueling farmwork, seeks romance in a tatty country dance hall, but reality doggedly whittles away at her dreams. "The Ballroom of Romance" establishes what was to become a persistent pattern in Trevor's Irish fiction: sympathetic portraits of sensitive characters, often children, whose consoling illusions are crushed by circumstances beyond their control: poverty, family demands, social narrow-mindedness.

Though for most of the 1970s Trevor continued to write primarily about English characters, including the chilling, darkly humorous portrait of a psychopathic youth, *The Children of Dynmouth* (1976), and most of the stories in *Angels at the Ritz* (1975) and *Lovers of Their Time* (1978), his fiction begins to show the impact of the sectarian violence and military occupation of Northern Ireland. Stories such as "The Distant Past" (in *Angels*) and "Another Christmas'' mournfully remind us that the ripples of violence shatter not only fragile human flesh but also the delicate web of human community. In "Attracta" and "Beyond the Pale," violent experiences shock two women into abortive attempts to heal politically induced wounds. Attracta, who long ago forgave the couple who killed her parents with a bomb intended for Black and Tans, is an elderly schoolteacher thwarted in her attempts to teach her students the necessity for forgiveness, the possibility that the violent can retrieve their humanity. Prodded to speak by the empathy she feels for an English soldier's widow whose own journey to forgiveness ends in rape and suicide, Attracta discovers that her pupils are calloused by violence, and their parents, astonished by her frankness, push her toward retirement.

Similarly ignored is Cynthia, an Englishwoman whose witnessing of a young Irishman's suicide catapults her into a realization of her own complicity in the Troubles, for she and her companions have for years vacationed in Antrim at an English-run resort yet remained completely detached from the Irish. When Cynthia decries their indifference and insularity, she is greeted with anger and disbelief.

Trevor's fiction about the Troubles is an expression of his humane deploring of violence's contagion and wastefulness. As Gregory Schirmer has noted, Trevor shares with E. M. Forster the yearning to "only connect" in a world where human communities, personal and public, repeatedly fail. Yet with "Beyond the Pale," Trevor first ventures into an exploration of the collisions between Irish and English cultures, and the result is a significant body of fiction probing Ireland's colonial legacy. When Cynthia exhorts her companions to see that their vacations in Antrim, during which they admire the Irish countryside but ignore the existence of the Irish, are part of a legacy of exploitation, she invokes Ireland's colonial history, but her English companions are angered and dismayed by her words. Beginning in the 1980s, when Ireland began to occupy a central place in Trevor's writing (including the travel book of literary places, *A Writer's Ireland*), the author, drawing on his early training as a historian, plumbs Ireland past to explain his often bleak vision of Ireland present.

Fools of Fortune (1983), Trevor's second novel about Ireland, continues the author's preoccupation with political violence's impact upon ordinary lives. Trevor both employs and reconstructs the Big House genre, for though the Quintons are of Ascendancy stock, their home, Kilneagh, is a haven for lonely souls, Catholic and Protestant alike; they abhor British injustice and support Irish independence. In this novel, which spans most of the twentieth century, Trevor eludes easy categorizations, for when politically motivated catastrophe strikes, this Anglo-Irish family is decimated not by Irish nationalists but by Black and Tans, who burn Kilneagh and cause the deaths of Mr. Quinton, his daughters, and three family servants, an act that later precipitates the suicide of Mrs. Quinton and psychologically damages her son, Willie. Raised on his mother's desire for vengeance, Willie savagely murders the soldier responsible for the Quintons' demise. Violence reverberates in the following generation, for while Willie is in exile his emotionally fragile daughter, Imelda, is driven mad by her English mother's graphic stories of the family's suffering. The novel ends on an elegiac note, as the now-elderly Willie is reunited with his lover and with the daughter he never knew existed. Happiest of all is Imelda, whom madness has granted a modicum of peace.

The title story of *The News from Ireland* (1985), Trevor's finest piece of short fiction, again explores Irish history against a Big House backdrop. Set in the famine years, the story employs multiple points of view to reveal the bigotry, moral blindness, and indifference that exacerbated this national catastrophe. The Ascendancy Pulvertafts do not comprehend that their comfortable lives are rooted in exploitation of the Irish, and they believe themselves generous in their distribution of soup and employment of the hungry to build famine roads. Their butler, Fogarty, urges the family's English governess, Anna Maria Heddoe, to speak up about the horrors that sicken and dismay her. But Heddoe is in effect a study in the genesis of bigotry, for ultimately, she "learns to live with things," keeping silent and eventually planning to marry the Pulvertaft's cruel, anti-Irish estate manager. Perceptive but impotent to effect change, Fogarty predicts that the Pulvertafts' descendants will suffer reversals in fortune.

The News from Ireland collection demonstrates Trevor's growing engagement with his native country, as more than half the stories concern Irish characters. He continues to explore the stifling effects of narrow environments on sensitive souls in such stories as "Music," "Virgins," and "The Property of Colette Nervi" (in *News*) as well as in the novella *Nights at the Alexandra* (1987). His concern with Ireland's colonial past persists in *The Silence in the Garden* (1988) and manifests itself with increasing subtlety in *Family Sins and Other Stories* (1990), *Reading Turgenev* (in *Two Lives*, 1991), and *Felicia's Journey* (1994).

Whereas much of Trevor's earlier Irish fiction suggested that Irish people's experience of disillusionment, violence, and loneliness was endemic to the human condition, his more recent works often grapple with the issue of Irish identity, symbolically linking individual Irish lives with Ireland's colonial history. The setting of *The Silence in the Garden*, Carriglas, an island whose name means "green rock," symbolizes Ireland itself, for its standing stones, ruined monastery, holy well, and Big House encapsulate Irish history. Its ruling family, the Rollestons, wrested the land from the Irish in Cromwell's time, offered relief in the Famine, witnessed the struggle for independence, and eventually become extinct, their once-lovely estate now a declining ruin linked to the mainland by a bridge named for the Irish nationalist who attempted to murder them.

In effect a sequel to "The News from Ireland," *The Silence in the Garden* suggests that the exploitation of power breeds violence and sterility. A cruel childhood prank by the young Rollestons unleashes an oil slick of violence, suffering, and masochistic guilt that smears Protestant and Catholic, rich and poor. Trevor implies that all of Ireland has been similarly bedeviled by injustice and exploitation.

In several of the predominantly Irish stories of *Family Sins*, Trevor sympathetically examines the impact of Irish culture on Irish women. In "Events at Drimaghleen," a deliberately ambiguous account of the aftermath of a murder/ suicide on a remote farm, two dead women lose their identities through the stereotyping of those trying to explain the horrific event. Mrs. Butler's personality vanishes in the Irish community's assertion that she is an obsessive mother of an only son; Maureen McDowd is transformed into a colleen gone bad by an unscrupulous English journalist. In "Kathleen's Field," Trevor subverts the male-invented myth of Ireland as dispossessed woman and provides a decidedly unromantic account of young woman whose family's poverty impels them to sell her youth for a piece of land. Similarly subversive is "August Saturday," whose protagonist, the mythically named Grania, is no tragic victim but rather a woman who boldly takes charge of her own future. Gender and colonialism are linked in many of these stories, particularly where poverty restricts the characters' choices.

In *Reading Turgenev*, one of the two novellas in *Two Lives*, Trevor constructs a parable about the provincial Protestant Ireland of his childhood. The Dallons and the Quarrys are a vanishing breed in newly powerful Catholic Ireland, and those who fail to adapt to this changing world are doomed to extinction: Mary Louise Dallon, having married one of the few available Protestant men, Elmer Quarry, seeks escape from her sexless marriage in a platonic romance with her dying cousin, and after his death lives an eccentric shadow-life in a mental asylum. Only Mary Louise's sister, Letty, continues the family line—and she does so by marrying a Catholic.

A symbolic reading of Ireland's colonial history likewise informs the important but uncollected story "Lost Ground," which appeared in *The New Yorker* in 1992. The aptly named Milton Leeson attempts the Miltonian task of justifying the ways of God to humanity when he attempts, like Attracta, to preach reconciliation. But this scion of a militantly Unionist family pays for his courage with his life, murdered by his own brother. The act is both ghastly and self-defeating, for with Milton dies the hope that the Leesons' beloved land will remain in the family.

Trevor's *Excursions in the Real World: Memoirs*, though often reticent and elusive about the author's personal life, provides valuable insights into his early years in Ireland. The essays about childhood are vividly realized recollections about Trevor's itinerant education, the slow disintegration of his parents' marriage, and the Irish locales and characters that inspired his fiction. His often hilarious accounts of his employment in an advertising firm in London are tinctured with the bitter scent of exile, as in the insistence of one bizarrely endearing employee who could not comprehend that Trevor could be both Irish *and* Protestant.

Continuing Trevor's exploration of Anglo-Irish relations, *Felicia's Journey* is a chilling account of a naive Irish woman's search for the father of her unborn child. Preyed upon by a superficially kindly serial killer, drawn into the grim world of the urban homeless, Felicia journeys to an English underworld that her Irish upbringing has left her ill prepared to endure.

William Trevor's brilliant manipulation of point of view, his profound understanding of conflicting perspectives, and his sympathy for alienated souls have rendered him a particularly astute observer of the Irish condition. Although he continues to link Irish characters with universal human themes of loneliness, miscommunication, and social restraint, his Irish fiction constitutes a sustained vision of his native country as a society thwarted and stunted by the effects of colonial occupation.

CRITICAL RECEPTION

Trevor's expatriate status and his early choice of England as subject matter undoubtedly have contributed to the critical downplaying of his Irishness in favor of thematic studies. Julian Gitzen's 1979 essay focused on the plight of "truth-tellers" in Trevor's fiction, whereas Gregory Schirmer's 1990 book contends that the author's prevalent theme, the yearning for, and failure of, human relationships, is based on E. M. Forster's "only connect." Suzanne Morrow Paulson, arguing the importance of Trevor's short fiction, emphasizes the author's "human insight," particularly his "sympathy for women, sensitive men, and adolescents who suffer from destructive stereotypes of feminine and masculine behavior."

Several critics perceive Trevor's Irishness as essential to an understanding of his fiction. In the 1980s Robert Rhodes (in Brophy and Porter's *Contemporary Irish Writing*) initiated serious consideration of Trevor as an Irish author, including the impact of political violence upon Trevor's Irish fiction and the author's use of secrets as a plotting device in his Irish stories. Kristin Morrison contends that the imprint of the author's nationality may be discovered in all of the fiction, including his use of the garden—"at once a lost Eden and a possible Paradise"—as a metaphor for Ireland and his "system of correspondences" whereby "[t]he various elements of space and time are intrinsically interrelated." Mary Fitzgerald-Hoyt notes Trevor's increasing concern with Irish identity, manifested in his subversion of nationalist stereotypes of women and his examination of the impact of Ireland's postcolonial history.

Trevor's status as one of the century's finest fiction writers is now assured; his contribution to Irish literature, though widely recognized, requires further serious assessment.

BIBLIOGRAPHY

Selected Works by William Trevor

The Ballroom of Romance. London: Bodley Head; New York: Viking, 1972.
Beyond the Pale. London: Bodley Head; Harmondsworth: Penguin; New York: Viking Penguin, 1981.

The Collected Stories. London: Bodley Head; New York: Viking Penguin, 1992.
The Distant Past. Swords, County Dublin: Poolbeg, 1979.
Ed. *The Oxford Book of Irish Short Stories.* Oxford: Oxford University Press, 1989.
Excursions in the Real World. London: Hutchinson; New York: Knopf, 1993.
Family Sins and Other Stories. London: Bodley Head; New York: Viking, 1990.
Felicia's Journey. Harmondsworth: Penguin, 1994.
Fools of Fortune. London: Bodley Head, 1983.
Mrs. Eckdorf in O'Neill's Hotel. London: Bodley Head, 1969.
The News from Ireland. London: Bodley Head, 1985.
The Silence in the Garden. London: Bodley Head; New York: Viking, 1988.
The Stories of William Trevor. Harmondsworth: Penguin, 1983.
Two Lives: Reading Turgenev; My House in Umbria. London: Bodley Head; New York: Viking Penguin, 1991.
A Writer's Ireland. London: Thames and Hudson, 1984.

Studies of William Trevor

Fitzgerald-Hoyt, Mary. "De-Colleenizing Ireland: William Trevor's *Family Sins.*" *Notes on Modern Irish Literature* 5 (1993): 28–33.
———. "William Trevor's Protestant Parables." *Colby Quarterly* 31.1 (March 1995): 40–45.
Gitzen, Julian. "The Truth-Tellers of William Trevor." *Critique* 21 (1979): 59–72.
Morrison, Kristin. *William Trevor.* New York: Twayne, 1993.
Paulson, Suzanne Morrow. *William Trevor: A Study of the Short Fiction.* New York: Twayne, 1993.
Schirmer, Gregory A. *William Trevor: A Study of His Fiction.* London and New York: Routledge, 1990.
Stout, Mira. "The Art of Fiction CVIII: William Trevor." *Paris Review* 110 (1989–1990): 119–51.

Katharine Tynan

(c. 1858–1931)

Anne Ulry Colman

BIOGRAPHY

Katharine Tynan's death certificate, the most legal document available, lists her age at death as seventy-three years. This indicates 1858 as the proper year of her birth. Alternate dates ranging from 1859 to 1861 have been given for her birth.

Katharine was born in Dublin, one of eleven children to survive infancy. The Tynan family moved to Whitehall, near Tallaght, about 1868. About that time Katharine developed eye problems, a type of chronic ulceration that left her with diminished sight. Tynan's term for her vision was "purblind."

Her mother became an invalid at an early age, and Katharine felt little attachment to her. In *Memories*, she says of her mother: "She counts for no more in my life that was full of him, than if she had been a person in a book" (390). The "him" at the center of Tynan's life, from birth until marriage, was her father. Their mutual devotion was such that other members of the household rarely entered into Katharine's sphere. Norah, her sister, reports their father insisted the other children assume Katharine's household responsibilities to ensure she had adequate time for writing and reading.

Katharine Tynan hosted a modest salon, frequented by W. B. Yeats, Susan L. Mitchell, and other familiar figures of the Celtic Revival. Tynan was a regular contributor to literary periodicals, particularly the *Irish Monthly*, edited by Father Matthew Russell. She idolized and idealized Rosa Mulholland, but their friendship did not survive Mulholland's marriage to Sir John T. Gilbert. Tynan always suspected Sir Gilbert thought her a mildly unsuitable friend for his wife. The Sigerson sisters, Dora and Hester, Alice Furlong, Rose Kavanagh, and John and

Ellen O'Leary were among Tynan's most intimate friends. She joined the Ladies' Land League in 1878, adding Anna Parnell to her circle of friends.

Tynan married relatively late in life, at approximately thirty-five years of age. Henry Albert Hinkson, her successful suitor, was a barrister living in London. Tynan seems to have been reluctant about leaving her father and her role as his constant companion. She married in 1893, traveling alone to London for the ceremony, which her family did not attend. The Hinksons settled in Ealing and were to remain in England for the next eighteen years. The couple's first two children died in infancy, but three living children were eventually born. The family returned to Ireland in 1911, when Hinkson was appointed resident magistrate for County Mayo.

In 1914, Katharine Tynan traveled to Rome, where she wrote a series of articles on the World Congress of Women. Henry Hinkson died in 1919, and thereafter his widow traveled extensively, staying in rented accommodations or in the homes of friends. Tynan was a popular houseguest whose facile conversation, literary reputation, and pleasant manner ensured her welcome. Tynan died on April 2, 1931 in Wimbledon, of cerebral thrombosis and congestion of the lungs.

MAJOR WORKS AND THEMES

Tynan's career total of 182 volumes makes it necessary to divide her works into three major categories for discussion: poetry, novels, and miscellaneous works. Tynan began publishing in 1885, with *Louise de la Vallière and Other Poems*, which was financially subsidized by her father. The collection was immediately successful and established Tynan as an up-and-coming new poet. Two other volumes, *Shamrocks* and *Ballads and Lyrics*, followed (1891). Tynan's last poetry volume was *Collected Poems* (1930). As a poet, Tynan's work is firmly, devoutly Catholic. She was not interested in mysticism or spiritual alternatives. She is at her poetic best in the rituals and symbols of Catholicism, which contributed to her popular appeal and success. Tynan also wrote of nature, particularly utilizing color and sound as focal points in her verse, perhaps as a result of her "purblind" state, which blurred nature's fine details. She wrote less about the myths and folk legends of Ireland, preferring to concern herself with the time in which she lived. Tynan wrote well and happily of families, mothers and children, and nature, and also wrote devotional verse. Infant mortality, maternal grief, and childless women are among Tynan's most effective topics for verse. It is interesting to note her fascination for trees, as evidenced by "The Tree-Lover" section in her *Collected Poems*.

Tynan's novels were primarily written to generate income and thus appeal to the widest possible audience. She was an immensely popular novelist, whose novels follow a standard romance story line. She demonstrates a capacity for particularly intricate plots and allows her personal beliefs to shine through the conventional characters. Tynan believed in, and personally adhered to, the practice of daily bathing, a policy that is recommended and practiced by characters in her novels. Tynan's heroines reflect the author's own religious views, firm in their faith and their morals.

The miscellaneous category of her writings presents a rather mixed bag: hagiography, history, character sketches and tales, stories for children, memoirs, and autobiography. Tynan's autobiography is a multivolume endeavor. While she provides insights into her contemporaries and inadvertently into her own character, Tynan tends to be repetitive in her recollections. Her personal prejudices and beliefs about social hierarchies are confidently stated. She fondly recalls accepting the label of a "Sinn Feiner" by her British friends, while realizing she would never fit that definition in Ireland. She refers to the 1916 Rising as a "rebellion" and wonders at the unfriendly attitude of the locals to her family during Henry Hinkson's tenure as a resident magistrate in County Mayo. Living for lengthy periods in England gave Tynan a comfortably colonized perspective. Although a dedicated Parnellite, she was never a dedicated nationalist.

One of Tynan's greatest contributions to the women's literary scene was her revised edition of the *Cabinet of Irish Literature*. Originally edited by Charles Read in 1880, Tynan's 1902–1903 edition added a substantial number of women authors and remains one of the best sources for women's biographical information.

CRITICAL RECEPTION

Katharine Tynan was an immensely popular writer. When her first poetry collections appeared, she was hailed as the best female poet in Ireland and potentially the best poet regardless of gender.

The *Irish Monthly*'s review of *Louise de la Vallière*, published in volume 13, strongly praises Tynan's first volume:

This, the first volume Miss Katharine Tynan has given to the world ... is a very remarkable one in itself, and doubly so as the production of a young girl; the quiet mastery over her art, the perfect strength and subdued richness of colouring, the holy tenderness of thought, and the perfection of rhythmic construction which this young poet shows, are as rare as delightful. ... we do find *real poetry*, and we mean by *real poetry, beautiful thought clothed in beautiful language.* (377)

The review continues for six pages. Such a lengthy and effusive review of a first collection of poetry was indeed rare. This sort of praise continued in subsequent reviews of Tynan's poetry and prose by the *Irish Monthly* and other literary magazines.

Ernest Boyd, writing in *Ireland's Literary Renaissance*, notes that "Seldom has the first effort of a beginner met with such encouragement as greeted Katharine Tynan's *Louise de la Vallière and Other Poems* in 1885" (103). Boyd disliked Tynan's poetry after the publication of *Ballads and Lyrics*, feeling that Tynan had exhausted both her poetic range and talent in her first three volumes. Boyd was interested in the Celtic Revival, judging Tynan's work on the basis of her contribution to that literary movement and her use of Celtic themes. Despite his obvious dislike of Tynan's later works, he calls her "almost unique in that she is the only writer of any importance whose Catholicism has found literary expression" (107). He sums up her literary career thus: "It is difficult, when reading her later verse, to remember that until the arrival of W. B. Yeats, Katharine Tynan was held to be the young poet of the greatest promise in Ireland" (107). Boyd closes his short review of her work by declaring, "Interesting though she may be as the only important Catholic poet in Ireland, Katharine Tynan will hardly rank with the best writers of the Literary Revival" (112).

There has been little response to Tynan's work by contemporary critics. In the most recent book—as far back as 1974—Marilyn Gaddis Rose reads Tynan from a feminist perspective:

Katharine Tynan, in short, is a woman writer who sees herself and expresses herself in terms of women's roles. . . . in her poetry, her most rigorously controlled genre by any set of standards, her low expectations of every man outside her own family are not completely sublimated, but they are so conventionally disguised that they would neither offend a male reader nor alarm a female reader. In her fiction, her least controlled genre, her plots and characterizations are woven with implicit criticism of men's inevitable inadequacies, with which women's resourcefulness must forever cope. (17)

Tynan's journalistic efforts were diverse and were written to demonstrate "how she succeeded in a man's world and how she proposed to make it easier for other women to succeed also" (Rose 18). Seamus Deane's introduction to her work in the *Field Day Anthology* (1991) is the only truly recent work on her and is worth consulting.

Tynan's contribution to Ireland's literary history has never been properly reassessed. Perhaps her status as a fringe contributor to the predominant literary movement headed by W. B. Yeats, coupled with her financial need to produce a steady stream of popular romance novels, has led to her marginalized status. Oddly enough, no full-length critical study of Katharine Tynan's life and works has been produced.

BIBLIOGRAPHY

Selected Works by Katharine Tynan

Poetry

Louise de la Vallière and Other Poems. London: Kegan Paul, 1885.
Ballads and Lyrics. London: Kegan Paul, Trench, 1891.

Cuckoo Songs. London: Elkin Mathews, 1894.
Poems. London: Lawrence and Bullen, 1901.
Twenty-One Poems by Katharine Tynan: Selected by W. B. Yeats. Dundrum: Dun Emer, 1907.
Experiences: Poems. London: A. H. Bullen, 1908.
New Poems. London: Sidgwick and Jackson, 1911.
Flower of Youth: Poems in War Time. London: Sidgwick and Jackson, 1915.
Late Songs. London: Sidgwick and Jackson, 1917.
Twilight Songs. Oxford: Basil Blackwell, 1927.
Collected Poems. London: Macmillan, 1930.

Novels

A Girl of Galway. London: Blackie and Son, 1902.
The Handsome Quaker. London: A. H. Bullen, 1902.
Dick Pentreath. London: Smith, Elder, 1905.
Peggy the Daughter. London: Cassell, 1909.
Honey, My Honey. London: Smith, Elder, 1912.
Pat the Adventurer. London and Melbourne: Ward, Lock, 1923.

Autobiographies

Twenty-Five Years: Reminiscences. London: Smith, Elder, 1913.
The Middle Years. London: Constable, 1916.
The Years of the Shadow. London: Constable, 1919.
The Wandering Years. London: Constable and Boston: Houghton-Mifflin, 1922.
Life in the Occupied Area. London: Hutchinson, 1925.

Further Volumes

Ed. *The Cabinet of Irish Literature*. Rev. ed. 4 vols. London: Gresham, 1902.
A Book of Memory: The Birthday Book of the Blessed Dead. London: Hodder and Stoughton, [1906].
The Book of Flowers (with Frances Maitland). London: Smith and Elder, 1909.
Lord Edward. London: Smith, Elder, 1916. (Study of Edward Fitzgerald)
Katharine Tynan's Book of Irish History. Dublin and Belfast: Educational Company of Ireland, [1918].
Memories. London: E. Nash and Grayson, 1924.

Studies of Katharine Tynan

Alspach, K. R. "The Poetry of Katharine Tynan Hinkson." *The Ireland America Review* 4 (1940): 121–26.
Gibbon, Monk, ed. "Introduction." *Poems of Katharine Tynan*. Dublin: Allen Figgis, 1963.
O'Mahony, Norah Tynan. "Katharine Tynan's Girlhood." *Irish Monthly* 59 (June 1931): 358–68.
Rose, Marilyn Gaddis. *Katharine Tynan*. Lewisburg, PA: Bucknell University Press, 1974.

Russell, George William [AE]. "Foreword." *Collected Poems* [by Katharine Tynan].
    London: Macmillan, 1930.
Yeats, W. B. *Letters to Katharine Tynan*. Ed. Roger McHugh. New York: McMullen,
    1953.

William Butler Yeats

(1865–1939)

Bernard McKenna

BIOGRAPHY

William Butler Yeats was born in Sandymount, County Dublin, on June 13, 1865, into a family whose origins lie deep in the Anglo-Irish community. The Yeatses came from Yorkshire in the seventeenth century and started a successful linen merchant's house. The Butlers were descendants of the family of the Duke of Ormond and had been in County Kildare for generations. W. B. Yeats's father was a successful portrait painter. His wife, Susan Mary Pollexfen, came from a family of ship and mill owners. They had two daughters. Susan Mary, better known as Lily, was born in 1866. Elizabeth Corbet, known as Lolly, was born in 1868. Another son, Jack, a noted artist and author in his own right, was born in 1871. William Butler Yeats was educated first by his father, then at the Godolphin School in Hammersmith, at Erasmus school in Dublin, and, finally, at Dublin's Metropolitan School of Art. During this time, Yeats lived in both Dublin and London but almost always spent his summers in County Sligo with his mother's family.

In 1886, Yeats abandoned his studies as an artist and dedicated himself to a literary career. He had been publishing some poetry, possibly as early as 1882 but certainly by 1885. Also in 1886, he published his first book, actually a long dramatic poem, titled *Mosada*. In the coming years, he published his *Fairy and Folk Tales of the Irish Peasantry, The Celtic Twilight*, and *Crossways*, works that marked him as a major new voice in the Celtic Revival. In the early 1890s, he lived in London and helped to found the Rhymers' Club and began an association with the artists of the fin de siecle. In the late 1890s, he returned to Ireland and founded, with Lady Gregory, the Irish Literary Theatre, later to become the Abbey Theatre; developed an interest in Irish politics and Maud

Gonne; and established relationships with John Synge, Olivia Shakespear, AE, and the writers and artists of the Irish Renaissance. Yeats continued to publish poetry and plays in the 1910s, establishing a friendship and working association with Ezra Pound. In 1917, after unsuccessful proposals to Maud Gonne and her daughter, Iseult, he married Georgie Hyde-Lees, with whom he had two children, Michael and Anne. In the 1920s, he served as a member of the Irish Senate, was awarded the Nobel Prize in literature, and received a D.Litt. from Trinity College, Dublin. In the 1930s, he began, for health reasons, to spend his winters away from Ireland in Italy and, later, France; continued his work for the Abbey; and composed some of his most remarkable poetry. He died on a Thursday, January 26, 1939, in France and was buried in Roquebrune. After the war, in 1948, his body was disinterred and brought home to Sligo and Drumcliffe Churchyard.

MAJOR WORKS AND THEMES

Poetry

Early Work

Critics generally consider Yeats's first creative phase to encompass his poetic production dating from his earliest publications through the 1904 edition of *In the Seven Woods* and his *Collected Poems*, although even in this later work Yeats's poetry begins to develop a more mature and public voice. Readers will discover in the work of this period some of his more famous poetic achievements, including "To an Isle in the Water" and "Down by the Salley Gardens" from his first major collection, *Crossways* (1889); "The Lake Isle of Innisfree," "When You are Old," and "The White Birds" from *The Rose* (1893); "The Hosting of the Sidhe," "The Song of Wandering Aengus," "The Cap and Bells," "The Valley of the Black Pig," and "The Fiddler of Dooney" from *The Wind among the Reeds* (1899); and "Never Give All the Heart" and "Adam's Curse" from *In the Seven Woods* (1904). The major factors that inform this production can be discovered in Yeats's prose work of the period, most notably, *The Celtic Twilight* and *The Tragic Generation* section of his *Autobiographies*, which articulate the influences of, respectively, the Celtic Revival and the aesthetic movement.

Celtic Revival

Yeats was born into an Anglo-Irish tradition separate from both the English experience and the Catholic native Irish experience. Intellectually, this Protestant, largely Anglican community reached its height in the mid-to-late nineteenth century in a movement known as the Gaelic or Celtic Revival, which was born as a reaction to industrialization and as a movement toward nationalism. The progenitors of the movement—among them James Clarence Mangan, William

Allingham, Aubrey de Vere, and Samuel Ferguson—sought both an alternative to the growing industrialization and secularization of Britain and a national identity independent of that imposed on them from England.

Significantly, the Anglo-Irish alternative to the modern was not fashioned from any direct contact with the reality of Ireland but rather with an idea of Ireland or a sometimes vague impression of what Ireland ought to be in order to meet certain undefined but intuitively sensed spiritual needs. Yeats, like the other Protestant writers of the Revival—significantly, only a few Catholic writers, among them Eoin Mac Neill and Ellen O'Leary, contributed to the movement—fashioned a dream of a rural Ireland uncorrupted by the faults of the industrialized, scientific world. They created an imaginative, bucolic retreat populated by figures of rather unreal romance and myth who had a strong and direct connection not only with the mythic past, not only with a fecund and mysterious landscape alive with preternatural possibilities, but with the deep meaning and purposefulness endemic to that past and to those landscapes, a meaning and purposefulness that eluded the industrial societies of the mid-to-late nineteenth century.

Aestheticism

Aestheticism and its predecessor, the Pre-Raphaelite movement, like the Celtic Revival, have their origins in German romanticism and a desire for an alternative to Victorian society. Its practitioners, like the French symbolists, advocate an extreme experience of passion and a highly refined expression of that passion in their writings. The authors of the fin de siècle—including Yeats, Rhys, Dowson, Moore, Symons, Johnson, Le Gallienne, Hillier, and sometimes Wilde—formed the Rhymers' Club to protect one another's reputation in the press and to cultivate, jointly, their ideas and philosophies. Yeats, initially concerned that he would be isolated from literary society in London, helped to form the club, excited by the prospect of meeting his contemporary writers and by the opportunity to cultivate his artistic technique.

Yeats's writings that demonstrate the influence of aestheticism speak to a transformation and representation of the real as something spiritual and permanent, a representation of the intensity of emotion the poet feels when confronted by the object. As in the writings of Blake, an edition of which Yeats put together in this period, there exist two possibilities—that of the mundane world and that of the spiritual, purified world. The artist's objective should not be one or the other but the experience of both simultaneously. Consequently, critics who condemn Yeats for objectifying women or even for "Orientalizing" the Irish find ample fodder for their argument in the work of this early period. However, the dramatic tension of Yeats's work, the quality that gives his poetry its force, comes from the interrelationship between these two worlds.

Second Phase

The influences that shape the poetic production of Yeats's second, more public, phase appeared as early as his association in the mid-to-late 1890s with the

Irish Literary Theatre and with the Irish nationalist cause and continued in one form or another until the development of his mature spirituality shortly after his marriage. The work of this period is characterized by a language more dramatically powerful than in his previous production and by themes that explore more of the reality of the human condition. Specifically, they take an interest in both the work of the Abbey Theatre and in the Irish political situation that developed in the years surrounding the Easter Rising through independence and partition. When reviewing Yeats's writings of this period, readers will recognize many commonly anthologized works, including "No Second Troy," "The Fascination of What's Difficult," and "All Things Can Tempt Me" from *The Green Helmet and Other Poems* (1910); "September 1913," "Running to Paradise," and "The Magi" from *Responsibilities* (1914); "The Wild Swans at Coole," "In Memory of Major Robert Gregory," "An Irish Airman Foresees His Death," and "Upon a Dying Lady" from *The Wild Swans at Coole* (1919); and "Easter, 1916," "The Second Coming," and "A Prayer for My Daughter" from *Michael Robartes and the Dancer* (1921).

John Unterecker discusses some of the major themes and epistemological influences of this period, including the theory of the mask, which is "a technique by which the personal could somehow be objectified, be given the appearance of impersonal 'truth' and yet retain the emotive force of privately felt belief" (16). Clearly, this dynamic represents a refinement of Yeats's earlier aesthetic between the spiritual and the real. However, the components of the mask are less rooted in an imagined experience than in direct interaction with the reality of experience—the people of Ireland, women, and the other subjects of Yeats's writing. The tension between mask and reality creates the dramatic power of Yeats's work and serves to explain the conflicting views of the Irish of "September 1913" and "Easter, 1916"; the women of Yeats's Helen/Maud Gonne poems; his dreams and fears for his daughter; and his reaction to the beauty and reality of the creative process. The mask is not restricted to the individual but is applied to a nation, a community, a family, any dynamic within or between people.

Final Phase

The poetry of Yeats's final period can be traced through the influences that shaped his *A Vision* through the poems finished in the weeks before his death. It includes work—"The Second Coming," "The Phases of the Moon"—that appeared in earlier collections and is characterized by an increasingly more articulate understanding of his personal spiritual vision that includes theories of history associated with gyres and phases of the moon; unity of being, unity of image, and unity of culture; Indian and Eastern philosophies; and ancient Greek and Latin models. In the 1920s Yeats began "a systematic study of Greek philosophy and read widely not only in Platonism . . . but also in the Presocratic philosophers" (Arkins 13). He was attracted to Platonic doctrines "of a transcendent reality" and of "the immortality of the soul" (Arkins 24). Yeats also explored Eastern spiritualities related to his articulation of this Western philosophy, including establishing, in the decade before his death, an association with Shri Purohit Swami, for whom Yeats wrote the introduction to *An Indian Monk*. Readers of the correspondence between Yeats and Swami discover a series of requests by Yeats for information on the rituals associated with the myriad religious traditions called Hinduism. Yeats mines Swami's experiences and memories for contributions to a symbolic storehouse. Significantly, the letters also demonstrate an annoyance with Swami the man, a hesitation to meet with him personally, and a reluctance to discuss anything other than philosophical issues. Clearly, Yeats's attitude was partially due to his wife's and his friends' dislike for Swami but also due to Yeats's still-lingering conflict between the spiritual and the real. A swami known only through a correspondence that emphasizes spiritual concerns can remain part of the ideal Eastern world.

The most profound influence of this later period involves Yeats's spiritualities associated with his wife's trials with automatic writing. Shortly after Yeats married Georgie Hyde-Lees, she began to experiment with automatic writing. Yeats was convinced that she was in direct contact with the supernatural world and encouraged her in her channeling efforts. Occasional episodes of automatic writing grew into regular sessions that brought about hours and days of work. Ultimately, she began to dictate the messages to her husband, who wrote them down carefully and diligently. Critics are rightly skeptical of a wife's motivation to interest a husband who clearly chose her only after his lifelong love and her daughter rejected him. Further, many of the principles that came from the experiments demonstrate the direct influence of Yeats's renewed study of Greek philosophy. However, Yeats thought the channeling genuine and incorporated many of the messages into his work. Two epistemological concepts are particularly important. Yeats based one of his systems on a "Great Wheel" with twenty-eight spokes, obviously making a connection with the lunar calendar. The twenty-eight phases stood for an individual's twenty-eight incarnations, the twenty-eight different types of personality, the twenty-eight phases of an individual's life, and the twenty-eight phases of history. The other symbolic system of primary importance to an understanding of Yeats's later aesthetic is the concept of the gyres of history. The gyres, roughly similar to Empedocles's theory of the cyclic alteration between harmony and discord, are representations of an individual's or an era's place and position on the wheel. Each person or time has two conflicting trends in operation at once, each fighting against the other, each growing or receding in a constant motion in relation to the other. Clearly, Yeats articulated sophisticated and oftentimes obscure personal theories of time and personality. Readers beginning an association with Yeats's work should be aware of Yeats's personal spirituality. However, they can appreciate the poetry of his final stage without a full understanding of his systems.

Significantly, many of the poems of this final period are considered the best of his work independent of an understanding of Yeats's epistemology. Specifically, those works that are most often cited include "Sailing to Byzantium,"

"Meditations in a Time of Civil War," "Nineteen Hundred and Nineteen," "Among School Children," and "Leda and the Swan" from *The Tower* (1928); "Blood and the Moon," "Byzantium," and the Crazy Jane sequence from *The Winding Stair and Other Poems* (1933); the Supernatural Songs from *Parnell's Funeral and Other Poems* (1935); "Lapis Lazuli" and "The Municipal Gallery Revisited" from *New Poems* (1938); and "Under Ben Bulbert," "The Statues," "Long-Legged Fly," and "The Circus Animals' Desertion" from *Last Poems*.

Drama and the National Theater

Yeats began to compose plays or, more correctly, dramatic poetry early in his career. However, only after a production in London of his *The Land of Heart's Desire* did he begin to take an interest in not just dramatic literature but dramatic theater. His philosophy of drama stands in sharp contrast to that of Ibsen or even Shaw. Early in Yeats's career, he felt that drama should have the characteristics of ritual. The scenery and the gestures of the play should be minimal and highly symbolic. The dialogue should follow a lyrical and poetic pattern. Informed by his early aesthetic, which valued a distance from the values of industrialized society, and the theatrical production of Maeterlinck, Yeats's plays of this period include not only *The Land of Heart's Desire* (1894) but also *The Countess Cathleen* (1892) and even *Cathleen ni Houlihan* (1904). Subsequently, Yeats's work with the Abbey Theatre, originally the Irish Literary Theatre, produced a drama more attentive to the demands of dramatic convention and necessity. His attentiveness was partially inspired by the simple gift, from Gordon Craig, of a model stage and scaled players. With these, Yeats was able to manipulate the actions of his imagination directly onto a small dramatic platform and subsequently developed more dramatically viable work somewhat less reliant on symbol and dialogue. However, Yeats still strongly supported and followed his early theories of drama, as any observer of Gordon Craig's designs that accompany Yeats's *Plays for an Irish Theatre* (1911) can clearly observe, simply revising them with a growing understanding and developing theory of characterization and form, believing that comedy is driven by character, and tragedy is driven by purified thought and intense emotions. Yeats's growing theatrical aesthetic found a resonance in the established form of Japanese Noh drama, introduced to Yeats by Ezra Pound, which valued sparse scenery, a ritualistic and symbolic chorus, a small number of players, the use of music to heighten a ritualistic sense, and masked figures incorporating the work of sculptures and artists into the stylized dramatic scene. The plays of this period, showing the growing influence not just of Noh drama but also of Yeats's later exposure to various spiritual disciplines, include *The Player Queen* (1922), *The Words upon the Window Pane* (1934), and *Purgatory* (1938), in addition to versions of Sophocles's *Oedipus the King* (1928) and *Oedipus at Colonus* (1934).

Yeats's work with the Abbey Theatre, the national theater, began in 1897, when he met with George Moore, Edward Martyn, and Lady Gregory with the idea of developing a school of Irish drama and an audience for Irish plays. In 1899, the Irish Literary Theatre produced the first of a series of annual spring plays importing actors and designers from England for a production of Yeats's *The Countess Cathleen* and Martyn's *The Heather Field*. Eventually, Yeats formed a partnership with a company of Irish players under the direction of the Fay brothers that enabled the development of a uniquely Irish drama. Touring England in 1904, the company achieved critical and popular success and the sponsorship of Miss A.E.F. Horniman, who secured a building that became the Abbey Theatre and gave the company financial security until it could develop its own fiscal stability. Yeats chronicled the early development of the theater in the journal *Samhain* and played an active role with the Abbey until his death, serving as director and encouraging young playwrights such as Sean O'Casey and John Synge. Further, the national theater has continued to produce Yeats's work, staging as recently as 1993 productions of *The Hour Glass, The Words upon the Window Pane*, and *The Cat and the Moon*.

Prose Works and Literary Criticism

Throughout his career, Yeats wrote remarkable commentaries on his life and work and wrote numerous important critical studies. Most notably, his essays on Spenser and Blake and an edition of Blake are important early critical studies of these authors. Further, Yeats's autobiographies, his prose essays, his spiritual writings, and his analysis of the emerging literary and theatrical trends of the late nineteenth and early twentieth centuries are an invaluable firsthand account not only of the major developments in Yeats's career but also of many of the major literary and artistic movements of the past century.

CRITICAL RECEPTION

Comments on Yeats's earliest poetic achievement express something less than admiration. In a letter to Coventry Patmore, Gerard Manley Hopkins writes that Yeats's earliest work, *Mosada*, is "strained and unworkable allegory" (*Further Letters* 226). Writing fifteen years later, William Archer suggests that Yeats "is becoming more and more addicted to a petrified, fossilised symbolism" (556). However, some early critics do recognize the seeds of later artistic genius and do appreciate the beauty of Yeats's early poetic achievement. Arnold Bennett, in a letter to George Stuart dated February 7, 1899, observes that Yeats is "intensely spiritual, and [writes] with a style which is the last word of simplicity and natural refinement" (*Letters of Arnold Bennett* 119). Further, writing in 1904, Arthur Symons admires "the extraordinary art which has worked these tiny poems, which seem as free as waves, into a form at once so monumental and so alive! Here, at last, is poetry which has found for itself a new form, a form really modern'' (235). One of the first extended studies of Yeats, published in 1915 and written by the Ulster novelist Forrest Reid, echoes the criticism of Symons and Bennett. Reid sees in Yeats a ''more or less perfect expression of a writer's individuality'' informed by a ''profound influence of a deep spiritual experience'' (9). However, Reid balanced these remarks with observations regarding what he saw as the limits of Yeats's appeal.

Shortly after Yeats's death, two important studies of his work appeared, including Louis MacNeice's *The Poetry of W. B. Yeats*, which still serves as a good introduction to the older poet's life and work and focuses on ''what Yeats was writing *about*, with the life and ideas from which the poetry came'' (16). The other influential work that appeared in the years following Yeats's death is the 1941–1942 number of *The Southern Review*, which includes fifteen important studies of Yeats's creative aesthetic and marks the beginnings of the modern critical industry focusing on Yeats's life and work, intricately examined in Richard Finneran's *Anglo-Irish Literature—A Review of Research* and its supplement, *Recent Research on Anglo-Irish Writers*. Currently, there are two annual publications devoted to Yeats studies—*Yeats: An Annual of Critical and Textual Studies* and *The Yeats Annual*—and one regular journal, *The Yeats/Eliot Review*. Recently, several important studies of Yeats have been published, including A. Norman Jeffares's *W. B. Yeats—A New Biography* and Augustine Martin's short study, *W. B. Yeats*. These two works, together with MacNeice's volume, John Unterecker's *A Reader's Guide to William Butler Yeats*, Micheal Mac Liammoir and Eavan Boland's *W. B. Yeats*, and Richard Ellmann's *The Identity of Yeats*, serve as ideal introductions to Yeats's life and career.

BIBLIOGRAPHY

Selected Works by William Butler Yeats

Autobiographies. London: Macmillan, 1955.

Collected Edition of the Works of W. B. Yeats. Gen. ed. Richard J. Finneran and George Mills Harper. London: Macmillan, 1989–. (continuing series, unless otherwise noted.)

Vol. 1: *The Poems of W. B. Yeats*. Ed. Richard Finneran.

Vol. 2: *The Plays*. Ed. David Clark.

Vol. 3: *Autobiographies*. Ed. Douglas Archibald, J. Fraser Cocks, and Gretchen Schwenker.

Vol. 4: *Early Essays*. Ed. Warwick Gould.

Vol. 5: *Later Essays*. Ed. William O'Donnell and Elizabeth Bergmann Loizeaux. New York: Scribner's, 1994.

Vol. 6: *Prefaces and Introductions*. Ed. William O'Donnell.

Vol. 7: *Letters to the New Island*. Ed. George Bornstein and Hugh Witemeyer.

Vol. 8: *The Irish Dramatic Movement*. Ed. Mary Fitzgerald.

Vol. 9: *Early Articles and Reviews*. Ed. John Frayne.

Vol. 10: *Later Articles and Reviews*. Ed. Colton Johnson.

Vol. 11: *The Celtic Twilight and The Secret Rose*. Ed. Warwick Gould, Philip Marcus, and Michael Sidnell.

Vol. 12: *John Sherman and Dhoya*. Ed. Richard Finneran.

Vol. 13: *A Vision* (1925). Ed. Connie Hood and Walter K. Hood.

Vol. 14: *A Vision* (1937). Ed. Connie Hood and Walter K. Hood.

The Collected Letters of W. B. Yeats. Vol. 1. 1865–1895. Ed. John Kelly and Eric Domville. Oxford: Clarendon, 1986.

The Collected Letters of W. B. Yeats. Vol. 3. 1901–1904. Ed. John Kelly and Ronald Schuchard. Oxford: Clarendon, 1995.

The Collected Plays of W. B. Yeats. New York: Macmillan, 1952.

A Critcal Edition of Yeats's A Vision (1925). Ed. George Mills Harper and Walter Kelly Hood. London: Macmillan, 1978.

Essays and Introductions. London: Macmillan, 1961.

Explorations. London: Macmillan, 1972.

Fairy and Folk Tales of Ireland. London: Macmillan, 1983.

The Letters of W. B. Yeats. Ed. Allen Wade. London: R. Hart-Davies, 1954.

Memoirs. Ed. Denis Donoghue. London: Macmillan, 1972.

Mythologies. London: Macmillan, 1959.

The Senate Speeches of W. B. Yeats. Ed. Donald Pearce. Bloomington: Indiana University Press, 1960.

The Variorum Edition of the Plays of W. B. Yeats. Ed. Russell K. Alspach. London: Macmillan, 1966.

The Variorum Edition of the Poems of W. B. Yeats. Ed. Peter Alt and Russell K. Alspach. London: Macmillan, 1966.

A Vision. London: Macmillan, 1937.

Studies of William Butler Yeats

Archer, William. *Poets of the Younger Generation*. London: Bodley Head, 1902, 531–59.

Arkins, Brian. *Builders of My Soul: Greek and Roman Themes in Yeats*. Gerrards Cross: Smythe, 1990.

Ellmann, Richard. *The Identity of Yeats*. Oxford: Oxford University Press, 1964.

Hopkins, Gerard. *Letters of Gerard Manley Hopkins*. Ed. C. C. Abbott. London: Oxford University Press, 1938.

Jeffares, A. Norman. *W. B. Yeats—A New Biography*. London: Century Hutchinson, 1989.

Jochum, K.P.S. *A Classified Bibliography of Criticism*. Urbana: University of Illinois Press, 1990.

Mac Liammoir, Micheal, and Eavan Boland. *W. B. Yeats*. London: Thames and Hudson, 1971.

MacNeice, Louis. *The Poetry of W. B. Yeats*. London: Oxford University Press, 1941.

Martin, Augustine. *W. B. Yeats*. Dublin: Gill and Macmillan, 1983.

Reid, Forrest. *W. B. Yeats, A Critical Study*. London: Martin Secker, 1915.

Symons, Arthur. *Studies in Prose and Verse*. London: Dent, 1904, 230–41.

Unterecker, John. *A Reader's Guide to William Butler Yeats*. New York: Farrar, Straus, and Giroux, 1959.

Wade, Alan. *A Bibliography of the Writings of W. B. Yeats*. London: Hut-Davies, 1968.

Bibliographies

MAIN BIBLIOGRAPHY

Literary Histories

Boyd, Ernest. *Ireland's Literary Renaissance*. New York: Alfred A. Knopf, 1916; rev. 1922; Barnes & Noble, 1968.

Cahalan, James M. *Modern Irish Literature and Culture: A Chronology*. New York: Macmillan, 1993.

Deane, Seamus. *A Short History of Irish Literature*. South Bend, IN: University of Notre Dame Press, 1986, 1994.

——, ed. *The Field Day Anthology of Irish Writing* Derry: Field Day, 1991.

Fallis, Richard. *The Irish Renaissance*. Syracuse: Syracuse University Press, 1977.

Harmon, Maurice. *Modern Irish Literature 1800–1967: A Reader's Guide*. Dublin: Dolmen, 1967.

Hyde, Douglas. *A Literary History of Ireland from Earliest Times to the Present Day*. London: Unwin, 1899. Repr. 1967.

Jeffares, A. Norman. *Anglo-Irish Literature*. Dublin: Macmillan; New York: Schocken, 1982.

McHugh, Roger, and Maurice Harmon. *A Short History of Anglo-Irish Literature from Its Origins to the Present Day*. Totowa, NJ: Barnes & Noble, 1982.

McCormack, W. J. *From Burke to Beckett: Ascendancy, Tradition, and Betrayal in Literary History*. Cork: Cork University Press, 1994.

Murphy, Maureen O'Rourke, and James MacKillop, eds. *Irish Literature: A Reader*. Syracuse: Syracuse University Press, 1987.

O'Connor, Frank. *A Short History of Irish Literature: A Backward Look*. New York: Putnam's, 1967.

Power, Patrick C. *A Literary History of Ireland*. Cork: Mercier, 1969.

Vance, Norman. *Irish Literature: A Social History*. Oxford: Blackwell, 1990.
Warner, Alan. *A Guide to Anglo-Irish Literature*. New York: St. Martin's, 1981.

General

Allen, Michael and Angela Wilcox, eds. *Critical Approaches to Anglo-Irish Literature*. Totowa, NJ: Barnes and Noble, 1989.

Barfoot, C. C., and Theo D'Haen, eds. *The Clash of Ireland: Literary Contrasts and Connections*. Amsterdam and Atlanta: Rodopi, 1980.

Bertha, Csilla, and Donald E. Morse. *Worlds Visible and Invisible: Essays on Irish Literature*. Debrecen, Hungary: Kosseth University Press, 1994.

Boyd, Ernest. *Appreciations and Depreciations: Irish Literary Studies*. Dublin: Talbot; London: Unwin, 1917.

Boylan, Henry. *A Dictionary of Irish Biography*. Dublin: Gill and Macmillan, 1978, rev. 1989.

Brady, Anne and Brian Cleeve. *A Biographical Dictionary of Irish Writers*. Mullingar: Lilliput, 1985.

Bramback, Birgit, and Martin Croghan, eds. *Anglo-Irish and Irish Literature: Aspects of Language and Culture*. Stockholm: Almqvist and Wiksell International, 1988.

Brophy, James, and Eamon Grennan, eds. *New Irish Writing: Essays in Memory of Raymond J. Porter*. Boston: Hall, 1989.

Brophy, James, and Raymond J. Porter, eds. *Contemporary Irish Writing*. Boston: Twayne, 1983.

Brown, Malcolm. *The Politics of Irish Literature from Thomas Davis to W. B. Yeats*. Seattle: University of Washington Press, 1972.

Brown, Roy B., William J. Roscelli, and Richard Loftus, eds. *The Celtic Cross*. West Lafayette, IN: Purdue University Studies, 1964.

Brown, Terence. *Ireland's Literature*. Mullingar: Lilliput, 1988.

Cairns, David, and Toni O'Brien Johnson, eds. *Gender in Irish Writing*. Philadelphia: Open University Press, 1990.

Carlson, Julia, ed. *Banned in Ireland: Censorship and the Irish Writer*. Athens, GA: University of Georgia Press, 1990.

Connolly, Peter, ed. *Literature and the Changing Ireland*. Totowa, NJ: Barnes and Noble, 1982.

Costello, Peter. *The Heart Grown Brutal: The Irish Revolution in Literature from Parnell to the Death of Yeats, 1891–1939*. Dublin: Gill and Macmillan, 1977.

Crone, John S. *A Concise Dictionary of Irish Biography*. Dublin: Talbot, 1928.

Cronin, Anthony. *Heritage Now: Irish Literature in the English Language*. Dingle: Brandon, 1982; New York: St. Martin's, 1983.

Dawe, Gerald, and Edna Longley, eds. *Across a Roaring Hill: The Protestant Imagination in Modern Ireland: Essays in Honour of John Hewitt*. Belfast: Blackstaff, 1985.

Deane, Seamus. *Celtic Revivals: Essays in Modern Irish Literature*. London: Faber and Faber, 1985.

Dumbleton, William. *Ireland: Life and Land in Literature*. Albany: State University of New York Press, 1984.

Dunn, Douglas, ed. *Two Decades of Irish Writing*. Cheadle: Carcanet; Chester Springs, PA: Dufour, 1975.

Ellmann, Richard. *James Joyce*. New York: Oxford, 1959. Rev. 1982.

Finneran, Richard J., ed. *Anglo-Irish Literature, a Review of Research*. New York: Modern Language Association of America, 1976.

————. *Recent Research on Anglo-Irish Writers*. New York: Modern Language Association of America, 1983.

Foley, Timothy, Lionel Pilkington, Sean Ryder, and Elizabeth Tilley, eds. *Gender and Colonialism*. Galway: Galway University Press, 1996.

Foster, John Wilson. *Essays in Irish Literature and Culture*. Syracuse: Syracuse University Press, 1992.

Genet, Jacqueline, ed. *The Big House in Ireland: Reality and Representation*. Dingle: Brandon, 1991.

Griffin, Gerald. *The Wild Geese: Pen Portraits of Famous Irish Exiles*. London: Jarrold's, 1938.

Gwynn, Stephen. *Irish Literature and Drama*. New York: Nelson, 1936.

Hall, Wayne. *Shadowy Heroes: Irish Literature of the 1890s*. Syracuse: Syracuse University Press, 1980.

Harmon, Maurice, ed. *The Irish Writer and the City*. Totowa, NJ: Barnes and Noble, 1983.

Hayley, Barbara, and Christopher Murray, eds. *Ireland and France, a Bountiful Friendship: Essays in Honour of Patrick Rafroidi*. Savage, MD: Barnes and Noble, 1992.

Heinz, Kosok, ed. *Studies in Anglo-Irish Literature*. Bonn: Bouvier, 1982.

Henn, T. R. *Last Essays*. New York: Harper and Row, 1976.

Hirsch, Edward. "The Imaginary Irish Peasant." *Publications of the Modern Language Association* (*PMLA*) 106.5 (October 1991): 1116–33.

Hogan, Robert, ed. *Dictionary of Irish Literature*. Westport, CT: Greenwood, 1979, Revised 1996.

Howarth, Herbert. *The Irish Writers: 1880–1940*. New York: Hill and Wang, 1958.

Hyland, Paul, and Neil Sammells, eds. *Irish Writing: Exile and Subversion*. New York: St. Martin's, 1991.

Imhof, Rüdiger, ed. *Ireland: Literature, Culture, Politics*. Heidelberg: Universitatsverlag C. Winter, 1994.

Innes, C. L. *Woman and Nation in Irish Literature and Society, 1880–1953*. Hemel Hempstead, UK: Harvester Wheatsheaf, 1993.

Jeffares, A. Norman. *Images of Invention: Essays on Irish Writing*. Gerrards Cross, UK: Colin Smythe, 1995.

Kain, Richard. *Dublin in the Age of Yeats and Joyce*. Norman: University of Oklahoma Press, 1962.

Kearney, Richard, ed. *The Irish Mind: Exploring Intellectual Traditions*. Dublin: Wolfhound, 1985.

————. *Transitions: Narratives in Modern Irish Culture*. Dublin: Wolfhound, 1988.

Kenneally, Michael, ed. *Cultural Contexts and Literary Idioms in Contemporary Irish Literature*. Gerrards Cross: Smythe, 1988.

————. *Irish Literature and Culture*. Savage, MD: Barnes and Noble, 1992.

Kenner, Hugh. *A Colder Eye: The Modern Irish Writers*. New York: Knopf, 1983.

Kenny, Herbert. *Literary Dublin*. New York: Taplinger, 1974.

Kiberd, Declan. *Inventing Ireland: The Literature of a Modern Nation*. Cambridge, MA: Harvard University Press, 1995.

Komesu, Okifumi, and Masaru Sekine, eds. *Irish Writers and Politics*. Totowa, NJ: Barnes and Noble, 1990.

Kosok, Heinz, ed. *Studies in Anglo-Irish Literature*. Bonn: Bouvier, 1982.

Krause, David. *The Profane Book of Irish Comedy*. Ithaca, NY: Cornell University Press, 1982.

Lane, Denis, and Carol McCrory Lane, eds. *Modern Irish Literature*. New York: Ungar, 1988.

Law, H. A. *Anglo-Irish Literature*. New York: Longmans, Green, 1926.

Lloyd, David. *Anomalous States: Irish Writing and the Post-Colonial Movement*. Dublin: Lilliput, 1993.

Longley, Edna. *Two Decades of Irish Writing*. Chester Springs, PA: Dufour, 1975.

———. *The Living Stream: Literature and Revisionism in Ireland*. Newcastle, UK: Bloodaxe, 1994.

Lyons, F. S. L. *Ireland since the Famine*. New York: Scribner's, 1971.

MacDonagh, Thomas. *Literature in Ireland*. Dublin: Talbot, 1916.

Marcus, Phillip. *Yeats and the Beginning of the Irish Renaissance*. Ithaca, NY: Cornell University Press, 1970.

Martin, Augustine. *Anglo-Irish Literature*. Dublin: Department of Foreign Affairs, 1980.

———, ed. *The Genius of Irish Prose*. Dublin: Mercier, 1984.

McCormack, William J. *Ascendancy and Tradition in Anglo-Irish Literary History from 1739 to 1939*. Oxford: Clarendon; New York: Oxford University Press, 1985.

McMinn, Joseph, ed. *The Internationalism of Irish Literature and Drama*. Savage, MD: Barnes and Noble, 1992.

Mercier, Vivian. *The Irish Comic Tradition*. New York: Oxford, 1992.

———. *Modern Irish Literature: Sources and Founders*. Edited by Eilís Dillon. Oxford: Clarendon, 1994.

Morash, Chris. *Writing the Irish Famine*. Oxford: Clarendon, 1995.

Morse, Donald E., Csilla Bertha, and Istvan Pallfy, eds. *A Small Nation's Contribution to the World: Essays on Anglo-Irish Literature and Language*. Gerrards Cross: Smythe, 1994.

Moynahan, Julian. *Anglo-Irish: The Literary Imagination in a Hyphenated Culture*. Princeton: Princeton University Press, 1995.

O'Connor, Theresa, ed. *The Defiant Spirit: Comedy in the Works of Irish Women Writers*. Gainesville: University of Florida Press, 1995.

O'Hanrahan, Brenda. *Donegal Authors*. Dublin: Irish Academic Press, 1982.

O'Leary, Philip. *The Prose Literature of the Gaelic Revival 1881–1921: Ideology and Innovation*. University Park, PA: The Pennsylvania State University Press, 1994.

O'Malley, Ernie. *On Another Man's Wound*. Dublin: The Sign of the Three Candles, 1936.

O'Malley, William T. *Anglo-Irish Literature: A Bibliography of Dissertations, 1873–1989*. Westport, CT: Greenwood, 1990.

O'Sullivan, Sean. *Folktales of Ireland*. Chicago: University of Chicago Press, 1969.

O'Sullivan, Seumas [James Starkey]. *Essays and Recollections*. Dublin: Talbot, 1944.

Ó Tuama, Seán. *Repossessions: Selected Essays on Irish Literary Heritage*. Cork: Cork University Press 1996.

Partridge, A. C. *Language and Society in Anglo-Irish Literature*. Totowa, NJ: Barnes and Noble, 1984.

Porter, Raymond, and James Brophy, eds. *Modern Irish Literature*. New York: Iona College Press, 1972.

Rauchbauer, Otto, ed. *Ancestral Voices: The Big House in Anglo-Irish Literature*. Hildesheim: Olms, 1992.

Rickard, John S. *Irishness and (Post) Modernism*. Lewisburg, PA: Bucknell University Press, 1994.

Ronsley, Joseph, ed. *Myth and Reality in Irish Literature*. Ontario: Wilfrid Laurier University Press, 1977.

Schleifer, Ronald, ed. *The Genres of the Irish Literary Revival*. Norman, OK: Pilgrim, 1980.

Sekine, Masaru, ed. *Irish Writers and Society at Large*. Gerrards Cross: Smythe, 1985.

Skelton, Robin. *Celtic Contraries*. Syracuse: Syracuse University Press, 1990.

Taylor, Estella. *The Modern Irish Writers*. Lawrence: University of Kansas Press, 1954.

Todd, Loreto. *The Language of Irish Literature*. New York: St. Martin's 1989.

Ussher, Arland. *The Face and Mind of Ireland*. London: Gollancz, 1949.

Wall, Richard. *A Dictionary and Glossary of the Irish Literary Revival*. Gerrards Cross, UK: 1995.

Walshe, Éibhear, ed. *Sex, Nation and Dissent in Irish Writing*. Cork: Cork University Press, 1997.

Waters, Maureen. *The Comic Irishman*. Albany: State University of New York Press, 1984.

Watson, George J. *Irish Identity and the Literary Revival*. Washington, DC: Catholic University of America Press, 1979; Repr. 1994.

Weekes, Ann Owens. *Irish Women Writers: An Uncharted Tradition*. Lexington: University of Kentucky Press, 1990.

Welch, Robert. *Changing States: Transformations in Modern Irish Writing*. London: Routledge, 1993.

———, ed. *Irish Writers and Religion*. Savage, MD: Barnes and Noble, 1992.

———, ed. *The Oxford Companion to Irish Literature*. Oxford: Oxford University Press, 1996.

Yeats, W. B. *The Autobiographies*. New York: Collier, 1965.

Fiction

Adams, Robert Martin. *After Joyce: Studies in Fiction after Ulysses*. New York: Oxford University Press, 1977.

Averill, Deborah. *The Irish Short Story from George Moore to Frank O'Connor*. Washington, DC: University Press of America, 1982.

Ben-Merre, Diana A., and Maureen Murphy, eds. *James Joyce and His Contemporaries*. Westport, CT: Greenwood, 1989.

Cahalan, James. *Great Hatred, Little Room: The Irish Historical Novel*. Syracuse: Syracuse University Press, 1983.

———. *The Irish Novel: A Critical History*. Boston: Twayne, 1988.

Cohn, Dorrit. *Transparent Minds*. Princeton: Princeton University Press, 1978.

Cronin, John. *The Anglo-Irish Novel*. Totowa, NJ: Barnes and Noble, 1980.

———. *The Anglo-Irish Novel*, vol. 2, 1900–1940. Belfast: Blackstaff, 1990.

DeSalvo, Louise, Kathleen Walsh D'Arcy, and Katherine Hogan, eds. *Territories of the Voice: Contemporary Stories by Irish Women Writers*. Boston: Beacon, 1989.

Farrow, Anthony. "Currents in the Irish Novel: George Moore, James Joyce, Samuel Beckett." *Dissertation Abstracts International (DAI)* 33 (1973).

Foster, John W. *Fictions of the Irish Literary Revival: A Changeling Art*. Syracuse: Syracuse University Press, 1987.

———. *Forces and Themes in Ulster Fiction*. Totowa, NJ: Rowman and Littlefield, 1974.

Imhof, Rüdiger, ed. *Contemporary Irish Novelists*. Tübingen: Gunter Narr Verlag, 1990.

Kiely, Benedict. *Modern Irish Fiction*. Dublin: Golden Eagle, 1950.

Kilroy, James F., ed. *The Irish Short Story: A Critical History*. Boston: Twayne, 1984.

Krans, Horatio. *Irish Life in Irish Fiction*. New York: AMS, 1966.

Lubbers, Klaus. "Irish Fiction: A Mirror for Specifics." *Eire-Ireland* 20.2 (Summer 1985): 90–104.

Mercier, Vivian. "Realism in Anglo-Irish Fiction 1916–1940." Diss., Trinity College, Dublin, 1943.

O'Connor, Frank. *The Lonely Voice*. Cleveland: World, 1963.

Rafroidi, Patrick, and Maurice Harmon, eds. *The Irish Novel in Our Time*. Lille: Publications de L'Universite de Lille, 1976.

Rafroidi, Patrick, and Terence Brown, eds. *The Irish Short Story*. Atlantic Highlands, NJ: Humanities, 1979.

Saul, George Brandon. *Rushlight Heritage*. Philadelphia: Walton, 1969.

Thompson, Richard J. *Everlasting Voices: Aspects of the Modern Irish Short Story*. Troy, NY: Whitston, 1989.

Titley, Alan. *An tUrscéal Gaeilge*. Baile Atha Cliath [Dublin]: Clochomar, 1991.

Drama

Bell, Sam Hanna. *The Theatre in Ulster*. Dublin: Gill and Macmillan, 1972.

Boyd, E. A. *The Contemporary Drama of Ireland*. Dublin: Talbot, 1918.

Clark, William Smyth. *The Early Irish Stage*. Oxford: Oxford University Press, 1955.

Courtney, Marie-Therese. *Edward Martyn and the Irish Theatre*. New York: Vantage, 1956.

Driver, Tom. *Romantic Quest and Modern Query: History of the Modern Theatre*. New York: Delacorte, 1970.

Ellis-Fermor, Una. *The Irish Dramatic Movement*. New York: Barnes and Noble, 1939; rev. 1954.

Fay, Gerard. *The Abbey Theatre, Cradle of Genius*. London: Hollis and Carter, 1958.

Feeney, William J. *Drama in Hardwicke Street: A History of the Irish Theatre Company*. Rutherford, NJ: Fairleigh Dickinson University Press, 1983.

Fitz-Simon, Christopher. *The Irish Theatre*. London: Thames and Hudson, 1983.

Genet, Jacqueline, and Richard Allen Cave, eds. *Perspectives of Irish Drama and Theatre*. Gerrards Cross, Bucks: Smythe, 1991.

Hogan, Robert. *After the Irish Renaissance*. Minneapolis: University of Minnesota Press, 1967.

———. *Laying the Foundations, 1902–1904*. Atlantic Highlands, NJ: Humanities, 1976.

Hogan, Robert, and Richard Burnham. *The Years of O'Casey, 1921–1926*. Newark: University of Delaware Press, 1992.

Hogan, Robert, Richard Burnham, and Daniel P. Poteet. *The Abbey Theatre: The Rise of the Realists, 1910–1915.* Atlantic Highlands, NJ: Humanities, 1984.

Hogan, Robert, and James Kilroy. *The Abbey Theatre: The Years of Synge 1905–09.* Dublin: Dolmen; Atlantic Highlands, NJ: Humanities, 1978.

———— (with James Kilroy). *The Irish Literary Theatre, 1899–1901.* Atlantic Highlands, NJ: Humanities, 1975.

Hunt, Hugh. *The Abbey, Ireland's National Theatre, 1904–1978.* Dublin: Gill and Macmillan, 1979.

Kavanagh, Peter. *The Story of the Abbey Theatre.* New York: Devin-Adair, 1950.

Krutch, Joseph W. *Modernism in Modern Drama.* Ithaca, NY: Cornell University Press, 1953.

Malone, Andrew E. *The Irish Drama.* 1929. New York and London: Blom, 1965.

Maxwell, D.E.S. *A Critical History of Modern Irish Drama, 1891–1980.* Cambridge: Cambridge University Press, 1984.

Murray, T. C. *The Irish Theatre.* London: Macmillan, 1939.

O'Driscoll, Robert, ed. *Theatre and Nationalism in Twentieth-Century Ireland.* Toronto: University of Toronto Press, 1971.

O'hAodha, Michael. *Theater in Ireland.* Oxford: Blackwell, 1974.

O'Mahoney, Mathew. *Guide to Anglo-Irish Plays.* Dublin: Progress House, 1960.

Rafroidi, Patrick, Ramonde Popot, and William Parker, eds. *Aspects of the Irish Theatre.* Lille: Publications de l' Universite de Lille, 1972.

Richtarik, Marilynn J. *Acting between the Lines: The Field Day Theatre Company and Irish Cultural Politics 1980–1984.* Oxford: Clarendon, 1994.

Robinson, Lennox, ed. *The Irish Theatre.* 1939. New York: Haskell House, 1971.

————. *Ireland's Abbey Theatre.* London: Sidgwick and Jackson, 1951.

Roche, Anthony. *Contemporary Irish Drama.* New York: St. Martin's, 1955.

Sekine, Masaru, ed. *Irish Writers and the Theatre.* Gerrards Cross, Bucks: Smythe, 1986.

Setterquist, Jan. *Ibsen and the Beginnings of Anglo-Irish Drama.* New York: Gordian, 1974.

Williams, Raymond. *Drama from Ibsen to Eliot.* London: Chatto and Windus, 1961.

Worth, Katherine. *The Irish Drama of Europe from Yeats to Beckett.* Atlantic Highlands, NJ: Humanities, 1978.

Poetry

Andrews, Elmer, ed. *Contemporary Irish Poetry: A Collection of Critical Essays.* London: Macmillan, 1992.

Brown, Terence. *Northern Voices: Poets from Ulster.* Dublin: Gill and Macmillan, 1975.

Brown, Terence, and Nicholas Grene, eds. *Tradition and Influence in Anglo-Irish Poetry.* London: Macmillan, 1989.

Colman, Anne, and Medbh McGuckian, eds. *The Grateful Muse: Poems by Irish Women, 1716–1939.* Derry: Field Day, 1995.

Corcoran, Neil, ed. *The Chosen Ground: Essays on the Contemporary Poetry of Northern Ireland.* Bridgend, Ireland: Seren, 1992.

Coughlan, Patricia, and Alex Davis, eds. *Modernism and Ireland: The Poetry of the 1930s.* Cork: Cork University Press, 1995.

Dawe, Gerald. *Against Piety—Essays in Irish Poetry.* Belfast: Lagan, 1995.

Deane, John F., ed. *Irish Poetry of Faith and Doubt: The Cold Heaven*. Dublin: Wolfhound, 1990.

Farren, Robert. *The Course of Irish Verse*. London: Sheed and Ward, 1948.

Fleming, Deborah, ed. *Learning the Trade: Essays on W. B. Yeats and Contemporary
Poetry*. West Cornwall, CT: Locust Hill, 1993.

Garratt, Robert F. *Modern Irish Poetry: Tradition and Continuity from Yeats to Heaney*.
Berkeley: University of California Press, 1986.

Gifford, Terry. *Green Voices: Understanding Contemporary Nature Poetry*. Manchester
and New York: Manchester University Press, 1995.

Haberstroh, Patricia. *Women Creating Women: Contemporary Irish Women Poets*. Syracuse: Syracuse University Press, 1995.

Haffenden, John. *Viewpoints: Poets in Conversation*. London and Boston: Faber and
Faber, 1981.

Harmon, Maurice. *Irish Poetry after Yeats*. Boston: Little, Brown, 1979.

Johnston, Dillon. *Irish Poetry after Joyce*. Notre Dame, IN: Notre Dame University Press,
1985, rev. 1997.

Kenneally, Michael, ed. *Poetry in Contemporary Irish Literature*. Gerrards Cross:
Smythe, 1995.

Loftus, Richard J. *Nationalism in Modern Anglo-Irish Poetry*. Madison: University of
Wisconsin Press, 1964.

Lucy, Sean, ed. *Irish Poets in English*. Cork: Mercier, 1973.

Power, Patrick C. *The Story of Anglo-Irish Poetry 1800–1922*. Cork: Mercier, 1967.

Smith, Michael. ''Irish Poetry since Yeats.'' *The University of Denver Quarterly* 5 (Winter 1971): 1–26.

———. *Irish Poetry: The Thirties Generation*. Dublin: Raven Arts, 1983.

Somerville-Arjat, Gillean, and Rebecca E. Wilson, eds. *Sleeping with Monsters: Conversations with Scottish and Irish Women Poets*. Edinburgh: Polygon, 1989.

Welch, Robert. *Irish Poetry from Moore to Yeats*. Gerrards Cross: Smythe, 1980.

Westendorp, Tjebbe A., and Jane Mallinson, eds. *Politics and the Rhetoric of Poetry:
Perspectives on Modern Anglo-Irish Poetry*. Amsterdam and Atlanta: Rodopi,
1995.

Wills, Clair. *Improprieties: Politics and Sexuality in Northern Irish Poetry*. Oxford: Clarendon, 1993.

Index

About the Editor and Contributors

ANN MARIE ADAMS specializes in twentieth-century British literature, with an emphasis in Irish studies and postcolonial literatures.

THOMAS AKSTENS is lecturer in English at Siena College. His articles have appeared in *Journal of Dramatic Theory and Criticism*, *Shakespeare Bulletin*, *New England Theatre Journal*, and *Philological Quarterly* and in a recent collection of essays, *Antonin Artaud and the Modern Theater*.

JANE BIONDI has specialized in Irish literature and culture, particularly Ireland's contemporary women poets.

RICHARD BONACCORSO has been a member of the English Department at Central Connecticut State University since 1975. His book, *Sean O'Faolain's Irish Vision*, was published in 1987. His chapters and articles on Irish subjects include studies of Daniel Corkery, Sean O'Faolain, Frank O'Connor, Brian Friel, William Trevor, and Seamus Heaney.

NOELLE BOWLES teaches at the University of Miami as a lecturer for the English Department and the women's studies program.

RAND BRANDES is Martin Luther Stevens Professor and professor of English at Lenoir Rhyne College, Hickory, North Carolina. In 1993 he was a Fulbright Senior Research Fellow and worked with Seamus Heaney in Dublin. He is currently completing a bibliography on Heaney's works.

REGINA M. BUCCOLA writes reviews of poetry and short fiction collections for *Another Chicago Magazine* and produced the entries on Jane Addams and Hull-House for *The Historical Dictionary of Women's Education*.

JAMES M. CAHALAN is professor of English at Indiana University of Pennsylvania, where he teaches graduate courses in Irish literature. He is the author of numerous articles and four books in this field: *Great Hatred, Little Room: The Irish Historical Novel* (1983); *The Irish Novel: A Critical History* (1988); *Liam O'Flaherty: A Study of the Short Fiction* (1991); and *Modern Irish Literature and Culture: A Chronology* (1993).

PHYLLIS CAREY is associate professor of English at Mount Mary College, Milwaukee, Wisconsin. She is coeditor (with Ed Jewinski) of *Re: Joyce 'n Beckett* (1992) and (with Catherine Malloy) *Seamus Heaney: The Shaping Spirit* (1996). In addition, she has published articles on Beckett, Joyce, and Václav Havel and interviews with Czeslaw Milosz and Seamus Deane.

LAURIE CHAMPION is a Sul Ross State University assistant professor of English and has edited two volumes for Greenwood's Critical Responses in Arts and Letters Series. Her essays and reviews appear in *American Literature, Explicator, Mississippi Quarterly, Southern Literary Journal, Southern Quarterly, Texas Review*, and other journals. Her short stories appear in the anthologies *New Texas '93* and *Texas Short Fiction: A World in Itself II*.

ANNE ULRY COLMAN is a research fellow at the Institute of Irish Studies, The Queen's University, Belfast. She specializes in pre-twentieth-century Irish women writers.

DEBORAH H. MCWILLIAMS, an independent scholar, explores inscriptions of cultural tradition, notably in Irish literature, and examines how idiomatic, dialectic, and vernacular manifestations evince a writer's sense of identity. Her research probes how paradigms of history, mythology, sociology, and anthropology combine to forge the cornerstones of selfhood and nationhood.

JOHN D. CONWAY is associate professor of English at Central Connecticut State University. He has published articles and reviews on Yeats, Joyce, A.E., O'Flaherty, and Paul Vincent Carroll.

ALBERT J. DEGIACOMO is assistant professor of English at Mount Aloysius College, Pennsylvania. His articles on T. C. Murray have appeared in *Eire-Ireland* and *Irish University Review*; at present he is working on a book-length study of Murray's work.

MARYANN DONAHUE's interests include poststructuralist literary theory and contemporary Irish poetry and fiction. She is book review editor for the *James Joyce Quarterly* and research assistant for poet Richard Murphy.

MARY E. DONNELLY has written on Irish adolescent and Oedipal narratives, has also published in *ARIEL: A Review of International English Literature*, and regularly reviews books for several journals.

MARYANNE FELTER is assistant professor of English at Cayuga Community College, Auburn, New York. She has been assistant editor of the *Journal of*

Irish Literature since 1978, has published articles and reviews in the *Journal* and *Eire-Ireland*, and is a contributor to the revised edition of the *Dictionary of Irish Literature*.

PATRICIA J. FERREIRA is assistant professor in the Department of English at James Madison University. Her focus is cultural studies, particularly the intersections between the Irish and African-American communities. She has published in the *African American Review, SAGE: A Scholarly Journal on Black Women, Canadian Journal of Irish Studies, Irish Literary Supplement*, and the *Review of Pedagogy/Education/Cultural Studies*.

MARY FITZGERALD-HOYT is professor of English at Siena College, where she teaches courses in Irish literature. She has published pieces on such contemporary Irish writers as Brian Friel, William Trevor, Julia O'Faolain, and Ciaran Carson and is currently working on a book on William Trevor's Irish fiction.

BARTON R. FRIEDMAN is professor of English at Cleveland State University. He is the author of two scholarly books, *Adventures in the Deeps of the Mind: The Cuchulain Cycle of W. B. Yeats* (1977) and *Fabricating History: English Writers on the French Revolution* (1988), and a book of poems, *You Can't Tell the Players* (1979). He has also written a number of articles on Yeats and on James Stephens.

PAULA GILLESPIE's current research and publications concern voice not only in fiction but in rhetoric and composition, and her writing-center work grounds her in student voices of all kinds. She is director of the Ott Memorial Writing Center at Marquette University.

CLAIRE GLEITMAN is assistant professor of dramatic literature at Ithaca College. She has published articles on the drama in *The Canadian Journal of Irish Studies* and *Comparative Drama* and delivered numerous papers on contemporary Irish theater. She is currently at work on a book-length study of contemporary Irish drama.

ALEXANDER G. GONZALEZ, professor of English, is the Irish literature specialist at Cortland College of the State University of New York. Educated at Queens College and at the University of Oregon, where he received his doctorate, he has also taught at both these institutions, as well as at The University of California at Santa Barbara, at The Ohio State University, and at The Pennsylvania State University as a Distinguished Scholar in Residence. He has authored two books, *Darrell Figgis: A Study of His Novels* (1992) and *Peadar O'Donnell: A Reader's Guide* (1997), and edited two more, *Short Stories from the Irish Renaissance: An Anthology* (1993) and *Assessing the Achievement of J. M. Synge* (1996). In addition he has published over thirty articles in journals such as *Studies in Short Fiction, Irish University Review, Eire-Ireland, Colby Library Quarterly, The Journal of Irish Literature*, and *Notes on Modern Irish Litera-*

ture. He is currently writing a monograph on Daniel Corkery and editing *Contemporary Irish Women Poets: Some Male Perspectives*.

NICOLE PEPINSTER GREENE, instructor in the English Department at the University of Southwestern Louisiana, directs the Developmental Writing Program and is writing on Somerville and Ross. She has read papers at the Conference on College Composition and Communication and the American Conference for Irish Studies.

ELIZABETH GRUBGELD is associate professor of modern British and Irish literature at Oklahoma State University. She is author of *George Moore and the Autogenous Self: The Autobiography and Fiction* (1994) and various articles on twentieth-century Irish literature. She is currently completing *Anglo-Irish Autobiography: A Critical History*.

ANDREW J. HAGGERTY is interested in modern Irish literature, having previously contributed an essay on Gerry Adams for *The Dictionary of Irish Literature*.

MICHAEL F. HART was associate professor of English at St. John's University, where he taught courses on modern Irish literature, the novel, Romanticism, and modern poetry. His publications include articles on Joyce, Yeats, Sterne, and Irish culture. He was writing a book on the early work of Joyce in the context of nineteenth-century intellectual history when he met his untimely death in January of 1997.

ALLISON T. HILD has published articles on Virginia Woolf and Sarah Orne Jewett and given numerous conference papers on Edna O'Brien, Elizabeth Bowen, and other Irish writers. Her areas of concentration are twentieth-century British literature and world literature (with specific focus on African writers).

SHAWN HOLLIDAY is teaching associate at Indiana University of Pennsylvania. His areas of specialization include colonial discourse and postcolonial theory, modern Irish literature, and American realism and naturalism.

PATRICIA KANE O'CONNOR is adjunct professor in the Department of Language and Literature at Bucks County Community College in Newtown, Pennsylvania.

EDWARD A. KOPPER, JR., Distinguished Commonwealth Professor of English at Slippery Rock University of Pennsylvania, is the author of over seventy-five publications, including twelve books, dealing with modern Irish, English, and American literature. He is the editor and publisher of *Notes on Modern Irish Literature* and, from 1976 through 1980, edited and published *Modern British Literature*.

MARGARET LASCH MAHONEY is adjunct professor of humanities at the Albany College of Pharmacy in Albany, New York. She has studied at St. Patrick's College in Maynooth, County Kildare, and at University College, Dublin.

MADELEINE MARCHATERRE is visiting teaching associate at the University of Illinois in Urbana–Champaign and is editing, with John Frayne, a forthcoming revised edition of the *Uncollected Prose of W. B. Yeats*.

BERNARD MCKENNA teaches in the English Department at the University of Miami. He is associate editor of the second edition of *The Dictionary of Irish Literature* and has published essays on Irish literature and colonialism for a variety of journals, including *Eire-Ireland* and *Nineteenth-Century Prose*.

BARBARA E. MCLAUGHLIN is instructor at Marquette University. She has been a member of the American Conference for Irish Studies since 1988.

MAUREEN MCLAUGHLIN is assistant professor in the Professional Communication Department at Alverno College in Milwaukee, Wisconsin. A former journalist, she has published articles in the *Chicago Tribune, The Milwaukee Journal, The Writer, Utne Reader*, and other publications. She is working on a manuscript about Irish-American journalist Anne O'Hare McCormick.

JAMES MCNAMARA is a member of the American Conference for Irish Studies and has presented papers at the Third Annual Virginia Woolf Conference and at A Harold Pinter Festival: An International Meeting.

JIM MCWILLIAMS, instructor of English at Western Nebraska Community College, has published a book, *Mark Twain in the St. Louis Post-Dispatch* (1997), and numerous articles about American and British literature in journals such as *Nineteenth-Century Literature, American Studies International, The Explicator*, and the *Walt Whitman Quarterly Review*.

JACK MORGAN is assistant professor of English, University of Missouri–Rolla. He is coeditor of *The Irish Stories of Sarah Orne Jewett* and has published in *Irish University Review, Eire-Ireland, The Irish Literary Supplement, Notes on Modern Irish Literature*, and *Working Papers in Irish Studies*.

KEVIN MURPHY is professor of English at Ithaca College and teaches both Irish and American literature. He has published essays on Eamon Grennan, Eavan Boland, and the Field Day Theater Company, as well as articles on Whitman, James, and Twain and reviews of contemporary poetry, both Irish and American.

TAURA S. NAPIER teaches in the School of English at Queen's University, Belfast. Her work has focused on literary autobiographies of twentieth-century Irishwomen and on the recovery of Mary Colum's writings. She has published on Colum in the *Canadian Journal of Irish Studies*.

JOHN O'BRIEN teaches English at Normandale Community College in the twin cities of Minneapolis-St. Paul. He has published articles on Denis Johnston and Irish theater in *The Canadian Journal of Irish Studies* and *The Journal of Irish Literature* and a book, *Milan Kundera and Feminism: Dangerous Intersections* (1995).

MARY O'CONNOR is associate professor of English literature at South Dakota State University. Born in Wexford, Ireland, she has been involved in women's issues through active work, publication, and the presentation of papers at national and international conferences since 1977.

LAUREN ONKEY is assistant professor of English at Ball State University in Muncie, Indiana, where she teaches twentieth-century British and Irish literature and postcolonial literature and theory. She has published essays on Brian Friel and Roddy Doyle and is currently completing a manuscript entitled *Embodying the Nation: Post-Colonial Irish Women's Fiction.*

COÍLÍN D. OWENS, associate professor of English at George Mason University, has edited *Family Chronicles: Maria Edgeworth's Castle Rackrent,* co-edited *Irish Drama: 1900–1980,* and written numerous articles on Irish drama, language, and literature.

ALAN I. REA, JR., has researched James Joyce and edited a collection on Russian history. He served on a ''Robert Cormier'' panel at a National Council of Teachers of English (NCTE) Conference and has presented at other conferences, including the Thirty-Seventh Annual Midwestern Modern Language Association (M/MLA). He is secretary of the M/MLA's Science Fiction Panel and upcoming secretary for the Literary Criticism and Theory Panel.

ANDREW J. SHIPE has presented papers at the Graduate Irish Studies Conference, the International James Joyce Symposium, and several other conferences. He is also an assistant editor of the *James Joyce Literary Supplement.*

REBECCA CREASY SIMCOE teaches philosophy and literature at Tulsa Junior College and has written on Samuel Beckett.

MICHAEL STEINMAN, associate professor of English at Nassau Community College (State University of New York), is the author of *Yeats's Heroic Figures: Wilde, Parnell, Swift, Casement* and *Frank O'Connor at Work.* He has edited *A Frank O'Connor Reader* and *The Happiness of Getting It Down Right: Letters of Frank O'Connor and William Maxwell, 1945–1966.*

SANFORD STERNLICHT, part-time professor of English at Syracuse University and professor emeritus of English and theater at the State University of New York at Oswego, is the author of *Padraic Colum* (1985) and editor of *The Selected Short Stories of Padraic Colum* (1985), *Selected Plays of Padraic Colum* (1986), and *Selected Poems of Padraic Colum* (1989).

BARBARA A. SUESS has written on the ritual aspects of modern verse drama and is active in the American Conference for Irish Studies, for which she serves on the New England region's executive board.

ROBERT SULLIVAN is currently a visiting professor at Brown University. He has taught at universities in Algeria and Ghana and is the author of *Christopher*

Caudwell (1987) and various articles and reviews on modern British literature. His monograph on Brian Moore, *A Matter of Faith: The Fiction of Brian Moore*, was published in 1996.

ANN OWENS WEEKES, director of the Humanities Program in the University of Arizona, researches Irish women writers and is the author of *Irish Women Writers: An Uncharted Tradition* (1990) and *Unveiling Treasures: Guide to Irish Women Writers* (1993).

KELLIE DONOVAN WIXSON is interested in gothic literature and is researching the way in which gothic conventions prefigure Anglo-Irish Big House literature.

ISBN 0-313-29557-3

EAN

9 780313 295577

HARDCOVER BAR CODE